Magic, Witchcraft, and Religion

Cover photograph by Terry Heffernan

The artifacts shown (from the Lowie Museum of Anthropology, University of California, Berkeley) were made by the Tlingit Indians of the Pacific Northwest. At top is a dance mask of carved and painted alder. At middle left is a carved and painted wooden rattle. At middle right is a shaman's piece, a "soul catcher," of carved ivory, probably representing a man killed by whales. At lower left is a wooden rattle with puffin beaks. At lower right is a dance baton of carved and painted red cedar.

Magic, Witchcraft, and Religion
An Anthropological Study of the Supernatural

Arthur C. Lehmann and James E. Myers

California State University, Chico

Mayfield Publishing Company

Palo Alto and London

Library of Congress Catalog Card Number: 84-061380
International Standard Book Number: 0-87484-685-4

Manufactured in the United States of America
10 9 8 7 6 5 4 3

Mayfield Publishing Company
285 Hamilton Avenue
Palo Alto, California 94301

The verse quotation on p. 372 is from "The Seven Spiritual Ages of Mrs. Marmaduke Moore," in *Verses from
1919 On* by Ogden Nash. Copyright 1933 by Ogden
Nash. Used by permission of Little, Brown and Company.

Sponsoring editor: Janet M. Beatty

Manuscript editor: Joy Dickinson

Managing editor: Pat Herbst

Art director: Nancy Sears

Designer (interior and cover): Marilyn Langfeld

Mask drawings: Betty Armstrong

Cover photograph: Terry Heffernan

Production manager: Cathy Willkie

Compositor: Auto-Graphics, Inc.

Printer and binder: Malloy Lithographing, Inc.

*This book is dedicated to the memory of
Alan P. Merriam and Allen Holmberg.*

Contents

Foreword

It has often been remarked that the challenge to anthropologists, as well as their opportunity, is to show the familiar in the strange and the strange in the familiar. Nowhere in anthropology are that challenge and opportunity more present than in the comparative study of religion. It is our task as anthropologists to encounter, study, record, understand, and interpret the social practices and cultural patterns of human groups, wherever and whenever they have gathered—from the Arctic to the tropics; from Neanderthal times to the present. We have thus brought together in our literature a vast collection of religious beliefs and practices, many of which may seem strange indeed to twentieth-century North Americans. Yet if we bring these beliefs and practices wisely under anthropological focus, as Professors Lehmann and Myers have done in this reader, they will be seen to be strangely familiar. They are beliefs, we discover, that under other circumstances we might have believed ourselves. They are ritual practices, we see, that we might have engaged in, as, often enough, did our own ancestors. In these beliefs and practices we come to recognize needs, desires, appetites, and satisfactions ultimately characteristic of all human experience.

It is not enough, then, to study strange practices unless that study somehow enables us to gain perspective on our own way of life—to understand better because we see as from a distance. That is what is meant by seeing the strange in the familiar. Anthropology, by taking us out to dwell, if only momentarily, among unfamiliar practices else-

where, should by that act alone give us perspective on our own lifeways when we return. It is the particular virtue of this collection of readings, however, to give a convincing additional twist to the distancing we obtain from contemplating strange religious practices elsewhere in the world: The editors have included in each section studies of practices taking place in modern Western societies today, mostly in North America. They show us the "strange" not only in exotic circumstances but also in a society with which we are extremely familiar. Although we may not always be familiar with the specific behavior described—the health food movement or contemporary Satanism, for example—the fact that such beliefs and practices are active among us today underscores the continuing relevance and vitality of the anthropological study of religion, wherever it is conducted. The religious impulse, with all its variegated manifestations, remains at work even in the so-called secular societies of present-day North America.

Why, especially, should we want to make the strange familiar and the familiar strange? What can we gain from the added perspective achieved by seeing ourselves as from a distance? At least three answers may be given to this question: tolerance, diversity, and adaptability. We now live in an increasingly interdependent world in which we are constantly being brought into contact with the strange and with strangers. Order in such a world demands an increased tolerance for lifeways that are strange to us. Moreover, familiarity with the exotic not only creates respect for, but may also help preserve, an enlivening diversity in the world, rather than the homogenized, consumption-oriented, worldwide popular culture toward which we seem to be irrevocably moving. A homogenized world culture gives us a much less interesting world in which to live. Finally, an increased perspective on our own beliefs and practices (which is not incompatible with continuing satisfaction in them) helps us avoid inert or fanatical overcommitment to them. (This is particularly the case with religious practices, which have so often been attended by intolerance, if not fanaticism.) The hallmark of the human career as compared with other creatures has been our adaptability: our ability to change our lifeways to fit into many diverse environments and to respond quickly and effectively to the challenge of changing circumstances. The maintenance of a balanced perspective on our own beliefs and practices—the avoidance of overcommitment to them because we have come to see them as strange in their own way —is part and parcel of our adaptability, our readiness to meet and master changing circumstances.

Beyond these values of tolerance, diversity, and adaptability that can emerge from the study of comparative religion lies the fact of religion itself.

Religion is a human universal: It is found in every culture known to anthropologists, in a great diversity and variety of forms of expression. No reader who embarks on an attentive reading of this rewarding selection of articles can fail to recognize the human creativity that lies in this diversity. Nor can he or she fail to recognize the particular power through which religion enables men and women to speak to and cope with the ultimate circumstances of human life: injustice, unpredictability, suffering, death. An attentive reading, then, will offer insight both into what makes us human and into some of the more effective ways we have of battling that frail humanity. Such insight and understanding are a main object of anthropological study of any aspect of culture, but the study of religion has been particularly rewarding in this respect. The anthropological study of comparative religion stretches out to embrace diversity, as does this collection of readings. It stretches out to diversity to try to show us not only what being human is but what it might be.

James W. Fernandez
Princeton University

Preface

We prepared this reader to fill an obvious void in the existing literature on comparative religion. Having taught the anthropology of religion for a number of years, we were repeatedly frustrated by the lack of adequate reading materials for our courses. Because of the complex nature of comparative religion, no single text covered the subject in such a way that it was generally applicable to a wide range of students. Existing volumes were either too complex or advanced for introductory courses or too narrowly focused to systematically deal with the cross-cultural aspects of religion.

Magic, Witchcraft, and Religion: An Anthropological Study of the Supernatural was thus designed both to reach a broad spectrum of students and to demonstrate a comparative approach to the major elements and categories of religion. The volume provides teachers and students with contemporary, provocative readings on both non-Western and Western subjects. These readings allow students not only to investigate their own religious belief systems but also to compare those systems with others outside their culture. We believe this text thus illustrates the importance of understanding religion in our own culture as well as in those of the non-Western world. Primarily designed to reach undergraduate students, it is appropriate as a supplemental reader for graduate students as well.

In designing this volume, we carefully searched through the literature of comparative religion, sociology, psychology, and anthropology, intensively screening hundreds of articles on the basis of their readability, academic quality and level, topical in-

terest, and subject matter (including geographical and cultural area). Our overall goal was to achieve a final collection that would introduce students to the main topics in the study of magic, witchcraft, and religion, while at the same time also introducing them to the major ethnographic areas of the world. Although the book does center on the non-Western world, we agreed early in the selection process to place in each chapter one article from contemporary North America, both to increase students' interest and to heighten their cross-cultural perspective.

Using the recommendations of students and the evaluations and suggestions of faculty from various universities who have taught a similar course over the years, we narrowed the field to the existing selections, which are organized topically into ten chapters: (1) the anthropological study of religion; (2) myth, ritual, symbolism, and taboo; (3) shamans, priests, and prophets; (4) the religious use of drugs; (5) witchcraft, sorcery, and other forces of evil; (6) demons, exorcism, divination, and magic; (7) ethnomedicine (religion and healing); (8) ghosts, souls, and ancestors; (9) old and new religions; and (10) the occult. To allow for this breadth of coverage, references from the original publication of the articles were intentionally deleted to provide additional space for readings.

We believe the resulting volume is unique, and especially valuable, because of the following features:

• The content not only covers every major traditional topic in comparative religion, but also features separate chapters on the religious use of drugs, old and new religions, ethnomedicine, and the occult.

• Each chapter includes both a core of non-Western articles and at least one reading from contemporary North America.

• Although the majority of the articles are the most recent available, classic readings are also included.

• The selections were chosen specifically for students on the basis of compelling subject matter and readability.

• The readings represent a broad sample of the world's geographic areas and economic levels.

• Each selection is preceded by a headnote that draws out the main theoretical and substantive points in the work.

• An introduction to each chapter presents a historical and theoretical overview of the major topics that follow, thus providing students with a framework for understanding the contemporary importance of the subject.

A number of people contributed significantly to the preparation and development of this volume. We acknowledge with thanks the comments and suggestions made by the following reviewers of preliminary drafts of the manuscript: H. Glynn Custred, California State University, Hayward; Jill Dubisch, University of North Carolina, Charlotte; Mark S. Fleisher, Washington State University; Bruce T. Grindal, Florida State University; David Hicks, State University of New York, Stony Brook; Edward J. Jay, California State University, Hayward; Helen H. Schuster, Iowa State University; and George Westermark, University of Santa Clara. In addition, we wish to thank Frank Graham for encouraging us to write this book, Pat Herbst for guiding the project through production, Pam Trainer for dauntless efforts to acquire reprint permissions, and Joy Dickinson for a rigorous and thoughtful editing of the final draft.

A.C.L.
J.E.M.

Magic, Witchcraft, and Religion

1
The Anthropological Study of Religion

Anthropologists have always been interested in the origins of religion, although the lack of both written records and archaeological evidence has made the subject speculative. It is reasonable to assume, however, that religion, like material culture, has a prehistory. Surely, uncertainty and change have always existed, exposing people in all ages to real and imagined threats and anxieties. The human animal alone senses a pattern behind the facts of existence and worries about life here and in the hereafter. We are born, we live, and we die. And although this is true of other animals, only humans are aware of the precariousness of life and the inevitability of death. As William Howells has observed, "Man's life is hard, very hard. And he knows it, poor soul; that is the vital thing. He knows that he is forever confronted with the Four Horsemen—death, famine, disease, and the malice of other men" (1962: 16).

The earliest surviving anthropological evidence of humans possibly expressing these concerns through religious practices dates from

Buffalo mask of the Bobo, Upper Volta.

1

the era of *Homo sapiens Neanderthalensis*, approximately a hundred thousand years ago. Because the Neanderthals buried their dead with tools, weapons, and other funerary objects, many anthropologists have held that they were the first humans to believe in an afterlife of some sort. The era of *Homo sapiens sapiens* (modern man in the biological sense), approximately thirty thousand years ago, has yielded increasing evidence of religious beliefs—more elaborate burials, carved figurines (''Venuses''), and magnificent cave art. And during the Neolithic period, which began about ten thousand years ago, burials indicate a deep respect for the power of the dead. It is likely that during this period, which is marked by the cultivation of crops and the domestication of animals, cycles of nature became an important feature of magic and religious beliefs. Drought, storms, and other natural perils of the farmer could have created a growing dependence on supernatural powers.

The antiquity of religion indirectly testifies to its utility; however, the usefulness of supernaturalism to contemporary societies is a clearer, more provable demonstration of its functions. The many forms of adversity facing individuals and groups require explanation and action; we are unwilling to let challenges to health, safety, and salvation go unchecked. Just as adversity is universal, so too is the use of religion as an explanation for and solution to adversity. Although the form religion takes is as diverse as its practitioners, all religions seek to answer questions that cannot be explained in terms of objective knowledge—to permit people reasonable explanations for often unreasonable events and phenomena by demonstrating a cause-and-effect relationship between the supernatural and the human condition. This may be its most important function.

In his article ''Religion: Problems of Definition and Explanation'' (1966: 109–17), Melford E. Spiro has distinguished three sets of basic desires (cognitive, substantive, and expressive), each of which is satisfied by a corresponding function of religion (adjustive, adaptive, and integrative). Spiro's first and second functions are basically those of explanation and solution: the adjustive function of religion, as he defines it, is to satisfy the cognitive desires we experience as we at-

tempt to understand what goes on around us (illness, natural phenomena); the adaptive function seeks to satisfy substantive desires (the desire for rain, or for victory in war). In his third category, however, Spiro moves to different territory: the often unconscious, expressive desires made up of what Spiro calls painful drives and painful motives.

According to Spiro, painful drives are anxieties concerning infantile and primitive fears (fears of destruction, or of one's own destructiveness). Painful motives are culturally forbidden—for example, types of aggressive or sexual behavior that result in feelings of shame, inadequacy, and moral anxiety. Because of the pain they create in an individual, these drives and motives are usually relegated to the unconscious, where, ''in the absence of other, or of more efficient means,'' religion becomes the vehicle ''by which, symbolically, they can be handled and expressed.'' Thus, in what Spiro calls the integrative function of supernaturalism, ''religious belief and ritual provide the content for culturally constituted projective mechanisms by which unconscious fears and anxieties may be reduced and repressed motives may be satisfied'' (1966: 115).

Over the years, scholars have taken several approaches in their attempts to understand the reasons for the existence of religious behavior. The most prominent of these approaches are psychological, sociological, and anthropological. Melford Spiro's belief that religious behavior serves to reduce unconscious fears typifies the psychological approach, which, briefly stated, sees religion as functioning to reduce anxiety. For example, the famous British social anthropologist Bronislaw Malinowski held that the proper use of religious rites reduced anxieties brought on by crisis. (Like all theorists who apply the psychological approach, Freud also believed that religion and ritual functioned to reduce anxieties, but, unlike others, he saw religion as a neurotic need that humans would eventually outgrow.) In contrast, the sociological viewpoint stresses the societal origins of religion. The French sociologist Emile Durkheim, for example, viewed religion as a manifestation of social solidarity and collective beliefs. According to Durkheim, members of society create religious objects, rituals, beliefs, and symbols in order to integrate their cultures. A. R.

Radcliffe-Brown, a British social anthropologist, agreed with Durkheim that participation in annual religious rites functioned to increase social solidarity.

Although their functional analyses of religious behavior and phenomena do explain, in part, the universality of religion, neither the psychological nor the sociological theorists adequately provide answers to the origin of religion. Both approaches are too limited in focus, centered as they are on human emotions and social structure respectively; neither explores the wide variety of cultural expressions of religion. Because religious experience, wherever it is observed, displays such great variation of cognitive and phenomenal expression, anything less than a wide-ranging holistic approach would not allow true comparisons; as a result, generalizations about the nature of religious systems would be incomplete as well as inaccurate.

The third, the anthropological approach to the study of religion, is by its very nature holistic, combining not only sociological and psychological, but historical, semantic, and evolutionary perspectives as well. As Clifford Geertz demonstrates in the lead article of this book, anthropologists attempt to go beyond the observable to the analysis of symbolic forms. In order to make generalizations on pan-human religious behavior, symbology, and ideology, however, anthropologists must work from the common basis of a definition of religion. Without an acceptable and accurate definition, anthropologists would be unable to establish a common basis for comparison of religion cross-culturally.

Many definitions of religion have been generated by anthropologists. Tylor, the father of modern anthropology, described religion as the belief in spiritual beings, what he called "animism," the most primitive form of religion. At the opposite extreme from Tylor's open-ended definition, which set no limits as to what the study of spiritual beings would embrace, are a majority of contemporary anthropologists who, like Spiro, define religion more narrowly as "an institution consisting of culturally postulated superhuman beings" (1966: 96). At first glance, Tylor's and Spiro's definitions appear similar, but Spiro's use of the term "superhuman," unlike Tylor's "spiritual beings," emphasizes an aura of omnipotence unknown to the living. Further, Spiro's position that religion is an "institution" places it in the realm of phenomena that can be empirically studied, as any other cultural institution can be. Still, similarities in Tylor's and Spiro's definitions are apparent: both show, for example, that religion is the study of the nature of the unnatural. Spirits are not of this world, nor are superhumans; indeed, both are "supernatural," which has been defined by the anthropologist Edward Norbeck "to include all that is not natural, that which is regarded as extraordinary, not of the ordinary world, mysterious or unexplainable in ordinary terms" (1961: 11).

Expanding the definition of religion beyond spiritual and superhuman beings to include the extraordinary, the mysterious, and unexplainable allows a more comprehensive view of religious behaviors among the peoples of the world and permits the anthropological investigation of phenomena such as magic, sorcery, curses, and other practices that hold meaning for both pre-literate and literate societies. For this reason, this book focuses on the concept of the "supernatural" and incorporates a wide variety of contemporary examples of religious beliefs and practices that demonstrate the breadth of human ideology.

Through their comparative research anthropologists have shown that religious practices and beliefs vary in part as a result of the level of social structure in a given society. In *The Birth of the Gods* (1960), Guy Swanson applied a statistical approach to support the argument that religious forms are related to social development, and in *Religion: An Anthropological View* (1966: 84–101), Anthony F. C. Wallace presented a provocative typology of religious behavior based on the concept of the cult institution—"a set of rituals all having the same general goal, all explicitly rationalized by a set of similar or related beliefs, and all supported by the same social group" (p. 75). Ranging from the simplest to the most complex, Wallace describes individualistic, shamanic, communal, and ecclesiastical cult institutions. Each succeeding or more complex level contains all components of those preceding it. The ecclesiastical, for example, contains all of the elements of the less complex individualistic, shamanistic, and communal cult institutions.

According to Wallace, in the simplist, *individu-*

alistic cult institution, each person functions as his or her own specialist without need for such intermediaries as shamans or priests. Examples occur in both modern and primitive societies (the dream cult among the Iroquois, sealing magic among the Trobriand Islanders, and various cults among the Americans). The next level, the *shamanic*, also found in cultures around the world, marks the beginning of a religious division of labor. Individual part-time practitioners are designated by experience, birth, or training to help lay clients enlist the aid of the supernatural. The *communal* cult institution is even more complex, with laypeople handling important religious rituals for people in such special categories as secret societies, kinship groups, and age groups. (Examples include the ancestor ceremonies of the Chinese and some African tribal groups, Iroquois agricultural rituals, and Australian puberty rituals.) Although specialists such as shamans, skilled speakers, and dancers may participate, the lay group assumes the primary responsibility for conducting the sacred performance; an extensive religious hierarchy is still not in evidence. It is in the fourth, *ecclesiastical* cult institution that a professional religious clergy is formally elected or appointed and the division of labor is sharply drawn, with the laymen usually passive participants instead of active performers. Ecclesiastical cult institutions have characteristically worshipped either an Olympian pantheon of gods (as among the ancient Greeks and Romans) or a monotheistic deity (as among the Judeo-Christian and Moslem religions).

The differences between religious behavior and belief in so-called primitive and modern cultures has been of great interest to anthropologists over the years. William Howells (1962: 5) observed several characteristics that he believed distinguished the major world religions from the belief systems of more primitive cultures. First, the "great faiths" are messianic, their origins stemming from such charismatic figures as Jesus, Buddha, and Muhammed. Second, they have a rigid ethical form. Third, each has a missionary, imperialistic aspect, seeing itself as the one and only religion. Finally, each displays an exclusiveness in its belief system to the degree of being intolerant of other faiths. Howells is quick to point out that he has been generalizing, reminding the

reader that the varied nature and heterogeneity of native cults may make an understanding of their nature arduous, especially for anyone aware only of the differences among Christian sects (1962: 6). His concluding remark is important to an understanding of all the articles in this book; referring to the "perfect legitimacy" of native cults, he states that the "primitive devotees are not people of another planet, but are essentially exactly like us, and are engaged with precisely the same kind of religious appetite as the civilized. And that appetite is fed and stilled by their own religions. This is very important; it is why we are taking those religions seriously. They are not toys. They are what we might be doing ourselves; and they are what most of our ancestors were indeed doing, two thousand years ago today" (1962: 7).

The four articles in this chapter have been selected to provide a basic understanding of the anthropological approach to the study of the supernatural. Each stresses the use of the comparative method, the very anchor for anthropological thought. In the first selection Clifford Geertz provides us with a taste of the comparative approach, not so much by comparing the religious behaviors of several different cultures— as occurs throughout the book—as by comparing various academic approaches to the study of the supernatural. What is the historical approach? How does it differ from the psychological approach? What are the sociological and semantic approaches, and how does the anthropological approach differ from all the above? In the second selection Robert Lowie discusses the importance of fieldwork in the understanding of the role of religion in the life of the individual and the community. Now we see the true comparative approach at work. Although Lowie comments on religion among the Choctaw, the Maori of New Zealand, the Eskimo, the Apinaye of Northern Brazil, and in medieval Europe, most of his article is devoted to a comparison of religious belief and behavior among the Hopi of Arizona and the Crow of Montana—both of whom Lowie had studied in the field for many years. Lowie ends his article with a provocative commentary on what has happened to modern societies that have tried to eliminate religion. The Nazis are used as a prime example. Finally, Lowie seeks to understand the nature of the conflict between science and religion.

Next, Dorothy Lee's article on religious perspectives in anthropology shows how religion is part and parcel of a pre-literate people's total way of life. Lee tells us about pre-literate societies in which ceremonies and their preparation occupy most of a year. The last reading in this introductory chapter is John R. Cole's "Anthropology Beyond the Fringe," which marks the beginning of a practice that will occur throughout the book: the inclusion of an article, always the last in the chapter, on a topic from contemporary United States. In this instance, Cole examines the role of anthropology in the examination of such popular phenomena as UFOs, Bigfoot, ESP, the paranormal, creationism, psychic archaeology, and the like. Cole discusses the need for anthropologists to be more critical in their acceptance of their informants' accounts of reality, forcefully arguing that anthropologists make greater use of empirical testing in their study of the paranormal world.

References Cited

Howells, William
1962 *The Heathens: Primitive Man and His Religions.* Garden City, N.Y.: Doubleday.

Norbeck, Edward
1961 *Religion in Primitive Society.* New York: Harper and Brothers.

Spiro, Melford E.
1966 "Religion: Problems of Definition and Explanation." In Michael Banton, ed., *Anthropological Approaches to the Study of Religion,* pp. 85–126. London: Tavistock Publications Limited for the Association of Social Anthropologists of the Commonwealth.

Swanson, Guy
1960 *The Birth of the Gods: The Origin of Primitive Beliefs.* Ann Arbor: University of Michigan Press.

Wallace, A. F. C.
1966 *Religion: An Anthropological View.* New York: Random House.

Religion
Clifford Geertz

In Clifford Geertz's classic work, "Religion as a Cultural System" (1966), the author argued for a broadened analysis of religion. This argument, aimed primarily at the narrowness of the British sociological approach to the study of comparative religion, was accepted by American ethnologists and reflected in their contemporary research. In the following 1972 article Geertz pursues his goal, demonstrating the importance of his historical, psychological, sociological, and semantic approaches to the study of religion, and concluding that a mature theory of religion will consist of an integration of them all into a conceptual system whose exact form remains to be discovered. In addition to extensive field work in Java, Professor Geertz has also conducted research in Bali and Morocco.

Reprinted by permission of the publisher from *International Encyclopedia of the Social Sciences*, David L. Sills, Editor. Vol. 13, pp. 398–406. Copyright © 1972 by Crowell Collier and Macmillan, Inc.

THE ANTHROPOLOGICAL STUDY OF RELIGION HAS been highly sensitive to changes in the general intellectual and moral climate of the day; at the same time, it has been a powerful factor in the creation of that climate. Since the early discussion by Edward Tylor, interest in the beliefs and rituals of distant, ancient, or simpler peoples has been shaped by an awareness of contemporary issues. The questions that anthropologists have pursued among exotic religions have arisen from the workings—or the misworkings—of modern Western society, and particularly from its restless quest for self-discovery. In turn, their findings have profoundly affected the course that quest has taken and the perspective at which it has arrived.

Perhaps the chief reason for the rather special role of comparative religious studies is that issues which, when raised within the context of Western culture, led to extreme social resistance and personal turmoil could be freely and even comfortably handled in terms of bizarre, presumably primitive, and thus—also presumably —fanciful materials from long ago or far away. The study of "primitive religions" could pass as the study of superstition, supposedly unrelated to the serious religious and moral concerns of advanced civilization, at best either a sort of vague foreshadowing of them or a grotesque parody upon them. This made it possible to approach all sorts of touchy subjects, such as polytheism, value relativism, possession, and faith healing, from a frank and detached point of view. One could ask searching questions about the historicity of myth among Polynesians; when asked in relation to Christianity, these same questions were, until quite recently, deeply threatening. One could discuss the projection of erotic wishes found in the "totemic" rites of Australian aborigines, the social roots and functions of African "ancestor worship," or the protoscientific quality of Melanesian "magical thought," without involving oneself in polemical debate and emotional distress. The application of the comparative method—the essence of anthropological thought—to religion permitted the growth of a resolutely scientific approach to the spiritual dimensions of human life.

Through the thin disguise of comparative method the revolutionary implications of the work of such men as Tylor, Durkheim, Robertson Smith, Freud, Malinowski, and Radcliffe-Brown soon became apparent—at first mainly to philosophers, theologians, and literary figures, but eventually to the educated public in general. The meticulous descriptions of tribal curiosities such as soul loss, shamanism, circumcision, blood sacrifice, sorcery, tree burial, garden magic, symbolic cannibalism, and animal worship have been caught up in some of the grander intellectual battles of the last hundred years—from those over evolutionism and historicism in the late nineteenth century to those over positivism and existentialism today. Psychoanalysts and phenomenologists, Marxists and Kantians, racists and egalitarians, absolutists and relativists, empiricists and rationalists, believers and skeptics have all had recourse to the record—partial, inconsistent, and shot through with simple error as it is—of the spiritual life of tribal peoples to support their positions and belabor those of their opponents. If interest in "primitive religion" among savants of all sorts has been remarkably high, consensus concerning its nature and significance has not.

At least three major intellectual developments have exercised a critical influence on the anthropological study of religion: (1) the emergence, in the latter half of the nineteenth century, of history as the sovereign science of man; (2) the positivist reaction against this sovereignty in the first decades of the twentieth century and the radical split of the social sciences into resolutely psychologically approaches, on the one hand, and resolutely sociological ones, on the other; and (3) the growth, in the interwar period, of a concern with the role of ideational factors in the regulation of social life. With the first of these came an emphasis on the nature of primitive reasoning and the stages of its evolution into civilized thought. With the second came an investigation of the emotional basis of religious ritual and belief and the separate examination of the role of ritual and belief in social integration. The concern with value systems and other features of the ideational realm led to an exploration of the philosophical dimensions of religious ideas, particularly the symbolic vehicles in terms of which those ideas are expressed.

Evolutionism and Its Enemies

Like so much else in anthropology, the study of the religious notions of primitive peoples arose within the context of evolutionary theory. In the nineteenth century, to think systematically about human affairs was to think historically—to seek out survivals of the most elementary forms and to trace the steps by which these forms subsequently developed. And though, in fact, Tylor, Morgan, Frazer, and the rest drew more on the synthetic social-stage theories of such men as Comte and Hegel than on the analytic random-variation and natural-selection ideas of Darwin, the grand concept of evolution was shared by both streams of thought: namely, that the complex, heterogeneous present has arisen, more or less gradually, out of a simpler, more uniform past. The relics of this past are still to be found scattered, like Galápagos turtles, in out-of-the-way places around us. Tylor, an armchair scholar, made no "voyage of the *Beagle.*" But in combing and organizing the reports of missionaries, soldiers, and explorers, he proceeded from the same general premise as did Darwin, and indeed most of the leading minds of the day. For them a comprehensive, historically oriented comparison of all forms of a phenomenon, from the most primitive to the most advanced, was the royal road to understanding the nature of the phenomenon itself.

In Tylor's view, the elementary form out of which all else developed was spirit worship—*animism*. The minimal definition of religion was "a belief in spiritual beings." The understanding of religion thus came down to an understanding of the basis upon which such a belief arose at its most primitive level. Tylor's theory was intellectualistic. Belief in spirits began as an uncritical but nonetheless rational effort to explain such puzzling empirical phenomena as death, dreams, and possession. The notion of a separable soul rendered these phenomena intelligible in terms of soul departure, soul wandering, and soul invasion. Tylor believed that the idea of a soul was used to explain more and more remote and hitherto inexplicable natural occurrences, until virtually every tree and rock was haunted by some sort of gossamer presence. The higher, more developed forms of "belief in spiritual beings," first polytheism, ultimately monotheism, were founded upon this animistic basis, the urphilosophy of all mankind, and were refined through a process of critical questioning by more advanced thinkers. For this earnest Quaker the religious history of the world was a history of progressive, even inevitable, enlightenment.

This intellectualistic, "up from darkness" strain has run through most evolutionist thought about religion. For Frazer, a nineteenth-century figure who lived for forty years into the twentieth century without finding it necessary to alter either his views or his methods, the mental progress involved was from magic to religion to science. Magic was the primordial form of human thought; it consisted in mistaking either spatiotemporal connection ("sympathetic magic," as when drinking the blood of an ox transfers its strength to the drinker) or phenomenal similarity ("imitative magic," as when the sound of drumming induces thunderheads to form) for true scientific causality. For Durkheim, evolutionary advance consisted in the emergence of specific, analytic, *profane* ideas about "cause" or "category" or "relationship" from diffuse, global, *sacred* images. These "collective representations," as he called them, of the social order and its moral force included such sacra as "mana," "totem," and "god." For Max Weber, the process was one of "rationalization": the progressive organization of religious concern into certain more precisely defined, more specifically focused, and more systematically conceived cultural forms. The level of sophistication of such theories (and, hence, their present relevance) varies very widely. But, like Tylor's, they all conceive of the evolution of religion as a process of cultural differentiation: the diffuse, all-embracing, but rather unsystematic and uncritical religious practices of primitive peoples are transformed into the more specifically focused, more regularized, less comprehensively authoritative practices of the more advanced civilizations. Weber, in whom both intellectualism and optimism were rather severely tempered by a chronic apprehensiveness, called this transformation the "disenchantment (*Entzauberung) of the world."

On the heels of evolutionism came, of course,

anti-evolutionism. This took two quite different forms. On one side there was a defense, mainly by Roman Catholic scholars, of the so-called degradation theory. According to this theory, the original revelation of a high god to primitive peoples was later corrupted by human frailty into the idol worship of present-day tribal peoples. On the other side there was an attack, mainly by American scholars of the Boas school, upon the "armchair speculation" of evolutionary thinkers and a call for its replacement by more phenomenological approaches to the study of tribal custom.

The first of these reactions led, logically enough, to a search among the most primitive of existing peoples for traces of belief in a supreme being. The resulting dispute, protracted, often bitter, and stubbornly inconclusive as to the existence of such "primitive monotheism," turned out to be unproductive—aside from some interesting discussions by Lang (1898) concerning culture heroes and by Eliade (1949) concerning sky gods—and both the issue and the theory that gave rise to it have now receded from the center of scholarly attention. The second reaction has had a longer life and great impact on ethnographic methodology, but it too is now in partial eclipse. Its main contributions—aside from some devastating empirical demolitions of evolutionist generalization—came in the field of cultural diffusion. Leslie Spier's study of the spread of the Sun Dance through the Great Plains (1921) and A. L. Kroeber's application of the age-area approach to aboriginal religion in California are good examples of productive diffusion studies. However, apart from their importance for culture history, the contribution of such distributional studies to our understanding of religious ideas, attitudes, and practices as such has not been great, and few students now pursue these studies. The call of the Boas school for thorough field research and disciplined inductive analysis has been heeded; but its fruits, insofar as religious studies are concerned, have been reaped by others less inhibited theoretically.

Psychological Approaches

The major reaction against the intellectual tradition of the cultural evolutionists took place not within anthropology, however, but in the general context of the positivist revolt against the domination of historicist modes of thought in the social sciences. In the years before World War I the rise of the systematic psychologism of psychoanalysis and of the equally systematic sociologism of the *Année sociologique* forced evolutionist theorizing into the background, even though the leaders of both movements—Freud and Durkheim—were themselves still very strongly influenced by it. Perhaps even more relevant, it introduced a sharp split into anthropological studies of religion which has resolved into the militantly psychodynamic and the militantly social-structural approaches.

Freud's major work in this field is, of course, *Totem and Taboo*, a book anthropologists in general have had great difficulty in evaluating—as Kroeber's two reviews of it, the first facilely negative, the second, two decades later, ambivalently positive, demonstrate. The source of the difficulty has been an inability or an unwillingness to disentangle Freud's basic thesis—that religious rituals and beliefs are homologous with neurotic symptoms—from the chimerical ethnology and obsolete biology within which he insisted upon setting it. Thus, the easy demolition of what Kroeber called Freud's "just so story" concerning primal incest, parricide, and guilt within some protohuman horde ("in the beginning was the deed") was all too often mistaken for total rejection of the rather more penetrating proposition that the obsessions, dreams, and fantasies of collective life spring from the same intrapsychic sources as do those of the isolated individual.

For those who read further in Freud's writings, however—especially in "Mourning and Melancholia" and "Obsessive Acts and Religious Practices"—it became apparent that what was at issue was the applicability of theories concerning the forms and causes of individual psychopathology to the explanation of the forms and causes of public myth and group ritual. Róheim (1950) analyzed Australian circumcision rites against the background of orthodox Freudian theories of psychosexual development, especially those clustered around the Oedipal predicament. However, he explicitly avoided recourse to speculations about buried memories of primordial occurrences. Bettelheim (1954) adopted a similar, though more systematic and less orthodox, approach to initiation practices generally, seeing them as socially instituted symbolic mechanisms for the definition and stabilization of sexual identity. Kardiner (1945), taking a neo-Freudian position, sought to demonstrate that the religious institutions of tribal peoples were projections of a "basic personality structure," formed not by the action of an unconsciously remembered historical trauma but by the more observable traumas produced by child-training practices, an approach later extended and cast into quantitative form by Whiting (Whiting and Child 1953). Erikson (1950), drawing upon developments in ego psychology which conceived the emergence of the adult personality to be a joint product of psychobiological maturation, cultural context, and historical experience, interpreted the religious notions of the Yurok and the Sioux in terms of certain basic modes of relating to the world. These relationships gradually developed during the whole course of childhood and adolescence. Others—notably Devereux (1951)—have attempted to use the autobiographical, case-history approach to determine the relations between personality dynamics and religious orientation in particular individuals; still others—notably Hallowell (1937–1954)—have employed projective tests, questionnaires, reports of dreams, or systematic interviews toward similar ends.

In all such studies, even when individual authors have dissented from many of Freud's specific views, the basic premise has been Freudian: that religious practices can be usefully interpreted as expressions of unconscious psychological forces—and this has become, amid much polemic, an established tradition of inquiry. In recent years, however, responsible work of this type has come to question the degree to which one is justified in subjecting historically created and socially institutionalized cultural forms to a system of analysis founded on the treatment of the mental illnesses of individuals. For this reason, the future of this approach depends perhaps more upon developments within psychoanalysis, now in a somewhat uncertain state, than within anthropology. So far, perhaps only Kluckhohn's pioneering *Navaho Witchcraft* (1944) has attempted to systematically relate psychological factors to social and cultural aspects of primitive religion. The great majority of psychoanalytic studies of tribal beliefs and rites remain willfully parochial.

In any case, not all psychological approaches to religion have been Freudian. Jungian influences have had a certain impact, especially on studies of myth. Campbell (1949), for example, has stressed the continuity of certain themes both cross-culturally and temporally. These themes have been interpreted as expressions of transpersonal constancies in unconscious mental functioning which are at the same time expressions of fundamental cosmic realities.

Simple emotionalist theories have also been extremely popular. There have been two main varieties of these: awe theories and confidence theories. Awe theories have been based on some usually rather vague notion of "religious thrill" experienced by human beings when brought face to face with cosmic forces. A wide range of ethnologists, from Max Müller through Lang and Marett to Lowie and Goldenweiser, have accepted such theories in one form or another. However, awe theories remain mere notations of the obvious—that religious experience is, in the nature of the case, touched with intense feelings of the grandeur of the universe in relation to the self and of the vulnerability of the self in relation to the universe. This is not explanation, but circular reasoning.

Confidence theories also begin with a notion of man's inward sense of weakness, and especially of his fears—of disease, of death, of ill fortune of all kinds—and they see religious practices as designed to quiet such fears, either by explaining them away, as in doctrines of the afterlife, or by claiming to link the individual to external sources of strength, as in prayer. The best-known confidence theory was that set forth by Malinowski. He regarded magic as enabling man to pursue uncertain but essential endeavors by assuring him of their ultimate success. Confidence, or anxiety-reduction, theories, like awe theories, clearly have empirical foundation but do not adequately explore the complex relationship between fear and religious activity. They are not rooted in any systematic conceptualization of mental functioning and so merely point to matters desperately in need of clarification, without in fact clarifying them.

Sociological Approaches

The sociological approach to the analysis of the religions of nonliterate peoples proceeded independent of, and even at variance with, the psychoanalytic approach, but it shared a concern with the same phenomenon: the peculiar "otherness,"

the extraordinary, momentous, "set apart" quality of sacred (or "taboo") acts and objects, as contrasted with the profane. The intense aura of high seriousness was traced by Freud to the projection of unacceptable wishes repressed from consciousness onto external objects. The dramatic ambivalence of the sacred—its paradoxical unification of the commanded and the forbidden, the pure and the polluted, the salutary and the dangerous—was a symbolic expression of the underlying ambivalence of human desires. For Durkheim, too, the extraordinary atmosphere surrounding sacred acts and objects was symbolic of a hidden reality, but a social, not a psychological one: the moral force of the human community.

Durkheim believed that the integrity of the social order was the primary requisite for human survival, and the means by which that integrity superseded individual egocentricity was the primary problem of sociological analysis. He saw Australian totemism (which he, like Freud, made the empirical focus of his work) as a mechanism to this end. For example, the collective rituals involving the emblems of the totemic beings—the so-called bull roarers—aroused the heightened emotions of mass behavior and evoked a deep sense of moral identification among the participants. The creation of social solidarity was the result of the common public veneration, by specific groups of persons, of certain carefully designated symbolic objects. These objects had no intrinsic value except as perceptible representations of the social identity of the individuals. Collective worship of consecrated bits of painted wood or stone created a moral community, a "church," upon which rested the viability of the major social units. These sanctified objects thus represented the system of rights and obligations implicit in the social order and the individual's unformulated sense of its overriding significance in his life. All sacred objects, beliefs, and acts, and the extraordinary emotions attending them, were outward expressions of inward social necessities, and, in a famous phrase, God was the "symbol of society." Few anthropologists have been able to swallow Durkheim's thesis whole, when put this baldly. But the more moderate proposition that religious rituals and beliefs both reflect and act to support the moral framework underlying social arrangements (and are in turn animated by it) has given rise to what has become perhaps the most popular form of analysis in the anthropological study of religion. Usually called "functionalism"—or sometimes, to distinguish it from certain variants deemed objectionable, "structuralism"—this approach found its champion in Radcliffe-Brown and its major development in Great Britain, though its influence has now spread very much more widely.

Radcliffe-Brown (1952) agreed with Durkheim's postulate that the main role (or "function") of religion was to celebrate and sustain the norms upon which the integration of society depends. But unlike Durkheim (and like Freud), Radcliffe-Brown was concerned with the content of sacred symbols, and particularly with the reasons why one object rather than another was absorbed into rite or woven into myth. Why here stones, there water holes, here camp circles, there personified winds?

Durkheim had held this to be an arbitrary matter, contingent upon historical accident or psychological proclivity, beyond the reach of and irrelevant to sociological analysis. Radcliffe-Brown considered, however, that man's need for a concrete expression of social solidarity was not sufficient explanation of the structure of a people's religious system. Something was needed to tie the particular objects awarded sacred status (or, in his terminology, "ritual value") to the particular social interests they presumably served and reflected. Radcliffe-Brown, resolute empiricist that he was, chose a solution Durkheim had already magisterially demolished: the utilitarian. The objects selected for religious veneration by a given people were either directly or indirectly connected to factors critical to their collective well-being. Things that had real, that is, practical, "social value" were elevated to having spiritual, or symbolic, "ritual value," thus fusing the social and the natural into one overarching order. For primitives at least (and Radcliffe-Brown attempted to establish his theory with regard to the sanctified turtles and palm leaves of the pre-agricultural Andaman Islanders and, later on, with regard to Australian totemism), there is no discontinuity, no difference even, between moral and physical, spiritual and practical relationships and processes. These people regard both men and things as parts of a single normative system. Within that system those elements which are critical to its effective functioning (or, sometimes, phenomena empirically associated with such elements, such as the Andaman cicada cycle and the shifting monsoons) are made the objects of that special sort of respect and attention which we call religious but which the people themselves regard as merely prudential.

Radcliffe-Brown focused upon the content of sacred symbols and emphasized the relation between conceptions of the moral order of existence and conceptions of its natural order. However, the claim that the sanctity of religious objects derives from their practical social importance is one of those theories which works when it works and doesn't when it doesn't. Not only has it proved impossible to find even an indirect practical significance in most of the enormous variety of things tribal peoples have regarded as sacred (certain Australian tribes worship vomit), but the view that religious concerns are mere ritualizations of real-life concerns leaves the phenomenon of sacredness itself—its aura of mystery, power, fascination—totally unexplained.

More recent structuralist studies have tended to evade both these questions and to concentrate on the role played by religion in maintaining social equilibrium. They attempt to show how given sets of religious practices (ancestor worship, animal sacrifice, witchcraft and sorcery, regeneration rites) do in fact express and reinforce the moral values underlying crucial processes (lineage segmentation, marriage, conflict adjudication, political succession) in the particular society under investigation. Arnold van Gennep's study of crisis rites was perhaps the most important forerunner of the many analyses of this type. Although valuable in their own right as ethnography and as sociology, these structural formulations have been severely limited by their rigid avoidance on the one side, of the kind of psychological considerations that could account for the peculiar emotions which permeate religious belief and practice, and, on the other, of the philosophical considerations that could render their equally peculiar content intelligible.

The Analysis of Symbolic Forms

In contrast to other approaches—evolutionary psychological sociological—the field of what we may loosely call "semantic studies" of religion is extremely jumbled. There is, as yet, no well-established central trend to analysis, no central figure around whom to order debate, and no readily apparent system of interconnections relating the various competing trends to one another.

Perhaps the most straightforward strategy—certainly the most disarming—is merely to *accept* the myriad expressions of the sacred in primitive societies, to consider them as actual ingressions of the divine into the world, and to trace the forms these expressions have taken across the earth and through time. The result would be a sort of natural history of revelation, whose aim would be to isolate the major classes of religious phenomena considered as authentic manifestations of the sacred—what Eliade, the chief proponent of this approach, calls hierophanies—and to trace the rise, dominance, decline, and disappearance of these classes within the changing contexts of human life. The meaning of religious activity, the burden of its content, is discovered through a meticulous, wholly inductive investigation of the natural modalities of such behavior (sun worship, water symbolism, fertility cults, renewal myths, etc.) and of the vicissitudes these modalities undergo when projected, like the Son of God himself, into the flux of history.

Metaphysical questions (here uncommonly obtrusive) aside, the weaknesses of this approach derive from the same source as its strengths: a drastic limiting of the interpretations of religion to the sort that a resolutely Baconian methodology can produce. On the one hand, this approach has led, especially in the case of a scholar as erudite and indefatigable as Eliade, to the uncovering of some highly suggestive clusterings of certain religious patterns with particular historical conditions—for example, the frequent association of sun worship, activist conceptions of divine power, cultic veneration of deified heroes, elitist doctrines of political sovereignty, and imperialist ideologies of national expansion. But, on the other hand, it has placed beyond the range of scientific analysis everything but the history and morphology of the phenomenal forms of religious expression. The study of tribal beliefs and practices is reduced to a kind of cultural paleontology whose sole aim is the reconstruction, from scattered and corrupted fragments, of the "mental universe of archaic man."

Primitive Thought

Other scholars who are interested in the meaningful content of primitive religion but who are in-

capable of so thoroughgoing a suspension of disbelief as Eliade, or are repelled by the cultic overtones of this somewhat mystagogic line of thought, have directed their attention instead toward logical and epistemological considerations. This has produced a long series of studies that view "primitive thought" as a distinctive mode of reasoning and/or a special body of knowledge. From Lévy-Bruhl through Lévi-Strauss, and with important contributions from members of the evolutionary, psychoanalytic, and sociological schools as well, this line of exploration has persisted as a minor theme in anthropological studies of religion. With the recent advances in linguistics, information theory, the analysis of cognition, semantic philosophy, modern logic, and certain sorts of literary investigation, the systematic study of symbolic activity bids fair to become, in a rather thoroughly revised form, the major theme for investigation. The "new key" Susanne K. Langer heard being struck in philosophy in the early 1940s—"the concern with the concept of meaning in all its forms"—has, like the historicist and positivist "keys" before it, begun to have its echo in the anthropological study of religion. Anthropologists are increasingly interested in ideational expression, increasingly concerned with the vehicles, processes, and practical applications of human conceptualization.

The development of this approach has come in two fairly distinct phases, one before and one after World War II. In the first phase there was a concern with "the mind of primitive man" and in particular with its capacity for rational thought. In a sense, this concern represented the evolutionists' interest in primitive reasoning processes detached from the historicist context. In the second phase, which is still in process, there has been a move away from, and in part a reaction against, the subjectivist emphasis of the earlier work. Ideational expression is thought of as a public activity, rather like speech, and the structure of the symbolic materials, the "language," in whose terms the activity is conducted becomes the subject of investigation.

The first, subjectivist, phase was animated by a protracted wrangle between those who used the religious beliefs and practices of tribal peoples as evidence to prove that there was a qualitative difference between the thought processes of primitives and those of civilized men and the anthropologists who considered such religious activity as evidence for the lack of any such differences. The great protagonist of the first school was the French philosopher Lévy-Bruhl whose theories of "prelogical mentality" were as controversial within anthropology as they were popular outside it. According to Lévy-Bruhl, the thought of primitives, as reflected in their religious ideas, is not governed by the immanent laws of Aristotelian logical reasoning, but by affectivity—by the vagrant flow of emotion and the dialectical principles of "mystical participation" and "mystical exclusion."

The two most effective antagonists of Lévy-Bruhl's theories concerning primitive religion were Radin and Malinowski. Radin, influenced by Boas' more general attacks on theories of "primitive mentality," sought to demonstrate that primitive religious thought reaches, on occasion, very high levels of logical articulation and philosophical sophistication and that tribal society contains, alongside the common run of unreflective doers ("men of action"), contemplative intellectuals ("men of thought") of boldness, subtlety, and originality. Malinowski attacked the problem on an even broader front. Using his ethnographic knowledge of the Trobriand Islanders, Malinowski argued that alongside their religious and magical notions (which he, too, regarded as mainly emotionally determined) the "savages" also had a rather well-developed and, as far as it went, accurate empirical knowledge of gardening, navigation, housebuilding, canoe construction, and other useful arts. He further claimed that they were absolutely clear as to the distinction between these two sorts of reasoning, between mystical-magical and empirical-pragmatic thinking, and never confused them in actual practice. Of these two arguments, the former seems to be today nearly universally accepted and was perhaps never in fact really questioned. But with respect to the latter, serious doubts have arisen concerning whether the lines between "science," "magic," and "religion" are as simple and clear-cut in the minds of tribal peoples (or any peoples) as Malinowski, never one for shaded judgments, portrayed them. Nevertheless, between them, Radin and Malinowski rather definitively demolished the notion of a radical qualitative gap between the thought processes of primitive and civilized men. Indeed, toward the end of his life even Lévy-Bruhl admitted that his arguments had been badly cast and might better have been phrased in terms of different modes of thinking common to all men. (In fact, Freud, with his contrast between primary and secondary thinking processes, had already made this distinction.)

Thus, the debate about what does or does not go on in the heads of savages exhausted itself in generalities, and recent writers have turned to a concern with the symbolic forms, the conceptual resources, in terms of which primitives (and non-primitives) think. The major figure in this work has been Claude Lévi-Strauss, although this line of attack dates back to Durkheim and Mauss's influential 1903 essay in sociological Kantianism, *Primitive Classification*. The writings of E. E. Evans-Pritchard on Zande witchcraft, Benjamin Whorf on Hopi semantics, and Gregory Bateson on Iatmul ritual and, among non-anthropologists, works by Granet, Cassirer, and Piaget have directed attention to the study of symbolic formulation.

Symbolic Systems

Lévi-Strauss, whose rather highly wrought work is still very much in progress, is concerned with the systems of classification, the "homemade" taxonomies, employed by tribal peoples to order the objects and events of their world (see Lévi-Strauss 1958; 1962). In this, he follows in the footsteps of Durkheim and Mauss. But rather than looking, as they did, to social forms for the origins and explanations of such categorical systems, he looks to the symbolic structures in terms of which they are formulated, expressed, and applied. Myth and, in a slightly different way, rite are systems of signs that fix and organize abstract conceptual relationships in terms of concrete images and thus make speculative thought possible. They permit the construction of a "science of the concrete"—the intellectual comprehension of the sensible world in terms of sensible phenomena—which is no less rational, no less logical, no more affect-driven than the abstract science of the modern world. The objects rendered sacred are selected not because of their utilitarian qualities, nor because they are projections of repressed emotions, nor yet because they reflect the moral force of social organization ritualistically impressed upon the mind. Rather, they are selected because they permit the embodiment of general ideas in terms of the immediately perceptible realities—the turtles, trees, springs, and caves—of everyday experience; not, as Lévi-Strauss says, apropos of Radcliffe-Brown's view of totems, because they are "good to eat," but because they are "good to think."

This "goodness" exists inherently in sacred objects because they provide the raw materials for analogical reasoning. The relationships perceived among certain classes of natural objects or events can be analogized, taken as models of relationships —physical, social, psychological, or moral—obtaining between persons, groups, or other natural objects and events. Thus, for example, the natural distinctions perceived among totemic beings, their species differentiation, can serve as a conceptual framework for the comprehension, expression, and communication of social distinctions among exogamous clans—their structural differentiation. Thus, the sharp contrast between the wet and dry seasons (and the radical zoological and botanical changes associated with it) in certain regions of Australia is employed in the mythology of the native peoples. They have woven an elaborate origin myth around this natural phenomenon, one that involves a rainmaking python who drowned some incestuous sisters and their children because the women polluted his water hole with menstrual blood. This model expresses and economizes the contrasts between moral purity and impurity, maleness and femaleness, social superiority and inferiority, fertilizing agent (rain) and that which is fertilized (land), and even the distinction between "high" (initiate) and "low" (noninitiate) levels of cultural achievement.

Lévi-Strauss contends that primitive religious systems are, like all symbolic systems, fundamentally communications systems. They are carriers of information in the technical Shannon-Weaver sense, and as such, the theory of information can be applied to them with the same validity as when applied to any physical systems, mechanical or biological, in which the transfer of information plays a central regulative role. Primitives, as all men, are quintessentially multichanneled emitters and receivers of messages. It is merely in the nature of the code they employ—one resting on analogies between "natural" and "cultural" distinctions and relationships—that they differ from ourselves. Where there is a distinguishing difference, it lies in the technically specialized codes of modern abstract thought, in which semantic properties are radically and deliberately severed from physical ones. Religion, primitive or modern, can be understood only as an integrated system of thought, logically sound, epistemologically valid, and as flourishing in France as in Tahiti.

It is far too early to evaluate Lévi-Strauss's work with any assurance. It is frankly incomplete and explorative, and some parts of it (the celebration of information theory, for example) are wholly programmatic. But in focusing on symbol systems as conceptual models of social or other sorts of reality, he has clearly introduced into the anthropology of religion a line of inquiry which, having already become common in modern thought generally, can hardly fail to be productive when applied to tribal myth and ritual.

Whether his own particular formulation of this approach will prove to be the most enduring remains, however, rather more of a question. His rejection of emotional considerations and his neglect of normative or social factors in favor of an extreme intellectualism which cerebralizes religion and tends to reduce it yet again to a kind of undeveloped (or, as he puts it, "undomesticated") science are questionable. His nearly exclusive stress on those intellectual processes involved in classification, i.e., on taxonomic modes of thought (a reflex of his equally great reliance on totemic ideas as type cases of primitive beliefs), at the expense of other, perhaps more common, and certainly more powerful styles of reasoning, is also doubtful. His conception of the critical process of symbolic formulation itself remains almost entirely undeveloped—hardly more than a sort of associationism dressed up with some concepts from modern linguistics. Partly as a result of this weakness and partly as a result of a tendency to consider symbol systems as entities functioning independently of the contextual factor, many of his specific interpretations of particular myths and rites seem as strained, arbitrary, and oversystematized as those of the most undisciplined psychoanalyst.

But, for all this, Lévi-Strauss has without doubt opened a vast territory for research and begun to explore it with theoretical brilliance and profound scholarship. And he is not alone. As the recent work of such diverse students as Evans-Pritchard, R. G. Lienhardt, W. E. H. Stanner, Victor W. Turner, Germaine Dieterlen, Meyer Fortes, Edmund R. Leach, Charles O. Frake, Rodney Needham, and Susanne K. Langer demonstrates, the analysis of symbolic forms is becoming a major tradition in the study of primitive religion—in fact, of religion in general. Each of these writers has a somewhat different approach. But all seem to share the conviction that an attempt must be made to approach primitive religions for what they are: systems of ideas about the ultimate shape and substance of reality.

Whatever else religion does, it relates a view of the ultimate nature of reality to a set of ideas of how man is well advised, even obligated, to live. Religion tunes human actions to a view of the cosmic order and projects images of cosmic order onto the plane of human existence. In religious belief and practice a people's style of life, what Clyde Kluckhohn called their *design for living*, is rendered intellectually reasonable; it is shown to represent a way of life ideally adapted to the world "as it 'really' ('fundamentally,' 'ultimately') is." At the same time, the supposed basic structure of reality is rendered emotionally convincing because it is presented as an actual state of affairs uniquely accommodated to such a way of life and permitting it to flourish. Thus do received beliefs, essentially metaphysical, and established norms, essentially moral, confirm and support one another.

It is this mutual confirmation that religious symbols express and celebrate and that any scientific analysis of religion must somehow contrive to explain and clarify. In the development of such an analysis historical, psychological, sociological, and what has been called here semantic considerations are all necessary, but none is sufficient. A mature theory of religion will consist of an integration of them all into a conceptual system whose exact form remains to be discovered.

Religion in Human Life

Robert H. Lowie

*In this article Robert H. Lowie demonstrates
the importance of anthropological field work in
understanding the role of religion in the life of the
individual and the community. The universality
of religious practice led Lowie, and other
anthropologists, to perceive religion as a cultural
phenomenon that clearly demanded their attention.
Referring to his own field work among the Hopi of
Arizona and the Crow of Montana, Lowie observes
that anthropologists must always understand the
belief system of the people they study if they are
to discover how a faith serves to integrate the
individual's behavior in society. Lowie also explores
the important relationship between religion and
science, noting several areas of conflict and
agreement. (Of long interest to anthropologists
before and after Lowie, this topic will be examined
extensively by Bronislaw Malinowski in Chapter 6.)
Although Lowie died in 1957, his work in
comparative religion, North American Indians, and
the history and theory of anthropology remains
important to contemporary scholars.*

Reproduced by permission of the American Anthropological Association, from *American Anthropologist*, Vol. 65 (1963), pp. 532–42 (abridged).

SINCE THIS ARTICLE IS CONCERNED WITH THE
moot matter of religion, I should perhaps begin
by making clear my own point of view and my
reasons for coming to the conclusions that I
have come to. My first awareness of religious
strife came from my grandfather before I left
Vienna at the age of ten; he had been an agnos-
tic from his medical student days, and he laid
the foundations for my own later attitudes.
From my parents I received no religious training
of any kind. By the time I was sixteen, I was
already reading the *philosophes* and imitating
their violent anti-clericalism and bitterness
toward all religion. This period continued, largely under the stimulus of and acquaintance with
Ernst Haeckel, until I was about 25. At this point
I was already going into the field as an ethnolo-
gist. It did not take long to discover that to the
primitive mind religion was of paramount importance. If I wanted to understand the Indians
of that period I simply had to study its values for
them. Moreover, my constant field trips brought
me into contact with dedicated men of all faiths
who were certainly deriving neither money nor
renown by being missionaries to a group of Indians on a remote reservation. They lived as other
members of the community did, in poverty, and
they remained with their charges through pesti-
lence and famine. One day it occurred to me
that both the Indians and the hardy souls who
were trying to convert them to Christianity had
some inner strength that I lacked. Nor was I
unique in this lack. I began to wonder how
many scientists would undergo for their science
the years of poverty that the priests and ministers willingly accepted for their religion.

Here clearly was a phenomenon of both
primitive and civilized life that warranted study.
So I began to collect information about native
religions on the same objective basis upon
which I assembled data on basket weaving, social organization, hunting, or any other aspect of

primitive life. Moreover, through my reading I discovered that no group of people had ever been found who did not have a religion of some kind. Since religion is a universal manifestation, it must have some value. I found also that despite the immense variations in the outward observances, the inner glow and the function of religion in the group were identical from one form to another. The Catholic priest, the Mormon missionary, the Eskimo shaman, the African witch doctor, and the Protestant clergyman were all alike in their sense of inner conviction, in their intense desire to help others, and in their dependence upon some force outside themselves that gave them courage. Fanatic, ignorant, or rigid they might be, but they were men of faith. I cannot say that I have become a religious man as the result of my study, but I have become an informed one; and I have seen too much to believe now in the dicta that I accepted in my youth. I no longer doubt that religion has a definite place in human life.

My position towards religion as a cultural phenomenon springs directly from my conception of anthropology as a *science*. Since it is a science it must take cognizance of values because these form an essential part of its subject matter; but it must treat these values objectively—that is, it must refrain from judgment. Thus, an anthropologist who is studying West African fetishism must stick to what he can see and hear for himself and what he can find out from informants as to the meaning of fetishism to them, but he must not judge it in terms of his own religious standards. Probably my own lack of religious training was an asset rather than a drawback, because I could not condemn any form of worship merely because it differed from mine. I could only view it as a human manifestation worthy of scientific investigation. This same point of view should certainly be extended to include the religions of one's own day. Yet I have known anthropologists who accorded a benevolent understanding to the Hopi but denied it to Catholics, Mormons, Buddhists, or Mohammedans. This dichotomy of viewpoint strikes me as ridiculous and completely unscientific. In short, I will study as many religions as I can, but I will judge none of them. I doubt if any other attitude is scientifically defensible.

To a modern intellectual, religion is probably the most unfamiliar subject in the world. He cannot, of course, remain wholly ignorant of its role in the past, but the sentiments of such men as St. Francis of Assisi, George Fox, or John Wesley are utterly remote and unintelligible. For many people the religious issue is intertwined with an adolescent revolt against parental authority or with a struggle for intellectual freedom. For others it has become a symbol of restriction, repression, and reaction. To still others it is either just plain mumbo jumbo or a narcotic. The former attitude is well illustrated by Voltaire's statement that religion began when the first knave duped the first fool. Marxians have their special brand of the second attitude: that it is an opiate with which exploiting capitalists lull the masses in order to fleece them with impunity. Most if not all of these attitudes are based upon a profound ignorance of what religion is and does.

While it is true that religion has lost ground during the past century, it has never ceased to sway the lives and fortunes of millions. And even if open allegiance to a church has become more rare as the decades have flowed past, the moral strength of religion has continued to influence people. During World War II many people either found religion for the first time or else returned to their former church for comfort and strength to bear the fears and pressures brought about by war. It should never be forgotten that all religions thrive on adversity. It is probable that the common attitude of indifference and apathy is caused primarily by too much prosperity.

The indifference is not confined to one church or to one country, as may be seen from the following two examples. In Italy the vast majority of the population is Catholic. Some of the people are certainly devout, but these come predominantly from the peasant class. The others—excluding a handful of freethinkers—are passive in their Catholicism. They have their children baptized by the Church; they are married and buried by the Church; but they seem to go through life without religious feeling or spiritual experience.

The situation is much the same in Protestant Sweden, where the people are overwhelmingly Lutheran and the king is constitutionally bound to profess the evangelical creed. But when one glances through a brief survey of Swedish life, one finds a good deal about the iron and match industries, about timbering and handicrafts, and about sports, but strangely little concerning the officially dominant faith as a force in shaping human lives. In the newspapers the sporting page, though shorter than in American dailies, is easily three times as long as the half-page or less that has to do with church or religion.

It was not of course like this in medieval Europe. Art, scholarship, philosophy, education, and crafts of every sort were all permeated by the Church. And the earlier crusades bear witness to the dynamic power of the Christian faith among the people. This all-pervasive character of religion has almost vanished from contemporary life, but in the days of my field work I found it still alive among the Indians whom I visited. For instance, when the Choctaw played an inter-village game, the performance started on the previous evening with 12 repetitions of a ceremonial dance by the players. The tribal prophets continued their magic rites throughout the night, and during the game itself the conjurers were almost as conspicuous as the players. The most matter-of-fact features in the daily routine of any primitive people are likely to be linked with magical observances, prayers, chants, or sacrifices. In New Zealand a Maori recited sacred spells when he began to build a canoe, when he launched it, when he planted his crops, when he harvested them; even when he taught a youngster to weave, he muttered a charm to increase the learner's receptiveness. During their farming period the Apinayé of Northern Brazil sang daily songs in honor of the sun. The Eskimo firmly believed that success in sealing hinged upon the favor of a powerful sea goddess. And so forth ad infinitum all over the savage world.

The field worker's business is always and everywhere to understand the true inwardness of the beliefs and practices of the people he studies. He is not content to record that infants are suffocated, aged parents abandoned, or enemies eaten. Unless he can also recover the accompanying sentiments, he has failed in his task. It is one thing if a parent throttles his newborn child from sheer brutality, another if he kills it because the mother died in delivery and a nurse cannot be found, and still another if his tribe has a superstitious fear of twins. And the field worker who consistently sees human civilization as one indivisible whole cannot logically apply a sympathetic attitude to Australian infanticide, Eskimo abandonment of old people, or

Tupinamba cannibalism, and a prejudiced attitude to Catholics, Baptists, or Methodists. The touchstone of his anthropological conscience is whether or not he treats the communicant of some other faith than his own with the consideration he professionally metes out to an Indian medicine man or an Eskimo shaman.

In my own field experience the Hopi of Arizona and the Crow of Montana both impressed upon me the integrating power of religion, but from two instructively antithetical angles. The Pueblos illustrate ceremonialism par excellence, with a profusion of outward observances and paraphernalia. What first of all amazes the observer among the Hopi is the incredible amount of time consumed by their religious activities. Apart from an infinitude of minor performances there is a fixed calendar of major festivals lasting nine days each. While there is a slight variation from year to year, the average amount of time devoted to religious ceremonial is one day in three. In the Hopi village of Walpi, for instance, the "year" starts with a nine-day initiation of youths into adult status. At the winter solstice there is a celebration in honor of the Kachina spirits, impersonated by mummers. In January the people play shinny as a magic fertility rite; moreover, several fraternities and sororities prepare the characteristic Pueblo offerings, such as feathered sticks to be smoked and prayed over before they are deposited in caves, springs, or other appropriate places. Follows the Bean festival, with secret planting of the vegetable, distribution of beans and of seed corn, burlesques, masqueradings, and a legion of other ritualistic rites. After a period of spirit-impersonating dances, March ushers in the drama of the Water Snakes, with suckling of serpent images as part of a fertility ceremonial. In April, there is the first corn planting "for the Kachina"; in May, the Skeleton God is represented and ritualistically slain; in June, prayer-sticks must be made for the sun; in July, the Kachina spirits have their farewell ceremony. In August comes either of two festivals in regular alternation, the famous Snake Dance or the Flute Dance. In September and the early part of the fall the several feminine organizations perform, and in November youths are once more initiated.

Not all members of the community participate in the series in equal measure. Large portions of the esoteric rituals, the prerogative of special organizations, are barred to nonmembers; and within a fraternity the functions of the priest differ from those of the rank and file. However, even the outsider is affected by the solemnity that invests the community during the whole of a festival. Further, in a sense, everyone's welfare is involved, for whatever may be the special objects of major ceremonials, they are all meant to bring rain. As my interpreter quaintly put it, "The Hopi have no streams to irrigate with, so they must perform their ceremonies." These expert farmers who make a go of corn-growing where many White agriculturists would despair nevertheless believe unshakably in the indispensableness of ritual for gaining their ends. By wheedling the spirits, by mimicking whatever is associated with showers, they expect to wring rain from the powers of the universe. Now they offer their feathered sticks, now they draw pictures of clouds dropping precipitation, now they whirl a board through the air to simulate thunder.

The heavy display of fixed ritual in Hopi supernaturalism does not easily yield up its meaning from the worshipper's point of view. Literally thousands of pages in print about Pueblo ceremonies have until fairly recently left the reader almost wholly in the dark on this crucial point of the subject. As late as 1942 appeared Sun Chief's autobiography, which tells at least how one believer felt about it all.

Among the Plains Indians there was also some emphasis upon ritual, but it was overshadowed by the importance of the subjective thrill in visions, auditions, or particularly vivid dreams. The contrast between the Crow and the Hopi corresponds roughly to that popularly conceived between an established church and lay evangelism. However, if there were a ritual of however simple a nature it was observed with the same punctilio. I shall not readily forget the ceremonial opening of Flat-head-woman's sacred bundle. First he divided live embers into two heaps, strewed incense on both, then alternately lowered each end of the bundle toward the nearer heap. With muttered words of prayer he opened the bundle, its cloth wrappings being carefully folded back on the sides without disturbance of their relative positions. When possibly ten coverings had been gradually unfolded, nothing was visible but a large bunch of feathers. Flat-head-woman next combined the two heaps of em-

bers, strewed more incense on top, then carefully arranged the feathers and extracted from among them, as the sacrosanct core, an arrow. This bundle was holy only because it had been revealed to the original owner (within Flat-head-woman's lifetime) by the Seven Stars. The arrow-spirit subsequently visited the first visionary's brother, Hillside, in his sleep. Hillside passed the bundle on to Flat-head-woman, who had never had a vision of his own; but after receiving the sacred bundle he began to have visions, seeing stalks of grass flying like arrows. For years he continued to receive revelations from the arrow-spirit. On one occasion it forbade him to throw ashes out of his lodge or to strike the lodge when removing snow from the tent cover. At another time it ordered him to visit the site of the original arrow revelation, where he was to find an eagle's feather in the cleft of a rock; and he found it.

The Crow, then, no less than the Hopi, attach extreme significance to things that we should regard as trivial. Both tribes insist upon a stereotyped procedure without the slightest deviation from the rules, lest you come to harm. Yet there is an immense difference between the tribes, for all those subjective experiences which are submerged in Hopi ritualism form the very warp and woof of Crow religion. The Crow Indians and their neighbors continually amazed me by their ever-recurring, face-to-face communication with the superhuman. It is such direct intercourse with the divine that is most distinctive of religion at its peak. As a veritable tyro I met Red-shirt, the Shoshone medicine man, who told me about his own death and resurrection. He had died, he said, because he had eaten salmon contrary to his familiar's orders and thus forever lost that spirit's protection. Fortunately, the Sun appeared to him in a dream, telling him he would die but promising resuscitation. This happened about 1880, and Red-shirt pointed out to me the spot where his tribesmen had built a special mortuary shelter for him. And now comes an illuminating detail. After his soul had stepped out of his thigh and taken a few steps forward, something suddenly descended clear through it, and it began to go downwards— not upwards, according to the general Shoshone belief. Red-shirt mistrusted the other Shoshone shamans no less than the Christian missionaries: Did he not have the direct evidence of his senses

that the soul descended after death instead of rising? They were only guessing, but he *knew*. This
adventure, though the most impressive in Red-
shirt's career, was by no means the only one. Traveling at night on one occasion, he saw an Indian
approaching; the face was invisible, but he was
wearing a striped vest. As the figure got close,
however, the stripes turned out to be bare ribs.
Red-shirt fled from the specter, whom he headed
off from pursuit by pronouncing a spell of exorcism: "You are only a ghost, leave me alone!" Then
the figure wheeled about and vanished into the
ground.

This type of experience was reported to me
wherever I went in the Northern Plains. The
Stoney Assiniboine attached great importance to
dreams. A man to whom a certain animal appeared in a dream would not kill or eat the flesh of
its fellows. Only very young Stoneys dreamed of
spirits, who would instruct them for several years
and then depart for good. Jim Crack may be cited
as an example: his benefactor, a dwarfish human,
had taught him how to pursue every kind of game,
so that Jim grew up to be a great hunter, after
which his guide was seen no more. In Montana a
blind Assiniboine recounted to me a series of personal revelations. Once he had been taken in a
dream to a tent with a sun design on the cover; an
old woman seated inside ordered him to decorate
his own tent in the same manner and promised
him that he and his family would enjoy good
health. He did, and they did! On another occasion
he received the right to doctor the sick. This was to
be done in a special kind of painted tipi, the model
being exhibited for his guidance; in it the practitioner was to be bound hand and foot and an invisible spirit would announce whether or not a cure
was possible, and if so, would untie the doctor.
Still another time my informant was shown a
procession of Fool Dancers and bidden, on pain of
premature death, to conduct their ceremony at
least once a year. In 1908 he was still obeying this
injunction, although total blindness had forced
him to rely on the aid of a proxy.

It would be an exaggeration to say that every
phase of a Crow's life was tinctured with religion,
but it is literally true that every situation of strain
or stress fused with the native concept of individual revelation. Thus, the young man who has been
jilted goes off at once to fast in loneliness, praying

for supernatural succor. An elk spirit may come
and teach him a tune on a flute, as a means of
luring the maiden back. The young man plays his
tune, ensnares the haughty girl, and turns her
away in disgrace, thus regaining his self-respect.
Similarly, a wretched orphan who has been
mocked by a young man of family hastens to the
mountains to be blessed by some being, through
whose favor he gains glory and loot on a raid, and
can then turn the tables upon his tormentor. A
woman big with child fasts and in a vision sees a
weed which she subsequently harvests and
through which she ensures a painless delivery. A
gambler who has lost all his property retrieves his
fortune through a revelation; and by the same
technique a sorrowing kinsman identifies the slay-
ers of his beloved relative and kills them. These are
all typical instances, amply documented in personal recollections of informants and in traditional
lore, showing the intrusion of religion into the
frustrations of everyday living.

Out of this general atmosphere blossomed the
notion that all conspicuous success in life is due to
visions and revelations. Contrariwise, failure is interpreted as equivalent to lack of superhuman favor. As one informant put it: "All who had visions
were well-to-do; I was to be poor, and that is why
I had no visions." Such a man could still, however,
tap hidden resources by borrowing a talisman—or
a replica of one—from a more fortunate relative or
friend. By its means he often managed to get a
start, and later he might begin to have revelations
of his own.

The question now arises as to how the ethnographer should appraise this faith in the reality, the
paramount value, of visions. A casual estimate
might suggest that the visionaries are all mystics or
fools, but after several years' acquaintance with
them, I am certain that they are neither. Every
young man automatically went out to seek a vision, and those who claimed success were precisely the leaders of the tribe. The question still
remains whether or not these men were intentional or unintentional frauds. My interpreter, a baptized Christian who was keenly aware of the
inherent improbability by modern criteria of visions, thought otherwise. As he said, "When you
listen to the old men telling their stories, you've
just *got* to believe them." And in this impression I
concur. Whatever the narrator's experiences may

have been, he himself conceived them as being as he represented them.

But it is not necessary to rely upon subjective impressions, since there are at least four bits of evidence to suggest that the speakers were sincere. First, why should they lie to a white man, when they perfectly well knew that the more flamboyant their story the less likely I would be to believe it? Therefore, a pretense of wonderful experiences would serve no useful purpose for them. Second, among their own people, the rise of kudos through a vision required a good deal more than the palming off of a convenient hoax. Normally, the aspirant for a vision would go to the mountains, refrain for four days from food and water, and mutilate himself, to convince the deities of his sincerity. These offerings of flesh are not figments of myth, for I have seen the mutilated fingers and the deep scars on back and chest. Even with such austerities, there were many who never succeeded in getting a vision. I doubt that sheer mountebanks would lacerate or starve themselves. Third, even assuming that a man's desire for status drove him to self-mutilation and the fabrication of a dream or vision, he would be no better off than before, because it was only the *demonstrably successful* healer or war leader who achieved a following. Until the revelation was backed up with results, and unless it were, the would-be-visionary was held up to endless ridicule. A deliberate imposter would, therefore, be far more likely to lose prestige than to gain it. And fourth, the man who received power through a revelation also received usually at least one and perhaps more life-long and onerous restrictions. One old man of my acquaintance had not ridden a horse since the day of his vision thirty-years earlier, for the spirits had forbidden him to do so. He had trudged on foot. Although the ownership of horses had great prestige value, he had sold the one he owned at the time of his vision and had never owned another. He would gain military renown by killing an enemy but not by the much simpler method of stealing an enemy's horse. Another Indian had been forbidden to eat eggs and was a constant nuisance because he would not eat anything unless he personally supervised its preparation, lest the cook slip in an egg without his knowledge. And a third was forbidden to touch salmon, one of the Crows' few delicacies; on one occasion he ate a mixture of prepared fish without knowing there was salmon there and attributed the following eleven years of rheumatism to his unwitting breaking of his taboo. So a vision was not an unmixed blessing, and a man could hardly hope to derive benefit from a fake.

The role of religion in the life of either community or individual has already been at least implied. A living faith serves to integrate the individual's behavior in society, to give him confidence in meeting the crises which life inescapably brings, and to introduce into his existence a stable central core in the light of which he can assign values. These same purposes are served by the religion of those more sophisticated than my Indian informants, although they may not show the basis of their integration in so clear a fashion. Religion should also provide the basis for ethics. It should enter into everything an individual does, every judgment he makes, every point of view he develops. It is admittedly true that religion is not the only integrator; the impulse may come from immersion in art, music, education, or science in the case of those who have the necessary abilities for such absorption. For the average citizen, however, religion is still the most available source of integration. This fact not only justifies its existence but also explains its universal appeal.

Perhaps it might be well to take a momentary look at what has happened in modern times to societies that have deliberately set about exterminating religion, at least in so far as they could. The Nazis are a case in point. It did not take Hitler long to discover that the churches and the clergy were his implacable enemies. Priests and ministers insisted upon doing what they considered right, they criticized him openly, they tried to rally their congregations to oppose him, they helped enemies of the state to escape, they harbored the persecuted. Hitler could not put his policies of suppression, incarceration, and extermination into effect until he had eliminated the clergy, who would not do as they were told and would not keep their mouths shut. Moreover, they were upheld by a power that he did not understand but which he feared. During the ten years of his dominance the one effective resistance that he could not completely eliminate came from organized religion. One main purpose of his "youth" groups was to bring up a generation that lacked the Christian virtues of compassion or mercy. The Soviets are attempting the same combination of repression and education of children without religious scruples. One *modus operandi* that has been used in totalitarian countries for the suppression of religion has been to carry away from each village as hostage one small child; thereafter, if any member of that village were caught at a secret religious gathering, if any gave aid to a member of the clergy, if any were seen saying his prayers, the child was killed. It is hard to imagine that in a country of even lukewarm Christianity such a method could be used. There are many people who might like to see the extermination of all religion, but perhaps they might take a closer look at what happens when religious attitudes are destroyed: the accompanying ethical standards also disappear, and one is left with a society not only without religion but also without restraining virtues. It is extremely doubtful that a nation can keep its ethics after it loses its religion.

For the last century at least much has been made of the conflict between religions and science and of the eventual and desirable substitution of the latter for the former. Perhaps before taking sides in this controversy one should consider to what extent the two systems of thought actually do contradict and interfere with each other. As soon as one stops to think it is clear that there are vast bodies of scientific facts and principles that have never been challenged by any religious group—the ontogeny of silkworms, the expansion of mercury by heat, the predictability of an eclipse, the distance of the moon from the earth, the chemical constitution of water, the antiquity of man, the distinction between tame and domesticated animals, the germ theory of disease, the laws of gravity, and so on. In fact, the points upon which there is conflict are extremely few when compared to the sum total of scientific knowledge.

Perhaps the basic difficulty in seeing the relation of religion and science is that the majority of people do not know in the least what a science is, much less what it can and cannot do. The man-in-the-street commonly regards scientific facts as eternal truths—things that cannot change. Nothing could be more incorrect. To take a very simple example: in my chemistry class I was taught that an atom was an absolutely indivisible particle of matter, but now it seems that it is not; and the theory of light waves, as expounded to me in my college

days, has long since been amended. And so on, in every field of science. The layman seems to think that because a scientific theory is derived from experiments it *must* be true; such a theory is true only until further experimentation shows wherein it must be altered. A theory is only a hypothesis that will have to do until a better one comes along. There is nothing fixed about it. Another misconception arises from the notion that science is independent of the social and economic pressures of the environment. Quite the reverse is true. Thus, the very problems that are attacked at a particular stage in history are selected by irrational considerations or outside economic pressures, rather than in the light of eternal fitness. This statement explains why classical Greece was so sterile in useful inventions. It was certainly not because of any dearth in acute thinkers or of any ineptitude for experimentation. The reason is to be sought rather in the predominant ideology, which exalted speculation over utilitarian application. Further, the social scheme allocated manual work to slaves, of which there was an ample supply. The tone-setting classes thus had no urge to minimize human effort by labor-saving devices. Those who were mechanically gifted accordingly lavished their ingenuity upon clever but useless toys, such as wooden pigeons that flew by compressed air.

Still another erroneous notion that one often hears expressed is the idea of the scientist as a person who dwells in an ivory tower, remote from the common pressures of mankind, and reaches his conclusions by the exercise of pure reason. This notion, made familiar by various forms of mass communication, is mostly poppycock, as may be shown by taking at random a few samples from the history of science. Ideally, of course, a scientist should be a man who is uniformly critical, willing to follow proof, and insistent upon the application of reason, but unfortunately he is a man like other men, with the same dependence upon tradition in his field, upon his own prejudices, upon his own social milieu. Thus we find Tycho de Brahe, one of the foremost observational astronomers in the history of the science, piquing himself above all upon the accuracy not of his observations but of his horoscopes. History shows us again and again the whole guild of scientists rejecting epoch-making discoveries and advances that did not fit in with their traditional ideas. The scientists of his day branded Harvey as a charlatan for announcing his discoveries about the circulation of the blood, they martyrized Semmelweiss for expounding the cause of child-bed fever, they ridiculed Boucher de Perthes when he declared that man had been a contemporary of extinct animals. These examples are taken from previous centuries, but the ability of a scientist to free himself from tradition and to embrace novel ideas has not increased greatly. Moreover, even a well-balanced, objective scientist is frequently mistaken in his conclusions, not because he does not reason but because he does not yet have all the facts he needs to reason with. Thus, a generation or two ago Lord Kelvin estimated the age of the earth at a figure absurdly low in the light of subsequent research.

To return to the original argument, there are of course points upon which science and religion collide, and the intensity of the clash naturally varies with the circumstances. Medical science is intransigent against religious cults that reject vaccination. Religious leaders may be equally determined to resist the principle of birth control. Both sides have argued endlessly and to no great profit about Christian Science. Medical men have attacked it as being both useless and dangerous. Its defenders can point to much good that has been done for individuals. Probably both sides are right; they are simply talking about different people and different problems. If a man is a diabetic, he will not be cured by Christian Science, and the period during which he tries to effect a cure by such means may postpone medical treatment until it is too late to do much good. But if a man has a psychosomatic condition, he cannot be cured by a doctor's prescription because the sickness in his body is only a symptom of the sickness in his emotional life. There is a chance that Christian Science can cure him; there is no chance that a pill can. I am reminded of a cousin who was unemployed, depressed, and down to her last hundred dollars, of which she spent fifty for a "course" given by a complete charlatan who actually sent her nothing but form letters, all encouraging her to have faith in the future. Everyone, including myself, thought she was out of her mind, but we were all wrong because the man cured her. She returned to work and remained emotionally adjusted and useful throughout the remainder of her life. This sort of thing illustrates one point about human nature

that is often not recognized: that what the average person wants is a workable solution, and he does not in the least care how many mistakes have been made in the computation.

There is thus no warrant for the notion that Science consists of a body of doctrine established once and for all time in the realm of Pure Reason. At any particular stage science is a sportsmanlike adventure in ferreting the truth out of a coy universe. And it is by no means the only method of approach. When we compare what is now known with what was known, say, four hundred years ago, there is every reason for good cheer. But even today research is not wholly a matter of earnest striving, specialized training, innate capacity for observation and deduction; it is the result of all these and of human frailty working under the handicap of a despotic heritage of traditional prejudice. The result is admittedly our best possible instrument for controlling physical environment and for formulating ideas of the material world. But it does not at all follow that it is soul-satisfying, or that it can serve as a basis for moral action.

If we keep before us the attitude of the man in the street, we shall understand why he can never be satisfied with science as a substitute for religion. That eternal striving for the truth without attaining it, which Lessing lauded as the highest good, has no appeal whatever for the generality of mankind. What the normal human being wants is peace, security, and relaxation. And he can never find these things in that dynamic, ever-growing, ever-disturbing thing that we have found science to be. In ringing words Ernst Mach has defined its nature: "The scientist's highest philosophy consists precisely in bearing an incomplete world view and preferring it to one that is apparently complete, but inadequate." This is precisely the scientist's philosophy, but most people are nonscientists, and it is of them that I am speaking. The contrast is well expressed by Goethe's oft-quoted quatrain:

> Wer Wissenschaft und Kunst besitzt
> Hat auch Religion;
> Wer jene beiden nicht besitzt,
> Der *habe* Religion.

Whatever one may think of the snobbish flavor of these lines, they adumbrate an essential psychological truth. If a man's being is *wholly* absorbed in intellectual and esthetic pursuits, his interests may assume for him the place of spiritual guidance; without immersion in such activity, man had better rely upon the traditional faith. What an average man wants above everthing else is security. But does science supply this? The answer is "No." That complete world view that science explicitly renounces is precisely what the layman cr ves. In this perilous universe he is forever beset with dangers beyond his control. He wants at all odds to survive, and here science leaves him in the lurch— not everywhere and always, but often enough to make him keenly sensible of its imperfections. If he is dying of an incurable disease, it cheers him little to be told that medical science has made great strides in the past decades and that a remedy will almost certainly be found a hundred years hence,

and probably sooner. Instead of running eagerly toward the latest scientific discovery, the average man is likely to wish the discovery had never been made, because it has proved so upsetting to his security. Science has achieved remarkable results, both practical and theoretical, but it has not made man a superman; so long as the enormous chasm yawns between man's rational control of nature and his biologico-psychological drives, there will still be room for belief in a Providence that grants not mere comfort, but security—not mere probability, but certainty. Religion and science thus perform different functions in the life of man, and it is not necessary that either should interfere with the other.

Religious Perspectives in Anthropology

Dorothy Lee

At first glance the study of the religion of non-Western cultures may appear somewhat esoteric, albeit interesting. In reality, however, religion is very much a part of everyday, practical activities in these cultures, and knowledge of a society's religion is essential for the successful introduction of social changes. In the following article Dorothy Lee dramatically shows how religion is part and parcel of pre-literate people's world view, or Weltanschauung: *the corpus of beliefs about the life and environment in which members of a society find themselves. Among pre-literate societies, economic, political, and artistic behavior is permeated by religion. Lee points out that anthropologists make every attempt to understand the insiders' "emic" view of their universe, which they share with other members of their group, and demonstrates that an outsider's "etic" view is too limited a base of cultural knowledge on which to introduce innovations that do not violate the religious tenets of the society and meet with acceptance.*

Reprinted from Lowell D. Holmes, ed., *Readings in General Anthropology* (New York: Ronald Press, 1971), pp. 416–27.

IN PRIMITIVE SOCIETIES, WE DO NOT ALWAYS find the worship of God or a god, nor the idea of the supernatural. Yet religion is always present in man's view of his place in the universe, in his relatedness to man and nonhuman nature, to reality and circumstance. His universe may include the divine or may itself be divine. And his patterned behavior often has a religious dimension, so that we find religion permeating daily life—agriculture and hunting, health measures, arts and crafts.

We do find societies where a Supreme Being is recognized; but this Being is frequently so far removed from mundane affairs, that it is not present in the consciousness of the people, except on the specific occasions of ceremonial or prayer. But in these same societies, we find communion with the unperceivable and unknowable in nature, with an ultimate reality, whether spirit, or power, or intensified being, or personal worth, which evokes humility, respect, courtesy or sometimes fear, on man's part. This relationship to the ultimate reality is so pervasive, that it may determine, for example, which hand a man will use in adjusting his loin cloth, or how much water he will drink at a time, or which way his head will point when he sleeps, or how he will butcher and utilize the carcass of a caribou. What anthropologists label "material culture," therefore, is never purely material. Often we would be at least as justified to call the operation involved religious.

All economic activities, such as hunting, gathering fuel, cultivating the land, storing food, assume a relatedness to the encompassing universe, and with many cultures, this is a religious relationship. In such cultures, men recognize a certain spiritual worth and dignity in the universe. They do not set out to control, or master, or exploit. Their ceremonials are often periods of intensified communion, even social affairs, in a broad sense, if the term may be extended to include the forces of the universe. They are not placating or bribing or even thanking; they are rather a formal period of concentrated, enjoyable association. In their relationships with nature, the people may see themselves as the offspring of a cherishing mother, or the guests of a generous hostess, or as members of a democratic society which proceeds on the principle of consent. So, when the Baiga in India were urged to change over to the use of an iron plow, they replied with horror that they could not tear the flesh of their mother with knives. And American Indians have hunted many animals with the consent of the generic essence of these—of which the particular animal was the carnal manifestation—only after establishing a relationship or reciprocity; with man furnishing the ceremonial, and Buffalo or Salmon or Caribou making a gift of the countless manifestations of his flesh.

The great care with which so many of the Indian groups utilized every portion of the carcass of a hunted animal, was an expression, not of economic thrift, but of courtesy and respect; in fact, an aspect of the religious relationship to the slain. The Wintu Indians of California, who lived on land so wooded that it was difficult to find clear land for putting up a group of houses, nevertheless used only dead wood for fuel, out of respect for nature. An old Wintu woman, speaking in prophetic vein, expressed this: "The White people never cared for land or deer or bear. When we Indians kill meat, we eat it all up. When we dig roots we make little holes. When we build houses, we make little holes. When we burn grass for grasshoppers, we don't ruin things. We shake down acorns and pinenuts. We don't chop down the trees. We only use dead wood. But the White people plow up the ground, pull up the trees, kill everything. The tree says, 'Don't. I am sore. Don't hurt me.' But they chop it down and cut it up. The spirit of the land hates them. They blast out trees and stir it up to its depths. They saw up the trees. That hurts them. The Indians never hurt anything, but the white people destroy all. They blast rocks and scatter them on the ground. The rock says, 'Don't! You are hurting me.' But the White People pay no attention. When the Indians use rocks, they take little round ones for their cooking. . . . How can the spirit of the earth like the white man? . . . Everywhere the White man has touched it, it is sore.' "

Here we find people who do not so much *seek* communion with environing nature as *find themselves* in communion with it. In many of these societies, not even mysticism is to be found, in our sense of the word. For us, mysticism presupposes a prior separation of man from nature; and communion is achieved through loss of self and subsequent merging with that which is beyond; but for many cultures, there is no such distinct separation between self and other, which must be overcome. Here, man is *in* nature already, and we cannot speak properly of man *and* nature.

Take the Kaingang, for example, who chops out a wild beehive. He explains his act to the bees, as he would to a person whom he considered his coordinate. "Bee, produce! I chopped you out to make beer of you! Yukui's wife died, and I am making beer of you so that I can cut his hair." Or he may go up to a hive and say simply, "Bee, it is I." And the Arapesh of New Guinea, going to his yam garden, will first introduce to the spirit of the land, the brother-in-law whom he has brought along to help him with the gardening. This is not achieved communication, brought about for definite ends. It implies an already present relatedness with the ultimate reality, with that which is accepted in faith, and which exists irrespective of man's cognition or perception or logic. If we were to abstract, out of this situation, merely the food getting or the operational techniques, we would be misrepresenting the reality.

The same present relatedness is to be found in some societies where the deity is more specifically defined. The Tikopia, in the Solomon Islands Protectorate, sit and eat their meals with their dead under the floor, and hand food and drink to them; the dead are all somewhat divine, progressively so as they come nearer to the original, fully divine ancestor of the clan. Whatever their degree of divinity, the Tikopia is at home with them; he is aware of their vague presence, though he requires the services of a medium whenever he wants to make this presence definite.

Firth describes an occasion when a chief, having instructed a medium to invite his dead nephew to come and chew betel with him, found himself occupied with something else when the dead arrived, and so asked the medium to tell the spirit—a minor deity—to chew betel by himself. At another time, during an important ceremonial, when this chief was receiving on his forehead the vertical stripe which was the symbol that he was now the incarnation of the highest god, he jokingly jerked his head aside, so that the stripe, the insignium of the presence of the god, went crooked. These are the acts of a man who feels accepted by his gods, and is at one with them. And, in fact, the Tikopia appear to live in a continuum which includes nature and the divine without defining bounds; where communion is present, not achieved; where merging is a matter of being, not of becoming.

In these societies, where religion is an everpresent dimension of experience, it is doubtful that religion as such is given a name; Kluckhohn reports that the Navaho have no such word, but most ethnographers never thought to inquire. Many of these cultures, however, recognized and named the spiritual ingredient or attribute, the special quality of the wonderful, the very, the beyondness, in nature. This was sometimes considered personal, sometimes not. We have from the American Indians terms such as *manitou*, or *wakan*, or *yapaitu*, often translated as power; and we have the well-known Melanesian term *mana*. But this is what they reach through faith, the other end of the relationship; the relationship itself is unnamed. Apparently, to behave and think religiously, is to behave and think. To describe a way of life in its totality is to describe a religious way of life.

When we speak of agricultural taboos and rites, therefore, we often introduce an analytical factor which violates the fact. For example, when preparing seed for planting, one of the several things a Navaho traditionally does is to mix ground "mirage stone" with the seed. And in the process of storing corn, a double-eared stalk is laid at the bottom of the storage pit. In actual life, these acts are a continuous part of a total activity.

The distinction between the religious and the secular elements may even separate an act from the manner of performance, a verb from its adverb. The direction in which a man is facing when performing a secular act, or the number of times he shakes his hand when spattering water, often have their religious implications. When the Navaho planted his corn sunwise, his act reflected a total world view, and it would be nonsense for us to separate the planting itself from the direction of the planting.

Those of us who present religion as separate from "everyday" living, reflect moreover the distinctions of a culture which will identify six days with the secular in life and only the seventh with religion. In many primitive societies, religion is rarely absent from the details of everyday living, and the ceremonials represent a formalization and intensification of an everpresent attitude. We have societies such as that of the Hopi of Arizona, where ceremonials, and the preparation for them, cover most of the year. Some years ago, Crowwing, a Hopi, kept a journal for the period of a year, putting down all events of ceremonial import. Day after day, there are entries containing some casual reference to a religious activity, or describing a ritual, or the preparation for a ceremonial. After a few weeks of such entries, we come to a sequence of four days' entries which are devoted to a description of a ball game played by two opposing groups of children and enjoyed by a large number of spectators. But, in the end, this also turns out to have been ceremonial in nature, helping the corn to grow.

Among many groups, agriculture is an expression of man's religious relatedness to the universe. As Robert Redfield and W. Lloyd Warner have written: "The agriculture of the Maya Indians of southeastern Yucatan is not simply a way of securing food. It is also a way of worshipping the gods. Before a man plants, he builds an altar in the field and prays there. He must not speak boisterously in the cornfield; it is a sort of temple. The cornfield is planted as an incident in a perpetual sacred contract between supernatural beings and men. By this agreement, the supernaturals yield part of what is theirs—the riches of the natural environment—to men. In exchange, men are pious and perform the traditional ceremonies in which offerings are made to the supernaturals. . . . The world is seen as inhabited by the supernaturals; each has his appropriate place in the woods, the sky, or the wells from which the water is drawn. The village is seen as a reflection of the quadrilateral pattern of the cosmos; the cornfield too is oriented, laid out east, west, north, and south, with reference to the supernaturals that watch over the cardinal points; and the table altars erected for the ceremonies again remind the individual of this pattern. The stories that are told at the time when men wait to perform the ceremony before the planting of the corn or that children hear as they grow up are largely stories which explain and further sanction the traditional way of life."

Art also is often so permeated with religion that sometimes, as among the Navaho, what we classify as art is actually religion. To understand the rhythm of their chants, the "plot" of their tales, the making of their sand paintings, we have to understand Navaho religion: the concept of harmony between man and the universe as basic to health and well being; the concept of continuity, the religious significance of the groups of four, the door of contact opened through the fifth repetition, the need to have no completely enclosing frame around any of their works so that continuity can be maintained and the evil inside can have an opening through which to leave.

The sand paintings are no more art than they are ritual, myth, medical practice or religous belief. They are created as an integral aspect of a ceremonial which brings into harmony with the universal order one who finds himself in discord with it; or which intensifies and ensures the continuation of a harmony which is already present. Every line and shape and color, every interrelationship of form, is the visible manifestation of myth, ritual and religious belief. The making of the painting is accompanied with a series of sacred songs sung over a sick person, or over someone who, though healed of sickness by emergency measures has yet to be brought back into the universal harmony; or in enhancing and giving emphasis to the present harmony. What we would call purely medical practices may or may not be part of all this. When the ceremonial is over, the painting is over too; it is destroyed; it has fulfilled its function.

This is true also of the art of the neighboring Hopi, where the outstanding form of art is the drama. In this we find wonderfully humorous clowning, involving careful planning and preparation, creation of magnificent masks and costumes, rehearsals, organization. Everyone comes to see and responds with uproarious hilarity. But this is not mere art. It is an important way of helping nature in her work of growing the corn. Even the laughter of the audience helps in this.

More than dramatic rehearsal and creation of costumes has gone into the preparation. The actors have prepared themselves as whole persons. They have refrained from sexual activity, and from any-thing involving conflict. They have had good thoughts only. They have refrained from anger, worry and grief. Their preparations as well as their performance have had a religious dimension. Their drama is one act in the great process of the cyclical growing of corn, a divinity indispensable to man's well being, and to whose well being man is indispensable. Corn wants to grow, but cannot do so without the cooperation of the rest of nature and of man's acts and thoughts and will. And, to be happy, corn must be danced by man and participate in his ceremonials. To leave the religious dimension out of all this, and to speak of Hopi drama as merely a form of art, would be to present a fallacious picture. Art and agriculture and religion are part of the same totality for the Hopi.

In our own culture, an activity is considered to be economic when it deals with effective utilization or exploitation of resources. But this definition cannot be used when speaking of Hopi economics. To begin with, it assumes an aggressive attitude toward the environment. It describes the situation of the homesteader in Alaska, for example, who works against tremendous odds clearing land for a dairy farm, against the inexorable pressure of time, against hostile elements. By his sweat, and through ingenuity and know-how and the use of brutally effective tools, he tames nature; he subjugates the land and exploits its resources to the utmost.

The Hopi Talayesua, however, describing his work on the land, does not see himself in opposition to it. He works *with* the elements, not *against* them. He helps the corn to grow; he cooperates with the thunderstorm and the pollen and the sun. He is in harmony with the elements, not in conflict; and he does not set out to conquer an opponent. He depends on the corn, but this is part of a mutual interdependence; it is not exploitation. The corn depends on him too. It cannot grow without his help; it finds life dull and lonely without his company and his ceremonials. So it gives its body for his food gladly, and enjoys living with him in his granary. The Hopi has a personal relationship with it. He treats it with respect, and houses it with the care and courtesy accorded to an honored guest. Is this economics?

In a work on Hopi economics we are given an account of the Hopi Salt Journey, under the heading, "Secondary Economic Activities." This expedition is also described in a Hopi autobiography, and here we discover that only those men who have achieved a certain degree of experience in the Hopi way, can go on this journey; and then, only if their minds are pure and they are in a state of harmony with the universe. There is a period of religious preparation, followed by the long and perilous journey which is attended by a number of rituals along the way. Old men, lowering themselves from the overhanging ledge onto the salt deposits, tremble with fear, knowing that they may be unable to make the ascent. The occasion is solemnly religious. This is no utilization of resources, in the eyes of the Hopi who makes the journey. He goes to help the growing corn; the Salt Journey brings needed rain. Twelve adult men will spend days and court dangers to procure salt which they can buy for two dollars from the itinerant peddler. By our own economic standards, this is not an efficient use of human resources. But Hopi ends transcend our economic categories and our standards of efficiency are irrelevant to them.

In many societies, land tenure, or the transference of land, operations involved in hunting and agriculture, are often a part of a religious way of life. In our own culture, man conceives of his relationship to his physical environment, and even sometimes his human environment, as mechanistic and manipulative; in other cultures, we often find what Ruth Benedict has called the animistic attitude toward nature and man, underlying practices which are often classified miscellaneously together in ethnographics, under the heading of superstitions or taboos. The courteous speech to the bear about to be killed, the offering to the deer world before the hunter sets out, the introduction of the brother-in-law to the garden spirit, or the sacrifice to the rice field about to be sold, the refraining from intercourse, or from the eating of meat or from touching food with the hand, are expressive of such an attitude. They are the practices we find in a democratic society where there is consideration for the rights of everyone as opposed to the brutal efficiency of the dictator who feels free to exploit, considering the rights of none. They reflect the attitude of people who believe in conference and consent, not in coercion; of people who generally find personality or mana in nature and man, sometimes more, sometimes less. In this framework, taboo and superstitious act mean that

man acts and refrains from acting in the name of a wider democracy which includes nature and the divine.

With such a conception of man's place in nature, what is for us land tenure, or ownership, or rights of use and disposal, is for other societies an intimate belongingness. So the Arapesh conceive of themselves as belonging to the land, in the way that flora and fauna belong to it. They cultivate the land by the grace of the immanent spirits, but they cannot dispose of it and cannot conceive of doing so.

This feeling of affinity between society and land is widespread and appears in various forms and varying degrees of intensity, and it is not found only among sedentary peoples. We have Australian tribes where the very spirit of the men is believed to reside in the land, where a bush or a rock or a peculiar formation is the present incarnation of myth, and contains security and religious value; where a social class, a structured group of relatives, will contain in addition to human beings, an animal and a feature of the landscape. Here, when a man moves away from the land of his group, he leaves the vital part of himself behind. When a magistrate put people from such societies in jail in a distant city, he had no idea of the terrifying severity of the punishment he was meting; he was cutting the tribesman off from the very source of his life and of his self, from the past, and the future which were incorporated and present in his land.

In the technology of such societies we are again dealing with material where the religious and secular are not distinct from each other. We have, for example, the description which Raymond Firth gives of the replacing of a wornout wash strake on a canoe, among the Tikopia. This operation is expertly and coherently carried out, with secular and religious acts performed without distinction in continuous succession or concurrently. A tree is cut down for the new wash strake, a libation is poured out to the deities of the canoe to announce this new timber, and a kava rite is performed to persuade the deities to step out of the canoe and on to a piece of bark cloth, where they can live undisturbed, while the canoe is being tampered with. Then comes the unlashing of the old wash strake, the expert examination of the body of the canoe in search of lurking defects, the discovery of signs indicating the work of a borer, the cutting of the body of the canoe with a swift stroke to discover whether the borer is there, accompanied by an appeal to the deities of the canoe by the expert, to witness what he is doing, and the necessity for doing it.

Now a kinsman of the original builde of the canoe, now dead and a tutelary deity, spontaneously drops his head on to the side of the canoe and wails over the wounding of the body of the canoe. The borer is discovered, in the meantime, to be still there; but only a specially consecrated adze can deal with him successfully. The adze is sent for, dedicated anew to the deity, invoked, and finally wielded with success by the expert.

All this is performed with remarkable expedition and economy of motion yet the Tikopia workers are not interested in saving time; they are concerned neither with time limits nor with speed in itself. Their concern is with the dispossessed deities whose home must be made ready against their return; and the speed of their work is incidental to this religious concern. The end result is efficiency; but unlike our own efficiency, this is not rooted in the effort to utilize and exploit material and time resources to the utmost; it is rooted in that profound religious feeling which also gives rise to the time-consuming rites and the wailing procedures which, from the purely economic point of view, are wasteful and interfering.

The world view of a particular society includes that society's conception of man's own relation to the universe, human and non-human, organic and inorganic, secular and divine, to use our own dualisms. It expresses man's view of his own role in the maintenance of life, and of the forces of nature. His attitude toward responsibility and initiative is inextricable from his conception of nature as deity-controlled, man-controlled, regulated through a balanced cooperation between god and man, or perhaps maintained through some eternal homeostasis, independent of man and perhaps of any deity. The way a man acts, his feeling of guilt and achievement, and his very personality, are affected by the way he envisions his place within the universe.

For example, there are the Tiv of Southern Nigeria who as described by one of them in the thirties, people the universe with potentially hostile and harmful powers, the akombo. Man's function in the maintenance of his own life and the moderate well-being of the land and of his social unit, is to prevent the manifestation of akombo evil, through performing rites and observing taboos. So his rites render safe through preventing, through expulsion and purging. His role is negative, defending the normal course against the interference. Vis-à-vis the universe, his acts arise out of negative motives. Thus what corresponds to a gift of first fruits to a deity in other cultures is phrased as a rite for preventing the deities from making a man's food go bad or diminish too quickly; fertility rites for a field are actually rites preventing the evil-intentioned from robbing the fields of their normal fertility.

In the writings of R. F. Barton, who studied the Ifugao of Luzon in the early part of this century, these people also appear to see deities as ready to interfere and bring evil; but their conception of man's role within the structure of the universe is a different one from that of the Tiv. In Barton's descriptive accounts, the Ifugao either accept what comes as deity-given, or act without being themselves the agents; they believe that no act can come to a conclusive end without the agency of a specific deity. They have a specific deity often for every step within an operation and for every part of the implement to be used. R. F. Barton recorded the names of 1,240 deities and believed that even so he had not exhausted the list.

The Ifugao associate a deity with every structured performance and at least a large number of their deliberate acts. They cannot go hunting, for example, without enlisting the aid of the deity of each step of the chase, to render each effective, or to nullify any lurking dangers. There is a deity for the level spot where "the hunter stands watching and listening to the dogs"; one for when the dogs "are sicced on the game"; one for when "the hunter leans on his spear transfixing the quarry"; twelve are listed as the deities of specific ways of rendering harmless to the hunter's feet the snags and fangs of snakes which he encounters. If he is to be successful in the hunt, a man does not ask the blessing of a deity. He pays all the particular deities of every specific spot and act, getting them to transitivize each act individually.

Even so, in most cases an Ifugao remains non-agentive, since the function of many of the deities is to save man from encounter, rather than to give him success in his dealing with it. For example, in the area of interpersonal relations, we have Tupya who is invoked so that, "the creditor comes for dun for what is owed, but on the way he forgets and goes about other business"; and Dulaiya, who is invoked so that, "the enemies just don't think about us, so they don't attack." His tools, also, are ineffective of themselves; so that, when setting a deadfall, he invokes and bribes such deities as that for the Flat Stone of the Deadfall, the Main Posts of the Deadfall, the Fall of the Deadfall, the Trigger of the Deadfall. Most of the Ifugao economy is involved in providing sacrifices to the deities, big or little according to the magnitude of the operation and the importance of the deities. There is no warmth in the sacrifices; no expression of gratitude or appeal or belongingness. As the Ifugaos see it, the sacrifice is a bribe. With such bribes, they buy the miraculous intervention and transitivization which are essential for achievement, health, and good personal relations.

The Ifugao show no humility in the face of this ineffective role in the universe; they merely accept it as the state of things. They accept their own failures, the frequent deaths, the sudden and disastrous flaring up of tempers, as things that are bound to happen irrespective of their own desires and efforts. But they are neither passive nor helpless. They carry on great undertakings, and, even now they go on forbidden head hunts. They know when and how and whom to bribe so as to perfect their defective acts. When however, a deity states a decision, they accept it as immutable. A Catholic priest tells a story about the neighboring Iloko which illustrates this acceptance. A Christian Iloko was on his deathbed, and the priest, trying to persuade him to repent of his sin, painted to him vividly the horrors of hell; but the dying man merely answered, "If God wants me to go to hell, I am perfectly willing."

Among the Wintu Indians of California we find that man sees himself as effective but in a clearly limited way. An examination of the myths of the Wintu shows that the individual was conceived as having a limited agentive role, shaping, using, intervening, actualizing and temporalizing the given, but never creating; that man was viewed as needing skill for his operations, but that specific skill was useless without "luck" which a man received through communion and pleading with some universal power.

It is to this limited role of man, geared to the working of the universe, that I referred when I spoke earlier of Hopi drama and agriculture. Without an understanding of this role, no Hopi activity or attitude or relationship can be understood. The Hopi have developed the idea of man's limited effectiveness in their own fashion, and have elaborated it systematically in what they call the "Hopi Way." Laura Thompson says of the Hopi, "All phenomena relevant to the life of the tribe—including man, the animals, and plants, the earth, sun, moon, clouds, the ancestors, and the spirits— are believed to be interdependent. . . . In this system each individual—human and non-human—is believed to have . . . a definite role in the universal order." Traditionally, fulfillment of the law of nature—the growth of the corn, the movements of the sun—can come only with man's participation, only with man's performance of the established ceremonials. Here man was effective, but only in cooperation with the rest of the phenomena of nature.

The Indians of the Plains, such as the Crow and the Sioux, have given a somewhat different form to this conception of man's circumscribed agency. The aggressive behavior for which they have been known, their great personal autonomy, their self-assurance and assertiveness and in recent years, their great dependence and apathy, have been explained as an expression of this conception. These societies envisioned the universe as pervaded by an undifferentiated religious force on which they were dependent for success in their undertakings and in life generally. The specific formulation different in the different tribes, but, essentially, in all it was believed that each individual and particularly each man, must tap this universal force if his undertakings were to be successful. Without this "power" a man could not achieve success in any of the valued activities, whether warfare or the hunt; and no leadership was possible without this power. This was a force enhancing and intensifying the being of the man who acted; it was not, as with the Ifugao, an effectiveness applied to specific details of activities. The individual himself prepared himself in the hardihood, self-control, skills and areas of knowledge necessary. Little boys of five or seven took pride in their ability to withstand pain, physical hardship, and the terrors of running errands alone in the night. The Sioux did not appeal for divine intervention; he did not want the enemy to forget to come. Yet neither was he fearless. He appealed for divine strength to overcome his own fears as well as the external enemy.

The relationship with the divine, in this case, is personal and intense. The Plains Indian Sioux did not, like the Hopi, inherit a specific relatedness when he was born in a specific clan. Each man, each pre-adolescent boy, had to achieve the relationship for himself. He had to go out into the wilderness and spend days and nights without food or drink, in the cold, among wild beasts, afraid and hungry and anxious, humbling himself and supplicating, sometimes inflicting excruciating pain upon himself, until some particular manifestation of the universal force took pity upon him and came to him to become his life-long guardian and power. The appeals to the universal force were made sometimes in a group, through the institution of the Sun Dance. But here also they were individual in nature. The relationship with the divine was an inner experience; and when the Dakota Black Elk recounted his autobiography, he spoke mainly of these intense, personal religious experiences. Within this range of variation in form and concept and world view, we find expressed by all the same immediate relatedness to the divine.

Anthropology Beyond the Fringe

John R. Cole

Basic to all cultural anthropology is the concept of cultural relativism, the belief that cultures everywhere have the right to their own beliefs. Unfortunately, too much zeal in the support of this concept has sometimes led the uncritical student to foresake all rules and standards of behavior. In this article John R. Cole explores the importance of anthropologists' endorsing cultural relativism without abandoning scientific logic, method, and skepticism in the observation and analysis not only of traditional religious practices but also of such current "paranormal" topics as psychic archaeology, the "ancient astronauts" theories, and Bigfoot. It is fitting that Cole's article appears in the first chapter of this book, for the viewpoint of respecting a cultural tradition without having to endorse its scientific validity is reflected in the work of every anthropologist contributing to this anthology.

Reprinted from *The Skeptical Inquirer*, Vol. 2, no. 2 (Spring/Summer 1978), pp. 62–71, by permission of the author and the Committee for the Scientific Investigation of Claims of the Paranormal.

ANTHROPOLOGISTS STUDY COUNTLESS TOPICS, A disproportionate number of which are alien to the general public and to other scientists. And we also study *ourselves*—belief in UFOs or Bigfoot or Creationism or ESP or witches is grist for the anthropological mill and can itself be studied scientifically. There *is* science in this ecumenicism, however; and however unorthodox our subject matter, most of us distinguish between our discipline and our subject. Without contempt for believers in strange explanations of the world, we fairly often distinguish between the explanations of "insiders" and the empirical evidence we try to explain scientifically. The doctrine of "cultural relativism" is like a scientific ACLU, arguing that everyone has the right to their beliefs without censure from a Western tradition "establishment."

Still, there are weird things afoot to worry even the most cautious anthropologist in the public perception of the things we study. When a folk tradition explains the origin of the world as the result of the actions of a Great Turtle creating heaven and earth, we can respect the tradition without endorsing its scientific reality. But when people invoke the name of science to prove such claims, we need to speak out as scientists skeptical of these claims without disrespect for the people outside the scientific tradition who believe them. We can argue that "sacred cows" are not literally sacred while recognizing the underlying adaptive values of Hindu "cow worship," which is an ideological rationalization of quite reasonable and realistic ecological forces: killing every cow in India might give everyone a hamburger, but it would eliminate that country's source of fuel for fires, traction, fertilizer, construction mortar, milk and cheese, and even methane electrical generators. Traditional Western ideology, then, does not have all the answers to the anthropologists familiar with alternate solutions.

But studying the question of what it means to be human leaves anthropology at the mercy of cranks, crackpots, and the politically inspired cynics—not to mention the perhaps naive sensationalists capitalizing upon irrational, antiscientific cultural currents.

Let us grant that "anything is possible," without rejecting as impossible even the weirdest claims about humanness, while retaining our demand as scientists that revolutionary claims prove themselves rather than be accepted simply because they are asserted.

Major themes of current unverified (to be charitable) anthropological science include several "paranormal" topics: "creationism" of various forms purporting to disprove Darwin; "psychic archaeology" finding sites and interpreting prehistory by séance rather than scientific excavation; acceptance at face value of ESP and magic; resuscitation of hoary Atlantis and Lemuria myths; the "ancient astronauts" syndrome popularized by von Däniken, despite dissections by Ronald Story and others; near-religious belief in pre-Columbian colonization of the Americas by Europeans and Middle Easterners as an explanation of everything noteworthy ever accomplished by Native Americans (and the cyclical "discovery" of American inscriptions and altars that "prove" such pre-Columbian contacts); claims that humans descend from an ancient amphibious female creature, for which there is no known evidence; arguments that contemporary "races" can be ordered hierarchically according to IQ when even the identification of races is an open question among anthropologists and biologists; claims such as Robert Ardrey's that humans are natural killers; and so forth. The list is nearly endless, but the political implications are often rather transparently ominous.

A final category of anthropology potentially awry is the uncritical acceptance of informants' versions of reality without empirical testing. At the 1977 meeting of the American Anthropological Association in Houston, for example, one paper reported on Haitian stories of a coffin traveling the streets under its own power. This paper said the "simplest" explanation of the "evidence" was that either it had happened or there was at least something going on unexplainable by normal science. This paper was the only one I saw reported in the Houston press. I suppose this made better news copy than hundreds of other more orthodox papers read at the meeting, but as "science" it was, to say the least, a bit lacking.

The cultural relativist viewpoint, which refuses to judge *people*, need not rule out scientific evaluations of their *claims* as objective reality. Like most scientists, anthropologists are simply not trained to judge alleged paranormal phenomena. I have this old-fashioned desire to see controlled experiments and empirical evidence rather than simple testimonials assuring me that rules of scientific evidence are outmoded or are a slavish misapplication of Western concepts to phenomena beyond the ken of brainwashed science-worshipers.

Like other sciences, and perhaps even more than some with longer traditions of "sciencing" rather than speculation, anthropology is vulnerable to exploitation by naive or crank claims and by speculations that ignore the criteria of scientific proof while still claiming the mantle of "science." Margaret Mead, for example, is one of my culture heroes, a pioneering and peerless writer and ethnographer, and a woman who has contributed immeasurably to our understanding of the world around us. But when as president of the American Association for the Advancement of Science she convinced that body to accept as an official affiliate the Parapsychological Association, I believe she gave in to the cultural relativist position of uncritical acceptance of *possibilities* rather than insisting on the scientific discipline that she has championed for half a century. Scientific claims simply cannot be voted upon, even if the voters are thoroughly respectable and sincere.

Not every strange claim in anthropology can be dealt with in a short paper, but I can at least stress that anthropology includes a strong scientific, empirical tradition: at the least, sensational claims do not represent "orthodoxy" in anthropology, for better or worse. However, I will discuss briefly two current themes in anthropology and on its fringes: the current fad for "hyperdiffusionism," which derives Native American cultures from Old World sources; and the perhaps more subtle claims for an extreme antiquity for American peoples (which sometimes go as far as to claim that humans evolved in America rather than Africa).

Erich von Däniken's claims of an extraterrestrial origin for human cultural florescence have been disproved devastatingly, but what of diffusionist claims that assert that American cultures did not evolve according to the apparent laws of cultural evolution because they were strongly influenced by European or Asian or African cultures long before Columbus? Without ruling out the possibility, or even probability, of rather small-scale transoceanic diffusion, there is simply no valid empirical evidence of claims for massive pre-Columbian diffusion between the Old and New Worlds, such as those recently revived by Barry Fell in his book *America, B.C.* (New York: Quadrangle, 1977) or Cyrus Gordon's *Before Columbus* (New York: Crown, 1971). They resuscitate centuries-old claims and arguments repeatedly disproven, to the point that anthropologists no longer bother to argue. "Indians" simply were not too dumb to pile up dirt or stones into mounds and pyramids, despite the prejudices of early European colonialists. Early missionaries tried to prove that Native Americans were descendents of even earlier Old World colonists, sometimes to prove that their charges were worthy of respect rather than annihilation. Today there seems to be a more directly racist tinge to such claims, and in fact claims that Europeans "owned" real estate in the Americas before they were displaced by "savages" has direct political utility in the burgeoning spate of Native American lawsuits challenging European usurpation of tribal lands. Less clear-cut than this perhaps unconscious but significant racism, advocates of "ancient inscriptions" appeal to a romantic idea that a European history for the Americas is somehow more exciting and mysterious than mundane reality based on serious archaeology and physical anthropology.

Fell and his friends have found inscriptions in Celtic, Ogham, Latin, Phoenician, Egyptian, Cretan, Minoan, Greek, Carthaginian, Iberian, Libyan, and many other languages in New Zealand, Ecuador, Canada, Oklahoma, Minnesota, Iowa, and other localities that they claim have been "ignored" by the professionals. At a 1977 "conference" in Castleton, Vermont, celebrating Fell's work, one speaker alluded to "dozens" of major Egyptian cities in Ohio systematically "covered up" by the closed-minded establishment—while offering no evidence beyond the description of some burial mounds! Fell himself said he had evidence (unrevealed) proving that Jesus was known in the Americas "as early as the fourth century

A.D." He also cited "evidence" such as Ecuadorian "gold tablets" whose source he could not reveal; when I pointed out that they were from the collection of one Padre Crespi of Cuenca, Ecuador (Erich von Däniken's major source for his *Gold of the Gods* book), discounted as a naive crank by people familiar with his collection (which includes a copper toilet-tank float identified as Inca gold!), Fell refused to answer questions.

He cites the "Iowa Tablets," known where I grew up as the "Davenport Conspiracy" because of actual confessions by the original hoaxers, who used steel tools to carve slate roof slabs traced to a Davenport, Iowa, building. The Minnesota "Kensington Stone" was exposed rather convincingly as a hoax by Erik Wahlgren's book *The Kensington Stone: A Mystery Solved.* "Mystery Hill," New Hampshire, *may* not be fully understood, but its stone buildings have been traced by professional archaeologists to early historic times with an underlay of Native American artifacts dating much earlier but unrelated to European "Megalithic" cultures such as Stonehenge. Its "sacrifice stone" seems to be identical to grooved stones used throughout New England for two centuries in the production of lye and potash from wood ashes. "Celtic inscriptions" prove to be in modern Celtic, not in the form of the language used thousands of years ago at the time of alleged Celtic colonization. American Ogham inscriptions (an Irish shorthand version of Latin, consisting of patterned hashmarks) seem to be plow scratches on rocks, natural geologic fault-fractures, or outright hoaxes, such as an engraved stone displayed at the conference with fresh scratches, which, given the type of stone, could not be older than a century or so. Other inscriptions and paintings on pottery are simply Native American pictographs or geometric designs that may resemble some Old World symbols but prove nothing. Something like a "starburst" pattern or asterisk is a worldwide design element depicting the sun or stars, not evidence of diffusion. A mark such as "////" *could* be a tally or just three lines, but certainly is not a definite Roman numeral three! Slashes, triangles, squares, and crosses are so simple to reinvent that their presence is meaningless as proof of diffusion from European languages using similar symbols.

Perhaps buried in all of this hodgepodge of "ancient inscription" claims there *are* some real Old

World inscriptions, but the vast majority are either hoaxes or misinterpretations. When Fell and his cohorts accept them all, they discredit possibly *valid* diffusionist arguments, and we should avoid simple guilt by association. Yet every inscription claim that has been investigated by archaeologists, linguists, and geologists seems so far to be spurious. How long must the burden of proof lie with the nonextremists? When Fell "deciphers" an "inscription" such as that on the Canadian "Sherbrooke Stones" in at least three radically different ways in one year—and even accepts the idea that they may be ancient wormholes in sedimentary mudstone!—how can his decipherments be taken seriously in general? How can one argue with a man who identifies frost-pocking of rocks as "cuppules" with religious significance? When oral tradition, historical memory, and archaeological evidence point to the conclusion that New England's "Megalithic shrines" are simply root cellars and other historic constructions, why should we accept the torturously reasoned claim that they are anything else?

Aside from the dubious nature of these alleged inscriptions and shrines, one must ask: Why did ancient voyagers leave behind nothing but inscriptions and religious structures? Where are the habitation sites and tools and pottery one would expect from the many centuries of claimed Old World colonization? (*Not* just contact, but ongoing settlement and trade networks are being claimed.) Native Americans needed horses, sheep, cows, and pigs much more than they needed inscriptions! Significant colonization should yield such domesticated animal bones in pre-Columbian times for the archaeological record, but they do not appear. Artifacts of subsistence and not just ideology should have been left behind, given what we know about the workings of culture. An early Libyan (or whatever) colony would have been in a real position of power if it could have introduced draft animals and domesticated protein sources, as demonstrated by the Spanish Conquest. And why is there no evidence of Old World diseases before the "official" conquest—or of clear genetic admixture with Native American populations, which would be identifiable from human bone remains? According to what we know about cultural and biological processes, any significant pre-Columbian contact (that is, not just a possible stray boat or very temporary settlement such as the Vikings') would simply have had to leave evidence other than religious artifacts.

The "Early Man in the New World" argument suffers some of the same problems. People clearly were in the Americas about 15,000 years ago and perhaps much earlier; fragmentary evidence much in dispute suggests the *possibility* of human occupation even 50,000 years ago. Even earlier dates are possible, but it is *not* possible that humans evolved in the Americas rather than in the Old World, because there are *no* humanlike or ape fossils in the Americas—only those of very primitive monkeys. No *human* remains such as those of Neanderthals or "Peking Man" types have ever been identified in the New World, while they are plentiful in the Old World. Claims of human antiquity of hundreds of thousands of years in America show up in tabloid news stories but not in scientific journals or museum collections that can be examined by skeptics.

There is a definite popular appeal for "Guinness records," such as earliest, best, biggest, and so on, but American claims for them tend to be reasoned about as well as Bermuda Triangle arguments and documented by claims from people who say "Trust me," rather than, "Here's the evidence and its theoretical explanation." *If* people lived in America during or before the latest Ice Age, what did they do for a living? How did they get here? The claim of an "Atlantic land bridge" has no support from the facts of geology. Sources in Atlantis or Lemuria are, if anything, even more ludicrous. When a supposed scientist says that mammals may have migrated to America as many as a million years ago to prove that humans could have done the same, perhaps he sounds convincingly aware of multidisciplinary data. But some of the oldest mammals known are from the Americas, and such a comment suggests ignorance of the data rather than proof of a good argument (and 60- and 120-million-year-old mammals have nothing to do with humans who have only been around for a few million years at most!).

Anyone claiming extreme antiquity for New World humans must answer several questions: What is the dating technique? In what controlled context were the artifacts found? Could they be "naturefacts," or natural objects? What were tools used for, and how do they fit into a cultural pattern and evolutionary sequence? What effect would human habitation have had upon other animals and the rest of the environment, and what evidence is there for such effects (slaughtered game, burned clearings, postholes in the ground, gathered plant remains, and so on)? And where did the people come from—and how—if there is no evidence for contemporary human occupation of Siberia, which would have been the only reasonable source for early Americans in the time before boats?

At first glance "early man" claims may not seem as "paranormal" as psychic archaeology or the semireligious inscription mania. But the subject tends to become a single-minded obsession, promoted as an argument of faith rather than scientific method and data. Such statements as, "We're working on a frontier; all we ask is that you accept our subject and evidence" (and then maybe we'll show you our data and methods) are romantic appeals in the tradition of ESP advocates. Another statement often heard is, "Maybe there's more out there than traditionally believed—that's really revolutionary." Well, who could argue with that? But when someone advocating a revolutionary approach says, "The burden of proof lies with our critics," adding that nothing is being *claimed*, but just suggested as a *possibility*, there is a classic paranormal-claim syndrome at work. It *is* tempting to give into the argument "You won't let us get to first base" until one realizes that such an a priori decision is an unwarranted decision to accept a previously ineligible baserunner! Just as in baseball, a "hit" or walk or error is a prerequisite to getting to first base, and errors do not reflect well upon either side!

What is most basic is how unorthodox claimants use scientific method and logic rather than simple claims upon belief. If claims are rejected by most scholars, why is this so? If the only answer is "dogmatism" and accusations of jealousy and persecution of pioneer thinkers, one can at least be a little wary. Denouncing "experts" in praise of noble "amateurs" is not the same as scientific proof. Conservatism *may* be in error regarding new claims, but it serves a real purpose in forcing the burden of proof upon new ideas, making them more rigorous—otherwise we would have to regard every idea that came along, however idiotic, as equal to all others, and science would spend all of its time disproving rather than proving.

Methodology and logic can be evaluated to some extent by non-specialists if they read carefully enough. Arguments such as those quoted above are giveaways that something may be wrong. Too often we all regard a claim as a valid hypothesis simply because it is in print, but hypotheses, unlike some "claims," are testable and suggest their own tests of verification of falsificaton. Simply requesting a priori belief in basic premises that contradict established premises is not scientific. While we cannot simply take a vote among experts to decide the "truth," the experts' criticisms need to be taken into account by would-be revolutionaries in their very proposals.

One can endorse cultural relativism without forsaking scientific logic, method, and skepticism. People may be equal, but their contradictory explanations of the empirical world are not. Anthropology deals with sensitive issues of "human nature" vulnerable to political, religious and ideological controversy in a way physics and astronomy no longer are. If humans are called "naturally aggressive," there are clear implications about the inevitability of war and authoritarianism. If civilization can only develop in the Americas as a result of Old World influences, serious racist overtones are at least possible in the argument. Treating culture and its diffusion simply in terms of inscribed symbols implies that ideology and belief are much more important than factors of subsistence and technology—a theoretical position with which I would argue and at least want made explicit.

Anthropology, used or misused, has practical implications that make the treatment of it as simply a collection of "mysteries" or details a mistake, even if it were *not* a science already. But far too often that seems to be its fate in the popular press, tantalized more by exotic things "out there" than by the scientific explanation of them. Explanations are far from complete, but anthropologists simply contribute to further misunderstanding when they sometimes remain aloof from their ultimate clients *and* subject matter, the general public.

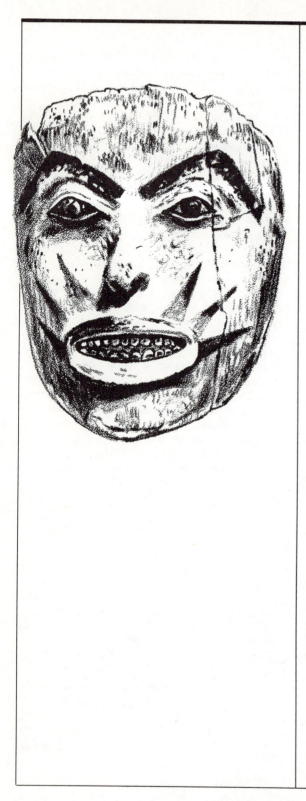

2

Myth, Ritual, Symbolism, and Taboo

Tales, legends, proverbs, riddles, adages, and myths make up what anthropologists call *folklore*, an important subject for the study of culture. Because of its sacred nature, myth is especially significant in the analysis of comparative religion. Myth functions in a society as a "charter," as Malinowski puts it—a model for behavior that also explains the origins of the world, life on earth, death, and all other experiences of human existence: "[Myth] is a statement of primeval reality which lives in the institutions and pursuits of a community. It justifies by precedent the existing order and it supplies a retrospective pattern of moral values, of sociological discriminations and burdens and of magical belief. . . . The function of myth is to strengthen tradition and to endow it with a greater value and prestige by tracing it back to a higher, better, more supernatural, and more effective reality of initial events" (1931: 640–41).

Some anthropologists apply a psychological approach to myth analysis and see myths as symbolic expressions of sibling rivalry, male-

Indian mask of painted wood, Northwest Coast, North America.

female tensions, and other themes. Others—structural anthropologists such as Claude Lévi-Strauss—view myths as cultural means of resolving critical binary oppositions (life-death, matrilineal-patrilineal, nature-culture) that serve as models for members of a society (1976: 280–81). Whether in Judeo-Christian and Moslem cultures, where myths have been transcribed to form the Tora, Bible, and Koran, or in other, less familiar cultures, these sacred narratives still serve their time-honored function for the bulk of humanity as the basis of religious belief. What is important to remember is that myths in traditional societies are considered to be truthful accounts of the past, just as are the writings of the so-called great religions.

Like myth, ritual and ceremony are of crucial significance to all human societies, and are important for the understanding of religion in culture. According to Victor Turner, in a definition widely quoted from his article that appears later in this chapter, "A ritual is a stereotyped sequence of activities involving gestures, words, and objects, performed in a sequestered place and designed to influence preternatural [magical] entities or forces on behalf of the actors' goals and interests." As described by Anthony Wallace, ritual is "the primary phenomenon of religion": "Ritual is religion in action; it is the cutting edge of the tool. Belief, although its recitation may be part of the ritual, or a ritual in its own right, serves to explain, to rationalize, to interpret and direct the energy of the ritual performance. . . . It is ritual which accomplishes what religion sets out to do" (1966: 102).

It is through ritual that religion is able to impress on people a commitment to their system of religious beliefs. Participants in a religious ritual are able to express group solidarity and loyalty. Indeed, Emile Durkheim argued that the true nature of religion was ritual participation. Of course, history abounds with examples of the importance of the individual experience in religion; yet there is no denying the overwhelming effect of group participation. As William Howells has pointed out, ritual helps individuals but does so by treating them as a whole group: "they are like a tangled head of hair, and ritual is the comb" (1962: 243).

Although in this chapter Max Gluckman urges

the rejection of any simple explanation of ritual as a response to anxiety, most anthropologists believe, along with Malinowski and other early functionalists, that ritual at least allays anxiety. Through the shared performance of group dances and ceremonies, humans are able to reduce the fears that often come when life's events threaten their security and sense of well-being. Other scholars, such as A. R. Radcliffe-Brown, have taken the opposite tack, claiming that ritual may actually create rather than allay anxiety and fears.

Most introductory textbooks in anthropology divide religious ritual into rites of passage and rites of intensification. Rites of passage mark transition points in the lives of individuals—for example, birth, puberty, marriage, and death. Rites of intensification occur during a crisis for a group and are thus more important in maintaining group equilibrium and solidarity. They are typically associated with natural phenomena, such as seasonal changes or a lack of rain, but other events, such as impending warfare, could also trigger a rite of intensification. Whatever precipitates the crisis, there is need of a ritual to lessen the anxiety that is felt by the group.

Although the division of rituals into this two-fold scheme is useful, it does not adequately represent the variety of ritual occurring in the world's cultures. Anthony Wallace, for example, has outlined five major categories of ritual (1966: 107–66).

1. *Technological rituals*, designed to control nature for the purpose of human exploitation, comprise three subdivisions:

   a. Divination rites, which help predict the future and gain hidden information.

   b. Rites of intensification, designed to help obtain food and alcohol.

   c. Protective rites, aimed at coping with the uncertainty of nature (for example, stormy seas, floods, crop disease, and bad luck).

2. *Therapy and anti-therapy rituals* are designed to control human health. Curative rites exemplify therapy rituals; witchcraft and sorcery, anti-therapy.

3. *Ideological rituals*, according to Wallace, are "intended to control, in a conservative way, the behavior, the mood, the sentiments and values of

groups for the sake of the community as a whole." They consist of four subcategories:

a. Rites of passage, which deal with role change and geographic movement (for example, marriages).

b. Rites of intensification, to ensure people adhere to values and customs (for example, Sunday church service).

c. Taboos (ritual avoidances), courtesies (positive actions), and other arbitrary ceremonial obligations, which serve to regulate human behavior.

d. Rites of rebellion, which provide a form of "ritualized catharsis" that contributes to order and stability by allowing people to vent their frustrations.

4. *Salvation rituals* aim at repairing damaged self-esteem and other forms of impaired identity. Wallace sees three common subdivisions in this category:

a. Possession, in which an individual's identity is altered by the presence of an alien spirit that occupies the body (exorcism is the usual treatment).

b. Ritual encouragement of an individual to accept an alternate identity, a process similar to the ritual procedure shamans undergo upon assuming a shamanic role.

c. The mystic experience—loss of personal identity by abandoning the old self and achieving salvation by identifying with a sacred being.

5. *Revitalization rituals* are aimed at what can be described as an identity crisis of an entire community. The revitalization movement may be seen as a religious movement (a ritual) that, through the help of a prophet, strives to create a better culture.

Just as myth and ritual are expressions of ideology, the study of symbolism too is vital to the study of religion. Anthropology has been less than clear in its attempt to define the meaning of this important concept. Minimally, a symbol may be thought of as something that represents something else. The development of culture, for example, was dependent on human beings having the ability to assign symbolic meanings to words—to create and use a language. Religion is also a prime example of man's proclivity to attach symbolic meanings to a variety of behavior and objects. "The object of symbolism," according to Alfred North Whitehead, "is the enhancement of the importance of what is symbolized" (1927: 63).

That anthropological interest in the topic of symbolism had its start with the study of religious behavior is not surprising, especially in light of the plethora of symbols present in religious objects and ceremonies. Reflect for a moment on any religious service. Immediately on entering the building, be it a church, synogogue, or mosque, one is overwhelmed by symbolic objects—the Christian cross, the Star of David, paintings, statues, tapestries, and assorted ceremonial paraphernalia—each representing a religious principle. Fittingly, Geertz has noted that a religious system may be viewed as a "cluster of sacred symbols" (1957: 424). Unlike the well-defined symbols in mathematics and the physical sciences, these religious symbols assume many different forms and meanings: witness Victor Turner's concept of the multivocalic nature of symbols (their capacity to have many meanings), outlined in his article in this chapter.

More than a simple reminder of some remote aspect of a religion's history, religious symbols are often considered to possess a power or force (*mana*) emanating from the spiritual world itself. The symbols provide people with an emotional and intellectual commitment to their particular belief system, telling them what is important to their society, collectively and individually, and helping them conform to the group's value system. Durkheim accounted for the universality of symbols by arguing that a society kept its value system through their use; that is, the symbols stood for the revered values. Without the symbols, the values and, by extension, the society's existence would be threatened.

Whereas symbols, like myths and rituals, prescribe thoughts and behaviors of people, taboos restrict actions. Because the term *taboo* (also known as *tabu* and *kapu*) originated in the Pacific Islands, beginning anthropology students often associate it with images of "savage" Polynesians observing mystical prohibitions. It is true that Pacific Islanders did cautiously regard these restrictions, being careful to avoid the supernatural retribution that was certain to follow violations.

Taboos are not limited to the Pacific, however: every society has restrictions that limit behavior in one respect or another, usually in association with sex, food, rites of passage, sacred objects, and sacred people. The incest taboo is unique in that it is found in all societies. Although anthropologists have yet to adequately explain why the incest taboo exists everywhere, they have demonstrated that most taboos are reinforced by the threat of punishments meted out by supernatural forces.

As anthropologists have pointed out, taboos are adaptive human mechanisms: they function to counter dangers of both the phenomenal and ideational world. It is possible to theorize that the existence of fewer real or imagined dangers would result in fewer taboos, but it is equally safe to argue that all societies will continue to establish new taboos as new threats to existence or social stability arise. Certainly taboos function at an ecological level, for example, to preserve plants, animals, and resources of the sea. Taboos also function to distinguish between and control social groups, threatening violators with supernatural punishments as severe as the denial of salvation. Depending on the culture, sacred authority is often as compelling as the civil codes to which people are required to comply. Simply stated, the breaking of a sacred taboo, as opposed to a civil sanction, is a sin. The impersonal power of *mana* made certain objects and people in Pacific cultures taboo. Although the concept of *mana* does not exist in contemporary Western cultures, certain symbols and objects are similarly imbued with such an aura of power or sacredness that they too are considered taboo.

Using both a case study and an encyclopedic approach to myth, ritual, symbolism, and taboo, the five articles selected for this chapter clearly show the importance of these topics to the study of comparative religion. Leach, Gluckman, Turner, and Douglas bring to the reader the results of their field work in the non-Western world; Dubisch, on the other hand, discusses the religious aspects evidenced in the American health food movement—a phenomenon that displays common elements of all of this chapter's major topics.

References Cited

Geertz, Clifford
      1957 "Ethos, World-View and the Analysis of Sacred Symbols," *Antioch Review* 17: 421–37.

Howells, William
      1962 *The Heathens*. Garden City, N.Y.: Doubleday.

Hunter, David E., and Phillip Whitten
      1976 *Encyclopedia of Anthropology*. New York: Harper and Row.

Malinowski, Bronislaw
      1931 "Culture." In David L. Sills, ed., *Encyclopedia of the Social Sciences*, Vol. 4, pp. 621–46. New York: Macmillan Free Press.

Wallace, A. F. C.
      1966 *Religion: An Anthropological View*. New York: Random House.

Whitehead, Alfred N.
      1927 *Symbolism*. New York: G. P. Putnam's Sons.

Genesis as Myth

Edmund R. Leach

Rather than analyze myths that have originated in non-Western societies, Edmund R. Leach here dissects a familiar story: the Old Testament recounting of the beginning of the world. Leach argues that although myths such as the Book of Genesis are repetitive, intricate, and contradictory, their construction is logical. He also shows how modern information theory throws new light on myths as a form of communication. Because to the true believer these mythic messages are the word of God, their very redundancy is reassuring. Each version confirms and reinforces the meaning of all the others and thereby reifies man's faith in the unknowable, making it the known. Leach explains the role of opposites as a basic construct of human minds, and maintains that the structure of binary opposites in myth reflects our natural cognitive map as we separate, for example, God from man. Myth not only creates the oppositions, but sets as a common mythic element how these separations are eliminated through supernatural intermediaries and rituals, which bring the opposites together.

Reprinted from *Discovery* (May 1982), pp. 30–35, by permission of the author.

A DISTINGUISHED GERMAN THEOLOGIAN HAS DEfined myth as "the expression of unobservable realities in terms of observable phenomena" (Bartsch 1953). All stories which occur in the Bible are myths for the devout Christian, whether they correspond to historical fact or not. All human societies have myths in this sense, and normally the myths to which the greatest importance is attached are those which are the least probable. The non-rationality of myth is its very essence, for religion requires a demonstration of faith by the suspension of critical doubt.

But if myths do not mean what they appear to mean, how do they come to mean anything at all? What is the nature of the esoteric mode of communication by which myth is felt to give "expression to unobservable realities"?

This is an old problem which has lately taken on a new shape because, if myth be a mode of communication, then a part of the theory which is embodied in digital computer systems ought to be relevant. The merit of this approach is that it draws special attention to precisely those features of myth which have formerly been regarded as accidental defects. It is common to all mythological systems that all important stories recur in several different versions. Man is created in Genesis (chapter I, verse 27) and then he is created all over again (II, 7). And, as if the two first men were not enough, we also have Noah in chapter VIII. Likewise in the New Testament, why must there be four gospels each telling "the same" story yet sometimes flatly contradictory on details of fact? Another noticeable characteristic of mythical stories is their markedly binary aspect; myth is constantly setting up opposing categories: "In the beginning God created the heaven and the earth," "they crucified Him and two others with him, on either side one, and Jesus in the midst," "I am the Alpha and the Omega, the beginning and the end, saith the Lord." So always it is in myth —God against the world and the world itself for ever dividing into opposites on either side—male and female, living and dead, good and evil, first and last . . .

Now, in the language of communication engineers, the first of these common characteristics of myth is called *redundancy,* while the second is strongly reminiscent of the unit of information—the *bit.* "Information" in this technical sense is a measure of the freedom of choice in selecting a message. If there are only two messages and it is arbitrary which you choose then "information is unity," that is = 1 bit (*bit* stands for "binary digit") (Shannon and Weaver 1949).

Communication engineers employ these concepts for the analysis of problems which arise when a particular individual (the sender) wishes to transmit a coded message correctly to another individual (the receiver) against a background of interference (noise). "Information" refers on the one hand to the degrees of choice open to the sender in encoding his transmission and on the other to the degrees of choice open to the receiver in interpreting what he receives (which will include noise in addition to the original transmitted signal). In this situation a high level of redundancy makes it easy to correct errors introduced by noise.

Now in the mind of the believer, myth does indeed convey messages which are the Word of God. To such a man the redundancy of myth is a very reassuring fact. Any particular myth in isolation is like a coded message badly snarled up with noisy interference. Even the most confident devotee might feel a little uncertain as to what precisely is being said. But, as a result of redundancy, the believer can feel that, even when the details vary, each alternative version of a myth confirms his understanding and reinforces the essential meaning of all the others.

Binary Structure of Myth

The anthropologist's viewpoint is different. He rejects the idea of a supernatural sender. He observes only a variety of possible receivers. Redundancy increases information—that is the uncertainty of the possible means of decoding the message. This explains what is surely the most striking of all religious phenomena—the passionate adherence to sectarian belief. The whole of Christendom shares a single corpus of mythology so it is surely very remarkable that the members of each particular Christian sect are able to convince themselves that they alone possess the secret of revealed truth. The abstract propositions of communication theory help us to understand this paradox.

But if the true believer can interpret his own mythology in almost any way he chooses, what principle governs the formation of the original myth? Is it random chance that a myth assumes one pattern rather than another? The binary structure of myth suggests otherwise.

Binary oppositions are intrinsic to the process of human thought. Any description of the world must discriminate categories in the form *"p is what not-p is not."* An object is alive or not alive and one could not formulate the concept "alive" except as the converse of its partner "dead." So also human beings are male or not male, and persons of the opposite sex are either available as sexual partners or not available. Universally these are the most fundamentally important oppositions in all human experience.

Religion everywhere is preoccupied with the first, the antinomy of life and death. Religion seeks to deny the binary link between the two words; it does this by creating the mystical idea of "another world," a land of the dead where life is perpetual. The attributes of this other world are necessarily those which are not of this world; imperfection here is balanced by perfection there. But this logical ordering of ideas has a disconcerting consequence—God comes to belong to the other world. The central "problem" of religion is then to reestablish some kind of bridge between Man and God.

This pattern is built into the structure of every mythical system; the myth first discriminates between gods and men and then becomes preoccupied with the relations and intermediaries which link men and gods together. This much is already implicit in our initial definition.

So too with sex relations. Every human society has rules of incest and exogamy. Though the rules vary they always have the implication that for any particular male individual all women are divided by at least one binary distinction, there are women of *our kind* with whom sex relations would be incestuous and there are women of the *other kind* with whom sex relations are allowed. But here again we are immediately led into paradox. How was it in the beginning? If our first parents were persons of two kinds, what was that other kind? But if they were both of our kind, then their relations must have been incestuous and we are all born in sin. The myths of the world offer many different solutions to this childish intellectual puzzle, but the prominence which it receives shows that it entails the most profound moral issues. The crux is as before. If the logic of our thought leads us to distinguish *we* from *they*, how can we bridge the gap and establish social and sexual relations with "the others" without throwing our categories into confusion?

So, despite all variations of theology, this aspect of myth is a constant. In every myth system we will find a persistent sequence of binary discriminations as between human/superhuman, mortal/immortal, male/female, legitimate/illegitimate, good/bad . . . followed by a "mediation" of the paired categories thus distinguished.

"Mediation" (in this sense) is always achieved by introducing a third category which is "abnormal" or "anomalous" in terms of ordinary "rational" categories. Thus myths are full of fabulous monsters, incarnate gods, virgin mothers. This middle ground is abnormal, non-natural, holy. It is typically the focus of all taboo and ritual observance.

This approach to myth analysis derives originally from the techniques of structural linguistics associated with the name of Roman Jakobson (Jakobson and Halle 1956) but is more immediately due to C. Lévi-Strauss, one of whose examples may serve to illustrate the general principle.

Certain Pueblo Indian myths focus on the opposition between life and death. In these myths we find a threefold category distinction: agriculture (means to life), war (means to death), and hunting (a mediating category since it is means to life for men but means to death for animals). Other myths of the same cluster deploy a different triad: grass-eating animals (which live without killing), predators (which live by killing), and carrion-eating creatures (mediators, since they eat meat but do not kill in order to eat). In accumulation this total set of associated symbols serves to imply that life and death are *not* just the back and the front of the same penny, that death is *not* the necessary consequence of life (Lévi-Strauss 1955).

My Figure 1 has been designed to display an analogous structure for the case of the first four chapters of Genesis. The three horizontal bands of the diagram correspond to (i) the story of the seven-day creation, (ii) the story of the Garden of Eden, and (iii) the story of Cain and Abel. The diagram can also be read vertically: column 1 in band (ii) corresponds to column 1 in band (i) and so on. The detailed analysis is as follows:

Upper Band

First Day (I, 1–5; not on diagram). Heaven distinguished from Earth; Light from Darkness; Day from Night; Evening from Morning.

Second Day (I, 6–8; col. 1 of diagram). (Fertile) water (rain) above; (infertile) water (sea) below. Mediated by firmament (sky).

Third Day (I, 9–10; col. 2 and I, 11–12; col. 3). Sea opposed to dry land. Mediated by "grass, herb yielding seed (cereals), fruit trees." These grow on dry land but need water. They are classed as things "whose seed is in itself" and thereby contrasted with bisexual animals, birds, etc.

The creation of the world as a static (that is, dead) entity is now complete and this whole phase of the creation is opposed to the creation of moving (that is, living) things.

Fourth Day (I, 13–18; col. 4). Mobile sun and moon are placed in the fixed firmament of col. 1. Light and darkness become alternations (life and death become alternates).

Fifth Day (I, 20–23; col. 5). Fish and birds are living things corresponding to the sea/land opposition of col. 2 but they also mediate the col. 1 oppositions between sky and earth and between salt water and fresh water.

Sixth Day (I, 24–25; col. 6). Cattle (domestic animals), beasts (wild animals), creeping things. These correspond to the static triad of col. 3. But only the grass is allocated to the animals. Everything else, including the meat of the animals, is for Man's use (I, 29–30). Later at Leviticus XI creatures which do not fit this exact ordering of the world—for instance, water creatures with no fins, animals and birds which eat meat or fish, etc.—are classed as "abominations." Creeping Things are

FIGURE 1. The first four chapters of Genesis contain three separate creation stories. Horizontal bands correspond to (a) 7-day creation; (b) Garden of Eden; and (c) Cain and Abel. Each story sets up opposition of Death versus Life, God versus Man. World is "made alive" by using categories of "woman" and "creeping thing" to mediate this opposition.

anomalous with respect to the major categories, Fowl, Fish, Cattle, Beast and are thus abominations *ab initio* (Leviticus XI, 41–42). This classification in turn leads to an anomalous contradiction. In order to allow the Israelites to eat locusts the author of Leviticus XI had to introduce a special qualification to the prohibition against eating creeping things: "Yet these ye *may* eat: of every flying creeping thing that goeth on all four which have legs above their feet, to leap withal upon the earth" (v. 21). The procedures of binary discrimination could scarcely be carried further!

(I, 26–27; col. 7), Man and Woman are created simultaneously. The whole system of living creatures is instructed to "be fruitful and multiply" but the problems of Life versus Death, and Incest versus Procreation are not faced at all.

Centre Band

The Garden of Eden story which now follows tackles from the start these very problems which have been evaded in the first version. We start again with the opposition Heaven versus Earth, but this is mediated by a fertilising mist drawn from the dry infertile earth (II, 4–6). This theme, which blurs the distinction life/death, is repeated. Living Adam is formed from the dead dust of the ground (II, 7); so are the animals (II, 19); the garden is fertilised by a river which "went out of Eden" (II, 10); finally fertile Eve is formed from a rib of infertile Adam (II, 22–23).

The opposition Heaven/Earth is followed by further oppositions—Man/Garden (II, 15); Tree of Life/Tree of Death (II, 9, 17); the latter is called the tree of the "knowledge of good and evil" which means the knowledge of sexual difference.

Recurrent also is the theme that unity in the other world (Eden, Paradise) becomes duality in this world. Outside Eden the river splits into four and divides the world into separate lands (II, 10–14). In Eden, Adam can exist by himself, Life can exist by itself; in this world, there are men and women, life and death. This repeats the contrast between monosexual plants and bisexual animals which is stressed in the first story.

The other living creatures are now created specifically because of the loneliness of Man in Eden (II, 18). The categories are Cattle, Birds, Beasts. None of these is adequate as a helpmeet for Man. So finally Eve is drawn from Adam's rib . . . "they are of one flesh" (II, 18–24).

Comparison of Band 1 and Band 2 at this stage shows that Eve in the seond story replaces the "Creeping Things" of the first story. Just as Creeping Things were anomalous with respect to Fish, Fowl, Cattle and Beast so Eve is anomalous to the opposition Man versus Animal. And, as a final mediation (chapter III), the Serpent, a creeping thing, is anomalous to the opposition Man versus Woman. Christian artists have always been sensitive to this fact; they manage to give the monster a somewhat hermaphrodite appearance while still indicating some kind of identification between the Serpent and Eve herself.

Hugo Van der Goes puts Eve and the Serpent in the same posture; Michelangelo makes Adam and Eve both gaze with loving adoration on the Serpent, but the Serpent has Eve's face.

Adam and Eve eat the forbidden fruit and become aware of sexual difference, death becomes inevitable (III, 3–8). But now for the first time pregnancy and reproduction become possible. Eve does not become pregnant until after she has been expelled from Paradise (IV, 1).

Lower Band

Cain the Gardener and Abel the Herdsman repeat the antithesis between the first three days of the creation and the last three days in the first story. Abel's living world is more pleasing to God (IV, 4–5). Cain's fratricide compares with Adam's incest and so God's questioning and cursing of Cain (IV, 9–12) has the same form and sequence as God's questioning and cursing of Adam, Eve and the Serpent (III, 9–19). The latter part of III, 16, is later repeated exactly (IV, 7) so Cain's sin was not only fratricide but also incestuous homosexuality. In order that immortal monosexual existence in Paradise may be exchanged for fertile heterosexual existence in reality, Cain, like Adam, must acquire a wife (IV, 17). To this end Adam must eliminate a sister; Cain a brother. The symmetry is complete.

Cross-Cultural Comparison

The issue here is the logical basis of incest categories and closely analogous patterns must occur in all mythologies regardless of their superficial content. Cross-cultural comparison becomes easier if we represent the analysis as a systematic pattern of binary discriminations as in Figure 2.

Adam/Eve and Cain/Abel are then seen to be variants of a theme which can also occur in other forms as in the well-known myth of Oedipus. The actual symbolism in these two cases is nearly identical. Oedipus, like Adam and Cain, is initially earthbound and immobile. The conclusion of the Athenian version of the Oedipus story is that he is an exiled wanderer, protected by the gods. So also is Cain (IV, 14–15). The Bible also includes the converse of this pattern. In Genesis XXVIII Jacob is a lonely exile and wanderer under God's protection but (XXXII, 24–32) he is renamed Israel and thus given the status of a first ancestor with a territorial autochthonous base, and he is lamed by God. Although Jacob dies abroad in Egypt he is buried on his own ancestral soil in Israel (XL, 29–32; L, 5–7).

In the Oedipus story, in place of Eve's Serpent we have Jocasta's Sphinx. Like Jocasta the Sphinx is female, like Jocasta the Sphinx commits suicide, like the Serpent the Sphinx leads men to their doom by verbal cunning, like the Serpent the Sphinx is an anomalous monster. Eve listens to the Serpent's words and betrays Adam into incest;

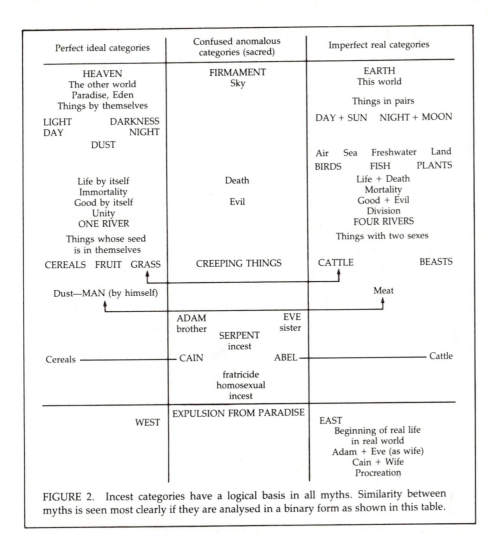

FIGURE 2. Incest categories have a logical basis in all myths. Similarity between myths is seen most clearly if they are analysed in a binary form as shown in this table.

Oedipus solves the Sphinx riddle and is led into incest. Again, Oedipus's patricide replaces Cain's fratricide—Oedipus, incidentally, meets Laius "at a cross roads."

Parallels of this kind seem too close to be accidental but this kind of algebra is unfamiliar and more evidence will be needed to convince the sceptical. Genesis contains several further examples of first ancestors.

Firstly, Noah survived the destruction of the world by flood together with three sons and their wives. Prior to this the population of the world had included three kinds of being—"sons of God,"

"daughters of men" and "giants" who were the offspring of the union of the other two (VI, 1–4). Since the forbears of Noah's daughters-in-law have all been destroyed in the Flood, Noah becomes a unique ancestor of all mankind without the implication of incest. Chapter IX, 1–7, addressed to Noah is almost the duplicate of I, 27–30, addressed to Adam.

Though heterosexual incest is evaded, the theme of homosexual incest in the Cain and Abel story recurs in the Noah saga when drunken Noah is seduced by his own son Ham (IX, 21–25). The Canaanites, descendants of Ham, are for this reason accursed. (That a homosexual act is intended is evident from the language "Ham saw the nakedness of his father." Compare Leviticus XVIII, 6–19, where "to uncover the nakedness of" consistently means to have sexual relations with.)

In the second place Lot survives the destruction of the world by fire together with two nubile daughters. Drunken Lot is seduced by his own daughters (XIX, 30–38). The Moabites and the Ammonites, descendants of these daughters, are for this reason accursed. In chapter XIX the men of Sodom endeavour to have homosexual relations with two angels who are visiting Lot. Lot offers his nubile daughters instead but they escape unscathed. The implication is that Lot's incest is less grave than heterosexual relations with a foreigner, and still less grave than homosexual relations.

Thirdly, the affair of the Sodomites and the Angels contains echoes of "the sons of God" and "the daughters of men" but links specifically with chapter XVIII where Abraham receives a visit from God and two Angels who promise that his ageing and barren wife Sarah shall bear a son. Sarah is Abraham's half-sister by the same father (XX, 12) and his relations with her are unambiguously incestuous (Leviticus XVIII, 9). Abraham loans Sarah to Pharaoh saying that she is his sister (XII, 19). He does the same with King Abimelech (XX, 2). Isaac repeats the game with Abimelech (XXVI, 9–11) but with a difference. Isaac's wife Rebekah is his father's brother's son's daughter (second cousin) and the relation is *not* in fact incestuous. The barrenness of Sarah is an aspect of her incest. The supernatural intervention which ultimately ensures that she shall bear a child is evidence that the incest is condoned. Pharaoh and Abimelech both suffer supernatural penalties for the lesser offence of adultery, but Abraham, the incestuous husband, survives unscathed.

There are other stories in the same set. Hagar, Sarah's Egyptian slave, bears a son Ishmael to Abraham, whose descendants are wanderers of low status. Sarah's son Isaac is marked out as of higher status than the sons of Abraham's concubines, who are sent away to "the east country" (c.f. wandering Cain who made his home in Nod "eastward of Eden"). Isaac marries a kinswoman in preference to a Canaanite woman. Esau's marriage to a Hittite woman is marked as a sin. In contrast his younger and favoured twin brother

Jacob marries two daughters of his mother's brother, who is in turn Jacob's father's father's brother's son's son.

All in all, this long series of repetitive and inverted tales asserts:

1. the overriding virtue of close kin endogamy;

2. that the sacred hero ancestor Abraham can carry this so far that he marries his paternal half-sister (an incestuous relationship). Abraham is thus likened to Pharaoh, for the Pharaohs of Egypt regularly married their paternal half-sisters; and

3. that a rank order is established which places the tribal neighbours of the Israelites in varying degrees of inferior status depending upon the nature of the defect in their original ancestry as compared with the pure descent of Jacob (Israel).

The myth requires that the Israelites be descended unambiguously from Terah, the father of Abraham. This is achieved only at the cost of a breach of the incest rule; but by reciting a large number of similar stories which entail even greater breaches of sexual morality the relations of Abraham and Sarah finally stand out as uniquely virtuous. Just as Adam and Eve are virtuous as compared to Cain and Abel, so Abraham's incest can pass unnoticed in the context of such outrageous characters as Ham, Lot's daughters, and the men of Sodom.

I have concentrated here upon the issue of sexual rules and transgressions so as to show how a multiplicity of repetitions, inversions, and variations can add up to a consistent "message." I do not wish to imply that this is the only structural pattern which these myths contain.

The novelty of the analysis which I have presented does not lie in the facts but in the procedure. Instead of taking each myth as a thing in itself with a "meaning" peculiar to itself it is assumed, from the start, that every myth is one of a complex and that any pattern which occurs in one myth will recur, in the same or other variations, in other parts of the complex. The structure that is common to all variations becomes apparent when different versions are "superimposed" one upon the other.

Whenever a corpus of mythology is recited in its religious setting such structural patterns are "felt" to be present, and convey meaning much as poetry conveys meaning. Even though the ordinary listener is not fully conscious of what has been communicated, the "message" is there in a quite objective sense. If the labour of programming could be performed the actual analysis could be done by a computer far better than by any human.

Furthermore, it seems evident that much the same patterns exist in the most diverse kinds of mythology. This seems to me to be a fact of great psychological, sociological, and scientific significance. Here truly are observable phenomena which are the expression of unobservable realities.

Ritual

Max Gluckman

Religious ritual is of crucial importance in all human societies. Ritual is the heart of religious behavior, or, as William Howells describes it, "the meat which goes on the bones of a cult's beliefs" (1962: 224). As a perusal of the literature makes clear, however, there is an endless variety not only in types of religious rituals, but also in modes of interpreting them. In this article, Max Gluckman briefly discusses various psychoanalytical, sociological, and anthropological explanations regarding the purpose and function of religious ritual. Using Swazi first-fruits rites and a Ndembu nubility ritual as ethnographic examples, Gluckman rejects any simple explanation of ritual as a response to anxiety, the transference of aggression into scapegoats, or the reinforcement of social sentiments. Rather, he prefers Victor W. Turner's more complicated analysis of the significance of ritual ceremonies. Briefly, Turner would collect from participants information on the meaning of ritual ceremonies and their symbols. Although the explanations given by the participants varied, Turner felt that in general they would stress the "socially valuable attributes of the symbol."

Reprinted from Richard Cavendish, ed., *Man, Myth, and Magic* (London, 1970), Vol. 17, pp. 2392–98, by permission of the author and BPCC/Phoebus Publishing.

MANY DIFFERENT KINDS OF PHENOMENA HAVE been described as ritual. The term has been applied, for example, to the mating habits of birds and animals, such as the dance on the water of the crested grebe; by psychoanalysts to the obsessive behaviour of neurotics, as when a man persistently checks whether he has turned off a tap, only to check anew after each check; and by anthropologists and sociologists to the established forms of behaviour of devotees of cults and religions. But while it is important to try to establish common explanations for the phenomena thus categorized, it is essential to grasp that there are fundamental differences between them and also between modes of interpreting them.

Freud himself argued that there were marked similarities between the obsessive "rituals" of neurotics and psychotics, and the "rituals" of what he called primitive society. Indeed, he postulated in *Totem and Tabu* (1913) from his theory of the development of the Oedipus complex (a theory derived from depth analyses of his patients), that the origin of sacrifice and religion in general was to be derived from a primordial killing and devouring of a patriarchal male, who dominated a group of females and their offspring, by the young males of the group. Overcome with guilt, they instituted a symbolic rekilling of the father-figure, now transformed into a god, and partaking of his being in a ritual of sacrifice and communion. If this be taken as what the anthropologist A. Kroeber called a "Just-so Story" (that is, a story which explains the origin of some well-known phenomenon), then there is no evidence for it, and more recent studies of the social life of the apes make it highly improbable. On the other hand, Kroeber allowed that it might represent a psychological process which most human males undergo, in symbolical form, in the course of their development. Then it might well be one of the springs of emotion which feed into social rituals. Even so, sociologists and anthropologists would argue that Freud's theory cannot be used to explain the development, and the complexity, of the social and cultural relationship involved in rituals.

Variations in Response

Similarly, anthropologists would reject any claim by psychoanalysts that, for example, circumcision ceremonies of boys near puberty can be "explained" by saying that they create castration anxiety and fix the incest taboo firmly in the boys' minds. While the above is the standard psychoanalytical explanation of circumcision, one psychoanalyst, B. Bettelheim, has argued from a study of four schizoid children who developed their own initiation ceremonies, that the practice of circumcision arises among males through envy of the productive wombs of females.

Anthropologists would concede that particular persons, passing through circumcision ceremonies, may feel castration anxiety or womb envy; but that this would have to be demonstrated by appropriate methods of research, and that the structure of the personalities of the persons enforcing, or undergoing, such ceremonial operations should be taken into account. It may well be that in all men and women, at very deep levels of the psyche, similar syndromes of feeling are to be found; but psychoanalysis itself shows that people vary in their degree of adjustment to those syndromes, in their more conscious feelings and their actions. Thus there is a considerable degree of variation in both the type and the intensity of individuals' reaction to participation in the same ritual.

Examples of this were noted by the present writer at circumcision ceremonies held among certain African tribes. At the ritual circumcision each candidate (aged from seven to 15), while being operated on, should be supported by his father, who is supposed to hold his son's penis and help the circumciser, a ritual adept, turn back the foreskin. On one occasion, the hands of the first father shook so much that it was impossible for the circumciser to act; and the father was replaced by his brother-in-law, the boy's mother's brother, who strictly was not appropriate. The hands of the second father were very steady, and he watched the operation steadily. The hands of the third father were steady, but he could not watch the operation

and turned his head away to look over his shoulder. One must draw the conclusion that the circumcision of each boy meant something quite different to each father, in terms of present relationships, of what each had felt and suffered when he himself as a boy underwent the operation, of the psychological syndromes established in each during infancy, and so on. Hence it seems that psychological analysis can only be effective if it is applied to bring out the significance of a particular ritual, or part of a ritual, for particular individuals, each with his own history of psychological development and his own established personality. Thereafter psychological analysis may feed into sociological-anthropological analysis; and of course the reverse is also true.

Swazi Songs of Hate

The Swazi of southern Africa, at the ripening of the first fruits, stage elaborate national ceremonies, at certain phases of which they are required to hurl insults at their king, who is the central figure of the rituals, and to sing sacred national songs stating how much the king is hated by his subjects. In social-anthropological analysis these rites have been successfully related to the low density of population as a result of the simple system of husbandry; the low variation in standards of living; and the delegation of authority from the king to subordinates ruling numbers of men who, because of the simplicity of weapons, are all warriors, constituting a private army which can help its leader in attempts to gain power. These leaders are of royal blood and may organize rebellions aimed at the kingship. There is therefore present in the national ceremony a symbolic representation of political processes built into the nation, which is riven by periodic armed civil wars.

The rites emphasize that while the kingship itself is sacred and is "strengthened" in the rites, the king is beset by internal enemies on whose loyalty he cannot rely. But this does not mean that each warrior who insults the king or who sings the songs of hatred against him, must necessarily have sentiments of disloyalty awakened, or go through a severe crisis of loyalty. For one warrior, though he may feel the sacredness of the occasion, it may be in some ways like a fete, a kind of carnival when licence is allowed. At the other extreme, other warriors may go through an emotional tur-moil in which strong resentments against authority are awakened, and perhaps a reliving of childhood difficulties in their relationships with their fathers. Again, analysis of individual, possibly variable, reactions to ritual is required.

One must similarly reject any simple direct ex-planation of ritual as the expression of tension, of despair, of anxiety or aggression, or as the trans-ference of stifled feelings of aggression onto scape-goats, or as simply and directly strengthening social sentiments. In the Swazi ceremony sum-marily analysed above, it is justified to say that the rites are calculated to arouse the sentiments that support national solidarity. Since we know that acting an emotion is likely to produce feelings of that emotion, it is probable that occasions of group celebration will arouse the sentiments which are appropriate to group solidarity and which support adherence to certain group values and morals, in most participants at least.

But we know equally well that the most com-plex and intensive reaction to a religious ceremony may come from the sinners in the congregation: they may be most deeply moved by emotions evoked by ritual, particularly ritual in which they have participated as children and as adolescents, and they may then feel determined during the ritu-al to sin no more. Their intensive emotional reac-tion may well be provoked by strong feelings of guilt and unworthiness. On the other hand, the man who conforms in his daily life with the pre-cepts of religion and morality is likely to worship with a much more restrained and consistent devo-tion, while those who are betwixt and between will respond in moderate degree. So in the Swazi ritual cited above, loyal men may have their sentiments of patriotism evoked less strongly than the poten-tial traitors.

Milk Tree Society

A much more complicated theory to relate rituals to emotional predispositions is therefore required, and the best as yet advanced is that of Victor W. Turner, in a series of analyses of the significance of ritual symbols. His highly complex argument[1] can be summarized as follows. Information on the meaning of ritual symbols can be collected from participants, who will give interpretations of vari-ous degrees of complexity, depending on whether they are ritual adepts or not. In general, explana-tions of this kind stress the harmonious, socially valuable attributes of the symbol. Thus, when the Ndembu of Zambia, whom Turner studied, are ini-tiating a nubile girl into womanhood, the key sym-bol is a tree which exudes a white substance, like milk. The Ndembu specifically compare the white sap of the "milk tree" with mother's milk, and state that it represents the tie between mother and child: it thus represents the tie between the girl being initiated and her own mother, and her fu-ture, nurturing tie with the children whom it is hoped she will produce.

Further, since the Ndembu are a matrilineal so-ciety (reckoning descent and succession and inher-itance from brother to sister's son), they are organized in groups of kinsfolk related to one an-other by descent through females. The milk tree therefore represents these groups, technically called matrilineages. As the matrilineages are the persisting groups of Ndembu society, and villages are to some extent combinations of matrilineages, the matrilineal principle in the abstract is vertebral to Ndembu society, and the milk tree symbolizes this, and symbolizes both the continuity of the so-ciety and its whole culture, its customs and its laws. In a graphic comparison, one of the Ndembu compared it with the Union Jack flying over the administrative headquarters of the district, then under British rule. He described the milk tree as "our flag."

But Turner showed that if one examined actions around the milk tree, in the ritual itself, these were not altogether harmonious, and did not reflect a continual state of harmony in accordance with the values stressed in the Ndembu's own account of the ritual. In practice, there was considerable com-petition and "strife" among the people assembled around the milk tree. Women were separated from the men, and had to behave "hostilely" towards them. Married women and unmarried girls, women of different matrilineages, and women of different villages, formed also competing pairs of contraposed groups. These alignments reflected the fact that while succession and inheritance passed through women, the women themselves dispersed, during their childbearing lives, to live at their husbands' villages—one example of the con-tradictory principles on which Ndembu society is built. These contradictory principles appear in the rituals and thus deny the very abstract harmony which is stated in the Ndembus' interpretation of them.

Duty Made Desirable

Turner shows that all the dominant ritual symbols of Ndembu society can be similarly analysed. His thesis is that two sharply different poles of reference for the symbols—the sensory and the ideological—must be distinguished. At the sensory pole are clustered meanings which refer to physiological facts and processes, such as mother's milk, blood, blood of menstruation and birth, semen, genitalia, copulation, excreta, death, and so on. While at the ideological pole are clustered social values and allegiances: conformity with the law, morality and custom; motherhood as a nurturing relationship; the established relationships between women and men, married women and girls, membership of matrilineages and villages, and so on. Symbols cover these diverse meanings because they can condense many meanings, can unify disparate meanings and can polarize meanings.

Turner argues that in the course of ritual, marked by feasting, drinking, dancing and music —all physiologically stimulating—as well as by fellowship, strong and varied emotions are evoked in response both to the feasting, drinking and so on, and to the sensory associations of the rites and symbols. The energy thus aroused is then transferred to, and fixed upon, the values evoked at the ideological pole. Thus there occurs a process in which the obligatory is felt also to be desirable.

Clearly this theory involves a much more complex approach to the relation between emotions evoked and forms of ritual, than the notions briefly criticized above. We can appreciate why it is that singing songs of hate and hurling insults at the king may act to strengthen, at least temporarily, sentiments of loyalty to him. Moreover, it is a theory which is in accord with the psychoanalytic theory of the sublimation of instinctual drives and demands towards socially approved ends.

If the step from psychological interpretation of ritual to understanding of its sociological functioning is so complicated, it is even more mistaken to relate ritual directly to the behaviour of animals, in mating dances, display, and the like.

Ritual from Relationships

Turner's theory was worked out on tribal rituals, but it seems that it could equally be applied to the ritual symbols of the great religions. These types of rituals, however, differ markedly from each other. Sociologists who have written on the general evolution of human society have all stressed that this development, associated with more complex technology and a greater division of labour, is marked by an increasing obsolescence of ritual and its replacement by what have been called universal religions, such as Christianity, Islam, and Buddhism, which any person can join as a convert, and in which any adherent can join any congregation assembled to worship. The examples above, of the Swazi first-fruits rites and the Ndembu nubility ritual, show that in tribal society rituals are constituted to specific social relationships according to the domestic, kinship, sexual, local, or political affiliations of the members of the cult. Only persons occupying specific positions in those relationships can participate, and they do so in terms of the specific ways in which they are related to one another. Moreover, in the ritual, apart from using special symbols (in the form of things, words, or actions), they act their specific roles in secular life, either directly, or sometimes invertedly (as in transvestism, by women dressing as men and men as women), or in some particular symbolic form. Hence an analysis of tribal rituals leads one into a detailed analysis of secular relationships because these are of the fabric of the ritual, and because it is believed that the symbolic representation of those relationships in some hidden, occult way creates and directs occult power so as to bless, purify, protect, strengthen, make fruitful, and otherwise successful, the persons involved in those relationships.

This type of analysis has shown that in some of the rituals the enactment of secular relationships involves a statement, in an exaggerated form, not only of the harmonious and unifying aspects of the relationships, but also of the conflicts which reside in them. This is one of the main means by which emotion is aroused, which is then fixed on socially approved values: out of the very conflicts which exist in normal life, on special occasions the value of an ideal of life without conflict is emotionally and intellectually established.

It has therefore been argued that ritual, occult beliefs, and practices will tend to occur in crisis situations in which the discrepant principles out of which social organization is formed, principles which are in conflict, produce actual or potential disputes which cannot be settled by judicial and other purely intellectual procedures. Ritual then may operate where there are fundamental disharmonies within the theoretical harmony of a social system.

This theory is based on the perception that in human, as against animal, society, there is a consistent tendency to exaggerate the differences between categories of persons. Thus belief in the occult contaminating effect of menstrual blood and its threat to things virile exaggerates the biological difference between women and men. There are other beliefs, and associated practices, of this kind, based on distinctions of age, the facts of locality, different kinds of relationship through birth and kinship, the relationship of ruler and subject, and so forth. This tendency is more marked in tribal society than in complex industrial societies where people's roles, the material things which they handle, the places they work and worship and play in, are more differentiated. This may explain why in tribal society we find a 'ritualization' of secular roles, while as society develops a more complex technology on which is based a more complex division of labour, there is a movement towards universal religions.

E. R. Leach and other anthropologists have argued from studies of tribal rituals that ritual is only a symbolic statement of status. This is undoubtedly one of the aspects of ritual, as has been shown. Others assert that rituals mainly manifest competition for power. This too is present in tribal rituals, and is also to be found within the congregations of universal religions. But there is clearly much more to ritual than these two aspects.

Complex problems are involved in the question of when actions referring to beliefs in occult power occur, and how they operate. It therefore seems advisable to use a more complicated vocabulary in discussing these problems. The term *ceremonial* may be used to describe all actions which involve symbolic statements of social status (for instance, All Saints' Day and the October Revolution parade). As a further distinction, *ceremoniousness* could be used to describe ceremonial where the practitioners have no idea of occult powers being involved (such as standing when "God Save the Queen" is played). Ritual describes ceremonial where ideas of occult power are present. Within the field of ritual in this sense, there is in tribal society a *ritualization* of secular social roles, of domestic places, and so forth. As this ritualization decreases with advancing civilization, some religions will be austere, while others will be marked by a high *ritualism*, symbolic itself, drawing on the same complex of emotions maybe, but not involving the enacting of everyday roles.

Symbols in African Ritual

Victor W. Turner

In the preceding article by Max Gluckman, reference is made to Victor Turner's analysis of the significance of ritual symbols. It is not unusual for even a scholar of Gluckman's stature to refer to Turner for assistance in an analysis of symbols, for Victor Turner has over the years established an excellent reputation in the field of symbolic analysis. In the present article, Professor Turner discusses three significant dimensions of symbols: the exegetic, the operational, and the positional. The exegetic involves any explanations given the field worker by the participants in a given ritual. The operational dimension is determined by the researcher seeking the relationship between a symbol's meaning and its use. In the last dimension, the positional, the anthropologist attempts to find the meaning of a symbol by studying the relationship between that symbol and other symbols in a given ritual.

Turner also applies Morris Opler's concept of cultural themes ("dynamic affirmations that can be identified in every culture") to an analysis of ritual, noting that ritual constitutes a base for the playing out of themes, while the themes themselves are passed along by the ritual symbols.

Interestingly, just as Edmund Leach used the technique of binary oppositions in the lead article of this chapter to help him analyze myths, so too does Turner apply this aspect of modern information theory to help him understand symbolism within ritual.

Reprinted from *Science*, Vol. 179 (1973), pp. 1100–1105, by permission of the author and the American Association for the Advancement of Science. Copyright © 1973 by the AAAS.

NO ONE WHO HAS LIVED FOR LONG IN RURAL sub-Saharan Africa can fail to be struck by the importance of ritual in the lives of villagers and homesteaders and by the fact that rituals are composed of symbols.

A ritual is a stereotyped sequence of activities involving gestures, words, and objects, performed in a sequestered place, and designed to influence preternatural entities or forces on behalf of the actors' goals and interests. Rituals may be seasonal, hallowing a culturally defined moment of change in the climatic cycle or the inauguration of an activity such as planting, harvesting, or moving from winter to summer pasture; or they may be contingent, held in response to an individual or collective crisis. Contingent rituals may be further subdivided into life-crisis ceremonies, which are performed at birth, puberty, marriage, death, and so on to demarcate the passage from one phase to another in the individual's life cycle, and rituals of affliction, which are performed to placate or exorcise preternatural beings or forces believed to have afflicted villagers with illness, bad luck, gynecological troubles, severe physical injuries, and the like. Other classes of rituals include divinatory rituals; ceremonies performed by political authorities to ensure the health and fertility of human beings, animals, and crops in their territories; initiation into priesthoods devoted to certain deities, into religious associations, or into secret societies; and those accompanying the daily offering of food and libations to deities or ancestral spirits or both. Africa is rich indeed in ritual genres, and each involves many specific performances.

Each rural African society (which is often, though not always, coterminous with a linguistic community) possesses a finite number of distinguishable rituals that may include all or some of the types listed above. At varying intervals, from a year to several decades, all of a society's rituals will be performed, the most important (for example, the symbolic transference of political authority from one generation to another, as among the Nyakyusa of Tanzania) being performed perhaps the least often. Since societies are processes responsive to change, not fixed structures, new rituals are devised or borrowed, and old ones decline and disappear. Nevertheless, forms survive through flux, and new ritual items, even new ritual configurations, tend more often to be variants of old themes than radical novelties. Thus it is possible for anthropologists to describe the main features of a ritual system, or rather ritual round (successive ritual performances), in those parts of rural Africa where change is occurring slowly.

The Semantic Structure of the Symbol

The ritual symbol is "the smallest unit of ritual which still retains the specific properties of ritual behavior . . . the ultimate unit of specific structure in a ritual context." This structure is a semantic one (that is, it deals with relationships between signs and symbols and the things to which they refer) and has the following attributes: (i) multiple meanings (significata)—actions or objects perceived by the senses in ritual contexts (that is, symbol vehicles) have many meanings; (ii) unification of apparently disparate significata—the essentially distinct significata are interconnected by analogy or by association in fact or thought; (iii) condensation—many ideas, relations between things, actions, interations, and transactions are represented simultaneously by the symbol vehicle (the ritual use of such a vehicle abridges what would verbally be a lengthy statement or argument); (iv) polarization of significata—the referents assigned by custom to a major ritual symbol tend frequently to be grouped at opposed semantic poles. At one pole of meaning, empirical research has shown that the significata tend to refer to components of the moral and social orders—this might be termed the ideological (or normative) pole of symbolic meaning; at the other, the sensory (or orectic) pole, are concentrated references to phenomena and processes that may be expected to stimulate desires and feelings. Thus, I have shown that the mudyi tree, or milk tree (*Diplorrhyncus*

mossambicensis), which is the focal symbol of the girls' puberty ritual of the Ndembu people of northwestern Zambia, at its normative pole represents womanhood, motherhood, the mother-child bond, a novice undergoing initiation into mature womanhood, a specific matrilineage, the principle of matriliny, the process of learning "women's wisdom," the unity and perdurance of Ndembu society, and all of the values and virtues inherent in the various relationships—domestic, legal, and political—controlled by matrilineal descent. Each of these aspects of its normative meaning becomes paramount in a specific episode of the puberty ritual; together, they form a condensed statement of the structural and communal importance of femaleness in Ndembu culture. At its sensory pole, the same symbol stands for breast milk (the tree exudes milky latex—indeed, the significata associated with the sensory pole often have a more or less direct connection with some sensorily perceptible attribute of the symbol), mother's breasts, and the bodily slenderness and mental pliancy of the novice (a young slender sapling of mudyi is used). The tree, situated a short distance from the novice's village, becomes the center of a sequence of ritual episodes rich in symbols (words, objects, and actions) that express important cultural themes.

Ritual Symbols and Cultural Themes

Opler has defined a theme as a part of a limited set of "dynamic affirmations" that "can be identified in every culture." In the "nature, expression, and relationship" of themes is to be found the "key to the character, structure, and direction of the specific culture." The term "theme" denotes "a postulate or position, declared or implied, and usually controlling behavior or stimulating activity, which is tacitly approved or openly promoted in a society." Every culture has multiple themes, and most themes have multiple expressions, some of which may be in one or more parts of the institutional culture. Ritual forms an important setting for the expression of themes, and ritual symbols transmit themes. Themes have multiple expressions, and ritual symbols, such as the mudyi tree (and thousands of others in the ethnographic literature of

African ritual), have multiple significata. The major difference between themes and symbols is that themes are postulates or ideas inferred by an observer from the data of a given culture, while ritual symbols are one class of such data. Ritual symbols are multivocal—that is, each symbol expresses not one theme but many themes simultaneously by the same perceptible object or activity (symbol vehicle). Symbols *have* significata, themes may *be* significata.

Themes, in their capacity as significata (including both conceptions and images), may be disparate or grouped, as we have seen, at opposed semantic poles. Thus the mudyi signifies aspects of female bodily imagery (milk, suckling, breasts, girlish slenderness) and conceptions about standards of womanhood and motherhood, as well as the normative ordering of these in relation to group membership, the inheritance of property, and succession to such political offices as chieftainship and village headmanship through matrilineal descent. These are rules of exclusion connected with the mudyi in this ritual context—all that is not concerned with the nurtural, procreative, and esthetic aspects of human femaleness and with their cultural control and structuring, is excluded from the semantic field of mudyi symbolism. This is a field of themes with varying degrees of concreteness, abstraction, and cognitive and orectic quality. The impulse that leads advanced cultures to the economical use of signs in mathematics finds its equivalent here in the use of a single symbol vehicle to represent simultaneously a variety of themes, most of which can be shown to be related, logically or pragmatically, but some of which depend for their association on a sensed likeness between variables rather than on cognitive criteria. One is dealing with a "mathematics" of sociocultural experience rather than with a mathematics of logical relationships.

Ritual symbols differ from other modes of thematic expression, particularly from those unformalized modes that arise in spontaneous behavior and allow for individual choice in expression. Indeed, it might be argued that the more ritualized the expression, the wider the range of themes that may be signified by it. On the other hand, since a ritual symbol may represent disparate, even contradictory themes, the gain in economy may be offset by a loss in clarity of communication. This would be inevitable if such symbols existed in a vacuum, but they exist in cultural and operational contexts that to some extent overcome the loss in intelligibility and to some extent capitalize on it.

Dominant Symbols in Ritual Cycles

Rituals tend to be organized in a cycle of performances (annual, biennial, quinquennial, and so on); even in the case of contingent rituals, each is performed eventually. In each total assemblage, or system, there is a nucleus of dominant symbols, which are characterized by extreme multivocality (having many senses) and a central position in each ritual performance. Associated with this nucleus is a much larger number of enclitic (dependent) symbols. Some of these are univocal, while others, like prepositions in language, become mere relations or function signs that keep the ritual action going (for example, bowings, lustrations, sweepings, and objects indicative of joining or separation). Dominant symbols provide the fixed points of the total system and recur in many of its component rituals. For example, if 15 separate kinds of ritual can be empirically distinguished in a given ritual system, dominant symbol A may be found in 10 of them, B in 7, C in 5, and D in 12. The mudyi tree, for example, is found in boys' and girls' initiation ceremonies, in five rituals concerned with female reproductive disorders, in at least three rituals of the hunters' cults, and in various herbalistic practices of a magical cast. Other dominant symbols of Ndembu rituals . . . recur almost as frequently in the ritual round. Each of these symbols, then, has multiple referents, but on each occasion that it is used—usually an episode within a ritual performance—only one or a related few of its referents are drawn to public attention. The process of "selectivity" consists in constructing around the dominant symbol a context of symbolic objects, activities, gestures, social relationships between actors of ritual roles, and verbal behavior (prayers, formulas, chants, songs, recitation of sacred narratives, and so on) that both bracket and underline those of its referents deemed pertinent in the given situation. Thus, only a portion of a dominant symbol's full semantic wealth is deployed in a single kind of ritual or in one of its episodes. The semantic structure of a dominant symbol may be compared with a ratchet wheel, each of whose teeth represents a conception or theme. The ritual context is like a pawl, which engages the notches. The point of engagement represents a meaning that is important in the particular situation. The wheel is the symbol's total meaning, and the complete range is only exposed when the whole cycle of rituals has been performed. Dominant symbols represent sets of fundamental themes. The symbol appears in many rituals, and its meanings are emphasized separately in many episodes. Since the settings in which the themes are ritually presented vary, and since themes are linked in different combinations in each setting, members of the culture who have been exposed to the entire ritual cycle gradually learn, through repetition, variation, and contrast of symbols and themes, what the values, rules, behavioral styles, and cognitive postulates of their culture are. Even more important, they learn in what cultural domains and with what intensity in each domain the themes should apply.

Positional Role of Binary Opposition

The selection of a given theme from a symbol's theme assemblage is a function of positioning—that is, of the manner in which the object or activity assigned symbolic value is placed or arranged vis-à-vis similar objects or activities. One common mode of positioning is binary opposition, the relating of two symbol vehicles whose opposed perceptible qualities or quantities suggest, in terms of the associative rules of the culture, semantic opposition. Thus when a grass hut is made at the Ndembu girls' puberty ceremony for the seclusion of the novice for several months, the two principal laths of the wooden frame are made respectively from mudyi and mukula (blood tree) wood. Both species are dominant symbols. To the Ndembu, mukula represents the husband whom the girl will marry immediately after the puberty rites, and the mudyi stands for the bride, the novice herself. Yet when mukula is considered as a dominant symbol of the total ritual system, it is found to have a wide range (what has aptly been called a "fan") of significata. Its primary and sensory meaning is blood—the Ndembu point to the dusky red gum secreted by the

tree from cracks in its bark to justify their interpretation. But some bloods, they say, are masculine and some feminine. The former include blood shed by warriors, hunters, and circumcisers in the call of duty; the latter represents blood shown at menstruation and parturition. Another binary opposition within the semantic field of blood is between running blood and coagulating blood. The latter is good, the former is dangerous. Thus, prolonged menstruation means that a woman's blood is ebbing away uselessly; it should coagulate to form fetus and placenta. But since men are the dangerous sex, the blood they cause to flow in hunting and war may be good—that is, beneficial for their own group.

Mukula symbolism is adroitly manipulated in different rituals to express various aspects of the human condition as the Ndembu experience it. For example, in the *Nkula* ritual, performed to placate the spirit of a dead kinswoman afflicting the female patient with menstrual troubles causing barrenness, mukula and other red symbols are contextually connected with symbols characteristic of the male hunting cults to convey the message: the patient is behaving like a male shedder of blood, not like a female conserver of blood, as she should be. It is her "masculine protest" that the ritual is mainly directed at overcoming and domesticating into the service of her female role. Mukula means many other things in other contexts, when used in religious ritual or in magical therapy. But the binary opposition of mudyi to mukula restricts the meaning of mudyi to young mature femininity and that of mukula to young mature masculinity, both of which are foundations of a hut, the prototypical domestic unit. The binding together of the laths taken from these trees is said to represent the sexual and the procreative union of the young couple. If these meanings form the sensory pole of the binary opposition as symbol, then the legitimated union by marriage represents the normative pole. In other words, even the binary opposition does not stand alone; it must be examined in the context of building the novice's seclusion hut and of the symbolic objects comprising the hut and its total meaning. There are, of course, many types of binary opposition. The members of pairs of symbols may be asymmetrical (A>B, A<B); they may be like or unlike but equal in value; they may be antithetical; one may be thought of as the product or

offspring of the other; one may be active, the other passive; and so on. In this way, the Ndembu are induced to consider the nature and function of relationships as well as of the variables being related, for nonverbal symbol systems have the equivalents of grammar, syntax, accidence, and parts of speech.

Sometimes binary opposition may appear between complexes of symbol vehicles, each carrying a system of dominant and secondary symbols. Thus, in the circumcision rites of the Wiko, in Zambia, one group of masked dancers may mime opposition to another group; each mask and headpiece is already a combination of multivocal symbols. Yet one team may represent protectiveness and the other, aggressiveness. It is, in fact, not uncommon to find complex symbol vehicles, such as statues or shrines, with simple meanings, while simple vehicles, such as marks drawn in white or red clay, may be highly multivocal in almost every ritual situation in which they are used. A simple vehicle, exhibiting some color, shape, texture, or contrast commonly found in one's experience (such as the whiteness of the mudyi or the redness of the mukula), can literally or metaphorically connect a great range of phenomena and ideas. By contrast, a complex vehicle is already committed, at the level of sensory perception, to a host of contrasts that narrow and specify its message. This is probably why the great religious symbol vehicles such as the cross, the lotus, the crescent moon, the ark, and so on are relatively simple, although their significata constitute whole theological systems and control liturgical and architectural structures of immense complexity. One might almost hypothesize that the more complex the ritual (many symbols, complex vehicles), the more particularistic, localized, and socially structured its message; the simpler the ritual (few symbols, simple vehicles), the more universalistic its message. Thus, ecumenical liturgiologists today are recommending that Christian ritual be essentially reduced to the blessing, distribution, and partaking of bread and wine, in order to provide most denominations with a common ground.

Actors Experience Symbols as Powers and as Meanings

The second characteristic of ritual condensation, which compensates in some measure for semantic obscurity, is its efficacy. Ritual is not just a concentration of referents, of messages about values and norms; nor is it simply a set of practical guidelines and a set of symbolic paradigms for everyday action, indicating how spouses should treat each other, how pastoralists should classify and regard cattle, how hunters should behave in different wild habitats, and so on. It is also a fusion of the powers believed to be inherent in the persons, objects, relationships, events, and histories represented by ritual symbols. It is a mobilization of energies as well as messages. In this respect, the objects and activities in point are not merely things that stand for other things or something abstract, they participate in the powers and virtues they represent. I use "virtue" advisedly, for many objects termed symbols are also termed medicines. Thus, scrapings and leaves from such trees as the mudyi and the mukula are pounded together in meal mortars, mixed with water, and given to the afflicted to drink or to wash with. Here there is direct communication of the life-giving powers thought to inhere in certain objects under ritual conditions (a consecrated site, invocations of preternatural entities, and so on). When an object is used analogously, it functions unambiguously as a symbol. Thus, when the mudyi tree is used in puberty rites it clearly *represents* mother's milk; here the association is through sight, not taste. But when the mudyi is used as medicine in ritual, it is felt that certain qualities of motherhood and nurturing are being communicated physically. In the first case, the mudyi is used because it is "good to think" rather than "good to eat"; in the second, it is used because it has maternal power. The same objects are used both as powers and symbols, metonymically and metaphorically—it is the context that distinguishes them. The power aspect of a symbol derives from its being a part of a physical whole, the ideational aspect from an analogy between a symbol vehicle and its principle significata.

Each symbol expresses many themes, and each theme is expressed by many symbols. The cultural weave is made up of symbolic warp and thematic weft. This weaving of symbols and themes serves as a rich store of information, not only about the natural environment as perceived and evaluated by the ritual actors, but also about their ethical, esthetic, political, legal, and ludic (the domain of play, sport, and so forth in a culture) ideas, ideals, and rules. Each symbol is a store of information, both for actors and investigators, but in order to specify just which set of themes any particular ritual or ritual episode contains, one must determine the relations between the ritual's symbols and their vehicles, including verbal symbolic behavior. The advantages of communication by means of rituals in non-literate societies are clearly great, for the individual symbols and the patterned relations between them have a mnemonic function. The symbolic vocabulary and grammar to some extent make up for the lack of written records.

The Semantic Dimensions

Symbols have three especially significant dimensions: the exegetic, the operational, and the positional. The exegetic dimension consists of the explanations given the investigator by actors in the ritual system. Actors of different age, sex, ritual role, status, grade of esoteric knowledge, and so forth provide data of varying richness, explicitness, and internal coherence. The investigator should infer from this information how members of a given society think about ritual. Not all African societies contain persons who are ready to make verbal statements about ritual, and the percentage of those prepared to offer interpretations varies from group to group and within groups. But, as much ethnographic work attests, many African societies are well endowed with exegetes.

In the operational dimension, the investigator equates a symbol's meaning with its use—he observes what actors do with it and how they relate to one another in this process. He also records their gestures, expressions, and other nonverbal aspects of behavior and discovers what values they represent—grief, joy, anger, triumph, modesty, and so on. Anthropologists are now studying several genres of non-verbal language, from iconography (the study of symbols whose vehicles picture the conceptions they signify, rather than being arbitrary, conventional signs for them) to kinetics (the study of bodily movements, facial expressions, and so forth as ways of communication or adjuncts and intensifiers of speech). Several of these fall under the rubric of a symbol's operational meaning. Non-exegetical, ritualized speech, such as formalized prayers or invocations, would

also fall into this category. Here verbal symbols approximate non-verbal symbols. The investigator is interested not only in the social organization and structure of those individuals who operate with symbols on this level, but also in what persons, categories, and groups are absent from the situation, for formal exclusion would reveal social values and attitudes.

In the positional dimension, the observer finds in the relations between one symbol and other symbols an important source of its meaning. I have shown how binary opposition may, in context, highlight one (or more) of a symbol's many referents by contrasting it with one (or more) of another symbol's referents. When used in a ritual context with three or more other symbols, a particular symbol reveals further facets of its total "meaning." Groups of symbols may be so arrayed as to state a message, in which some symbols function analogously to parts of speech and in which there may be conventional rules of connection. The message is not about specifications and circumstances, but about the given culture's basic structures of thought, ethics, esthetics, law, and modes of speculation about new experience.

In several African cultures, particularly in West Africa, a complex system of rituals is associated with myths. These tell of the origins of the gods, the cosmos, human types and groups, and the key institutions of culture and society. Some ritual episodes reenact primordial events, drawing on their inherent power to achieve the contemporary goals of the members of the culture (for example, adjustment to puberty and the healing of the sick). Ritual systems are sometimes based on myths. There may coexist with myths and rituals standardized schemata of interpretation that may amount to theological doctrine. But in wide areas of East and Central Africa, there may be few myths connected with rituals and no religious system interrelating myths, rituals, and doctrine. In compensation, there may be much piecemeal exegesis of particular symbols.

Foundations of Meaning

Most African languages have terms for ritual symbol. The Nyakyusa, for example, speak of *ififwani* (likenesses); the Ndembu use *chijikijilu* (a landmark, or blaze), which is derived from *kujikijila* (to blaze a trail or set up a landmark). The first connotes an association, a feeling of likeness between sign and signified, vehicle and concept; the second is a means of connecting known with unknown territory. (The Ndembu compare the ritual symbol to the trail a hunter blazes in order to find his way back from unexplored bush to his village.) Other languages possess similar terms. In societies that do not have myths, the meaning of a symbol is built up by analogy and association of three foundations—nominal, substantial, and artifactual—though in any given instance only one of these might be utilized. The nominal basis is the name of the symbol, an element in an acoustic system; the substantial basis is a symbol's sensorily perceptible physical or chemical properties as recognized by the culture; and its artifactual basis is the technical changing of an object used in ritual by human purposive activity.

For example: At the start of a girl's puberty ritual among the Nyakyusa of Tanzania, she is treated with a "medicine" called *undumila*. This medicine is also an elaborate symbol. Its nominal basis is the derivation of the term from *ukulumila*, meaning "to bite, to be painful." The substantial basis is a natural property of the root after which the medicine is named—it is pungent-tasting. As an artifact, the medicine is a composite of several symbolic substances. The total symbol involves action as well as a set of objects. Wilson writes that the root "is pushed through the tip of a funnel or cup made of a leaf of the bark-cloth tree, and salt is poured into the cup. The girl takes the tip of the root in her mouth and pulls it inward with her teeth, thus causing the salt to trickle into her mouth." The root and leaf funnel, together with their ritual use, constitute an artifact. These three bases of significance are substantiated by the Nyakyusa Wilson talked to. One woman told her: "The pungent root is the penis of the husband, the cup is her vagina, the salt, also pungent, is the semen of her husband. Biting the root and eating the salt is copulation." Another woman confirmed this: "The *undumila* is put through the leaf of a bark-cloth tree, shaped into a cup, and it is a sign of man and woman, the penis in the vagina. It is similar to the plantains which we give her when we wash her. The plantains are a symbol of the husband. If we do not give her . . . the *undumila*, she constantly has periods and is barren." A third informant said:

"It is the pain of periods that we symbolize in the sharpness of the *undumila* and salt." Thus *undumila* is at once a symbol of sexual intercourse, a prophylactic against pain in intercourse and against frequent or painful periods, and (according to other accounts) a ritual defense against those who are "heavy"—that is, those actively engaged in sexual intercourse, especially women who have just conceived. If a heavy person steps over the novice's footprints, the novice will not bear a child, but will menstruate continually. These explanations also demonstrate the multivocality and economy of reference of a single dominant symbol. The same symbol vehicles can represent different, even disparate, processes—marital intercourse and menstrual difficulty—although it may be argued that the Nyakyusa, at an unconscious level, regard a woman's "distaste" for intercourse as a cause of her barrenness or menorrhagia.

Symbols and Cosmologies

Similar examples abound in the ethnography of subsaharan Africa, but in the great West African cultures of the Fon, Ashanti, Yoruba, Dahomeyans, and Dogon, piecemeal exegesis gives way to explicit, complex cosmologies. Among the Dogon, for example, a symbol becomes a fixed point of linkage between animal, vegetable, and mineral kingdoms, which are themselves regarded as parts of "ungigantesque organisme humaine." The doctrine of correspondences reigns—everything is a symbol of everything else, whether in ritual context or not. Thus the Dogon establish a correspondence between the different categories of minerals and the organs of the body. The various soils in the area are conceived of as the organs of "the interior of the stomach," rocks are regarded as the bones of the skeleton, and various hues of red clay are likened to the blood. Sometimes these correspondences are remarkably precise: one rock resting on another represents the chest; little white river pebbles stand for the toes of the feet. The same *parole du monde* principles hold true for the relationship between man and the vegetable kingdom. Man is not only the grain of the universe, but each distinct part of a single grain represents part of the human body. In fact, it is only science that has emancipated man from the complex weave of correspondences, based on analogy, metaphor, and mystical participation, and that enables him to regard all relations as problematical, not preordained, until they have been experimentally tested or systematically compared.

The Dogon further conceive of a subtle and finely wrought interplay between speech .nd the components of personality. The body constitutes a magnet or focus for man's spiritual principles, which nevertheless are capable of sustaining an independent existence. The Dogon contrast visible and invisible ("spiritual") components of the human personality. The body is made up of four elements: water (the blood and bodily fluids), earth (the skeleton), air (breath), and fire (animal warmth). There is a continuous interchange between these internal expressions of the elements and their external aspects. The body has 22 parts: feet, shins, thighs, lumbar region, stomach, chest, arms, neck, and head make up nine parts (it would seem that Dogon reckon double parts, as they do twins, as a unit); the fingers (each counting as a unit), make up ten parts; and the male genitals make up three parts. Further numerical symbolism is involved: there are believed to be eight symbolic grains—representing the principal cereal crops of the region—lodged in the collarbones of each Dogon. These grains represent the mystical bond between man and his crops. The *body* of speech itself is, like the human body, composed of four elements: water is saliva, without which speech is dry; air gives rise to sound vibrations; earth gives speech its weight and significance; and fire gives speech its warmth. There is not only homology between personality and speech, but also a sort of functional interdependence, for words are selected by the brain, stir up the liver, and rise as steam from the lungs to the clavicles, which decide ultimately whether the speech is to emerge from the mouth.

To the 22 parts of the personality must be added the 48 types of speech, which are divided into two sets of 24. Each set is under the sign of a supernatural being, one of the androgynous twins Nommo and Yourougou. Here I must draw on Griaule and Dieterlen's extensive work on the Dogons' cosmogonic mythology. The twins are the creations of Amma. Yourougou rebelled against Amma and had sexual relations with his mother—he was punished by being changed into a pale fox. Nommo saved the world by an act of self-sacrifice, brought humans, animals, and plants to the earth, and became the lord of speech. Nommo's speech is human and can be heard; the Fox's is silent, a sign language made by his paw marks, and only diviners can interpret it. These myths provide a classification and taxonomy of cosmos and society; explain many details of ritual, including the forms and color symbolism of elaborate masks; and, indeed, determine where and how houses are constructed. Other West African cultures have equally elaborate cosmologies, which are manifested in ritual and divinatory symbolism. Their internal consistency and symmetry may be related to traditions of continuous residence and farming in a single habitat, combined with exposure to trans-Saharan cultural elements, including religious beliefs, for thousands of years—ancient Egyptian, Roman, Christian, Neo-Platonic, Gnostic, Islamic. The history of West Africa contrasts with that of Central Africa, where most societies descend from groups that migrated in a relatively short period of time across several distinct ecological habitats and that were then exposed to several centuries of slave raiding and slave trading. Groups were fragmented and then combined with the social detritus of other societies into new, temporary polities. There were conquests, assimilations, reconquests, the rise and fall of "kingdoms of the savannah," and temporary centralization followed by decentralization into localized clans. Swidden (slash-and-burn) agriculture kept people constantly on the move; hunting and pastoralism compounded the mobility. Because of these circumstances, there was less likelihood of complex, integrated religious and cosmological systems arising in Central Africa than in West Africa. Yet the needs and dangers of social and personal survival provided suitable conditions for the development of rituals as pragmatic instruments (from the standpoint of the actors) for coping with biological change, disease, and natural hazards of all kinds. Social action in response to material pressures was the systematic and systematizing factor. Order, cosmos, came from purpose, not from an elaborate and articulated cosmology. It is an order that accords well with human experience at pre-industrial technological levels; even its discrepancies accurately reflect the "facts of life"—in contrast to consistent and harmonious cosmologies whose symbols and myths mask and cloak the basic contradictions between wishes and facts.

The Continuing Efficacy of African Ritual Symbols

Nevertheless, from the comparative viewpoint, there are remarkable similarities among symbols used in ritual throughout sub-Saharan Africa, in spite of differences in cosmological sophistication. The same ideas, analogies, and modes of association underlie symbol formation and manipulation from the Senegal River to the Cape of Good Hope.

The same assumptions about powers prevail in kingdoms and nomadic bands. Whether these assemblages of similar symbols represent units of complex orders or the debris of formerly prevalent ones, the symbols remain extraordinarily viable and the themes they represent and embody tenaciously rooted. This may be because they arose in ecological and social experiences of a kind that still prevails in large areas of the continent. Since they are thus sustained and since there is a continuous flux and reflux of people between country and city, it is not surprising that much of the imagery found in the writings of modern African novelists and in the rhetoric of politicians is drawn from ritual symbolism—from which it derives its power to move and channel emotion.

Taboo

Mary Douglas

*One of the most difficult tasks anthropologists face
in their study of non-Western cultures is isolating
the bases for rules of right conduct. In the following
article, Mary Douglas succinctly demonstrates that
unlike modern industrialized nations, which have
shared common experiences for centuries, primitive
cultures have remained separated by distance and
language and have developed unique world views.
Pointing out, for example, that Westerners'
separation of the natural and the supernatural is
peculiar to us, Douglas explains how our reality
and, therefore, our taboos are so different from those
of the non-Western world.*

*Douglas's functional analysis of taboos shows
that they underpin social structure everywhere.
Anthropologists, studying taboos over extensive
periods of time, have learned that taboo systems are
not static and forever inviolate; on the contrary,
they are dynamic elements of learned behavior that
each generation absorbs. Taboos, as rules of
behavior, are always part of a whole system and
cannot be understood outside their social context.
Douglas's explanation of taboos holds as much
meaning for us in the understanding of ourselves as
it does for our understanding of rules of conduct in
the non-Western world. Whether considering the
taboos surrounding a Polynesian chief's* mana *or
the changing sexual taboos in the Western world, it
is apparent that taboo systems function to maintain
cultural systems.*

Reprinted from Richard Cavendish, ed., *Man, Myth,
and Magic* (London, 1979), Vol. 20, pp. 2767–71,
by permission of the author and BPCC/Phoebus
Publishing.

A TABOO (SOMETIMES SPELT TABU) IS A BAN
or prohibition; the word comes from the Polynesian languages where it means a religious restriction, to break which would entail some
automatic punishment. As it is used in English,
taboo has little to do with religion. In essence it
generally implies a rule which has no meaning,
or one which cannot be explained. Captain Cook
noted in his log-book that in Tahiti the women
were never allowed to eat with the men, and as
the men nevertheless enjoyed female company
he asked the reason for this taboo. They always
replied that they observed it because it was
right. To the outsider the taboo is irrational, to
the believer its rightness needs no explaining.
Though supernatural punishments may not be
expected to follow, the rules of any religion rate
as taboos to outsiders. For example, the strict
Jewish observance forbids the faithful to make
and refuel the fire, or light lamps or put them
out during the Sabbath, and it also forbids them
to ask a Gentile to perform any of these acts. In
his book *A Soho Address*, Chaim Lewis, the son
of poor Russian Jewish immigrants in London's
Soho at the beginning of this century, describes
his father's quandary every winter Sabbath: he
did not want to let the fire go out and he could
not ask any favour outright. Somehow he had to
call in a passerby and drop oblique hints until
the stranger understood what service was required. Taboos always tend to land their observers in just such a ridiculous situation, whether it
is a Catholic peasant of the Landes who abstains
from meat on Friday, but eats teal (a bird whose
fishy diet entitles it in their custom to be counted as fish), or a Maori hairdresser who after he
had cut the chief's hair was not allowed to use
his own hands even for feeding himself and had
to be fed for a time like a baby.

In the last century, when the word gained
currency in European languages, taboo was understood to arise from an inferior mentality. It
was argued that primitive tribes observed countless taboos as part of their general ignorance

about the physical world. These rules, which seemed so peculiar to Europeans, were the result of false science, leading to mistaken hygiene, and faulty medicine. Essentially the taboo is a ban on touching or eating or speaking or seeing. Its breach will unleash dangers, while keeping the rules would amount to avoiding dangers and sickness. Since the native theory of taboo was concerned to keep certain classes of people and things apart lest misfortune befall, it was a theory about contagion. Our scholars of the last century contrasted this false, primitive fear of contagion with our modern knowledge of disease. Our hygiene protects from a real danger of contagion, their taboos from imaginary danger. This was a comfortably complacent distinction to draw, but hygiene does not correspond to all the rules which are called taboo. Some are as obviously part of primitive religion in the same sense as Friday abstinence and Sabbath rest. European scholars therefore took care to distinguish on the one hand between primitive taboo with a mainly secular reference, and on the other hand rules of magic which infused the practice of primitive religion. They made it even more difficult to understand the meaning of foreign taboos by importing a classification between true religion and primitive magic, and modern medicine and primitive hygiene; and a very complicated web of definitions was based on this misconception.

In the Eye of the Beholder

The difficulty in understanding primitive taboo arose from the difficulty of understanding our own taboos of hygiene and religion. The first mistake was to suppose that our idea of dirt connotes an objectively real class from which real dangers to health may issue, and whose control depends on valid rules of hygiene. It is better to start by realizing that dirt, like beauty, resides in the eye of the beholder. We must be prepared to put our own behavior under the same microscope we apply to primitive tribes. If we find that they are busy hedging off this area from that, stopping X from touching Y, preventing women from eating with men, and creating elaborate scales of edibility and inedibility among the vegetable and animal worlds, we should realize that we too are given to this ordering and classifying activity. No taboo can ever make sense by itself. A taboo is always part of a whole system of rules. It makes sense as part of a classification whose meaning is so basic to those who live by it that no piecemeal explanation can be given. A native cannot explain the meaning of a taboo because it forms part of his own machinery of learning. The separate compartments which a taboo system constructs are the framework or instrument of understanding. To turn round and inspect that instrument may seem to be an advanced philosophic exercise, but it is necessary if we are to understand the subject.

The nineteenth-century scholars could not understand taboo because they worked within the separate compartments of their own taboo system. For them religion, magic, hygiene, and medicine were as distinct as civilized and primitive; the problem of taboo for them was only a problem about native thought. But put in that form it was insoluble. We approach it nowadays as a problem in human learning.

First, discard the idea that we have anything like a true, complete view of the world. Between what the scientists know and what we make of their knowledge there is a synthesis which is our own rough-and-ready approximation of rules about how we need to behave in the physical world. Second, discard the idea that there can ever be a final and correct world view. A gain in knowledge in one direction does not guarantee there will be no loss or distortion in another; the fullness of reality will always evade our comprehension. The reasons for this will become clear. Learning is a filtering and organizing process. Faced with the same events, two people will not necessarily register two identical patterns, and faced with a similar environment, two cultures will construe two different sets of natural constraints and regular sequences. Understanding is largely a classifying job in which the classifying human mind is much freer than it supposes itself to be. The events to be understood are unconsciously trimmed and filtered to fit the classification being used. In this sense every culture constructs its own universe. It attributes to its own world a set of powers to be harnessed and dangers to be avoided. Each primitive culture, because of its isolation, has a unique world view. Modern industrial nations, because and insofar as they share a common experience, share the same rules about the powers and dangers aroused. This is a valid difference between "Us" and "Them," their primitive taboos and ours.

For all humans, primitive or not, the universe is a system of imputed rules. Using our own distinctions, we can distinguish firstly, physical Nature, inorganic (including rocks, stars, rivers) and organic (vegetable and animal bodies, with rules governing their growth, lifespan and death); secondly, human behaviour; thirdly, the interaction between these two groups; fourthly, other intelligent beings whether incorporeal like gods, devils and ghosts or mixtures of human and divine or human and animal; and lastly, the interaction between this fourth group and the rest.

The use of the word supernatural has been avoided. Even a small amount of reading in anthropology shows how very local and peculiar to our own civilization is the distinction between natural and supernatural. The same applies even to such a classification as the one just given. The fact that it is our own local classification is not important for this argument as the present object is to make clear how taboos should be understood. Taboos are rules about our behaviour which restrict the human uses of things and people. Some of the taboos are said to avoid punishment or vengeance from gods, ghosts and other spirits. Some of them are supposed to produce automatically their dreaded effects. Crop failures, sickness, hunting accidents, famine, drought, epidemic (events in the physical realm), they may all result from breach of taboos.

The Seat of Mana

Taboos can have the effect of expressing political ideas. For example, the idea of the state as a hierarchy of which the chief is the undisputed head and his officials higher than the ordinary populace easily lends itself to taboo behaviour. Gradings of power in the political body tend to be expressed as gradings of freedom to approach the physical body of the person at the top of the system. As Franz Steiner says, in *Taboo* (1956):

> In Polynesian belief the parts of the body formed a fixed hierarchy which had some analogy with the rank system of society. . . . Now the backbone was the most important part of the

body, and the limbs that could be regarded as continuations of the backbone derived importance from it. Above the body was, of course, the head, and it was the seat of mana. When we say this, we must realize that by "mana" are meant both the soul aspect, the life force, and a man's ritual status. This grading of the limbs concerned people of all ranks and both sexes. It could, for example, be so important to avoid stepping over people's heads that the very architecture was involved: the arrangements of the sleeping rooms show such an adaptation in the Marquesas. The commoner's back or head is thus not without its importance in certain contexts. But the real significance of this grading seems to have been in the possibilities it provided for cumulative effects in association with the rank system. The head of a chief was the most concentrated mana object of Polynesian society, and was hedged around with the most terrifying taboos which operated when things were to enter the head or when the head was being diminished; in other words when the chief ate or had his hair cut. . . . The hands of some great chiefs were so dangerous that they could not be put close to the head.

Since the Polynesian political system was very competitive and chiefs had their ups and downs, great triumphs or total failures, the system of taboo was a kind of public vote of confidence and register of current distributions of power. This is important to correct our tendency to think of taboo as a rigidly fixed system of respect.

We will never understand a taboo system unless we understand the kind of interaction between the different spheres of existence which is assumed in it. Any child growing up learns the different spheres and interactions between them simultaneously. When the anthropologist arrives on the scene, he finds the system of knowledge a going concern. It is difficult for him to observe the changes being made, so he gets the wrong impression that a given set of taboos is something hard-and-fast handed down the generations.

In fact, the classifying process is always active and changing. New classifications are being pushed by some and rejected by others. No political innovation takes place without some basic reclassification. To take a currently live issue, in a stratified society, if it is taboo for lower classes or Negroes to sit down at table or to join sporting events with upper classes or whites, those who assert the rule can make it stronger if they find a basis in Nature to support the behaviour they regard as right. If women in Tahiti are forbidden to eat with men, or in Europe to enter certain male occupations, some ultimate justification for the rule needs to be found. Usually it is traced back to their physical nature. Women are said to be constitutionally feeble, nervous or flighty; Negroes to smell; lower classes to be hereditarily less intelligent.

Rules of the Game

Perhaps the easiest approach is to try to imagine what social life would be like without any classification. It would be like playing a game without any rules; no one would know which way to run, who is on his side or against him. There would be no game. It is no exaggeration to describe social life as the process of building classification systems. Everyone is trying to make sense of what is happening. He is trying to make sense of his own behaviour, past and present, so as to capture and hold some sense of identity. He is trying to hold other people to their promises and ensure some kind of regular future. He is explaining continually, to himself and to everyone else. In the process of explaining, classifications are developed and more and more meanings successfully added to them, as other people are persuaded to interpret events in the same way. Gradually even the points of the compass get loaded with social meanings. For example, the west room in an Irish farmer's house used to be the room where the old couple retired to, when the eldest son married and brought his wife to the farm. West meant retirement as well as sundown. In the Buddhist religion, east is the high status point; Buddha's statue is on a shelf on the east wall of the east room; the husband always sleeps to the east of his wife. So east means male and social superior. Up and down, right and left, sun and moon, hot and cold, all the physical antitheses are able to carry meanings from social life, and in a rich and steady culture there is a steady core of such agreed classifications. Anyone who is prepared to support the social system finds himself impelled to uphold the classification system which gets meaning from it. Anyone who

wants to challenge the social system finds himself up against a set of manifold classifications which will have to be rethought. This is why breach of taboo arouses such strong feeling. It is not because the minor classification is threatened, but because the whole social system (in which a great investment has been made) looks like tottering, if someone can get away with challenging a taboo.

Classification involves definition; definition involves reducing ambiguity; ambiguity arises in several ways and it is wrong to think that it can ever be excluded. To take the classification of animal species, they can be classified according to their obvious features, and according to the habitat they live in, and according to how they behave. This gives three ways of classifying animals which could each place the same beasts in different classes. Classed by behaviour, using walking, swimming or flying as basic types, penguins would be nearer to fish; classed by bone structure and egg laying, penguins would count more clearly as birds than would flying fish, which would be birds in the other classification. Animal life is much more untidy and difficult to fit into a regular system of classification than at first appears. Human social life is even more untidy. Girls behave like boys, there are adults who refuse to grow up, every year a few are born whose physical make-up is not clearly male or female. The rules of marriage and inheritance require clear-cut categories but always there will be some cases which do not fit the regularities of the system. For human classifications are always too crude for reality. A system of taboos covers up this weakness of the classification system. It points in advance to defects and insists that no one shall give recognition to the inconvenient facts or behave in such a way as to undermine the acceptability and clarity of the system as a whole. It stops awkward questions and prevents awkward developments.

Sometimes the taboo ban appears in ways that seem a long way from their point of origin. For example, among the Lele tribe, in the Kasai district of the Congo, it was taboo to bring fishing equipment direct into the village from the streams or lakes where it had been in use. All round the village fishing traps and baskets would be hung in trees overnight. Ask the Lele why they did this and they replied that coughs and disease would enter the village if the fishing things were not left out one night. No other answer could be got from them except elaboration of the danger and how sorcerers could enter the village if this barrier were not kept up. But another kind of answer lay in the mass of other rules and regulations which separated the village and its human social life from the forest and streams and animal life. This was the basic classification at stake; one which never needed to be explained because it was too fundamental to mention.

Injecting Order into Life

The novelist William Burroughs describes the final experiences of disgust and depression of some forms of drug addiction. What he calls the "Naked Lunch" is the point where all illusions are stripped away and every thing is seen as it really is. When everyone can see what is on everyone's fork, nothing is classed as edible. Meat can be animal or human flesh, caterpillars, worms, or bugs; soup is equally urine, lentils, scotch broth, or excreta; other people are neither friends nor enemies, nor is oneself different from other people since neither has any very clear definition. Identities and classifications are merged into a seething, shapeless experience. This is the potential disorder of the mind which taboo breaks up into classes and rules and so judges some activities as right and proper and others as horrifying.

This kind of rationality is the justification for the taboos which we ourselves observe when we separate the lavatory from the living room and the bed from the kitchen, injecting order into the house. But the order is not arbitrary; it derives from social categories. When a set of social distinctions weakens, the taboos that expressed it weaken too. For this reason sex taboos used to be sacred in England but are no longer so strong. It seems ridiculous that women should not be allowed in some clubs or professions, whereas not so long ago it seemed obviously right. The same for the sense of privacy, the same for hierarchy. The less we ourselves are forced to adopt unthinking taboo attitudes to breaches of these boundaries, the easier it becomes to look dispassionately at the taboos of other societies and find plenty of meaning in them.

In some tribal societies it is thought that the shedding of blood will cause droughts and other environmental disasters. Elsewhere any contact with death is dangerously polluting, and burials are followed by elaborate washing and fumigation. In other places they fear neither homicide nor death pollution but menstrual blood is thought to be very dangerous to touch. And in other places again, adultery is liable to cause illness. Some people are thickly beset with taboos so that everything they do is charged with social symbolism. Others observe only one or two rules. Those who are most taboo-minded have the most complex set of social boundaries to preserve. Hence their investment of so much energy into the control of behaviour.

A taboo system upholds a cultural system and a culture is a pattern of values and norms; social life is impossible without such a pattern. This is the dilemma of individual freedom. Ideally we would like to feel free to make every choice from scratch and judge each case on its merits. Such a freedom would slow us down, for every choice would have to be consciously deliberated. On the one hand, education tries to equip a person with means for exercising private judgement, and on the other hand, the techniques of education provide a kind of mechanical decision-making, along well-oiled grooves. They teach strong reactions of anxiety about anything which threatens to go off the track. As education transmits culture, taboos and all, it is a kind of brainwashing. It only allows a certain way of seeing reality and so limits the scope for private judgement. Without the taboos, which turn basic classifications into automatic psychological reflexes, no thinking could be effective, because if every system of classification was up for revision at every moment, there would be no stability of thought. Hence there would be no scope for experience to accumulate into knowledge. Taboos bar the way for the mind to visualize reality differently. But the barriers they set up are not arbitrary, for taboos flow from social boundaries and support the social structure. This accounts for their seeming irrational to the outsider and beyond challenge to the person living in the society.

You Are What You Eat: Religious Aspects of the Health Food Movement

Jill Dubisch

In this article Jill Dubisch shows that the health food movement in this country may be seen as more than a way of eating and more than an alternative healing system. Using Clifford Geertz's definition of religion as a "system of symbols," Dubisch maintains that the health food movement has many of the characteristics of a religion. For example, the anthropological concepts of mana *and* taboo *are used in a discussion of the merits of "health foods" (mana) versus the detrimental nature of "junk foods" (taboo). The health food movement, like religion, offers its adherents salvation of the body, psyche, and even society itself. Followers strive to gain new values and a new world view. Comparing health food devotees to people undergoing a religious revitalization, Dubisch describes how converts learn to criticize prevailing social values and institutions. She notes the process of conversion that individuals entering the movement undergo, their concern for the maintenance of purity, the "temples" (health food stores), the "rabbis" (health food experts), and the sacred writings that establish the movement's principles. Provocative and entertaining, Dubisch's analysis of the religious aspects of the health food movement is sound anthropology and is certain to remind each of us of our own, or an acquaintance's, "religious" involvement with health food.*

Reprinted from Susan P. Montague and W. Arens, eds., *The American Dimension: Culture Myths and Social Realities*, 2nd ed. (Palo Alto, Calif., 1981), pp. 115–27, by permission of the author and Mayfield Publishing Company.

Dr. Robbins was thinking how it might be interesting to make a film from Adelle Davis' perennial best seller, *Let's Eat Right to Keep Fit.* Representing a classic confrontation between good and evil—in this case nutrition versus unhealthy diet—the story had definite box office appeal. The role of the hero, Protein, probably should be filled by Jim Brown, although Burt Reynolds undoubtedly would pull strings to get the part. Sunny Doris Day would be a clear choice to play the heroine, Vitamin C, and Orson Welles, oozing saturated fatty acids from the pits of his flesh, could win an Oscar for his interpretation of the villainous Cholesterol. The film might begin on a stormy night in the central nervous system. . . .

—Tom Robbins, *Even Cowgirls Get the Blues*

I INTEND TO EXAMINE A CERTAIN WAY OF EATING; that which is characteristic of the health food movement, and try to determine what people are communicating when they choose to eat in ways which run counter to the dominant patterns of food consumption in our society. This requires looking at health foods as a system of symbols and the adherence to a health food way of life as being, in part, the expression of belief in a particular world view. Analysis of these symbols and the underlying world view reveals that, as a system of beliefs and practices, the health food movement has some of the characteristics of a religion.

Such an interpretation might at first seem strange since we usually think of religion in terms of a belief in a deity or other supernatural beings. These notions, for the most part, are lacking in the health food movement. However, anthropologists do not always consider such beliefs to be a necessary part of a religion. Clifford Geertz, for example, suggests the following broad definition:

> A *religion* is (1) a system of symbols which acts to (2) establish powerful, pervasive, and long-lasting moods and motivations in men by (3) formulating conceptions of a general-order of existence and (4) clothing these conceptions with such an aura of factuality that (5) the moods and motivations seem uniquely realistic. (Geertz 1965: 4)

Let us examine the health food movement in the light of Geertz's definition.

History of the Health Food Movement

The concept of "health foods" can be traced back to the 1830s and the Popular Health movement, which combined a reaction against professional medicine and an emphasis on lay knowledge and health care with broader social concerns such as feminism and the class struggle (see Ehrenreich and English 1979). The Popular Health movement emphasized self-healing and the dissemination of knowledge about the body and health to laymen. One of the early founders of the movement, Sylvester Graham (who gave us the graham cracker), preached that good health was to be found in temperate living. This included abstinence from alcohol, a vegetarian diet, consumption of whole wheat products, and regular exercise. The writings and preachings of these early "hygienists" (as they called themselves) often had moral overtones, depicting physiological and spiritual reform as going hand in hand (Shryock 1966).

The idea that proper diet can contribute to good health has continued into the twentieth century. The discovery of vitamins provided for many health food people a further "natural" means of healing which could be utilized instead of drugs. Vitamins were promoted as health-giving substances by various writers, including nutritionist Adelle Davis, who has been perhaps the most important "guru" of health foods in this century. Davis preached good diet as well as the use of vitamins to restore and maintain health, and her books have become the best sellers of the movement. (The titles of her books, *Let's Cook It Right*,

Let's Get Well, Let's Have Healthy Children, give some sense of her approach.) The health food movement took on its present form, however, during the late 1960s, when it became part of the "counterculture."

Health foods were "in," and their consumption became part of the general protest against the "establishment" and the "straight" life-style. They were associated with other movements centering around social concerns, such as ecology and consumerism (Kandel and Pelto 1980: 328). In contrast to the Popular Health movement, health food advocates of the sixties saw the establishment as not only the medical profession but also the food industry and the society it represented. Food had become highly processed and laden with colorings, preservatives, and other additives so that purity of food became a new issue. Chemicals had also become part of the food-growing process, and in reaction terms such as "organic" and "natural" became watchwords of the movement. Health food consumption received a further impetus from revelations about the high sugar content of many popular breakfast cereals which Americans had been taught since childhood to think of as a nutritious way to start the day. (Kellogg, an early advocate of the Popular Health movement, would have been mortified, since his cereals were originally designed to be part of a hygienic regimen.)

Although some health food users are members of formal groups (such as the Natural Hygiene Society, which claims direct descent from Sylvester Graham), the movement exists primarily as a set of principles and practices rather than as an organization. For those not part of organized groups, these principles and practices are disseminated, and contact is made with other members of the movement, through several means. The most important of these are health food stores, restaurants, and publications. The two most prominent journals in the movement are *Prevention* and *Let's Live*, begun in 1920 and 1932 respectively (Hongladarom 1976).

These journals tell people what foods to eat and how to prepare them. They offer advice about the use of vitamins, the importance of exercise, and the danger of pollutants. They also present testimonials from faithful practitioners. Such testimonials take the form of articles that recount how the author overcame a physical problem through a health food approach, or letters from readers who tell how they have cured their ailments by following methods advocated by the journal or suggested by friends in the movement. In this manner, such magazines not only educate, they also articulate a world view and provide evidence and support for it. They have become the "sacred writings" of the movement. They are a way of "reciting the code" —the cosmology and moral injunctions—which anthropologist Anthony F. C. Wallace describes as one of the important categories of religious behavior (1966: 57).

Ideological Content of the Health Food Movement

What exactly is the health food system? First, and most obviously, it centers around certain beliefs regarding the relationship of diet to health. Health foods are seen as an "alternative" healing system, one which people turn to out of their dissatisfaction with conventional medicine (see, for example, Hongladarom 1976). The emphasis is on "wellness" and prevention rather than on illness and curing. Judging from letters and articles found in health food publications, many individuals' initial adherence to the movement is a type of conversion. A specific medical problem, or a general dissatisfaction with the state of their health, leads these converts to an eventual realization of the "truth" as represented by the health food approach, and to a subsequent change in life-style to reflect the principles of that approach. "Why This Psychiatrist 'Switched'," published in *Prevention* (September 1976), carries the following heading: "Dr. H. L. Newbold is a great advocate of better nutrition and a livelier life style. But it took a personal illness to make him see the light." For those who have experienced such conversion, and for others who become convinced by reading about such experiences, health food publications serve an important function by reinforcing the conversion and encouraging a change of life-style. For example, an article entitled "How to Convert Your Kitchen for the New Age of Nutrition" (*Prevention*, February 1975) tells the housewife how to make her kitchen a source of health for her family. The article suggests ways of reorganizing kitchen supplies and reforming cooking by substituting health foods for substances detrimental to health, and also offers ideas on the preparation of nutritious and delicious meals which will convert the family to this new way of eating without "alienating" them. The pamphlet *The Junk Food Withdrawal Manual* (Kline 1978), details how an individual can, step by step, quit eating junk foods and adopt more healthful eating habits. Publications also urge the readers to convert others by letting them know how much better health foods are than junk foods. Proselytizing may take the form of giving a "natural" birthday party for one's children and their friends, encouraging schools to substitute fruit and nuts for junk food snacks, and even selling one's own baking.

Undergoing the conversion process means learning and accepting the general features of the health food world view. To begin with, there is great concern, as there is in many religions, with purity, in this case, the purity of food, of water, of air. In fact, there are some striking similarities between keeping a "health food kitchen" and the Jewish practice of keeping kosher. Both make distinctions between proper and improper foods, and both involve excluding certain impure foods (whether unhealthful or non-kosher) from the kitchen and table. In addition, a person concerned with maintaining a high degree of purity in food may engage in similar behavior in either case— reading labels carefully to check for impermissible ingredients and even purchasing food from special establishments to guarantee ritual purity.

In the health food movement, the basis of purity is healthfulness and "naturalness." Some foods are considered to be natural and therefore healthier; this concept applies not only to foods but to other aspects of life as well. It is part of the large idea that people should work in harmony with nature and not against it. In this respect, the health food cosmology sets up an opposition of nature (beneficial) versus culture (destructive), or, in particular, the health food movement against our highly technological society. As products of our industrialized way of life, certain foods are unnatural; they produce illness by working against the body. Consistent with this view is the idea that healing, like eating, should proceed in harmony with nature. The assumption is that the body, if allowed to function naturally, will tend to heal itself. Orthodox medicine, on the other hand, with its drugs and surgery and its non-holistic approach to health, works against the body. Physicians are frequently criticized in the literature of the movement for their narrow approach to medical problems, reliance on drugs and surgery, lack of knowledge of nutrition, and unwillingness to accept the validity of the patient's own experience in healing himself. It is believed that doctors may actually cause further health problems rather than effecting a cure. A short item in *Prevention*, "The Delivery Is Normal—But the Baby Isn't," recounts an incident in which drug-induced labor in childbirth resulted in a mentally retarded baby. The conclusion is "nature does a good job—and we should not, without compelling reasons, try to take over" (*Prevention*, May 1979: 38).

The healing process is hastened by natural substances, such as healthful food, and by other "natural" therapeutic measures such as exercise. Vitamins are also very important to many health food people, both for maintaining health and for healing. They are seen as components of food which work with the body and are believed to offer a more natural mode of healing than drugs. Vitamins, often one of the most prominent products offered in many health food stores, provide the greatest source of profit (Hongladarom 1976).

A basic assumption of the movement is that certain foods are good for you while others are not. The practitioner of a health food way of life must learn to distinguish between two kinds of food: those which promote well-being ("health foods") and those which are believed to be detrimental to health ("junk foods"). The former are the only kind of food a person should consume, while the latter are the antithesis of all that food should be and must be avoided. The qualities of these foods may be described by two anthropological concepts, *mana* and *taboo*. Mana is a type of beneficial or valuable power which can pass to individuals from sacred objects through touch (or, in the case of health foods, by ingestion). Taboo, on the other hand, refers to power that is dangerous; objects which are taboo can injure those who touch them (Wallace, 1966: 60–61). Not all foods fall clearly into one category or the other. However, those foods which are seen as having health-giving qualities, which contain *mana*, symbolize life, while *taboo* foods symbolize death. ("Junk food is . . . dead. . . . Dead food produces death," proclaims one health food manual [Kline 1978: 2–4].) Much of the space in health food publications is devoted to

telling the reader why to consume certain foods and avoid others ("Frozen, Creamed Spinach: Nutritional Disaster," *Prevention*, May 1979; "Let's Sprout Some Seeds," *Better Nutrition*, September 1979).

Those foods in the health food category which are deemed to possess an especially high level of *mana* have come to symbolize the movement as a whole. Foods such as honey, wheat germ, yogurt, and sprouts are seen as representative of the general way of life which health food adherents advocate, and Kandel and Pelto found that certain health food followers attribute mystical powers to the foods they consume. Raw food eaters speak of the "life energy" in uncooked foods. Sprout eaters speak of their food's "growth force" (1980: 336).

Qualities such as color and texture are also important in determining health foods and may acquire symbolic value. "Wholeness" and "whole grain" have come to stand for healthfulness and have entered the jargon of the advertising industry. Raw, coarse, dark, crunchy, and cloudy foods are preferred over those which are cooked, refined, white, soft, and clear. (See chart.)

Thus dark bread is preferred over white, raw milk over pasteurized, brown rice over white. The convert must learn to eat foods which at first seem strange and even exotic and to reject many foods which are components of the Standard American diet. A McDonald's hamburger, for example, which is an important symbol of America itself (Kottack 1978), falls into the category of "junk food" and must be rejected.

Just as the magazines and books which articulate the principles of the health food movement and serve as a guide to the convert can be said to comprise the sacred writings of the movement, so the health food store or health food restaurant is the temple where the purity of the movement is guarded and maintained. There individuals find for sale the types of food and other substances advocated by the movement. One does not expect to find items of questionable purity, that is, substances which are not natural or which may be detrimental to health. Within the precincts of the temple adherents can feel safe from the contaminating forces of the larger society, can meet fellow devotees, and can be instructed by the guardians of the sacred area (see, for example, Hongladarom 1976). Health food stores may vary

HEALTH FOOD WORLD VIEW

	Health Foods	Junk Foods	
cosmic oppositions	LIFE NATURE	DEATH CULTURE	
basic values and desirable attributes	holistic, organic harmony with body and nature natural and real harmony, self- sufficiency, independence homemade, small scale layman competence and understanding	fragmented, mechanistic working against body and nature manufactured and artificial disharmony, dependence mass-produced professional esoteric knowledge and jargon	undesirable attributes
beneficial qualities of food	whole coarse dark crunchy raw cloudy	processed refined white soft cooked clear	harmful qualities
specific foods with mana	yogurt* honey* carob soybeans* sprouts* fruit juices herb teas foods from other cultures: humus, falafel, kefir, tofu, stir-fried vegetables, pita bread	ice cream, candy sugar* chocolate beef overcooked vegetables soft drinks* coffee,* tea "all-American" foods: hot dogs, McDonald's hamburgers,* potato chips, Coke	specific taboo foods
	return to early American values, "real" American way of life	corruption of this original and better way of life and values	

*Denotes foods with especially potent mana or taboo.

in their degree of purity. Some sell items such as coffee, raw sugar, or "natural" ice cream which are considered questionable by others of the faith. (One health food store I visited had a sign explaining that it did not sell vitamin supplements, which it considered to be "unnatural," i.e., impure.)

People in other places are often viewed as living more "naturally" and healthfully than contemporary Americans. Observation of such peoples may be used to confirm practices of the movement and to acquire ideas about food. Healthy and long-lived people like the Hunza of the Himalayas are studied to determine the secrets of their strength and longevity. Cultures as yet untainted by the food systems of industrialized nations are seen as examples of what better diet can do. In addition, certain foods from other cultures—foods such as humus, falafel, and tofu—have been adopted into the health food repertoire because of their presumed healthful qualities.

Peoples of other times can also serve as models for a more healthful way of life. There is in the health food movement a concept of a "golden age," a past which provides an authority for a better way of living. This past may be scrutinized for clues about how to improve contemporary American society. An archaeologist, writing for *Prevention* magazine, recounts how "I Put Myself on a Caveman Diet—Permanently" (*Prevention,* September 1979). His article explains how he improved his health by utilizing the regular exercise and simpler foods which he had concluded from his research were probably characteristic of our prehistoric ancestors. A general nostalgia about the past seems to exist in the health food movement, along with the feeling that we have departed from a more natural pattern of eating practiced by earlier generations of Americans (see, for example, Hongladarom 1976). (Sylvester Graham, however, presumably did not find the eating habits of his contemporaries to be very admirable.)

The health food movement is concerned with more than the achievement of bodily health. Nutritional problems are often seen as being at the root of emotional, spiritual, and even social problems. An article entitled "Sugar Neurosis" states "Hypoglycemia (low blood sugar) is a medical reality that can trigger wife-beating, divorce, even suicide" (*Prevention,* April 1979: 110). Articles and books claim to show the reader how to overcome depression through vitamins and nutrition and the movement promises happiness and psychological well-being as well as physical health. Social problems, too, may respond to the health food approach. For example, a probation officer recounts how she tried changing offenders' diets in order to change their behavior. Testimonials from two of the individuals helped tell "what it was like to find that good nutrition was their bridge from the wrong side of the law and a frustrated, unhappy life to a vibrant and useful one" (*Prevention,* May 1978: 56). Thus, through more healthful eating and a more natural life-style, the health food movement offers its followers what many religions offer: salvation—in this case salvation for the body, for the psyche, and for society.

Individual effort is the keystone of the health food movement. An individual can take responsibility for his or her own health and does not need to rely on professional medical practitioners. The corollary of this is that it is a person's own behavior which may be the cause of ill health. By sinning, by not listening to our bodies, and by not following a natural way of life, we bring our ailments upon ourselves.

The health food movement also affirms the validity of each individual's experience. No two individuals are alike: needs for different vitamins vary widely; some people are more sensitive to food additives than others; each person has his or her best method of achieving happiness. Therefore, the generalized expertise of professionals and the scientifically verifiable findings of the experts may not be adequate guides for you, the individual, in the search of health. Each person's experience has meaning; if something works for you, then it works. If it works for others also, so much the better, but if it does not, that does not invalidate your own experience. While the movement does not by any means disdain all scientific findings (and indeed they are used extensively when they bolster health food positions), such findings are not seen as the only source of confirmation for the way of life which the health food movement advocates, and the scientific establishment itself tends to be suspect.

In line with its emphasis on individual responsibility for health, the movement seeks to deprofessionalize knowledge and place in every individual's hands the information and means to heal. Drugs used by doctors are usually available only through prescription, but foods and vitamins can be obtained by anyone. Books, magazines, and health food store personnel seek to educate their clientele in ways of healing themselves and maintaining their own health. Articles explain bodily processes, the effects of various substances on health, and the properties of foods and vitamins.

The focus on individual responsibility is frequently tied to a wider concern for self-sufficiency and self-reliance. Growing your own organic garden, grinding your own flour, or even, as one pamphlet suggests, raising your own cow are not simply ways that one can be assured of obtaining healthful food; they are also expressions of independence and self-reliance. Furthermore, such practices are seen as characteristic of an earlier "golden age" when people lived natural lives. For example, an advertisement for vitamins appearing in a digest distributed in health food stores shows a mother and daughter kneading bread together. The heading reads "America's discovering basics." The copy goes on, "Baking bread at home has been a basic family practice throughout history. The past several decades, however, have seen a shift in the American diet to factory-produced breads. . . . Fortunately, today there are signs that more and more Americans are discovering the advantage of baking bread themselves." Homemade bread, home-canned produce, sprouts growing on the window sill symbolize what are felt to be basic American values, values supposedly predominant in earlier times when people not only lived on self-sufficient farms and produced their own fresh and more natural food, but also stood firmly on their own two feet and took charge of their own lives. A reader writing to *Prevention* praises an article about a man who found "new life at ninety without lawyers or doctors," saying "If that isn't the optimum in the American way of living, I can't imagine what is!" (*Prevention*, May 1978: 16). Thus although it criticizes the contemporary American way of life, (and although some vegetarians turn to Eastern religions for guidance—see Kandel and Pelto 1980) the health food movement in general claims to be the true faith, the proponent of basic Americanness, a faith from which the society as a whole has strayed.

Social Significance of the Health Food Movement for American Actors

Being a "health food person" involves more than simply changing one's diet or utilizing an alternative medical system. Kandel and Pelto suggest that the health food movement derives much of its popularity from the fact that "food may be used simultaneously to cure or prevent illness, as a religious symbol and to forge social bonds. Frequently health food users are trying to improve their health, their lives, and sometimes the world as well" (1980: 332). Use of health foods becomes an affirmation of certain values and a commitment to a certain world view. A person who becomes involved in the health food movement might be said to experience what anthropologist Anthony F. C. Wallace has called "mazeway resynthesis." The "mazeway" is the mental "map" or image of the world which each individual holds. It includes val-

ues, the environment and the objects in it, the image of the self and of others, the techniques one uses to manipulate the environment to achieve desired end states (Wallace 1970: 237). Resynthesis of this mazeway—that is, the creation of new "maps," values, and techniques—commonly occurs in times of religious revitalization, when new religious movements are begun and converts to them are made. As individuals, these converts learn to view the world in a new manner and to act accordingly. In the case of the health food movement, those involved learn to see their health problems and other dissatisfactions with their lives as stemming from improper diet and living in disharmony with nature. They are provided with new values, new ways of viewing their environment, and new techniques for achieving their goals. For such individuals, health food use can come to imply "a major redefinition of self-image, role, and one's relationship to others" (Kandel and Pelto 1980: 359). The world comes to "make sense" in the light of this new world view. Achievement of the desired end states of better health and an improved outlook on life through following the precepts of the movement gives further validation.

It is this process which gives the health food movement some of the overtones of a religion. As does any new faith, the movement criticizes the prevailing social values and institutions, in this case the health-threatening features of modern industrial society. While an individual's initial dissatisfaction with prevailing beliefs and practices may stem from experiences with the conventional medical system (for example, failure to find a solution to a health problem through visits to a physician), this dissatisfaction often comes to encompass other facets of the American way of life. This further differentiates the "health food person" from mainstream American society (even when the difference is justified as a return to "real" American values).

In everyday life the consumption of such substances as honey, yogurt, and wheat germ, which have come to symbolize the health food movement, does more than contribute to health. It also serves to represent commitment to the health food world view. Likewise, avoiding those substances, such as sugar and white bread, which are considered "evil" is also a mark of a health food person. Ridding the kitchen of such items—a move often advocated by articles advising readers on how to "convert" successfully to health foods—is an act of ritual as well as practical significance. The symbolic nature of such foods is confirmed by the reactions of outsiders to those who are perceived as being inside the movement. An individual who is perceived as being a health food person is often automatically assumed to use honey instead of sugar, for example. Conversely, if one is noticed using or not using certain foods (e.g., adding wheat germ to food, not eating white sugar), this can lead to questions from the observer as to whether or not that individual is a health food person (or a health food "nut," depending upon the questioner's own orientation).

The symbolic nature of such foods is especially important for the health food neophyte. The adoption of a certain way of eating and the renunciation of mainstream cultural food habits can constitute "bridge-burning acts of commitment" (Kendel and Pelto 1980: 395), which function to cut the individual off from previous patterns of behavior. However, the symbolic activity which indicates this cutting off need not be as radical as a total change of eating habits. In an interview in *Prevention*, a man who runs a health-oriented television program recounted an incident in which a viewer called up after a show and announced excitedly that he had changed his whole life-style—he had started using honey in his coffee! *(Prevention*, February 1979: 89). While recognizing the absurdity of the action on a practical level, the program's host acknowledged the symbolic importance of this action to the person involved. He also saw it as a step in the right direction since one change can lead to another. Those who sprinkle wheat germ on cereal, toss alfalfa sprouts with a salad, or pass up an ice cream cone for yogurt are not only demonstrating a concern for health but also affirming their commitment to a particular life-style and symbolizing adherence to a set of values and a world view.

Conclusion

As this analysis has shown, health foods are more than simply a way of eating and more than an alternative healing system. If we return to Clifford Geertz's definition of religion as a "system of symbols" which produces "powerful, pervasive, and long-lasting moods and motivations" by "formulating conceptions of a general order of existence" and making them appear "uniquely realistic," we see that the health food movement definitely has a religious dimension. There is, first, a system of symbols, in this case based on certain kinds and qualities of food. While the foods are believed to have health-giving properties in themselves, they also symbolize a world view which is concerned with the right way to live one's life and the right way to construct a society. This "right way" is based on an approach to life which stresses harmony with nature and the holistic nature of the body. Consumption of those substances designated as "health foods," as well as participation in other activities associated with the movement which also symbolize its world view (such as exercising or growing an organic garden) can serve to establish the "moods and motivations" of which Geertz speaks. The committed health food follower may come to experience a sense of spiritual as well as physical well-being when he or she adheres to the health food way of life. Followers are thus motivated to persist in this way of life, and they come to see the world view of this movement as correct and "realistic."

In addition to its possession of sacred symbols and its "convincing" world view, the health food movement also has other elements which we usually associate with a religion. Concepts of mana and taboo guide the choice of foods. There is a distinction between the pure and impure and a concern for the maintenance of purity. There are "temples" (health food stores and other such establishments) which are expected to maintain purity within their confines. There are "rabbis," or experts in the "theology" of the movement and its application to everyday life. There are sacred and instructional writings which set out the principles of the movement and teach followers how to utilize them. In addition, like many religious movements, the health food movement harkens back to a "golden age" which it seeks to recreate and assumes that many of the ills of the contemporary world are caused by society's departure from this ideal state.

Individuals entering the movement, like individuals entering any religious movement, may undergo a process of conversion. This can be dramatic, resulting from the cure of an illness or the reversal of a previous state of poor health, or it can be gradual, a step-by-step changing of eating and other habits through exposure to health food doctrine. Individuals who have undergone conversion and mazeway resynthesis, as well as those who have tested and confirmed various aspects of the movement's prescriptions for better health and a better life, may give testimonials to the faith. For those who have adopted, in full or in part, the health food world view, it provides, as do all religions, explanations for existing conditions, answers to specific problems, and a means of gaining control over one's existence. Followers of the movement are also promised "salvation," not in the form of afterlife, but in terms of enhanced physical well-being, greater energy, longer lifespan, freedom from illness, and increased peace of mind. However, although the focus is this-worldly, there is a spiritual dimension to the health food movement. And although it does not center its world view around belief in supernatural beings, it does posit a higher authority—the wisdom of nature—as the source of ultimate legitimacy for its views.

Health food people are often dismissed as "nuts" or "food faddists" by those outside the movement. Such a designation fails to recognize the systematic nature of the health food world view, the symbolic significance of health foods, and the important functions which the movement performs for its followers. Health foods offer an alternative or supplement to conventional medical treatment, and a meaningful and effective way for individuals to bring about changes in lives which are perceived as unsatisfactory because of poor physical and emotional health. It can also provide for its followers a framework of meaning which transcends individual problems. In opposing itself to the predominant American life-style, the health food movement sets up a symbolic system which opposes harmony to disharmony, purity to pollution, nature to culture, and ultimately, as in many religions, life to death. Thus while foods are the beginning point and the most important symbols of the health food movement, food is not the ultimate focus but rather a means to an end: the organization of a meaningful world view and the construction of a satisfying life.

3

Shamans, Priests, and Prophets

In Chapters 1 and 2 the reader was introduced to the anthropological approach to the study of religion and to the complex variety of symbols, rites, ceremonies, and belief structures that constitute the heart of supernatural belief systems everywhere. We now turn to the role and place of the supernatural leader. Where and how do religious leaders get their power? What is the distinction between a shaman and a priest, or a prophet and a priest? How do sorcerers, diviners, and magicians differ? In short, this chapter introduces the topic of religious specialists.

Any member of society may approach the supernatural on an individual basis; for example, a person may kneel to the ground, all alone, and recite a prayer for help from the spiritual world. But the religions of the world, whether small animistic cults or the "great faiths," also have intermediaries: religious people who, acting as part-time or full-time specialists, intervene on behalf of an individual client or an entire community. Paul Radin (1937: 107) argued that the development of religion can be traced to the social roles undertaken by each of these "priest-thinkers"—at once, a philosopher of religion, a theologian of be-

Eskimo mask, Ingalik, Alaska.

liefs, a person who is the recognized master of worship.

If all religions appear to have specialists, anthropologists have also found that some societies place more emphasis on these religious experts than others do. Robert Textor has noted, for example, that the societies that are more likely to have religious specialists tend to produce food rather than collect it, use money as a medium of exchange, and display different social classes and a complex political system (1967). In other words, the more complex the society, the greater is the likelihood of having religious intermediaries.

Early anthropologists were drawn to the view of unilineal evolution: how institutions progressed from savagery to barbarism, finally achieving a civilized state. As societies advance, all institutions become more complex and specialized. In his classic work *Primitive Culture* (1871), E. B. Tylor posited an early definition of religion that prompted his colleagues to concern themselves with religious specialization. Describing religion as the belief in spiritual beings, what he called "animism," Tylor implied that a society's degree of religious specialization was directly related to its position on the evolutionary scale. Unilineal evolutionary theory was pockmarked with faulty premises, of course: although cultures do evolve, they do not necessarily follow a prescribed series of stages. What is important to note here, however, is that Tylor and his contemporaries began to look carefully at religious specialization and categories of religious phenomena. J. G. Frazer, in the *Golden Bough* (1890), distinguished between magic and religion and described the role of specialists. And Herbert Spencer's approach, in the *Principles of Sociology* (1896), that religious stages could only be comprehended if the functions of religion and the interrelationships of religion with other institutions were known, demanded that religious specialization be studied in terms of its functions in society —an approach that anthropologists still adhere to today. Anthropological data have shown the importance of shamans, priests, prophets, and other specialists to the maintenance of economic, political, social, and educational institutions of their societies.

The anthropological literature devoted to religious specialists is extensive; much work remains, however, to adequately define and distinguish between the actual functions they perform for members of their societies. Shamans, for example, have duties and religious obligations that differ from society to society, although their basic duty of curing through the use of the supernatural is accepted by anthropologists. The same kinds of differences exist in the tasks performed by prophets, priests, sorcerers, and others designated as "intermediaries" with the supernatural. Without a clear understanding of these distinctions, systematic cross-cultural comparisons would be impossible. Differentiation of specialists through an analysis of their functions tells anthropologists a great deal about the structure of society.

In addition to the definitional problem associated with specialists, anthropologists must also determine whether or not to place the tasks performed by these experts under the rubric of "the religious" or to create other categories for such activities. Is the performance of magic, witchcraft, and sorcery "religious" behavior, or are these examples of non-religious, indeed anti-religious acts? If those who practice these acts are outside the religious realm, then what, if any, connection do they have with the sacred? The real question becomes, What is religion? In Western culture witchcraft, magic, and sorcery are assigned to the occult and are considered outside of and, ordinarily, counter to religion. In the non-Western world, however, specialists who take part in these kinds of activities are often considered to be important parts of the total religious belief system. It is a common view in Africa south of the Sahara that people are often designated witches by God, and that sorcerers and magicians receive their power from the spirit world, that is, from supernatural agencies controlled by God. In these terms, is drawing upon supernatural aid from shamans, priests, or prophets more "religious" than turning to magicians, sorcerers, and other specialists who also call upon supernatural agents but for different ends? In light of these questions, anthropologists have found it necessary to consider all specialists whose power emanates from supernatural agents and power to be in the realm of the religious, although some specialists serve while others harm society through their actions.

Because not all societies contain identical religious specialists, determining why certain specialists exist and others do not is important to our understanding both of the structure of a society and its supernatural world, and of the causal forces behind good and bad fortune. In societies where witches do not exist, for example, it is frequently malicious ghosts or ancestors who are believed to bring misfortune and illness. In such cases elders may play an important role as diviners, in contrast to the diviner specialists that exist in other groups. Such data not only aid our understanding of supernatural causation and specialization but also demonstrate the connection between the social structure of the living—the position of the elder in society—and that of the ancestor or ghost in the afterworld. The example of the elder as religious specialist is problematic in some societies. Eugene Mendonsa, in speaking of the Sisala of Ghana, for example, makes clear that not all elders have the ability to divine and those who can are only specialists in a part-time sense (1976).

The difficulty inherent in making distinctions among non-Western specialists may be further realized by considering the position of the religious lay person in this country. Although not a specialist in the traditional sense, this individual is nevertheless more involved and usually more knowledgeable than the typical church member. Is the lay person significantly different from one of the more traditional part-time specialists? Immediately, the problem of the degree of participation comes to mind—part-time versus full-time—accompanied by the complicating factor of training—formal versus "on-the-job" learning. Making distinctions such as these is an important part of analytic accounts of religious functionaries.

The four excellent articles that follow tell us much about the religious specialist. Victor Turner's lead-off essay provides a broad-spectrum account of the various specialists who appear in ethnographic descriptions of religions around the world. Next, C. Von Furer-Haimendorf delineates the role of priests, and Douglas Barnes discusses the phenomenon of charismatic religious leaders. How do these leaders arise? What personality traits do they share? Are there any social situations responsible for their popularity? Finally, John Hall provides the closing contemporary Western article. Building on the social, political, and economic problems surrounding the success and failure of cults, Hall describes the tragedy at Jonestown—a religious event that is easier to comprehend after having read the previous material in this and the preceding chapter.

References Cited

Frazer, J. G.
  1890 *The Golden Bough.* London: MacMillan.

Mendonsa, Eugene L.
  1976 "Characteristics of Sisala Diviners." In *The Realm of the Extra-Human: Agents and Audiences*, pp. 179–95. World Anthropology Series, ed. Agehananda Bharati. The Hague: Mouton Publishers.

Radin, Paul
  1937 *Primitive Religion: Its Nature and Origin.* New York: Dover Publications.

Spencer, H.
  1896 *Principles of Sociology.* New York: D. Appleton.

Textor, Robert
  1967 *A Cross-Cultural Summary.* New Haven: HRAF Press.

Tylor, E. B.
  1871 *Primitive Culture: Researches into the Development of Mythology, Philosophy, Religion, Language, Art and Custom.*

Religious Specialists
Victor W. Turner

Noted for his specialization in the study of symbolism and symbolic behavior, Victor Turner here presents an outstanding general discussion of religious specialists and lays the groundwork for the more specialized articles to follow, which deal specifically with shamans, priests, and prophets. Turner not only deals with these avocations but includes other, less prominent but often equally important religious specialists—diviners, seers, mediums, witches, sorcerers, and magicians. Unlike many theorists of the past, Turner stresses that all should be included under the umbrella of the term "religion," for all, in special ways, manipulate the supernatural to their own or society's ends.

Turner's is no small theoretical accomplishment, for controversy over the definition of the term "religion" has long occupied anthropologists. His discussion illuminates the subtle but important differences among specialists, without which religions of the non-Western world would remain unintelligible.

Reprinted by permission of the publisher from the *International Encyclopedia of the Social Sciences*, David L. Sills, Editor. Vol. 13, pp. 437–44. Copyright © 1972 by Crowell Collier and Macmillan.

A RELIGIOUS SPECIALIST IS ONE WHO DEVOTES himself to a particular branch of religion or, viewed organizationally, of a religious system. "Religion" is a multivocal term whose range of meanings varies in different social and historical contexts. Nevertheless, most definitions of religion refer to the recognition of a transhuman controlling power that may be either personal or impersonal. A religious specialist has a culturally defined status relevant to this recognition. In societies or contexts where such power is regarded as impersonal, anthropologists customarily describe it as *magic*, and those who manipulate the power are magicians. Wherever power is personalized, as deity, gods, spirits, daemons, genii, ancestral shades, ghosts, or the like, anthropologists speak of *religion*. In reality, religious systems contain both magical and religious beliefs and procedures: in many of them the impersonal transhuman (or mystical, or non-empirical, or supernatural) power is considered to be a devolution of personal power, as in the case of the mystical efficacy of rites established *in illo tempore* by a deity or divinized ancestor.

Priest and Prophet

Scholars have tended to distinguish between two polarities of religious specialization. Max Weber, for example, although well aware of numerous historical instances of their overlap and interpenetration, contrasts the roles of priest and prophet. He begins by making a preliminary distinction between priest and magician. A priest, he writes, is always associated with "the functioning of a regularly organized and permanent enterprise concerned with influencing the gods—in contrast with the individual and occasional efforts of magicians." Accordingly, the crucial feature of priesthood is that it represents the "specialization of a particular group of persons in the continuous operation of a cultic enterprise, permanently associated with particular norms, places and times, and related to specific social groups." In Weber's view, the prophet is distinguished from the priest by "personal call." The priest's claim to religious authority derives from his service in a sacred tradition; the authority of the prophet is founded on revelation and personal "charisma." This latter term has been variously defined by Weber (in some contexts it seems almost to represent the *Führerprinzip)*, but it may broadly be held to designate extraordinary powers. These include, according to Weber, "the capacity to achieve the ecstatic states which are viewed, in accordance with primitive experience, as the preconditions for producing certain effects in meteorology, healing, divination and telepathy." But charisma may be either ascribed or achieved. It may be an inherent faculty ("primary charisma") or it may be "produced artificially in an object or person through some extraordinary means." Charisma may thus be "merited" by fastings, austerities, or other ordeals. Even in such cases, Weber asserts, there must be some dormant capacity in the persons or objects, some "germ" of extraordinary power, already vested in them. The prophet, then, is a "purely individual bearer of charisma," rather than the representative of a sacred tradition. He produces discontinuity in that cultic enterprise which it is the priest's major role to keep "in continuous operation." Weber's prophet feels that he has a "mission" by virtue of which he "proclaims a religious doctrine or divine commandment." Weber refuses to distinguish sharply between a "renewer of religion" who preaches "an older revelation, actual or suppositious" and a "founder of religion" who claims to bring completely new "deliverances," for, he says, "the two types merge into one another." In Weber's view, the charisma of a prophet appears to contain, in addition to ecstatic and visionary components, a rational component, for he proclaims "a systematic and distinctively religious ethic based upon a consistent and stable doctrine which purports to be a revelation" [(1922)].

Weber's distinction between priest and prophet has its main relevance in an analytical frame of reference constructed to consider the relationship between religion as "a force for dynamic social change" and religion as "a reinforcement of the stability of societies" (Parsons 1963). It has been found effective by such anthropologists as Evans-Pritchard (1949; 1956) and Worsley (1957a; 1957b)

who are dealing directly with social transitions and "the prophetic break," or what Parsons calls "the primary decision point [between] a direction which makes for a source of evolutionary change in the . . . established or traditional order, and a direction which tends either to reinforce the established order or at least not to change it drastically" (1963; p. xxix in 1964 edition).

Priest and Shaman

Anthropologists who are less concerned than Weber with the genesis of religions and with internal developments in complex societies or their impact on the "primitive" world are inclined to contrast priest not with prophet but with shaman or spirit medium and to examine the relationship between these statuses as part of the normal working of the religious system in the simpler societies. In their excellently representative *Reader in Comparative Religion* (1958), the editors W. A. Lessa and E. Z. Vogt devote a whole section to this distinction.

Often, where there is a priest the shaman is absent, and vice versa, although both these roles may be found in the same religion, as among the Plains Indians. According to Lowie (1954), a Plains Indian shaman is a ritual practitioner whose status is acquired through a personal communication from a supernatural being, whereas a priest does not necessarily have a face-to-face relationship with the spirit world but must have competence in conducting ritual. Lessa and Vogt ([1958] 1965, p. 410) expand these differences: a shaman's powers come by "divine stroke," a priest's power is inherited or is derived from the body of codified and standardized ritual knowledge that he learns from older priests and later transmits to successors. They find that shamanism tends to predominate in food-gathering cultures, where the shaman most frequently performs a curing rite for the benefit of one or more patients and within the context of an extended family group. Shamanistic rites are "non-calendrical," or contingent upon occasions of mishap and illness. The priest and priestly cult organization are characteristically found in the more structurally elaborated food-producing—usually agricultural—societies, where the more common ceremonial is a public rite performed for the benefit of a whole village or community. Such rites are often calendrical, or performed at critical points in the ecological cycle.

Shaman and Medium

Raymond Firth (1964*a*, p. 638) regards shamanism as itself "that particular form of spirit mediumship in which a specialist (the *shaman*) normally himself a medium, is deemed to exercise developed techniques of control over spirits, sometimes including mastery of spirits believed to be possessing another medium." This definition, like that of Howells (1948), stresses the *control* exercised over spirits. Howells describes the shaman as "bullyragging" gods or spirits and emphasizes his intellectual qualities as a leader. This element of mastery makes the shaman a distinctive type of spirit medium, one who is believed to be "possessed by a spirit (or closely controlled by a spirit) [and who] can serve as a means of communication between other human beings and the spirit world" (Firth 1964*b*, p. 689). The spirit medium per se need not exert mastery; he is rather the vessel or vehicle of the transhuman entity.

Thus, although we sometimes find the two functions of priest and shaman combined in the same individual (Piddington 1950), mediums, shamans, and prophets clearly constitute subtypes of a single type of religious functionary. The priest communicates with transhuman entities through ritual that involves cultural objects and activities. The medium, shaman, and prophet communicate in a person-to-person manner: they are in what Buber (1936) would describe as an I-thou relationship with the deities or spirits. The priest, on the other hand, is in what may be called an I-it relationship with the transhuman. Between the priest and the deity intervenes the institution. Priests may therefore be classified as institutional functionaries in the religious domain, while medium, shaman, and prophet may be regarded as subtypes of inspirational functionaries. This distinction is reflected in characteristically different modes of operation. The priest presides over a rite; the shaman or medium conducts a seance. Symbolic forms associated with these occasions differ correlatively: the symbols of a rite are sensorily perceptible to a congregation and have permanence in that they are culturally transmissible, while those of a seance are mostly in the mind of the entranced function-

ary as elements of his visions or fantasies and are often generated by and limited to the unique occasion. The inspirational functionary may describe what he has clairvoyantly perceived (or "been shown" as he might put it), but the institutional functionary manipulates symbolic objects with prescribed gestures in full view of this congregation.

Sociocultural Correlates

Since the priest is an actor in a culturally "scripted" drama, it is but rarely that priests become innovators, or "dramatists." If they do assume this role it is mainly as legislative reformers—by altering the details of liturgical procedure—that they do so. If a priest becomes a radical innovator in religion, he is likely to become a prophet to his followers and a heretic to his former superiors. From the priestly viewpoint it is the office, role, and script that are sacred and "charismatic" and not the incumbent of priestly office. The priest is concerned with the conservation and maintenance of a deposit of beliefs and practices handed down as a sacred trust from the founders of the social or religious system. Since its symbols at the semantic level tend to condense the critical values, norms, and principles of the total cultural system into a few sensorily perceptible representations, the sanctification of these symbols is tantamount to a preservative of the entire culture. What the priest is and does keeps cultural change and individual deviation within narrow limits. But the energy and time of the inspirational functionary is less bound up with the maintenance of the total cultural system. His practice has more of an ad hoc flavor; he is more sensitive and responsive than the priest to the private and personal, to the mutable and idiosyncratic. This type of functionary thrives in loosely structured food-gathering cultures, where he deals individually with specific occasions of trouble, or during periods of social turbulence and change, when societal consensus about values is sharply declining and numerically significant classes of persons and social groups are becoming alienated from the orthodox social order. The shaman subtype is completely a part of the cultural system of the food-gatherers; the prophet may well stand outside the cultural system during such a period of decomposition and propose new doctrines, ethics, and even economic values.

The shaman is not a radical or a reformer, since the society he services is traditionally flexible and mobile; the prophet is an innovator and reformer, for he confronts a tightly structured order that is moribund and points the way to religious forms that will either provide an intensified cognitive dynamic for sociocultural change or codify the new moral, ideational, and social structures that have been inarticulately developing.

There are of course significant differences in the scale of the societies in which shaman and prophet operate. The shaman enacts his roles in small-scale, multifunctional communities whose religious life incorporates beliefs in a multitude of deities, daemons, nature spirits, or ancestral shades—societies that Durkheim might have described as possessing mechanical solidarity, low moral density, and segmental organization. The prophet tends to come into his own when the division of labor is critically replacing "mechanical" by "organic" solidarity, when class antagonisms are sharpened, or when small-scale societies are decisively invaded by the powerful personnel, ideas, techniques, and cultural apparatus (including military skills and armaments) of large-scale societies. The shaman deals in a personal and specific way with spirits and lesser deities; the prophet enters into dialogue, on behalf of his whole community, with the Supreme Being or with the major deities of a traditional pantheon, whose tutelary scope embraces large numbers of persons and groups, transcending and transecting their traditional divisions and animosities. Alternatively he communicates with the generalized ancestors or *genii loci*, conceived to be a single anonymous and homogeneous collectivity rather than a structure of known and named shades, each representing a specific segment of society. Whereas the shaman's function is associated with looseness of structure in small-scale societies, the prophet's is linked with loosening of structure in large-scale societies or with incompatibilities of scale in culture-contact situations.

Divination and Religious Specialists

In its strict etymological sense the term "divination" denotes inquiry about future events or matters, hidden or obscure, directed to a deity who, it is believed, will reply through significant tokens. It usually refers to the process of obtaining knowledge of secret or future things by mechanical means or manipulative techniques—a process which may or may not include invoking the aid of non-empirical (transhuman) persons or powers but does not include the empirical methods of science.

In the analysis of pre-literate societies divination often is concerned with the immediate problems and interests of individuals and subgroups and but seldom with the destinies of tribes and nations. It is this specificity and narrowness of reference that primarily distinguishes divination from prophecy. Nadel (1954, p. 64) has called the kind of guidance it offers "mechanical and of a case-to-case kind." The diviner "can discover and disentangle some of the hidden influences which are at work always and everywhere. . . . He cannot uncover any more embracing design. . . . Yet within the limits set to it divination has a part to play, providing some of the certainty and guidance required for provident action." Thus, although its range and scope are more circumscribed than those of prophecy, divination is believed to reveal what is hidden and in many cases to forecast events, auspicious and inauspicious.

Divination further refers to the analysis of past events, especially untoward events; this analysis often includes the detection and ascription of guilt with regard to their perpetrators, real or alleged. Where such untoward events are attributed to sorcerers and witches the diviner has great freedom of judgment in detecting and determining guilt. Diviners are frequently consulted by victims' relatives and show intuitive and deductive virtuosity in discovering quarrels and grudges in their clients' kin groups and local communities. Social anthropologists find important clues to areas and sources of social strain and to the character and strength of supportive social norms and values in the diviners' diagnoses.

There is evidence that mediums, shamans, and priests in various cultures have practiced divination. The medium and shaman often divine without mechanical means but with the assistance of a tutelary spirit. In the work of Lessa and Vogt there is a translation of a vivid first-person account by a Zulu informant of a diviner's seance. This mediumistic female diviner

> dramatically utilizes some standard procedures of her art—ventriloquism, prior knowledge of the

clients, the overhearing of the client's unguarded conversation, and shrewd common sense—to enable her spirits to provide the clients with advice. In this example, . . . a boy is suffering from a convulsive ailment. The spirits discover that an ancestral spirit is spitefully causing the boy's illness: the spirits decree that the location of the family's village must be moved; a goat must be sacrificed to the ancestor and the goat's bile poured over the boy; the boy must drink *Itongo* medicine. The treatment thus ranges from physical to social actions—from propitiation of wrathful ancestors to prescription of a medicinal potion (Lessa & Vogt [1958] 1965, p. 340).

Similar accounts of shamanistic divinatory seances have been recorded by anthropologists working among North and South American Indians, Eskimos, and Siberian tribes, in many parts of Africa, and among Afro-Americans.

Divination was a function of members of the priesthood in many of the complex religious systems of Polynesia, west Africa, and ancient Mexico; in the religions of Israel, Greece, Etruria, and Rome; in Babylonia, India, China, Japan, and among the Celts. According to Wach,

> The Etruscans made these practices so much a part of their culture that the discipline has been named after them (*disciplina Etrusca* or *auguralis*). Different phenomena and objects were used as media to ascertain the desires of the gods (regular and irregular celestial events, lightning, fire, and earthquakes, the shape or utterances of animals, flights of birds, movements of serpents, barking of dogs, forms of liver or entrails). Both in Etruria and Rome a numerous and well-organized hierarchy of functionaries existed for the practice of the sacred arts (1958, p. 111 in 1961 edition).

Indeed, diffused through the Roman world, many of these techniques passed into medieval and modern culture.

Diviner and Doctor

Callaway's account (1868–1870) of the combined divinatory and curative seance in Zululand emphasizes the close relationship believed to hold in many preliterate societies between the functions of divination and therapy. Sometimes, as in the case cited, the diviner and "doctor" are the same person, but more often the roles are specialized and performed by different individuals. Modern therapy is taking increasingly into account the psychosomatic character of many maladies and the importance of sociological factors in their etiology. In most pre-literate societies bodily symptoms are regarded as signs that the soul or life principle of the patient is under attack or has been abstracted by spiritual forces or beings. Furthermore, it is widely held that these attacks are motivated by animosities provoked by breaches of cultural, mainly religious, prescriptions and/or by breaches of social norms regarded as binding on members of kin groups or local communities. Thus, to acquire a comprehensive understanding of why and how a patient was afflicted with certain symptoms by a spirit or witch, primitives seek out a diviner who will disclose the secret antagonisms in social relations or the perhaps unconscious neglect of ritual rules (always a threat to the cultural order) that incited mystical retribution or malice. The diviner is a "diagnostician" who refers his clients to his colleague, the doctor or "therapist." The doctor in question has both shamanistic and priestly attributes. The division of labor which in more complex societies segregates and institutionalizes the functions of priest and medical man has hardly begun to make its influence felt. The diviner-doctor dichotomy does not depend, as does the priest-shaman dichotomy, upon contrasting roles in regard to the transhuman realm but upon different phases in a social process which involves *total* human phenomena—integral personalities, many psychosomatic complexes, multiple social relationships, and multiform communities.

Modes of Religious Specialization

As the scale and complexity of society increase and the division of labor develops, so too does the degree of religious specialization. This process accompanies a contraction in the domain of religion in social life. As Durkheim stated with typical creative exaggeration in his *Division of Labor in Society* ([1893] 1960, p. 169): "Originally [religion] pervades everything; everything social is religious; the two words are synonymous. Then, little by little, political, economic, scientific functions free themselves from the religious function, constitute themselves apart and take on a more and more acknowledged temporal character."

Simple Societies

In the simplest societies every adult has some religious functions and the elders have most; as their capacity to hunt or garden wanes, their priestlike role comes into ever greater prominence. Women tend to receive more recognition and scope as religious functionaries than in more developed societies. There is some tendency toward religious specialization in such societies, based on a variety of attributes, such as knowledge of herbalistic lore, skill in leechcraft, the capacity to enter a state of trance or dissociation, and sometimes physical handicap that compels a man or woman to find an alternative means of support to subsistence activities. (I have met several diviners in central Africa with maimed hands or amputated limbs.) But such specialization can hardly be defined, in the majority of cases, as more than part-time or even spare-time specialization. Michael Gelfand's description of the Shona *nganga*, variously translated in the ethnographic literature as "medicine man," "doctor," or "witch doctor," exemplifies the socio-cultural situation of similar practitioners in very many pre-literate societies (1964). The Shona *nganga* is at once a herbalist, a medium, and also a diviner who, possessed by a spirit of a dead relative, diagnoses both the cause of illness and of death. Yet, reports Gelfand,

> when he is not engaged in his medical practice he leads exactly the same life as the other men of his village. He cultivates his land, looks after his cattle, repairs his huts, makes blankets or other equipment needed by his family. And the same applies to a woman *nganga*, who busies herself with the tasks expected of every Shona woman. . . . The amount the *nganga* does in his village depends, of course, on the demands of his patients, but on the average he has a fair amount of spare time. . . . A fair guess would be [that there is a *nganga*] to every 800 to 1,000 persons. . . . The *nganga* is given no special status in his village, his chances of being appointed headman are the same as anyone else's (1964, pp. 22–23).

Complex Societies

To bring out best the effects of increase in scale and the division of labor it is necessary to examine religious systems at the opposite end of the gradient of complexity. Religion no longer pervades all social domains; it is limited to its own domain. Furthermore, it has acquired a contractual and associational character; people may choose both the form and extent of their religious participation or may opt out of any affiliation. On the other hand, within each religious group a considerable amount of specialization has taken place. Much of this has been on the organizational level. Processes of bureaucratization, involving rationality in decision making, relative impersonality in social relations, routinization of tasks, and a hierarchy of authority and function, have produced a large number of types, grades, and ranks of religious specialists in all the major religious systems.

For example, the Catholic clerical hierarchy may be considered as (1) the hierarchy of order, whose powers are exercised in worship and in the administration of the sacraments, and (2) as the hierarchy of jurisdiction, whose power is over the members of the church. Within the hierarchy of jurisdiction alone we find such manifold statuses as pope and bishop (which are held to be of divine institution); cardinal, patriarch, exarch, and primate (whose powers are derived by delegation expressed or implied from the holy see); metropolitan and archbishop (who derive their powers from their patriarch, exarch, or primate); archdeacon, vicar general, vicar forane, rural dean, pastor, and rector (who derive their powers from their diocesan bishop).

In addition to the clerical hierarchy there are in the Catholic church numerous institutes of the religious, that is, societies of men and women approved by ecclesiastical superiors, in which the members in conformity with the special laws of their association take vows, perpetual or temporary, and by this means aspire to religious perfection. This is defined as "the heroic exercise of the virtue of supernatural charity" and is pursued by voluntary maintenance of the vows of poverty, chastity, and obedience, by ascetical practices, through charitable works, such as care of the poor, sick, aged, and mentally handicapped, and by contemplative techniques, such as prayer. Within each religious institution or congregation there is a marked division of function and gradation of office.

Thus there are many differences of religious status, rank, and function in a developed religious system such as the Catholic church. Differences in charismata are also recognized in such terms as "contemplative," "ascetic," "mystic," "preacher," "teacher," "administrator." These gifts may appear in any of the major divisions of the church: among clergy or laity, among hermits, monks, or friars, among female as well as male religious. Certain of these charismata are institutionalized and constitute the devotional pattern particular to certain religious institutions: thus there are "contemplative orders," "friars preachers," and the like.

Medium-Scale Societies

Other developed religions, churches, sects, cults, and religious movements exhibit degrees of bureaucratic organization and specialization of role and function. Between the situational specialization of religious activities found in small-scale societies and the full-time and manifold specialization in large-scale societies falls a wide variety of intermediate types. A characteristic religious dichotomy is found in many of the larger, politically centralized societies of west and east Africa, Asia, Polynesia, and pre-Columbian Central and South America. National and tribal gods are worshiped in the larger towns, and minor deities, daemons, and ancestral shades are venerated in the villages. At the village level we find once more the multifunctional religious practitioner. But where there are national gods there are usually national priests, their official servants, and worship tends to take place in temples or at fixed and elaborate shrines. Parrinder writes:

> In the cults of the West African gods [for example, in Dahomey, Yoruba, and Ashanti] there are priests who are highly trained to do their work. These priests are often set aside from birth, or they may be called to the service of the god by being possessed by his spirit. They will then retire from their families and public life, and submit to the training of an older priest. The training normally lasts several years, during which time the novice has to apply himself to learn all the secrets of consulting and serving the god. The training of a priest is an arduous matter. . . . [He] has to observe chastity and strict taboos of food and actions. He frequently has to sleep on a hard floor, have insufficient food, and learn to bear hardship. He is regarded as married to the god, though later he may take a wife. Like an Indian devotee, he seeks by self-discipline to train himself to hear the voice of his god. He

learns the ritual and dances appropriate to the cult, receives instruction in the laws and taboos of the god, and gains some knowledge of magical medicines (1954, pp. 100–101).

In these west African cults of deities there is a formal division of function between priests and mediums. In general, priests control mediums and carefully regulate their experience of possession. This situation is one solution to the perennial problem posed for priesthoods by what Ronald Knox (1950) has termed "enthusiasm," that is, the notion that one can become possessed by or identified with a god or God and that one's consequent acts and words are divinely inspired, even if they transgress religious or secular laws. In Dahomey, for example (Herskovits 1938), there are communal training centers, called cult houses or "convents," for mediums and assistants to priests. Here the novices are secluded for considerable periods of time. Part of their training involves the attempt to induce the return of the initial spirit possession that marked their calling. They learn later to produce coherent messages in a state of trance. During this period they are under the surveillance of priests. The Catholic church has similarly brought under its control as members of contemplative orders mystics and visionaries who claim "experiential knowledge of God's presence."

Religious and Political Specialization

In many primitive societies an intimate connection exists between religion and politics. If by politics we denote those behavioral processes of resolution of conflict between the common good and the interests of groups by the use of or struggle for power, then religion in such societies is pragmatically connected with the maintenance of those values and norms expressing the common good and preventing the undue exercise of power. In centralized political systems that have kings and chiefs, these dignitaries themselves have priestly functions; in many parts of Africa, for example, they take charge of observances which safeguard many of the basic needs of existence, such as rainmaking, sowing, and harvest rites, ritual to promote the fertility of men, domestic and wild animals, and so on. On the other hand, even where this is the case, there are frequently other specialized religious functionaries whose duties are bound up with the office of kingship. An illustration of this occurs among the Bemba of Zambia, where the *Bakabilo*

> are in charge of ceremonies at the sacred relic shrines and take possession of the *babenye* when the chief dies. They alone can purify the chief from the defilement of sex intercourse so that he is able to enter his relic shrine and perform the necessary rites there. They are in complete charge of the accession ceremonies of the paramount and the bigger territorial chiefs, and some of their number are described as *bafingo,* or hereditary buriers of the chief. Besides this, each individual *mukabilo* has his own small ritual duty or privilege, such as lighting the sacred fire, or forging the blade of the hoe that is to dig the foundations of the new capital (Richards 1940, p. 109 in 1955 edition).

The *Bakabilo* constitute a council that exerts a check on the paramount's power, since the members are hereditary officials and cannot be removed at will. They are immune to the paramount's anger and can block the implementation of decisions that they consider to be detrimental to the interests of the Bemba people by refusing to perform the ritual functions that are necessary to the exercise of his office. A priesthood of this type thus forms a constituent part of the interior structure of the government of a primitive state.

In stateless societies in Africa and elsewhere, incumbents of certain ritual positions have similar functions in the maintenance of order and the resolution of conflict. The "leopard-skin chief" or "priest of the earth" (as this specialist has been variously called) among the Nuer of the Nilotic Sudan is a person whose ritual relationship with the earth gives him power to bless or curse, to cleanse a killer from the pollution of bloodshed, and, most important, to perform the rites of reconciliation between persons who are ready to terminate a blood feud. A similar role is performed by the "masters of the fishing spear" among the Dinka and the *tendaanas,* or earth priests, among the Tallensi and their congeners in the northern territories of Ghana. Similar religious functionaries are found in many other regions of Africa. They serve to reduce, if not to resolve, conflict within the society. As against sectional and factional interests they posit the commonweal. In these contexts, moreover, the commonweal is regarded as part of the cosmic order; breach, therefore, is mystically punished. The religious specialists are accorded the function of restoring the right relation that should obtain between society, the cosmos, and the deities or ancestral shades.

Priests

C. Von Furer-Haimendorf

In the following article Von Furer-Haimendorf, a specialist in the ethnology of Asian societies, calls on his own field data to demonstrate the important roles of priests in society. Utilizing case studies of the aboriginal Hill Reddis and the Saora tribe of India, the Ifugao of the Philippines, and West African societies, he focuses on the functions of priests as experts on ritual, preservers of myths and religious belief systems, and conduits for communication with the supernatural.

Distinguishing between priests, shamans, magicians, and prophets, Professor Von Furer-Haimendorf also demonstrates that the functions of these religious specialists often overlap. Unlike other specialists, the position of priest is more precarious and constantly threatened with loss of power from a variety of sources, both human and superhuman. As a result, taboos evolved into important protective mechanisms for priests, functioning to guard them against innumerable forms of pollution that could drain away the priestly powers necessary to properly serve society. The respect given priests and the awe surrounding their station can be, in part, correlated with their quality of charisma, the subject of Douglas Barnes's article, which follows this one.

Reprinted from Richard Cavendish, ed., *Man, Myth and Magic* (London, 1970), Vol. 16, pp. 2248–55, by permission of the author and BPCC/Phoebus Publishing.

The priests, medicine men, or shamans of primitive societies are "specialists in the supernatural" who provide a channel of communication between human beings and the divine: more sophisticated societies also have specialist priesthoods.

AT MOST LEVELS OF CIVILIZATION PRIESTS ACT as the socially recognized mediators between men and supernatural beings. They are the experts in the performances of rituals, and in pre-literate societies it is they who preserve, by oral tradition, the myths and the body of religious concepts and ideas which constitute a people's intellectual heritage. The functions, selection, training, and social position of priests differ widely even within simpler societies, and the designation "priest" has been applied to a large variety of religious practitioners, who may have little in common except for their alleged ability to establish contact with gods and spirits, or to manipulate supernatural forces.

In some societies there is a distinction between priests, who are the official religious leaders and representatives of the community, and magicians, shamans, and prophets, whose power derives from individual supernatural experiences or what is presumed to be direct inspiration by deities or spirits. In practice, the functions of these two types of religious practitioners often overlap, and the distinction is not universal.

At the lowest level of economic development, there is little scope for the emergence of ritual experts or any other form of occupational specialization. Most societies of nomadic food gatherers and hunters lack religious specialists comparable to the priests of more advanced peoples. All adults are considered capable of invoking gods or spirits and of soliciting their favour by way of prayers and offerings. Cult acts involving all the members of a group may be conducted by old men experienced in the performance of ritual, but no training or hereditary qualification is required for such activity, nor do those engaging in the organization of religious rites enjoy any special privileges.

Priest and Magician

Where larger and more stable social groups have developed, increased economic efficiency enables man to divert some energies to the elaboration of religious practices. In most societies of some complexity the task of establishing contact with transcendental powers tends to be vested in individuals who act as the representatives of their clan or village. Such individuals need not possess outstanding intellectual gifts, but the ability and the right to perform priestly functions may be hereditary in certain families, lineages or clans. Another claim to priesthood is derived from psychological states interpreted as possession or selection by a divinity or spirit, who is supposed to invest the priest with powers and knowledge not accessible to other men. Priests who base their position on hereditary rights and priests called to their vocation by the gods may coexist in the same society.

The Hill Reddis, an aboriginal tribe of southern India, for instance, depend on two classes of intermediaries in their relations with the supernatural world: the hereditary priest of the local group or village and the magician who derives his powers from an intimate connection with a specific god or spirit. The hereditary priest is normally a descendant of the village-founder, and membership of the lineage of the man who first settled in the locality is sufficient qualification for his office. He is regarded as the head of the village, and as the appropriate mediator between man and the deities and spirits who dwell in the area.

As representative of the village he performs those rites and ceremonies that are believed to secure the prosperity of the community as a whole. And since this prosperity is intimately linked with the thriving of the crops, it is above all the agricultural rites that call for the intercession of the priest. He must inaugurate the sowing of the grain, propitiate the earth deity with sacrifices, and perform the rites at the great seasonal feasts. No special intuition or skill is required for these tasks.

Less simple are those that fall to the magician. While the hereditary spiritual head of the community follows the broad and well-trodden path of long-established ritual, the magician must battle through the wilderness of the supernatural world to discover the cause of disease and threatening disaster, and must devise the means of placating the wrath of malignant spirits. The priest acts, so to speak, while all is well; his offerings are tendered to gods while their mood is benevolent, and his prayers are designed to solicit their favour for the welfare of the community, and their protection against dangers not yet arisen. It is only when misfortune is rife that the magician is called in to restore the disturbed relations with supernatural powers, to draw the sick from the jaws of death or to counteract the black magic of an enemy. This power, which he could not wield unless he himself possessed a thorough knowledge of magical practices, justifies his being called a "magician."

Every Reddi village must have a priest, but there may or may not be a magician in the community. Being a magician is an art, acquired by learning or bestowed by supernatural beings on an eager apprentice. It is an art and a power within reach only of those men and women who are predisposed towards it by particular mental qualities. Naturally these may occur in a priest as well as in any other man, and his frequent performance of ritual acts is bound to favour their development. Nothing debars a priest from learning the practices of a magician, and the combination of both functions is fairly common.

No Reddi is born a magician and aptitude for the work does not manifest itself in childhood. A magician frequently owes his knowledge to the instruction of his father or an older kinsman, but not every son of a famous magician has the talent or the desire to assimilate his parent's teaching. The cooperation of a deity is indispensable to the process of becoming a magician, and it is not only men who seek the gods; on occasion the gods themselves take the initiative. Reddi magicians agree that they receive their inspiration and knowledge from the gods, either while in a state of trance or through the medium of dreams. When a magician is called on to treat a sick person, it is usually his guardian deity who tells him what medicines to apply and what animals to sacrifice.

Married to a Spirit

While the roles of priest and magician are clearly distinguished in some of the simpler societies, they overlap in others and a distinction between the functions of priests and magicians is hardly perceptible. Both deal with the control of supernatural forces and priests are generally expected to influence the gods through prayer and ritual performances, while magicians exert their power through spells and the manipulation of certain material objects possessed of mysterious efficacy. But as the principal duty of priests is to mediate between mankind and the higher powers, the faculty of communicating with gods and spirits is a primary qualification for the priesthood in many societies. This ability may be proved in different ways. When a person falls into a state of trance or ecstasy, people think that he or she is under the influence of a supernatural power, and therefore suitable for the role of mediator between men and gods. Or the supposed connection between priests and the spirit world may be that they have one or more tutelary deities of their own who assist them when required.

A striking example of this type of link between priests and supernatural beings occurs among the Saora tribe of Orissa in India. Among these primitive hill farmers, placating the vast otherworld of invisible and often hostile beings occupies the energy of a small band of dedicated men and women. Armed with a few fragile implements, and devoting themselves to supplication of spirits and the sacrifice of animals, these people strive bravely to protect mankind.

There are two types of religious practitioner among the Saoras, the village priest and the shaman or magician. The priest's special function is to maintain the cult of the local shrines and to guard the village lands from the interference of hostile spirits and sorcerers. When a new priest is to be appointed a shaman is called and, falling into a trance, he asks the gods and ancestors whether the proposed candidate is acceptable to them. If they agree that he is, the shaman summons the ghost of the last priest to hold office in the village. If he too approves, the shaman—possessed by, and representing, the dead man—puts his hands on the head of the new priest and tells him to do his work

well. This selection and installation of a Saora village priest demonstrates the coexistence and friendly cooperation of two quite different types of ritual expert.

For practical purposes, however, the shaman, who may be male or female, is the most important religious figure in a Saora village. He has the power not only to diagnose the source of trouble or disease, but to cure it. He is doctor as well as priest, psychologist as well as magician, the repository of tradition, the source of sacred knowledge. His primary duty is that of divination; in case of sickness he seeks the cause in trance or dream. Every male shaman has a spirit-wife in the underworld and every female shaman has a spirit-husband, whom she visits in her dreams. These tutelary spouses are the strength and inspiration of Saora shamans. The marriages are absolutely real in their own minds, and they believe themselves to be chosen by the direct intervention of the guardian spirit, through whom they subsequently have immediate access to the world of spirits and deities. A female shaman may have to be wooed by a spirit for a long time before she consents to accept him as husband. Usually such calls from the spirit world come as hallucinations or dream experiences, and a girl may appear to be deranged and ill until the 'marriage' to her suitor from the underworld has been performed.

After the marriage, the shaman's spirit-husband visits her regularly and lies with her till dawn. He may even take her away into the jungle for days at a time. In due course a spirit-child is born, and the ghostly father brings it every night to be nursed by the human wife. This imaginary marriage is no bar to marrying a human husband, but the dream-spouse seems as real to a Saora shaman as her husband of flesh and blood, and it is believed that she will become a spirit herself after death.

The Master of Ecstasy

The term "shaman," now widely current in anthropological literature, was first applied to the religious practitioners of central and northern Asia, where the magico-religious life of most of the indigenous population traditionally centres on the shaman. He is the dominating figure, though in many tribes there are also priests concerned with the performance of animal sacrifices, and every head of a family is also the head of the domestic cult. The ecstatic state is considered to be the supreme religious experience, and the shaman is the great master of ecstasy. Unlike persons possessed by spirits and temporarily in their power, the shaman controls spirits. He is able to communicate with the dead, or with demons and Nature spirits, without becoming their instrument.

Shamans are separated from the rest of society by the intensity of their religious experience, and in this sense they resemble the mystics of historic religions. The mental disposition which qualifies a person for the functions of a shaman points to an important feature of early priesthood. Among many peoples, priests must display a certain excitability of temperament, which in modern Western society might be considered as bordering on a psychopathic condition. The ability to fall into trance may be an essential prerequisite for the performance of certain rites, in which case only those capable of such psychological states are suitable as priests.

The importance attached to ectasy as a visible means of divine inspiration is shown in the numerous instances of priests obtaining their initiation by inducing a state of delirium or trance through the use of narcotics or fasting. The convulsive movements and seemingly irrational utterances of the inspired person suggest that his own controlling will is in abeyance, and that an external force or being has taken possession of his body. In many cases a god or spirit is supposed to speak through his mouth and determine his actions.

Not all priests need to undergo a formal course of training, or be initiated into the mystery of relations with supernatural powers by a specific ritual. Those who succeed to the priesthood through inheritance, for example, are usually believed to have powers acquired by birth into a family or clan. On the other hand, there are many pre-literate societies which require potential religious practitioners to be subjected to a rigorous training in self-control and in the sacred lore of the tribe. Among the Eskimo, for instance, the priests are trained in their profession from childhood.

Where priests receive formal instruction, their education often consists of two different phases. During the first period the novice is under the care of an experienced practitioner, who initiates him

into the body of religious beliefs and teaches him how to perform various rites. A later phase is devoted mainly to self-training, in the course of which the novice seeks mystic experiences, and through them a direct relationship with supernatural powers. During this preparation for the priesthood he may have to live in seclusion or submit himself to austerities such as prolonged fasting or exposure to the elements.

In some primitive societies the period of instruction and training culminates in an elaborate initiation ceremony which confirms upon the candidate the full status of an ordained priest.

In many societies, however, priests are trained in a much more casual way. Among the Ifugao tribe of the Philippines, for instance, there is no institutionalized method of initiating priests into the labyrinth of an immensely rich and complicated mythology. There is no organized priesthood recruited from a special social class. Any Ifugao possessing intellectual ability and a good memory may attach himself to an experienced priest of his kin-group or locality as an apprentice; but in many cases sons follow in the footsteps of fathers enjoying a reputation as knowledgeable and successful priests. Ifugao priests also act as chroniclers and genealogists, for the frequently repeated incantations of ancestors give them an unrivalled knowledge of genealogies. The ministrations of priests form an essential part of all the innumerable rituals by which Ifugaos mark social as well as religious occasions.

Some of these rituals may extend over a whole day or even over several days, and the demands they make on the memory can be prodigious. The priests are of supreme importance to the Ifugao, for only they are thought to be capable of manipulating the gods and coaxing them to aid human endeavour. The relation between man and deities is looked upon as one of bargaining and of give and take, and the priests must exert all their skill to get favourable terms for their clients. Ifugao gods are regarded as morally neutral and unconcerned with the ethical conduct of men, and the priests do not take any stand on moral questions. They do not feel any need to behave in an exemplary way in their private lives, nor do they attempt to influence the moral conduct of their clients and fellow villagers.

Unlike Christian priests or other holy men who

regard themselves as representatives of a moral order that derives its sanction from a supreme deity,
most priests in primitive societies act simply as the
agents of their fellow men, and are intent only on
obtaining material benefits for them. They have no
interest in giving them any guidance in moral matters. Priests of this kind do not preach to men, but
address themselves solely to the deities they seek
to influence.

In addition, whatever the circumstances in
which a priest acts as an intermediary between
men and gods, the quality which makes his mediation effective often resides in his office rather than
in himself as an individual. Consequently it may
not greatly matter what sort of person he is, socially, psychologically, or morally.

A Sense of Awe

Because of his usefulness and power a priest may
enjoy considerable prestige and authority, but his
position is so precarious and easily damaged that
he tends to be surrounded with taboos to protect
him against harmful contacts with forces that
might render him ineffective. The social position of
priests varies greatly from one society to another.
The ability to experience states of trance and spirit-
possession is usually not combined with great economic efficiency or political acumen, and priests
who on ritual occasions will act as the mouthpiece
of gods may be withdrawn and comparatively ineffective personalities in ordinary life. On the other
hand, someone who holds the position of clan
priest by hereditary right, and functions as the sole
mediator between a powerful clan and its protective deities, may derive considerable prestige and
material advantages from his office.

In some societies, as among certain West African tribes for instance, priests tend to increase the
respect in which they are held by enveloping their
proceedings in mystery. They often create a sense
of awe and fear among the laity, in order to enhance their power. The special and sometimes fantastic attire donned by some priests is intended
partly to distinguish them from the rest of the
population, and partly to impress deities and
spirits or avert malignant forces. Masks worn by
priests have similar purposes, and occasionally signify a mystical connection between the priest and
an ancestor spirit or deity whom he embodies.

In primitive societies priesthood is not exclusively a male occupation, and there are many instances of women functioning as priestesses and
magicians. It is rare for them to be debarred from
marriage, just as male priests are usually expected
to marry and lead a life not basically different from
that of other members of their society. Though
their priestly status may provide them with certain
privileges and material benefits, occupational specialization among primitive populations normally
does not go far enough to free religious practitioners from the need to till the soil or herd cattle.
At that level of material development priesthood is
seldom an exclusive profession, and a priest does
not diminish his spiritual status or prestige by engaging in normal secular occupations.

Restrictions on the sexual life of priests and
priestesses are usually found in the more advanced
civilizations. Primitive peoples rarely place any
value on celibacy and chastity, and priests are expected to have normal family lives. They may be
obliged to abstain from sexual activities during
periods of training or at the time of major rituals,
in the same way as fasting is regarded as a preparation for spiritual experiences; but in general
primitive priests are not expected to lead a life basically different from that of laymen.

Charisma and Religious Leadership: An Historical Analysis

Douglas F. Barnes

"Charisma" is a Greek word that means divine gift. We speak of a charismatic person as one who is able to attract and lead a popular group movement. Some names that immediately spring to mind in religious history are Muhammad, Buddha, Calvin, Joseph Smith, Jesus, and Gandhi. In this article Douglas Barnes has selected fifteen religious leaders from history after determining that each possessed the special qualities of a charismatic leader. After understandably admitting the difficulty inherent in categorizing the charismatic personality, especially in religion, where leaders have run the gamut from "frenzy-creating preachers to quiet, meditating sages," Barnes goes on to hypothesize that charismatic leaders live in periods of radical social change, are typically isolated from the mainstream of society, regard religious tradition as relative, and are innovative in their teachings.

Barnes's article is attractive to anthropologists because of his insistence on the cross-cultural approach in the selection of his fifteen leaders. Each of the leaders on his list was a prophet, each deeply involved in a reactive movement that proposed a drastic change in an existing social and religious system. Later in this book, in Chapter 9, we will examine religious-based social movements, such as millenarism, revivalism, and nativism. It would be profitable at this point to look ahead there to the articles by Anthony F. C. Wallace and Peter Worsley, to see how Barnes's hypothesis fits the leaders of such movements as the Ghost Dance among the North American Indians, the Paliau Movement in the Admiralty Islands, and the "cargo cults" of New Guinea and adjacent islands.

Reprinted from the *Journal for the Scientific Study of Religion*, Vol. 17 (1978), pp. 1–18, by permission of the author and the Society for the Scientific Study of Religion, Inc.

MAX WEBER INCORPORATED BOTH PSYCHOLOGICAL and sociological elements in his definition of charisma. He defined charisma (1922a: 48, 1968 reprint) as a "certain quality of an individual's personality by virtue of which he is set apart from ordinary men and treated as endowed with supernatural, superhuman, or at least specifically exceptional powers or qualities." This individualistic or psychological orientation towards charisma aligns itself with the more popular conception which holds that charisma originates from an inner, dynamic force of the leader's personality. Sociologically, Weber conceived of charisma as a form of authority which is dependent upon the recognition of a group of people. In this regard, he (1922a: 49, 1968 reprint) stated, "It is the recognition on the part of those subject to authority which is decisive for the validity of charisma. This is freely given and guaranteed by what is held to be a "sign" or proof, originally always a miracle, and consists in devotion to the coresponding revelation, hero worship, or absolute trust in the leader." Thus, leaders depend upon the perceptions of people for their charismatic authority, but nonetheless they also must be exceptional to gain such recognition (Willner and Willner 1975: 79).

Charisma is a pivotal concept for Weber's three pure types of authority because it is employed to explain radical social change. Charisma is personalistic, non-rational, and dynamic; whereas traditional and legal-rational authority are more impersonal and stable. Although Weber explained in great detail the routinization of charisma into these other more stable forms of authority, except for a few references to social change he neglected the problem of the origin of charismatic leadership. This paper proposes a theory of charismatic leadership and institutionalized religion which more thoroughly explores the socio-historical conditions under which charisma will originate. Secondly, the methodology utilized for investigating charismatic leaders has usually been case studies. In this investigation biographical data of fifteen religious founders who are recognized by historians as charismatic leaders have been compiled in order to test the proposed theory. Whenever possible, information was also gathered for the leaders' immediate successors.

A Theory of Religious, Charismatic Leadership

The distinction between charisma and charismatic leadership is very important. There can be many different types of charismatic leaders who display a wide range of possible behavior, but charisma is limited to a particular authority relationship between the leaders and their followings. Willner and Willner (1965: 79) have developed a definition of charisma which captures this distinction. They state that charisma can be redefined "without departing from Weber's intrinsic intention—as a leader's capacity to elicit from a following deference, devotion and awe toward himself as the source of authority. A leader who can have this effect upon a group is charismatic for that group." In agreement with Willner and Willner, charisma is defined here as that authority relationship which arises when a leader through the dynamics of a set of teachings, a unique personality, or both elicits responses of awe, deference, and devotion from a group of people.

Categorizing the unique personalities requisite for charisma is very difficult because leaders have ranged from frenzy-creating preachers to quiet, meditating sages. Various personal styles which demonstrate a capacity for charismatic leadership may include strategies such as rhetoric, use of simile and metaphor, allusions to myth and history, appropriate gestures, use of ritual, handling crises appropriately, and dealing with anxieties (Willner and Willner 1965: 83). But regardless of the variety of personal styles, the teachings of a religious, charismatic leader must deal with the ultimate concerns of a group of people. Clifford Geertz (1966) states that meaning, morality, and suffering are three points where chaos threatens to break upon man, and any religion which hopes to persist must cope with these problems. Likewise,

any religious, charismatic leaders who wish to maintain their authority over a following must also espouse an ideology to cope with these three basic points where chaos threatens to impinge on the consciousness of man.

The following theory of religious, charismatic leadership contains four basic propositions which suggest that certain variables or conditions must coincide within and around the same individual in order for charisma to exist. These characteristics in no way define charisma, but rather they stipulate certain relationships between charisma as a form of authority and other social and psychological variables. The four basic propositions are that (1) charismatic leaders will be de-alienated because they perceive sacred symbols as subject to change or verification by their own personal experience with the divine; (2) they will live during a period of social change or be members of a minority group; (3) they will have an innovative set of teachings if their religion is to be institutionalized; and, finally, (4) they can exist either within or outside of the context of traditional religion. Each of these propositions will be examined in order.

The Perception of Objective Symbols

The perception of objective symbols is one key concept for differentiating institutionalized religion and charismatic leadership. Two different ways to perceive objective symbols are alienation and de-alienation. Alienation is a term which has been used in many different ways in the sociological literature. In this paper, Peter Berger's assertion (1967: 81–101) that religion is generally alienated will be accepted. Charismatic leadership, on the other hand, tends to be de-alienated. De-alienation is the conscious realization that the social world is humanly constructed and therefore unstable (Berger 1967: 96–101). Charismatic leaders usually have an intimate connection with a transcendent or immanent divine source. This intense connection with a force or being beyond everyday or normal reality enables the leader to perceive religious symbols in a de-alienated fashion. Secondly, because charismatic leaders manipulate religious symbols, they recognize that they are subject to change. Charismatic leaders who preach a "return to the true faith" do so because they have received private confirmation that the symbols of the "true faith" are an adequate manifestation or representation of the divine. The experience of or communication with a divine source will always take precedence over or complement previously revealed religious tradition. One common mechanism for religious change involves the claim that a leader has received from a divine source an updated version of previously established, religious doctrine. However, a leader whose personal experience does not take precedence over religious tradition would be classified as alienated.

There are two different ways in which charismatic leaders may be de-alienated based on their differing relationships to the divine. The first is a mystical de-alienation in which the leaders realize that their own teachings are of the same fleeting nature as all other systems of thought. They realize that no meaning systems are absolute. Weber's (1922: 55, 1964 reprint) ideal type of the exemplary prophet is one kind of charismatic leader who is de-alienated. This type of charismatic leader is completely aware of the tension between consciousness and its symbolic projections. The second type of de-alienation is prophetic. The leaders may reject or accept the traditional sacred symbols and institutionalized religion of their times, yet they present their own teachings or interpretation of tradition as representing the word of God or some other divine source. In this case the divinely inspired word of the leader is to be followed without question. Weber's (1922a: 55, 1964 reprint) conception of ethical prophecy would be associated with this type of de-alienation. Prophetic de-alienation assumes a transcendent deity or force which is revealing its will through the leader. But, the followers of the leader in this case are alienated because they are asked to obey the will of the god and the leader. Thus, the first hypothesis is that charismatic leaders are either prophetically or mystically de-alienated because of their intense connection with an immanent or transcendent divine source.

A Period of Social Change

A period of radical social change which causes distress and dissatisfaction among a segment of the population or a group of people cut off from the mainstream of society is generally acknowledged as the typical environment within which a charismatic leader will arise (Friedland 1964; Tucker 1968; Willner and Willner 1965; Jones and Ans-

ervitz 1975). Institutionalized religion has a well-developed tradition or ideology and has been dealing with the problem of meaning in life for generations, but at times it can be resistant to change. The individual stream of consciousness is more flexible, but the answers which ordinary individuals formulate for their ultimate concerns in life are usually not very creative. Charismatic leaders on the other hand face the threat of chaos which is disruptive to a particular social segment of the community, and resolve this confrontation by formulating their own answers to the problem of meaning in life. Because their problems turn out to be widespread among the populace, the charismatic leaders' individual solutions to their ultimate concerns in life may meet the standards of many others in the same society. People in the society begin to notice that the charismatic leader provides answers to the same problems which had been bothering them.

A breakdown in traditional authority is precisely the appropriate socio-historical circumstance which is necessary for charismatic leaders to gain acceptance for their authority. Without proper social conditions the society would regard the potential leader as an eccentric getting excited over nothing. In this regard, Friedland (1964: 21) indicates that "while charismatics are continually being generated, their 'charisma' can frequently be unrecognized or indeed be considered peculiar, deviant, or perhaps insane." Several studies of charisma (Willner and Willner 1965; Apter 1968; Friedland 1964) have been carried out within the context of the breakdown of authority in ex-colonial, new states in Africa. Revivalist charismatic leaders are also known to spring up in the inner cities or rural areas where there is no institutionalized religion which intimately understands the needs of the local residents. In each of these cases charismatic leaders will attract followings based on their ideological and emotional support for a group of people. Thus, the second hypothesis is that the charismatic leader will arise in a period of social change or within a group of people who are cut off from the mainstream of society.

Institutionalization and the Leader's Teachings

A religion based on charismatic authority is usually inherently unstable. Charismatic leaders as individuals have two relevant means through which they can appeal to a group of followers: their unique personal style and the content of their teachings (Jones and Anservitz 1975: 1097). With the death of charismatic leaders, the dynamics of their personality are no longer a major factor. The extraordinary quality resulting from the leaders' personal confrontation with chaos dies with them, and all that remains is their legacy and a group of followers. In a word, with the leader absent, the quality of their teachings are left exposed without refuge to their creator's personality or defense, and they must pass the test of time. Describing this critical period in a neophyte religion's existence, O'Dea (1966: 37) uses the term "crisis of continuity" which is essentially similar to what Weber (1922a: 55, 1968 reprint) calls the problem of succession. However, Weber would not limit the problems of routinization only to the time of the leader's death.

The two crucial variables for the institutionalization of a religion are the quality of the leaders' teachings and the organization of their followers. Weber (1922a: 55–61, 1968 reprint) presents an elaborate typology for routinizing charismatic authority which includes six different ways through which the leaders' followers can designate a successor. The motives for routinizing charisma are based on the material and ideal interests of the followers and the members of the administrative staff for keeping the community alive. However, not enough attention has been given to the institutionalization of a religion during the lifetime of a leader. One proposition which was developed during the historical research is that religions may have three different agents of institutionalization which are not mutually exclusive—the founder himself, a follower of the founder or his successor, and finally a religious council.

The quality of the leader's teachings may also be an important variable for institutionalizing a religion, although this is not clearly developed in Weber's work on routinization. Tucker (1968: 743) identifies charismatic leadership as "specifically salvationist or messianic in nature." Without the leader's unique personal style, the desire for a group to continue to adhere to the salvational purpose contained in the leader's message may be partially dependent on the innovativeness of those teachings. The teachings may be couched in terms of traditonal mythology as is suggested by Willner and Willner (1965: 83) who investigated charisma in the context of ex-colonial, new states in Africa, or they may be a revolutionary ideology as is indicated by Tucker (1968: 75) in his study of Lenin and the Russian Revolution. However, for a religion to be institutionalized the leader's teachings must be innovative enough so that the religious community can identify unique salvational goals towards which to strive. Innovative teachings will enable the followers to clearly differentiate their religion from any other religious group. Thus, the third hypothesis is that the teachings of charismatic leaders must be innovative if their religion is to institutionalize.

The Relationship Between Charismatic Leaders and Traditional Religion

Earlier theoretical treatments of charisma have generally assumed an anti-institutional character. The prophet versus the priest dichotomy helped to further the bifurcation between the charismatic leader and the institutional order. Weber, for instance, has stated that "In order to do justice to their mission, the holders of charisma, the master as well as his disciples and followers, must stand outside of ties to this world, outside routine occupations, as well as outside the routine occupations of family life." Weber qualifies this statement by indicating that this is charisma in its pure form. Talcott Parsons and Peter Berger for different reasons argue that Weber's conception of the prophet as radically breaking with societal institutions is misleading. Parsons (1964; lxiv) criticizes Weber's ideal type methodology for its tendency to atomize traits instead of interrelating them. As a result, this atomization leads to a typological rigidity which characterizes the prophet as breaking with tradition. Berger (1963: 950) indicates that some of the historical data upon which Weber relied were found to be in error, and he concludes that the prophets of Israel were more connected to the institutional order of society than had previously been assumed by religious, historical scholarship. Accordingly, the prophet may emerge from the institutions or offices of society rather than be located primarily as a force outside the accepted institutional order.

The charismatic leader does not necessarily represent a force which is completely outside of institutionalized religion. In agreement with Parsons and Berger, the present theory of charismatic leadership allows the possibility that an individual within the social organization of a religion may possess charismatic authority. Berger (1963: 950) indicates that a charismatic leader who occupies an institutional office may attempt to change the religion by a "radicalization from within rather than of challenge from without." Secondly, charismatic leaders may also be within a religious tradition such as Christianity, and yet form their own religious organization as was common during the Protestant reformation. Finally, leaders may also break with both the institutional structure and the religious tradition and found their own religion. The advantage of viewing charisma as one form of legitimizing social values is that it may be a very useful concept for investigating social change both within or outside of the framework of institutionalized religion. Thus, the final hypothesis is that charismatic leaders can occupy an office within a religious organization, they may be inside of the religious tradition exclusively, or they can be the founder of a completely new religious tradition and institution.

Methods

Sample

The theory of charismatic leadership presented in this paper seeks to be universal, and therefore, a cross-cultural and cross-time sample must be employed to test the theory. An historical methodology has been used to analyze both the charismatic leaders and their immediate successors or seconds (whenever possible) according to available biographical information.

Fifteen religious founders were chosen from history on the basic assumption that they all were endowed with charisma. None of the theoretical points delineated above were utilized in the selection of the leaders. Unfortunately no list of charismatic religious founders exists from which the leaders could be randomly chosen. Therefore, the religious founders were chosen according to the following criteria. (1) They had to be recognized by historians as charismatic figures. (2) They must be chosen from different cultural areas of the world. (3) If possible, they should be from different historical periods. (4) Finally, there should be adequate biographical data available so that a valid judgment is possible for all variables in the investigation. Table 1 presents a list of religious, charismatic leaders and their seconds who were chosen for evaluation in this study.

The biographies of the leaders and the religious history of the movement with which they were associated were examined, and from this information the leaders were coded on specific variables suggested by the theory. The sample was admittedly limited to those leaders who are prominent figures in history; otherwise, not enough detailed biographical information would exist for making a knowledgeable decision in coding the variables.

To test the proposed theory, a comparison group without charisma is also necessary in order to ensure that the charismatic leaders actually differ systematically from non-charismatic figures. In this study the second leaders of the religious movement were chosen for this purpose because they lived during similar time periods and within the same cultures as the primary leaders. Although the distinct possibility exists that second leaders could have charismatic qualities, they most likely will not have the same degree of charisma as the original founder. Also, the second leaders when compared to the founders should be identical on all variables with the exception of those measured in the study. One problem encountered, however, is that although a wealth of historical information exists for the primary leader, a conspicuous lack of information was found for the second leaders who followed him. For this reason only eight out of fifteen charismatic leaders can be compared to the second leader. A second problem for testing the proposed theory involves the question of why the religions of some charismatic leaders become institutionalized and others do not. The ideal research design for testing this aspect of the theory would involve having one group of charismatic leaders whose religions are institutionalized, and another group of leaders whose religions fail the crisis of continuity. However, most religious sects which fail to institutionalize fall into obscurity and adequate historical information is unavailable.

Data

Several different methodologies were considered at the inception of this study. First, a panel

TABLE 1   THE SAMPLE: RELIGIOUS FOUNDERS, THEIR SECONDS, AND MAIN REFERENCES

Religion	Religious Founders	Second Leaders	Main References
Jainism	Mahavira		Taylor, 1970; Goplan, 1973
Hasidism	Bal Shem Tov	R. Dov Ber	Aron, 1969; Buber, 1960; Dresner, 1968; Rabinowicz, 1960
Sikhism	Guru Nanak	Guru Angad	Macauliffe, 1963; Court, 1959; Grewal, 1969; Gupta, 1969
Bahai Faith	Baha'O'Llah	A. Baha	Esselmont, 1970; Miller, 1931 Nabil-i-A'zam, 1932; Remey, 1912
Islam	Muhammad	A. Bakr	Irving, 1850; Abulteda, 1940; Ali, 1954; Jeffrey, 1958
Buddhism	Buddha	Kacyapa	Burtt, 1955; Wickremesinghe, 1972; Rockhill, 1972; Thapar, 1966
Nichiren Buddhism	Nichiren	Niko	Anesaki, 1916; Murata, 1969
Calvinism	Calvin	Theodore Beza	Harkness, 1931; Wendel, 1950; Schaff, 1892; McNeill, 1954; Baird, 1899; MacKinnon, 1936
Lutheranism	Luther		Erikson, 1958; Jorgensen, 1953; Bergendoff, 1967; Pascal, 1971
Mormons	Joseph Smith	Brigham Young	Hirshson, 1969; Gates and Widtsoe, 1930; Smucker, 1856; Beardsley, 1931; Smith, 1969
Quakers	George Fox		Barbour, 1964; Braithwaite, 1961; Russell, 1942; Fox, 1919
Confucianism	Confucius		Smith, 1973; Lin, 1938; Creel, 1949; Fung, 1948
Christianity	Jesus	Peter	Kidd, 1922; MacKinnon, 1931; Foakes-Jackson, 1927; Fofick, 1949; Hitchcock, 1907; Cullman, 1953
Gandhi's Religion	Gandhi		Rudolph, 1967; Erikson, 1969; Gandhi
SCLC	Martin Luther King		Lewis, 1970; Miller, 1968; Lincoln, 1970

of experts intimately familiar with one or more of the charismatic leaders could objectively code the charismatic leaders. Subsequent interviews and only random success in attempting to contact scholars through the mail proved this method inadequate. The second method involved contacting religious historians who could rate at least part of the sample on the variables important for the study. Although the few historians contacted were very interested in the project, the information which they could provide proved to be very sporadic. It was finally decided that quotes and appropriate summaries for each leader and successor on all the variables would provide the most accurate and useful information. Blind ratings of the accumulated summaries and quotes were con-

sidered, but the leaders for this project are so well known that they could not truly be rated blindly. The inherent difficulties in obtaining a representative sample and accurate information for any group of charismatic leaders were countered by selecting appropriate leaders and developing a strict procedure for coding the variables.

The procedure for coding the variables included gathering information from several sources in order to increase the reliability and accuracy of the information concerning the leaders. The information was then categorized according to the variables suggested by the theory of charismatic leadership. The variables coded for this project were the leaders' perception of objective symbols, the social environment of the leaders' ministry, their position within the traditional religious structure, the quality of their teachings, and finally how they succeeded the crisis of continuity.

The perception of objective symbols was divided into three mutually exclusive categories: alienation, mystical de-alienation, and prophetic de-alienation. The leaders who strictly believed that the sacred symbols of their religion are absolute were alienated. In this case the sacred symbols were divine and outside of the individual. Secondly, leaders who saw beyond the sacred beliefs of their time, including their own teachings, were mystically de-alienated. Such persons rejected any form of dogmatism, but they may have believed in a force power, or order which is beyond religious ideology. Finally, the prophetically de-alienated leader was an individual who may have accepted or rejected the prevailing religious ideology, but the beliefs which they espoused were verified or passed through the leaders by their contact with some divine being, spirit, or inspiration. Thus, the perception of objective symbols was divided into three categories which measured the leader's relative awareness of the tension between consciousness and its symbolic projections.

The social environment within which the leader lives is a very important variable for the proposed theory. The theory predicts that the leader will live during a period of radical social change or be cut off from the mainstream of society. If during the ministry of the leader a period of social upheaval or war was described by the historians and biographers, then the leader was coded as having lived during a period of radical social change. Secondly, being cut off from the mainstream of society was operationalized by ascertaining whether or not the leader was a member of a subordinate minority group. In both of the above cases groups of individuals may exist for whom traditional values of a religion do not adequately explain their spiritual needs. Finally, a period of stability was coded as a period of time in which there was no social upheaval or armed conflict. Coding the seconds presented somewhat of a problem because they usually lived during the lifetime of the leaders. Therefore, both the primary and the second leaders were coded for that period of time in which they were actually the head of a group of followers.

The quality of the leaders' teachings was oper-

ationalized by determining the extent of innovation within their teachings. If the biographers and historians regard the leaders' teachings as creative or innovative, then they were coded as having a high quality of teachings. The specific question to be answered was did the leaders' teachings deviate markedly from those of the religion of their times? If they did not then the leader was classified as espousing a rather uninnovative religious doctrine. The seconds were coded as innovative only if their teachings deviated markedly from those of the charismatic leader. Thus, if the seconds merely repeated or organized the teachings of the religious founder, then they were classified as uninnovative.

The position of the charismatic leader within the traditional religious structure was coded in three possible ways. The leaders may have occupied a religious office within a religious tradition; they may have remained within the tradition, but established a new religious institutional structure, and finally, the leaders may have rejected both the religious tradition and the institutional structure and formed their own new religion. In most cases, the biographers and historians were explicit concerning whether the founder broke with religious tradition and institutional structure, accepted the tradition and rejected the institution, or remained within both the structure and the tradition. In addition, the leaders' teachings provided some indication of whether they felt that they were founding a new religion. However, in coding this variable, the actual historical course of events was given precedence over the leader's own perception of the situation. The seconds were not coded on this variable because they all by definition fell into just one of the categories.

In the early stages of this study it was realized that the procedures for institutionalizing a religion vary considerably from leader to leader. Because this study is limited to religious founders and their seconds, all of them established a religious tradition and passed the crisis of continuity. However, the means through which the charismatic authority of the leader was transferred into institutional authority differed in many instances. Although this variable was not formally coded, because it was an unanticipated finding, a discussion of some of the different agents of institutionalizing a religion is also presented.

Results

The reliability of the historical data utilized in this investigation may be questioned. After all, the biographers of the various leaders and the historians of the religious movements may not have been objective in describing the life of the founder. Embellishments and half truths inevitably seep into the objective framework of the actual historical course of events. For some of the leaders, the authors had scant reliable factual data with which to work. Another factor distorting the findings is that the author personally had to code all of the variables and all of the leaders.

These sources of error were minimized by several procedures. First, several different biographies or histories were consulted in order to check the reliability of the data. Also, information regarding the leaders has been coded from the best possible sources. Finally, the method employed to code the leaders was to compile quotes from various sources under the heading of different variables. A sampling of these quotes is presented in this section. It might be added that first assumptions concerning a leader were frequently proven wrong by the actual research. But while an attempt has been made to eliminate error from the study, eradicating all distortion from the study is impossible because the sample is of historical, charismatic leaders around whom many myths have been woven.

The general hypothesis of this paper is that religious, charismatic leaders differ significantly from their successors on the variables which are specified by the proposed theory. Tables 2 and 3 present a summary of the findings of the research. In these Tables both the number and the percent of the total are presented for leaders by variables. A category of selected charismatic leaders had to be created because information was not available for second leaders in many instances. This category contains only those religious founders for whom seconds were also coded. Using Fischer's exact probability test, the selected leaders vary significantly from the followers on the perception of objective symbols, nature of teachings, and institutional setting (after collapsing adjacent cells so the test was possible), but only approach the .05 level of significance for periods of social change. Although charismatic leaders definitely lived in periods of social change, a high percentage of sec-

ond leaders tend to share this quality with the primary leaders.

The charismatic leader's perception of objective symbols is according to the findings de-alienated. Out of the fifteen leaders coded none were classified as alienated. Although this result may be due to the choice of religious founders as the subset of charismatic leaders to be investigated by this project, it is complemented by the finding that five out of a possible nine second leaders were found to be alienated. In all, eight leaders fell in the mystically de-alienated category. Gandhi is an example of this kind of de-alienation. Concerning Gandhi's perception of the relativity of objective symbols, Erikson (1969: 410–1) states, "The truth (for Gandhi) can only be revealed in the kind of appraisal which is in our action. . . . Gandhi commits himself only to 'the relative truth as I have conceived it,' but he also clings firmly to the dictum that only insofar as we can commit ourselves on selected occasions 'to the death' to test such truth—only to that extent can we be true to ourselves and others." Confucius, centuries before Gandhi, also demonstrates a mystical de-alienation by denying the absolute nature of laws. In this regard, Smith (1963: 68) states, "Confucius never refers to fixed unchangeable law or to a divine fiat which lays down what men can or cannot do in any particular circumstance, because he realizes that what is fitting on one occasion may be inappropriate to another." Because of similar reasons, eight out of fifteen charismatic leaders were placed in the mystical de-alienation category.

The remaining seven charismatic leaders were classified as prophetically de-alienated. John Calvin, the Swiss reformer, believed that the original authority of the gospel had been lost through confusion and obfuscation by the Roman Catholic church. In Calvin's own words, his conversion was produced by "God himself" (Schaff 1892: 310). According to McNeill (1954: 216) "Calvin saw the Reformation as the restoration of the true Catholic church that had been almost completely suppressed and undiscoverable in the previous era." Concerning controversy, "He (Calvin) ordinarily reveals no doubt that the truth is on his side" (McNeill 1954: 228). Nichiren, who has often been called Japan's Luther, is also classified as prophetically de-alienated. He lived during the thirteenth century and claimed to be the Buddha who by

Table 2   NUMBER OF LEADERS ACCORDING TO PERCEPTION OF OBJECTIVE SYMBOLS AND SOCIAL CONDITIONS[a]

		Perception of Objective Symbols			Social Conditions	
		Alienation	Mystical De-Alienation	Prophetic De-Alienation	Social Change	Period of Stability
All Charismatic	N	0	8	7	14	1
Leaders	%	0%	53%	47%	93%	7%
Selected Charismatic[b]	N	0	3	6	7	1
Leaders	%	0%	33%	67%	87%	13%
Second	N	5	2	2	4	4
Leaders	%	56%	22%	22%	50%	50%

[a]All percentages are row rather than column percentages.
[b]Selected Charismatic Leaders are those for whom information for coding the second leader was available.

Table 3   NUMBER OF LEADERS ACCORDING TO NATURE OF TEACHINGS AND INSTITUTIONAL SETTING[a]

		Nature of Teachings		Institutional Setting		
		Innovative	Uninnovative	Within Institution	Within Tradition	Outside Institution and Tradition
All Charismatic	N	14	1	4	6	5
Leaders	%	93%	7%	27%	40%	33%
Selected Charismatic[b]	N	9	0	1	4	4
Leaders	%	100%	0%	11%	44%	44%
Second	N	1	8	9	0	0
Leaders	%	11%	89%	100%	0%	0%

[a]All percentages are row rather than column percentages.
[b]Selected Charismatic Leaders are those for whom information for coding the second leaders was available.

prophecy was to appear in the Age of Mappo. Nichiren taught that the Lotus Sutra and his simple interpretation of it are the fundamental truth. According to Kiyoaki Murata (1969: 30), "Nichiren meant that the canon of every other Buddhist sect was fake, and they must accept the supremacy of his own Buddhist canon, the Lotus Sutra." Thus, all fifteen charismatic leaders were de-alienated with approximately half falling into each of the two possible categories.

The social environment of the religious founders can be described as a period of social upheaval. In fourteen out of fifteen cases, the leaders were cited by biographers to have existed during an era of social change. This finding, however, should be tempered with the knowledge that most biographers and social historians have a propensity for describing charismatic leaders as living during times of general unrest and tumult. Often the leaders were characterized as dynamic personalities who were able to forge order out of chaos. For example, George Fox, the founder of the Quakers, lived during a period of social unrest and spent much of his time in prison for conducting religious meetings. Rufus Jones (in Fox: 1919), in the preface to Fox's autobiography, states that "religious authority ceased to count as it had in the past. Existing religious conditions were no longer accepted as final. There was widespread restlessness which gradually produced a host of curious sects." The only leader who was not coded as living during a period of social change was Joseph Smith of the Mormons. He began his ministry during the 1820s, and none of the biographies reviewed refer to any condition of social unrest. Although the group he founded was persecuted and Joseph Smith was assassinated in a jail in Illinois, his followers were not members of a minority group. The results of this variable are strengthened by the finding that out of the eight second leaders coded, four of them conducted their ministry during a period of relative stability.

The religious founders were randomly scattered throughout the three possible categories which define his relationship with the traditional religious structure. This finding radically challenges the contention that charisma is a force which must exist outside of the institutional structure. Out of fifteen religious founders, four were within a religious institutional office; six were within a religious tradition, but not within the institutional structure; and, finally, five had broken with both the religious tradition and the institution in order to found a new religion. Martin Luther, paradoxically, is classified as within a religious institutional office. Much of his life was spent within the Catholic church fighting for reform, and after he split with the church his credentials as a theologian permitted him to reenter a religious office almost immediately as the leader of a previously established religious group. Mahatma Gandhi is an example of a leader who was well within the tradition of Hinduism, but did not fit within any institutionalized religious framework. Gandhi reinterpreted traditional Hinduism to meet the needs of an independence seeking India, but he never occupied any pre-existing religious office. The Buddha is a religious leader who broke both with the tradition and the institutional religion of his times. he ran away from his life as a noble much to the discontent of his father and became an ascetic. After having become disillusioned with the life of an ascetic, he finally attained enlightenment and began to preach the new doctrine of the middle way. Thus, the religious founders in this study tentatively confirm the hypothesis that charisma

can be found both inside and outside of a religious institution or tradition. (The fact that the second leaders were all within a religious institution is probably a function of how they were defined.)

The teachings of the religious founders in all but one case were coded as innovative. Fourteen leaders espoused a set of teachings which differed systematically from those of the traditional religion of their times. This finding suggests that an innovative set of teachings is an important variable for the institutionalization of religion. Once again, it should be cautioned that most biographers and historians of the leaders and their sects tend to extoll and expound on their respective virtues, and this bias may be reflected in the high number of leaders classified with innovative teachings. Jesus is an example of a leader classified as innovative. According to MacKinnon (1931: 305–6), "Whilst granting this dependence on inherited Hebrew thought, it is none the less evident that he (Jesus) moulds it in the crucible of his own mind and religious experience and has impressed on it the stamp of his own personality and genius." Joseph Smith's teachings, although not radically breaking with tradition, nevertheless contain many new elements. Referring to Smith's teachings Schmucker (1856: 67–8) states, "His doctrine was both old and new. It had sufficient of the old to attract those who would have been repelled by a creed entirely new, and it had sufficient of the new to rivet attention and inflame the imagination of those [on] whose minds an old ... creed ... would have fallen and taken no root." George Fox is the only religious founder who was cited as having an uninnovative set of teachings. None of the biographies reviewed stated that his teachings were innovative. Jones (in Fox 1919: 33) represents a typical sampling when he states, "His originality ... lies ... not so much in the discovery ... of the principle (of Divine Guidance) as in the fearless application of it. Other men had believed in Divine guidance, other Christians had proclaimed the impenetration of God in the lives of men." The finding that fourteen out of fifteen religious founders espoused an innovative set of teachings is buttressed by the contrasting results of the second leaders. Only one out of the nine second leaders coded was found to have teachings which differed significantly from the founder of the religion. Thus, innovative teaching is an important variable in distinguishing the religious founders from their seconds.

The procedure for institutionalizing charisma has always been a controversial subject in the sociology of religion. Although this variable was not coded per se, a summary of how each of the fifteen religions was institutionalized was compiled during the research. From these summaries it was found that a religion may be institutionalized by three different agents: the religious founder himself, a second or later follower, or finally a religious council. Each of the following cases represents one of these different forms of institutionalization. First, in several instances the religious founder himself is instrumental in the institutionalization of his own religion. For instance, George Fox, the founder of the Quakers, during his lifetime set up annual meetings of the clergy in which church doctrine and other matters were decided. Gradually, other meetings of laymen as well as clergy firmly institutionalized the religion well before Fox's death in 1691. In the second instance, a second or later leader organizes the founder's teachings and institutionalizes the religion. In such a case, the leader will usually justly or unjustly claim to have been designated by the charismatic leader to take over the reigns of control within the neophyte religion. Within Islam a split occurred immediately after Muhammad's death when Abu Bakr was approved as the second by the political powers, and Ali was chosen as the rightful heir to Muhammad because of his hereditary ties with the prophet. Eventually two religious traditions, the Sunnis and the Shi'ite, were established tracing their authority to Muhammad through two different means. Finally, the third type of agent of institutionalizing a religion is not through any individual, but through a religious council whose task is to unify the religion. In the case of Martin Luther, his Church began to fragment after his death in 1546. The secular authorities, who could not abide such disharmony caused by the conflicting factions, appointed a consistory to resolve the problems which were dividing the Lutherans. Thus, after Luther's death, no individual institutionalized the religion, but rather a council of secularly appointed theologians decided on matters concerning church doctrine. These three types of insti-

tutionalizing agents are not mutually exclusive categories and, in fact, different combinations of them may be instrumental in the institutionalization of a religion.

Discussion

The comparison of the religious founders to their second leaders is important for determining the unique characeristics of the charismatic leader. The seconds act as a comparison group in that they are expected to demonstrate a different pattern of attributes when compared with the founder. Because information was available for only nine second leaders, the comparisons, although stimulating, must not be understood as a rigorous test of the proposed theory. In general, the religious founders were de-alienated, lived during a period of radical social change, were inside or outside of the traditional and institutional structure of the religion, and their teachings were innovative. The second leaders were found to be alienated, lived during a period of social change or stability, were definitely within an institutional office, and generally their teachings were uninnovative. These findings suggest that the religious founder does systematically differ from the second on the variables which were deemed important by the proposed theory.

The findings of this study indicate that charisma is not an individualistic phenomena hinging only on the extraordinary quality of a leader's personality. Rather, charisma stems from a complex of factors meeting in and around the same individual. For instance, the leader is likely to live during a period of radical social change in which the values of the society have changed leaving an opening for a new formulation of religious beliefs. Although social factors determine the relative likelihood of the emergence of charismatic leaders, they do not determine that they will arise or what their teachings will be. In this respect the leader has a freedom of the will upon which Weber insisted. Although all of the conditions indicated above must converge in order to have the possibility for the existence of charisma, this does not diminish the chemistry which occurs between the charismatic leaders and their followers once all of these factors have been combined.

Apocalypse at Jonestown

John R. Hall

The tragic end of the People's Temple utopian experiment in Guyana is unparalleled in the history of humankind. Hall's article is more than an exploration of a religion gone mad, however: by viewing the Reverend Jim Jones and his followers through an anthropological lens, Hall has been able to compare charismatic leadership and prophetism in the West with non-Western examples (discussed both in this chapter and in Chapter 9, on "Old and New Religions"). Hall challenges the labeling of the People's Temple as a "cult," and demonstrates that the apostolic character of the Reverend Jones fits the profile of charismatic leaders the world over. Using a social psychological, structural approach, Hall discusses the membership of the sect, why they were attracted to it, and how Jones's leadership was vital to the subordination of individual rights that ended with the death of the nine hundred adherents at Jonestown. The rapid erosion of traditional values is but one of the many prerequisites necessary to precipitate a revitalization movement, that rapid and intentional process of socio-cultural change that has occurred so frequently in the non-Western world and for which Jones offered a Western alternative.

Reprinted by permission of Transaction, Inc., from *Society*, Vol. 16, no. 6 (September/October 1979), pp. 52–61. Copyright © 1979.

THE EVENTS OF NOVEMBER 1978 AT JONESTOWN, Guyana, have been well documented, indeed probably better documented than most incidents in the realm of the bizarre. Beyond the wealth of "facts" which have been drawn from interviews with survivors of all stripes, there remain piles of as yet unsifted documents and tapes; if they can ever be examined, these will perhaps add something in the way of detail. But it is unlikely they will change very much the broad lines of our understanding of Jonestown. The major dimensions of the events and the outlines of various intrigues are already before us. But so far we have been caught in a flood of instant analysis; some of this has been insightful, but much of the accompanying moral outrage has clouded our ability to comprehend the events themselves. We need a more considered look at what sort of social phenomenon Jonestown was, and why (and how) Reverend Jim Jones and his staff led the 900 people of Jonestown to die in mass murder and suicide. On the face of it, the action is unparalleled and incredible.

"Crazy Like a Fox"

The news media have sought to account for Jonestown largely by looking for parallels "in history"; yet we have not been terribly enlightened by the ones they have found, usually because they have searched for cases which bear the outer trappings of the event, but which have fundamentally different causes. Thus, at Masada, in 73 A.D., the Jews who committed suicide under siege by Roman soldiers knew their fate was death, and chose to die by their own hands rather than at those of the Romans. In World War II, Japanese kamikaze pilots acted with the knowledge that direct, tangible, strategic results would stem from their altruisitc suicides, if they were properly executed. And in Hitler's concentration camps, though there was occasional cooperation by Jews in their own executions, the Nazi executioners had no intentions of dying themselves.

Besides pointing to parallels which don't quite fit, the news media have targeted Jim Jones as irrational, a madman who had perverse tendencies from early in his youth. They have labelled the Peoples Temple as a "cult," perhaps in the hope that a label will suffice when an explanation is unavailable. And they have quite correctly plumbed the key issue of how Jones and his staff were able to bring the mass murder/suicide to completion, drawing largely on the explanations of psychiatrists who have prompted the concept of "brainwashing" as the answer.

But Jones was crazy like a fox. Though he may have been "possessed" or "crazed," both the organizational effectiveness of the Peoples Temple for more than 15 years, and the actual carrying out of the mass murder/suicide show that Jones and his immediate staff knew what they were doing.

Moreover, the Peoples Temple only became a "cult" when the media discovered the mass suicide. As an Indiana woman whose teenager died at Jonestown commented, "I can't understand why they call the Peoples Temple a cult. To the people, it was their church. . . ." It is questionable whether the term "cult" has any sociological utility. As Harold Fallding has observed, it is a value-laden term most often used by members of one religion to describe a heretical or competing religion, of which they disapprove. Of course, even if the use of the term "cult" in the press has been sloppy and inappropriate, some comparisons, for example to the Unification Church, the Krishna Society, and the Children of God, have been quite apt. But these comparisons have triggered a sort of guilt by association; in this view, Jonestown is a not-so-aberrant case among numerous exotic and weird religious "cults." The only thing stopping some people from "cleaning up" the "cult" situation is the constitutional guarantee of freedom of religion.

Finally, "brainwashing" is an important but incomplete basis for understanding the mass murder/suicide. There can be no way to determine how many people at Jonestown freely chose to drink the cyanide-laced Flav-r-ade distributed after Jonestown received word of the murders of U.S. Congressman Leo Ryan and four other visitors at the airstrip. Clearly over 200 children and an undetermined number of adults were murdered. Thought control and blind obedience to authority ("brainwashing") surely account for some additional number of suicides. But the obvious cannot be ignored: a substantial number of people—"brainwashed" or not—committed suicide. Insofar as "brainwashing" occurs in other social organizations besides the Peoples Temple, it can only be a necessary and not a sufficient cause of the mass murder/suicide. The coercive persuasion involved in a totalistic construction of reality may explain in part *how* large numbers of people came to accept the course proposed by their leader, but it leaves unanswered the question of *why* the true believers among the inhabitants of Jonestown came to consider "revolutionary suicide" a plausible course of action.

In all the instant analysis of Jones' perversity, the threats posed by "cults" and the victimization of people by "brainwashing," there has been little attempt to account for Jonestown sociologically, and as a religious phenomenon. The various facets of Jonestown remain as incongruous pieces of seemingly separate puzzles; we need a close examination of the case itself to try to comprehend it. In the following discussion based on ideal type analysis and *verstehende* sociology, I will suggest that the Peoples Temple Agricultural Project at Jonestown was an apocalyptic sect. Most apocalyptic sects gravitate toward one of three ideal typical possibilities: (1) preapocalyptic Adventism, (2) preapocalyptic war, or (3) postapocalyptic otherworldly grace. Insofar as the Adventist group takes on a communal form, it comes to approximate the postapocalyptic tableau of other-worldly grace. Jonestown was caught on the saddle of the apocalypse: it had its origins in the vaguely apocalyptic revivalist evangelism of the Peoples Temple in the United States, but the Guyanese communal settlement itself was an attempt to transcend the apocalypse by establishing a "heaven-on-earth." For various reasons, this attempt was frustrated. The Peoples Temple at Jonestown was drawn back into a preapocalyptic war with the forces of the established order. "Revolutionary suicide" then came to be seen as a way of surmounting the frustration, of moving beyond the apocalypse, to "heaven," albeit not "on earth."

In order to explore this account, let us first consider the origins of Jonestown and the ways in which it subsequently came to approximate the ideal typical other-worldly sect. Then we can consider certain tensions of the Jonestown group with respect to its other-worldly existence, so as to understand why similar groups did not (and are not likely to) encounter the same fate as Jonestown.

"A Prophet Calls the Shots"

An other-worldly sect, as I have described it in *The Ways Out*, is a utopian communal group which subscribes to a set of beliefs based on an apocalyptic interpretation of current history. The world of society-at-large is seen as totally evil, and in its last days; at the end of history as we know it, it is to be replaced by a community of the elect—those who live according to the revelation of God's will. The convert who embraces such a sect must, perforce, abandon any previous understanding of life's meaning and embrace the new worldview, which itself is capable of subsuming and explaining the individual's previous life, the actions of opponents to the sect, and the demands which are placed on the convert by the leadership of the sect. The other-worldly sect typically establishes its existence on the "other" side of the apocalypse by withdrawing from "this" world into a timeless heaven-on-earth. In this millennial kingdom, those closest to God come to rule. Though democratic consensuality or the collegiality of elders may come into play, more typically, a preeminent prophet or messiah, legitimated by charisma or tradition, calls the shots in a theocratic organization of God's chosen people.

The Peoples Temple had its roots in amorphous revivalistic evangelical religion, but in the transition to the Jonestown Agricultural Mission, it came to resemble an other-worldly sect. The Temple grew out of the interracial congregation Jim Jones had founded in Indiana in 1953. By 1964, the Peoples Temple Full Gospel Church was federated with the Disciples of Christ. Later, in 1966, Jones moved with 100 of his most devout followers to Redwood Valley, California. From there they expanded in the 1970s to San Francisco and Los Angeles—more promising places for liberal, interracial evangelism than rural Redwood Valley. In these years before the move to Guyana, Jones engaged himself largely in the manifold craft of revivalism. Jones learned from others he observed—Father Divine in Philadelphia and David Martinus de Miranda in Brazil, and Jones himself became a purveyor of faked miracles and faith healings. By the California years, the Peoples Temple was prospering financially from its somewhat shady "tent meeting" style activities, and from a variety of other petty and grand money-making schemes; it was also gaining political clout through the deployment of its members for the benefit of various politicians and causes.

These early developments give cause to wonder why Jones did not establish a successful but relatively benign sect like Jehovah's Witnesses, or, alternatively, why he did not move from a religious base directly into the realm of politics, as did the Reverend Adam Clayton Powell, from his Harlem congregation to the U.S. House of Representatives. The answer seems twofold. In the first place, Jim Jones seems to have had limitations both as an evangelist and as a politician. He simply did not succeed in fooling key California observers with his faked miracles. And for all the political support he peddled in California politics, Jones was not always able to draw on his good political "credit" when he needed it. A certain mark of political effectiveness concerns the ability to sustain power in the face of scandal. By this standard, Jones was not totally successful in either Indiana or California: there always seemed to be investigators and reporters on the trails of various questionable financial and evangelical dealings.

Quite aside from the limits of Jones' effectiveness, the very nature of his prophecy directed his religious movement along a different path from either "worldly" politics or sectarian Adventism. Keyed to the New Testament Book of Revelation, Adventist groups receive prophecy about the apocalyptic downfall of the present evil order of the world and the second coming of Christ to preside over a millennial period of divine grace on earth. For all such groups, the Advent itself makes social action to reform "this" world's institutions irrelevant. Adventist groups differ from one another in their exact eschatology of the last days, but the groups that have survived, like the Seventh Day Adventists and Jehovah's Witnesses, have juggled their doctrines which fix an exact date for Christ's appearance. Thus they have moved away from any intense chiliastic expectation of an imminent appearance, to engage in more mundane conversionist activities which are intended to pave the way for the Millennium.

"Apocalypse Now"

Reverend Jones himself seems to have shared the pessimism of the Adventist sects about reforming social institutions in this world (for him, the capitalist world of the United States). True, he supported various progressive causes, but he did not put much stake in their success. Jones' prophecy was far more radical than those of contemporary Adventist groups; he focused on imminent apocalyptic disaster rather than on Christ's millennial salvation, and his eschatology therefore had to resolve a choice between preapocalyptic struggle with "the beast" or collective flight to establish a postapocalyptic kingdom of the elect. Up until the end, the Peoples Temple was directed toward the latter possibility. Even in the Indiana years, Jones had embraced an apocalyptic view. The move from Indiana to California was in part justified by Jones' claim that Redwood Valley would survive nuclear holocaust. In the California years, the apocalyptic vision shifted to Central Intelligence Agency persecution and Nazi-like extermination of blacks. In California too, the Peoples Temple gradually became communalistic in certain respects; it established a community of goods, pooled resources of elderly followers to provide communal housing for them, and drew on state funds to act as foster parents by establishing group homes for displaced youth. In its apocalyptic and communal aspects, the Peoples Temple more and more came to exist as an ark of survival. Jonestown, the Agricultural Project in Guyana, was built beginning in 1974 by an advance crew that by early 1977 still amounted to less than 60 people, most of them under 30 years old. The mass exodus of the Peoples Temple to Jonestown really began in 1977, when the Peoples Temple was coming under increasing scrutiny in California.

In the move to Guyana, the Peoples Temple began to concertedly exhibit many dynamics of other-worldly sects, though it differed in ways which were central to its fate. Until the end, Jonestown was similar in striking ways to contemporary sects like the Children of God and the Krishna So-

ciety (ISKCON, Inc.). Indeed, the Temple bears a more than casual (and somewhat uncomfortable) resemblance to the various Protestant sects which emigrated to the wilderness of North America beginning in the seventeenth century. The Puritans, Moravians, Rappites, Shakers, Lutherans, and many others like them sought to escape religious persecution in Europe in order to set up theocracies where they could live out their own visions of the earthly millennial community. So it was with Jonestown. In this light, neither disciplinary practices, the daily round of life, nor the community of goods at Jonestown seem so unusual.

"The Jungle Is Only a Few Yards Away"

The disciplinary practices of the Peoples Temple—as bizarre and grotesque as they may sound, are not uncommon aspects of other-worldly sects: these practices have been played up in the press in an attempt to demonstrate the perverse nature of the group, so as to "explain" the terrible climax to their life. But as Erving Goffman has shown in *Asylums,* sexual intimidation and general psychological terror occur in all kinds of total institutions, including mental hospitals, prisons, armies, and even nunneries. Indeed, Congressman Leo Ryan, just prior to his fateful visit to Jonestown, accepted the need for social control: ". . . you can't put 1,200 people in the middle of a jungle without some damn tight discipline." Practices at Jonestown may well seem restrained in comparison to practices of, say, seventeenth-century American Puritans who, among other things, were willing to execute "witches" on the testimony of respected churchgoers or even children. Meg Greenfield observed in *Newsweek* in reflecting on Jonestown, "the jungle is only a few yards away." It seems important to recall that some revered origins of the United States lie in a remarkably similar "jungle."

Communal groups of all types, not just other-worldly sects, face problems of social control and commitment. Rosabeth Kanter has convincingly shown that successful communal groups in the nineteenth-century United States often drew on mechanisms of mutual criticism, mortification, modification of conventional dyadic sexual mores, and other devices in order to decrease the individual's ties to the outside or personal relationships within the group, and increase the individual's commitment to the collectivity as a whole.

Such commitment mechanisms are employed most often in religious communal groups, especially those with charismatic leaders. Other-worldly communal groups, where a special attempt is being made to forge a wholly new interpretation of reality, where the demand for commitment is especially pronounced (in a word, where it is sectarian) —these groups have tremendously high stakes in maintaining commitment. These groups are likely to seek out the procedures most effective at guaranteeing commitment. After all, defection from "the way" inevitably casts doubt on the sanctity of the way, no matter how it is rationalized among the faithful. Thus, it is against such groups that the charges of "brainwashing," chicanery, and mistreatment of members are most often leveled. Whatever their basis in fact, these are the likely charges of families and friends who see their loved ones abandon them in favor of committing material resources and persona to the religious hope of a new life. Much like other-worldly sects, families suffer a loss of legitimacy in the "defection" of one of their own.

The abyss that comes to exist between other-worldly sects and the world of society-at-large left behind simply cannot be bridged. There is no encompassing rational connection between the two realities, and, therefore, the interchange between the other-worldly sect and people beyond its boundaries becomes a struggle either between "infidels" and the "faithful" from the point of view of the sect, or between rationality and fanaticism from the point of view of outsiders. Every sectarian action has its benevolent interpretation and legitimation within the sect and a converse interpretation from the outside. Thus, from inside the sect, various practices of "confession," "mutual criticism," or "catharsis" sessions seem necessary to prevent deviant worldviews from taking hold within the group. In the Peoples Temple, such practices included occasional enforced isolation and drug regimens for "rehabilitation" akin to contemporary psychiatric treatment. From the outside, all this tends to be regarded as "brainwashing," but insiders will turn the accusation outward, claiming that it is those in the society-at-large who are "brainwashed." Though there

can really be no resolution to this conflict of interpretations, the widespread incidence of similar "coercive persuasion" outside Jonestown suggests that the fact it was practiced at Jonestown is not so unusual, at least within the context of other-worldly sects, or total institutions in general, for that matter.

What is unusual is the direction which coercive persuasion or "brainwashing" took. Jones worked to instill devotion in unusual ways—ways which fostered the acceptibility of "revolutionary suicide" among his followers. During "white nights" of emergency mobilization, he conducted rituals of proclaimed mass suicide, giving "poison" to all members, saying they would die within the hour. According to one defector, Deborah Blakey, Jones "explained that the poison was not real and we had just been through a loyalty test. He warned us that the time was not far off when it would be necessary for us to die by our own hands." This event initially left Blakey "indifferent" to whether she "lived or died." A true believer in the Peoples Temple was more emphatic: disappointed by the string of false collective suicides, in a note to Jones he hoped for "the real thing" so that they could all pass beyond the suffering of this world. Some people yielded to Jim Jones only because their will to resist was beaten down; others, including many "seniors"—the elderly members of the Peoples Temple—felt they owed everything to Jim Jones, and provided him with a strong core of unequivocal support. Jones allowed open dissension at "town meetings" apparently because, with the support of the "seniors," he knew he could prevail. Thus, no matter what they wanted personally, people learned to leave their fates in the hands of Jim Jones, and accept what he demanded. The specific uses of coercive persuasion at Jonestown help explain how (but not why) the mass murder/suicide was implemented. But it is the special use, not the general nature of "brainwashing" which distinguishes Jonestown from most other-worldly sects.

Meat Eaters and Bean Eaters

Aside from "brainwashing," a second major kind of accusation about Jonestown, put forward most forcefully by Deborah Blakey, concerns the work discipline and diet there. Blakey swore in an affidavit that the work load was excessive and the food served to the average residents of Jonestown inadequate. She abhorred the contradiction between the conditions she reported and the privileged diet of Reverend Jones and his inner circle. Moreover, because she had dealt with the group's finances, she knew that money could have been directed to providing a more adequate diet.

Blakey's moral sensibilities notwithstanding, the disparity between the diet of the elite and of the average Jonestowner should come as no surprise: it parallels Erving Goffman's description of widespread hierarchies of privilege in total institutions. Her concern about the average diet is more the point. But here, other accounts differ from Blakey's report. Maria Katsaris, a consort of Reverend Jones, wrote her father a letter extolling the virtues of the Agricultural Project's "cutlass" beans used as a meat substitute. And Paula Adams, who survived the Jonestown holocaust because she resided at the Peoples Temple house in Georgetown, expressed ambivalence about the Jonestown community in an interview after the mass murder/suicide. But she also remarked, "My daughter ate very well. She got eggs and milk every day. How many black children in the ghetto eat that well?" The accounts of surviving members of Reverend Jones' personal staff and inner circle, like Katsaris and Adams, are suspect, of course, in exactly the opposite way as those of people like the "Concerned Relatives." But the inside accounts are corroborated by at least one outsider, *Washington Post* reporter Charles Krause. On his arrival at Jonestown in the company of U.S. Congressman Leo Ryan, Krause noted, "contrary to what the Concerned Relatives had told us, nobody seemed to be starving. Indeed, everyone seemed quite healthy."

It is difficult to assess these conflicting views. Beginning early in the summer of 1977, Jones set in motion the mass exodus of some 800 Peoples Temple members from California to Jonestown. Though Jonestown could adequately house only about 500 people by then, the population quickly climbed well beyond that mark, at the same time ballooning way past the agricultural base of the settlement. The exodus also caused Jonestown to become "top heavy" with less-productive seniors and children. Anything close to agricultural self-sufficiency then became a more elusive and long-range goal. As time wore on during the group's last year of existence, Jones himself became ever more fixated on the prospect of a mass emigration from Guyana, and in this light, any sort of long-range agricultural development strategy seemed increasingly irrational. According to *The New York Times*, the former Jonestown farm manager, Jim Bogue, suggested that the agricultural program at Jonestown would have succeeded in the long run, if it had been adhered to. But with the emerging plans for emigration, it was not followed, and thus became merely a charade for the benefit of the Guyanese government. This analysis would seem to have implications for *internal* conflicts about goals within Jonestown: for example, Jim Jones' only natural son, Stephan Jones, as well as several other young men in the Peoples Temple, came to believe in Jonestown as a socialist agrarian community, not as an other-worldly sect headed up by Jim Jones. Reflecting about his father after the mass murder/suicide, Stephan Jones commented, "I don't mind discrediting him, but I'm still a socialist, and Jim Jones will be used to discredit socialism. People will use him to discredit what was built. Jonestown was not Jim Jones, although he believed it was."

The "seniors" who provided social security checks, gardened, and produced handicraft articles for sale in Georgetown in lieu of heavy physical labor, as well as the fate of agricultural productivity—these both reinforce the assessment that Jim Jones' vision of the Peoples Temple approximates the "other-worldly sect" as an ideal type. In such sects, as a rule, proponents seek to survive *not* on the basis of productive labor (as in more "worldly" utopian" communal groups), but on the basis of patronage, petty financial schemes, and the building of a "community of goods" through proselytism. This was just the case with Jonestown: the community of goods which Jones built up is valued at more than $12 million. As a basis for satisfying collective wants, any agricultural production at Jonestown would have paled in comparison to this amassed wealth.

But even if the agricultural project itself became a charade, it is no easy task to create a plausible charade in the midst of relatively infertile soil reclaimed from dense jungle; this would have required the long hours of work which Peoples Temple defectors described. Such a charade could serve as yet another effective means of social control. In the first place, it gave a purposeful role to those who envisioned Jonestown as an experimental socialist agrarian community. Beyond this, it monopolized the waking hours of most of the populace in exhausting work, and gave them only a minimal (though probably adequate) diet on which to do it. It is easy to imagine that many city people, or those with bourgeous sensibilities in general, would not find this their cup of tea in any case. But the demanding daily regimen, however abhorrent to the uninitiated, is widespread in other-worldly sects. Various programs of fasting and work asceticism have long been regarded as signs of piety and routes to religious enlightenment or ecstacy. In the contemporary American Krishna groups, an alternation of nonsugar and high-sugar phases of the diet seems to create an almost addictive attachment to the food which is communally dispersed. And we need look no later in history than to Saint Benedict's order to find a situation in which the personal time of participants is eliminated for all practical purposes, with procedures of mortification for offenders laid out by Saint Benedict in his *Rule*. The concerns of Blakey and others about diet, work, and discipline may have some basis, but they have probably been exaggerated, and in any case, they do not distinguish Jonestown from other-worldly sects in general.

Community of Goods

One final public concern with the Peoples Temple deserves mention because it so closely parallels previous sectarian practice: the Reverend Jim Jones is accused of swindling people out of their livelihoods and life circumstances by tricking them into signing over their money and possessions to the Peoples Temple or its inner circle of members. Of course, Jones considered this a "community of goods" and correctly pointed to a long tradition of such want satisfaction among other-worldly sects; in an interview just prior to the mass murder/suicide, Jones cited Jesus' call to hold all things in common. There are good grounds to think that Reverend Jones carried this philosophy into the realm of a con game. Still, it should be noted that in the suicidal end, Jones did not benefit from all the wealth the way a good number of other self-declared prophets and messiahs have done.

As with its disciplinary practices and its round of daily life, the community of goods in the Peoples Temple at Jonestown emphasizes its similarities to other-worldly sects—both the contemporary

ones labelled "cults" by their detractors, and historical examples which are often revered in retrospect by contemporary religious culture. The elaboration of these affinities is in no way intended to suggest that we can or should vindicate the duplicity, the bizarre sexual and psychological intimidation, and the hardships of daily life at Jonestown. But it must be recognized that the Jonestown settlement was a good deal less unusual than some of us might like to think: the things which detractors find abhorrent in the life of the Peoples Temple at Jonestown prior to the final "white night" of murder and suicide are the core nature of other-worldly sects. It should come as no surprise that practices like those in Jonestown are widespread, both in historical and contemporary other-worldly sects. Granted that the character of such sects—the theocratic basis of authority, the devices of mortification and social control, and the demanding regimen of everyday life—predispose people in such groups to respond to the whims of their leaders, whatever fanatic and zealous directions they may take. But given the widespread occurrence of other-worldly sects, the other-worldly features of Jonestown are in themselves insufficient to explain the bizarre fate of its participants. If we are to understand the unique turn of events at Jonestown, we must look to certain distinctive features of the Peoples Temple—things which make it unusual among other-worldly sects, and we must try to comprehend the subjective meanings of these features for various of Jonestown's participants.

Race and Ideology

If the Peoples Temple was distinctive among other-worldly sects, it is for two reasons: first, the group was far and away more thoroughly racially integrated than any other such group today. Second, the Peoples Temple was distinctively proto-communist in ideology. Both of these conditions, together with certain personal fears of Jim Jones (mixed perhaps with organic disorders and assorted drugs), converged in the active mind of the reverend to give a special twist to the apocalyptic quest of his flock. Let us consider these matters in turn.

In the Peoples Temple, Jim Jones had consistently sought to transcend racism in peace rather than in struggle. The origins of this approach, like most of Jones' early life, are by now shrouded in myth. But it is clear that Jones was committed to racial harmony in his Indiana ministry. In the 1950s, his formation of an interracial congregation met with much resistance in Indianapolis, and this persecution was one impetus for the exodus to California. There is room for debate on how far Jones' operation actually went toward racial equality, or to what degree it simply perpetuated racism, albeit in a racially harmonious microcosm. But the Peoples Temple fostered greater racial equality and harmony than that of the society-at-large, and in this respect, it has few parallels in present-day communal groups, much less mainstream religious congregations. The significance of this cannot easily be assayed, but one view of it is captured in a letter from a 20-year-old Jonestown girl. She wrote to her mother in Evansville, Indiana, that she could "walk down the street now without the fear of having little old white ladies call me nigger."

Coupled with the commitment to racial integration, and again in contrast with most other-worldly sects, the Peoples Temple moved strongly toward ideological communism. Most other-worldly sects practice religiously inspired communism—the "clerical" or "Christian" socialism which Marx and Engels railed against. But few, if any, to date have flirted with the likes of Marx, Lenin, and Stalin. By contrast, it has become clear that, whatever the contradictions other socialists point to between Jones' messianism and socialism, the Reverend Jim Jones and his staff considered themselves socialists. In his column "Perspectives from Guyana," Jim Jones maintained, "neither my colleagues nor I are any longer caught up in the opiate of religion. . . ." Though the practice of the group prior to the mass murder/suicide was not based on any doctrinaire Marxism, at least some of the recruits to the group were young radical intellectuals, and one of the group's members, Richard Tropp, gave evening classes on radical political theory. In short, radical socialist currents were unmistakably present in the group.

Preaching Atheism

It is perhaps more questionable whether the Peoples Temple was religious in any conventional sense of the term. Of course, all utopian communal groups are religious in that they draw together true believers who seek to live out a heretical or heterodox interpretation of the meaningfulness of social existence. In this sense, the Peoples Temple was a religious group, just as Frederick Engels once observed that socialist sects of the nineteenth century paralleled the character of primitive Christian and Reformation sects. Clearly, Jim Jones was more self-consciously religious than the socialist sects were. Though he "preached atheism," and did not believe in a God that answers prayer, he did embrace reincarnation, and a surviving resident of Jonestown remembers him saying, "Our religion is this: your highest service to God is service to your fellow man." On the other hand, it seems that the outward manifestations of conventional religious activity—revivals, sermons, faith healings—were, at least in Jim Jones' view, calculated devices to draw people into an organization which was something quite different. It is a telling point in this regard that Jones ceased the practice of faith healings and cut off other religious activities once he moved to Jonestown. Jones' wife Marceline once noted that Jim Jones considered himself a Marxist who "used religion to try to get some people out of the opiate of religion." In a remarkable off-the-cuff interview with Richard and Harriet Tropp—the two Jonestown residents who were writing a book about the Peoples Temple—Jones reflected on the early years of his ministry, claiming, "what a hell of a battle that [integration] was—I thought 'I'll never make a revolution. I can't even get those fuckers to integrate, much less get them to any communist philosophy.' " In the same interview, Jones intimated that he had been a member of the U.S. Communist party in the early 1950s. Of course, with Jones' Nixonesque concern for his place in history, it is possible that his hindsight, even in talking with sympathetic biographers, was not the same as his original motives. In the interview with the Tropps, Jones hinted that the entire development of the Peoples Temple down to the Jonestown Agricultural Project derived from his communist beliefs. This interview and Marceline Jones' comment give strong evidence of an early communist orientation in Jones. Whenever this orientation originated, the move to Jonestown was in part predicated on it. The socialist government of Guyana was generally committed to supporting socialists seeking refuge from capitalist societies, and they apparently thought

Jones' flexible brand of Marxism fit well within the country's political matrix. By 1973, when negotiations with Guyana about an agricultural project were initiated, Jones and his aides were professing identification with the world-historical communist movement.

The Persecution Complex

The convergence of racial integration and crude communism gave a distinctly political character to what in many other respects was an other-worldly religious sect. The injection of radical politics gave a heightened sense of persecution to the Jonestown Agricultural Project. Jim Jones seems to have both fed this heightened sense of persecution to his followers, and to have been devoured by it himself. Jones manipulated fears among his followers by controlling information and spreading false rumors about news events in the United States. With actual knowledge of certain adversaries, and fed by his own premonitions, Jones spread premonitions among his followers, thereby heightening their dedication. In the process, Jones disenchanted a few, who became Judas Iscariots, in time bringing the forces of legitimate external authority to "persecute" Jones and his true believers in their jungle theocracy.

The persecution complex is a stock-in-trade of other-worldly sects. It is naturally engendered by a radical separation from the world of society-at-large. An apocalyptic mission develops in such a way that "persecution" from the world left behind is taken as a sign of the sanctity of the group's chosen path of salvation. Though racial and political persecution are not usually among the themes of other-worldly persecution, they do not totally break the other-worldly way of interpreting experience. But the heightened sense of persecution at Jonestown did reduce the disconnection from society-at-large which is the signature of other-worldly sects.

Most blacks in the United States have already experienced "persecution": if Jim Jones gave his black followers some relief from a ghetto existence (which many seem to have felt he did), he also made a point of reminding the blacks in his group that persecution still awaited them back in the ghettos and rural areas of the United States. In the California years, for example, the Peoples Temple

would stage mock lynchings of blacks by the Ku Klux Klan as a form of political theater. And according to Deborah Blakey, Jones "convinced black Temple members that if they did not follow him to Guyana, they would be put into concentration camps and killed."

Similarly, white socialist intellectuals could easily develop paranoia about their activities: as any participant in the New Left movement of the 1960s and early 1970s knows, paranoia was a sort of badge of honor to some people. Jones fed this sort of paranoia by telling whites that the CIA listed them as enemies of the state.

Jones probably impressed persecution upon his followers to increase their allegiance to him. But Jones himself was caught up in a web of persecution and betrayal. The falling out between Jones and Grace and Tim Stoen seems central here. In conjunction with the imminent appearance of negative news articles, the fight over custody of John Victor Stoen—Grace's son whom both Jones and Tim Stoen claimed to have fathered—triggered Jones' 1977 decision to remove himself from the San Francisco Temple to Guyana.

We may never know what happened between the Stoens and Jones. According to Terri Buford, a former Jonestown insider, Tim Stoen left the Peoples Temple shortly after it became known that in the 1960s he had gone on a Rotary-sponsored speaking tour denouncing communism. Both sides have accused the other of being the progenitors of violence in the Peoples Temple. To reporters who accompanied Congressman Ryan, Jones charged that the Stoen couple had been government agents and provocateurs who had advocated bombing, burning, and terrorism. This possibility could have been regarded as quite plausible by Jones and his staff, for they possessed documents about alleged similar Federal Bureau of Investigation moves against the Weather Underground and the Church of Scientology. The struggle between Jones and the Stoens thus could easily have personified to Jones the quintessence of a conspiracy against him and his work. It certainly intensified negative media attention on the Temple.

For all his attempts to garner favor from the press, Jones failed in the crucial instance. The San Francisco investigative reporters gave horror stories about the Peoples Temple and Jones' custody battle a good deal of play. Jones may well have been correct in his suspicion that he was not being treated fairly in the press. After the mass murder/suicide, the managing editor of the *San Francisco Examiner* proudly asserted in a January 15, 1979, letter to the *Wall Street Journal* that his paper had not been "morally neutral" in its coverage of the Peoples Temple.

The published horror stories were based on the allegations by defectors, the Stoens and Deborah Blakey foremost among them. How true, widespread, exaggerated, or isolated the incidents reported were, we do not know. Certainly they were generalized in the press to the point of creating an image of Jones as a total ogre. The defectors also initiated legal proceedings against the Temple. And the news articles began to stir the interest of government authorities in the operation. These developments were not lost on Jim Jones. The custody battle with the Stoens seems to have precipitated Jones' mass suicide threat to the Guyanese government. Not coincidentally, according to Jim Jones' only natural son, Stephan Jones, at this point the first "white night" drills for mass suicide were held (Stephan Jones connects these events with the appearance of several negative news articles).

With these sorts of events in mind, it is not hard to see how it came to be that Jim Jones felt betrayed by the Stoens and the other defectors, and persecuted by those who appeared to side with the defectors—the press and the government foremost among them. In September 1978, Jones went so far as to retain well-known conspiracy theorist and lawyer Mark Lane to investigate the possibility of a plot against the Peoples Temple. In the days immediately after he was retained by Jones, Mark Lane (perhaps self-servingly) reported in a memorandum to Jones that "even a cursory examination" of the available evidence "reveals that there has been a coordinated campaign to destroy the Peoples Temple and to impugn the reputation of its leader." Those involved were said to include the U.S. Customs Bureau, the Federal Communications Commission, the Central Intelligence Agency, the Federal Bureau of Investigation, and the Internal Revenue Service. Lane's assertions probably had little basis in fact: though several of the named agencies independently had looked into certain Temple activities, none of them had taken any direct action against the Temple, even though they may have had some cause for doing so. The

actual state of affairs notwithstanding, with Lane's assertions, Jones had substantiation of his sense of persecution from a widely touted theorist of conspiracies.

The sense of persecution which gradually developed in the Peoples Temple from its beginning and increased markedly at Jonestown must have come to a head with the visit there of U.S. Congressman Leo Ryan. The U.S. State Department has revealed that Jones had agreed to a visit by Ryan, but withdrew permission when it became known that a contingent of "Concerned Relatives" as well as certain members of the press would accompany Ryan to Guyana. Among the Concerned Relatives who came with Ryan was the Stoen couple; in fact, Tim Stoen was known as a "leader" of the Concerned Relatives. Reporters with Ryan included two from the *San Francisco Chronicle*, a paper which had already pursued investigative reporting on the Peoples Temple, as well as Gordon Lindsay, an independent newsman who had written a negative story on the Peoples Temple intended to be (but never actually) published in the *National Enquirer*. This entourage could hardly have been regarded as objective or unbiased by Jim Jones and his closer supporters. Instead, it identified Ryan with the forces of persecution, personified by the Stoens and the investigative press, and it set the stage for the mass murder/suicide which had already been threatened in conjunction with the custody fight.

The ways in which the Peoples Temple came to differ from more typical other-worldly sects are more a matter of degree than of kind, but the differences together profoundly altered the character of the scene of Jonestown. Though the avowed radicalism, the interracial living, and the defector-media-government "conspiracy" are structurally distinct from one another, Jim Jones drew them together into a tableau of conspiracy which was intended to increase his followers' attachment to him, but ironically brought his legitimacy as a messiah into question, undermined the other-worldly possibilities of the Peoples Temple Agricultural Project, and placed the group on the stage of history in a distinctive relationship to the apocalypse.

Virtuosi of the Collective Life

Other-worldly sects by their very nature are permeated with apocalyptic ideas. The sense of a decaying social order is personally experienced by the religious seeker in a life held to be untenable, meaningless, or both. This interpretation of life is collectively affirmed and transcended in other-worldly sects, which purport to offer "heaven-on-earth," beyond the effects of the apocalypse. Such sects promise the grace of a theocracy in which followers can sometimes really escape the "living hell" of society-at-large. Many of Reverend Jones' followers seem to have joined the Peoples Temple with this in mind. But the predominance of blacks and the radical ideology of the Temple, together with the persistent struggle against the defectors and the "conspiracy" which formed around them in the minds of the faithful each gave the true believers' sense of persecution a more immediate and pressing, rather than "other-worldly" cast. Jones used these elements to heighten his followers' sense of persecution from the outside, but this device itself may have drawn into question the ability of the supposed charismatic leader to provide an other-worldly sanctuary. By the middle of October, a month before Congressman Ryan's trip in November 1978, Jones' position of preeminent leadership was beginning to be questioned not only by disappointed religious followers, but also by previously devoted "seniors" who were growing tired of the ceaseless meetings and the increasingly untenable character of everyday life, and by key virtuosi of collective life who felt Jones was responsible for their growing inability to deal successfully with Jonetown's material operations. Once those who were dissatisfied circumvented Jones' intelligence network of informers and began to establish solidarity with one another, the "conspiracy" can truly be said to have taken hold within Jonestown itself. If the times were apocalyptic, Reverend Jones was like the revolutionary millenarians described by Norman Cohn and Gunther Levy. Rather than successfully proclaiming the postapocalyptic sanctuary, Jones was reduced to declaiming the web of "evil" powers in which he was ensnared, and searching with chiliastic expectation for the imminent cataclysm which would announce the beginning of the kingdom of righteousness.

Usually, other-worldly sects have a sense of the eternal about them: having escaped "this" world, they adopt the temporal trappings of "heaven," which amounts to a timeless bliss of immortality. But Jim Jones had not really established a post-apocalyptic heavenly plateau. Even if he had promised this to his followers, it was only just being built in the form of the Agricultural Project. And it was not even clear that Jonestown itself was the promised land. Jones did not entirely trust the Guyanese government, and he was considering seeking final asylum in Cuba or the Soviet Union. Whereas other-worldly sects typically assert that heaven is at hand, Jones could only hold it out as a future goal, and one which became more and more elusive as the forces of "persecution" tracked him to Guyana. Thus, Jones and his followers were still within the throes of the apocalypse, still, as they conceived it, the forces of good battling against the evil and conspiratorial world which could not tolerate a living example of a racially integrated American socialist utopia.

In the struggle against evil, Jones and his true believers took on the character of what I have termed a "warring sect"—fighting a decisive Manichean struggle with the forces of evil. Such a struggle seems almost inevitable when political rather than religious themes of apocalypse are stressed, and it is clear that Jones and his staff at times acted within this militant frame of reference. For example, they maintained armed guards around the settlement, held "white night" emergency drills, and even staged mock CIA attacks on Jonestown. By doing so, they undermined the plausibility of an other-worldly existence. The struggle of a warring sect takes place in historical time, where one action builds on another, where decisive outcomes of previous events shape future possibilities. The contradiction between this earthly struggle and the heaven-on-earth Jones would have liked to proclaim (for example, in "Perspectives from Guyana") gave Jonestown many of its strange juxtapositions—of heaven and hell, of suffering and bliss, of love and coercion. Perhaps even Jones himself, for all his megalomaniacal ability to transcend the contradictions which others saw in him (and labelled him an "opportunist" for), could not endure the struggle for his own immortality. If he were indeed a messianic incarnation of God, as he sometimes claimed, presumably Jones could have either won the struggle of the warring sect against its evil persecutors or delivered his people to the bliss of another world.

In effect, Jones had brought his flock to the point of straddling the two sides of the apocalypse. Had he established his colony beyond the unsympathetic perview of defectors, Concerned Relatives, investigative reporters, and governmental agencies, the other-worldly tableau perhaps could have been sustained with less-repressive methods of social control. As it was, Jones and the colony experienced the three interconnected limitations of group totalism which Robert Jay Lifton described with respect to the Chinese Communist revolution: (1) diminishing conversions, (2) inner antagonism (that is, of disillusioned participants) to the suffocation of individuality, and (3) increasing penetration of the "idea-tight milieu control" by outside forces. As Lifton noted, revolutionaries are engaged in a quest for immortality. Other-worldly sectarians in a way short-circuit this quest by the fiat of *asserting* their immortality—positing the timeless heavenly plateau which exists *beyond* history as the basis of their everyday life. But under the persistent eyes of external critics, and because Jones himself exploited such "persecution" to increase his social control, he could not sustain the illusion of other-worldly immortality.

On the other hand, the Peoples Temple could not achieve the sort of political victory which would have been the goal of a warring sect. Since revolutionary war involves a struggle with an established political order in unfolding historical time, revolutionaries can only attain immortality in the wide-scale victory of the revolution over the "forces of reaction." Ironically, as Lifton pointed out, even the initial political and military victory of the revolutionary forces does not end the search for immortality: even in victory, revolution can only be sustained through diffusion of its principles and goals. But as Max Weber observed, in the long run, it seems impossible to maintain the charismatic enthusiasm of revolution; more pragmatic concerns come to the fore, and as the ultimate ends of revolution are faced off against everyday life and its demands, the quest for immortality fades, and the immortality of the revolutionary moment is replaced by the myth of a grand revolutionary past.

The Peoples Temple could not begin to achieve revolutionary immortality in historical time, for it could not even pretend to achieve any victory against its enemies. If it had come to a pitched battle, the Jonestown defenders—like the Symbionese Liberation Army against the Los Angeles Police Department S.W.A.T. (strategic weapons and tactics) Team—would have been wiped out.

But the Peoples Temple could create a kind of "immortality" which is really not a possibility for political revolutionaries. They could abandon apocalyptic hell by the act of mass suicide. This would shut out the opponents of the Temple: they could not be the undoing of what was already undone, and there could be no recriminations against the dead. It could also achieve the other-worldly salvation Jones had promised his more religious followers. Mass suicide united the divergent public threads of meaningful existence at Jonestown—those of political revolution and religious salvation. It was an awesome vehicle for a powerful statement of collective solidarity by the true believers among the people of Jonestown—that they would rather die together than have the life that was created together subjected to gradual decimation and dishonor at the hands of authorities regarded as illegitimate.

Most warring sects reach a grisly end: occasionally, they achieve martyrdom, but if they lack a constituency, their extermination is used by the state as proof of its monopoly on the legitimate use of force. "Revolutionary" suicide is a victory by comparison. The event can be drawn upon for moral didactics, but this cannot erase the stigma that Jonestown implicitly places on the world that its members left behind. Nor can the state punish the dead who are guilty, among other things, of murdering a U.S. Congressman, three newsmen, a Concerned Relative, and how ever many Jonestown residents that did not willingly commit suicide. Though they paid the total price of death for their ultimate commitment, and though they achieved little except perhaps sustenance of their own collective sense of honor, still those who won this hollow victory cannot have it taken away from them. In the absence of retribution, the state search for living guilty, as well as the widespread outcry against "cults," takes on the character of scapegoating. Those most responsible are beyond the reach of the law: unable to escape the hell of their own lives by creating an other-worldly existence on earth, they instead sought their "immortality" in death, and left it to others to ponder the apocalypse which they have unveiled.

4

The Religious Use of Drugs

Because the peoples of the world have such a myriad of uses for and attitudes toward what we call "drugs," it is impossible to define the term to the satisfaction of all. In the West, for example, chemical substances are prescribed to alleviate disease, but they are also used, often illegally, to provide "kicks" for the user; in many non-Western societies religious specialists utilize these materials as a vehicle for entry into the realm of the supernatural. Perhaps Marston Bates has most correctly defined the term, as "almost all materials taken for other than nutritional reasons" (1971: 113). Using this definition, one can count an extraordinary number of substances as falling into the category of "drugs."

Every culture, whatever the level of technological accomplishment, has an inventory of drugs and a medical system. The use of drugs is so ancient that Weston La Barre has posited the theory that shamanism itself developed from the use of hallucinogens (1972). The aim of this chapter is to describe the religious functions of drugs. This purpose almost totally eliminates the role of drugs in the West, where they are either medicinal or used for pleasure. At varying periods in Western history, most recently in the social ferment

Zapotec mask representing life and death, from Oaxaca, Mexico.

of the 1960s, drug usage was proclaimed by some people to have religious overtones, but few fool themselves today by believing that drugs provide the taker with a religious experience. Hedonism and escapism leading to addiction are the most prominent characteristics of Western drug use, and pose immense problems for governments that recognize the changing values that have encouraged the availability of illicit drugs. Certainly anthropologists have found the pleasure and escape motivation for drug use in non-Western societies as well, but the interrelationship of drugs and religion is dominant in traditional societies, where specialists such as shamans utilize plant and animal substances to contact the spirit world. Cross-cultural comparison demonstrates not only that drugs are perceived differently but also that they may actually have different effects on the users from one society to the next (despite having identical chemical makeup). Indeed, physiological and psychological reactions to drugs vary among individuals in the same society, a phenomenon that is often explained in terms of supernatural intervention.

Because most of us know little of the scientific properties of drugs, it is worthwhile to categorize them as to their effects on users. Lewis Lewin, the famous German toxicologist, whose drug classification is still basically sound and continues to be used by pharmacologists, offered the following categories (after Lewin as quoted by Bates [1971]: 115–16):

I. *Euphoria:* sedatives which reduce mental activity and induce mental and physical comfort, such as morphine, cocaine and the like.

II. *Phantastica:* hallucinogens, bringing on visions and illusions which vary greatly in chemical composition, but may be followed by unconsciousness or other symptoms of altered brain states. This group includes: mescal buttons, hashish and its source, marijuana.

III. *Inebriantia:* drugs which produce an initial phase of cerebral excitation followed by a state of depression which sometimes leads to unconsciousness. Chloroform, alcohol, ether, and others are members of this group.

IV. *Hypnotica:* sedatives or sleep producers such as chloral, sulphonol and some recent synthetic barbiturates.

V. *Excitania:* mental stimulants today referred to as analeptics. Coffee, tea, betel, and tobacco; that is, all plants containing caffeine, nicotine and the like.

Today we would add a sixth category to the above—the tranquilizers, sometimes termed "ataraxics." In reality none are new drugs; rather, they are relatively newly discovered.

Interestingly, none of the first five categories, indeed, even the sixth (ataraxics), was unknown to so-called primitive people. Although the history of the use of these drugs is so ancient as to make attempts at tracing their origins academic exercises, it wasn't until the development of synthetics, prompted by the shortages of natural products during World War II, that hunting and gathering societies knew of and used the same basic chemical substances of medicines as modern technological cultures. For their knowledge of the chemical properties of the plants and animals in their environments, modern man's debt to "primitive man" is great.

The focus of drug use in traditionally based non-Western cultures is on the religious specialist, particularly the shaman, whose duty it is to control the spirit world for the benefit of the members of his society. Of all the categories of drugs, it is the hallucinogens, Lewin's "phantastica," that command our attention, for it is these psychotropic plant and animal substances that provide the shamans with their visions of the supernatural realm. Importantly, what one society considers to be real or unreal is not always shared by another society. Michael Harner's article in this chapter demonstrates, for example, that the Jívaro of the Ecuadorian Amazon consider reality to be what is found in the hallucinogenic state that results from drinking a tea made from the Banisteriopsis vine; the non-hallucinogenic, ordinary state is considered to be an illusion. Indeed, some drugs not considered hallucinogens in Western pharmacology do cause a visionary state; such is the case of the Warao shamans' use of tobacco. The point is that whether we agree or not with the folk categories of drugs in other societies, the mainspring of shamanistic power is centered on drugs that produce visual hallucinations as well as hallucinations of the other senses.

The shamanistic use of a variety of hallucinogenic drugs for trance inducement has not in itself guaranteed that a shaman's patient would recover, or that an enemy would suffer. To this end many other, non-hallucinogenic drugs and practices have also been used, some of which involved effective chemical properties or constituted successful non-drug techniques, such as the sucking-out of evil forces. Even substances having only inert chemicals were often effective in the hands of the shaman. Surely, other reasons must be offered for those successes. The illnesses of non-Western traditional societies have sometimes been described as being due to imbalances or disruptions of the patients' social environment. Physical and mental illnesses are difficult to separate, particularly in groups where belief systems are shared by a high percentage of the population. The treatment offered by shamans is relatively standard and almost always considered correct by patients, as well as by their families and friends, who are often present for the curing process and ceremony. The anxiety of the patient, on the one hand, and the confidence of the shaman, on the other, work to develop a level of suggestibility that literally sets the stage for effective treatment. Shamans, with their secret formulas, chants, and personal contact and control over spirit helpers—knowledge and power the patient does not possess—appear omnipotent and inordinately powerful. The encouragement and support of family and friends in a familiar environment all count toward the eventual cure. Westerners have learned much from shamanistic treatment, for it treats the physical and the psychological, both of which are irrevocably intertwined with the supernatural causes of illness.

The first three articles in this chapter were chosen because each one focuses on a different aspect of drug use in traditional societies. Francis Huxley takes a broad approach to the subject, discussing the general use of drugs in primitive societies. Furst and Coe's work on "Ritual Enemas" is an ethnohistorical reconstruction of Maya drug usage through an analysis of their pottery. In "The Sound of Rushing Water," Michael Harner offers an insight to Jívaro reality, a state that can be achieved only through consumption of the hallucinogenic tea, natema. Finally, in the fourth article, Raziel Abelson, Allen Ginsberg, and Michael Wyschogrod, as members of a symposium on drugs, demonstrate that the functions of hallucinogenic drugs in the West are highly disputed and draw attention to the changes in Western attitudes toward drugs in the 1960s and today.

References Cited

Bates, Marston
  1971 *Gluttons and Libertines: Human Problems of Being Natural.* New York: Vintage Books.

La Barre, Weston
  1972 "Hallucinogens and the Shamanistic Origins of Religion." In Peter T. Furst, ed., *Flesh of the Gods: The Ritual Use of Hallucinogens*, pp. 261–78. New York: Praeger.

Wilbert, Johannes
  1972 "Tobacco and Shamanistic Ecstasy Among the Warao Indians of Venezuela." In Peter T. Furst, ed., *Flesh of the Gods: The Ritual Use of Hallucinogens*, pp. 55–83. New York: Praeger.

Drugs

Francis Huxley

Field workers' interest in religious specialists inevitably drew anthropologists' attention to the religious use of drugs. The important role of drugs in human life, particularly in aboriginal South America where they are used in the most traditional manner, has prompted Marston Bates to refer to us as Homo medicans, *man the drug taker. His definition of drugs as almost all materials taken for other than nutritional reasons may be vague, but it does demonstrate the extraordinary variety of substances that are eaten, drunk, smoked, chewed, or rubbed on the skin but lack food value as their primary function (1971: 112–13). Francis Huxley's article discusses uses of drugs the world over, but focuses on such religious purposes as curing illnesses of the soul and body, divining, gaining supernatural knowledge, and contacting spirits. Huxley argues that drugs used in many religious rites tend to be hallucinogenic rather than those that suppress mental and physical activity. Unlike users of hallucinogens in contemporary society, however, primitive groups have long recognized the need for a ritual setting to channel the dangerous forces contained in drugs.*

Reprinted from Richard Cavendish, ed., *Man, Myth and Magic* (London, 1970), Vol. 5, pp. 711–16, by permission of the author and BPCC/Phoebus Publishing.

THE POET BAUDELAIRE DESCRIBED DRUGS WHICH affect the mind as "artificial paradises." The phrase is apt and Lewis Lewin, the German biochemist, repeated it in his pioneering study of these drugs (*Phantastica*, 1924), where he divided paradise into categories: five of them in all, the paradises of narcosis, stimulation, euphoria, intoxication and hallucination. More simply we might say: of dreaming sleep, energetic wakefulness, well-being, drunkenness and the inspired imagination.

In palmistry, a certain small line near the bottom edge of the palm is called the paradise line. Some people, however, call it the poison line, because it indicates the capacity to enjoy a private and rarefied pleasure which in large doses cuts a man off from reality and infects him with an unattainable hope. A substance known as a drug in the pejorative sense of that word also has the characteristic of being paradisiacal and poisonous, as though it were one product of the serpent coiled about the Tree of Life.

One cannot read widely about drugs these days without coming across persistent references to the "drug problem." Drugs are indeed a problem in that they are addictive and encourage strange forms of narcissism which, though they may end fatally, are still attempts to regain paradise. The desire to do so is one of the fundamental ambitions of human nature which nearly every religion encourages, and this illuminates the drug problem from another aspect. If drugs can be used to enter paradise, what are the uses of paradise itself?

Drugs are used the world over, sometimes for entertainment, often for therapy or as a religious observation. Thus the soma plant celebrated in the early Vedic hymns of the East gave such bliss to those who took its juices that it was regarded as a divinity, and the visionary worlds of splendour praised by its devotees are certainly descriptions of the images which it induced. Opinions are divided as to what plant soma was originally; at one time it was thought to be a species of either *Asclepias* or of *Sarcostemma*, though it has recently been identified as *Amanita muscaria*, the fly agaric.

The use of this toadstool and of other hallucinogenic (hallucination-producing) mushrooms may have been much more widespread in the past than we realize, and its effects quite possibly helped to give form to a number of traditional descriptions of heaven. Indeed, the most famous mysteries of antiquity, those of Eleusis, may have used the fly agaric in order to initiate the worshippers into a realization of the divine, which could well account for the veneration in which the mysteries were held. In Mexico before and after the Spanish Conquest several plants were held sacred because of their illuminating properties, ranging from the peyote cactus from which mescalin is derived to a species of *ipomea* containing a relative of lysergic acid (LSD); the *psilocybe* mushroom which was called *teonanactl* or "god's flesh," whose active principle is psilocybine, and *Datura stramonium* or thornapple with its scopolamine and atropine.

Such plants were used to cure illnesses of the soul and of the body, to divine the future and to gain a sense of supernatural knowledge. In South America other plants are used for similar purposes: one Brazilian curer has tracked down some 80 such plants in his own country, including a hallucinatory tree-toadstool. These plants include lianas like *Banisteria caapi*, peppers like *Piptadenia*, cocaine in the Andes, and at least one hallucinogenic animal, a caterpillar found inside bamboo stems.

In Africa, Asia, Siberia and Australia the list of plants which produce psychotropic (mind-changing) effects is long, and where no such plant is available alcohol may be used instead. Modern pharmacology has added to the number of psychotropic substances with highly potent and dangerous derivatives of opium, with anaesthetics, synthetic narcotics, tranquillizers—the original one being a synthetic based on the active principle of *Rauwolfia*, a plant used for centuries in India to calm the mind—pep pills, hallucinogens, and others. However, no modern doctor considers such substances to be sacred, as they would be amongst traditional cultures and as they are, up to a point, among those who use these products for their own enjoyment. This fact in itself has much to do with the existence of a drug problem.

The Religious Use of Drugs

The widespread use of drugs around the world, and especially in our society, makes it plain that man is a discontented animal beset by psychological and physical troubles, by boredom and spiritual ambitions. He uses drugs to relieve pain and illness, and also to change his entire way of looking at things. In religious language, human nature is always wishing to transcend its usual limitations. For waking consciousness is by no means the only kind which it is possible or desirable to experience, and other states can be reached by the use of psychophysical techniques and also by drugs.

Because they change the degree of alertness of the mind in one way or another, it seems probable that drugs interfere with the sleep cycle, either by allowing one to dream while still awake or by using the force of dreams to power action. It seems hardly credible, however, that maté tea, made from the leaf of a South American shrub and containing caffeine, could ever be used to induce trance. Tea, which contains tannin as well as caffeine in quite large quantities, certainly does not have this effect normally, and it was originally celebrated in India and China for its refreshing qualities that allowed the mind to stay awake during meditation. By itself maté could not bring about an oracular state of trance—as it does amongst Indians still living in the Mato Grosso—unless its actions reinforce a process already set in motion by the seer and, by this working together of a psychological technique with a physiological agent, bring about a state of dissociation in which the mind finds a new faculty of expression.

The religious use of drugs, in fact, usually accompanies the practice of shamanism, though shamanism often does without drugs. Shamanism is a technique by which a man, and sometimes a woman, prepares himself by singing, dancing, training and long periods of seclusion during which he meditates, for an influx of untoward inspiration that can carry him into the world of spirits where events on earth are ordained and carried out. It is often a hereditary calling, but may equally well be embraced by those who have either a surplus of mental energy or who have suffered from what we would call a nervous complaint of some severity. Such unsatisfied or unbalanced states of mind are continually looking for a resolution of their frustrations and ambitions, and they do so by using traditional methods which articulate their powers coherently.

Drugs can help to do this because their effects are so similar to those produced by other methods of shamanistic training. An instructive case concerns tobacco, which like maté was used for getting into trance. Throughout the Americas this plant was used much as we use it today, for pleasure and to aid concentration, though it was sometimes accounted a fault in an ordinary man if he smoked it in private. But its most significant use was by shamans who smoked large amounts at one sitting to achieve their ecstatic experiences. The combination of tobacco smoke and overbreathing (causing oxygen intoxication) produces that kind of giddiness and nausea which most people experience with their first cigarette. Giddiness is one of the universal symptoms of ecstasy—the word giddy comes from the Old English *gidig*, meaning possessed by a god—and it is by entering into this giddiness and following down the physiological pathways which it opens up that a shaman is able to dissociate himself from his normal waking self and arrive at a place in his mind where all is certain and a quite different conscious process begins.

What such people have done is to use the forces within the paradisiacal experience for definite ends. The lack of such ends in modern society, as has already been implied, is one reason why we have a drug problem: without a ritual support the mind is often not strong enough to resist the effects of a drug, and so loses its sense of direction. When we consider the power of some drugs, this is not surprising. The incredibly small quantity of 100 microgrammes of lysergic acid is enough to bring about a psychedelic experience in which the mind is profoundly altered in its normal functioning and of which it previously had but the barest suspicion. Indeed many investigators have been so taken aback by these changes that they prefer to call the drug a psychosomimetic, one which produces a condition resembling madness.

The purpose of a ritual setting for the taking of a drug is to prevent madness, by directing the energies which the drug releases into a number of specific channels, and to put paradise into relation with objects in the outside world by establishing a dogmatic plan within the imagination, through

which social events can be seen as psychological ones, psychological as physical ones, and physical ones as spiritual.

By such a method even opium, the grandmother of all narcotics, has occasionally been used not merely to enjoy its sumptuous and pearly visions but to carry out a conscious intention. Such is the habit of shamans in parts of Southeast Asia, who take opium to increase the ecstatic effects of dancing and through them to send their spirits upon a supernatural adventure for the curing of illness or the foretelling of the future. The soporific effect of opium is such, however, that its devotees are much more liable to become physically passive, which must be why it is so seldom used in an active and practical manner. It is true that opium is used in the East for conviviality, but its solitary use is difficult to control. Coleridge, who first took laudanum, a derivative of opium, to dull a particularly ferocious toothache and eventually became addicted to it, did manage to write at least one great poem under its influence: or perhaps we should say that *Kubla Khan* composed itself when his mind, still active in its poetic function, directed the opium into a creative activity. But such feats are rare, for the mind's ability to hold its own against the sweetly insidious effects of opium in large quantities is limited, and the drug soon brings about that passive state in which, as Henri Michaux, the modern French poet, has said, "One no longer dreams, one is dreamed."

"O just, subtle and all-conquering opium!" cried de Quincey, author of *Confessions of an English Opium Eater* (1822), who took laudanum as an elixir for his neurasthenia and declared it to be the centre of the true religion of which he was the high priest. But religions have hells as well as heavens, and the last stages of his addiction were marked, as they always are, by psychic and physical horrors from which he at last managed to free himself. What is this paradise, as Baudelaire said of hashish, which one buys at the price of one's eternal damnation? But this progression from paradise to the inferno allows one to draw a most interesting parallel between the possessive effects of a drug and those of a spirit, as in Voodoo.

In Voodoo ceremonies we might say that a pact has been entered into with any one of the many gods or spirits of the Haitian pantheon, which are called *loa*. The worshipper is possessed by the loa in such a way that he no longer has conscious control of his actions, and has no memory of what passed when he was possessed. The loa who rides him, as the phrase goes, always has a definite way of behaving—a stereotype, we might say, or schema—and this ability to act out the character of a loa is only achieved after training and initiation. Those who feel the influx of divine energy before they are initiated into Voodoo suffer not only from unfortunate accidents but often from manic outbursts ending in madness. It is the business of Voodoo to avoid this outcome and to see that its initiates can become possessed by this energy and still remain sane.

A Pact with the Devil

We might thus call an addict one who has been possessed by a drug after a private initiation which has no aim other than the desire continually to be possessed, unlike a Voodoo ceremony with its definite beginning and end. The addict cannot but wish his experience will continue for ever, even if he realizes that his body will disintegrate under the impact of the drug and that he then can no longer call his soul his own. The narcotic drugs, which slow down physical activity, and the excitants like amphetamine which speed it up, are particularly apt to bring about this state of living on borrowed time; this is presumably not only because they bring out long-term metabolic changes but also because the will cannot detach itself from the pleasures it seeks.

The question of whether it is ethical to take drugs is a difficult one to answer. They have been and still are being used as an aid to meditation, but the masters of this art are unanimous in condemning them, since they tend to inflame the imagination and give it a wrong idea of its powers. From his own experience, Jean Cocteau has said that no one becomes an opium addict unless he has made a pact with it: a pact in which he dedicates his will to the power of the drug. There is no doubt that the mythology surrounding drug-taking reflects certain basic notions about black magic for this reason. Black magic is rightly regarded as a dangerous pastime because it provides immediate gains without immediate payment: it is a pact with the Devil, who comes later when it suits him and presents a

bill on which are written the ominous words, One Soul.

What does it mean, to enter into a pact with the Devil? Freud was much interested in the subject and wrote a study of it at the time when he was still taking cocaine, which he did for ten years. The traditional reasons for such a pact include the obtaining of wealth, of power over men and Nature, and over the hearts of women. But Freud concluded from the case he studied that the central reason was to overcome depression and to find a father-substitute. About cocaine he wrote: "One senses an increase of self-control and feels more vigorous and more capable of work," and he suggested that its effects were due, not to direct stimulation but to the removal of anxiety symptoms, which produced a return to a state of normal euphoria. Anxiety has to do with the superego in his system, and we can enlarge this description by remarking that by removing the "censor" cocaine also removes anxiety. Because of this cocaine may have been an indispensable tool for Freud during his self-analysis: it allowed him to follow the lines of his reasoning into the subconscious without his mental censor putting up a resistance. That Freud escaped from addiction while one of his friends, to whom he had recommended it, died from its effects, suggests that he only did so because he had found a method by which the effects of the drug became subservient to the force of his intellectual drive. He had created a special form of ritual.

Separating Mind from Body

Without this drive cocaine is undoubtedly a danger, as we may see from the religious taking of coca amongst the Kogi of Colombia. This tribe uses it ceremonially to learn the lengthy genealogies and liturgies of their worship, and to fill their minds with the proper religious awe and sense of significance. Coca however has the unfortunate effect of making its takers impotent after a while, and the Kogi are suspicious of their womenfolk (who are not allowed to chew it) and so inefficient as farmers that their children are undernourished. Ironically, the atheists of the tribe who have dropped out of the religion altogether are much healthier and happier, though their neighbours scorn them for losing their chance of immortality. This petrifying effect of coca, even with a religious system to direct it, is certainly partly caused by the fact that the Kogi way of life is beset on all sides by the creole population and has withdrawn into a state of apathy.

Coca is used elsewhere in the Andes to ward off hunger and fatigue, and it does so by numbing these sensations and dissociating the mind from anxieties arising in the body. But anxiety may persist even if its symptoms disappear with the use of a drug. These symptoms emerge again after a long time in an even more disagreeable form, as the nightmare effects of addiction show. When at such a time the use of the drug is stopped, this anxiety must be at least one of the constituents of the most unpleasant withdrawal symptoms.

Attacking the Self

The drugs used in other religious rites tend to be hallucinogenic rather than narcotic or stupefying, and these have a quite different effect upon anxiety. Common to plants with such different active principles as *Banisteria*, *Amanita* and *Datura* is the production of a sudden and violent surge of energy with visions in which terror and splendour may be equally present. The Viking berserkers seem to have used *Amanita* to endow themselves with a blind and warlike frenzy no opponent could withstand, a frenzy that might last more than a day and after which they sank into a long torpor of exhaustion.

In South America the Indians who take *Banisteria* and other plants fall victim to a similar frenzy (though they do not use it when on war parties), and European travellers who have tried the drug in their company report experiencing the traditional visions, amongst which are those of beasts of prey about to tear them into pieces. Such drugs seem to work by putting psychological anxieties into touch with the musculature, and what is dissociated is the ego from the imagination rather than, as in narcotics, the imagination from anxiety. There may be a connection between the fact that hallucinogens are not physically addictive and that they do not inhibit anxiety.

All these drugs, however, can be used for delicate purposes as well as frenzied ones. One must remember that all shamanistic traditions speak of an initiatory experience in which the body is felt to be torn apart, after which a crystalline body is given by the spirits. Both the dismemberment and the illumination of the body are commonly felt under hallucinogens, even if in a mild fashion, and one can understand dismemberment as the outcome of a drug-induced dissociation in which the normal persona or expression of the personality, is forced to give up its defensive reactions. What is known as a "bad trip" is caused by the anxiety which the approach of such a psychological dismemberment evokes, and which generates an increasing feeling of loss and horror when it cannot be properly discharged. From all accounts a really bad trip has certain similarities to a schizophrenic attack, and hospitals report many instances of bad trips which last for days or even months. The taking of tranquillizers is certainly one way of bringing such an episode to an end, but the traditional method is to accept the attack which the drug makes on the self without fear, an acceptance which transforms anxiety into knowledge and makes it give up its energy to a higher faculty.

But no two drugs attack the self in quite the same way, and they activate different parts of the same underlying process and give rise to different types of anxiety. The drug found in *Amanita* seems to be particularly effective in putting the motor system into spasm, and the shamans who use it must go through a long education in this experience and have grappled with the startling visions it produces before they can master its immediate effects and use them according to their will. *Datura* also activates a sense of physical power together with a pyschic ambition that may lead a man so far out of his normal range that a spasm of timidity at the wrong moment may leave him stranded upon an ungovernable activity. Different is the effect of the *psilocybe* mushroom which clinically is said to be that of depersonalization. But there are two sides of every coin, and what is depersonalization to one man may be dematerialization to another: tribal practitioners in fact call upon this effect when they wish to penetrate material obstacles, to free consciousness from its bodily entanglements and allow it to inhabit bodies other than its own.

Drug of the Aztecs

Peyote traditionally used has yet other consequences. It was one of the first hallucinogens to be experimented with in Europe, and is famous for its visions of fantastic and grotesque architecture, of prodigious landscapes and giant figures striding about or petrified into ancient statuary, and of jewels shining with abundant colour. All these visions occur without apparent reason, and the Indians phrase this by saying that peyote is a power in itself that works from the outside, a teacher who can show a man the right way to live and answer his questions by giving him an experience to live through.

This quality of the peyote experience allows one to qualify the remark of Michaux that under such drugs one does not dream, one is dreamed. If used correctly peyote has the power of personifying a dream in such a way that it allows the dreamer to keep some part of his self-awareness intact and still questioning. The consequence of searching for a meaning within the visions which inhabit one is that they become increasingly full of meaning themselves.

Peyote is of particular interest because it is the sacrament of the Native American Church, a religion based upon Indian practices and having Christianity for its justification. It was used by the Aztecs for divinatory purposes, and by the Tarahumara and Huichot of northern Mexico as the body of divinity on which all their beliefs centred. This religion was picked up by the Plains Indians at the time of their defeat by the whites and used to rally the wisdom of the Indian past to cope with the degrading changes that overcame them. It was in fact a type of cult such as we often find springing into existence when old ways of life are being destroyed by a powerful and technically more advanced culture, and it is also the only surviving one of several such cults which arose in the Plains.

The Search for Power

The drug problem in the West should probably be seen in the same light: the popularity of drugs is at least partly due to the very rapid changes now occurring in our society. Drugs have always been used to search for power, a power which can be used to enlarge the capacity of the imagination and to bring about change in society. When society itself changes, drugs give a certain kind of life to the imagination which is being stripped of its ancient forms, and a confidence in its ability to live in a strange world. Cannabis has certainly been used in this way from time to time: in Jamaica, for instance, the Rastafari smoke it both for religious and political reasons in the hope that they may soon return to their promised land—Abyssinia, where the Lion of Judah still reigns. Half a century ago or more, cannabis was also the motive cause for a new religion being set up by the Baluba of the Congo: they destroyed their fetish houses, and proclaimed the drug to be a power under which they could live in perpetual friendship and protected from calamity. The drinking of alcohol was forbidden, and those who had committed misdeeds were condemned to smoke a number of pipes of cannabis in order to reform their misconceptions.

Wherever a drug is used by a religion to gain a view and foretaste of divinity, it is treated as though it were a god itself. "We have drunk Soma, we have become immortals, we have arrived at the light, we have reached the gods: what power has malevolence over us now, what can the perfidy of mortals do to us, O Immortal?" So runs one of the hymns of the *Rig Veda*, one of the sacred texts of the East. Opium has been called the hand of God and anchor of salvation, though Cocteau has remarked that it resembles religion as an illusionist resembles Jesus. Tobacco has been called the blessed plant, honour of the earth and gift from Olympus, and both wine and beer have been similarly praised down the centuries. "Our glass was the full moon, the wine is the sun. If the grave is moistened with such a wine, the dead man will rediscover his soul and the corpse will revive," said Ibn al Farid, the medieval Arabian poet. But the wine he talks of here is that of the Spirit, which also descended upon the Apostles at Pentecost so that they spoke with tongues and were accused of being drunk.

A drug is nothing unless it kindles the spirit in a man, though this spirit may be thought of as divine or demoniacal according to predilection. Whichever it may be, the spirit is not man's possession but a gift made to him, and as a gift it has a nature and a morality of its own which must be both wrestled with and obeyed if it is not to bring harm to its host. Every religion has its own way of experiencing and ordering this power, and their often stringent ritual requirements are the product of a long experience in bringing the spirit in touch with the world of men. The religious taking of drugs is one particular example of this: it says plainly enough that amateurism in these matters does little but create a problem, and that if the mind is to reach beyond itself by the use of a drug it must be placed in the service of an idea and a method that makes for wisdom and communion rather than folly and isolation.

Ritual Enemas

Peter T. Furst
Michael D. Coe

As we have seen in earlier articles, many of the world's cultures contain religious specialists and lay people who routinely undergo, for ritual purposes, an altering of their normal state of consciousness. Although this state can be obtained by non-drug related methods, it is not uncommon to find ethnographic accounts of drugs being used to enhance and quicken an altered state of consciousness. This article is about the religious use of various psychoactive substances among the Mayan Indians of Central Mexico. The authors note that although hallucinogenic mushrooms, morning glories, and other psychedelic plants were known and used by the Maya, yet another substance seems to have been employed—intoxicating enemas. This phenomenon quite clearly appears in Maya art as early as the first millennium A.D.; it is curious that it has not been described in the literature over the years. Ritual enemas were well known in South America, where rubber-tree sap was used for bulbed syringes. Furst and Coe reason that a rectal infusion of intoxicants could result in a more quickly and more radically changed state of consciousness, with fewer negative side effects.

Reprinted with permission from *Natural History*, Vol. 86, no. 3 (1977), pp. 88–91. Copyright the American Museum of Natural History, 1977.

WHEN THE SPANIARDS CONQUERED MEXICO IN the sixteenth century, they were at once fascinated and repelled by the Indians' widespread use not only of alcoholic beverages but also of numerous hallucinogenic plants.

From the Spaniards' point of view, however, both served the same purpose—to conjure up visions of demons and devils and to take imbibers from their daily life to supernatural realms.

Distillation was unknown in the New World before the conquest, but Mesoamerican Indians were making, as they still do, a variety of intoxicating ritual drinks, principally by fermenting cactus fruit; agave, or century plant, sap; or maize kernels. Among the Maya, the ritual beverage was balche, made from fermented honey mixed with a bark extract from the balche tree, *Lonchocarpus longistylus*. These concoctions were all taken orally.

But according to a Spanish writer known only as the Anonymous Conqueror, the Huastec people of northern Veracruz and southern Tamaulipas had pulque (fermented agave sap) "squirted into their breech," meaning that they used intoxicating enemas. There are indications that the Aztecs, as well as several other Mesoamerican groups, also followed this practice.

Mesoamerican Indians generally used liquor only on sacred occasions, when, according to such sixteenth-century observers as Bishop Diego de Landa of Yucatán, the Indians often drank themselves into states approaching oblivion. Similarly, the use of many botanical hallucinogens, first described by Fray Bernardino de Sahagún and his contemporaries, was strictly limited to occasions when direct communication with the otherworld was required. Today, the best known of these is peyote, *Lophophora williamsii*, a small, spineless cactus native to the north-central desert of Mexico and southern Texas. The plant now serves as sacrament for 225,000 adherents of the Native American

Church and also plays an important role in the religious life of the Huichol Indians of western Mexico. Before the conquest, peyote was widely traded throughout Mexico, where the Aztec priests numbered it among their important magical and medicinal plants.

At the time of the conquest the seeds of the white-flowered morning glory *Turbina corymbosa* were a widely used hallucinogen. In 1960, Albert Hofmann, the Swiss discoverer of LSD (a synthetic hallucinogenic drug), isolated the active alkaloids in this morning glory species and a related species, the purple- or blue-flowered *Ipomoea violacea*, and found them to be lysergic acid derivatives closely resembling LSD-25. The latter species is often referred to as "heavenly blue" in the United States.

Mushrooms also played an important role in preconquest Mesoamerican Indian life. Certain species, most of them now known to belong to the genus *Psilocybe*, were perhaps the most extraordinary natural hallucinogens in use in Mexico. The Aztecs called them *teonanácatl*, or "God's flesh." Psychedelic fungi were widely employed in Mexico when the Spaniards came, and their use in divination and supernatural curing survives to this day in central Mexico, as well as in the state of Oaxaca (*see* "Drugs, Chants, and Magic Mushrooms," *Natural History*, December 1975). The Indians even used tobacco to induce ecstatic trance states, which the Spanish only saw as diabolic communication.

While Spanish writers of the sixteenth and seventeenth centuries left us relatively detailed accounts of the use of hallucinogens in central Mexico, there is little mention of this intriguing aspect of native religion among the Maya, who lived farther to the south. The silence is the more puzzling because we have circumstantial evidence of a very early cult of sacred mushrooms in the Maya highlands of Guatemala and the adjacent lowlands, in the form of more than 250 mushroom effigies made of carved stone, many dating to the first millennium B.C.

The Maya were an integral part of Mesoamerican civilization and shared many of its basic assumptions about the nature of the universe and the relationship of humans to the natural and supernatural environment. Like the central Mexicans, they divided the cosmos into upperworlds and underworlds with their respective gods, believed in the cyclical destruction and regeneration of the earth and its inhabitants, and followed the 260-day ritual calendar.

In view of these many similarities, as the Maya scholar J. Eric Thompson has written, it was hard to believe that the Maya did not use intoxicating plants. Thompson searched the pages of sacred traditional books of the Yucatec Maya, set down in the European alphabet in the colonial period, for hints of ecstatic visionary trances through which the priests made their prophecies. In the *Books of Chilam Balam* (jaguar-priest) of Tizimín and Mani, he found mention of trancelike states but no hint whatever of any hallucinogenic plants. He also discovered scattered scenes in Maya relief sculpture that suggested visionary experiences characteristic of hallucinogenic ritual.

This is slim evidence, however, compared with the data from central Mexico, and some Maya scholars are not convinced that the Maya practiced the kinds of ecstatic shamanistic rituals or vision quests with botanical hallucinogens that played so pervasive a role in central Mexico, or among the Zapotecs, Mixtecs, Mazatecs, and other peoples of Oaxaca.

The silence of Spanish colonial writers on the subject of hallucinogenic plants or rituals among the Maya accords well with the view, once widely held among scholars, that the Maya were quite unlike their Mexican contemporaries in temperament, being less preoccupied with warfare and the Dionysian excesses than with the contemplative interpretation of the heavens and the passage of time. But the discovery at Bonampak, Chiapas, of mural paintings that depict, among other events, a fierce battle among Maya warriors, indicate that this traditional view is very wide of the mark.

As specialists have more closely examined Maya art and iconography in recent years, they have accumulated increasing evidence that among the classic Maya, ecstatic ritual was important. One suggestion for this is that some of the major Mexican hallucinogens—among them the morning glories and the hallucinogenic mushroom *Stropharia cubensis*—occur in the Maya country. These and other psychedelic plants were undoubtedly known to the Maya.

Had Maya specialists looked more closely at the earliest dictionaries of the Quiché and Cakchiquel languages, compiled in the first centuries after the conquest of highland Guatemala, they would have discovered mention of several varieties of mushrooms with hallucinogenic properties. One is called *xibalbaj okox* (*xibalba* means "underworld," or "land of the dead," and *okox*, "mushroom"), said by the sixteenth-century compiler to give those who eat it visions of hell. If the association of this species with the Maya underworld left any doubt of its psychedelic nature, it is dispelled by a later reference to the same species in Fray Tomas Coto's dictionary of the Cakchiquel language. According to him, *xibalbaj okox* was also called *k'aizalah okox*, which translates as the "mushroom that makes one lose one's judgment." Still another fungus, *k'ekc'un*, had inebriating characteristics, and another, *muxan okox*, apparently brought on insanity or caused one to "fall into a swoon."

We have recently come across a wholly unexpected use of psychoactive substances among the Maya—the ritual use of intoxicating enemas, unmistakably depicted in classic Maya art of the first millennium A.D., but not mentioned either in the colonial or the modern literature. This practice is well documented among the inhabitants of South American tropical forests as well as among the Inca and their contemporaries in the Andes, where archeologists have discovered enema syringes.

Sixteenth-century sources describe the Incas as regularly intoxicating themselves with infusions of *willka*, now known to be the potent hallucinogenic seeds of the acacialike *Anadenanthera colubrina* tree. Lowland Indians also used tobacco enemas.

South American Indians were the first people known to use native rubber tree sap for bulbed enema syringes. While medical enemas had a long history in the Old World, having been used by ancient Sumerians and Egyptians, as well as by Hindus, Arabs, Chinese, Greeks, and Romans, the rubber bulb syringe was unknown in Europe until two centuries after the discovery of the New World.

The native Amerindian enema was distinguished from its Old World counterpart in that its primary purpose was to introduce medicines and intoxicants into the body, while the Old World enema was employed principally to clear the bowels. During the seventeenth and eighteenth centuries, the enema as a relief for constipation, real or imagined, became a craze in Europe—so much so, that Louis XIV had more than 2,000 enemas administered to him during his reign, sometimes

even receiving court functionaries and foreign dignitaries during the procedure.

The wide dissemination of the intoxicating enema in South America suggests the discovery by Indians that the rectal administration of intoxicants could radically alter one's state of consciousness more rapidly, and with fewer undesirable side effects, such as nausea, than oral administration. The physiological reason is simple: Substances injected into the rectum enter the colon, the last segment of the large intestine; the principal function of the large intestine is the reabsorption of liquids into the system and the storage of wastes until they can be evacuated. The absorbed liquid immediately enters the bloodstream, which carries it to the brain. An intoxicant or hallucinogen injected rectally closely resembles an intravenous injection in the rapidity of its effects.

The first evidence that not only the Huastecs, whose language is related to the Maya languages, but also the classic Maya knew of and employed the intoxicating enema came to light this past year through the examination of a painted vase in a private collection in New York. This polychrome jar, with a high, vertical neck and flaring rim, was probably painted in the heavily forested Petén district of northern Guatemala during the classic Maya phase, which dated from the third century A.D. to the first decades of the seventh century. Seven male-female pairs, the women easily distinguished by their robes and long hair, are depicted in two horizontal rows. That one woman is fondling a child suggests a familial setting. The activity being portrayed would have brought blushes to the cheeks of the traditional Maya specialist, for while one man is inserting a syringe into his rectum, this delicate task is being carried out for another male by his consort. One male also has a bulbed enema syringe tucked into his belt.

Nine vases, identical in shape to the actual vessel, are painted between the couples, and painted dots at the mouth of each represents a foaming, fermented liquid that is probably balche, the common alcoholic drink among the Maya at the time of the conquest. We must conclude that the people on the vase are taking intoxicating enemas, a practice previously unrecorded for this culture.

An understanding of the scenes depicted on the Maya vase was only the first link in a chain of iconographic discovery of the Mesoamerican enema phenomenon. Suddenly, several previously enigmatic scenes and objects in classic Maya art had new meaning. A small clay figurine from a burial excavated in 1964 by Mexican archeologists on the island of Jaina, in the Gulf of Campeche, depicts a male in squatting position, his hand reaching back to his rectum. For a long time Maya experts were puzzled because the figure's position seemed to represent defecation. But would the Maya have interred such a scene as an offering to their dead?

A small hole in the anus suggested that a piece was missing—that some small object previously inserted there had either become lost during excavation or had been made of some perishable material, long since decayed. The discovery of the enema vase from the Petén district seems to have solved the riddle. The little Maya was probably not defecating but was in the act of giving himself an enema.

The gods themselves were also depicted as indulging in the enema ritual. One Maya vase has the figures of thirty-one underworld deities painted on it. A naturalistically designed enema syringe dangles from the paw of one of the principal figures. Maya experts did not recognize the significance of the object until they had examined the enema vase in New York. As another example, a polychrome bowl from Yucatán, now in the National Museum of Anthropology in Mexico City, shows a naked being with a pointed head injecting himself with liquid.

The ritual importance of the intoxicating enema is highlighted by the involvement in the rite of one of the greatest underworld deities, an old lord associated with earth, water, and agricultural fertility. The Maya may have believed that this god—now identified by Mayanists only by the letter N, but very likely the same deity as the ancient Yucatecan god Pauhatun—consisted of four parts, each part living in the underworld and supporting the four corners of the earth.

The quadripartite god is depicted on a fine vase in a private collection in Chicago. Each of the four parts has a characteristically chapfallen face. Four young and fetching consorts are apparently preparing each of the god's representations for the enema rite. Enema pots with syringes on top are in front of two of the consorts. The female consorts may well represent the important Mother Goddess

of the Maya, known as Ixchel, as several figurine examples of the god N embracing this goddess have been found.

The same association of the god N, females and enemas is depicted on another pottery vase, with a consort shown standing behind each god representation and untying his loincloth. Again, the same enema pots are in front of the consorts. So often are the pottery forms and syringes encountered together that we must conclude that they were commonly used in the enema rite.

The explicit depiction of enema rituals on Maya vases has led us to take a new look at a hitherto puzzling type of clay figurine from central Veracruz, which also dates from the classic Maya period. Some archeologists have interpreted these curious sculptures as representing human sacrifice. They are usually of males whose facial expressions suggest pleasure or ecstatic trance, not death. Their legs are raised, either draped over a high pillow or some other type of support or else slightly spread, with the feet up in the air. The posture—and the enraptured look—suggest the intoxicating enema. The reclining position also conforms to the Anonymous Conqueror's description of the method of enema intoxication among the Huastecs.

The hallucinogenic, or intoxicating, enema has apparently not disappeared altogether from Middle America. While conducting linguistic research in the Sierra Madre Occidental in western Mexico some years ago, ethnographer Tim Knab was shown a peyote apparatus reportedly used by an elderly woman curer. The bulb was made from a deer's bladder and the tube from the hollow femur of a small deer. The curer prepared peyote by grinding it to a fine pulp and diluting it with water. Instead of taking the peyote by mouth, as for example, the Huichols normally do, either whole or ground (see "An Indian Journey to Life's Source," *Natural History*, April 1973), she injected it rectally, experiencing its effects almost at once while avoiding its bitter and acrid taste and the nausea that even some experienced Indian *peyoteros* continue to feel as they chew the sacred plant.

We do not know what materials the ancient Maya used for their syringes. The deer was sacred to the Maya, as it still is to Indians in western Mexico. Still, to make the transition from contemporary western Mexico to the Maya requires an enormous jump in time and space. Fish bladders and the bones of birds, which are prominent in Maya art, might have served for the syringe, as might rubber from the latex tree, which is native to the Maya region. More important than the precise technology, however, is the discovery that, no less than the simpler folk of the South American tropical rain forests, the creators of the most flamboyant and intellectually advanced native civilization in the New World hit upon the enema as a technique of intoxication or ecstasy—a practical means of ritually altering or transforming the ordinary state of consciousness.

The Sound of Rushing Water

Michael Harner

Amazonian Indians, as in the case of forest dwellers everywhere, have a tremendous depth of understanding of the chemical properties of plants indigenous to their habitats. Extracts of plants are prepared as medicines that are used both in the Western pharmacological sense and in the supernatural sense. Preparations take a variety of forms and range from ebene, *the snuff used by the Yanomamo of Brazil and Venezuela, to the tea-like drink* natema, *used by the Jívaro of Ecuador. Both contain hallucinogenic properties, provide the taker entry into the spirit world, and offer powers otherwise unattainable without ingestion of potent alkaloid compounds. Yet, elsewhere, as among the Warao of South America, non-hallucinogenic drugs such as tobacco are consumed by shamans to achieve a similar ecstatic state, which, as in the case of* ebene *and* natema, *provides visions of spirit helpers and other agents of the supernatural world (Wilbert 1972). Comparisons such as these give anthropologists insight into the importance of shared belief systems and suggestibility. Describing the use of the Banisteriopsis vine by Jívaro shamans, Michael Harner draws on his field data to illustrate the use of the hallucinogenic drink* natema. *Called by a variety of names in other Amazonian societies, this drug gives extraordinary powers to cure or bewitch, and shamans specialize in either one or the other.*

Reprinted with permission from *Natural History*, Vol. 77, no. 6 (June/July 1968), pp. 28–33. Copyright the American Museum of Natural History, 1968.

HE HAD DRUNK, AND NOW HE SOFTLY SANG. Gradually, faint lines and forms began to appear in the darkness, and the shrill music of the *tsentsak*, the spirit helpers, arose around him. The power of the drink fed them. He called, and they came. First, *pangi*, the anaconda, coiled about his head, transmuted into a crown of gold. Then *wampang*, the giant butterfly, hovered above his shoulder and sang to him with its wings. Snakes, spiders, birds, and bats danced in the air above him. On his arms appeared a thousand eyes as his demon helpers emerged to search the night for enemies.

The sound of rushing water filled his ears, and listening to its roar, he knew he possessed the power of *tsungi*, the first shaman. Now he could see. Now he could find the truth. He stared at the stomach of the sick man. Slowly, it became transparent like a shallow mountain stream, and he saw within it, coiling and uncoiling, *makanchi*, the poisonous serpent, who had been sent by the enemy shaman. The real cause of the illness had been found.

The Jívaro Indians of the Ecuadorian Amazon believe that witchcraft is the cause of the vast majority of illnesses and non-violent deaths. The normal waking life, for the Jívaro, is simply "a lie," or illusion, while the true forces that determine daily events are supernatural and can only be seen and manipulated with the aid of hallucinogenic drugs. A reality view of this kind creates a particularly strong demand for specialists who can cross over into the supernatural world at will to deal with the forces that influence and even determine the events of the waking life.

These specialists, called "shamans" by anthropologists, are recognized by the Jívaro as being of two types: bewitching shamans or curing shamans. Both kinds take a hallucinogenic drink, whose Jívaro name is *natema*, in order to enter the supernatural world. This brew, commonly called *yagé*, or *yajé*, in Colombia, *ayahuasca* (Inca "vine of the dead") in Ecuador and Peru, and *caapi* in Brazil, is prepared from segments of a species of the vine *Banisteriopsis*, a genus belonging to the Malpighiaceae. The Jívaro boil it with the leaves of a similar vine, which probably is also a species of *Banisteriopsis*, to produce a tea that contains the powerful hallucinogenic alkaloids harmaline, harmine, d-tetrahydroharmine, and quite possibly dimethyltryptamine (DMT). These compounds have chemical structures and effects similar, but not identical, to LSD, mescaline of the peyote cactus, and psilocybin of the psychotropic Mexican mushroom.

When I first undertook research among the Jívaro in 1956–57, I did not fully appreciate the psychological impact of the *Banisteriopsis* drink upon the native view of reality, but in 1961 I had occasion to drink the hallucinogen in the course of field work with another Upper Amazon Basin tribe. For several hours after drinking the brew, I found myself, although awake, in a world literally beyond my wildest dreams. I met bird-headed people, as well as dragon-like creatures who explained that they were the true gods of this world. I enlisted the services of other spirit helpers in attempting to fly through the far reaches of the Galaxy. Transported into a trance where the supernatural seemed natural, I realized that anthropologists, including myself, had profoundly underestimated the importance of the drug in affecting native ideology. Therefore, in 1964 I returned to the Jívaro to give particular attention to the drug's use by the Jívaro shaman.

The use of the hallucinogenic *natema* drink among the Jívaro makes it possible for almost anyone to achieve the trance state essential for the practice of shamanism. Given the presence of the drug and the felt need to contact the "real," or supernatural, world, it is not surprising that approximately one out of every four Jívaro men is a shaman. Any adult, male or female, who desires to become such a practitioner, simply presents a gift to an already practicing shaman, who administers the *Banisteriopsis* drink and gives some of his own supernatural power—in the form of spirit helpers, or *tsentsak*—to the apprentice. These spirit helpers, or "darts," are the main supernatural forces believed to cause illness and death in daily life. To the non-shaman they are normally invisible, and even shamans can perceive them only under the influence of *natema*.

Shamans send these spirit helpers into the victims' bodies to make them ill or to kill them. At other times, they may suck spirits sent by enemy shamans from the bodies of tribesmen suffering from witchcraft-induced illness. The spirit helpers also form shields that protect their shaman masters from attacks. The following account presents the ideology of Jívaro witchcraft from the point of view of the Indians themselves.

To give the novice some *tsentsak*, the practicing shaman regurgitates what appears to be—to those who have taken *natema*—a brilliant substance in which the spirit helpers are contained. He cuts part of it off with a machete and gives it to the novice to swallow. The recipient experiences pain upon taking it into his stomach and stays on his bed for ten days, repeatedly drinking *natema*. The Jívaro believe they can keep magical darts in their stomachs indefinitely and regurgitate them at will. The shaman donating the *tsentsak* periodically blows and rubs all over the body of the novice, apparently to increase the power of the transfer.

The novice must remain inactive and not engage in sexual intercourse for at least three months. If he fails in self-discipline, as some do, he will not become a successful shaman. At the end of the first month, a *tsentsak* emerges from his mouth. With this magical dart at his disposal, the new shaman experiences a tremendous desire to bewitch. If he casts his *tsentsak* to fulfill this desire, he will become a bewitching shaman. If, on the other hand, the novice can control his impulse and reswallow the first *tsentsak*, he will become a curing shaman.

If the shaman who gave the *tsentsak* to the new man was primarily a bewitcher, rather than a curer, the novice likewise will tend to become a bewitcher. This is because a bewitcher's magical darts have such a desire to kill that their new owner will be strongly inclined to adopt their attitude. One informant said that the urge to kill felt by bewitching shamans came to them with a strength and frequency similar to that of hunger.

Only if the novice shaman is able to abstain from sexual intercourse for five months, will he have the power to kill a man (if he is a bewitcher) or cure a victim (if he is a curer). A full year's abstinence is considered necessary to become a really effective bewitcher or curer.

During the period of sexual abstinence, the new

shaman collects all kinds of insects, plants, and other objects, which he now has the power to convert into *tsentsak*. Almost any object, including living insects and worms, can become a *tsentsak* if it is small enough to be swallowed by a shaman. Different types of *tsentsak* are used to cause different kinds and degrees of illness. The greater the variety of these objects that a shaman has in his body, the greater is his ability.

According to Jívaro concepts, each *tsentsak* has a natural and supernatural aspect. The magical dart's natural aspect is that of an ordinary material object as seen without drinking the drug *natema*. But the supernatural and "true" aspect of the *tsentsak* is revealed to the shaman by taking *natema*. When he does this, the magical darts appear in new forms as demons and with new names. In their supernatural aspects, the *tsentsak* are not simply objects but spirit helpers in various forms, such as giant butterflies, jaguars, or monkeys, who actively assist the shaman in his tasks.

Bewitching is carried out against a specific, known individual and thus is almost always done to neighbors or, at the most, fellow tribesmen. Normally, as is the case with intratribal assassination, bewitching is done to avenge a particular offense committed against one's family or friends. Both bewitching and individual assassination contrast with the large-scale headhunting raids for which the Jívaro have become famous, and which were conducted against entire neighborhoods of enemy tribes.

To bewitch, the shaman takes *natema* and secretly approaches the house of his victim. Just out of sight in the forest, he drinks green tobacco juice, enabling him to regurgitate a *tsentsak*, which he throws at his victim as he comes out of his house. If the *tsentsak* is strong enough and is thrown with sufficient force, it will pass all the way through the victim's body causing death within a period of a few days to several weeks. More often, however, the magical dart simply lodges in the victim's body. If the shaman, in his hiding place, fails to see the intended victim, he may instead bewitch any member of the intended victim's family who appears, usually a wife or child. When the shaman's mission is accomplished, he returns secretly to his own home.

One of the distinguishing characteristics of the bewitching process among the Jívaro is that, as far

as I could learn, the victim is given no specific indication that someone is bewitching him. The bewitcher does not want his victim to be aware that he is being supernaturally attacked, lest he take protective measures by immediately procuring the services of a curing shaman. Nonetheless, shamans and laymen alike with whom I talked noted that illness invariably follows the bewitchment although the degree of the illness can vary considerably.

A special kind of spirit helper, called a *pasuk*, can aid the bewitching shaman by remaining near the victim in the guise of an insect or animal of the forest after the bewitcher has left. This spirit helper has his own objects to shoot into the victim should a curing shaman succeed in sucking out the *tsentsak* sent earlier by the bewitcher who is the owner of the *pasuk*.

In addition, the bewitcher can enlist the aid of a *wakani* ("soul," or "spirit") bird. Shamans have the power to call these birds and use them as spirit helpers in bewitching victims. The shaman blows on the *wakani* birds and then sends them to the house of the victim to fly around and around the man, frightening him. This is believed to cause fever and insanity, with death resulting shortly thereafter.

After he returns home from bewitching, the shaman may send a *wakani* bird to perch near the house of the victim. Then if a curing shaman sucks out the intruding object, the bewitching shaman sends the *wakani* bird more *tsentsak* to throw from its beak into the victim. By continually resupplying the *wakani* bird with new *tsentsak*, the sorcerer makes it impossible for the curer to rid his patient permanently of the magical darts.

While the *wakani* birds are supernatural servants available to anyone who wishes to use them, the *pasuk*, chief among the spirit helpers, serves only a single shaman. Likewise a shaman possesses only one *pasuk*. The *pasuk*, being specialized for the service of bewitching, has a protective shield to guard it from counterattack by the curing shaman. The curing shaman, under the influence of *natema*, sees the *pasuk* of the bewitcher in human form and size, but "covered with iron except for its eyes." The curing shaman can kill this *pasuk* only by shooting a *tsentsak* into its eyes, the sole vulnerable area in the *pasuk's* armor. To the person who has not taken the hallucinogenic drink, the *pasuk* usually appears to be simply a tarantula.

Shamans also may kill or injure a person by using magical darts, *anamuk*, to create supernatural animals that attack a victim. If a shaman has a small, pointed armadillo bone *tsentsak*, he can shoot this into a river while the victim is crossing it on a balsa raft or in a canoe. Under the water, this bone manifests itself in its supernatural aspect as an anaconda, which rises up and overturns the craft, causing the victim to drown. The shaman can similarly use a tooth from a killed snake as a *tsentsak*, creating a poisonous serpent to bite his victim. In more or less the same manner, shamans can create jaguars and pumas to kill their victims.

About five years after receiving his *tsentsak*, a bewitching shaman undergoes a test to see if he still retains enough *tsentsak* power to continue to kill successfully. This test involves bewitching a tree. The shaman, under the influence of *natema*, attempts to throw a *tsentsak* through the tree at the point where its two main branches join. If his strength and aim are adequate, the tree appears to split the moment the *tsentsak* is sent into it. The splitting, however, is invisible to an observer who is not under the influence of the hallucinogen. If the shaman fails, he knows that he is incapable of killing a human victim. This means that, as soon as possible, he must go to a strong shaman and purchase a new supply of *tsentsak*. Until he has the goods with which to pay for this new supply, he is in constant danger, in his proved weakened condition, of being seriously bewitched by other shamans. Therefore, each day, he drinks large quantities of *natema*, tobacco juice, and the extract of yet another drug, *pirípiri*. He also rests on his bed at home to conserve his strength, but tries to conceal his weakened condition from his enemies. When he purchases a new supply of *tsentsak*, he can safely cut down on his consumption of these other substances.

The degree of illness produced in a witchcraft victim is a function of both the force with which the *tsentsak* is shot into the body, and also of the character of the magical dart itself. If a *tsentsak* is shot all the way through the body of a victim, then "there is nothing for a curing shaman to suck out," and the patient dies. If the magical dart lodges within the body, however, it is theoretically possible to cure the victim by sucking. But in actual practice, the sucking is not always considered successful.

The work of the curing shaman is complementary to that of a bewitcher. When a curing shaman is called in to treat a patient, his first task is to see if the illness is due to witchcraft. The usual diagnosis and treatment begin with the curing shaman drinking *natema*, tobacco juice, and *pirípiri* in the late afternoon and early evening. These drugs permit him to see into the body of the patient as though it were glass. If the illness is due to sorcery, the curing shaman will see the intruding object within the patient's body clearly enough to determine whether or not he can cure the sickness.

A shaman sucks magical darts from a patient's body only at night, and in a dark area of the house, for it is only in the dark that he can perceive the drug-induced visions that are the supernatural reality. With the setting of the sun, he alerts his *tsentsak* by whistling the tune of the curing song; after about a quarter of an hour, he starts singing. When he is ready to suck, the shaman regurgitates two *tsentsak* into the sides of his throat and mouth. These must be identical to the one he has seen in the patient's body. He holds one of these in the front of the mouth and the other in the rear. They are expected to catch the supernatural aspect of the magical dart that the shaman sucks out of the patient's body. The *tsentsak* nearest the shaman's lips is supposed to incorporate the sucked-out *tsentsak* essence within itself. If, however, this supernatural essence should get past it, the second magical dart in the mouth blocks the throat so that the intruder cannot enter the interior of the shaman's body. If the curer's two *tsentsak* were to fail to catch the supernatural essence of the *tsentsak*, it would pass down into the shaman's stomach and kill him. Trapped thus within the mouth, this essence is shortly caught by, and incorporated into, the material substance of one of the curing shaman's *tsentsak*. He then "vomits" out this object and displays it to the patient and his family saying, "Now I have sucked it out. Here it is."

The non-shamans think that the material object itself is what has been sucked out, and the shaman does not disillusion them. At the same time, he is not lying, because he knows that the only important thing about a *tsentsak* is its supernatural aspect, or essence, which he sincerely believes he has removed from the patient's body. To explain to the layman that he already had these objects in his mouth would serve no fruitful purpose and would prevent him from displaying such an object as proof that he had effected the cure. Without incontrovertible evidence, he would not be able to convince the patient and his family that he had effected the cure and must be paid.

The ability of the shaman to suck depends largely upon the quantity and strength of his own *tsentsak*, of which he may have hundreds. His magical darts assume their supernatural aspect of spirit helpers when he is under the influence of *natema*, and he sees them as a variety of zoomorphic forms hovering over him, perching on his shoulders, and sticking out of his skin. He sees them helping to suck the patient's body. He must drink tobacco juice every few hours to "keep them fed" so that they will not leave him.

The curing shaman must also deal with any *pasuk* that may be in the patient's vicinity for the purpose of casting more darts. He drinks additional amounts of *natema* in order to see them and engages in *tsentsak* duels with them if they are present. While the *pasuk* is enclosed in iron armor, the shaman himself has his own armor composed of his many *tsentsak*. As long as he is under the influence of *natema*, these magical darts cover his body as a protective shield, and are on the lookout for any enemy *tsentsak* headed toward their master. When these *tsentsak* see such a missile coming, they immediately close up together at the point where the enemy dart is attempting to penetrate, and thereby repel it.

If the curer finds *tsentsak* entering the body of his patient after he has killed *pasuk*, he suspects the presence of a *wakani* bird. The shaman drinks *maikua* (Datura sp.), an hallucinogen even more powerful than *natema*, as well as tobacco juice, and silently sneaks into the forest to hunt and kill the bird with *tsentsak*. When he succeeds, the curer returns to the patient's home, blows all over the house to get rid of the "atmosphere" created by the numerous *tsentsak* sent by the bird, and completes his sucking of the patient. Even after all the *tsentsak* are extracted, the shaman may remain another night at the house to suck out any "dirtiness" (*pahuri*) still inside. In the cures which I have witnessed, this sucking is a most noisy process, accompanied by deep, but dry, vomiting.

After sucking out a *tsentsak*, the shaman puts it into a little container. He does not swallow it because it is not his own magical dart and would therefore kill him. Later, he throws the *tsentsak* into the air, and it flies back to the shaman who sent it originally into the patient. *Tsentsak* also fly back to a shaman at the death of a former apprentice who had originally received them from him. Besides receiving "old" magical darts unexpectedly in this manner, the shaman may have *tsentsak* thrown at him by a bewitcher. Accordingly, shamans constantly drink tobacco juice at all hours of the day and night. Although the tobacco juice is not truly hallucinogenic, it produces a narcotized state, which is believed necessary to keep one's *tsentsak* ready to repel any other magical darts. A shaman does not even dare go for a walk without taking along the green tobacco leaves with which he prepares the juice that keeps his spirit helpers alert. Less frequently, but regularly, he must drink *natema* for the same purpose and to keep in touch with the supernatural reality.

While curing under the influence of *natema*, the curing shaman "sees" the shaman who bewitched his patient. Generally, he can recognize the person, unless it is a shaman who lives far away or in another tribe. The patient's family knows this, and demands to be told the identity of the bewitcher, particularly if the sick person dies. At one curing session I attended, the shaman could not identify the person he had seen in his vision. The brother of the dead man then accused the shaman himself of being responsible. Under such pressure, there is a strong tendency for the curing shaman to attribute each case to a particular bewitcher.

Shamans gradually become weak and must purchase *tsentsak* again and again. Curers tend to become weak in power, especially after curing a patient bewitched by a shaman who has recently received a new supply of magical darts. Thus, the most powerful shamans are those who can repeatedly purchase new supplies of *tsentsak* from other shamans.

Shamans can take back *tsentsak* from others to whom they have previously given them. To accomplish this, the shaman drinks *natema*, and, using his *tsentsak*, creates a "bridge" in the form of a rainbow between himself and the other shaman. Then he shoots a *tsentsak* along this rainbow. This strikes the ground beside the other shaman with an explosion and flash likened to a lightning bolt. The purpose of this is to surprise the other shaman so that he temporarily forgets to maintain his guard over his magical darts, thus permitting the other shaman to suck them back along the rainbow. A shaman who has had his *tsentsak* taken away in this manner will discover that "nothing happens" when he drinks *natema*. The sudden loss of his *tsentsak* will tend to make him ill, but ordinarily the illness is not fatal unless a bewitcher shoots a magical dart into him while he is in this weakened condition. If he has not become disillusioned by his experience, he can again purchase *tsentsak* from some other shaman and resume his calling. Fortunately for anthropology some of these men have chosen to give up shamanism and therefore can be persuaded to reveal their knowledge, no longer having a vested interest in the profession. This divulgence, however, does not serve as a significant threat to practitioners, for words alone can never adequately convey the realities of shamanism. These can only be approached with the aid of *natema*, the chemical door to the invisible world of the Jívaro shaman.

Psychedelics and Religion: A Symposium

Raziel Abelson
Allen Ginsberg
Michael Wyschogrod

The primary purpose of this article is to discuss the religious and philosophical aspects of the so-called consciousness-expanding drugs. Allen Ginsberg assumes the position that there is a positive value in using such drugs as marijuana and LSD to attain a more intensive religious experience, while Professor Wyschogrod emphasizes the "artificiality" of any religious experience based on drugs. Wyschogrod is not basing his argument on the question of the legality or morality of drugs, but rather on his belief that a drug-induced religious experience results only in a synthetic or "illusory" religious experience.

As we have seen in the preceding articles of this chapter, psychotropic (mind-changing) drugs are used throughout the world to bring about or enhance religious experiences. In the United States today, however, as well as in other countries, drug usage is considered a major social problem. The amount of popular media coverage devoted to the topic of drugs in this country is staggering, reflecting the deep social, philosophical, and moral conflict over their use. This article stemmed from a 1967 drug symposium held at New York University. It is not difficult to understand why the symposium was convened. In the 1960s, millions of young Americans turned to drugs as one aspect of their rejection of what they felt was an unsuccessful system of American values. Difficult as it was for an older generation to cope with the sudden popularity of such drugs as marijuana and LSD in the profane world of the streets and the college campus, to many the thought of their use in the sacred world was frightening, even terrifying.

This article first appeared in the *Humanist* issue of Fall 1967 (September/December), pp. 153–56 and 190–91, and is reprinted by permission.

Introduction: Raziel Abelson

The purpose of this symposium is to discuss the religious and philosophical aspects of the so-called "consciousness expanding" drugs, particularly LSD and marijuana. It occurs to me that the title of this symposium is much too pretentious and stuffy; I would prefer to call it something simpler and more cozy. I suggest we call this a "Trip-in," for a reason not quite what you would naturally think. My reason is a personal one: it has to do with various trips I have made recently and a new one I am reluctant to take until I can see a good reason for it.

I am particularly interested in the subject of our discussion because of my feeling of closeness to the generation that has made it an issue, the generation that came of age or will come of age in the 1960s. I consider it an extraordinarily interesting generation, the most exciting that I have had contact with. My own generation of the 40s was, I think, not a bad one; it was interested in its fellowmen, it was dynamic and hard working, it fought a world war against barbarism, but it was not as free as the present one because it was enslaved to ideologies. For the conservative prejudices of our parents we substituted the radical and neo-Puritanical prejudices of Marxism and Freudianism. I began to teach in the 1950s, and the generation of students who attended my lectures in that decade was, I think, the dullest, most boring of my time. It was enslaved to things far worse than ideologies: to chrome-plated Cadillacs, large houses, good jobs and social status. Its heroes were McCarthy on the "right" and Eisenhower on the "left." I first began to enjoy teaching in the 60s, because only then did I feel a rapport with students, whom I found so remarkably free that I felt myself liberated by them—free of pretentious ideology, free of mechanical rules of grammar, spelling, etiquette and sexual behavior, free of parental authoritarianism, of superstitions and phobias, willing to explore and appreciate any kind of human experience, able to say, like Marsiglio of Padua: "Nothing human is alien to me." Unfortunately, my age disqualifies me from full, card-carrying membership in this new generation, but, unlike Lewis Feuer and Ronald Reagan, I recognize its superiority to my own and I would like to be at least an honorary or associate member. For this reason I have tried to share its experience by taking various "trips" with it. In 1963 I took a trip on a rickety old school bus at four in the morning, to the Washington March for civil rights legislation. The following summer I took a trip to Mississippi to observe the Freedom Schools and voter registration drive; although I wasn't there long, I did get a taste of the "agony and the ecstasy"of the students who fought non-violently and valiantly for reason and decency. I believe that summer of 1964 was the most glorious moment in the history of American youth; it was the moment at which the older generations began to look to the youth for the leadership they did not have the courage to assume. Two summers later I took another trip on a rickety old school bus, full of students, to march on Washington to end the war in Viet Nam, and this year I marched with them in New York, surrounded by Viet Cong banners and hippies with bananas, flowers, and electric guitars. Up to that point, the generation of the 60s had always turned me on. Their skeptical rebelliousness and their intense social involvement seemed to me to promise a far better world when they would take control. But something very disturbing has been happening in the last two years. This generation, that created in me and many others so much hope for the future, has itself lost hope and nerve, and has turned from social concern inward toward its own private experience: it has turned from iconoclasm to quietism, from humanistic liberalism to passivity and drugs. The revolutionary generation is "copping out."

The "trips" I had taken with it were all outward, other-centered, and to get things done that needed doing. Now, if I listen to the proselytes of Liberation Through Drugs, I am to take a trip in the exact opposite direction—inward, toward passivity, hallucination, inconsequence. Maybe I can understand the motives for this shift into reverse gear—disappointment at the snail's pace of social reforms, moral revulsion and despair about the abominable, uncontrollable and endless war in Viet Nam—but motives are not reasons, and I would like to know the *reason* why, before I take this trip backward into darkness. I am in search of enlightenment: why are drug induced fantasies better than the light of cool reason; why is sensual over-stimulation more worthwhile than the pursuit of rational social ideals? I look to two extremely well-qualified experts to enlighten me on these questions. From Mr. Ginsberg I hope for a clear answer to the question, "Why?" and from Professor Wyschogrod, an equally clear explanation of "Why not?"

Turning On with LSD and Pot: Allen Ginsberg

I would like to begin by introducing some data from comparative religion. Those who have done any dilettanting around in Tantric Hinduism or its esoteric erotic sexual practices will no doubt know of the book, *The Serpent Power*, by Arthur Avalon. It is a translation of an ancient Hindu text, the *Mahanirvana tantra*, one of the older, more conservative texts of the Shaivite school of Hinduism. This text deals with ritual, prayer, and the formal religious use of marijuana. If one reads just a few sentences from the text, he can get an appreciation of the importance of the use of marijuana in the religious rituals. One who engages in mantra prayer and chanting will use this narcotic hemp in his ceremonies.

I should point out that I am a formally initiated member of the Shiva sect, and I assume that my presentation of its rituals is protected by the First Amendment of the U.S. Constitution. Since I have a central preoccupation within my heart with religious matters, I wish to stay off legal problems and to focus upon the actual subject matter on a more realistic level, without worrying about whether it's going to be against the law, whether it's moral or immoral to break the law, whether you'll go mad or you won't go mad. I want to deal with the phenomenology of LSD and pot and their philosophical implications. Professor Elia Rubichek of Prague, who has done a lot of work on LSD, defines it in Pavlovian and Marxian terminology, the terminology the "Iron Curtain" would use in dealing with the effects of LSD. The phraseology is really interesting. What he said was, "It inhibits conditioned reflexes." Now that's a big deal out there in Russia where there's a Pavlovian conception of consciousness, because it means that there is a way of reversing or wiping out the conditioning that would make a member of the former upper class no longer eligible to be condemned by the bureaucrat. Anybody could take LSD and say that he had his conditioned reflexes wiped out and was now just as good as the proletariat.

What it means in terms of our country is something you have been digging lately—Marshall McLuhan's generalizations about the effects of the conditioning of our technology on our consciousness. He's saying that the media or environment we have created around us is a giant conditioning mechanism, a giant teaching machine. We are hardly aware of it as a teaching machine. We are hardly aware of its effect. We are hardly aware that consciousness is not necessarily a conceptual or verbal matter, that there are other levels of consciousness, depths of consciousness, that there is feeling consciousness, that there is touch consciousness, that there is smelling, seeing, hearing, and levels of memory consciousness that we are not generally aware of. But McLuhan has been saying recently that the verbal and language consciousness that we have been conditioned to over the last centuries has atrophied our other senses. That is, the universe into which we have projected ourselves and developed has atrophied our other sense—smell, touch, taste—in a way that he could even quantify. McLuhan told me that he wanted to work out a way to quantify in scientific terminology the difference caused by our preoccupation with visual consciousness; that is, the difference caused to the other senses. There is a quantitative mode of measurement that he could apply. What has this to do with LSD? McLuhan didn't know the connection because he hasn't taken LSD or read much about it. Yet given a chemical which can reverse conditioning, we have a kind of open consciousness which receives almost all of the data present to us and takes account of it all, as if that which we usually are not aware of or is uncon-

scious within us is presented to our awareness during the time that we are high on LSD. This goes on without any screening structure—something that Leary has been saying over and over—to the point where something is either understood and is boring or is not understood and is still a koan for people to solve.

What good is that kind of consciousness? I don't know if I have presented it clearly enough to have any value for you. It involves a consciousness that is not socially conditioned (though conditioned by our bodies surely), a consciousness where the social conditioning is reversed, and where we had eight hours to look around us as newborn babes to see our bodies, to see our relationships, to see our architecture around us, to see our relationships to other forms of life. It involves eight hours of experience of ourselves as mammalian sentient beings. Is that a socially useful experience?

I think it always has been considered a socially useful experience. I think that the LSD experience approximates the mystical experience, as it is called, the religious experience, or the peak experience, as Maslow calls it. It approximates the kind of experience that one reads about in William James's *The Varieties of Religious Experience*. I'm not sure it's identical with what people would call the classical religious experience, but then in William James one also finds that very few of those experiences are identical experiences. Their common quality is that there is a break in the normal mode of consciousness, an opening up of another universe of awareness, so that from one description to another in any of the books describing mystical experiences the forms are not the same. One thing that everybody cries out in delight at is that the universe they had taken for granted had suddenly opened and revealed itself as something much deeper and fuller, much more exquisite, something more connected with a divine sense of things—a Self perhaps. So I would say that the LSD experience does approximate what we humans have been recording over millenia as a flight of higher imagination or a flight of higher awareness. Now that experience has always been accorded a very honored status in society. A few people have been burned at the stake or crucified for attempting to manifest the insights that they've experienced. But at least in the academies, in religion, in the church, and even among truck drivers, there is a respect for the non-conditioned, non-verbal, non-conceptual opening up of the mind to all of the data of experience flooding in at once, newly perceived, or perceived as a newborn babe or early child.

Its usefulness in our society is extra. That's why I began talking about McLuhan, inasmuch as we have arrived at sort of a Buck Rogers space age, science-fiction society in which everybody is electronically intercommunicated, in which visual images and verbal images are multiplied, stereotyped and implanted in everybody's brain so that it is very difficult to escape the automatic, mechanistic forms that are constantly being played on our bodies by radio, television, newspapers, by our own university, or by our own parents.

In a world now facing apocalypse, in the sense that America, the largest world power, is perhaps preparing for a war on the Asiatic life form, it becomes important not only to see what we have in common with the Asiatic life form and what we actually have distinct and separate from it but also to find those points, to control the angers built up in us, to measure the actual universe around, to lose the conditioning that brought us to this path of anger, fear and paranoia, to experience what is original in our nature as distinct from what has been educated into our nature since our birth. The problem, however, that still arises, particularly when people have had religious experience and have not had LSD experience, is this question: "Is this experience like an evil specter or is it something that can be reconciled with the older religious experience? Does it have any relationship to the norms of human experience, or at least the high norms of human experience, that are described in the religious books?

Of these we have neither enough experiments nor enough data. My own experience is as follows: When I was younger (when I was about 28) I had a series of visionary or religious or illuminative experiences which are best categorized as the aesthetic experience, since they became catalyzed by reading poems of Blake. I had an auditory hallucination of Blake's voice and also experienced a number of moments of guilelessness about the world around me and feeling that the father of the universe had existed all along but I had not realized it, that the father of the universe loved me and that I was identical with the father. So this was

an experience of bliss. I realized that I had my place in the universe. I tried to describe this a few times in poetry or in prose but it's very difficult to describe. At the time that I had it (it was about in 1948) this kind of experience was, at least in the circles where I ran (Columbia University), an experience which was practically unknown and was considered madness. I remember that when this happened I went to Lionel Trilling and said, "I've seen light." And he looked at me and seemed to be wondering, "What am I going to do with this?" He looked as if he wondered where I was going to wind up. There were two people at Columbia at the time who had enough inner experience to be able to understand, to talk to me, to reassure me. One was Raymond Weaver who had been the first biographer for Herman Melville and who had lived in Japan and was for those at Columbia in the forties *the* great light, a secret light because he was a cranky cat. He used to know Hart Crane and Wanda Landowska. He was the most eminent professor at Columbia. He shared an office with Mark Van Doren. Weaver could deal with this kind of experience without slipping out and becoming anxious. Mark Van Doren also could deal with it. When I went to him in an overexcited and totally disoriented state and said, "I have seen some light, I heard Blake's voice!" he said, "What kind of light was it?" Then he began questioning me about the quality of the experience, asking for data. Everybody else thought I was nuts. However I am what I am. So I'll stand in my own body and believe my own senses and experiences.

Later I found that LSD catalyzed a variety of consciousness that was very similar to the natural experience. I've used a variety of other hallucinogenics—maybe about thirty times over a fifteen-year period. This is very small actually compared to the usage now being made by the younger people. I found that there has not been any contradiction between the kind of consciousness I had under LSD and my height of rapture of consciousness in natural moments. I also found that I faced the same difficulties with LSD as I had faced with my original visionary experience. Those difficulties were that, having gotten into a state of high perception, how to maintain my normal life, my awareness on a higher level, incorporating in my daily experience some of the concrete perceptions that I had in a moment of ecstasy. Specifically I had had a non-drug vision in the Columbia book store. I'd gone in there for years, and I went in there this day and suddenly I saw that everybody looked like tortured animals. I was reading Blake's poem about—

> I wander through London's chartered streets
> Near where the chartered Thames doth flow
> On every face I meet I see
> Marks of weakness
> Marks of woe

Well, in those moments I saw marks of suffering on the faces of the bookstore clerks, the enormous-like mammalism sexual deliciousness of their being and the contrary stultified, rigid, unsexualized, non-feeling, day-to-day commerce over the books with a few camp jokes mixed in to refer to the unknown. I asked, How, in coming down to a day-to-day dealing with the bookstore people or anyone on the campus, how to deal with such persons, such deep persons as exist in everybody? And that took very slow practice and continuous awareness of the fact that everyone was a deep person and a divine mammal rather than a bookstore clerk. The same problem exists in relation to LSD. Having had a vision on LSD of either your parents' or your own role, how do you manifest that in your school life or whatever life you are pursuing? Henri Michaud, a great French poet who did a lot of early experiments, finally told me that he had concluded that what was important was not the visions, but what people did with the visions afterward, and how they manifested them in their daily life. I think that the really basic practical problem to be faced is the problem common to all mysticism. How is one in day-to-day life to keep continuous high consciousness of the eternal which he had experienced in separated moments of a larger consciousness? What good is it if they are separated moments; if they are not totally, distinctly integrated into everyday life? Having experienced only separated moments of divine consciousness without drugs, I find that the drugs do make possible a return to more native awareness which is useful when I have to take stock of my activities. For instance, a year and a half ago I was involved in the Viet-Nam Day Committee in Berkeley. There was a great deal of anger and outrage about the war. I found myself being swept along into that

outrage and vowing vengeance on the murderers of innocent children; and my wits were astray because of all of that senseless tumult; and I all but cried for vengeance on the murderers. I took some LSD the day the President went for his gall bladder operation and I realized that he was another suffering deep person, perhaps one almost ignorant of his own state of consciousness and so suffering a great deal more because of that ignorance, one however entering the valley of the shadow. My hatred simply disappeared. What was left was a funny kind of compassion for him in his ignorance, a prayer for him for his return from the valley of the shadow. In a state of awareness, less hostile, less fearful, less paranoid than his entrance, I found myself praying for him, praying for his own understanding. The thing that I did realize was that my piling up my own hatred on top of the general hatred of the Pentagon and the *New York Daily News* and the military and industrial complex only added to the anti-Vietnam War reaction. Piling up my hatred and my curses and my magic on top of that was going to make the situation worse. I wanted to move to liquidate the anger hallucination that was controlling everybody.

Finally, we have a few other details that might interest you. A poet friend of mine has worked for ten years in Zen monasteries, has done formal meditation, and is an accomplished Zen student. He was here in America a few months ago, and we had several conversations about the rising LSD culture and the Haight-Ashburys. He felt that the LSD experience was not contradictory to the experience of Satori as described by Zen. The younger, qualified, completely trained Zen masters in Japan who had tried LSD were interested in it and considered it a useful tool for education in relation to their own discipline. They were not against its use and were themselves beginning to employ it. The Roshi Suzuki—Roshi means master—who is the head of the meditation sect in San Francisco, said he felt the LSD experience is not the same as Zazen sitting meditation. However he finds that most of the meditators in his group are people who are originally turned on by LSD. As far as he can see, it does open people up to a widening area of consciousness, which can then be worked in with other disciplines. I find the same report coming in now from the schools of Tibetan

Buddhism. There is a Geshe who has a monastery in New Jersey. He has some American disciples who have been equally experienced in Tibetan meditation and psychedelics. Wanga and his disciple, Tenjin, who is an ex-Harvard student, have prepared translations of old Tibetan meditation texts and are preparing them for publication with the foreword note that the Tibetan prayers, methods and procedures may be found useful in collaboration with psychedelic experiments. Thus it seems clear to me that there is a close relationship between psychedelic drugs and mystical experience.

Instant Mysticism: Michael Wyschogrod

I think the point of view expressed by Allen Ginsberg is a very good one—an attitude of reason, of peace, of affection, of understanding, and therefore, I am not in a polemical spirit. I do not wish to disagree, to forbid, to outlaw, or to consider LSD and marijuana evil or immoral. They exist like many other things in the world, and it's very superficial to take a simple "no" attitude to what one finds in the world.

Nevertheless there are a number of issues that deserve deeper analysis. I think the two issues we do not want to discuss are these: first, I think it a mistake to approach this problem from the point of view of the dangers involved. The dangers, of course, are not irrelevant. I think anyone who contemplates taking psychedelic drugs deserves to have all of the knowledge necessary so that he can make an intelligent choice as to just what risk is involved; but that is not a final word because many things in life involve risk and yet we don't shun them. In this country the automobile kills forty thousand people a year, and yet I have not heard anyone advocate the abolition of the automobile. For some reason we feel that the advantages of the automobile outweigh the disadvantages. In any case if the psychedelic substances have substantial spiritual and religious advantages, then I would be prepared to say that this outweighs a great many perils and disadvantges. So the element of peril, though relevant, in my opinion is not crucial and is not the final consideration. Secondly, I think that this problem ought not to be approached essential-

ly from the legal point of view, because whether we ought or ought not to outlaw something is again a secondary question.

The first consideration is, is this a good thing or a bad thing? Outlawing is only secondary. Even if we decide that this is a bad thing, it does not necessarily follow that it ought to be outlawed. The heart of the matter is the question: what good are these drugs? And the moment we ask this question we are in the religious realm. My thesis can be stated very simply: it's a thesis of wonder and surprise. I find that the younger generation to which Professor Abelson referred senses that there is something wrong with the technological mode of existence into which we have been projected in the middle of the twentieth century. There is something wrong with the artificiality of our existence. We no longer experience reality. We live through artificial media such as the television and radio, which have a life of their own and stand as a screen between man and reality. Life in our times is in essence artificial. And because it is artificial there are those people who want to break through this artificiality on all levels, who want to live as a man ought to live and was intended to live, in serenity and peace, with direct contact with reality, not in a life of instant coffee, instant pudding, instant bake mixes, and instant this and that and the other thing—but a wholesale life of cooking vegetables as they grow and taking flour and using it for baking, of brewing coffee, instead of getting it out of an instant mix. Our lives are nightmares of instant experiences. And this, of course, is a profound truth. But then something amazing has happened and I am genuinely amazed—suddenly there is instant mysticism, there is technological mysticism, instead of patience, serenity, humility and waiting for enlightenment and praying for it and loving our fellow man. Instead we look to chemistry: "better living through better things through chemistry."

It seems to me that the genuinely religious person cannot want to buy his relationship to God in a sugar cube, a bottle, or a chemical. It is true that these substances are not yet mass-produced by the pharmaceutical companies. But perhaps that won't take long, if this thing catches on and if people go for it. I assure you that in a few years *Life* and *Time* will be full of ads and every drug company will be selling the stuff and holding out the hope of a quick road to God. And there will be competition, there will be the jingles. I don't want that. I think that would be a travesty on genuine religion, genuine mysticism, and genuine religious experience.

The real thing is always harder and more difficult to achieve than the imitation. And with the real thing you run the risk of never quite making it. There is one element and thought that is universally agreed on among scholars of religion, and that is this: there is a profound distinction between magic and religion. The distinction is simple: Magic is power; religion is prayer. The magician is of the opinion that there is some secret formula which, when discovered, gives him power over the spirit. Once he has that, the spirit cannot refuse his demands. The spirit of magic and the spirit of modern technology are very close indeed because both see man in the driver's seat. Both see man as the power that controls the world around him, and human destiny as a destiny with ever greater control over human existence. Just as through technology we control our environment, the heat and the cold, and the world around us, so by means of magic was the same attempted. The only difference was that we think that science works better than magic. But the spirit is the same; and against science and against magic stands genuine religion. Genuine religion is prayer. Prayer is asking God, and he can say "no."

There is the story of the little kid who prayed; and his cynical uncle said, "Well God didn't answer you, did he?" And the little kid answered, "Yes, he did. He said, 'No.'"

This is the spirit of true religion. In genuine religion we hand ourselves over to the greater spirit, whether one calls it "God," "the Father," or "the spirit of the universe." Fundamentally it doesn't matter. But you see yourself as worshipping that being, that spirit, loving Him. He loves you in return. And you live in peace and union with Him.

Drug mysticism is the conversion of mysticism into magic. It is the illusion that one can have power over the spirit; and this never has happened and never will happen. What comes in a bottle or in a chemical is not the spirit of God. What comes in a bottle or a chemical is an illusion. It is the epitome of just that technological threat against which well-meaning people are fighting and suc-

cumbing to through drugs and narcotics. It is the victory of the slogan of the chemical industry, and I don't want to see that happen.

Ginsberg Replies to Wyschogrod

For all I know perhaps Professor Wyschogrod is right! I have no idea about the victory of the chemical industry, or victory of artificial madness, or black magic technology. Burroughs, a former teacher of mine and someone I respect a great deal, has had considerable experience with hallucinogens and has stopped using them. Occasionally he turns on; but lately he has taken to saying, "No, I'd better watch out. The Pentagon is going to poison us all. Things have gotten too Orwellian."

As to religious reality, I don't agree with Professor Wyschogrod as to what constitutes a valid religious experience. The spirit of religion is investigation and practice, of which prayer is only an element. But there isn't a pre-supposition, or what I call a hang-up on a Jehovah, that you've got up there that you've got to be humble to, that you've got to pray to, or to be said "no" by. Jehovah is within in Buddhism and Hinduism and in some aspects of Christianity and actually in some Hebraic traditions also. The external Jehovah is just high camp. In some schools that sense of an external authority is not relied on, certainly not in Buddhism where one of the major koans is that Buddha is not a divine being to be worshipped. The saying is that, "If you meet the Buddha on the way to enlightenment and he bars your way, cut him down!"

As to LSD coming in a bottle and whether or not it is the spirit of God, it all depends on the way we are using the term "god." If there were a Jehovah I wouldn't put it past him to come through a bottle any way. Certainly it would be within his power. Certainly a God would see it as equally charming to come through a bottle as through prayer. So I don't think there is anything to be feared in that sense. What might be feared is dependence on the drug and lack of ritual or lack of prayer or lack of humility or lack of earnestness in the yoga of the drug. I tried to provide the suggestions for ritual, the suggestions for prayer, the suggestions for the application of the drug vision to daily life. But I think that purely verbal terminologies are a bit over-dramatized in speaking of

LSD as merely "magic" as opposed to religion. I think those are verbal distinctions. I think they are basically stereotypes of thought. I don't think they fit the enormity and eloquence of the experience which many of us have felt.

Wyschogrod Replies to Ginsberg

I agree with Mr. Ginsberg that these are very serious matters and it's presumptuous for anyone to say what is the case and what is not the case. Yet each of us talks from his own experience. I do not speak out of LSD experience but I talk out of religious experience and I think that I am reporting what I see. I don't think that I have the last word. I don't think that I am right, but do feel deeply that there is profound danger here.

I would add just one word. I don't know much about eastern religion. I deeply respect it. I have an intuitive sense that there is something very real and very deep there, but I'm not a Japanese, Chinese or a Far Easterner. I'm a Westerner. What goes on in the Far East in the setting of that civilization over the thousands of years of art, poetry, and history, and what has gone into the development of those religions I cannot enter into. Therefore I think it is spiritually dangerous for men of New York, for example, to take one aspect of foreign or eastern civilization and transport it here and to think that we have the same thing here that they have. We are Jews or Christians and there is very much to Judaism and Christianity, and we must be what we are. I think there is something very sad about a person trying to be something that he is not and never can be.

Mr. Ginsberg advises people to take pot and LSD. Now I grant an individual the full freedom to act as he wishes and to be what he wishes and I'd be the last person to take that away. But at the same time I must express my convictions. Life poses a peculiar problem: to become what you are. Now this sounds paradoxical, because if you are what you are, why do you need to become what you are? Here there is always tension between becoming what you are, and becoming what you are meant to be. And that's the job for each of us to find. All I can do for you is to say, Look once more before you embark on this strange new path of psychedelic religion. Look once more at your heritage. Just give it a second look and after that you're on your own.

Post Mortem: Raziel Abelson

I must confess that I do not feel I have received the enlightenment I had hoped for—I am not exactly in a state of Satori. The trouble with this discussion is that both participants have assumed something to be the case which, it seems to me, is even more doubtful than the qualities of the drugs they have argued about. Both Ginsberg and Wyschogrod have assumed that religious experience is necessarily good, and I do not see any reason for accepting that assumption. Ginsberg has argued that, because religious experience is always good, and (he claims) LSD and marijuana help produce religious experience, these drugs are very good and useful things. Wyschogrod has argued, to the contrary, that drugs cannot *possibly* (later he modified his claim to the effect that they do not, so far as he can see) produce genuine religious experience, but only spurious, synthetic, "instant," "bottled," in a word, *illusory* religious experience. Thus he takes it for granted that there is a clear distinction between illusion and reality in religious experience. On this point, it seems to me, Ginsberg has much the better of the argument. To Wyschogrod's claim "You can't get God out of a bottle" Ginsberg replied, very sensibly, "Why not?"

Why not, indeed? I am reminded of Philip Roth's story, *The Conversion of the Jews*, in which the Rabbi pontificates to his Hebrew school class that Christianity is more irrational than Judaism, because it (Christianity) claims that Jesus was born without sexual intercourse; and little Ozzie then demands to know why an omnipotent God, who can divide the Red Sea and send plagues over Egypt, cannot make a woman become pregnant without any sexual intercourse. Once we begin talking about the transcendental (a fancy word for supernatural) anything goes—each one makes up his own rules. One says you can't find God in a bottle, but you can in a burning bush; another says God can't make a woman pregnant without intercourse but that the Holy Ghost in the form of a dove can. How adjudicate such theological claims, and why bother? How one can find God depends very much on just what one means by "God," and it is not at all clear what either Ginsberg or Wyschogrod means, and still less clear whether whatever they mean exists. And if He doesn't exist, you can no more find Him through prayer than through drugs or in a bottle.

Now it seems to me that the distinction between real and unreal, whether it is applied to religious experience, to God, or to the beauty and goodness allegedly revealed by psychedelic drugs, is crucial to this discussion. And my own objection to the claims made for such drugs is on the philosophical ground that this distinction is being applied to a type of experience to which it cannot properly be applied, because there are no established criteria for making the distinction. Indeed, the experience, being hallucinatory, is that there cannot possibly be criteria for distinguishing the real from the apparent. Mr. Ginsberg made this clear in describing how, under LSD, he felt compassion for everyone and anything, for President Johnson (he said to me later) for Adolph Hitler. Now what sense is there in compassion that does not distinguish the executioner from his victims? How can one have real compassion for the sufferer without hating the agent who makes him suffer? What good is such compassion; indeed, is it really compassion, or is this feeling of compassion not as hallucinatory as everything else in the state of being drugged? To be more exact, the trouble here is that there is no objective way of distinguishing what is real from what is imaginary, hallucinatory, apparent, spurious, or in any sense unreal. The psychedelic experience is one that, by its very nature, leads one beyond (or below) all criteria of reality. One can, of course, easily say that it leads one to a "higher reality," but this verbalism is empty because "real" makes no sense where it cannot be distinguished from unreal. And this breakdown of the distinction is, of course, typical of all modes of irrationality, including religious mysticism. Consequently, it is impossible to judge whether psychedelic experience and religious experience are the same or different. All we can say is that they are equally hallucinatory. Why the speakers should assume that that is a very good thing is still a mystery to me.

In effect, Mr. Ginsberg has made two claims: first that psychedelic drugs are good in an instrumental sense because they have beneficial effects on one's personality and abilities, and second, that the experience they induce is intrinsically good. The first claim, it seems to me, cannot be authoritatively established by Mr. Ginsberg or anyone else who testifies only from personal experience, any more than the therapeutic value of psychoanalysis can be established by brainwashed patients who have been persuaded by their analyst that they are much improved (when no one else can see any difference in their behavior). Such a claim can only be proved by carefully controlled scientific studies, and no conclusive studies have yet been made. So I would discount this claim completely, just as anyone with sense would discount the claims made by Krebiozin enthusiasts, and just as Freud came close to discrediting himself as a doctor when he made premature claims for the therapeutic value of cocaine.

The second claim, that the psychedelic experience is intrinsically good, is more difficult to assess, for the reason that its value has to be judged within the experience (I am frequently rebuked by students when I question the value of taking drugs. I am told I haven't tried them, so I can't possibly know whether they are good or bad). Yet the experience is such that within it, all established criteria of good or bad are dissolved, just as, in a dream, the criteria for distinguishing real from apparent cease to apply. One dreams that something is real and something else is not, but this distinction is itself dreamt, and therefore ineffectual. Consequently, it makes no more sense to say that what one experiences is bad than to say that it is good. We simply have no standards for evaluating the hallucinatory objects of a psychedelic experience, for we have no standards for evaluating any hallucinatory objects. So far, the human race is a reality-oriented species. If enough people take drugs, this may change, and then the philosophical premises of a discussion such as this will be different, but it is as useless to speculate on such a state of affairs as to try to imagine what the world would be like if the laws of physics ceased to hold.

I do not mean to question the right of anyone, including Mr. Ginsberg, to express a preference for any type of experience he chooses to enjoy. If someone likes to smoke pot or take acid, and injures no one else in doing so, that so far as I am concerned, is his affair; and I no more support legislation against such activities than I support legislation against suicide. But to say that one likes something is not the same as to say that that something is good. I do very strongly object to the proselytizing of drugs, because, as I have tried to explain, there are no objective grounds for making a claim either to intrinsic value or to instrumental value with respect to such drugs. I still see one rather compelling reason not to take them, a reason that I tried to indicate in my opening remarks. To steep oneself in illusion is to escape from the irksome necessity to distinguish illusion from reality—in a word, to cop out. My conclusion from this discussion is: there's a lot of work to be done in the real world, and a lot of real beauty to enjoy—let's get on with it.

5

Witchcraft, Sorcery, and Other Forces of Evil

All societies recognize the frailness of the human condition; wherever pain, illness, injury, and unjustness exist, so too do culturally prescribed explanations. In many parts of the world, where opportunities for formal education are limited to an elite whose numbers are small, although their economic and political power may be considerable, explanations of events and phenomena are still rooted deeply in traditional interpretations passed from generation to generation by word of mouth. In rural Africa, for example, where between 70 and 90 percent of the population is not covered by public health services (Shehu 1975: 29), mental and physical illnesses are often accounted for in terms of a formidable array of supernatural sources, including witchcraft, sorcery, magic, curses, spirits, or a combination of these. The point is that, whether explanations for illness are "scientific" or "mystical," all societies must have explanations for crises. Mental and physi-

Devil mask from the Tyrol.

cal illness cannot be permitted to go unchecked.

In pre-literate societies a vast number of daily crises are attributed to witchcraft, particularly in sub-Saharan Africa, where the highest level of belief in witchcraft exists today. Here witchcraft explanations are logical, indeed, some say indispensable. In short, witchcraft is an integral part of traditional African belief systems, as are sorcery and magic, and it is considered by many anthropologists to be essential to African religions.

Lucy Mair, a British social anthropologist and a leading authority on African witchcraft, points out that the belief in witchcraft is universal. Around the world, greed and sexual motifs are commonly associated with witches, as is the "nightmare" witch that prowls at night and is distinguished from the everyday witch by nocturnal habits (1969: 36–37). Women are more often labeled witches than men, and societies frequently associate particular types of personalities with individuals whom they feel have the highest probability of becoming witches. According to Mair (1969: 43), many of the qualities associated with being a poor neighbor, such as unsociability, isolation, stinginess, unfriendliness, and moroseness, are the same qualities ascribed to the everyday witch. Nothing compares in terms of sheer evil, however, to the nightmare witch, whose hatred of the most basic tenets of human decency earns it a special place of infamy.

Witches, wherever they exist, are the antithesis of proper behavior. Their antisocial acts, moreover, are uncontrollable. A final commonality of witch beliefs is that their powers are innate, unlike those of the sorcerer, whose powers are learned; the witch inherits the power for evil or is given the power by God.

To the beginning student in anthropology, witchcraft surely must appear to effect a society negatively; a careful analysis of belief systems demonstrates more positive than negative functions, however. In his analysis of the functions of witchcraft among the Navaho, Clyde Kluckhohn evaluated the belief more positively than negatively in terms of economic and social control and the psychological states of a group (1967; Kluckhohn and Leighton, 1962). Beliefs in witchcraft act to level economic differences, for example. Among the Navaho, the rich are believed to have gained their wealth by secret supernatural techniques. In such cases, the only way to quell this kind of rumor is through a variety of forms of generosity that may take the form of redistribution of wealth among relatives and friends (Kluckhohn and Leighton 1962: 247). In his later work, Kluckhohn demonstrated that witchcraft beliefs help reinforce social values. For example, the belief that uncared-for elderly will turn into witches demands that the Navaho treat the aged with proper care. The worry that the death of a close relative may cast suspicion of witchcraft on survivors, particularly siblings, also reinforces their social values regarding obligations to kin. Ironically, because leaders are thought to be witches, people were hesitant to be disobedient for fear of supernatural retribution (1967: 113).

Kluckhohn maintained that at the psychological level witchcraft was an outlet for hostility because frustrated individuals used witches, rather than relatives or neighbors, as scapegoats. Anxiety and neglect could also be accommodated through commonly held witchcraft beliefs, for people showing symptoms of witchcraft-caused illnesses, usually those neglected or of low status, would have their importance to kinsmen and the group reaffirmed at the public curing ceremonies (1967: 83–84).

The terms *witchcraft* and *sorcery* are often used interchangeably to mean any kind of evil magic; however, E. E. Evans-Pritchard's (1937) analysis of Azande witchcraft and sorcery resulted in a distinction between the two terms that is accepted by most anthropologists today. Generally speaking, a sorcerer intentionally seeks to bring about harm. Sorcerers have learned how to cast spells and use certain formulas and objects to inflict evil. The sorcerer's methods are real, not psychic like those of the witch. Sorcery is conscious and an acquired skill, whereas witchcraft is unconscious and innate. Contrary to witchcraft, sorcery is not always antisocial or illegitimate, and occurs with a higher frequency than does witchcraft.

Interestingly, some scholars believe that witchcraft does not, in truth, exist despite the strong beliefs of those in the culture. Witchcraft, they argue, exists only in the minds of the people, whereas sorcery is proven by the presence of paraphernalia, medicines, and the identification of sorcerer specialists in the community. The point is, however, that witchcraft serves so many functions it is hard to believe its importance can be whittled away by the difficulties involved in trying to prove its existence or in distinguishing it from sorcery. Everywhere there is social conflict: people become angry, get insulted, or perhaps become jealous of someone's success; it is during such uncomfortable times that witches may be found at fault and sorcerers may be called upon for help.

When someone in North American culture thinks of witches and witchcraft, the usual association is with early modern European witchcraft and the Salem trials in New England in 1692. Yet, these European-based witch beliefs, including the Salem case, were quite different from those of the pre-literate societies in which witchcraft occurs, where it functions as an everyday, socially acceptable way of managing tension, explaining the otherwise unexplainable, leveling disparities in wealth and status, and resolving social conflict. In contrast, early modern European witchcraft was a response to the strains of a time of profound change, marked by immense political and religious conflict. Although witch beliefs had been a feature of European culture since the Dark Ages, the Church managed to keep the situation under control until the turmoil of the sixteenth and seventeenth centuries, when the practice of labeling Church heretics as witches became popular and the witchhunt craze became a terrifying fact of history. Naturally, the Salem witchhunt of 1692 is of the greatest interest to Americans, but Salem's 200 arrests and 19 executions pale in comparison with the approximately 500,000 people who were executed in Europe during the fifteenth, sixteenth, and seventeenth centuries after having been convicted of witchcraft.

Ethnographic reports on witchcraft and sorcery dominate the literature, but other forces of evil are also responsible for much unjust suffering. One such power, but certainly not the only one, is the evil eye—widely known in the Middle East, parts of Europe, Central America, and Africa, areas characterized by Islamic and Judeo-Christian as well as so-called pagan religious traditions. The evil eye was believed to be a voluntary power brought about by the malicious nature of the possessor, on the one hand, or an involun-

tary but still dangerous, uncontrolled power, on the other. Strangers, dwarfs, old women, certain types of animals, menstruating women, and people with one eye have been often viewed as being particularly dangerous. Children and farm animals, the most precious of one's possessions, were thought most vulnerable to the evil eye, which could cause various disasters to occur immediately or in the future, particularly by asserting control over the victim. A variety of protective measures have been prescribed to ward off the evil eye. Glass evil eyes and various shaped metal amulets, for example, are sold to tourists and residents alike in modern Greece. Plants, certain avoidance actions, colors, and magical words and gestures have also at different times and places been felt to be effective against the evil eye.

In addition to the evil eye, anguish can be created by malicious ghosts, spirit possession, attacks by enemy shamans, curses of the envious, and the spells of evil magicians and other specialists who have learned how to manipulate power to harm others. Each of these causes harm and creates fear in a community and as such is an index of social strain; however, each may also function positively by allowing individuals to blame supernatural agencies rather than kinsmen and neighbors for illness or misfortunes that befall them.

In societies where no other explanations are available or satisfactory, belief in witchcraft, sorcery, and other forces of evil still accounts for the occurrence of disease, death, injustice, and other unpleasant and tragic events. In the lead article of this chapter, Daniel Offiong discusses the causes of contemporary witchcraft among the Ibibio of Nigeria. Harry Eastwell updates previous research on "voodoo deaths," arguing that some Australian aborigine deaths by magic or sorcery resembling classic cases of "voodoo death" may be more accurately diagnosable as orthodox medical conditions. In the third article Ronald Reminick describes the evil eye among the Amhara of Ethiopia. It is Reminick's belief that the Amhara use the evil eye to maintain their social system by displacing threats and projecting them onto an outgroup of strangers known as the *buda* people. The final article, by Edward J.

Moody, is about witchcraft in contemporary United States. Through his fieldwork with a group of Satanists in San Francisco, Moody shows how some people use witchcraft today to help them understand the world in which they live and to help them adjust to their personal inadequacies.

References Cited

Cannon, Walter B.
  1942 "Voodoo Death." *American Anthropologist* 44: 169–81.

Evans-Pritchard, E. E.
  1937 *Witchcraft, Oracles and Magic Among the Azandi*. Oxford: Clarendon Press.

Kluckhohn, Clyde
  1967 *Navaho Witchcraft*. Boston: Beacon Press (first published, 1944).

Kluckhohn, Clyde, and Dorthea Leighton
  1962 *The Navaho*. Cambridge, Mass.: Harvard University Press (first published, 1946).

Mair, Lucy
  1969 *Witchcraft*. New York: McGraw-Hill.

Shehu, U.
  1975 *Health Care in Rural Areas*. AFRO Technical Papers, No. 10.

Warner, W. Lloyd
  1964 *A Black Civilization: A Study of an Australian Tribe*, rev. ed. New York: Harper Torchbooks.

Witchcraft Among the Ibibio of Nigeria

Daniel Offiong

A recent witch purge among the Ibibio of Nigeria is the focus of Daniel Offiong's encyclopedic article on contemporary witchcraft in West Africa. Contrary to popular belief, the Ibibio have increased their reliance on witchcraft as an explanation for misfortunes, despite a higher level of scientific training throughout the country. Offiong's view is that people use witchcraft explanations to account for the frustration that accompanies their failure to achieve expected successes through education—an example of a manifest function of witchcraft. (One can only hypothesize on the latent functions of witchcraft, but no doubt they exist.) Professor Offiong demonstrates that although the Ibibio are predominantly Christian, elements of their faith are taken out of the Christian context and "synchronized" with traditional spirits and symbols in what is believed to result in a more certain method of combating all malicious supernatural forces. The Ibibio's distinction between white and black witches is a familiar use of symbolism among Westerners, who commonly associate various colors with good and evil, an association whose origin is so ancient and diverse as to make it impossible to trace.

Reprinted from the *African Studies Review*, Vol. 26, no. 1 (March 1983), pp. 107–24, by permission of the author and the African Studies Association.

IN NOVEMBER 1978 A WITCH-PURGE CRUSADE LED by Edem Edet Akpan (alias Akpan Ekwong) took place among the Ibibio people of the Cross River State in Nigeria. Edem claimed that all the evils which afflicted the Ibibio were attributable to the malevolent forces of witches and that he possessed supernatural powers to detect witches. Assisted by a few lieutenants, Edem began his crusade to eradicate witches and witchcraft. He would send messengers to a village to inform its residents that on a certain day of the week all were to assemble at the public square. Members of the village were forbidden to leave, and letters were sent out to those who were already out to return.

On the appointed day Edem or one of his lieutenants would arrive and go around picking out those he believed were witches. The suspects had their hands tied together and red pepper (which the villagers referred to as powder) sprayed all over their bodies and into their eyes, ears, and noses. In addition, large quantities of black ants were poured on the suspected witches. Under agonizing pain, they were asked to confess all those they had killed, those whose money or other property they had bewitched, their rank in the witch society, and so on. They were untied after they confessed. There were others, not selected by the crusaders, who voluntarily went to the village council to confess that they were witches and paid the fine stipulated for them. In this way they were able to avoid the ordeal meted out to those accused of witchcraft by the crusaders.

The meetings in which witches were selected were held simultaneously in several villages, since the leader of the crusade or any of his lieutenants (who had acquired the supernatural powers of the leader) could preside. People moved from one village to the other to watch witches confess.

The Police Commissioner moved to suppress

the witch purge, issuing orders to the police to shoot on sight and arresting Edem. Yet, despite these measures, the purge continued into 1979, for the crusade was extremely popular and villagers defiantly fought against the police who tried to disperse or prevent such gatherings. In most cases the police became ordinary spectators, an indication of their approval of the exercise. Even the arrested leader publicly stated that he was given excellent treatment and that he was allowed to make anti-witchcraft charms for people, including the police, while still in detention. The later trial and acquittal (on technical grounds) of Edem merely confirmed to the people the righteousness of their course of action. Traders, farmers, barren and pregnant women, and even taxi drivers were jubilant because they believed that the annihilation of witches and witchcraft in the area would usher in a new era in which people would go about their daily activity without worrying about being bewitched. These men and women stormed houses or compounds of "identified" witches to search for the witchcraft substance that made witches so powerful; in some cases they set such houses or compounds ablaze. Many suspected or identified witches were tortured to death, some were beaten to death, still others mysteriously disappeared from their homes and have never been seen again (presumably murdered); and at least three committed suicide rather than stand the shame and torture, and many others were maimed for life.

Events of that witch crusade suggested that the Ibibio see witches as posing a serious threat to the entire community; that witchcraft is an antisocial act that goes against what Durkheim calls collective conscience; that witches are humans with mysterious or supernatural power with which they can and do harm their fellow human beings. They attribute to witchcraft almost every social evil, political and social backwardness; even personal failures are regularly explained with the idiom and logic of witchcraft. In other words, witchcraft is the psychic act through which socially disapproved supernatural techniques influence events, and this perception is central to the cosmological ideas of the Ibibio.

Despite the obsession with the diabolical machinations of witches and witchcraft, highlighted by the traumatic events of 1978–79, there has not been any systematic ethnographic study of the factors responsible for the phenomenon and the dynamics of the art and its possible effect on the social, political, and economic life of the people of the more than two million Ibibio (1963 census). This study seeks to fill this gap through three objectives: to categorize witches and witchcraft; to describe the behavior and practices ascribed to witches; to describe the techniques for coping with their attacks as well as preventive measures against possible attacks.

Collection of the data for this paper occurred mainly among the Eastern and Delta Ibibio, two of the six very broad sub-cultural groups of the Ibibio, during the time of the Akpan Ekwong witch-eradication crusade in 1978–79. During the meetings in which crusaders picked out witches, their confessions and any other occurrences of interest were recorded. Six assistants working in pairs provided coverage for the simultaneous meetings. By having two assistants attend to each meeting it was possible to check the accuracy of their information as each recorded his observations separately. On the days without meetings there were informal conversations with people, often in bars with the researcher buying palm wine, to find out what people thought about the crusade and the confessions. Since the crusade and witch confessions were the talk of the moment, the researcher used to stop wherever he ran into people sitting by the roadside or elsewhere to talk about those things. Another common meeting-place was the village market, where almost every conversation was about the crusade and its events.

Further research to follow up the original collection of data took place in 1981. This consisted of interviews with confessed as well as suspected witches and with non-witches to get their views concerning the taxonomy of witches and witchcraft enunciated during the witch eradication crusade. Numerous discussions with people from other sub-cultural groups—areas that were not involved in the witch eradication crusade—were also held. Witchcraft is a very sensitive matter, and its investigation requires good personal rapport and confidence. Thus these interviews took the form of personal conversation and always began on a very informal note and advanced as long as the respondent was willing to cooperate. There was no set of specific questions except that each interviewee was asked if he or she had witnessed the 1978–79 witch purge and what were his or her impressions. Respondents were further asked if they believed in witches. A total of sixty interviews were conducted over a period of three months. Among those interviewed were eight male self-confessed witches, two suspected male witches, thirty-two male non-witches (including six whose mothers were suspected to be witches), fourteen female non-witches, two traditional doctors, and two spiritualists. The ages of the forty-six non-witches ranged from sixteen to forty-eight, and none had less than primary education. It should be emphasized that the primary interest in these interviews was to see if the taxonomy of witches and witchcraft collected during the 1978–79 witch purge would rhyme, and whether or not the respondents believed in witches and witchcraft. Without exception all agreed in various degrees that witches and witchcraft exist.

Witches and Witchcraft

Without attempting a comprehensive description of the Ibibio theology and world view, it suffices to say that most Ibibio "worship an all-powerful deity *(Absi)* who rules over the physical universe, other supernatural entities of lesser stature and mankind" (Messenger, 1959: 280). A host of spirits *(ndem)* aid Abasi by serving as intermediaries with mankind. They are his assistants or messengers rather than deities in their own right, and perform a variety of economic, social, political, and religious tasks for the deity. They inhabit shrines *(iso idem)* where prayers and sacrifices are offered, which they deliver to Abasi, who responds by sending power *(odudu)* to achieve the desired ends if the supplicants deserve it. In the economic realm, spirits promote the successful growth of crops and so forth, while politically they protect members of the village or lineage and aid the elders in their decisions. Socially, there are spirits responsible for fostering reproduction, health, and longevity. Most spirits perform religious tasks by maintaining contact between the religious practitioners and the deity, by installing souls and fates upon conception, and by observing the behavior of each human being and reporting it to Abasi for subsequent reward or punishment (Messenger, 1959: 281).

The Ibibio further believe that the prognostication can alter the course of a life. A person wishing to have knowledge of events to come consults a diviner *(Abia Idiong, Mbia Idiong,* plural) who gains his insights from Abasi through intercession of the spirit of divination. The ability of the Abia Idiong to foretell the future depends upon previous acts of the client as well as upon ritualistic perfection exercised by the diviner. Further once somebody takes ill, an Abia Idiong is consulted to find out the cause of illness as well as prescribe treatment. Mbia Idiong, as we shall see, are well versed in both good and bad medicines and may as well be witches. The ethic of their profession, however, compels them not to use bad medicine against their clients. They depend for their livelihood on their ability to provide good medicine and attract customers. Because of the fear posed by witchcraft and other malevolent forces, most Ibibio—young and old, male and female, wealthy and poor, educated and uneducated—resort to the use of good medicine (or turn to spiritualists) for charms to protect themselves from jealous foes.

The Ibibio distinguish between good *(eti)* and evil *(idiok)*. Evil represents the adversities that befall a person as the result of a fate which decrees them, the machinations of malevolent supernatural beings, or the attacks of a worker of evil magic (Messenger, 1959: 282). Evil can also befall somebody as the result of filial impiety, that is, disregard for the ancestors, or the violation of a taboo. On the other hand, good is viewed as the absence of misfortunes induced by the above agents.

Presently the Ibibio are predominantly Christians. Extremely few profess Islam, while fewer still are pagans. Yet virtually all still engage in pre-Christian and pre-Islamic beliefs and practices, although modifying some considerably to accommodate Islamic and Christian practice. For example, the Christian Holy Spirit *(Edisana Odudu)* is dissociated from the Trinity and conceived as the most powerful of the spirits, capable of curing every disease and injury, insuring longevity, bringing wealth, combatting all malicious supernatural forces, and rendering infinite other services. The Christian God *(Ata Abasi)* is syncretized with the Ibibio Abasi, and the Holy Spirit is thought to inhabit the church altar, which is regarded as a shrine where prayers and sacrifices could be made to Abasi. It is believed that the Holy Spirit could possess souls of communicants; thus the denominations such as Christ Army, Salvation Army, Apostolic Church, Seventh Day Adventist, Assembly of God, Cherubim and Seraphim, the Brotherhood of the Cross and Star, and others countenancing this kind of worship are called spiritualist churches.

Among members of the spiritualist churches are men and women (spiritualists) who are believed to be endowed with special powers by God. They, with the help of Edisana Odudu, heal people of all kinds of infirmities, foretell the future, pray for people to get promotion, rescue people from witchcraft attack, and so on. Basing their belief on the Biblical statement that "with God all things are possible," they believe there is no limit to what they can do. Most spiritualist churches designate Wednesday and Friday of every week as their healing and "request" days. These prayer meetings are always filled to capacity with people from all walks of life asking God for one favor or another. Of all the non-orthodox beliefs among the Ibibio, witches pose the greatest threat.

The Ibibio word for both witch and witchcraft is *ifot*, which they use in two senses. In the first usage, a witch is any person who behaves abnormally; that is, outside the expected patterns of behavior. Parents might thus refer to a child who behaves badly as a witch. Among abnormal behaviors likely to earn one the stigma of being a witch are manifestations of antisocial behavior such as: not being fond of greeting people; living alone in an isolated area; enjoying adultery; exacting too much for sales of anything; committing incest; walking about in the night; crying at night (in cases of children); not showing adequate sorrow at the death of a relative or somebody from within the community; not taking proper care of one's parents (particularly aged parents), children, wife or wives; hard-heartedness. In general, witches are mean-looking, mean-acting, or otherwise socially disruptive people whose behavior deviates significantly from cultural or community norms. What is obvious here is that deviance is not an attribute inherent in certain forms of a behavior; it is an attribute conferred upon these forms by social definitions. It is thus obvious that groups create deviance by making rules, the infraction of which they then assign the definition of deviance. By the same token, the Ibibio define what constitutes proper behavior, and those who significantly deviate from such patterns are generally referred to as witches, that is, wicked or anti-social or even asocial people. It should also be noted that these characteristics are also associated with sorcerers (*ifot*), but the Ibibio distinguish between witchcraft and sorcery.

In the second usage, a witch refers to the person that the community suspects of practicing witchcraft, a person who has confessed to practicing the art, or a person who has been identified by traditional doctors, spiritualists, or fellow witches to be a witch. A witch usually possesses the qualities described in the first usage of the term. Thus, once somebody confesses to being a witch or is identified as one, people are usually not surprised since the person will possess many anti-social and/ or asocial characteristics. Since the characteristics believed to be associated with witches are well understood, anybody who possesses them is labeled as such. Thus, long before the confession or accusation of being a witch occurs, people gossip about the behavior of the person. They will have talked about seeing the individual make any surreptitious visits to people who are known witches; they will say the person chased, flogged, or whipped them in dreams. As far as the Ibibio are concerned, all this confirms that the person is a witch. What this suggests is that witchcraft accusation follows a process of discussion and affirmation among relatives and friends before the accuser actually makes the accusation.

The Ibibio define witchcraft as some mystical or supernatural power that causes harm, including death. This power is purely psychic. Those involved in the art of witchcraft practice a form of incorporeal vampirism by removing the soul of their victim and transforming it into a goat, sheep, or cow (or any animal of their choice), thus causing a slow, wasting disease. According to the witches and others interviewed, and the confessions at the 1978–79 witch purge, once the animal into which the soul of their victim has been transferred is slaughtered and eaten by them, the victim dies instantly. The symbolic cannibalism is done invisibly, and only witches know what transpires. Witches, however, unlike sorcerers, do not perform rites and do not use bad medicine. Essentially, witchcraft is a psychic act that bridges the distance between the person of the witch and the person of his or her victim, even though the originators may not voluntarily wish to bewitch their victims.

The Ibibio conception of witchcraft is similar to that of the Azande (Evans-Pritchard, 1937), except that the Ibibio do not believe in the "inherent quality" of witchcraft. Both the Azande and the Ibibio believe that witches perform no rites, cast no spells, and possess no medicines; they view it as purely a psychic act. Like the Ibibio, the Nupe of Bida in northern Nigeria believe witchcraft is not hereditary but must be acquired from a person who already has it. It is interesting to note that while the Nupe say that witches are mostly women the Ibibio see witches as being mostly men, but both agree that women are the most dangerous witches (Nadel, 1954; 1952).

Like the Azande, the Ibibio believe that every witch has a physical substance, witchcraft, existing in his other body that allows the soul to engage in errands to harm their fellow beings. The Azande conceive of the witchcraft substance as a "round, hairy ball with teeth" which is passed on from parent to child, with all the sons of a male witch and all the daughters of a female witch being witches (Evans-Pritchard, 1937). Since witchcraft substance is organic, the Azande believe its existence can be determined through a post-mortem examination. While the Ibibio believe that witches have witchcraft substance, wherein lie their mysterious powers, they do not believe that it can be inherited. Every witch must get the substance from an established witch by physically swallowing the substance. The witchcraft substance of the Ibibio is a special concoction embodying red, white, and black thread, along with needles and other ingredients which the witch-to-be swallows. There are local variations in the substance. Taking the substance opens eyes, so to speak, and enables the person to move about mysteriously and perform many of the things that witches are believed to accomplish.

The Ibibio, like the Azande and the Mende of Sierra Leone, believe in the physicality of the substance in the stomach, but only renowned traditional doctors or spiritualists can use some supernatural powers to bring it out. They give the witch a substance that neutralizes the witchcraft substance in the stomach and forces the witch to vomit it out. Occasionally, at the death of a known witch, the children may ask a traditional doctor or

spiritualist to remove the substance by cutting the stomach open. It is not everybody who can see this, since certain supernatural powers have to be used on the substance to make it visible to the uninitiated. The Tiv also believe in the existence of the substance (called *tsav*), which they say grows on the hearts of human beings and some animals. It is said to look like the liver, and it may be rounded or notched at the edges. This substance is believed to be red, black, or white, and it can be good or bad (Parrinder, 1963: 136). The good and bad witchcraft are similar to the Ibibio black and white counterpart to which we shall turn later.

Witches, with the help of the substance, can change themselves into animals and birds such as dogs, cats (particularly black ones), and owls, and give off a glowing light like fireflies. This belief is quite similar to that of the Akan peoples of Ghana and Ivory Coast (Parrinder, 1963: 135). Witches leave their physical bodies during sleep. They can even change into rats and eat up the crops, and can spread diseases among people. They can suck the blood of their victims, thereby making the person look dry or suffer from anemia. Like the Ga of Ghana, the Ibibio believe that witches meet in companies at night while their mortal or physical bodies remain on their bed. They travel to the assembly by flying in their planes, or by canoes or bicycles. They can change into owls and fly to the assembly; or into cats, frogs, or dogs and change into human beings at the assembly. They meet at a particular spot where their victims are said to be transformed into various kinds of animals, killed, cooked, and eaten. Once this is done the victims die.

As the last paragraph suggests, witches are organized. This, in fact, was what the witches said during the 1978–79 witch-eradication meetings. They are hierarchically arranged—some witches are more powerful than others. One's power depends on the ability of the individual to locate an established witch who can provide the most potent power. Having become a witch, an individual knows who has the most powerful substance and can acquire it in addition to that he or she already has. Starting as a novice, a witch aspires to a higher position over the years. The highest rank consists of those who have been in the practice for a considerable number of years and have bewitched very many people. It is from this rank that the president of the chapter comes (each village constitutes a chapter, with the clan chapter as the supreme body). The headship of the witch society is the exclusive right of males, but the most experienced female witch is the recognized leader of all female witches and is referred to as Eka Iban. Women leaders in Ibibio churches are known by the same title. Among the Nupe, on the other hand, a woman is the acknowledged head witch (Nadel, 1954: 195).

The second rank consists of witches who have established themselves in the art and will in due course move into the top-most rank. The third rank consists of the novices. Finally comes the fourth rank, consisting of those who do not know that they are witches. They were given the substance without knowing it and the substance was not properly constituted, so that their eyes are not opened properly. They do bewitch people and also attend witch meetings, but they are not aware of what they do. Apart from the president, chapters have other officers such as the clerk who puts down names of people to be killed and those who have bewitched them; messengers who summon people to meetings and run errands; preachers, who are preachers in the real world—they open every meeting with prayers and a sermon; police officers who act as orderlies and also arrest and bring to the meeting stubborn victims—that is, souls of bewitched victims who hesitate to appear. The police are also responsible for torturing those the witches do not want to kill immediately.

Of great significance was the revelation during the witch-eradication crusade that witches take an oath of secrecy never to reveal anything to non-initiates, particularly the names of chapter members. At their meetings, witches do not answer to their real names; instead, they take on new and funny names, such as Ofim (air, suggesting the incomprehensibility of the person's power); Eyop Ekpo (ghost's oil palm, suggesting his invincibility); Asabo (python, dreaded snake because of its poison and power); Itiat (stone, suggesting invincibility). During the witch purge meetings, before members of any chapter confessed or named others in the society, the president performed a neutralization ceremony of the oath.

The Ibibio identify two kinds of witchcraft—Black (Obubit) and White (Afia). The purpose of Black witchcraft is to commit evil. Those who possess it are the ones who engage in destructive and diabolical acts, such as bewitching and killing their victims, bewitching their victims' money or even changing into rats and eating up the victims' crops. They can do almost any evil, and thus the Ibibio attribute almost anything evil to them.

On the other hand, those who possess White witchcraft are harmless. They are true witches but they do not kill or harm people. People also believe them to be more powerful than their Black counterparts. Although they attend witches' meetings, they do not practice the ceremonial cannibalism as do Black witches. Asked during interviews why they became White witches, they replied that it made them powerful. This is another way of saying that it gave them status within the community, because witches are feared and non-witches avoid conflict with them. This is probably one of the reasons why people confess to being witches. People also said they became White witches in order to protect themselves and their family from Black witches. During the crusade of 1978–79, witches said that they often try victims as they do in law courts, and that fellow witches argue as to whether the victim should be killed immediately, tortured, often for lengthy periods, deformed and let go, or be discharged and acquitted. White witches claimed that they defended certain victims whom they thought should be left alone. They do not always succeed but they have recorded successes. One Black witch said he answered Iboto (umbrella) at their assembly because he spent most of his time defending victims who otherwise would have been killed. His name signifies protection for people.

White witches remain harmless as long as they do not join in the ceremonial cannibalism of their Black counterparts. They said at interviews that when attending meetings they carry a piece of meat or some stockfish so that when Black witches are eating their human victims they too will be eating their meat or fish. Once a White witch eats the meat from Black witches he or she must give his or her own meat, which means bewitching somebody. In the usual way, the soul of the person will be commandeered and turned into a goat or any other animal which they kill and eat, and the person dies. Once this happens, the White witch becomes a Black one.

People become witches in several different ways. People may decide to become witches because of their natural tendency to do evil. They are envious or jealous, or may have had some conflict with their relatives or some other persons within the family or community and want to hurt them or other enemies. Enemies can be co-wives, brothers, or sisters, a former husband of a man's wife, somebody with whom a man became involved in a land case, or somebody who took away a girlfriend. In fact, the enemy can be anyone, including one's mother or father, and vice versa.

A person can turn into a witch because he suspects another person who is in a state of enmity with him is about to bewitch him, or that the person is a witch and the only way he can prevent being bewitched is to become a witch himself.

One can become a Black witch accidentally. One way is through seeking to purchase White witchcraft but instead acquiring the Black type. Another way, as one interviewee from a village not affected by the 1978–79 witch purge noted about several people in his and other neighboring villages who were Black witches without their being aware of it, was that the persons who prepared the witchcraft substance made a mistake. The result was that instead of being White witches the initiates are Black witches. Furthermore, since the substance was improperly concocted, these witches do not really know what they are, even though they attend witch meetings and also give their people to be killed and eaten. There is a third accidental way of becoming a witch in which the witch did not seek to become one. He or she may have approached a traditional doctor who was also a witch to provide some medicine or other assistance that will ward off witchcraft. One might then end up at a meeting of witches where he or she partakes in symbolic cannibalism. Once this happens the initiate must also bring a victim, whose soul is mysteriously transferred into an animal and then slaughtered, cooked, and eaten. A fourth way is through gift. In such a case the giver out of love gives someone the witchcraft substance to make him or her powerful so that no other person can bewitch or harm the recipient. The person who receives this gift may be unaware of it at the time but with certainty will one day find himself or herself in a meeting with other witches and begin to act as they do.

On the other hand, an individual may receive the substance out of hatred. In this case the proper concoctions are not given to him or her; the com-pounds are not complete so that his eyes are not properly opened. He is a very clumsy witch, lacks the proper power, does not eat at the table with other witches and behaves very much like a scavenger. During the witch purge exercise and interviews with witches from areas not affected by the purge, it was admitted that this kind of witchcraft is a form of punishment by the witch who gave the person the substance. Established witches say that the dresses of such scavenger-like witches are used in wiping their hands after eating during their meetings. Further, such witches are very dangerous, according to the other witches, because the powerful and clever witches command them to bring their children and other relatives to be killed and eaten. They are not aware that they are witches except that they dream about being involved in all kinds of witch activities. In fact, during the witch eradication purge the other witches recommended to the communities not to punish or fine such persons because they were not responsible for their actions.

Although not themselves witches, since they have not swallowed the substance, drummers, dancers, singers, and other such people are commandeered by witches to entertain their assemblies. Through supernatural means such people are brought to entertain witches without being conscious of their role except for dreaming about their activities. During the witch purge many spectators who were drummers and dancers confirmed that they had been engaging in long, drawn-out dreams of how they were entertaining people they did not know.

The Ibibio believe that even in death a witch continues in his art until the substance is removed. Those who voluntarily want to give up the practice go to traditional doctors who prepare for them certain medicines which they drink in order to force out the substance. During interviews the respondents confirmed without exception that they had heard about or personally know of certain people who brought out the substance after being treated by a traditional doctor or spiritualist. One interviewee said that he witnessed a relative bring out an egg which, when broken, contained needles, red, white, and black thread, and a host of other things. Another interviewee also said that he had personally witnessed the removal of the substance from the stomach of a dead witch who had told his children and other close relatives that they all had been earmarked for extinction. The only way to avoid this was to invite a traditional doctor at the death of the man to cut open his stomach and remove the substance, which turned out to be two live snakes (one of which was a python), bundles of black, red, and white thread, and other such items. Another interviewee, who was selected because he was close to an uncle believed to be a witch, said he had refused accepting the substance from his uncle before the latter died. He narrated the story of how, after the uncle's death, other relatives began to die in mysterious circumstances. According to the young man, an oracle was consulted and it was revealed that the dead uncle was the one killing those people—that he was still active as a witch even in death. The only remedy was the exhumation and burning of the skull. The young man said he participated in the exercise, and that it required superior supernatural powers before the attending traditional doctor could get out the skull. The right side of the head was still alive while all the other parts had decayed—the man had been buried for more than three years. The head was burned and from then on the family of the witch was at peace. Similar stories were repeated numerous times by those interviewed. The implication here is that even if all the living witches were to be eliminated, witchcraft would still exist—practiced by the dead.

Behavior of Witches

Behaviors ascribed to witches include metamorphosis into various animal forms and the ability to travel at unusual speed, sometimes over vast distances. During the witch-eradication exercises the witches themselves claimed to have various means of transportation, including airplanes. Thus they can travel to any place in the world to haunt their victims, and thus distance is not a problem for witches. No wonder that even when an Ibibio dies overseas the death is still attributed to witchcraft.

It was noted earlier that witches, through their supernatural powers, transfer the souls of their victims into any kind of animal and then kill and eat the animal. The result is the death of the victim. Witches can kill victims through accidents, childbirth, drowning, and disease, although they do not kill all of them. Some may decide just to torture. In such a case they remove the soul of the victim and put it in water, hang it on a tree or over a fireplace, or flog it every evening. As a result the person remains in ill health all the time and can only be rescued if the witches are given what they want. At times they refuse to accept anything until compelled by a supernatural power to let the victim go.

Witches decide at their nighttime meetings who should bring the next meat; they have a right to reject what is offered and order better meat. Interviews as well as confessions made during the witch purge crusade stated that in order to attend a meeting the soul of a witch escapes from the body and turns into a familiar bird or animal. If the husband is a witch and the wife is not, and if both of them sleep together, to attend the night assembly he touches his wife, which will make her sleep until he returns. Respondents said that if the wife has some supernatural power in her she can know when the husband's soul leaves the body, and if she wants to kill the husband all she needs to do is to rub his body with red pepper so that when the soul returns from the meeting it will not be able to penetrate the body. The husband then dies. The interviewees said that they had heard of this experiment being performed with success. However, they never showed or named the woman or man who had done this.

We already noted that Ibibio witches are organized, that they have officers, that all cases of victims of witches are brought up at their meetings, and that they are united through taking an oath to keep everything secret. Similarly, Ga witches belong to companies which meet at night to hold discussions and eat human flesh. The company is very much like a court and has a chief, a messenger, and an executioner (Parrinder, 1963: 143). According to confessions by Ga witches, they rival each other at their meetings in performing marvels, and the one with the most demons or marvels is made chief. As with Ibibio witches, since they are believed to meet together, they are believed to be able to recognize one another in the daytime and to be able to tell who are other witches.

Ibo witches are said to form guilds, enabling them to work together to procure victims. Parrinder (1963) notes that when an Ibo is accused of having bewitched somebody he or she marches around the village calling on members of his or her guild to surrender the parts of their victim they had taken. This is exactly what happens among the Ibibio, except that the request that members surrender their portions of meat is done at the night meetings. Similarly, Azande witches also meet together, with elders who are selected from the older and more experienced witches, assembling to the beating of drums made of human skin. The leaders advise the younger witches and also consider their proposals, for no witch is allowed to kill a man on his own; his suggestions have to be discussed and accepted by the whole assembly, as with Ibibio witches. While Ibibio and witches from other societies go out invisibly, those of the Lovedu are believed to go out at night with their whole being, and not just their souls.

Age is of as great significance in the behavior of witches as it is in the real and material world. Age is associated with wisdom. Most of the identified and confessed witches in the Akpan Ekwong crusade were old men and women. Their victims were mostly young, enterprising men and women. If they did not kill them the witches bewitched and stole their money. This is what the Ibibio refer to as *ino ekpu*. Or they cause them hard luck by preventing them from getting a job or, if they already have a job, profession, or trade, involve them in all kinds of situations where they will waste away their money. They may also cause failures in examinations. The fact of the matter is that the young pose a serious threat to the old people in a fast-changing, traditional society and there is a natural hostility between the two groups; this becomes expressed in witchcraft accusation. By accusing old people of bewitching them, young people provide a theory of causation as far as misfortune, death, and illness are concerned. As Crawford (1967: 104) has noted, "Belief in witchcraft is an attempt by man to rationalize and understand the malevolent forces of nature and the misfortunes of life."

The Ibibio are not alone in attributing almost every malevolent occurrence to witchcraft. Among the Xhosa, for instance, ill fortune traditionally was ascribed to witches and there was a "smelling out" process. After reviewing a vast literature on African witchcraft, Parrinder (1963: 128–29) concludes: "In modern times lack of success, failure in examinations, inability to gain promotion in office or shop, any strange disease, and especially barrenness in women and impotence in men, is attrib-

uted to witchcraft." In emphasizing the persistence of witchcraft belief among contemporary Africans, Parrinder notes further that "there is little sign of a decrease in witchcraft belief with increasing education." Conversations with fellow colleagues at the University of Calabar and at professional conferences suggest that most Nigerians still tenaciously hold to belief in witchcraft, as have similar conversations with colleagues from East and Central Africa about such beliefs in these areas. One colleague pointed out, for instance, that President Julius Nyerere in 1980 asked social scientists in Tanzania to investigate the impact of witchcraft belief on the national economy. In January 1969, President Kenyatta "urged a crowd of 40,000 Kenyans . . . to give up witchcraft" (Davidson, 1969: 121). Every now and then one reads in the newspapers of football matches being held up because one team has accused the other of using charms against them. All this suggests that Africans still very strongly believe in witchcraft.

Coping with Witchcraft

By now it is abundantly clear that the Ibibio view witchcraft as being irrationally vindictive or inexplicably persistent, and thus quickly attribute overwhelming, inexplicable, or irrational misfortune to witchcraft. Parents whose children die one after the other suspect witchcraft as the cause. Sudden illness in children as well as adults is attributed to witchcraft. Once somebody takes ill there is always an attempt to find out what the cause of the illness is. This happens even when the patient is in a hospital where traditional doctors frequently are smuggled in by relatives of the patient in order to perform certain sacrificial rites for the quick recovery of the sick. There are numerous cases in which patients have been removed from hospital beds because a traditional doctor or spiritualist has said that the patients are bewitched and no hospital can treat such cases. Further, there are cases in which sick people have been rushed to hospitals at the point of death after all attempts at traditional healing have failed.

Spiritualists claim to have the power to determine the cause of ill health, as do traditional doctors. In fact, every traditional doctor is believed to be either a Black or White witch; most confessed to being White witches during the white purge exercise. Traditional doctors consult oracles whom they claim tell them the causes and nature of the illness. On the other hand, spiritualists determine the causes of illness through spirit possession. Having determined the cause, the spiritualists and traditional doctors state what is to be done in order for the patient to be rescued from the witch attack.

The data for this study overwhelmingly point to the fact that most Ibibio go to either or both spiritualists and traditional doctors in spite of also perhaps receiving treatment in hospitals. The two traditional doctors and two spiritualists interviewed claimed to be making lots of money from highly educated clients. One of the spiritualists who had resided in Lagos said that such was the case there as well. Discussions among students in a social change class of almost one hundred students from all parts of Nigeria indicated that such practices are not peculiar to the Ibibio.

Traditional doctors, otherwise known as Abia Ibok or Abia Mfa, are those Westerners pejoratively refer to as witch-finders. The term witch-doctor emphasizes witch-finding, but in actual fact this is just one of their functions. The traditional doctor may as well be a witch, especially the White type, and thus claims to be able to determine easily and accurately if illness is due to witchcraft. One infers that by being a witch the doctor should have seen the sick person brought to a witch meeting. A witch, by way of emphasis, may be a traditional doctor well versed in the medicinal properties of herbs and roots and therefore a practitioner of good medicine. The witch may also be a sorcerer. Sorcery involves the use of spells, medicines, and rituals to harm others. Further, a spiritualist may himself be a witch. Many spiritualists, as well as those from established churches like Methodist, Catholic, and Lutheran, were identified as witches. Many also voluntarily confessed.

The Ibibio use the term Abia Ibok or Abia Mfa to include the practitioner of good (both curative and preventive) medicine as well as a sorcerer (ifot) whose medicine is used to harm people. Thus the Ibibio generally fear traditional doctors since they are versed in both good and bad medicine. But the ethic of their profession prevents them from harming their clients. The Ibibio could not afford to stop seeing a traditional doctor or a spiritualist because in almost every illness they are likely to suspect the involvement of the supernatu-

ral; only the traditional doctors and spiritualists can treat such cases. It is a common practice to travel out of one's community for treatment by a traditional doctor or spiritualist. This is because the witch who is the cause of the illness is in most cases likely to be a member of one's family or community. It is better to be far away from the area.

Once the spiritualist or traditional doctor diagnoses the cause of the illness to be witchcraft (if it is not witchcraft it must be the result of filial impiety or some other thing that will demand traditional or spiritual treatment), the relatives of the sick person will not only seek the cure but will also try to discover who is responsible. The belief is that a witch launches his attacks when motivated by hatred, envy, greed, or jealousy. What the victim or his people do is to review the list of those who are likely to feel such emotions toward him and then set about trying to discover who is actually the guilty person, who usually turns out to be in a state of enmity with the sick person. Often the suspected witch is within the extended family.

Traditional doctors frequently name witches responsible for illnesses. Some doctors have informants all over the area who, when they learn of illness, approach the family of the sick person or the person himself and encourage a would-be client to go with them to consult a renowned traditional doctor. Before they take the client to the traditional doctor, however, they first brief him about the person. Thus as soon as the patient arrives the doctor tells him his or her name and then begins to describe how the illness worries the client. In such cases the client readily believes that the doctor is really an expert, especially when he names an already suspected witch in the extended family of the client to be the cause of his or her misfortune.

Three informants claimed to have personal knowledge of how certain traditional doctors obtain their clients. These quacks have become very famous through the ingenious use of modern technology for long-established tricks of the trade. A tape recorder is hidden in a particular room, and as soon as clients arrive an attendant takes them to that room. The attendant secretly turns it on and then asks the client to pour a libation telling the gods and deities their names and their problems and then to pray for them to reveal these things to the doctor, who is soon to take on the role of diviner. While this is going on the attendant pretends to inform the doctor that the clients have arrived. By the time the attendant returns the people have completed their prayers. He then takes them to another room to wait for the arrival of the doctor. The attendant then secretly removes the tape and passes it on to the doctor, who thus learns all that has happened to the clients, even the names of their suspected witches. The doctor then appears, sits in his shrine, and the operation begins. All that he does is to recount what he had gathered from the tape, but to the clients he is an expert because he merely confirms what they had suspected all along.

The next and crucial stage is how to rescue the sick. Once the doctor confirms that witchcraft is the cause, he will, as a matter of necessity, describe what is to be done to rescue the sick person. If a spiritualist was consulted and also confirms the same cause, he too will equally prescribe the steps to take. In the old days the practice was for the relatives of the sick person to walk up to the suspected witch and demand that their son or daughter be de-witched, that is, for his or her soul, now with the witches and about to be killed and eaten, be returned to the sick person. The suspected witch would be given an ultimatum and a certain number of days, after which the relatives would take action. If the person did not recover by then, the relatives would machete the suspected witch to death. Although the killing of witches is not as common as it was, there are still cases in which this happens today. In yesteryears, should the accused witch deny the accusation, he or she was given an *esere* bean—*Physostigma Venemosum*—to eat. If he did not die then he was not a witch, but very few ever survived the effect of the poisonous bean. Today a suspected witch is asked to take an oath.

Witchcraft curers are of three categories: (1) those who cast out Beelzebub by using Beelzebub, (2) those who use spiritual means, and (3) those who use White witchcraft (Parrinder, 1963: 182). In the first category, the doctor, who may or may not be a witch, begs and pleads with the witches to spare the life of the bewitched. Usually the doctor makes sacrifices to witches to release the soul of the patient which they have hidden away, often on top of a silk-cotton tree. This frequently consists of placing some rice, yam, groundnuts (peanuts),

sugar, crayfish, salt, banana, a shilling, a penny (now kobo), a half-penny (one half-kobo), and goat meat on a white plate and then putting it on a table at the foot of a tree (often silk-cotton), where witches are believed to gather. The hope is that the witches will devour the meal and will in turn release the soul they hang on the tree, pending their killing and eating it. If they decide to release him or her the person recovers, but the release of the soul this time does not mean that the same person cannot be bewitched again; there are many cases in which rescue from witchcraft is for some people a perennial affair.

In the second category, the spiritualists use the all-powerful name of Jesus and his angels forcibly to wrest the bewitched person from the witches. The spiritualists constitute the Elijahs who rival the priests of Baal—the priests of Baal representing the witches. While the orthodox Christian churches do not, in theory, recognize the belief in witchcraft, data for this paper showed that a staggering number of members of these churches turn either to traditional doctors or spiritualists for rescue from witchcraft. African Christian sects such as Christ Army, Cherubim and Seraphim, Mount Zion, Apostolic Faith, Brotherhood of the Cross and Star, on the other hand, spend most of their time rescuing people from witch attack and other malevolents. Most spiritualists have syncretized certain aspects of traditional religious practices with those of the Christian faith. While it is more prestigious to attend an orthodox church than a spiritual church, highly established Ibibio will surreptitiously steal into a spiritualist's home at night to consult about personal problems, witch attacks, and so on. Similarly, others secretly sneak into a traditional doctor's house at night for consultation. When collecting data for this paper, arrangements were made with spiritualists and traditional doctors to stop at their residences at specified days and times. Each time their residences were filled with cars and people waiting to consult them. A bishop from a spiritualist church said that one of his clients bought his car for him and that others built him a house, wired it and purchased a generator; clients have built him houses in several parts of the country.

It should be noted that spiritualists, particularly those who are believed to be renowned in their trade, are greatly respected. They have better status in the community than the traditional doctors. During the witch-eradication crusade, witches, some of whom were traditional doctors, confessed that they fear the spiritualists because they rarely can stand their power. These witches also said that for other powers they could seek out answers, but with spiritual powers there was nothing they could do. One interviewee, a traditional doctor, said that with other supernatural powers you can give them what they want and then they let you do what you intend to do or you can forcefully neutralize them, but God does not take bribes and you cannot neutralize His powers: all powers originate from Him.

In the third situation, the person who possesses White witchcraft is believed to be more powerful than those who practice Black witchcraft. The most important thing is to be able to locate who possesses it, and the person must be located before the symbolic cannibalism of the witches is carried out. In this instance all that the possessor of White witchcraft does is to order the witches to release the person and his order is carried out.

Prevention of Witchcraft

Spending money trying to rescue oneself from witchcraft attack is not something that the Ibibio like. Just as the Tonga of Zambia consider a person a fool who fails first to acquire charms that would protect against evil persons filled with envy (Swartz, Turner, and Tuden, 1966), the Ibibio strongly believe in protection against witchcraft and other malign contingencies of fate. Their approach to protection against witchcraft and other evil forces is similar to that of the Wolof of the Gambia. In his study of witchcraft, David Ames (1959) categorized personal protective means against witchcraft into amulets, solutions applied internally and/or externally, and magical devices planted within the home or compound yard. With the exception of an insignificant few, the Ibibio people either possess charms from a traditional doctor or from a spiritualist. Some highly educated individuals may in conversations with others, particularly foreigners, pretend not to believe in the existence of witchcraft. Pretending disbelief is a mark of education and sophistication, but the fact is that most educated Ibibio do secretly visit traditional doctors and/or spiritualists for potent charms

against witchcraft. One traditional doctor said during an interview that election times are usually periods of lucrative business as politicians throng to him for charms against supernatural attacks by their opponents. A bishop stated to the interviewer that he had healed a politician who at the time of this writing is a governor of a state. A politician who is currently a member of the National Assembly consulted a spiritualist as to whether or not he should resign his position as a senior lecturer and acting head of a political science department in a Nigerian university. The spiritualist assured him of winning the election. He resigned, contested, and won the election.

The charms from spiritualists consist mainly of the cross on which Jesus was crucified, blessed handkerchiefs, and gravel that David used in killing Goliath. Amulets are carried about on the person of the believer; they may be hung around the neck, tied on the wrist, placed inside the shoes or on the finger, or tied around the waist. The L. W. de Lawrence Company of Chicago, Illinois, specializes in such amulets, and hundreds of Nigerians order them annually. This company has agents in several places in Nigeria—Ijebu Ode and Munshin in Western Nigeria are examples. All kinds of advertisements for charms against witchcraft and ill luck appear in Nigerian dailies. Certain compounds are believed to immunize people against witchcraft and other malicious attacks by supernatural forces. The commonest immunization is black powder (ekim). The skin of the client is cut open at several places with a razor blade by the traditional doctor, and while blood gushes out the powder is rubbed into the wounds. The preparation of the black powder is accompanied by special rites and incantations. Once a person is inoculated, the powder leaves indelible marks on the skin, reminiscent of inoculation against smallpox. The belief is that the powder produces an antidote or anti-toxin that prevents witches from excising the soul of the individual concerned. In other instances, concoctions, both spiritual and otherwise, are put in pots or other containers and buried or hung somewhere in the compound. These protect the compound and the inhabitants from witches' assault. Indeed, preventive charms are a big industry for both the traditional doctors and spiritualists who claim to make such charms. Needless to say, people believe them to be efficacious.

A wide variety of animal and plant materials are placed in amulets or made into solutions. Muslims often write on pieces of what they describe as virgin paper potent verses of the Koran for amulets. Christians, on their part, write potent verses of the Bible, particularly psalms, along with names of certain angels, spirits and saints, on virgin paper for amulets. A religious body known as Life-Study Fellowship, located in Noroton, Connecticut, lists potent verses in the Bible in their monthly magazine called *Faith*, and these verses are to be used each day. The Ibibio love this, as they write the verses on paper and carry them about as protection against witchcraft and other charms. The virgin paper mentioned above is made out of certain sacred animals like ram. These amulets, covered with leather, cloth, or brightly-colored plastic, along with rings, are carried about, as already noted, by those who believe they are vulnerable to witch attack, including those who believe they were once attacked and were rescued.

Medicines are buried in bottles or pots with the necks protruding just above the surface of the ground. Others are hung on the ceiling of houses or on doors. A very famous type of medicine among the Ibibio is known as *nim etim*. A red piece of cloth of about one square yard, a metal gong, and a decorated gourd with some concoctions in it are placed on the wall. Beneath it is a big stone and other substances unknown to the non-initiate. The owner has to make regular sacrifices, usually chicken, to it. Various other medicines require regular sacrifices. Besides these sacrifices, possessors of these protective medicines are made to observe certain rules including not trying to harm others and not having sexual intercourse with twin mothers. Since the possession of protective medicines calls for moral purity on the part of the possessor, one can detect some unanticipated functions. First, the possessors try to behave according to popular norms—they do not bewitch others or try to hurt other people in any way. If they do, it will surely return to them like a boomerang. Second, the rules the possessors have to maintain provide the traditional doctor with excuses for the failure of his medicine. If the medicine fails to work its possessor must have violated some rules in the form of a taboo. This prevents the client from asking the traditional doctor to return the money paid.

Conclusion

From the above analysis, it is clear that witchcraft beliefs form part of the Ibibio cosmology. Because of this, it is essential to see such beliefs against the background of religion and other ideas of the people. Religious beliefs are relevant not only because witchcraft beliefs are, in some aspects, an inversion of Ibibio beliefs, but also because religious beliefs provide alternative explanations for the cause of misfortune. As discussed in this paper, evil can befall a person as the result of fate, filial disobedience, or the violation of a taboo. As explanations for misfortune, all these have negative connotations and one does not elicit as much sympathy as when witchcraft is said to be the cause of the misfortune. Thus witchcraft becomes the scapegoat of every misfortune.

Increasing scientific knowledge does not necessarily destroy witchcraft beliefs. It is obvious to the Ibibio that if lightning strikes a man or a snake bites him he is likely to die. However, "this knowledge does not solve the problem as to why the lightning or snake should have killed the particular person in question. The knowledge that disease is caused by bacteria still does not solve the problem as to why the disease was 'sent'" (Crawford, 1967: 67). As Parrinder (1963: 168) has noted, "A man is killed by an animal, but the animal may be a witch in disguise, or he was acting under the influence of a spell. Rainfall may ruin one field and not another. The rain is the agent, but witchcraft is seen as the cause." Once sickness or misfortune strikes, the first question that people ask is why this has happened. Certainly there are many potential witches, but they have to be actuated by hatred or jealousy. The sufferer of misfortune begins to think of those who might have a grudge against him, either for some offense or through envy at this achievement or success.

It therefore follows that witchcraft is often suspected among a person's closest acquaintances. It is natural that those we know best are the ones with whom there may be the greatest friction. Thus accusations of witchcraft are often levelled against close relatives and rarely against those who live far away. When a person feels that a witch is responsible for his or her misfortune or sickness, he or she will have recourse to a traditional doctor or a spiritualist to find out who is responsible.

Once it is confirmed that a witch is responsible, the afflicted will seek to neutralize that diabolical power and to prevent a future attack.

As already noted, higher education and increasing scientific knowledge have not destroyed beliefs in witchcraft. Modernization has resulted in the disintegration of traditional societies and one repercussion arising from this has been insecurity. There is a great disparity between the aspirations of the people and their real chances of success; this has led to a high rate of failure. People tend to respond to these failures through extra-punitive measures; the individual does not blame his own short-comings but shifts the responsibility to external agents. The commonest of all the agents is witchcraft. This is not common just among the Ibibio.

In the Cornell survey at Abeokuta in Western Nigeria, one-half of all those suffering certain or probable mental disorders believed that they had been bewitched; close to a quarter believed that sorcery was being used against them (Leighton, 1963). Quite a few of them said that the talismans they had purchased to ensure success were "not strong enough" to counter other evil forces. A few of them blamed their failures on the neglect of traditional deities, the omission of sacrifices or infringement of taboos. The fear of witchcraft and other malevolent forces is still prevalent all over Nigeria. As Lloyd (1967: 254) has observed, witchcraft is not feared just by people who fail but perhaps even more so by the successful. The young man or woman who has his or her education financed by a large number of near kin fears the envy of his less fortunate half-brothers, half-sisters, and cousins—or, more especially, that of their mothers. The wealthy man suspects that his relatives and close friends expect greater benefits from his affluence than he is willing to share with them. The usual answer to these situations is to consult a traditional doctor or a spiritualist for a protective charm.

Finally, witchcraft belief provides a theory of causation as far as misfortune, death, and illness are concerned. Thus, despite the generalized anxiety witchcraft causes, its operation among the Ibibio provides an explanation for what would otherwise be unexplainable and hence potentially disruptive. Witchcraft consists of a set of moral judgments, hence it helps to reinforce ideas of what is good and what is bad or evil, and also who is good and who is bad. Generally, people whose behavior conflicts with the social norms is likely to be accused of being witches. Thus witchcraft helps make the Ibibio conform with accepted standards of behavior. The tendency is to equate witchcraft with the sentiments that provoke it, such as envy, greed, and hatred, in other words, the sentiments that are socially disapproved. Since a jealous person can be suspected of witchcraft, he is likely to minimize his jealousy. On the other hand, those he is jealous of may be witches themselves and may try to hurt him; thus, he is likely to control his jealousy. In this way sanctions against witchcraft help maintain the social order.

Voodoo Death and the Mechanism for Dispatch of the Dying in East Arnhem, Australia

Harry D. Eastwell

Among the Murngin of Australia, if a person commits a particularly heinous act—incest, for example—a possible response may be punishment by sorcery. The perpetrator may have a supernatural curse leveled at him and as a result shortly sicken or die. Cases of illness or death caused by witchcraft or sorcery are common in the ethnographic literature, with many documented accounts coming from aboriginal Australia. Several terms have been applied to this phenomenon—"psychosomatic," "magical," "psychogenic"—but "voodoo death" appears to be the most popular usage. In a classic article, Walter Cannon (1942) reasoned in physiological terms that a victim of sorcery may experience fear to the extent that he or she will die from the prolonged shock. W. Lloyd Warner (1964) believed a person who fell victim to a sorcerer's witchcraft could become ill or die because the community withdrew its support from the already "half-dead" person. Although Cannon's and Warner's theories on the subject have prevailed over the years, Harry D. Eastwell, a senior lecturer in psychiatry at the University of Queensland, Australia, provides in this article a much-needed update. Professor Eastwell does not deny the role of sorcery in "voodoo deaths"; rather, he takes issue with explanations that place the mechanism of the illness or death on "psycho-physiological reactions." It is Eastwell's belief that sorcery-induced phenomena such as those described in this article are more accurately diagnosable as orthodox medical conditions—specifically, dehydration by confiscation of fluids. With this explanation, Eastwell believes much of the mystique of voodoo death will fade.

Reproduced by permission of the American Anthropological Association from the *American Anthropologist*, Vol. 84, no. 1 (March 1982), pp. 5–17.

PIONEER ARNHEM ANTHROPOLOGIST W. LLOYD Warner, working with the "Murngin" people in and around Milingimbi Mission in 1926–29, thought that social practices involving direct suggestion caused certain deaths. In *A Black Civilization* he describes this sequence:

> The attitude is taken that the man is "half-dead" and will shortly die. The effect on a suggestible individual . . . is sufficient to set up certain psychophysiological reactions which tend to destroy him. Pressure is then applied through the mortuary rites which perform the function of attempting to remove him from the society of the living to that of the dead, further destroying his desire to live and frequently bringing about his ultimate death. [1958:9]

Together with other sections of Warner's account, this statement is regarded by Landy (1975) as a most useful description of the involvement of the social system in voodoo death which it helps define. Another early Arnhem anthropologist, Donald Thompson, also believed that suggestion could kill. He records: ". . . to the individual the prediction of death is sufficient ultimately to bring it to pass" (1939: 20).

The term "voodoo death" is time-hallowed, although Yap (1974) prefers "thanatomania," but also uses "psychosomatic" or "magical," and Lex (1974) uses "death by suggestion" but considers "psychocultural" as more appropriate. "Psychogenic" is also used, as by Lewis (1977). By implying a nonphysical cause, all these terms beg the question as to the mode of death, which characteristically occurs among native peoples after putative sorcery, from taboo violation, or while anticipating avengers. Barber (1961) notes the scarcity of satisfactorily documented case material, and Lewis comments that "it would require very special circumstances to be able to provide such information" (1977: 136). He concludes that most reports are anecdotal, not having been observed first-hand. Thus it has always been difficult to study actual cases scientifically, and this problem may become more acute in the future. Because medical services are now within call, to observe in Australia today is to intervene.

It is the nature of Warner's "psycho-physiological reaction," the mechanism of death, which is under debate. The classic contribution is by physiologist W. B. Cannon (1942), who uses Warner's descriptions. Cannon's conclusions are summarized by ethnopsychiatrist P. M. Yap, who defines voodoo death as "progressive psychophysiological disorganization with surgical shock from terror in catastrophic situations" (1974: 95), thus dispelling any ambiguity lingering around the term. Yap here follows Cannon in implicating dysfunction of the automatic nervous system, translating this concept as "surgical shock," which is a well-known clinical entity associated with many conditions other than surgery, and which is often terminal. The autonomic nervous system adjusts the body to emotional stimuli, of which hearing the prediction of one's own imminent demise is an extreme example. Other forceful proponents of an autonomic cause are Richter (1957) and Lex (1974). Lewis stresses the inconclusive aspect of this work of Cannon, Richter, and Lex: "[this] area of the subject is uncertain, holding a morbid fascination to find if it is true or not" (1977: 111).

Alternatively, the psychology of voodoo death is stressed by other authors, without specifying precisely the bodily mode of death. Thus Engel (1971) coined the term "giving up—given up complex" for the mental state involved. Lester (1972) describes it as hopelessness or helplessness, reinforced by social process. Another school of thought rejects the whole concept of psychogenic death. Barber (1961) favors physical illness or poison, but admits the possibility of terminal dehydration. Clune (1973), in a short comment unsupported by cases, also believes that poisoning is the mechanism, but this is criticized by Yap (1977), who regards it unlikely to be used by relatively unsophisticated peoples. Medical anthropologist G. Lewis is also skeptical: "Is it really the case that healthy people have died in a day, or three days, because they know they were victims of sorcery? Who has seen this happen with his own eyes? Is there no explanation for it but sorcery?" (1977: 111). In the face of discord and questioning, Yap (1977) appeals for concrete findings from ethnologists and medical field-workers that can be appraised critically.

Deaths in Times of Transition

Local Whites refer to this region with no roads to the outside world as "a backwater within a backwater," but White imperialism is nevertheless pervasive. In the northeast there is a small mining community, Nhulunbuy, where the hotel acts as a magnet for Aboriginal men on drinking sprees. The administration of the area is from the state capital, Darwin (population 50,000), 650 km. west of Nhulunbuy. Here the White coroner records and scrutinizes the details of each death. The Aboriginal population centers around five ex-mission settlements and one government settlement, each with 500 to 1,000 people. More traditional life styles are preserved in the 30 or so small outstations in the bush (populations from about 30 to 70). These are on clan territory and are an Aboriginal reaction to White encroachments. The total Aboriginal population is approximately 6,000.

Materially, White technology drastically changes death practices. Bush vehicles and aircraft now transport corpses and are then ritually decontaminated. At one settlement there are two mobile freezers, one for each moiety, so the corpse can be preserved in the deceased's house while distant relatives forgather (Reid 1979), some of them hiring aircraft for the journey. Above all, the behavior of relatives and health caretakers around the dying person is an amalgam of custom and intruding modern medical interventions, the latter increasingly carried out by trained Aboriginal health workers. White nurse practitioners organize small clinics at centers of over 200 people, and the Flying Doctor makes routine visits. The missionary pastor commonly sits on the sand with the dying patients. The juxtaposition of cultures makes the events under discussion more outstandingly incongruous and more difficult to describe with the minimum of bias.

Method

Since 1969 I have collected data during visits that were primarily for the purpose of conducting psychiatric clinics among the people. During the years 1970–76, I spent six weeks in the field; in other years I made two visits of two weeks each. The data were compiled from patients' medical records kept at the bush hospitals and outstation clinics, and from 15 Aboriginal health workers; 12 females and 3 males who were mostly in their 30s. All came from different clans: they were selected widely to gain community acceptance for their unsupervised work at night and weekends when, among other tasks, they attend the dying. They were not particularly acculturated, and most were not Christians. I have known many of them for a couple of years, some for a decade. All found these topics about death highly distasteful. All female informants were questioned in groups of two or three. Five spoke of the deaths of close relatives in the recent past. All responses were in Aboriginal English, and where relevant, these are recorded verbatim. Older male informants were deliberately not sought out for two reasons: they found the topics even more disagreeable, regarding the discussion as personally ominous, and the language problem was greater.

The Sorcery Syndrome: A Forerunner of Voodoo Death?

The third most common "psychiatric" syndrome in East Arnhem is a gross fear state. Fear of death from sorcery is the dominant symptom, with intense agitation and restlessness, gross sleeplessness and increased vigilance at night, terror, sweating, and other physiological accompaniments of fear. Many patients attempt to arm themselves with guns, knives, or spears, or to flee to the protection of Whites. Illusory misperceptions are common, such as hearing malefactors prowling outside their huts. The syndrome is similar whether or not sorcery has actually been performed; it is the belief of the patient and the patient's kin that establishes the diagnosis. It is treated pragmatically using tranquilizing drugs, with or without referral to traditional healers. Commonly, the syndrome exists for some weeks before diagnosis and treatment;

because sorcery is suspected, it is not immediately referred for Western treatment. The syndrome understandably refuses to fit readily into Western classificatory molds. I treated 39 such East Arnhem patients between 1969 and 1980; all but 1 were men. The syndrome is a reaction to specific life events that conform to the ethnographic situations preceding classical voodoo death, as listed in Table I. Most commonly, the evidence for sorcery is the sudden death of a clan relative, where all clan members regard themselves endangered by sorcery; when one patient recovers, another clan member may show the same symptoms. Three patients showed the overwhelming extent of their fear by an unusual autonomic reaction—marked protrusion of the eyeballs with widely dilated pupils. All these patients can be considered prime risks for voodoo death because of the ethnographic precipitants and because of the extreme autonomic reaction (Table I).

Only two patients died; their cases will be considered individually. The first died three months after the onset of his symptoms. He was 27 years old in 1973, and his father was accused of a mistake in a ceremony. His family moved to Numbulwar to minimize the sorcery risk. The son feared retribution, becoming so tremulous that he could not place tranquilizing tablets in his mouth and his pupils were widely dilated from autonomic activity. He died in the company of his parents, an Aboriginal health worker, and his tribal practitioner, in a panic attack with froth issuing from his mouth, similar to the description of one of Cannon's cases. A chest radiograph one month before death was normal. Arguments for the reality of voodoo death are not advanced in this case, because the patient suffered from a syndrome of psychosexual infantilism with a hormonal basis, with sex characteristics very poorly developed. This may have predisposed him to sudden death under stress, possibly because of abnormality of the adrenal glands, which mediate responses to stress as well as male sexual characteristics.

The second fatality was a 20-year-old Numbulwar man, newly married to an attractive girl. Within months of his marriage in 1979 he began losing weight and became impotent. He was dismayed when his wife began consorting with a rival who had been interested in her in the past but who had

TABLE 1   EVIDENCE OF SORCERY

Life Event Precipitating Fear-of-Sorcery Syndrome	Number of Patients
Sudden death of close clan relative	8
Serious illness of close clan relative	5
Disputes over acquisition of second or third wives	5
Promiscuity with married women	5
Life-threatening accident to patient (motor vehicle, electric shock, lightning strike)	3
Dispute with wife's lover	2
Promiscuity by sons	1
Murder of opponent in interclan spear fight	1
Unwitting desecration of ceremony ground	1
Ceremonial "mistakes" by father	1
Severe physical illness	1
Tribal healers accused of causing deaths	2
Unknown (precipitants not investigated)	4
	39

not negotiated successfully for her. The patient was more dismayed when his parents, seeking to explain his obvious physical decline, asserted that his rival was ensorcelling his beer. When referred for treatment, he was a well-developed case of the syndrome described above, convinced that nothing could save him. At this time, medical tests at the settlement clinic suggested an alternative explanation for his physical decline: kidney function was failing. He was transported by Flying Doctor aircraft to Darwin for treatment in a fully equipped hospital, where the diagnosis was chronic nephritis and treatment involved correcting the imbalance of chemicals in his body by intravenous therapy, with tubes inserted into veins, mouth, and bladder. In his frightened state he misinterpreted these tubes into and out of his body, fearing that his vital essence was draining away through them, a recurrent Aboriginal fear in this situation. He escaped from the hospital, borrowed air fare, and returned home to the care of his parents who were already making plans to avenge his death. Here his kidney failure was complicated by heart failure, and he died one month after the initial diagnosis. (The young wife remarried the rival af-

ter the unseemly lapse of only four months. Thereupon the patient's uncles, who lived on a large island off the coast, hired an aircraft to mount a revenge expedition to Numbulwar. The new husband was wounded but escaped with his life, and the uncles retired with honor, reboarded their aircraft, and headed back home.)

In these 39 syndrome cases both patient and relatives expected death, but when it did occur it was explainable by orthodox Western medicine. These data cannot be used to argue that terror can never cause death, but its rarity here poses significant questions. It implies we may have adopted the native belief system too readily and unquestioningly that in accepting sorcery as a sufficient cause. Fear states such as this Arnhem example are widely distributed among native peoples. The Latin American variant, *susto*, meaning "fright," is mentioned by Rubel (1964) as not being associated with dramatic death. Despite Lewis's familiarity with sorcery cases during his two years in New Guinea, he also found the absence of dramatic deaths noteworthy: "I did not witness illnesses or deaths more devastating and intrinsically mysterious than illnesses and deaths I had seen in English hospitals" (1977: 112). As Western medical services extend into regions where voodoo deaths were reported, so the possibility diminishes of detecting a death in which psychosocial factors operate to the exclusion of physical causes. The two cases already described would serve as good models of voodoo death if the physical substratum remained undisclosed. From his study of historical and ethnographic sources, Ellenberger (1965) elaborates the concept of psychogenic death into rapid and slow varieties. The above cases conform to his rapid variety and to his Australo-Melanesian type which is characterized by paralyzing fear. This is contrasted with his Polynesian type, in which the emotion of shame is predominant.

Voodoo Death Averted

To establish the cause of voodoo death in bodily terms, a series of victims should be examined just prior to death. Cannon recommends a set of simple but valuable observations to test the validity of his theory, for example: "The pulse towards the end would be rapid and thready. The skin would be cool and moist" (1942: 180). That such observations are not available attests to the difficulty of examining even isolated cases. In practical terms of fieldwork, once the sequence is set in motion, the major difficulty in making observations is lack of preexisting rapport with the relatives who must tolerate the intrusion and potential intervention of the observer. The voodoo death sequence of Warner where "all the members of the society act in a manner exactly opposite to the ordinary" (1958: 9) was interrupted in the following two cases.

G., an unmarried mother aged 24, lived in a tribally oriented outstation 30 km. from Milingimbi. She refused marriage to a tribal elder and his third wife, and there was speculation, even expectation, that he would retaliate with sorcery because he had paid the bride price, which could not now be repaid. In 1974, her mother, an attractive widow, decided to remarry, threatening to end G.'s notably dependent relationship with her. G. was supported by her mother's welfare payments, which would cease when she remarried. G. responded to these twin threats of losing mother and losing financial support with a series of dramatic hysterical trances, treated first by a tribal practitioner. These trances were misinterpreted by her

relatives as evidence of sorcery from her spurned husband. After one trance, they responded by commencing the ancestral songs, withdrawing from her, and restricting her water. This was an effort to salvage her soul, which would then be available to animate later generations of her clan, as Warner describes. Hearing of these events, the White nurse at Milingimbi demanded that G. be brought to her clinic. After two days G. was carried in, close to death from dehydration, with a fungal growth in her mouth from the drying up of salivary flow. At that time she was anuric (experiencing kidney failure from severe dehydration), a state akin to Yap's "surgical shock." She was beyond help in the bush and was flown to the Darwin Hospital, 450 km. away, against the wishes of relatives who acted as if she were dead already and so should remain near clan territory. In the hospital she was still anuric, clear evidence of dehydration, despite intravenous fluids given in the bush. After lengthy resuscitation in hospital, hysterical blindness remained, easily interpreted as reaction to her recent victim status. I examined the patient in the hospital and took her full history later from her mother at Milingimbi. Her sight recovered in four months and she is presently quite well. It is clear that had this patient died, the mode of death would have been dehydration.

M. of Yirrkala was 35 years old in 1972 when he suffered a radiographically demonstrated artery occlusion to the brain (the basis of a severe stroke). This occurred while he was dancing in a ceremony, clear evidence of sorcery. A year later I found him lying in the sun, socially isolated, with chanting relatives withdrawn to the shade of a nearby hut. Against the wishes of relatives, but at his own request, he was removed by air to Darwin Hospital 650 km. away. He drank copiously before boarding the plane. In the hospital I treated him with major tranquilizing drugs. After a good recovery he chose not to return to Yirrkala for one year for fear of further "singing" (his own word). For him this was a year of lonely existence in Darwin, so he relented and returned to his clan. He died at his clan outstation one month later but the circumstances are unknown. The precipitant of the previous mortification is known in this case: his stroke induced disinhibited behavior in which he made sexual advances to his caretaker, a classificatory mother.

The death of M. of Milingimbi (born 1929, died 1955) is recounted here, not because of relevance to the dehydration hypothesis, but because it provides additional information about the relatives' reactions, necessary for the presentation of a more complete model of the voodoo death sequence. The information comes from her medical file and from the White nurse who was in attendance. Three weeks before death, relatives began chanting her clan songs, wailing in grief, and withdrawing from her, saying she was "dead," the sequence described by Warner. She attended the clinic daily in an agitated state, spending most of her time in the company of White nurses, a most un-Aboriginal behavior, which is otherwise observed only in the fear state described above. She was not immediately diagnosed as pregnant but she went into labor and delivered a small, stillborn baby of perhaps 24 weeks gestation. She remained in postpartum care because of grossly disturbed behavior unrelated to any signs of fever, in which she screamed repeatedly and attacked White staff. Then three days postpartum, a fever of 39°C was recorded and she died with copious frothing of saliva and mucus. Her relatives then arranged burial within hours, while her body was still warm, with no chanting or rites. Her brother asked the White linguist to write to absent relatives giving the time of death as three weeks previously, the time when the chanting and wailing was heard. From the Aboriginal viewpoint, the cause of death was sorcery by a cowife, using the patient's urine patch. From the Western viewpoint, the sudden rise of temperature preceding death is typical of a well-known complication of childbirth, abnormal blood clots in the lung, which occurs with greatest frequency two to four days postpartum, as here, and with a temperature of the order recorded. This does not imply that psychosomatic factors were completely absent. The case is included as "voodoo death averted" because her death in the manner described probably preempted the usual voodoo death sequence with terminal dehydration had she returned to her relatives.

A model for mortification in voodoo death can now be presented. The relatives and victim conclude that sorcery-induced death is inevitable. The relatives withdraw, wailing in grief, and the songs begin. The victim is socially dead and fluid is withheld. After death there is no wailing and burial takes place promptly, for fear of the victim's trickster spirit, the *mokwuy*.

The Psychosocial Sequence for the Dispatch of the Dying

The predeath events surrounding certain old, enfeebled patients are described in this section. The majority of the patients have diagnosable medical conditions that sooner or later will cause death. All are regarded by relatives as loosely integrating body and soul. It is the concern for timely salvage of the soul that precipitates the sequence. Because of the difficulty of recording a series of voodoo deaths, it is proposed to argue by analogy, with the inference that if the mode of expediting bodily dying can be established in these cases, then it is likely that the same holds for voodoo death. The conclusion is that dehydration from confiscation of fluids is the common factor and the ultimate cause of death. The components of the sequence follow.

Beginning the Funeral Rites

Health-worker informants are adamant that chanting is requested by the dying person. H., a Rembarrnga woman, says: "Sick person asks his sons to start that singing." This is not always so, as Warner implies, because in the two cases cited previously where voodoo death was averted, and in the one following, the victims were not expecting the songs to begin and it was against their wishes, but they were powerless to prevent the sequence from continuing. These cases conform closely to the situation that Warner and Cannon discuss. Some local Whites mistakenly believe that the rites themselves are meant to hasten death, as mentioned by Reid (1979). That the rites alone are not a major factor is shown by the large number of patients who recover after the chants are begun, as Reid also notes. These recovering patients sometimes dismiss their mourners with some vexation, a comment on the power ascribed to the sequence, of which the songs are harbingers.

J. (born 1925, died 1976) was a man from the Arnhem bush. He underwent lengthy hospital stays in Darwin for leprosy, which became complicated by failure of major organs. When nothing more could be done, hospital authorities discharged him on November 29 to his clan outstation where it was expected he would live for a few weeks or months. He himself anticipated renewing associations with brothers, sons, ex-wives, and seeing for the last time places in the bush of significance to him (so stated to hospital staff). Relatives hired a small plane to take him to the nearest airstrip, Ramangining. He alighted unassisted from the plane to confront a situation he was totally unprepared for. As witnessed by resident anthropologist J. P. Reser, his clansmen were chanting his ancestral songs, and they remained at a distance from the plane. This is an example of Warner's "looking at the man as one already dead" (1958: 241). J. was conveyed by truck to his outstation, where he died within three days, on December 2.

The Acquiescence of the Dying

"The victim on his part reciprocates this feeling" (that his proper position is in the world of the dead) (Warner 1958: 242). Once the mortification gains momentum, when the body is regarded as weakly animated by the spirit of a guiding forefather, the patient develops a fatalistic acceptance of death. Health worker H. comments that her grandmother said emphatically in the vernacular, "This is time for me to die." Many patients are still capable of walking for nourishment if they so desired, but medical aid is rejected from this point on, and death occurs within days. Engel's complex of "giving up—given up" applies to this psychological state rather better than Lester's "hopelessness or helplessness." The ideology of clanship in Arnhem includes the concept of recycling the individual soul through future generations of the clan. This implies a quality of timelessness to individual life which aids the acceptance of death. Terminal patients often show great relief once the rites have begun, as White nurses comment.

The components of this psychosocial sequence are summed up by the senior nurse discussing a death at Yirrkala in 1972, of a woman I examined.

> Maku was an old widow, probably in her late 50s. After a vertebra collapsed (probably from tuberculosis) she was hospitalized for bedrest. We did not think she would die. One morning an old man appeared and said he dreamt she was going to die. He brought singers and dancers who began outside but she was left alone in the room. From that time she was not given water and we were asked not to help her.

The health workers did what the old man ordered. Her tongue was misshapen from thirst and she died the next day. There was running water in the hospital room but she made no attempt to reach it, although she could have if she tried.

This sequence was encountered again in a death at Galiwinku in 1978. G. was born in the bush around 1930 and became the second of four wives, with five grown children. When infection supervened on her chronic lung disease she became bedridden but was not considered moribund. She was moved on her blanket into the open where she remained day and night, until her death three days later. To the local missionary she said: "This is time for me to die." Relatives requested the White nurse to discontinue antibiotic injections. Twenty people were sitting in the shade 5 m. away. While she was still alert, one of her sons delivered a large bolt of red cloth in which her body was to be wrapped. This was ceremoniously placed beside her on the blanket. At this time the songs were begun and all fluid was withdrawn for her last two days. The cause of her death was listed as dehydration, not chest infection.

These three cases show an element of isolation by the relatives which brings them closely into line with the voodoo death sequence. This factor with its negation of lifelong social bonds must suggest strongly to the dying person the role he or she is expected to play.

The Death Mechanism: Dehydration by Confiscation of Fluids

With the establishment of this mechanism, much of the mystique of voodoo death will fade, at least for Arnhem. In this permaheat region which is 12° south latitude, where day temperatures below 27°C occur only once or twice a year, deaths were observed to take place 24 to 36 hours after total restriction of fluids. The deaths range from a desirable euthanasia where the sequence prevents prolonged dying, to an occasional avoidable death. In this circumstance the term "senilicide" is appropriate, signifying active intervention by the relatives in the confiscation of fluids. Jones and Horne (1972) believe that dehydration is the cause of similar deaths in the Australian Western Desert, but their case material, gathered from White nurses, is not given in detail. Two Melanesian voodoo deaths from dehydration are recorded in the literature (Barber 1961: Simon et al. 1961). Cannon quotes his medical correspondent W. E. Roth of Queensland, Australia, who says of the victim: ". . . he will actually lie down to die . . . even at the expense of refusing food and succour within his reach" (1942: 172). Other commentators record the refusal of food without specifically mentioning fluid: Gelfand's reliable African account is an example (1957: 539), as is Elkin's Arnhem case of 1956 (1977: 153). Cannon himself mentions of the victim: "In his terror he refuses both food and drink, a fact which many observers have noted. . . ." (1942: 176), and he quotes a Spanish Civil War death from "malignant anxiety" in which: "The lack of food appears to have attended lack of water for the urine was concentrated . . ." (1942: 180).

In Arnhem, the health workers are explicit that fluid is actually confiscated. Health worker H. states, "We take that water away from him—no need for water or food. We just don't give food or water." P., a Burada clanswoman living in Galiwinku: "The relatives say no more water." Male health worker D. of the Warramirri at Galiwinku: "If real close up finish, take water away so spirit goes." M., a Djapu woman at Yirrkala: "We take the water and food from the sick one." They reveal that it is a common practice which can be discussed openly.

Deaths at Two Settlements

Recent deaths at the compact settlement of Milingimbi, population 700, are well documented for two reasons. First, the nurse practitioner has been resident for nearly 30 years; she knows all the aged, and personally ministers to them at their deaths. Second, because Aboriginal houses have no refrigeration to store milk drinks, a system of distributing them to the dying has been arranged. When a container is used, it is returned to the clinic where it is refilled and sent back to the patient again. Thus the regularity of refilling gives some check on probable fluid intake. Between 1978 and mid-1980 there were eight deaths of patients over the age of 50, with terminal dehydration observed in seven, and brief case descriptions of these follow.

L., female, was born about 1915 and led a healthy life until an episode of heart failure developed, which would normally respond to therapy allowing a prolongation of life. The Flying Doctor was hopeful of recovery but finally annotated her medical file: "I cannot be held responsible if relatives refuse to give my patient food or fluid." The last note in her file reads: "Not eating or drinking. Deceased."

D., female was born about 1926. She suffered from the common obstructive airways disease, not necessarily fatal. Toward the end of her life she lived in the household of her son, a traditional healer. She was befriended by White staff members for many years. One of them, a graduate teacher, had this to say of her last illness: "Her relatives became upset when I gave fluids and her son threatened to knock me down. Later she herself became negativistic and refused water. She died of thirst." White concern had been increased by the patient's role in caring for an eight-year-old waif not directly related to her.

M., male, was born about 1922. He was a traditional painter on bark, which brought him an adequate income. Eventually he developed severe heart failure, which required hospital treatment away from his home, but which he refused. The senior nurse commented: "He would have died anyhow, but he was not given water for his last 24 hours." This was the most prompt death in the series, and one which was unquestionably a desirable euthanasia.

D., male, born about 1892, showed great tenacity for life, recovering from repeated chest infections. He was a sought-after informant as one of the last men to remember the annual visits of Indonesian traders to this coast. Warner mentions him by name. He was mentally alert up to his final year when senility supervened. The senior nurse commented on his mode of death: "His mouth was so dry, and the milk container left unused in the same room."

M., male, born about 1917, suffered from lung cancer. He died within days of receiving news of the death of his favorite son. The file reads: "Sept. 12: Told about son's death, deteriorating. Sept. 13: Fluid intake—minimal oral. Has not passed urine. Sept. 14: Died." The psychological aspect of "giving up—given up" was particularly prominent.

D., female, born about 1911, is mentioned in Warner as the femme fatale of the day. She later became a respected traditional healer. She suffered from obstructive airways disease but her last days were marked by temporary recovery when fluids were given by nurses. The file reads: "August 28. More alert. Taking drinks when offered. Aug. 30. Flying Doctor orders intravenous fluids. 2 litres given. Sept. 2. Refused fluids. Sept. 7. Died." Initially ambivalent about the prospect of death, she later became resigned and succumbed when additional relatives gathered.

D., male, born around 1900. Warner mentions him as embarking on a political career in which he acquired eight wives. Five of these were sitting at a respectful distance from him in his dying days. his physical disease was prostate cancer. "May 16: No fever. Given only very small amounts of fluid. May 18: Very little water. May 20: No fever. Died." The aspect of euthanasia with the prevention of suffering was paramount in his case. Three hundred people attended his funeral, with burial five days after death.

The Darwin coroner's conclusions are quoted for the following two deaths in 1978 at the remote Lake Evella settlement of 300 people. The first was D., male, born about 1915, who was in unskilled employment until his final illness, which was a potentially treatable heart ailment. The coroner recorded this finding: "He continued to refuse food and would drink only sips of water. He deteriorated rapidly and deceased." The second was M., female, born about 1920. She was reported to the nurse as suffering from diarrhea, but no evidence for this could be found. The coroner concluded: "While her condition improved she became reluctant to eat and drink and refused further medical treatment. Her condition stabilized but due to her refusal to eat or drink she gradually wasted away, deceasing June 19th." The coroner's findings were more detailed than usual for tribal deaths for the following reason. The only White nurse at this outpost became alarmed when he observed the confiscation of fluids from patients whom he judged capable of recovery. He gave sufficient evidence in writing to enable the coroner to absolve him from responsibility in these deaths.

Ritual Nullification of the Thirst Drive

According to Yap (1977), voodoo death takes place too rapidly to be due to dehydration, but he refers to no case material. The most rapid death reported here is that of M. from Milingimbi, 1978, when death took place in 24 hours in the absence of any fluid intake. Lex (1974) concedes that dehydration may sometimes be a factor, but she takes the view that autonomic dysfunction prevents the victim swallowing fluid or absorbing it. The evidence of the health workers is that fluid is actively withheld to expedite dying, and this also applied to the two cases in which voodoo death was averted. This confiscation of fluids explains the observed dehydration more parsimoniously; Lex's hypothesis regarding difficulty in swallowing is not a major factor, but in terminal dehydration it is true that water cannot be absorbed without aggravating the imbalance of minerals and salts in the body fluids. Among these people there is the cultural rationalization that the mortified individual is animated only by the spirit of the forefather, which does not require fluid: "It is then too late for food or drink." This ideology explains why some relatives actively promote dehydration while others passively allow it to occur. A unitary hypothesis for voodoo death is not proposed: what is proposed is that psychological factors are secondary to the basic physical process of dehydration, but both are involved. The continuing concept of voodoo death as caused by suggestion, that is, by the victim's belief in sorcery and the conviction of the victim's own demise, speaks to total involvement in his or her assumptive world. The notion of the psychological causation has persisted because "it would seem to show such final and tragic evidence of true belief" (Lewis 1977: 139).

The social behavior of beginning the obsequies while the patient-victim is alert defines the role of the dying person and prescribes the person's behavior. The ancestral songs in which he or she silently participates become self-referential, and the induced mental state of "giving up—given up" is sufficient to suppress the physiological drive for fluid. It allows dehydration its final action and prevents active efforts to obtain fluid. In this fatalistic state of mind the person truly regards death as a rite of passage and is oriented to the next world. Significantly, as the health workers say, it is a "water world and has spirits in it," in the depths of the clan waterhole. As Warner says "[he] returns to his totemic well, and the circle is complete" (1958: 5).

The Evil Eye Belief Among the Amhara of Ethiopia

Ronald A. Reminick

The evil eye belief maintains that the eyes of gods, demons, and even humans can be extremely dangerous to a person upon whom they are directed. The effect of a gaze from an evil eye upon a hapless victim could be death, impotence, frigidity, or perhaps infliction of some terrifying disease. The French call the evil eye the mauvais oeil, *while in Italy and Germany it is known respectively as* malocchio *and* bose blick. *The biblical proverb "Eat thou not the bread of him that hath an evil eye" (Proverbs 26:3) is evidence of a religious concern for the belief. In the following article Ronald Reminick examines the evil eye among the Amhara, a group of settled agriculturalists who live in the central highlands of Ethiopia. The Amhara believe evil power is not attributed to people within their own social structure, but is practiced by people who are not part of their society. The* buda, *or evil eye people, are believed to be a completely different population. Reminick holds that the internal solidarity of the Amhara is preserved by the displacement of the threat of the evil eye and its projection onto an outgroup of strangers.*

Reprinted from *Ethnology*, Vol. 13 (July 1974), pp. 279–91, by permission of the author and the Department of Anthropology, University of Pittsburgh.

VARIATIONS OF THE BELIEF IN THE EVIL EYE are known throughout much of the world, yet surprisingly little attention has been given to explaining the dynamics of this aspect of culture (cf. Spooner 1970; Foster 1972; Douglas 1970). The Amhara of Ethiopia hold to this belief. Data for this study were gathered among the Mänze Amhara of the central highlands of Shoa Province, Ethiopia. Their habitat is a rolling plateau ranging in altitude from 9,500 to 13,000 feet. The seasons vary from temperate and dry to wet and cold. The Amhara are settled agriculturists raising primarily barley, wheat, and a variety of beans and importing teff grain, cotton, and spices from the lower and warmer regions in the gorges and valleys nearby. Amhara technology is simple, involving the bull-drawn plow, crop rotation, soil furrowing for drainage, and some irrigation where streams are accessible. The soil is rich enough to maintain three harvests annually. Other important technological items include the sickle, loom, and the walking and fighting stick for the men; the spindle, large clay water jug, grindstone, and cooking utensils for the women. The most highly prized item of technology is the rifle, which symbolizes the proud warrior traditions of the Amhara and a man's duty to defend his inherited land.

The homestead is the primary domain of authority within the larger political structure. The homestead varies in size from that of a nuclear family to a large hamlet consisting of several related families and their servants, tenants, and former slaves. The system of authority can be characterized in terms of Weber's patriarchalism, where a group is organized on the basis of kinship and economics with authority exercised by a particular person controlling the resources upon which the group depends (Weber 1948: 346 ff). Obedience and loyalty are owed to the person rather than to the role or the rule, and this person rules only by the consent of the group members who stand to gain a portion of their patriarch's wealth as a legacy upon his death. This institution of patriarchal authority is reinforced by a cultural emphasis on male qualities of aggressiveness oriented around the acquisition and defense of land. Land is the fundamental requirement of the patriarchal system, for without it a man cannot fulfill his basic role of supporting his dependents and providing a legacy for his children as a reward for their loyalty and service. But land is a scarce resource, and there are often more claims to land than can be supported. Thus, closest siblings may unite against a more distant relative to maintain land among themselves or siblings may compete for scarce land among themselves, becoming bitter enemies and dividing the kinship or domestic group.

The Amhara peasant's supernatural world includes both Christian and pagan elements. Although Monophysite Christianity is the legitimate religion of the Amhara people, who in fact define their tribal identity largely in terms of their Christian God, the pagan or "nonlegitimate" systems of belief also play an important role in the everyday routine of the peasant's social and cultural life. There are essentially four separate realms of supernatural beliefs. First, there is the dominant Monophysite Christian religion involving the Almighty God, the Devil, and the saints and angels in Heaven. Second, there are the *zar* and the *adbar* spirits, "protectors" who exact tribute in return for physical and emotional security and who deal out punishments for failure to recognize them through the practice of the appropriate rituals. Third is the belief in the *buda*, a class of people who possess the evil eye, and who exert a deadly power over the descendants of God's "chosen children." The fourth category of beliefs includes the *čiraq* and *satan*, ghouls and devils that prowl the countryside, creating danger to unsuspecting persons who cross their path.

The Status of the Evil Eye People

In contrast to much of sub-Saharan Africa, evil power is not attributed to a person occupying a status at a point of social disjunction within the structure of social relations. Rather, those people who are believed to have a dangerous power are not a part of Amhara society. The *buda* or evil eye people are a completely separate category of population of different ethnic origin, with a rather minimum amount of interaction with the Amhara people. The *buda* own no land and therefore work in handicrafts, making pots from clay, fashioning tools from iron, and weaving cloth from handspun cotton and sheep's hair. They are known generally as *ṭayb*. The term is derived from the noun *tebib* which means "craftsman." It is also associated with an idea which means "to be wise" or "to be very clever." The terms *ṭayb* and *buda* are synonymous. To be *buda* is to have the evil eye. The term "evil eye" is also known as *ayn og* and sometimes *kifu ayn*. It designates the power to curse and destroy and reincarnate, harnessing the labor of the dead for one's own ends.

The beautiful craftsmanship of the *buda's* work is one sign of his status. The finely made, well-proportioned water pots with their black finish are unmatched by any Amhara peasant who would deign to make one in the first place. Fashioning tools from iron takes considerably more skill and is not practiced by anyone but the *ṭayb* people. Although weaving is associated with the *ṭayb* people, many Mänze peasants have also taken up the skill, not as a trade but to accumulate needed cash. Yet the peasants say the *ṭayb* know a special form of weaving that the Amhara cannot learn. There is, though, a critical distinction made by the Amhara peasant that frees him from the stigma of the craft, *viz.*, that he did not inherit the trade from his father.

There are, then, two major social categories. The *rega* are those people whose ancestry are *niṣu atint*, of "clean bone," unblemished by social stigma or bodily catastrophe, such as leprosy. They are the "noble people." Most Amhara trace their lineages to a near relative or ancestor who had wealth and status and who was patron of many who worked the land of their estates. A *rega* person is known by his community; his relatives and ancestors are known, and hence he cannot be suspected of being "impure." The *buda* person, on the other hand, is one who has inherited through his line the lower status. One may inherit status through either the mother's or the father's line, or both. One cannot avoid the status of *buda*. It is his destiny to be born into the tradition.

Anyone whose ancestry or kin are unknown

may be suspect. If one is suspected of being *buda*, he may be liable to accusation by a family that fears that he "attacked" or "ate" or "stabbed" one of their members. Accusation must be carried out on one's own without the sanction of the courts. If one marries a person whose family is unknown, and it is later learned that the relatives were of *buda* status, the *rega* spouse will be forced to effect a divorce and another spouse of "clean bone" will then be found as a substitute. Sometimes the spouse who is *buda* will be driven from the community, or more rarely killed, for attempting to taint a family's line.

There is no sure way to recognize a *buda*, for their physical qualities may not differ discernibly from other people. They may be thinner than usual, because their blood is believed to be thinner than a normal Amhara person's blood. They may have an eye deformity or suffer discharge of tears or pus from their eyes. They may tend to look sidewise at people, or they may have very light skin, or they may be believed to have an ashen substance in their mouths and be unable to spit saliva. But these qualities are not, in themselves, sufficient to arouse suspicion. There are other more convincing characteristics, such as occupation. If a stranger comes to town and is overly friendly, suspicion may be aroused that he is too eager to befriend others, and hence, possibly over-anxious about concealing his true identity. The relations of *buda* people with *rega* people are in *status quo*, being neither overly peaceful nor overly combative. They mix with each other easily, as in court, in the shops, and in market places without repercussions, as long as their social relations are on a superficial basis.

The Attack of the Evil Eye

The real threat of the *buda* people to the *rega* people is the ever-present possibility of attack. Most people are fearful of even mentioning the *buda*, especially at night, because if they are overheard by a *buda* he will become angry and one of the family may be "eaten," thereby causing sickness or death. A person is most vulnerable to being "eaten" when the *buda* sees fear, worry, or anxiety in his potential victim. Therefore, it helps to maintain one's composure when in the presence of a *buda*, acting naturally as if the *buda* did not matter at all.

The peasant who is especially good looking or whose child is considered beautiful, or someone who does something extraordinary, may fear the attack of the evil eye because of the envy believed to be kindled in the *buda*. The attack is not limited to human beings. The evil eye can attack any living object. When a person is "eaten" he may know immediately that he has been attacked, for the consequences may occur at the same time as the strike. But the symptoms can just as easily be delayed for a few hours, a day, or a week, rarely longer. If a *buda* has planned an attack on some victim, but this victim suddenly falls ill before the strike is to be made, then the *buda* may merely wait patiently to see the outcome of the patient's illness. If the person recovers, the *buda* may then attack. If he dies, the *buda* will then attend to the activity that involves *buda* people with the dead. It is believed that when one is feeling ill the body is more vulnerable than ever to an attack by the evil eye.

The process of attack may occur in one of several different manners. Because of the power of the evil eye, *buda* people can change into hyenas and roam the countryside at night. It is convenient for a *buda* to attack a victim in this form in order to conceal his human identity. The Amhara attach great salience to the hyena, partly because they believe in both the natural and the supernatural forms of this animal. If the *buda*, in seeking out a victim, assume the form of the hyena, the transformation takes place by his first taking off the hair and then rolling in the ashes of the hearth. Once transformed into a hyena, he then searches for a victim, and on finding one, fixes the unfortunate person with an evil gaze, returns home, rolls in the ashes to turn back into human form, and waits for the victim to die. The second method of attack involves the evil eye person finding a victim, twisting the root of a certain plant and forming a loop with this root as if one were tying a knot. The loop is then drawn smaller very slowly, and while this is being done, the victim dies. After the victim is buried, the *buda* squats by the graveside and slowly loosens the knot while shouting to the corpse to arise. The body is exhumed and the grave is then closed up again by retightening the knot. The third method of attack involves giving the evil eye gaze to the victim and then waiting for his death. After burial the body is exhumed by carrying two round, thin, lentil-pancake breads to the grave, one lying flat and the other folded twice. Unfolding the one bread opens the grave and brings out the body. Folding up the other recloses the grave.

The people most liable to attack are those who have a bit more wealth than the average person, who are handsome, and who are proud of their beautiful children. Those who become especially liable to attack are those who become too familiar with the *buda* person, which heightens one's chances of succumbing to the gaze of the evil eye. One comes into physical proximity with *buda* people in daily affairs, but social distance is usually maintained. A likely danger to the *rega* people is the presence of a beautiful *buda* woman or handsome *buda* man. A *rega* who sleeps with a *buda* will grow thinner and thinner because the eye of the *buda* will suck the blood out of the victim, causing the victim to lose his or her appetite and to become weak and helpless. When a *rega* is attracted to a *buda* and the *buda* wishes to draw the *rega* nearer, the *buda* will wait for a moment of privacy and then will utter to the *rega* something about seeing the genitals revealed through the *rega's* clothes. This will fill the *rega* with excitement and then the *rega* will "fall with" the *buda* lover. The warm affectionate relationship can be maintained without serious danger; but when there is a quarrel, the *rega*, already weakened by the blood given up to the *buda*, will be "eaten" and become seriously ill.

However the attack is effectuated and however the corpse is taken from the grave, the ultimate goal of the *buda* is to use the victim as a slave. After being exhumed, the corpse is taken to the house of the *buda* where it is brought back to life in order to serve the *buda*. But the slave is mute, unable to utter a single sound. The *buda* owns two switches. One switch is used to turn the slave into a pot when visitors come; and then when the outsiders have left, a rap on the pot with the other switch transforms the pot into a slave again. In this way outside interference is prevented. When the slave is treated cruelly, it will shed silent tears, desperately trying to weep. (It is interesting to note that to be silent in the presence of one's superiors and to suffer indignities in silence is the obligation of children and the traits attributed to the despised dog.) The slave of the *buda* does not go on indefinitely in its risen state. After seven years the body

begins to disintegrate, finally turning into ashes and leaving the *buda* without a "helper."

The *buda's* distinctive activities are not fully intentional. The *buda* has within his body a quality or power known as *qalb*. *Qalb* is a subtle, internal, unconscious desire to perform those activities which make the *buda* so notorious. In the *buda's* daily interactions with the *rega* people of the community, there is really little difference between the two groups, both sharing feelings of love and hate, envy and covetousness, anger and aggression. But the *buda* has this additional power gained from the association with the devil that creates an illegitimate advantage over those of higher status and greater legitimate advantage. The *buda*, by his very nature, must "eat" others. He does this in order to better his chances for gaining opportunities and achieving success in his daily life among the *rega* people. He uses his power, then, to make himself equal with others who have more land, more "helpers" such as tenants, servants, and former slaves, and thus he attempts to acquire those objects, persons and, services that he covets among the *rega* Amhara people. There is a difference of opinion as to whether or not the *buda* himself can be the object and victim of evil eye attack. Some Amhara say that just as the *rega* fight among themselves for the wealth of the lineage, so the *buda* people fight and attack each other with the evil eye for more equal shares of wealth. But other Amhara say that this is not true; that the *buda* people have much more to gain from the *rega*, and furthermore, know how to protect themselves from each other's attack.

Precautions Against Evil Eye Attack

Since amorous relations with *buda* are not condoned by the Amhara, especially by the clergy, the priests teach that one's only protection against a *buda* lover is to crawl to church on one's hands and knees for seven days, the priest's intent being to frustrate the beginnings of such a relationship. Parents who fear their child is weak and vulnerable to the influence of the evil eye may, on the advice of a *däbtärä* (lower order clergyman), adopt the custom of addressing their child in the gender opposite to the child's actual sex. The custom of shaving the heads of children, leaving only a tuft of hair over the former fontanelle of the boys and a ring of hair around the heads of the girls, provides protection against minor attacks of lice, most often considered initiated by an envious *buda*. If an Amhara is worried about a child's imminent danger from an evil glance, a light, rapid spitting into the child's face provides a short-term protection. Compliments are always suspect if not accompanied with the invocation, "Let God protect you from the evil eye!" And at feasts all must be served equally lest someone deprived becomes envious and curses the food, making the participants sick.

Another precaution taken by the Amhara peasant against the possibility of attack is to be silent and guarded. When one expresses his emotions too freely and becomes too outgoing with others, he places himself in a position of vulnerability to the evil eye. This disposition is fairly generalized. When one is seen laughing and joking freely with others it is usually with close and trusted friends and relatives. At most other times the peasant presents a facade of stolidity and silence. In this way one does not attract the attention of an envious *buda*, who may resent persons enjoying themselves while he is not invited to share in the mirth. The custom of hiding one's face behind the large soft cloak, concealing especially the mouth and the nose, is one common way to avoid the penetration of the evil eye.

If a person succumbs to the attack of the evil eye, the family of the deceased may intercede and prevent the *buda* from wresting the corpse from its grave. A member of the family must watch the grave for forty days and forty nights (some say twelve days and twelve nights) after the body has been interred, allowing sufficient time to elapse so that the body will be adequately decomposed and thereby deprive the *buda* of a body to possess. If the grave is watched the *buda* will not come. In this way the family saves their relative from seven years of slavery.

Diagnosis and Cures for the Evil Eye Attack

Diagnosis of the symptoms and subsequent treatment may be carried out in one of four ways. In the first method, if the family is poor and they know a *däbtärä* of the local church, they may take the patient to him. For a modest fee, he performs a rite over holy water, praying and pronouncing

words in the ancient language of Giiz used in the Christian religious ceremonies. The patient then drinks the holy water and breathes in the smoke of a burning root. The *däbtärä* may find the diagnostic answer in his magic star book, while the holy water and inhaled smoke may effect a cure.

A second alternative is to bring the patient to a wizard, one who has powers gained through agents of the devil, to communicate with the *zar* spirits and to effect cures for many kinds of illness. First, a silver bracelet is placed on the patient's left wrist. The wizard then goes into a trance, seeking possession by a devil who may reveal the appropriate cure for the illness. In seeking out the attacker, a very hot fire is made in the hearth and a piece of metal, a sickle or knife blade is put into the flames and heated until glowing. The hot metal is applied to the patient's face, making a small pattern of burns. As the wounds heal, the scars will become transferred onto the face of the attacker in the same place and with the same pattern. The family must then seek out the guilty party.

A third method does not involve the use of specialists outside of an elder member of the family who knows the procedures and whose age gives him a bit better judgment. When a person begins biting his lip it is the first sign that he has been attacked by the evil eye, although this symptom does not always appear. If relatives are around they will first tie the victim's left thumb with string. Then the victim will be made to breathe the smoke from the dung fire. After taking in sufficient dung smoke, the victim gains the power to speak in the spirit and voice of his attacker. The victim begins recounting the chain of events of his attacker that led to the confrontation and the attack. Then the relatives ask the possessed victim what form of compensation should be given to counteract the attack. The victim, speaking in the voice of the attacker, demands some filthy matter such as beer dregs, ashes, a dead rat, or human or animal excrement. The victim eats this and soon cries, "I've left him! I've left my victim!" or something of this order. Then the family knows that the devil has left the body, and the stricken person may now recover. The cure involves active vocal participation. If the victim cannot speak, he will surely die.

The fourth method of diagnosis and counter-action involves the evil eye person in a more direct, mundane way. When the victim is attacked and he begins to bite his lip and to act strangely, he may appear to go into a daze and begin to jump and shout "in tongues." At this point, a relative must try to get the victim to utter the name of his attacker. If he does not, the family may tie a rope to the victim and then have the victim lead the relatives to the house of his attacker. If neither of these tactics are successful, they may have one other indication. If the victim begins crying suddenly, it is a sign that the attacker is in close proximity and that the relatives must only scout the area and seize the *buda* person they come across. If the suspect is found, he is brought to the bedside of the victim, by gunpoint if need be. The relatives take a lock of hair and a bit of clothing from the *buda*, preferably without his knowledge, and then the *buda* is made to spit on the victim and walk over him. A fire is built with the hair and cloth and the victim then breathes in the smoke. He continues inhaling the smoke until he cries, in the voice of the spirit, that the illness has left his body.

No matter what the method, if the *buda* gives up his victim there will be no reprisals by the victim's family. If the victim dies, the *buda* may be ejected from the community or killed.

The Mythology of the Origin of the Buda People

According to the Amhara, the beginnings of *buda* status go back to Creation. It is said that Eve had thirty children, and one day God asked Eve to show Him her children. Eve became suspicious and apprehensive and hid fifteen of them from the sight of God. God knew her act of disobedience and declared the fifteen children she showed God as His chosen children and cursed the fifteen she hid, declaring that they go henceforth into the world as devils and wretched creatures of the earth. Now some of the children complained and begged God's mercy. God heard them and, being merciful, made some of them foxes, jackals, rabbits, etc., so that they might exist as Earth's creatures in a dignified manner. Some of the hidden children he left human, but sent them away with the curse of being agents of the devil. These human counterparts of the devil are the ancestors of the *buda* people. There occurs a pleat in time and

the story takes up its theme again when Christ was baptized at age thirty. As told by an old Amhara peasant farmer:

> The angry devils, envious of God's favoring Christ while they suffered God's curse, tried to kill Christ. But Christ ran and fled his enemies. He hid in the crevice of a great cliff, sharing it with the giant *gabalo* lizard. While hidden, many children were killed by the devils in their search for "God's child," but they were unsuccessful in finding Christ. All the animals were asked to betray the whereabouts of Christ, but they refused and they were beaten and tortured to no avail. But the lizard waved his head from side to side showing Christ's pursuers where he hid. Christ saw this and cursed the lizard so that to this day this lizard still sways his head so. No one could get Christ down out of the crevice in the cliff. They tried with ropes and ladders to no avail. Then, the clever *buda* people made giant tongs of wood and plucked Jesus Christ out of the crevice. The blacksmiths made the nails and the carpenters made the cross and while Christ hung on the cross he cursed those people whose skills made it possible to crucify him.

Some Amhara claim that the devil is the sole source of *buda* qualities and power. Others say the origin of *buda* existence is different from the source of their power. Although their existence is associated with the devil, their power comes from a different source only questionably related to the devil. Although there are several versions of the myth, the following example narrated by an adolescent Amhara student is typical:

> The source of *buda* power is an ancient man who has immortality. He has no arms and no legs. He is like a lump of flesh and just sits at a place called Yerimma which is a cave of extremely great depth. He is, indeed, endowed with supernatural powers. Each year the *buda* people make their annual visit to this lump of man with their small children who are just learning to walk and to talk. This ancient man can distinguish between the *rega* who may come and the *buda* themselves. He rejects the former and accepts the latter. The ancient man then teaches the *buda* children all the "arts" to the *buda* trade and then presents the child with the leaf from an *iṣ* plant (also used by devils to make themselves invisible so as to avoid being eaten by the hyena). And

every year each *buda* must make a sacrifice to this ancient man of one human being. The sacrifice is like a tax, and if the *buda* cannot find a suitable victim by the time the sacrifice is due, he must sacrifice his own child.

Interpretation

There are essentially three analytically separable levels of behavior upon which to focus. First, there is the overt and manifest level of verbal behavior that expresses the configuration of ideas and feelings recognized as the evil eye belief system. This level of behavior is explicated through ethnographic description. Second, there is the analysis of values and psychological predispositions, areas of positive attraction, indifference, anger, and fear or dread. The symbols in the cultural configurations, as expressed through the narratives of the Amhara point out these areas of emotional salience and foci of concern. Through a symbolic analysis particular kinds of themes become evident. Some of these themes are based in the manifest functions of the belief, while others point to covert symbolic and latent functions of the belief system. Third, there is the social context that the symbols express and the social context of the actual behavior that expresses the evil eye belief.

With this approach it is possible to examine "the relationship between explicit cultural forms (symbols) and underlying cultural orientations" (Ortner 1973: 49), where these symbolic forms provide the vehicle for the analysis of the relationships between underlying cultural orientations and observable patterns of sociocultural behavior. Foster (1972: 166) offers a caveat that must be taken into consideration when analyzing the motivational significance of a particular belief or custom, which is, that original motives often disappear with the institutionalization of the belief or custom, and in its place, habit becomes the primary source for the reinforcement of the pattern. Also Kennedy (1969) argues against the more familiar teleological functional interpretations offered by social anthropologists when he proposes that these institutionalized beliefs and customs may themselves be the source of fears, or pathological responses to situations that present no real threat and could conceivably be defined in more innocu-

ous terms. In his discussion of witchcraft belief, Kennedy (1969: 177) states:

> Witchcraft systems are forms of institutionalized patterns of psychopathology which tend to be pathogenic and which create built-in self-perpetuating stress systems . . . (and) tend to regularly generate the hate and aggression which they allegedly function to relieve.

Including the evil eye belief within the purview of the problem of witchcraft is not without justification, for, although there are quite noticeable differences, the similarities demand some scrutiny. Spooner (1970: 311) notes how well known the evil eye belief is to us all, yet how little attention has been given to it by ethnographers:

> The concept of the Evil eye is reported throughout Europe, the Middle East, and North Africa, and in so many cultures elsewhere that it may be regarded as a universal phenomemon. Further, it is reported in circumstances which show it to be undoubtedly of the same order of phenomena as witchcraft.

Douglas, in agreement with Spooner, identifies the evil eye belief as a special case of witchcraft belief which becomes expressed at critical social disjunctions between persons who hold structurally generated enmity toward each other. Her definition (Douglas 1970: xxx) of a witch can be generalized to the Amhara's conception of the *buda*:

> The witch is an attacker and deceiver. He uses what is impure and potent to harm what is pure and helpless. The symbols of what we recognize across the globe as witchcraft all build on the theme of vulnerable internal goodness attacked by external power.

Douglas fits the evil eye belief into a typology she develops from the cases written up in the volume she edited. She (Douglas 1970: xxvii) proposes two general categories of witches: (a) the witch as outsider, and (b) the witch as internal enemy, Each of these categories has subtypes. The outsider type can be either (1) a witch not identified or punished, or (2) a witch expelled from the community. In this outsider type, the primary function of accusation is to redefine the boundaries of social solidarity. The witch as internal enemy appears in the more complexly organized societies, where two or more factions are involved within the community. The body of the victim is usually symbolized in the image of the betrayed community, where the internal strength is sapped or polluted by one in very close contact with the other members of the community. Where the witch is conceived as an internal enemy, the witch can be identified (1) as a member of a rival faction, where the function of the accusation is to redefine faction boundaries or the faction hierarchy; (2) as a dangerous deviant, where the function of the accusation is to control the deviant in the name of community values, or (3) as an internal enemy with outside liaisons, where the function of accusation is to promote factional rivalry, split the community, and/or redefine the hierarchy. Given this typology, Douglas (1970: xxx) then suggests an hypothesis for further testing:

> When the source of witchcraft power is thought to come from inside the witch, particularly from an area beyond conscious control, the social situation will correspond to type 3 above, where the witch is seen as an internal enemy, not as a member of a rival faction.

In the Amhara case, we can recognize similar qualities between the witch defined by Douglas and the *buda* as conceived by the Amhara peasant. However, the correspondence that Douglas suggests is not borne out in the Amhara case. The *buda* with internal and somewhat uncontrollable powers is not conceived of as a person internal to the Amhara group. The Amhara conceive of the *buda* as an outsider who nevertheless lives, geographically but not integrally, within the social networks of the Amhara people. Thus, the *buda* does not quite fit into any of the categories that Douglas has proposed. This exception to her typology suggests that much wider comparison is still necessary.

The dominant theme expressed in the Amhara evil eye belief system is one which is shared by possibly all those societies that maintain a belief in the evil eye: the fear of being envied and the interpretation of certain misfortunes as the consequences of another's envy. In Spooner's (1970: 314) discussion of the evil eye belief in the Middle East, this theme is especially salient:

> The concept of the Evil Eye appears to be an institutionalized psychological idiom for the . . . personification of misfortune, . . . insofar as misfortune, or the fear of it, may relate to the fear of outsiders and their envy.

In his careful analysis of the concept of envy Foster (1972: 167) defines envy as the act of looking maliciously upon someone; looking askance at; casting an evil eye upon; feeling displeasure and/or ill-will in relation to the superiority of another person. Foster (1972: 168) states that envy, along with the closely associated feeling of jealousy, "involves a dyad . . . whose relationship is mediated, or structured, by an intervening property or object." Thus, a jealous person is jealous of what he possesses and fears he might lose, while an envious person does not envy the thing, but rather envies the person who has it. Foster considers the predisposition to envy to be most apparent in peasant societies, or in what he calls "deprivation societies" of scarce resources where people hold to the "image of limited good" and where social interaction and transaction is defined and perceived as a "zero-sum" game, and where one's advantage derives from the other's loss. Foster (1972: 169) maintains that in those societies where the "zero-sum" game is the definition of the situation, it is the relative differences between two parties that triggers the omnipresently latent envy into overt expression. He further notes that in primitive and peasant societies, food, children and health, those things most vital for the survival of the family, rank at the top as objects of envy. Cattle and crops have some, but lesser, salience.

Congruent with sub-Saharan witchcraft belief in the context of well-defined and enforced rules and norms, envy and its consequences are mitigated to a considerable degree, primarily because both the structures of the family and of the class/caste system involve cultural definitions stipulating that the relationships between status classes or between the generations are noncompetitive. Foster (1972: 171) maintains that the function of this kind of definition is to eliminate or mitigate rivalry between persons in different categories of status or between persons in different social classes, thereby lubricating interclass and interpersonal transactions. Among the Amhara, the principle of patriarchal domination maintains order in domestic and political groups. The absence of the patriarch or of a mediating superior authority generates, or is believed to generate, anarchy within a group having no mediating authority among equals. Although this principle holds among the Amhara, the *buda* people are of non-Amhara tribal identity, and hence can only pose a threat to the Amhara by virtue of their being different. This difference, I maintain, is symbolic of what the Amhara detest, fear, or dread.

The *buda* people are "strangers" to the land of the Amhara. Originating from a different region, they are landless and make a living with their manual skills of smithing, tanning, weaving, and pottery-making. *Buda* status contrasts with *rega* or "nobility" status. Both statuses are inherited consanguineally on a bilateral basis. The origin myth of the *buda* people expresses the basic themes found in the belief system in general and in certain actual social situations: envy and conflict between siblings who are treated differentially by a superior authority. In the myth, envy and conflict are generated by the curse of God for the sins of the mother Eve. Added to this is God's favoring of His child, Christ, the "chosen" son of God. The story of the envious siblings' hunting down of Christ in order to attain equality among siblings has a strong parallel in real-life situations where a father favors one child with the lion's share of land, creating sibling conflict over the equalization of their rights to their father's land. The myth and the belief have it that the *buda* people inherit their *qalb*, a power gained from the devil which gives them the uncontrollable drive to "eat" the *rega* people, who happen to be the Amhara, to cause their death and to bring them back to life as slaves. It is a conception that expresses a dominant theme of envious status inferiors using illegitimate means to gain an advantage over status superiors who possess a legitimate means of domination.

The *buda* belief suggests that the *buda* are the symbolic expression of the latent consequences of unmediated equal status relationships between men and between a man and a woman. Without pyramidal control mechanisms, this form of relationship generates the anxiety of unstable and unpredictable consequences between two dependent and self-oriented egos, the ultimate consequences of which are symbolized in the logically extended extreme of domination—the relationship of master and slave. The function of the evil eye belief in maintaining the social system can be teleologically interpreted as the displacement of a threat and its projection onto an outgroup. The threat of equal status rivalry between kin and siblings outside of well-defined situations is projected onto the *buda* people, thereby preserving the internal solidarity (what there is of it) of the Amhara people. *Buda* belief appears to be a function of a power superiority among status equals based on the model of the eldest son as the object of envy by his less fortunate younger siblings, for it is the eldest son, in Mänz, who normally is the favored one and who inherits the lion's share of the father's land.

Belief in the evil eye among the Mänze Amhara, then, has a projective function which, through the transformation from personality trait to cultural configuration, becomes manifest as a form of domination anxiety expressed through culturally legitimated ideas of reference. This projective process is by no means complete, for it is known that the most serious concerns of the Amhara involve sibling and other kin conflicts over unequal usufructory rights to land. The landless *buda*, who is dependent upon others for his livelihood, is the symbolic reflection of the threat of becoming landless and without authority, *ergo*, without identity, because of the ambitions of a more powerful relative or the father's curse of disinheritance.

Urban Witches

Edward J. Moody

Starting in the mid-1960s, contemporary America began to witness a revival of witchcraft. In this article, Edward J. Moody examines a particular offshoot of witchcraft known as Satanism. As might be expected, the Satanic belief system described by Moody is the opposite of Christianity. Using the participant-observation research technique common to anthropological field investigation, Moody joined a group of Satanists in San Francisco, California, and sought answers to such questions as why people join the group, why Satanists persist in spite of their denouncement and persecution, and what benefits do they derive from membership. Interestingly, unlike witchcraft proper, where the witch may practice white (good) or black (bad) magic, the Satanists believe all magic is black magic. White or altruistic magic does not exist for the Satanist. Although brief mention is made in the article to the Satanist's leader, the so-called Prince of Darkness or, as he is sometimes known, the "Black Pope of Satanism," there is no reference to any prolonged interview with him. However, John Fritscher's fascinating interview with the high priest and founder of the Church of Satan, Anton Szandor La Vey, is recounted in Chapter 10 of this book.

Reprinted from *Conformity and Conflict: Readings in Cultural Anthropology*, 3rd ed. (Boston, 1977), pp. 427–37, by permission of the author.

EVERY FRIDAY EVENING JUST BEFORE MIDNIGHT, a group of men and women gathers at a home in San Francisco; and there, under the guidance of their high priest, a sorcerer or magus sometimes called the "Black Pope of Satanism," they study and practice the ancient art of black magic. Precisely at midnight they begin to perform Satanic rituals that apparently differ little from those allegedly performed by European Satanists and witches at least as early as the seventh century. By the dim and flickering light of black candles, hooded figures perform their rites upon the traditional Satanic altar—the naked body of a beautiful young witch—calling forth the mysterious powers of darkness to do their bidding. Beneath the emblem of Baphomet, the horned god, they engage in indulgences of flesh and sense for whose performance their forebears suffered death and torture at the hands of earlier Christian zealots.

Many of these men and women are, by day, respected and responsible citizens. Their nocturnal or covert practice of the black art would, if exposed, make them liable to ridicule, censure, and even punishment. Even though we live in an "enlightened" age, witches are still made a focus of a community's aggression and anxiety. They are denounced from the pulpit, prosecuted to the limit of the law, and subjected to extralegal harassment by the fearful and ignorant.

Why then do the Satanists persist? Why do they take these risks? What benefits do they derive from membership in a Satanic church, what rewards are earned from the practice of witchcraft? What indulgences are enjoyed that they could not as easily find in one of the more socially acceptable arenas of pleasure available in our "permissive" society?

The nearly universal allegation of witchcraft in the various cultures of the world has excited the interest of social scientists for years and the volume of writing on the topic is staggering. Most accounts of witchcraft, however, share the common failing of having been written from the point of view of those who do not themselves practice the black art. Few, if any, modern authors have had contact with witches, black magicians, or sorcerers, relying instead on either the anguished statements of medieval victims of inquisition torture, or other types of secondhand "hearsay" evidence for their data. To further confuse the issue, authoritative and respected ethnologists have reported that black magic and witchcraft constitute an imaginary offense because it is impossible—that because witches cannot do what they are supposed to do, they are nonexistent.

Witches and Magicians

But the witches live. In 1965 while carrying out other research in San Francisco, California, I heard rumors of a Satanic cult which planned to give an All-Hallows Eve blessing to a local chamber of horrors. I made contact with the group through its founder and high priest and thus began over two years of participant-observation as a member of a contemporary black magic group. As a member of this group I interacted with my fellow members in both ritual and secular settings. The following description is based on the data gathered at that time.

The witches and black magicians who were members of the group came from a variety of social class backgrounds. All shades of political opinion were represented from Communist to American Nazi. Many exhibited behavior identified in American culture as "pathological," such as homosexuality, sadomasochism, and transvestism. Of the many characteristics that emerged from psychological tests, extensive observations, and interviews, the most common trait, exhibited by nearly all Satanic novices, was a high level of general anxiety related to low self-esteem and a feeling of inadequacy. This syndrome appears to be related to intense interpersonal conflicts in the nuclear family during socialization. Eighty-five percent of the group, the administrative and magical hierarchy of the church, reported that their childhood homes were split by alcoholism, divorce, or some other serious problem. Their adult lives were in turn marked by admitted failure in love, business, sexual, or social relationships. Before entering the group each member appeared to have been battered by failure in one or more of the areas mentioned, rejected or isolated by a society frightened

by his increasingly bizarre and unpredictable behavior, and forced into a continuing struggle to comprehend or give meaning to his life situation.

Almost all members, prior to joining the group, had made some previous attempt to gain control over the mysterious forces operating around them. In order to give their environment some structure, in order to make it predictable and thus less anxiety-provoking, they dabbled in astrology, the Tarot, spiritualism, or other occult sciences, but continued failure in their everyday lives drove them from the passive and fatalistic stance of the astrologer to consideration of the active and manipulative role of sorcerer or witch. In articles in magazines such as *Astrology* and *Fate*, the potential Satanist comes into direct contact with magic, both white and black. Troubled by lack of power and control, the pre-Satanist is frequently introduced to the concept of magic by advertisements which promise "Occult power . . . now . . . for those who want to make real progress in understanding and working the forces that rule our Physical Cosmos . . . a self-study course in the practice of Magic." Or, Ophiel will teach you how to "become a power in your town, job, club, etc.," how to "create a familiar [a personal magic spirit servant] to help you through life," how to "control and dominate others." "The Secret Way" is offered free of charge, and the Esoteric Society offers to teach one how herbs, roots, oils, and rituals may be used, through "white magic," to obtain love, money, power, or a peaceful home. They will also teach one self-confidence and how to banish "unwanted forces." The reader is invited to join the Brotherhood of the White Temple, Inc.; the Monastery of the Seven Rays (specializing in sexual magic); the Radiant School; and numerous other groups that promise to reveal the secrets of success in business, sex, love, and life—the very secrets the potential or pre-Satanist feels have eluded him. Before joining the group, the pre-Satanist usually begins to perform magic ceremonies and rituals whose descriptions he receives for a fee from one of the various groups noted above, from magical wholesale houses, or from occult book clubs. These practices reinforce his "magical world view," and at the same time bring him in contact with other practitioners of the magical arts, both white and black.

Although most of the mail-order magic groups

profess to practice "white" magic—benevolent magic designed only to benefit those involved and never aggressive or selfish, only altruistic—as opposed to "black," malevolent, or selfish magic, even white magic rituals require ingredients that are rare enough so they can be bought only at certain specialty stores. These stores, usually known to the public as candle shops although some now call themselves occult art supply houses, provide not only the raw materials—oils, incenses, candles, herbs, parchments, etc.—for the magical workings, but serve as meeting places for those interested in the occult. A request for some specific magic ingredient such as "John the Conqueror oil," "Money-come powder, "crossing" powder, or black candles usually leads to a conversation about the magical arts and often to introductions to other female witches and male warlocks. The realization that there are others who privately practice magic, white or black, supports the novice magician in his new-found interest in magical manipulation. The presence of other witches and magicians in his vicinity serves as additional proof that the problems he has personally experienced may indeed be caused by witchcraft, for the pre-Satanist has now met, firsthand, witches and warlocks who previously were only shadowy figures, and if there are a few known witches, who knows how many there might be practicing secretly?

Many witches and magicians never go beyond the private practice of white or black magic, or at most engage in a form of magic "recipe" swapping. The individual who does join a formal group practicing magic may become affiliated with such a group in one of several ways. In some cases he has been practicing black magic with scant success. Perhaps he has gone no further than astrology or reading the designs on the ancient Tarot cards, a type of socially acceptable magic which the leader of the Satanic church disparagingly calls "god in sport clothes." But the potential Satanist has come to think of the cosmos as being ordered, and ordered according to magical—that is, imperceptible—principles. He is prompted by his sense of alienation and social inadequacy to try to gain control of the strange forces that he feels influence or control him and, hearing of a Satanic church, he comes to learn magic.

Others join because of anxiety and inadequacy of a slightly different nature. They may be homo-sexual, nymphomaniac, sadist, or masochist. They usually have some relatively blatant behavioral abnormality which, though they personally may not feel it wrong, is socially maladaptive and therefore disruptive. As in many "primitive" societies, magic and witchcraft provide both the "disturbed" persons and, in some cases, the community at large with a ready and consistent explanation for those "forces" or impulses which they themselves have experienced. Seeking control, or freedom, the social deviants come ultimately to the acknowledged expert in magic of all kinds, the head of the Satanic church, to have their demons exorcised, the spells lifted, and their own powers restored.

Others whose problems are less acute come because they have been brought, in the larger religious context, to think of themselves as "evil." If their struggle against "evil" has been to no avail, many of the individuals in question take this to mean that the power of "evil" is greater than the power of "good"—that "God is dead"—and so on. In their search for a source of strength and security, rather than continue their vain struggle with that "evil" force against which they know themselves to be powerless, they seek instead to identify themselves with evil, to join the "winning" side. They identify with Satan—etymologically the "opposition"—and become "followers of the left-hand path," "walkers in darkness."

Finally, there are, of course, those who come seeking thrills or titillation, lured by rumors of beautiful naked witches, saturnalian orgies, and other strange occurrences. Few of these are admitted into the group.

Black Magic

For the novice, initial contact with the Satanists is reassuring. Those assisting the "Prince of Darkness" who heads the church are usually officers in the church, long-term members who have risen from the rank and file to positions of trust and authority. They are well-dressed, pleasant persons who exude an aura of confidence and adequacy. Rather than having the appearance of wild-eyed fanatics or lunatics, the Satanists look like members of the middle-class, but successful middle-class. The Prince of Darkness himself is a powerfully built and striking individual with a shaven head and black, well-trimmed beard. Sitting among the implements of magic, surrounded by books that contain the "secrets of the centuries," he affirms for those present what they already know: that there is a secret to power and success which can and must be learned, and that secret is black magic.

All magic is black magic according to the Satanists. There is no altruistic or white magic. Each magician intends to benefit from his magical manipulation, even those workings performed at someone else's behest. To claim to be performing magic only for the benefit of others is either hypocrisy—the cardinal sin in Satanic belief—or naiveté, another serious shortcoming. As defined by the Satanists, magic itself is a surprisingly common-sense kind of phenomenon: "the change in situations or events in accordance with one's will, which would, using normally accepted methods, be unchangeable." Magic can be divided into two categories: ritual (ceremonial) and nonritual (manipulative).

Ritual, or "the greater magic," is performed in a specified ritual area and at a specific time. It is an emotional, not an intellectual act. Although the Satanists spend a great deal of time intellectualizing and rationalizing magic power, they state specifically that "any and all intellectual activity must take place *before* the ceremony, not during it."

The "lesser magic," nonritual (manipulative) magic, is, in contrast, a type of transactional manipulation based upon a heightened awareness of the various processes of behavior operative in interaction with others, a Satanic "games people play." The Satanist in ritual interaction is taught to analyze and utllize the motivations and behavioral Achilles' heels of others for his own purposes. If the person with whom one is interacting has masochistic tendencies, for example, the Satanist is taught to adopt the role of sadist, to "indulge" the other's desires, to be dominant, forceful, and even cruel in interaction with him.

Both the greater and the lesser magic is predicated upon a more general "magical" world view in which all elements of the "natural world" are animate, have unique and distinctive vibrations that influence the way they relate to other natural phenomena. Men, too, have vibrations, the principal difference between men and inanimate objects being that men can alter their pattern of vibrations,

sometimes consciously and at will. It is the manipulation and the modification of these vibrations, forces, or powers that is the basis of all magic. There are "natural magicians," untrained and unwitting, manipulators of magic power. Some, for example, resonate in harmony with growing things; these are people said to have a "green thumb," gardeners who can make anything grow. Others resonate on the frequency of money and have the "Midas touch" which turns their every endeavor into a profit-making venture. Still others are "love magnets"; they automatically attract others to them, fascinate and charm even though they may be physically plain themselves. If one is a "natural magician," he does some of these things unconsciously, intuitively, but because of the intellectual nature of our modern world, most people have lost their sensitivity to these faint vibrations. Such individuals may, if they become witches, magicians or Satanists, regain contact with that lost world just as tribal shamans are able to regain contact with another older world where men communicated with animals and understood their ways. It is this resensitization to the vibrations of the cosmos that is the essence of magical training. It takes place best in the "intellectual decompression chamber" of magic ritual, for it is basically a "subjective" and "non-scientific" phenomenon.

Those who have become members of the inner circle learn to make use of black magic, both greater and lesser, in obtaining goals which are the antithesis of Christian dogma. The seven deadly sins of Christian teaching—greed, pride, envy, anger, gluttony, lust, and sloth—are depicted as Satanic virtues. Envy and greed are, in the Satanic theology, natural in man and the motivating forces behind ambition. Lust is necessary for the preservation of the species and not a Satanic sin. Anger is the force of self-preservation. Instead of denying natural instincts the Satanist learns to glory in them and turn them into power.

Satanists recognize that the form of their ritual, its meanings, and its functions are largely determined by the wider society and its culture. The novitiate in the Satanic cult is taught, for example, that the meaning of the word "Satan" etymologically is "the opposition," or "he who opposes," and that Satanism itself arose out of opposition to the demeaning and stultifying institutions of Christianity. The cult recognizes that had there been no Christianity there would be no Satanism, at least not in the form it presently takes, and it maintains that much of the Satanic ritual and belief is structured by the form and content of Christian belief and can be understood only in that larger religious context. The Satanists choose black as their color, not white, precisely because white is the symbol of purity and transcendence chosen by Christianity, and black therefore has come to symbolize the profane earthy indulgences central to Satanic theodicy. Satanists say that their gods are those of the earth, not the sky; that their cult is interested in making the sacred profane, in contrast to the Judeo-Christian cults which seek to make the profane sacred. Satanism cannot, in other words, be understood as an isolated phenomenon, but must be seen in a larger context.

The Satanic belief system, not surprisingly, is the antithesis of Christianity. Their theory of the universe, their cosmology, is based upon the notion that the desired end state is a return to a pagan awareness of the mystical forces inhabiting the earth, a return to an awareness of their humanity. This is in sharp contrast to the transcendental goals of traditional Christianity. The power associated with the pantheon of gods is also reversed: Satan's power is waxing; God's, if he still lives, waning. The myths of the Satanic church purport to tell the true story of the rise of Christianity and the fall of paganism, and there is a reversal here too. Christ is depicted as an early "con man" who tricked an anxious and powerless group of individuals into believing a lie. He is typified as "pallid incompetence hanging on a tree." Satanic novices are taught that early church fathers deliberately picked on those aspects of human desire that were most natural and made them sins, in order to use the inevitable transgressions as a means of controlling the populace, promising them salvation in return for obedience. And finally, that substantive belief, the very delimitation of what is sacred and what is profane, is the antithesis of Christian belief. The Satanist is taught to "be natural; to revel in pleasure and in self-gratification. To emphasize indulgence and power in this life."

The opposition of Satanists to Christianity may be seen most clearly in the various rituals of greater magic. Although there are many different types of rituals all aimed at achieving the virtues that are the inverted sins of the Christian, we shall examine briefly only two of these: blasphemy and the invocation of destruction. By far the most famous of Satanic institutions, the Black Mass and other forms of ritual blasphemy serve a very real and necessary function for the new Satanist. In many cases the exhortations and teachings of his Satanic colleagues are not sufficient to alleviate the sense of guilt and anxiety he feels when engaging in behavior forbidden by Judeo-Christian tradition. The novice may still cower before the charismatic power of Christian symbols; he may still feel guilty, still experience anxiety and fear in their presence. It is here that the blasphemies come into play, and they take many forms depending on the needs of the individuals involved.

A particular blasphemy may involve the most sacred Christian rituals and objects. In the traditional black Mass powerful Christian symbols such as the crucifix are handled brutally. Some Black Masses use urine or menstrual flow in place of the traditional wine in an attempt to evoke disgust and aversion to the ritual. If an individual can be conditioned to respond to a given stimulus, such as the communion wafer or wine, with disgust rather than fear, that stimulus's power to cause anxiety is diminished. Sexuality is also used. A young man who feared priests and nuns was deliberately involved in a scene in which two witches dressed as nuns interacted with him sexually; his former neurotic fear was replaced by a mildly erotic curiosity even in the presence of real nuns. The naked altar —a beautiful young witch—introduces another deliberate note of sexuality into a formerly awe-inspiring scene.

By far the most frequently used blasphemy involves laughter. Awe-inspiring or fear-producing institutions are made the object of ridicule. The blasphemous rituals, although still greater magic, are frequently extremely informal. To the outsider they would not seem to have any structure; the behavior being exhibited might appear to be a charade, or a party game. The Satanists decide ahead of time the institution to be ridiculed and frequently it is a Christian ritual. I have seen a group of Satanists do a parody of the Christmas manger scene, or dress in clerical garb while performing a satire of priestly sexual behavior. The target of blasphemy depends upon the needs of the various

Satanists. If the group feels it is necessary for the well-being of one member, they will gladly, even gleefully, blaspheme anything from psychiatry to psychedelics.

In the invocation of destruction black magic reaches its peak. In some cases an individual's sense of inadequacy is experienced as victimization, a sense of powerlessness before the demands of stronger and more ruthless men. The Satanic Bible, in contrast to Christian belief, teaches the fearful novice that "Satan represents vengeance instead of turning the other cheek." In the Third Chapter of the Book of Satan, the reader is exhorted to "hate your enemies with a whole heart, and if a man smite you on one cheek, SMASH him on the other . . . he who turns the other cheek is a cowardly dog."

One of the most frequently used rituals in such a situation is the Conjuration of Destruction, or Curse. Contrary to popular belief, black magicians are not indiscriminately aggressive. An individual must have harmed or hurt a member of the church before he is likely to be cursed. Even then the curse is laid with care, for cursing a more powerful magician may cause one's curse to be turned against oneself. If, in the judgment of the high priest and the congregation, a member has been unjustly used by a non-Satanist, even if the offender is an unaffiliated witch or magician, at the appropriate time in the ritual the member wronged may step foward and, with the aid and support of the entire congregation, ritually curse the transgressor. The name of the intended "sacrifice" is usually written on parchment made of the skin of unborn lamb and burned in the altar flame while the member himself speaks the curse; he may use the standard curse or, if he so desires, prepare a more powerful, individualistic one. In the curse he gives vent to his hostility and commands the legions of hell to torment and sacrifice his victim in a variety of horrible ways. Or, if the Satanist so desires, the High Priest will recite the curse for him, the entire group adding their power to the invocation by spirited responses.

The incidence of harmful results from cursing is low in the church of Satan because of two factors: first, one does not curse other members of the church for fear that their superior magic might turn the curse back upon its user; second, victims outside the congregation either do not believe in the power of black magic or do not recognize the esoteric symbols that should indicate to them they are being cursed.

On only one occasion was I able to see the effect of a curse on a "victim." A member attempted to use the church and its members for publicity purposes without their permission. When the leader of the group refused to go along with the scheme, the man quit—an action that would have normally brought no recrimination—and began to slander the church by spreading malicious lies throughout San Francisco social circles. Even though he was warned several times to stop his lies, the man persisted; so the group decided to level the most serious of all curses at him, and a ritual death rune was cast.

Casting a death rune, the most serious form of greater magic, goes considerably beyond the usual curse designed to cause only discomfort or unhappiness, but not to kill. The sole purpose of the death rune is to cause the total destruction of the victim. The transgressor's name is written in blood (to the Satanist, blood is power—the very power of life) on special parchment, along with a number of traditional symbols of ceremonial magic. In a single-minded ritual of great intensity and ferocity, the emotional level is raised to a peak at which point the entire congregation joins in ritually destroying the victim of the curse. In the case in question, there was an orgy of aggression. The lamb's-wool figurine representing the victim was stabbed by all members of the congregation; hacked to pieces with a sword, shot with a small calibre pistol, and then burned.

A copy of the death rune was sent to the man in question, and every day thereafter an official death certificate was made out in his name and mailed to him. After a period of weeks during which the "victim" maintained to all who would listen that he "did not believe in all that nonsense," he entered the hospital with a bleeding ulcer. Upon recovery he left San Francisco permanently.

In fairness, I must add that the "victim" of the curse had previously had an ulcer, was struggling with a failing business, and seemed hypertense when I knew him. His knowledge of the "curse" may have hastened the culmination of his difficulties. The Satanic church, however, claimed it as a successful working, a victory for black magic, and word of it spread among the adherents of occult subculture, enhancing the reputation of the group.

Conclusion

Contemporary America is presently undergoing a witchcraft revival. On all levels, from teenagers to octogenarians, interest in, or fear of, witchcraft has increased dramatically over the past two years. It is hardly possible to pass a popular magazine rack without seeing an article about the revival of the black arts. Covens and cults multiply, as does the number of exorcisms and reconsecrations. England, France, Germany, and a host of other countries all report a rebirth of the black art. Why? Those who eventually become Satanists are attempting to cope with the everyday problems of life, with the here and now, rather than with some transcendental afterlife. In an increasingly complex world which they do not fully understand, an anxiety-provoking world, they seek out a group dedicated to those mysterious powers that the sufferers have felt moving them. Fearful of what one witch calls "the dark powers we all feel moving deep within us," they come seeking either *release* or *control*. They give various names to the problems they bring, but all, anxious and afraid, come to the Satanic cult seeking help in solving problems beyond their meager abilities. Whatever their problem— bewitchment, business failure, sexual impotence, or demonic possession—the Satanists, in the ways I have mentioned and many more, *can* and *do* help them. Witchcraft, the witches point out, "is the most practical of all beliefs. According to its devotees, its results are obvious and instantaneous. No task is too high or too lowly for the witch." Above all, the beliefs and practices provide the witch and the warlock with a sense of power, a feeling of control, and an explanation for personal failure, inadequacy, and other difficulties.

Moreover, a seeker's acceptance into the Inner Circle provides a major boost for his self-esteem; he has, for the first time, been accepted into a group as an individual despite his problems and abnormalities. Once within the Inner Circle that support continues. The Satanic group is, according to the cultural standards of his society, amoral, and the Satanist frequently finds himself lauded and rewarded for the very impulses and behavior that once brought shame and doubt.

Each Satanist is taught, and not without reason, that the exposure of his secret identity, of the fact that he is a powerful and adequate black magician, means trouble from a fearful society. Therefore, in keeping with the precepts of lesser magic, he learns to transform himself magically by day (for purposes of manipulation) into a bank clerk, a businessman, or even a college professor. He wears the guise and plays the role expected by society in order to manipulate the situation to his own advantage, to reach his desired goals. Members of society at large, aware only of his "normal" role behavior and unaware of the secret person within, respond to him positively instead of punishing him or isolating him. Then, in the evening, in the sanctity of his home, or when surrounded by his fellow magicians, he reverts to his "true" role, that of Satanic priest, and becomes himself once again. Inadequate and anxious persons, guilty because of socially disapproved impulses, are accepted by the Satanists and taught that the impulses they feel are natural and normal, but must be contained within certain spatial and temporal boundaries—the walls of the ritual chamber, the confines of the Inner Circle.

6
Demons, Exorcism, Divination, and Magic

Demons, spirits, ancestors, and gods all exist as realities in the human mind, and possess the power to harm and harass the living. Good and evil are counter-balanced in every society through a variety of rituals and other forms of protection; yet this balance is inevitably broken by human weaknesses and transgressions that invite the evil nature of supernatural agents. The malicious acts of these agents inflict pain and anguish on the innocent as well as on those deserving of punishment. Although all supernaturals can possess an individual and cause an unending variety of harm, the most commonly known agent of possession is the demon. Demons may aid their human consorts from time to time, but generally they are seen as being responsible for diseases, injuries, or a myriad of major and minor personal and group disasters. More powerful than mere humans, they are also generally believed to be less pow-

Tsham mask from Tibet.

erful than gods and ancestral spirits (Collins 1978: 195).

Possession by demons is ordinarily considered dangerous, but this is not always the case. For the Aymara Indians of Bolivia, for example, possession results in serious consequences for the victims and their community, whereas among the Haitians it is actively sought at Voodoo ceremonies in order to obtain the supernatural knowledge of the spirits. Haitians, however, conceive of both good and evil spirits, and all fear possession by the latter.

The functions of possession commonly go unnoticed, overshadowed as they are by the dramatic expressive actions of the possessed and those in attendance. Stanley and Ruth Freed (1964: 71) showed that spirit possession in a north Indian village functioned primarily to relieve the individual's intropsychic tensions while simultaneously giving the victim the attention and sympathy of relatives and friends. The possession itself and its overt demonstration was only a vehicle for these functions. Even rules designed to avoid demons, such as the *jinns* of Islamic countries, can promote individual self-discipline and propriety in behavior, both, as Howells has pointed out, desirable qualities (1962: 202). The prohibitions promoted to avoid *jinns* do direct behavior toward socially approved goals, but despite these positive functions, the fact remains that demons cause suffering and pain to members of both Western and non-Western societies and every society is forced to cope with their devious nature.

Exorcism—the driving away of evil spirits such as demons by chanting, praying, commanding, or other ritual means—occurs throughout the world and is invoked when an evil spirit has caused illness by entering a person's body. (A belief in exorcism assumes a related belief in the power of ritual to move an evil spirit from one place to another.) Although the idea that foreign objects can enter the body and cause illness has been widespread, it was especially prevalent among American Indians, where curers, shamans, and sometimes a specialist known as a "sucking doctor," had the ability to remove these materials by such techniques as rubbing and kneading the patient's body, gesturing over the diseased area, or directly sucking out the evil object. Shamans,

because of the "trick" aspect of their rituals, are especially well versed in the intricacies of exorcism as a means of removal of disease-causing objects. Typically, a sleight-of-hand maneuver is used to show the patient that the harmful substance has been removed.

William Howells (1962: 92–94) has described several techniques used around the world for exorcising evil spirits and diseases: using sweatbaths, cathartics, or emetics to flush out the offending spirits; trephining; manipulating and massaging the body; sucking-out of the disease objects; scraping or sponging the illness off the body; reciting magical spells, coaxing, or singing songs to lure the spirit away; tempting the spirit to evacuate the body by laying out a sumptuous meal for it; keeping the patient uncomfortable, sometimes by administering beatings, so the spirit will be discontented with the body and want to depart; building a fire under the patient to make it uncomfortably warm for the spirit; placing foul-smelling, overripe fruit near the patient; and scandalizing the demon by having the patient's naked wife jump over the patient.

There is considerable evidence to support the belief that trephination among pre-Columbian Peruvians was a supernatural-based method of exorcism. A technique of skull surgery, trephining involved cutting a hole in the skull with a type of small saw or knife known as a trephine. Although the primary reason for the procedure was generally believed to be the physical easing of pressure on the brain, the supernatural reasons for the practice cannot be overlooked.

Until the recent popularity of movies, television shows, and novels about possession by demons, the American public was largely unaware that exorcism has been practiced throughout the history of Western religions. Somewhat alarming to many Americans was the realization that the Catholic church continued to approve exorcisms in twentieth-century America. The following seventeenth-century conjuration was recited by priests in order to exorcize evil spirits from troubled houses. The words may be different, as are the names for the supernatural beings referred to, but the intent of the conjuration is identical to incantations uttered by religious specialists in preliterate societies during exorcism rites for similar purposes:

I adjure thee, O serpent of old, by the Judge of living and the dead; by the Creator of the world who hath power to cast into hell, that thou depart forthwith from this house. He that commands thee, accursed demon, is He that commanded the winds and the sea and the storm. He that commands thee, is He that ordered thee to be hurled down from the height of heaven into the lower parts of the earth. He that commands thee is He that bade thee depart from Him. Hearken, then, Satan, and fear. Get thee gone, vanquished and cowed, when thou art bidden in the name of our Lord Jesus Christ who will come to judge the living and the dead and all the world by fire. Amen. (Crehan 1970: 873)

William James saw religion as the belief in an unseen order. If one important aspect of religion is helping believers to come to know that unknown, it then follows that divination is important to religion. Divination means learning about the future or about things that may be hidden. Although the word itself may be traced to "divinity," which indicates its relationship to gods, the practice of divination belongs as much to magic as it does to religion proper. From the earliest times, human beings have wanted to know about such climatic changes as drought and heavy rainfall. Without scientific information to help predict natural events, early humans looked for "signs" in the flight of birds, or the entrails of small animals, or perhaps the positions of coals in a fire or pebbles in a stream. To this day the methods of divination in the world's cultures are far too varied and numerous to mention here. However, John Collins (1978: 56–58), following a classification scheme conceived by H. J. Rose, has listed ten basic varieties of divination techniques:

1. *Dreams*, probably the most prevalent form of divination, with the dream's meaning either obvious or requiring analysis.

2. *Presentiments*, a more personal type of divination in which an individual develops a feeling, or presentiment, about something.

3. *Body actions*, such as sneezing, twitching, and hiccupping, which may be interpreted as predictions of rainfall, good or bad luck, drought, or some other particular event.

4. *Ordeals*, painful and often life-threatening tests that a person suspected of guilt may be forced to undergo, such as dipping a hand into hot oil, swallowing poison, or having a red-hot knife blade pressed against some part of the body. Although the ordeal is usually used to help resolve conflict situations, the likelihood that an innocent person may be found guilty is potentially as great as "divining" the actual guilty individual.

5. *Possession* by spirits, enabling the diviner better to reveal the future by discovering hidden knowledge.

6. *Necromancy*, similar to possession, a technique of seeking "signs" from spirits of the dead, or perhaps by close observation of a corpse.

7. *Animal types*, a form of divination in which knowledge is derived either from the observation of living animals or from the inspection of the entrails of dead animals.

8. *Mechanical types*, a form of divination (the most comprehensive category of all) that involves seeking answers by manipulating an innumerable number of objects (for example, a sandal flipped in the air may be interpreted as meaning yes if it lands on its sole, no if on the straps).

9. *Nature types*, in which answers are determined by looking for signs in nature (for example, a particular pattern of mushrooms in the ground, the way leaves tumble from a tree, astrological signs such as the position of the stars and moon).

10. *Miscellaneous divination*, a large category including divination techniques that do not fit into the previous types (for example, death always strikes in threes).

Up to this decade controversy has surrounded the definition of magic and religion by anthropologists. Only recently have they come close to agreement that the dichotomy is a false one or that, if a dichotomy does exist, its ramifications are not significant to the study of the practitioners of each. Both magic and religion deal directly with the supernatural, and our understanding of the cultural applications of each provides deeper insights into the world view of the people practicing them.

Magic is usually divided into types, depending on the techniques involved. For example, Frazer distinguished "imitative magic," in which the magician believes that the desired result could be achieved by imitation, from "contagious magic," in which materials or substances once in contact with the intended victim are used in the magical attack. Other scholars would include "sympathetic magic," a form of magic in which items associated with or symbolic of the intended victim are used to identify and carry out the spell. Obviously, sympathetic magic contains elements of both imitative and contagious magic.

These forms of magic, still in use today, have been important methods of reducing anxiety regarding problems that exceeded the ability of people to understand and control them, especially because of a lack of technological expertise. Divination, special formulas and incantations, spells and curses, all are considered magical, and all can be used for good or evil. Since these activities are learned, they should be differentiated from witchcraft, which is considered innate and, most believe, uncontrollable.

It is logical to assume that non-Western reliance on explanations of events in terms of magic, sorcery, and witchcraft is a natural outcome of a lack of scientific training. But it is equally important to note that Westerners also rely on religious beliefs, with faith playing a strong role in determining actions and behaviors in our daily lives. Our ethnocentrism still blinds us to the similarities between ourselves and our fellow humans in the underdeveloped regions of the world. The great questions concerning the human condition are asked by all peoples, and despite the dispa-

rate levels of technology our sameness is demonstrated by the universality of religion.

In the first article of this chapter, Colleen Ward and Michael Beaubrun explore the psychodynamics of demon possession in contemporary Trinidad. E. Mansell Pattison's article is concerned with the widespread renewal of social interest in the supernatural, mystical, magical, and "irrational" in contemporary Western society. The article is a good choice for this chapter because of its focus on exorcism, demonology, and possession. Eugene Mendonsa shows how divination acts as a social control mechanism among the Sisala of northern Ghana. The Malinowski essay is a classic analysis of the distinction preliterate peoples make between magic and science. In the last article, George Gmelch cleverly applies Malinowski's ideas on magic and science to modern baseball.

References Cited

Collins, John J.
    1978 *Primitive Religion*. Totowa, N.J.: Littlefield, Adams and Co.

Crehan, J. H.
    1970 "Exorcism." In Richard Cavendish, ed., *Man, Myth and Magic*, Vol. 7, pp. 869–73. London: BPCC/Phoebus Publishing.

Freed, Stanley A., and Ruth S. Freed
    1964 "Spirit Possession as Illness in a North Indian Village." *Ethnology* 3: 152–71.

Howells, William
    1962 *The Heathens*. Garden City, N.Y.: Doubleday.

The Psychodynamics of Demon Possession

Colleen A. Ward
Michael H. Beaubrun

Demons come in many varieties. In terms of power, they are usually categorized above humans but below gods and ancestral spirits. Some demons, Irish leprechauns, for example, are generally pranksters, while others are completely evil. There are many ways in which they can cause trouble for humans; indeed, throughout the world possession by demons is common. This paper examines the psychodynamics of demon possession in contemporary Trinidadian society and focuses on the predisposing, precipitating cultural factors that contribute to the possessed state. Colleen Ward and Michael Beaubrun demonstrate that possession affords positive advantages to the victim—direct escape from a conflict situation and the diminution of guilt by projecting blame onto spirits. Proper behavior and avoidances can help direct demons away from people, and thus guarantee that the tenets of society are observed.

Reprinted from the *Journal of the Scientific Study of Religion*, 1980, Vol. 19, no. 2 (1980), pp. 201–207, by permission of the author and the Society for the Scientific Study of Religion, Inc.

MENTAL ILLNESS HAS OFTEN BEEN ATTRIBUTED to supernatural powers. Although a conception of man as the supernatural battleground of eternal demonic war for the possession of his soul was most prevalent in the Middle Ages, archeological and anthropological evidence indicates that even Stone Age man had a demon-ridden cosmos and a sorcerous treatment of madness. With modification, this "evil spirit" theory has endured for centuries, and instances of demon possession are still apparent in both primitive and advanced twentieth century societies.

This paper seeks to examine the psychodynamics of demon possession in contemporary Trinidadian society, and focuses on the predisposing, precipitating and cultural factors which contribute to this condition. This includes analysis of Trinidadian folk beliefs and superstitions as well as isolation of specific stress factors in individual case histories. The paper also comments on the pragmatic nature of the possession-reaction and the advantages afforded by allowing the individual to escape from unpleasant reality as well as projecting feelings of blame or guilt on to the intruding spirit.

Defining Possession

Various types and definitions of possession are cited in anthropological and psychiatric literature, differentiated on ritual-non-ritual, good-evil, and voluntary-involuntary dimensions. This paper deals specifically with demon possession, as distinguished from both bewitchment, in which some agent casts a spell or charm over the victim (Galvin & Ludwig, 1961), and ritual possession, a temporary, generally voluntary and usually reversible form of trance exhibited in the context of religious ceremonies and attributed to the power of sympathetic spirits (Walker, 1972). Demon possession, by contrast, refers to a relatively long term state in which the individual believes he is unwillingly possessed by one or more intruding spirits and exhibits contingent (usually maladaptive) behavioural responses which he attributes to the spirits' influence. Although possession of this type may be somewhat uncommon, cases have been reported in psychiatric literature in the United States (Galvin & Ludwig, 1961; Ludwig, 1965; Warner, 1977) Hong Kong (Yap, 1960) and India (Freed & Freed, 1964), as well as more primitive tribal societies (Leiris, 1968; Kiev, 1964).

The Cultural Background

Research reported here was undertaken in Trinidad, one of the wealthiest islands in the West Indies. Trinidadian society is a society of racial blends and mixtures, with the one and one quarter million population composed of African descendents, particularly of the Nigerian Yoruba tribe (43%), East Indian migrants who arrived as indentured servants in the mid-nineteenth century (40%), mixed races (14%), and a smaller number of Chinese, Syrians and Europeans. Caribbean supernaturalism, then, is a complex, syncretic phenomenon. Ethnically, it is a composite of European demonology, African ancestor worship and fetishism, Asian mysticism, and several minor systems of metaphysical phenomena which have evolved as native forms within the larger body of supernaturalism in the Caribbean as a whole (Elder, 1970).

While some practices (such as the East Indian Kalipuja, a common form of divination and revenge sorcery) are specific to particular cults or religious persuasions, other folk beliefs and superstitions, such as astrology, use of bush medicine and necromancy, are more widely accepted. Lower class Trinidadians frequently consult "Lookermen" and "Lookerwomen" to learn about their future as well as "Obeahmen" for guards, charms, cures and revenge. Beliefs in souciyants, women who fly at night sucking the blood of their victims, abound. All in all, despite the predominantly Christian nature of Trinidadian society, the populace is very superstitious at all social levels (Beaubrun, 1975).

The case studies reported here were obtained from interviews with various members of a local Pentecostal church who were initially observed undergoing exorcism at a weekly miracle service. The Pentecostal sect has a Christian-based theology and is particularly reliant on vibrant preaching, manifestations of the Holy Spirit, including speaking in tongues, and faith healing. The Pentecostal following in Trinidad is similar to the charismatic movement in North America, but services appear even more dynamic and emotionally charged. The congregation is predominantly composed of lower- and lower-middle-class blacks and East Indians.

The Psychodynamics of Possession: Case Studies

Case No. 1: Sonia, a fair-skinned, 32-year-old Negro woman, reported suffering from a variety of aches and pains, particularly headaches, stomach pains and abdominal swelling, as well as suicidal tendencies, for more than 15 years. She attributed her pains, as well as her lack of motivation and domestic problems, to demons who she believed acted as incubi coming to her in the night to engage in sexual intercourse. Sonia had a long history of seeking relief from these disorders in various forms of folk healing. Her first attacks occurred about the age of 16, when her suitor, with whom she had had sexual relations and who had promised marriage, ultimately rejected her. At that time, Sonia consulted an obeahman who prescribed a bush bath. Soon after, Sonia began work, and her condition improved. After refusing to marry as her mother planned, and thus being asked to leave home, Sonia moved into her uncle's residence to help with the housework and to attend to his sick wife. She eventually became involved in sexual relations with the uncle, and it was then that Sonia's stomach pains and headaches returned and she consulted a second obeahwoman, who offered her a bush bath and temporary relief.

After the death of her aunt, Sonia became pregnant by her uncle but was forced to have an abortion to save her life. Soon afterward she experienced abdominal swelling, diagnosed as inflammation of the womb, and began to believe she was being tormented by demons desiring sexual intercourse with her.

In addition to these experiences, Sonia has had several dealings with obeahmen and believes herself to be the victim of assorted spells and charms.

In one instance, a local healer discovered symbolic objects, a pair of slippers, a toothbrush and a hair tie, which had been purposefully buried under Sonia's house. Sonia also believes in dreams, visions and precognition.

Sonia was brought to the Pentecostal Church at the age of 31 and has reported 32 exorcisms in a one-year period. She is currently cohabiting with a married man and believes she is still plagued by demons which she attributes to the workings of jealous family members.

Case No. 2: Salina, a 32-year-old woman of East Indian descent, reported suffering from sleeplessness, headaches, chest pains, consumption, swollen feet, and constipation. She also complained of bitter domestic problems; she eventually came to attribute these difficulties to demons.

At the age of 15, Salina was married against her will. She experienced strong discontentment with married life and was also forced to suffer the stern disapproval of her father-in-law. Three months after marriage, Salina began to experience a variety of physical complaints, depression, and lack of motivation.

Four years later, Salina sought help from an obeahwoman, received a bush bath, but got no relief. The symptoms continued, her home life worsened, and her husband discontinued sexual relations. Doctors diagnosed rheumatism and a nervous condition, but medication did not improve her situation. According to Salina, she suffered consistently with these complaints for more than 15 years and many days did not even bother to leave her bed.

At the age of 30, Salina came to the Pentecostal Church and after four months of attendance received her first exorcism. In a two year period, she has reported over 100 exorcisms and believes herself to have been possessed by at least twenty different demons. Salina believes her father-in-law is responsible for these possessions and that her husband and daughter are also possessed.

Case No. 3: Phil, a 17-year-old male of East Indian descent, reported periods of dissociation, headaches, malaise, depression, and serious family difficulties. He attributes these problems to demons which he believes were invoked by his step-father's first wife.

Phil's mother and step-father both left their original spouses, and although they have three children of their own, there is considerable marital strife. The prime difficulty lies with Phil's step-father, who frequently wavers between Phil's mother and his first wife. At times, the step-father will leave the home for days, while in other instances, he may assume the loving father role. The step-father also drinks regularly, has a violent temper, and frequently beats the wife and children. Phil has been separated from his mother and sisters because his step-father will not allow him to remain at home.

About the time that the domestic problems became intense, Phil was hospitalized for an abdominal pain. While the cause of the complaint was never diagnosed, Phil experienced periods of dissociation, in addition to selective amnesia. He reports loss of recognition of his immediate family, as well as "feeling peculiar." After release from the hospital, Phil was taken to an obeahman by his mother, given a bush bath and various charms to wear, but reported no substantial relief.

In the following month, Phil was taken to the Pentecostal services and was exorcised immediately. He has reported three exorcisms in a three-month period. He believes that his mother and sister are also possessed and that their home is ridden with evil spirits.

Case No. 4: Nan, a 25-year-old East Indian woman, experienced her first symptoms at 15 in the form of extended, heavy menstrual bleeding, accompanied by dreams of blood. Nan was taken to an obeahman, who told her she was demon possessed, and attempted to release her by ritual ceremony. Although Nan claims that she did not believe in possessions at that time, she reported that the bleeding lessened, although she felt weak, lazy, inactive, and suffered with headaches and melancholia.

At 17, Nan found a serious boyfriend who was several years older than she. Although they engaged in sexual relations, her parents did not approve of the boy and insisted that the relationship end. Nan reports depression and guilt feelings at that time as well as a reluctance to "get involved again." At that time, Nan was treated for a nervous condition, still suffering with headaches and melancholia. Assessing the situation retrospectively, Nan believes she was demon possessed.

Nan's condition worsened at the age of 24 in connection with a second boyfriend who proposed marriage. After a serious quarrel, Nan became extremely depressed, and a second demon immediately manifest. She began to shake and tremble, exhibiting alternate fits of laughter and tears, as well as speaking in unknown tongues. She reports subsequent loss of appetite, weakness, visions, and black menstrual flow. Nan believes she is possessed by a demon who loves her and appears as a handsome man at night to seduce her. The demon, called Peter, is also very jealous and does not allow Nan to maintain close relationships with other men. Nan believes the demon lives in her womb.

Nan was exorcised at her first visit to the Pentecostal Church and reports three exorcisms in a two month period.

Discussion

As Ludwig (1965) maintains, belief in witchcraft and demonology *per se* is not intrinsically pathological unless symptoms interfere with adequate social and interpersonal functioning. Cases reported here were isolated during field observations of exorcism performed at a Trinidadian Pentecostal Church. These individuals had neither been institutionalized nor previously referred for psychiatric consultation, but their histories reflect maladaptive behavioural patterns. It is important to note that the Pentecostal congregation, as a whole, professes a profound belief in both demon possession and faith healing, but few have had personalized experiences (Glazier, in press). As Kiev (1964) has noted, the predominance of religious/magical beliefs in hospitalized West Indians is similar to that of other West Indians, but the former overpersonalize a distorted significance of mysticism in what seems to be an unsuccessful restitutive effort to explain their experiences.

Although individuals interviewed here show a tendency toward hysterical features, both conversion and dissociation, no consistent clinical picture of psychopathology is apparent. Similarly, while Yap (1960) reported a predominance of hysterics (48.5%) in an institutionalized Chinese sample, he also found in it a fair proportion of schizophrenics (24.3%) and depressives (12.2%), with additional diagnoses of mania, delirium, senile and epileptic confusion. Likewise, in five cases reported by Ludwig (1965), possession appeared as minor symptoms, a complex of symptoms, a syndrome, and as a major feature of a psychiatric disorder. It is important to distinguish these cases from the

Trinidadian cases, however, which were neither institutionalized nor referred for psychiatric consultation.

Cultural factors appear to play a crucial role in the belief and susceptibility to witchcraft. As previously elaborated, Trinidadian society is rich in superstition. The cases reported here reflect three basic forms of magical thinking: imitative magic, low magic, and necromancy (Cavendish, 1977). Imitative magic is based on the premise that anything which was once a part of a man's body or in close contact with him retains the connection even after it has been physically separated from him. This is the magic link between the spell and the victim. In case No. 1, the possessed woman found a pair of slippers, a toothbrush and a hair tie buried under her house. She related these items to her various complaints; lack of motivation (inability to move around), loss of appetite, and severe headaches.

Low magic includes numerous processes of a comparable vulgar order such as charms, guards and cures. The most common form of low magic in Trinidad (reported in three out of four cases here) is the bush bath, wherein the individual is bathed in various roots and herbs in conjunction with prayer and ritual in the intention of treating a supernatural condition (maljo). Low magic also encompasses the use of guards as apparent in case No. 3. It should be noted that each individual sought relief from folk medicine before coming to the Pentecostal church.

Necromancy, divination by the dead, is also apparent, with the primary aim being the summoning of spirits for purposes of harm or mastery. In cases one, two and three, the possessed person clearly attributes the spirit's invocation to specific individuals, usually for purposes of revenge or jealousy. In exorcism practices, the individual may even describe the invocation ceremony, naming the specific cemetery in which it occurred.

That stress precipitates possession has been a common finding (Douyon, 1966; Freed & Freed, 1964; Leiris, 1958; Pressel, 1974; Warner, 1977). Freed and Freed (1964) have postulated that possession is a basic condition in response to an individual's intra-psychic tension and a precipitating situation due to an event involving unusual stress or emotion. According to their paradigm, stress arises if the victim is involved in difficulties with relatives or in a situation where expectations for aid or support are low. In addition, Ludwig (1965) has noted that incestuous conflicts as well as emotional crises, guilt, feelings of rejection, strong unmet dependency needs, or feelings of inadequacy also act as precipitating factors.

In these Trinidad cases, sexual conflicts and domestic difficulty appear as the primary stress factors. In cases one and four, the women experience intense guilt over incestuous or illicit love affairs, case one being further compounded by an unwanted abortion. In cases two and four, domestic difficulties seem to predominate, with an unwanted and unhappy marriage and a lack of a stable home situation, respectively. But in each case, feelings of rejection, unmet dependency needs, and a sense of inadequacy may also be recognized.

While their symptoms may differ, all individuals share a susceptibility to possession; that is, possession, unlike any other psychological defense, is ideally suited to coping with their conflicts. Possession affords two positive advantages: escape from unpleasant reality, and diminution of guilt by projecting blame onto an intruding agent. In the first instance, escape may be provided by dissociation or conversion, which furnishes the most direct and explicit means of escape. In fact, Douyon (1966) has previously demonstrated a strong relationship between stress and loss of consciousness in possession-prone individuals. The dissociation reported here in case three affords the afflicted young man the opportunity to avoid a stressful household situation, both by momentary relief from domestic constraints, and by denial of painful familial bonds. By contrast, psychosomatic disorders induced by conversion may diminish emotional tension by shifting focus from fundamental stress factors to secondary somatic symptoms. Cases one and two, which include complaints of headaches, stomach pains, abdominal swelling, sleeplessness and constipation, illustrate the conversion phenomenon. In these instances, somatic complaints generally occupy the possessed individual (and family and friends) to

such an extent that the prime source of emotional conflict may be largely ignored.

In addition, the possession-complex allows release from guilt through a sense of diminished responsibility. Under these circumstances, the intruding demon, rather than the unwilling sufferer, becomes responsible for the person's thoughts and actions. Consequently, the possessed individual assumes no liability or guilt. This is particularly prominent in case four, the instance of a young woman experiencing emotional conflict of a sexual nature. The incubus both forces her into involuntary sexual relations, alleviating her of the guilt of consent, and also restricts her emotional ties with potential lovers, allowing her to deny responsibility for these fruitless relationships.

Finally, when viewed in the specific context of Pentecostal worship, possession also offers strong social bonds and group support within a well-defined subculture. Possession-prone individuals are treated with deference and concern; they generally merit certain privileges in the Pentecostal community as well as individual recognition and cure by the pastor and other leading members in the church hierarchy. In one sense, possessed individuals are accorded a sense of dignity and prestige in their subculture, and, even more importantly, they may be given the affection and emotional support lacking in their daily lives.

Conclusion

The case histories of four individuals in the context of Trinidadian Pentecostal services suggest that the predisposing cultural mores, beliefs, traditions, and superstitions, coupled with highly emotional stress situations, constitute the precipitating factors of demon possession. Although possessed individuals exhibited hysterical features, a single psychiatric diagnosis was not readily apparent. The possession reaction did, however, afford similar advantages in all cases: (1) escape from unpleasant situations, (2) diminution of responsibility and guilt, and (3) group support in a clearly defined subculture.

Psychosocial Interpretations of Exorcism

E. Mansell Pattison

E. Mansell Pattison, a professor of psychiatry and human behavior, begins this article with an examination of the contemporary interest in demonology and exorcism in Western society. Agreeing with Claude Lévi-Strauss, Pattison observes that primitive ideas of reality result in a more coherent and cohesive model of the world than do Western scientific explanations. He traces the present renewal of interest in demonology and exorcism in contemporary scientific cultures to certain social situations that support an oppressive social structure. Pattison believes modern psychiatry's failure to provide meaning and understanding of reality has caused people to abandon the psychoanalyst in favor of the exorcist. The author demonstrates how modern psychoanalytic psychotherapy is like exorcism, discusses the differences between "scientific healers" and "folk healers," and analyzes the implications for psychotherapeutic practice.

Reprinted from the *Journal of Operational Psychiatry*, Vol. 8, no. 2 (1977), pp. 5–19, by permission of the author and the University of Missouri-Columbia, Department of Psychiatry.

"The power of magic defeats the demons of scientific technology" (advertisement for the movie "Wizards," 1977).

THIS PAPER IS CONCERNED WITH THE WIDE-spread renewal of social interest in the supernatural, mystical, magical, and "irrational" in contemporary western society. This is reflected in the rapid shift among young people from the iconoclastic social activism of the 1960s toward an internal personal quest for peace and meaning in the 1970s. This latter quest is seen in the popularity of non-conventional religiosity, mystical experience, and eastern philosophies. The tip of the iceberg of this social revolution of consciousness is our manifest fascination with demonology and exorcism.

Corollary to society in general, the mental health professions have begun to closely examine the beliefs and practices of indigenous healers. Therefore, my inquiry begins with the general social phenomenon and leads into a comparative examination of "scientific healers" versus "folk healers" and the implications for psychotherapeutic practice.

Naturalistic Versus Supernaturalistic Systems

Our western views of health and illness, cause and effect, reality and fantasy are, of course, the product of an evolving construction and explanation of reality, in large part determined by the empirical rationalism of experimental science, its adoption by medicine, and thence to psychiatry. The western mode of thought and its construction of reality has often been the measure against which all other cultural constructions of reality were assessed; while so-called primitive cultures were considered to be unrealistic, irrational, simplistic, and naive. From this point of view, it seems absurd that sophisticated western people should evince interest, much less belief, in magical, mystical, and metaphysical ideas that western culture has long since given up for more realistic views and explanations of the world. In particular the belief in demons, possession, and exorcism seems especially atavistic.

What the western mind does not see, is that western science and its construction of reality is terribly fragmented. The naturalistic system of the world of the west, rooted in the empirical rationalism of latter day humanism, provides proximate and limited explanations of isolated fragments of human life. It fails to provide western mankind with a cohesive picture of human life. Further, without ontological grounding it does not provide a rationale, nor purpose, nor meaning to life. The optimistic world view of 19th-century scientific humanism has become the 20th-century world view of cynicism, despair, existential ennui and a cosmos of the absurd.

Sartre states the dilemma of modern western man succinctly:

The existentialist . . . thinks it very distressing that God does not exist, because all possibility of finding values in a heaven of ideas disappears along with him. . . . Everything is permissible if God does not exist, and as a result man is forlorn, because neither within him nor without does he find anything to cling to. . . . We find no values or commands to turn to which legitimize our conduct. So, in the right realm of values, we have no excuse behind us, nor justification before us. We are alone, with no excuses.

Or consider the conclusion of psychoanalyst Allen Wheelis:

At the beginning of the modern age science did, indeed, promise certainty. It does no longer. Where we now retain the conviction of certainty we do so on our own presumption, while the advancing edge of science warns that absolute truth is a fiction, is a longing of the heart, and not to be had by man. . . . Our designations of evil are as fallible now as they were ten thousand years ago; we simply are better armed now to act on our fallible vision.

My point is that the superiority of western consciousness and the western construction of reality as a mode of existence has failed to be demonstrated. That western empirical technology has achieved greater creature comforts and longevity of life is indisputable, but what of the quality, meaning, and value of life?

These considerations only briefly intimate the conclusion that in the west we have entered a new age of irrationalism. Yet at the same time, we continue to misinterpret other world views of reality.

As Lévi-Strauss has demonstrated so well in "The Savage Mind," so-called primitive constructions of reality provide a much more coherent, cohesive, and explanatory model of the world and human behavior than does the western scientific construction of the cosmos. Science does not provide a very comprehensive description and explanation of human behavior. *The Savage Mind* had an explanation and intervention for everything.

Foster has compared naturalistic versus supernaturalistic systems of thought about health and illness. He finds that naturalistic systems (western) view misfortune and illness in atomistic terms. Disease is unrelated to other misfortune, religion and magic are unrelated to illness; and the principal curers lack supernatural or magical powers, for their function is solely an instrumental technical task performance. On the other hand, supernaturalistic systems integrate the totality of all life events. Illness, religion, and magic are inseparable. The most powerful curers are astute diagnosticians who employ both technical and symbolic means of therapeusis.

Early students of supernaturalistic systems of healing such as Ackerknecht and Rivers emphasized the particular magical beliefs and rituals of shamans and other folk healers; thus they overlooked the complex integrated view of nature and mankind, and the complex refined distinctions that were made between different kinds of misfortunes, their causes, and cures.

Loudon comments:

This reduces the study of health and disease to studies of witchcraft, sorcery, magic, and in general curative or socially readjustive ritual practices, with herbalist and empirically rational treatment and prophylaxis as residual categories.

In brief, supernaturalistic systems encompass the totality of life, which integrates man and nature. Careful ethnographic studies of folk healers reveal a complex and sophisticated description of reality, in which there is indeed differentiation between accidents, distortions of natural process such as a malformed fetus, hazards such as snake-bites, psychosomatic disorders, and existential disorders of impaired human relations. Similarly, within the supernaturalistic system there are a range of interventions practiced by a variety of healers with skills suitable to the curing of the misfortune.

In sum, I have attempted to illustrate that the distinction between the naturalistic and the supernaturalistic is not so wide a gulf as we might suppose. Our rationalistic culture is absurd and irrational; while the supernaturalistic cultures possess a sophisticated, coherent construction of reality, with attendant differentiated diagnostic and therapeutic concepts. The fundamental difference may lie rather in our differing construction of what reality is.

Demonology as Part of Supernaturalism

Beliefs in demonology, possession, and exorcism can be adequately interpreted only within the framework of supernaturalistic systems. Anthropologist Erika Bourguignon has organized the variety of trance behaviors and associated beliefs into convenient chart form, as shown in Figure 1. As illustrated, the same phenomena can be explained in either naturalistic or supernaturalistic systems. And also evident is that demon possession is only one sub-type of many concepts of man and spirits.

Abundant ethnographic data have shown that although there may be widespread tacit acceptance and private belief in demonology, the actual practice of witchcraft and experience of possession states is limited. That is, the particular emergence of demon possession and exorcism can be shown to relate to rather particular socio-cultural milieux. The general conclusion is that the eruption of demonology is coincident with social situations where there is an oppressive social structure, a loss of trust in the efficacy of social institutions, and a seeming inability to cope with the evils of the social structure. In this situation, then, we see the personification of social evil in evil demons, and a displaced social protest in the form of accusations of witchcraft and personal experiences of possession. Being possessed of social evil is personified, while accused, accuser, and exorcist act out the

symbolization of the social dilemma in safely displaced form, since active social protest and reform seem impossible.

For example, Bourguignon finds the distribution of demonic possession in folk societies to be correlated with conditions of social oppression and stagnation. Wijesinghe, et al. report a high incidence of possession in a low status sub-community of Sri Lanka; and Carstairs and Kapur note that in an Indian community it was in the most oppressed case that they found possession.

Socio-cultural studies have thus emphasized the social dynamics that produce demonology. Yet at the same time we must account for the psychological dimensions which have played such a large part in typical psychiatric interpretations of demonology.

Freud stated the classic psychological formulation: "The states of possession correspond to our neuroses. . . . The demons are bad and reprehensible wishes." But this interpretation reduces demonology to nothing but individual neurosis, and may lead to the conclusion that the actors in the drama of demonology are dealing with individual neuroses.

In contrast the eminent medical historian George Rosen observes:

> Witch hunting expresses a dis-ease of society, and is related to a social context. . . . To be sure, some individuals involved in witch trials were mentally and emotionally disordered. Most of those involved were not. In part, their reactions were learned, in part, they conformed because of fear-producing pressures.

Similarly the historian Russell concludes:

> But it will not do to assume that the witches were on the whole mentally ill. They were responding to human needs more universal than those of individual fantasy: universal enough to be described in terms of myth. . . . The phenomenon of witchcraft, whether we are talking about the persecutors or the witches, was the result of fear, expressed in supernatural terms in a society that thought in supernatural terms, and repressed by a society that was intolerant of spiritual dissent. In most respects a variety, or at least an outgrowth, of heresy, witchcraft was one manifestation of alienation.

We cannot gainsay that the belief and practice of demonology was not and is not a defensive and

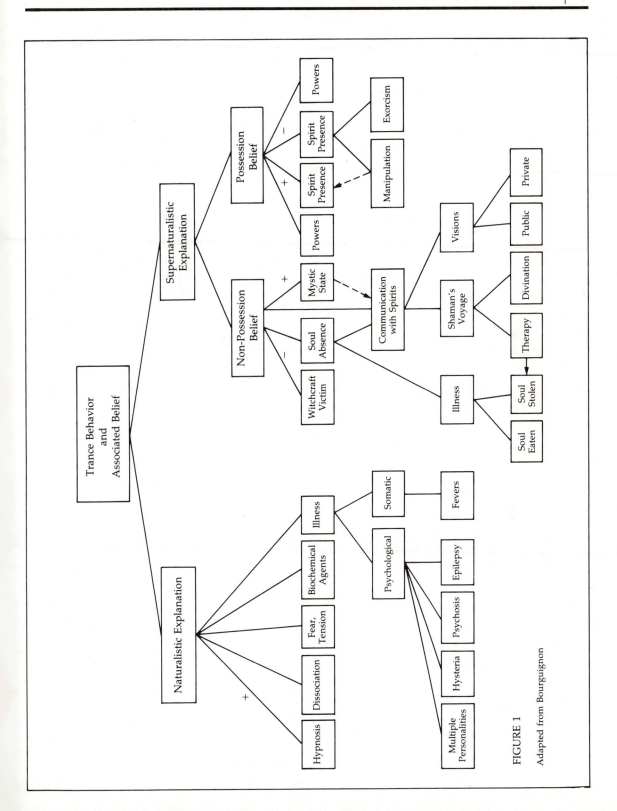

FIGURE 1

Adapted from Bourguignon

adaptive psychological maneuver. But from the viewpoint of culture this is not neurosis. As Spiro says: "There is a third category of defense mechanisms—culturally constituted defenses—which are not only not disruptive of, but rather serve to perpetuate, the socio-cultural system."

Robert LeVine has pointedly synthesized the issue by describing a *psychosocial* interpretation of demonology. That is, within the general culture of belief there will be degrees of potential, for more or less individuals, to act out the beliefs of demonology. And where the general belief of demonology is culturally no longer a modal belief, only those with specific psychological propensities (i.e., neurotic) are likely to use such beliefs in their ego defense.

With this summary at hand, we can now see that Freud and other psychiatric observers could readily reduce demonology to nothing but neurosis, for they were observing persons acting out beliefs not modal to the culture. But where demonology is modal, we must look beyond neurosis for our understanding.

Contemporary Demonology

With an understanding of the social conditions which give rise to demonology, it is possible to see that contemporary social conditions are ripe in the western world for the re-emergence of supernaturalistic belief systems, and even demonology. Society has been perceived as oppressive, trust in social institutions has disintegrated, social protest has been realistically dangerous, and a mood of helpless impotence has emerged. New hope, new meaning, and new purpose can be seen in the myriad of supernaturalistic systems now gaining devotees. So it should not surprise us that the evil society should again be personified and symbolized in demonology.

In his analysis of medieval demonology the Spanish anthropologist Baroja notes that western rationalism ousted the belief in witchcraft from its place in the collective consciousness of man, to survive only in the marginal circles of cranks and neurotics. Yet he finds us coming full circle with the breakdown of rationalism:

> We are in a better position nowadays to appreciate the feelings of the people involved, who discovered one day that they had a devilish

power in them, or were subject to the devilish power of a close enemy who had lived near them for years, watching and hating. For ours is no period of calm, with an optimistic view of public morality and religious philosophy and beliefs. It is an age of existentialism and an existentialist way of life, which leads man to break down the barriers and conventions and face up to his own angst.

Following along the existential consciousness of our day is the stark sense of alienated and singular responsibility for everything. Historian Judith Neaman finds it not surprising that psychiatry is becoming more biological just at the time when our society is becoming more metaphysical. She recalls that in every culture hyper-rationalism has been followed by a renewal of supernaturalism. For with the rationalism and ultimately the existentialism comes too much responsibility—too much to bear. Psychiatry brought man from outer reality into himself and only himself, and left man there. Neaman concludes:

> The legacy of the Middle Ages was the increasing interiorization of the self and a concomitant increase in responsibility for human action. These ideas were consummated in the twentieth century belief that we are responsible not only for our own actions but also for our own guilts, fears, and obsessions. The fantasy of the 1970s has been a wish to return to an age of exorcism.

Bourguignon similarly finds: "There is a wish to find alternative ways of living; and thus not only modify the society, but to modify the self."

Thus, we see that rather than unexpected, it is most consonant with history that supernaturalism and demonology should again appear in our time. The nadir of scientific psychiatry offers least to western man in terms of meaning, and people turn from the psychoanalyst to the exorcist.

Psychoanalytic Demonology

The demons out there that possessed us, have been gradually deanthropomorphized. Healing which was exorcism of the personal spirit became gradually more an exorcism of bad thoughts and feelings. Pattison et al. found that modern seekers of faith healing seek a spiritual cure of the self, which is but a step from the final abstraction of evil into pure thought in Christian Science, where evil, misfortune, and illness exist only in thought and have no reality.

But demonology has been resurrected in new form in the object relations theory of psychoanalysis. Possession is not to be left behind, but only redefined. We are possessed of good and bad objects—ego introjects. So we find twentieth century demonology interpreted by Fairbairn thusly:

> It is to the realm of these bad objects . . . that the ultimate origin of all psychopathological developments is to be traced; for it may be said of all psychoneurotic and psychotic patients that, if a True Mass is being celebrated in the chancel, a Black Mass is being celebrated in the crypt. It becomes evident, accordingly, that the psychotherapist is the true successor to the exorcist, and that he is concerned, not only with the "forgiveness of sins," but also with "the casting out of devils."

From the same object-relations theory, Henderson concludes that the therapist is not successor to the exorcist, just different in technique:

> The religious view of emotional pain contains an important if imperfect truth which has been too long disregarded. The psychotherapist differs from the exorcist not so much in theory, although his terminology is different, but in his belief that the therapeutic process to be effective is apt to require a more painstaking process to dissolve the persecuting forces.

This quote is interesting from several points of view, which all reflect typical western cultural biased assumptions. One, that the supernatural description of possession is less accurate than the naturalistic. Two, that folk healers are less painstaking than psychoanalysts. Three, that psychotherapy, western style, is more efficacious than folk healing. These assumptions are clearly challenged in the volumes cited in the bibliography; here I wish only to highlight the above assumptions, which lead to the next issue.

Modes of Relations Between Scientific and Folk Healers

In our time it has become fashionable to talk about providing psychotherapy to ethnic and minority groups, the poor and the working class, and the application of western psychotherapy to other cultures. But the limits of application of western style psychotherapy have yet to be clearly determined. Up to this point most of such interest has led to the notion of developing working relations between scientific psychotherapists and indigenous folk healers. Again what those working relations should or can consist of, remains vaguely defined. I propose that there are three current modes of working relations.

The first mode is *cooperation*. This mode is frequently found in developing countries where western psychiatrists establish friendly cooperative relations with native healers. Each retains his own assumptive world view, provides treatment within separate spheres of action, and transfers or triages mutual clients between each other. Carstairs and Kapur and Kiev have documented many examples of this type.

The second mode is *syncretistic*. That is, there is an attempt to functionally use indigenous healers as part of the psychiatric mental health care system. This mode functionally fuses two worlds of existence that have no necessarily logical relation. In this view the indigenous healer becomes coopted as a new style mental health "para-professional."

The third mode is *collaborative*. Here I have in mind a working relationship that involves sharing and participating in two worlds of consciousness and action.

In some cases documented by Carstairs and Kapur western psychotherapists have gradually given up western psychiatry and become healers within the folk tradition. It is hard to live in two worlds! Even to begin to move into collaborative modes requires real immersion into non-western modes of existence. Jilek and Jilek describe their efforts:

> "We found it is possible to bridge the cultural gap by first making oneself known to the people through participation in the activities of the non-western community. We strove to inform ourselves on the belief system, myths, rituals, social customs and organizations; we attended feasts, social, religious and political functions, seeking discussion with leading community figures and traditional healers."

In sum, I suggest that the popular enthusiasm to "work with the natives" does not do justice to the profound differences in consciousness and construction of reality involved. It would appear

that we are just beginning to appreciate the cul-
ture-boundedness of our western psychiatric
thinking.

A Case Study

To illustrate some issues raised thus far, the following case from my own experience highlights
the psychological meaning of possession and the
function of exorcism from a comparative therapeutic view.

This experience occurred during a period when
I served as the psychiatric consultant to the public
Health Service Clinic serving the Yakima Indian
reservation. The Yakima are located on several
thousand acres of farming and lumbering land in
central Washington amidst the rich agricultural
Yakima valley. As on many Indian reservations,
these Indian people live in close proximity to white
Western culture. Although they have relatively
good economic resources, life on the reservation is
isolated from the world in which it is located. The
reservation culture is in the midst of cultural disintegration. The "long hair" Indians cling to the traditional Yakima mores, while their middle-aged
children flounder in bewilderment, not part of the
white culture, not part of the Indian. Meanwhile
the grandchildren attend the local white schools
and watch television in the homes of their grand-
parents. Here in the middle of two cultures we
find our case.

Upon arrival at the reservation one snowy
December morning, the young public health doctor grabbed me for an emergency consultation. He
had been called to the home of an Indian family
the previous night to see an adolescent girl. The
family stated that she was crying, frightened, incoherent, running around the house in a state of
panic. He reported that upon arrival at the home
he found the girl incoherent, babbling, agitated,
muttering about ghosts and stated that she was
afraid of dying. He gave her an intramuscular injection of chlorpromazine which calmed her down,
and she went to sleep. He made a diagnosis of
acute schizophrenic psychosis. Since I was due to
arrive the next day, he requested that the family
bring the girl to the clinic for my evaluation and
recommendation for further treatment.

Precisely at the appointed time, the mother and
daughter appeared. I had worked on the reserva-

tion for several years at this time, and was known
to the Indian people. I had found good rapport
and little difficulty in establishing working relationships with my Indian clientele. But this was a
different situation from my usual clinical consultations. Both mother and daughter were sullen,
guarded, withdrawn. The girl was a pretty, well
developed, adolescent, thirteen years old. She was
dressed like a typical high school girl. But she
hunched herself over, eyes downcast, speaking in
barely audible tones. With great difficulty and
much patience her story was told.

The problems began the prior August when
Mary (her pseudonym) had gone off to a week-
long summer camp for Indian girls, sponsored by
the local O.E.O. program. One night, as children
are wont to do at a summer camp, after lights were
out and the counselors were in bed, Mary and several of her girl friends went sneaking out of their
cabin to frolic in the moonlight among the tall fir
trees. As they ran about in the moonlight they
looked up in the trees and saw human figures.
These ghost-like figures drifted down from the
trees, and the girls recognized them as their tribal
ancestors. The girls talked to the ghosts and the
ghosts talked to the girls. But after a few minutes
the girls became frightened, ran back to their cabin, jumped into bed, and hid under their covers.

All seemed safe now. Except for Mary. A ghost
followed her into the cabin, jumped on her as she
lay in bed, and tried to choke her. She fought and
struggled against the ghost, she gasped for breath,
she screamed for help. The counselors came running into the cabin, but they could not calm her.
Mary was sure the ghosts would kill her, she
sobbed and screamed. Finally, the counselors bun-
dled her up in a car and drove back home to the
local hospital. When seen in the emergency room
she was still in an agitated state and was given an
intramuscular tranquilizer shot before being taken
home to her parents.

The stage was set, and the pattern from then on
to December was rather routine. Mary would go
off to high school everyday with ratted hair and
teenie-bopper clothes. She would participate in her
daily high school activities like any teenager. She
was on the honor roll, was a cheerleader, and a
student body officer. But when she came home a
different Mary appeared. She combed her hair into
long Indian braids. She put on long-skirted tradi-

tional Indian clothes, and wandered about the house as if in a daze. She would see ghosts at the window and cry out in startled fright. She went walking in the fields and saw blood on the ground. She thought the ghosts had killed one of her girl friends. She thought the ghosts would attack and kill her younger brothers and sisters. She would become so frightened and worried that at times she would cry, and scream, and run around the house. At times the parents could not calm her, and they would take her to the hospital for a shot to calm her down. But the next morning she would always get up and go to school like a normal adolescent girl.

The mother and the girl had no explanation for this behavior. They were bewildered. The mother turned to me and asked what I, as a psychiatrist, thought of this behavior. Was her daughter crazy? What I observed was a withdrawn sullen girl. But she spoke in a coherent manner; she was logical and realistic in her conversation with me. I stated that I did not know what this all meant, but perhaps the mother might have some ideas.

The mother said she had heard that psychiatrists did not believe in religion. Did I believe in religion? I told her that I thought religion was very important in the lives of people. Did I believe that she had been healed? I told her that many people experience healing, and that she too might have had a healing experience. She smiled, relaxed and leaned toward me. Look at my face! Do you see any scars? No, I don't. Well, my father healed me. Do you believe that? Yes. Well he was a witchdoctor; he used to care for the whole tribe. And when I was a girl I fell in a fire and burned my face. And he made a pack of mud with his spittle, and anointed my face and said his prayers. And said I would be healed and have no scars. He said I would have a beautiful face. Do you think he was right? Is my face beautiful? Yes.

The mother was satisfied. She sat back. Then she tensed up again. Doctor? Yes? Should I say this? Maybe I shouldn't. I've never talked about this before. My daughter doesn't know about this. I've never told her. Well. You see, my father, the witchdoctor, he told me that his powers would be passed on when he died. But not to his children, not to me. His powers would be passed on to his grandchildren. And the oldest, this daughter, this girl, would have his powers.

By this time my thoughts about the clinical situation had been stirred. Do you think that Mary's experience has something to do with your father? Oh yes, she answered. But we don't talk about those things anymore, because, you know, we're Presbyterians now, and people don't believe in witchcraft anymore. But what if they did, I asked. How would you handle something like this?

The mother was now animated, and the daughter was listening intently. Well, we knew what to do. You see, in the old times, when someone was going to be given the powers of the spirits, was to be given the gifts of the witchdoctor, you had to struggle with the spirits. You had to prove you could rule them. Well, what would you do? I asked. Oh, there's nothing we can do. If this were the old times we would just open the door and let Mary wander out of the house at night. And she would go out and meet the spirits. And she would have to fight with them. And then she would come back with the powers . . . or maybe we would just find her out there after a few days, but that's the way it happens. . . .

I see, Well, what do you think about this now? Since this is not the old days, what do you think might be the best way to help Mary now?

Well, you know doctor, I've been thinking about that. You can't really practice much as a witchdoctor these days. It might be better if Mary were a Presbyterian and didn't accept the gift her grandfather left her.

Well, how would you work that out?

You see, doctor, we have to get rid of the spirits. We have to tell them that Mary doesn't want to fight with them. And then they'll go away and leave her alone. And she'll be O.K.

H'm. Well what do you have to do?

Oh, I don't know how to do that.

Who does?

Oh, Grandma does. She and some of the other old women know the ceremony. We all have to get together. And we would dress Mary up in the ceremonial dress, and we have to have prayers, and offerings, and we would anoint her, and say the prayers . . .

Lest I leave the reader in suspense, at the end of one of the most fascinating experiences in my professional life, I reached an agreement with Mary and her mother. We agreed that it was not appropriate for Mary to attempt to achieve the mantle of power of her grandfather had bequeathed her. That would be looking backward. So we agreed that Mary should renounce the legacy and look forward to becoming part of the modern world. The mother agreed to call the grandmother and see if she and the other tribal women could conduct a ritual of exorcism that night. I would return in one month. They agreed to see me again at that time.

Now it was January. With some trepidation I awaited their arrival. They came early! They were delighted to see me. I was a great doctor. They had followed my advice. The ceremony of exorcism had been conducted. It had been successful. Mary was healed.

Indeed, since that night of exorcism, the strange behavior had disappeared. The mother was happy, Mary was happy, I was happy. Because of my on-going contact with this tribe, I had the opportunity to follow this family for many months thereafter. Mary remained healthy and happy. No more was she bothered. In contrast to her mien that first cold snowy December morning, when I saw her there-after she was bright and bouncy, talkative and en-thusiastic, like any other energetic adolescent girl beginning to become a woman.

Some Religious Observations

As I listened to this story, I thought of an Old Testament story that was almost identical, and I thought of the universality of human experience.

In the following passage, we read of Jacob wres-tling with the angel of the Lord, in order to obtain power over the spirits:

> "And Jacob was left alone; and there wrestled a man with him until the breaking of the day. And when he saw that he prevailed not against him, he touched the hollow of his thigh; and the hollow of Jacob's thigh was out of joint, as he wrestled with him. And he said, Let me go, for the day breaketh. And he said, I will not let thee go, except thou bless me. And he said unto him, What is thy name? And he said, Jacob. And he said, Thy name shall be called no more Jacob, but Israel: for as a prince hast thou power with God and with men, and hast prevailed.... And Jacob called the name of the place Peniel: for I have seen God face to face, and my life is preserved ... and he halted upon his thigh. (Genesis 32:24–31)

What is remarkable is that over a span of perhaps six thousand years and over three continents we find the same interpretation. The man gains power over spirits by fighting with the spirits. If man wins, he then has special powers, he can com-mand the spirits. He is a shaman, a healer, a witch-doctor. But it is a dangerous business, for to acquire the special powers requires a mortal com-bat. Jacob won, but he was crippled for life. And as for Mary, she feared her own death, or that of her siblings, if they got in the way of the combat.

In this case, we have the reenactment of an age-old saga: Man in quest of power over the forces of his life.

Some Psychodynamic Observations

Although we have limited clinical material, we may rough out the following possible interpreta-tions. The mother presents herself as the favored daughter of her father. Father heals her, using his spittle (semen?). Mother continues to frame her ac-ceptability as a person around her external appear-ance, her beauty, her sexuality. She asks for acceptance as a desirable object from the therapist (father symbol). Daughter Mary appears on the scene at the time of adolescence as a maturing woman, hence competitor to mother. Mother does not give approval to daughter to become a sexually mature woman, for that poses a threat to mother. Mary projects the disapproving mother into the hallucinatory ghost object who would kill her. But also the projected forbidden object is the father fig-ure who lies upon her in bed—the incestuous fa-ther. Mary wanders in the field and finds blood in the fields (menstrual blood?) where her girl friend was killed. While the sibling competitive rivalry between mother and daughter is projected onto the fear of Mary's siblings being killed by the spirits.

The conflict is resolved. The mother is reaf-firmed in her role as woman. She in turn, in con-cert with her own mother, participates in a symbolic ritual which gives daughter, mother, granddaughter the sanction and approval to ma-ture, to grow up, to become a sexually mature woman. Daughter Mary is no longer a competitive rival, seeking to gain the exclusive rights and affec-tions of the witchdoctor grandfather (oedipal fa-ther). So mother can now allow daughter Mary to become a woman in her own right. Result: daughter no longer acts out the mother-daughter conflict.

A Trans-Cultural Perspective

Our observations are in concert with the work of Melford Spiro who has shown how one can look at various possession states and methods of healing from both the Western psychodynamic perspective and from the cultural perspective of the indigenous healer. It is of note that, in Spiro's work on possession, the most common conflict was sexual conflict. Spiro notes that the dissociative state of possession deals with the fear of retaliation, which is certainly true in this case.

But given the fact that we deal with a dissociative state, can we consider this an abnormal state? Here we have an instance in which the particular psychodynamic of family life was acted out in a pattern provided by the culture. Within the culture set, the behavioral pattern exhibited by Mary was not unusual nor unexpected. In fact, she acted out the cultural norm.

In this instance we can note that the diagnosis of acute schizophrenia is understandable, but inappropriate. However, the family itself was caught in an interesting and pathetic cultural bind. If they had been living within the traditional Indian culture, they would have followed the prescribed patterns of response. We may assume that the deviant behavior would have been appropriately resolved. However, the family was caught between two cultures, between two belief systems. And so the family was immobilized. The behavior of the patient, Mary, was congruent with the belief system of the old culture, while the treatment of the hospitals was congruent with the new belief system.

What provided a significant intervention in this impasse was a sanction by a scientific professional psychotherapist to an indigenous cultural healer. And that collaborative support enabled this natural system to function and to restore a person to function.

A psychodynamic interpretation of this case intervention might include the possibility of a "transference cure." In this instance the mother experiences reaffirmation of her beauty, her wholeness, her person, from the psychiatrist (witchdoctor-transferential father). She need not feel threatened by her daughter's emerging sexuality, for

mother is still the favored one. Then too, the psychiatrist (transference father symbol) enlists the aid of mother (herself now the successful oedipal competitor) to help daughter grow up. And this is allowed because daughter will not be stronger than mother.

Although these psychodynamic speculations may be appropriate and accurate, I do not think that one can conclude that this explains the total interaction.

In my opinion, these psychoanalytic motifs may indicate why this particular intervention was so rapidly catalytic of a therapeutic resolution. The psychodynamic cards were stacked in my favor.

On the other hand, the family had sought medical treatment on many occasions before they came to see me. The medical interventions could have been given the same symbolic ascriptions, which I propose were ascribed to me. And the failure of medical treatment, or the knowledge of the tribal beliefs could have resulted in the family going ahead and conducting the exorcism ceremonies. Yet they have not ostensibly even thought about exorcism.

If this family were fully participant in the Western thought world of the psychiatrist, then I would have considered a typical family therapy model of intervention. But this family was not in my thought world—it only looked like they were thinking and living within the Western scientific tradition of medicine. Indeed, they themselves were only conscious of their Western world thought and beliefs. Whether one can consider this solely an intrapsychic repression is an interesting problem. My own inclination is to conclude that this family had a higher than usual level of repressive defense structures. But also that idiosyncratic family style was reinforced by the transitional Indian culture in which they live, in which repression of the "old" belief systems is built into the experiential world of living on the reservation.

I seriously doubt that a scientific style psychotherapy intervention would have been of any value at all. Not that one cannot conduct rather typical psychotherapy with Indians living on the reservation. For I did conduct a great deal of straightforward psychodynamic interpretive psychotherapy. But the problem of Mary and her mother was embedded in the traditional Indian belief system. I think that psychotherapy with either Mary or her mother around other issues might have been possible and appropriate within the Western scientific frame of thought. But with the acting out of the problem within the framework of the traditional Indian belief system, in order to conduct a scientific psychotherapy, one would have to translate the whole problem from one belief system to another belief system.

The alternative which I followed was to take the traditional Indian belief system for real. To accept the interpretation of cause and effect within that system for real also. And to support an intervention within that system that would indeed be real.

Healing Symbols and the Future

It has long been recognized that there are many similarities if not identities between the western psychotherapist and the folk healer. Jerome Frank has elegantly summarized the non-specific *extrinsic* factors common to all psychotherapeutic healers; while Prince has recently reviewed evidence for the fact that there are common *intrinsic* self-healing factors in the client, which any healer may catalyze. Thus, there may be common extrinsic and intrinsic factors in psychotherapy regardless of the particular cultural context, language, or belief system. Thus, it might seem that moving across cultural systems of belief would be relatively simple, if one could make the necessary translations and understand the idioms.

But I propose that the matter of therapeutic healing is more profound than just the extrinsic factors of healing alluded to above. We see clearly in the healing rituals of folk healers a rich symbolization. What we do not see so clearly is that western psychotherapy is also a healing ritual with its own symbols.

Symbols are vital aspects of our existence. As Rollo May notes:

> The symbol draws together and unites experience. It bridges the inescapable antinomies of life—conscious and unconscious, reason and emotion, individual and society, history and the present. . . . A symbol is real and efficacious only to those who commit themselves to it.

It is noteworthy that in folk society, anthropologists such as Turner and Lévi-Strauss, have shown that the healing rituals symbolize not only personal conflict and resolution, but at the same time mirror

the cultural conflict and its resolution. The symbols of the rituals unite the person and his culture. The client and the healer both communicate effectively through the symbolic modes which are given them in their culture.

Now Perry London has pointed out that all psychotherapies have three common elements: (1) a theory of the nature of man, (2) a superordinate moral code, (3) healing techniques which symbolically evoke a healing transformation in accord with the first two elements.

In this light I suggest that western modes of psychotherapy are extremely limited to a small segment of our current society—at least as widely practiced. Henri Ellenberger notes the sub-cultural consciousness within which psychotherapy has been symbolized:

> By the end of the nineteenth century the upper classes could no longer be content with the existing method of hypnotic and suggestive therapy and demanded a new, nonauthoritarian psychotherapy that would explain to the patient what was going on in his own mind.

And again:

> One had to find a psychotherapy for educated people; it would be a non-authoritarian method, which would keep personal liberty intact, explain to the patient what was going on in his own mind, and guarantee that all the methods employed acting only through his own psyche.

Furthermore, it is widely recognized that the linguistic verbal content of psychotherapy may not be the most pertinent aspect of therapy, but rather there is a therapeutic transaction that symbolizes rationalistic construction of reality for "psychotherapeutic man." I find it interesting that the most recent symbolic-linguistic study of psychotherapy is aptly titled "The Structure of Magic."

In his history of psychotherapy, Jan Ehrenwald begins with the magical encounter (which is symbolization) and leads us finally to encounter groups (which, too, is symbolization). Is the history of psychotherapy then not linear but circular?

Returning to Ellenberger, he concludes his magnum opus aware of the fact that the history and evolution of psychotherapy may be circular, for he says:

> The dynamic psychotherapist is thus dealing . . . with psychic realities . . . . But what exactly are

psychic realities? . . . there are many kinds of psychic realities, and they often are contradictory and incompatible with each other, though endowed with the same character of certainty for those who are working with them. . . . The coexistence of two mutually incompatible approaches to the cognition of the human psyche shocks the scientist's yearning for unity.

Western psychoanalytic psychotherapy, I submit, has emerged as a healing ritual, based upon a particular western rationalistic, deterministic, and empiricist image of man. It has its own existentialist morality. And its therapeutic technique symbolizes this modern reality. Martin Grotjahn, the eminent psychoanalyst grasps this latter point well in his most recent book, "The Voice of the Symbol." Therein Grotjahn describes psychoanalytic technique as fundamentally a process for symbolizing reality:

He seeks the outline of the future in which "free creative symbol integration" will fulfill the only demand, the only duty which man has to life: to live to the fullest capacity of his potential, to experience life with all his courage, to become literate in terms of understanding himself and to integrate his unconscious with his intelligence.

The problem inherent in Grotjahn's description of psychoanalytic symbolizing is his assumption that Freud was the first to discover a method for understanding the symbol and the unconscious and thereby create a symbolizing therapy that integrates conscious man with unconscious realities of his socio-cultural development.

I suggest that the same discovery and process of integrating symbolization can be found in the therapies of indigenous folk healers. I believe the ethnographic evidence indicates that we have sold the folk healers short. We have interpreted their therapies solely as simple-minded magic rituals; whereas the potency and efficacy of their therapies may be every bit as efficacious with their culture as psychoanalytic therapy is in our culture. And perhaps with the same failures, as well!

In turn, there seems to be an almost romantic fascination with folk healers today. But belief in supernatural demonology and exorcism is not an unmixed blessing, even if supernatural rites of exorcism may be effective. For the particular forms of supernaturalism that become distilled as witchcraft and demonology contain a virulent disguise of the social ills of the society, and invite the acting out of personalized destructiveness.

Thus, Geoffrey Parrinder concludes:

"Belief in witchcraft is one of the great fears from which mankind has suffered. It has taken its toll literally in blood. . . . Witchcraft must be symbolic. It is a belief which helps to interpret and canalize the disease of society . . . (witchcraft beliefs) resolve certain conflicts or problems: but I did not say that this is a good solution. The aggression invited by witchcraft beliefs is as harmful as anything a society can produce in the way of disruptive practices; the relief offered by witch-hunting and witch-punishing is no more than temporary and their capacity to allay anxieties no more illusory: for if witchcraft beliefs resolve certain fears and tensions, they also produce others . . . the kind of remedy which both becomes a drug and poisons the system."

The personalization of social evil into demonology is the transformation to be avoided, not supernaturalism.

Paul Pruyser states it well: "The great question is: if illusions are needed, how can we have those that are capable of correction, and how can we have those that will not deteriorate into delusions." Similarly, Becker says: "If men live in myths and not absolutes, there is nothing we can do or say about that. But we can argue for nondestructive myths."

It is appropriate now, to examine the future of psychoanalytic western psychotherapy, both in relation to other folk healing systems and unto itself.

First, I have alluded to the data which allow us to conclude that psychoanalytic psychotherapy is part of a mythic system of western man, that its view of man, its morality, and its symbolizing techniques are relevant and efficacious only within the symbolizing mythic culture out of which it has developed. Therefore, we face a major task of reevaluating the structure and future of the interface between this symbolizing psychotherapy and other cultural views of man and the attendant symbolizing therapies of those cultures. Even within western culture there are widely divergent sub-cultures, such as the various religious associations of America for whom the psychoanalytic construction of reality is by no means easily made relevant. I only make passing note of the many modifications of psychotherapy underway today in

America to provide effective therapeutic services to other than the educated well-to-do intelligentsia of America.

Second, let us turn to the future of psychoanalytic psychotherapy itself. As we have seen, psychoanalysis and its derivative dynamic therapies are an integral part of the scientific epoch of western civilization—the time of the humanistic rational man.

As noted herein, we live in the twilight of the scientific age—we have moved on to the age of existential man. Accordingly, it is not surprising that there is widespread disillusionment with the psychoanalytic model of man.

S. K. Pande, a non-western psychiatrist, observes how the western cosmology created "deficits in the Western way of life . . . negative psychological implications . . . and Western psychotherapy, especially the psychoanalytic model, as a symbolic and substantive undertaking to correct them." But the psychoanalytic model becomes increasingly irrelevant as a symbolically effective force as it addresses a vanishing breed of humanistic rational men. Indeed irrational man, or at least existential man, is creating a new view of man, a new morality, and therefore new symbolizing therapeutic techniques, as represented in the existential psychotherapies, the humanistic psychotherapies, and direct experiential encounters of sundry form.

In all of this we are gradually becoming aware of the fact that the ontological underpinnings of any psychotherapy is critical to its relevance, acceptance, and efficacy. Psychotherapy in the western world is indeed a supernaturalistic system, that parades itself as a naturalistic system. Consider the trenchant observations of Ernest Becker:

Often psychotherapy seems to promise the moon: a more constant joy, delight, celebration of life, perfect love, and perfect freedom . . . psychotherapists are caught up in modern culture and forced to be part of it. Commercial industrialism promised western man a paradise on earth, . . . that replaced the paradise in heaven of Christian myth. And now psychology must replace them both with the myth of paradise through self-knowledge. This is the promise of psychology, and for the most part psychotherapists are obliged to live it and embody it.

At issue is the fact that over history and centuries of time, folk healers, the psychotherapists of societies and cultures were unabashedly part of the supernaturalistic system. Thus, they moved easily between the treatment of accident, illness, misfortune, interpersonal conflict and existential malaise.

But as Ellenberger has so nicely illustrated, the historical development of western psychotherapy has led it to a fragmented, isolated, and naturalistic position within society. The crisis of modern psychiatry is reflected in the fact that medical science cannot provide a belief system to live by, nor can psychiatry as a branch of medicine. Thus, we see a return of "psychiatry to medicine"—as a limited enterprise. Meanwhile, the psychotherapeutic side of psychiatry has been increasingly vulnerable to competing systems and persons each offering discipleship.

The problem is this: that the *atomization* and *particularization* of misfortune in western society leads to the *fragmentation* of healing. We have a seeming paradox. We see that psychotherapeutic healing deeply involves ideology, belief, and symbolization of reality. Yet in western society we have attempted to create a non-ideological, belief-free psychotherapy. I suggest that psychotherapy in the west has survived thus far because it has been based on a covert belief system. As we have unmasked that covert belief system, psychotherapists are now making unabashed pitches for their method of psychotherapy, which is a belief system.

Again Becker pertinently observes:

Now there are only three ways, I think, that psychology itself can become an adequate belief system. One of them is to be a creative genius as a psychologist and to use psychology as the immorality vehicle for oneself—as Freud and subsequent psychoanalysts have done. Another is to use the language and concepts of psychotherapy in much of one's waking life, so that it becomes a lived belief system. . . this is one of the reasons that psychotherapy has moved away from the Freudian intellectual model to the new experiential model. . . . The third and final way is merely an extension and sophistication of this. It is to take psychology and deepen it with religious and metaphysical associations so that it becomes actually a religious belief system with some breadth and depth. At the same time, the psychotherapist himself beams out the steady quiet power of transference and becomes the guru-figure of religion.

In conclusion, the symbolizing power of psychoanalytic psychotherapy is waning as the society out of which it sprang changes. I suggest that psychoanalytic psychotherapy is a supernaturalistic system of belief. (In this case the God and cosmos of science.) But its ontological grounding, its fundamental commitment to humanistic rational man, its method of experimental empiricism, is melting away. We can see the truth pointed out sometime ago by the French anthropologist Lévi-Strauss, that the psychoanalyst and the shaman are structurally the same. Both engage in powerful rituals that are symbolizing exercises of their culture. *Both are exorcists.*

My interpretation of all the foregoing data is that the reemergence of demonology and exorcism in our current society is symptomatic of an ontological crisis in western society. Psychoanalytic psychotherapy is losing its symbolic power because the society no longer strongly invests in the symbols of a scientific cosmos. And where the symbols have lost their power, the accompanying techniques become vapid. Accordingly, we see the search for a new cosmos, a new symbolic integration of life, and new healers invested with therapeutic powers because they participate in the new symbolization. One solution is regressive, a return to the ancient forms and symbols of demonology. Another solution, that of a scientific psychotherapy has been tried and is failing because of loss of its symbolic community and the erosion of its ontology. I propose that the future may produce psychotherapies that are much more explicit in their ontology; that there will be a delineation of the limited goals of treatment that can be offered by psychiatry as a universal science; that the more overarching existential problematics of life may well be addressed within a diversity of socio-culturally specific psychotherapeutics, which are part of specific supernaturalistic communities.

It appears to me that western psychotherapy has engaged in the self illusion that we offer a culture-free, value free, ideology-free cure, under the universal rubric of mental health. But a philosopher Joseph Margolis acutely observes:

> Psychotherapy, then, is primarily concerned with a technical goal, the preservation and restoration of mental health; nevertheless its own development leads it, inevitably, to take up the role of moral legislator.

Thus, it may be that we are on the edge of a new interpretation of psychotherapy. The notion of a scientific psychotherapy may be a chimera. The challenge for tomorrow is to explore the relationship between universalistic dimensions of psychotherapy which are naturalistic and particularistic dimensions of psychotherapy that must be supernaturalistic, naturalistic.

Summary

This study started with an exploration of the current social interest in demonology and exorcism in western society. We have seen that beliefs in demonology are part of a larger supernaturalistic cosmology. However, acting out of demonology beliefs occurs only in times where there is social oppression and loss of social integration. Modern demonology can be seen to be part of the social repudiation of the scientific determinism of rational man, coincident with the rise of existential irrationalism. The practice of exorcism is but one example of the powerful use of symbolic transformations in healing rituals. Seen in terms of symbolic actions, psychoanalytic psychotherapy is also a practice of exorcism. This leads us then to examine the symbolic systems of society that incorporate both the client and healer. It is seen that western psychotherapy is just as much a part of its culture as other healing systems. We close with an eye to the future, can there be a psychotherapy that is not supernaturalistic?

Characteristics of Sisala Diviners

Eugene Mendonsa

Divination is a mystical technique for acquiring knowledge about past, present, or future events that is unobtainable using ordinary explanatory methods. Rituals of divination have a vast variety. The Azande use at least four different oracles to gain information and answers without the use of empirical data. Unlike the use of oracles by the Azande, the Sisala divination techniques stress the power and intervention of ancestors in their daily lives. Mendonsa demonstrates that for the Sisala, divination is a customary method of communicating with the ancestors, who are thought to control the power of the universe and who use this power to afflict the living. It is through necromancy that the Sisala can determine the cause of and remedy for problems originating with ancestors. To a lesser degree the Sisala use other forms of divination techniques, but contact with the ancestors is of primary importance and illustrates the roles of ancestors and divination as mechanisms of social control.

Reprinted from *The Realm of the Extra-Human: Agents and Audiences*, World Anthropology Series (The Hague, 1976), pp. 179–95, by permission of the author and Mouton Publishers (Division of Walter de Gruyter and Co.).

Sisala Social Structure

THE SISALA LIVE MAINLY IN THE TUMU DISTRICT IN northern Ghana. The environment is African savanna, which is primarily bush, due to the relatively low population density. The Sisala show cultural uniformity with the other tribes of the Ashanti hinterland, that is, they are patrilineal, with a social structure of the Guinea type, and they practice hoe horticulture to produce a subsistence diet of millet, sorghum, maize, yams, and rice. Cattle are kept in small numbers for sacrificial purposes and bridewealth.

Agnatic descent is the keystone of Sisala social structure. Their society is divided into a number of patri-clans (*-viara*), which form localized ritual units having a common interest. The clan is an exogamous unit made up of several villages or sometimes village segments. The village (*tang* or *jang*) is the important focal point of identification for an individual. Patrilocal residence dictates, therefore, a divided sense of identification for the women, while men remain firmly rooted in their natal villages. A village is normally divided into a seris of lineages (*jechiking*) which are arranged to form two reciprocal burial groups—that is, the village is divided in two. While the entire village considers itself to be one body of kinsmen, kinship increases in intensity as the units of the segmentary system become smaller, and therefore the reciprocal burial groups are felt to be "brother" groups. The lineage (*jechiking*) is the important corporate unit. It is the subsistence-residential homestead or walled enclosure normally inhabited by an agnatic extended family. This unit is further divided into compounds or yards (*kaala*) made up of joint families who farm together. Each *kaala* is divided into houses (*diasang*) and rooms (*dia*). In this segmentary system the developmental cycle is a continual enlargement of the single room (*dia*), through marriage and childbirth, into higher-order units which may eventually result in fission and a repetition of the process.

Today the Isalung-speakers are governed by a paramount chief (the *Tumukuoro*) and various village chiefs *(kuoro)*, of whom twelve are divisional chiefs. This system was initiated by the British during their colonial efforts in northern Ghana, and although these political units did not correspond to traditional ones, they have since become realities. The most important precolonial political unit was the village *(jang)*, under the leadership of the village *tinteintina* (custodian of the earth) and the elders *(nihising)*. Because there were no "chiefs," the *tinteintina* wielded politico-ritual power based on his control of the ancestral shrines. Today the village chief *(kuoro)* has taken on the political functions, while the *tinteintina* has remained concerned with ritual matters such as the fertility of the earth and the fecundity of women.

Sisala society is a gerontocracy, and life is a series of age-based stages or grades. There are two important rites of passage for a man or woman, namely, marriage *(jaanung)* and death *(suunung)*. The first allows the passage from the status of small boy *(henmie)* or girl *(hantolowie)* to adult *(niwang)*. This transition is further enhanced when the marriage produces living offspring. The second rite of passage comes at a person's death, necessitating the performance of elaborate funerary rites marking passage from the status of elder *(nihiang)* to that of a remembered ancestor *(lelung)*.

Kinds of Sisala Divination

For the Sisala, divination is not so much a way of knowing the future, as a way of knowing *fa fa*— that is, knowing which occult entity has afflicted them—although it can also be used to determine whether affliction lies ahead. There are five major ways in which this is accomplished: (1) necromancy, (2) ordeal, (3) throwing cowries, (4) fairy-calling, and (5) traditional divination.

Necromancy

If a death is thought to be due to witchcraft, the members of the family in which the death has occurred may perform necromancy at the funeral. In former times this involved three men carrying the dead body on their shoulders; it was thought that as the men wandered around the crowded funeral,

the body would point out the dead person's killer. However, during colonial times the British stressed immediate burial of the body, and now the Sisala have substituted for the body a bundle of ebony sticks tied with the cover cloth of the dead person. If this bundle does not point out an individual who is responsible for the death, it may point to a shrine. This type of divination is practiced infrequently, and is most likely to be performed when the person has died mysteriously, e.g., by drowning or in the bush.

Ordeal

Ordeals are infrequent, possibly owing to the low level of witchcraft accusation but also because the Sisala prefer a less public means of sanction. Many times I noticed that persons would avoid taking their grevances to a public forum or ordeal. At first I thought this was a function of their guilt, but soon I learned that the Sisala prefer private means to public means. One day I was sitting with the *nihiang nihiang* [oldest man] of Bujan, and we were discussing the fact that his son's wife had had one *cedi* stolen while at the Tumu market. I suggested that she swear by the rain *(gmiese duong)* in order to punish the thief or force him to come forward, but everyone present was shocked at the suggestion. The *nihiang nihiang* explained that the Sisala do not like to do such things, and when I asked why this was so, he related a story:

> A long time ago in Kasana [a Kasena village to the north] an old woman had just pounded some *dawa-dawa* flour, and a woman of another lineage came and took part of it. When the old lady returned to discover the theft, she swore by the rain, calling it to kill the thief. Meanwhile the thief had put some of the flour in every cooking pot in her lineage. Every lineage member ate of it except one man who had just gone to the farm. The rain sent the lightning and killed all the lineage members except the one man at the farm. This is why we now hesitate to swear by the rain, although we don't taboo it. The Kasena still do this frequently, but we do not. Even if a chicken were to eat some of the flour, the rain would kill it. Many innocent people can die from such an act.

Nevertheless, some people do swear by the rain to discover a hidden thing, since doing hidden things *(luore)* is considered bad and is akin to witchcraft—as indicated by the word *luore*, which is cognate with the word for stomach, *luorung*, which is the seat of witchcraft. Since witchcraft is such a bad thing, some people feel justified in swearing by the rain to find a witch, but more commonly a sacrifice will be made on the earth shrine to determine whether a given individual is a witch.

The scorpion ordeal is another form of divination. It is usually used to divine a petty theft or some other minor delict—e.g., a man may determine which of his wives put her hand into his compound granary *(viribalung)*. Suspects are lined up and the scorpion is allowed to crawl over their arms, and the sting is both the proof and the punishment. When persons are accused of a petty crime, they often expose themselves to a kind of ordeal. When confronted, a person may deny the deed and add, "If I am guilty, let a snake bite me." The Sisala greatly fear the bite of a snake, and also believe that such a bite is often a punishment by the ancestors.

Although these institutions have judicial functions, they can be viewed as divinatory devices as well. Reynolds (1963: 121) has pointed out that an ordeal can be considered a legal device when administered to one person, whereas it is a divinatory device when several persons are involved. Yet there is an element of divination even in an accusation of witchcraft. A ritual formula is allowed to stimulate an answer from the occult world, and this is precisely what the traditional diviner does when he divines. When looking at divination, one should therefore consider the entire range of devices used to receive feedback from *fa fa* [the occult world].

Throwing Cowries

Diviners who throw cowrie shells *(vuge ari mo-wribie)* are also known and consulted, but this practice is not indigenous to the Sisala and has probably diffused into the Sisala area from the Islamic peoples to the north. There are relatively few Sisala who actually practice this kind of divination. Mostly cowrie-shell-throwers are found in the northwest section of Sisala-land, which is more heavily influenced by Islamic culture, and they are strangers who practice as wandering diviners. Many of the Sisala who practice throwing cowries are innovators who have made several earlier attempts to achieve prestige by nontraditional

means. In my experience, the same individuals who have tried throwing cowries have also tried calling fairies—which is also a practice that has been borrowed from the neighboring Awuna and Kasena to the north. Pagan Sisala who consult traditional diviners tend to look down on cowrie-throwing as less reliable than traditional divination, and traditional diviners have told me that if their verdict was too different from that of a cowrie-thrower, the latter would die from ancestral anger. Cowrie-throwers are sometimes consulted if they happen to be passing through the village— e.g., when a Wangara cowrie-thrower came through Bujan, many persons consulted him merely because he was there, and they hoped he would tell them something good. In general, however, when a Sisala suffers an affliction, he will seek out the traditional diviner to ascertain the occult cause. Cowrie-throwers are not viewed as being in the same class. One informant (a diviner) told me the following story, which is biased, but nonetheless reflects a general feeling:

> The divining bag [of the traditional diviner] came from God. It was here prior to those who throw cowries and who only profess to see things. Anyone can become a cowrie-thrower by going to another cowrie-thrower and asking to share his medicine. His face is washed with the medicine after he pays a fee, and he can start throwing cowries.

Fairy-Calling

The fairy-caller *(kantonngo yirang)* is a relatively recent introduction from the neighboring Awuna-Kasena peoples. There are only a few Sisala men who have learned this technique of divining, and the technique does not seem to be gaining much ground. Of the 272 Sisala males I interviewed about their consulting habits, only 7.3 percent had ever been to a fairy-caller in their entire lifetime, while 86 percent had consulted a traditional diviner at least once in the month prior to the interview. It is commonly held that Sisala men do not know the proper technique for calling fairies, therefore those who wish to consult a fairy-caller often make a rather long journey across the border into Upper Volta to do so. Some of the Sisala fairy-callers have fallen into outright disrepute as fakes and charlatans, and the people speak of them with contempt. They are usually individuals of some drive, who greatly desire public recognition, but who lack any traditional role in the public eye. Some fairy-callers even try throwing cowries as well.

The Sisala say that in former times (*fa fa*) there were no fairy-callers among them, although there have always been fairies (*kantonngo*). Fairies are beings of the wild, that dwell in trees or in the rivers of the bush. They are perceived as having access to both *fa fa* and *lele* [ancestors], and they can communicate with God and bring these messages back to man. At times they capture a man while he is walking through the bush and teach him secrets of one kind or another. But the Sisala have never had any way of initiating contact with the fairies, and have remained in a position of passively waiting for the fairies to communicate with them. The Awuna-Kasena, on the other hand, have developed a technique whereby the diviner calls the fairies, who then communicate by voice with assembled clients. Several persons consult such a diviner each night, and he calls the fairies to come into a dark room and speak to each of them about their troubles or wishes. The fairy-caller is the link between man and the fairies, and the fairies are the link with God (*Wia*), whereas the traditional diviner is a link with the ancestors (*lele*).

The institution of calling fairies is most widespread among those Sisala who live to the north and border on the Awuna-Kasena; Sisala people there tend to consult fairy-callers more often, and Islam is more entrenched there. Moslems use fairy-callers as a means of divining the wishes of Allah. Most of the Sisala men who have attempted to learn to call fairies live in these northern clans. The institution does not greatly affect the Sisala to the south—for example, the Crocodile Clan forbids any of its members from becoming a fairy-caller, although it is not taboo to consult one. Needless to say, traditional diviners are quite scornful of fairy-callers, and one frequently hears a diviner make reference in the course of his divining to "those fairy-callers who make so much noise."

Traditional Divination

A traditional diviner (*vugura*) is a man who occupies an accepted, traditional status in Sisala society. Neither the fairy-caller nor the cowrie-thrower has such a status. The office of diviner was instituted by God for the sake of the ancestors, who have perpetuated divination as a means of maintaining control over the living and thereby insuring the continuity of the moral order. It is the link *par excellence* with the occult world, and is the method most used when affliction strikes.

Myth of Origin

The first diviner was thought to have descended from God shortly after man descended to earth via the baobab tree. God gave shrines to men, but men did not understand what their function was nor did they know how to sacrifice on them, therefore affliction abounded in those first days (e.g. children were continually sick, wives died in childbirth, crops failed). God saw that man was confused, and sent down the diviner to help man in the proper use of shrines.

The first diviner was the chief of all diviners, the black ant (*chungchusunung*), which today remains a symbol of divination. The black ant is seen as being similar to God, and therefore serves as a link with God. When a diviner tells someone that he must "apologize to God" or to "pray to God," the person will be instructed to take items (e.g. three kola nuts and fifty cowries) to do so. If the decision is left to the client, he can do one of two things: he can take the objects to a black anthill and leave them on top of it, or he can take them to a real diviner. Also, when people purchase medicine from a medicine man (*dalusungtina*), they must throw away any remaining medicine on a black anthill—which is symbolic of returning the medicine to God. Black ants are like God because both are omnipresent, and both are dangerous if certain precautions are not taken. Black ants never sleep, and anyone who has walked through the African bush at night with a torch focusing on a black anthill has noticed that the ants are busy at work. Black ants are also very strong, and can destroy an entire millet harvest in one night if it is not properly protected. One informant made the following statement:

> Black ants are like God and Moslems. Have you ever seen a pile of millet after black ants have finished with it? They enter, and leave nothing but the chaff. That is what Moslems do, too.

Myth (*namaka*) explains that it was God who sent down the black ant to instruct the first human diviners in the beginning, and black ants taught the diviners to teach the people the purpose of their shrines. Man had received the blacksmith shrine prior to the divining shrine, and yet he did not know how to use it to prevent affliction; because he had no way of knowing when to sacrifice on it, affliction was rampant in the land.

Myth relates that God gave the divining shrine to man so that he could have a link with the occult world. It allowed man to communicate with *fa fa*, and provided a feedback mechanism. When affliction struck, man had some way of knowing the occult reason behind the affliction, and, more importantly, he had a mechanism for ameliorating the affliction through shrine sacrifice. The Sisala verbalize this as a link with God *(Wia)*, but it must be emphasized that this is somewhat misleading, because when they say this they are using God as a general symbol of *fa fa*—an occult mythical state which includes not only *Wiajang* [God's village], which is in the sky, but also *lelejang* [the ancestor's village], which is in the earth, as well as the "mystical" side of all shrines, rivers, rocks, trees, and farms. The diviner deals with the whole range of occult entities, but most consultations reveal an ancestral cause of affliction. The Sisala do not always verbalize about the ancestors as causative agents, but will do so if pressed; and they may substitute the word "God" or "shrine"—e.g. "a shrine has afflicted me," or "God has done it."

The Power of the Ancestors

Almost every consultation deals directly or obliquely with the power of the ancestors as guardians of the moral order. Much of the work of Meyer Fortes among the nearby Tallensi has pointed to this power in the daily lives of the living. Cultures in northern Ghana exhibit a pattern of ancestor worship, and the Sisala are no exception. The following two cases illustrate the importance of the ancestors and the belief in their power.

My informant said:

> In the village of Pulima a man named Baton decided to go to Tumu. He went to the lineage of Tokurojang and told lies, saying that he was asked by the elders of his compound to collect twenty *cedis* in bridewealth from Baduong. He collected this money and went home, but when he returned home he did not inform anybody, and spent the whole amount himself.

In about three months' time, when the people of Pulima came to collect the bridewealth *(hajarikiaa)*, they were told that Baton had already collected it. The members of Tokurojang informed the Pulima party that Baton had said that the Pulima elders had sent him to fetch the money for them. The Pulima elders returned immediately to their village and confronted Baton with the facts. They asked him if he had done this thing but he denied it. The elders could not prove him guilty, so they dropped the matter. Not long afterwards Baton became seriously ill, and his parents went from place to place trying to find medicines to cure him. None of the medicines worked, and they finally took him to the government health center in Tumu where he was given many injections, but he still did not recover. On the way home from the health center he died, and his body was taken home and buried.

The elders came together and called in a diviner. They consulted to know the cause of death. They asked if he was killed by the ancestors because he went to Tumu and told lies. It was determined that this was the case, and Baton's father was required to bring a cow, goat, and sheep to sacrifice at the ancestor *(lele)* shrine. If they had not done this, the ancestors would have brought great harm to the family (lineage) of Baton in the future. Because he told lies, he was killed by the ancestors.

Another informant related the following account:

> At Tuorojang in Tumu there was a young man named Cedu. He caught a goat that was for the ancestor of his house *(dia)*, and killed it to sell the meat. When the day came for the sacrifice, the elders searched for the goat so that they could kill it at the *lele* shrine. They could not find it, and asked to know who might have caught the goat. They could not decide who had taken the goat, so they caught another and used it for the sacrifice instead. During the sacrifice, the elders begged the ancestors to forgive them for not sacrificing the proper goat. The elders asked the ancestors to find and punish the thief. After the sacrifice, when all the elders had gone to their various houses, they heard that Cedu had died. They summoned a diviner to determine the cause of death, and found that Cedu had been the thief. He had been killed by the ancestors because he was the person who stole the goat

which belonged to the ancestors. Cedu's father was required to bring a cow to be sacrificed to the ancestors so that they might not do further harm to the family in the future.

These two cases clearly illustrate that the Sisla believe the ancestors have the power of affliction. When an individual goes contrary to the moral order, he stands the chance of suffering the wrath of the ancestors. In both of these cases a wrong was discovered and the ancestors were called upon to afflict the deviant. When a serious affliction befell a person who might have been the culprit, the elders consulted a diviner to determine whether this had been the case. Divination is the only method whereby the living can determine the actions of the ancestors, and by linking an affliction and a delict, divination reinforces belief in the power of the ancestors.

Affliction and Death Divination

In both of the above cases, death divination revealed that the ancestors had been the cause of death. Other afflictions, such as illness and accident, can also be caused by the ancestors, but death is the ultimate affliction.

After death, two consultations take place. The first is called *vuge na yoho* [literally, "divine to see the funeral"], and takes place before the funeral, as soon after death as possible; but since it is best to call a diviner from another village in cases of death determination, sometimes a day passes before this divination takes place. If the deceased was the lineage elder, his heir will consult; if not, the *jechikintina* will consult just outside the lineage gateway *(peke)* in the shade area *(biling)*. This is the only divining session that is held out of doors, as a public affair which anyone may attend, although, unless the death was an unusual one, usually only the family and close friends do attend. The primary function of this consultation is to determine whether the upcoming funeral will be free from conflict and quarrel—that is, whether it will be a "cool funeral" *(yoho fiala)*. At this time the family may also ask the occult cause of death (although most omit the question until the second consultation after the funeral); this is usually done only if the family suspects witchcraft or poisoning. In any

case, the main reason for this initial consultation is to determine whether any sacrifices need to be performed prior to the funeral to ensure that no conflict will erupt there. After the funeral, a second consultation takes place, which is called *vuge ne wi la siti suung suri* [literally, "divine to uncover the truth about death"]. This usually takes place shortly after the funeral. Some persons postpone making the second consultation for a week or so, but it should not be put off for long. Whereas the first consultation is public, the second is private, and is attended only by the lineage elders of the death lineage. Again, the *jechikintina* calls in an outside diviner and consults to know the occult cause of death, which nearly always involves the ancestors —that is, some delict is uncovered and used as a rationale of death. It may be determined that the ancestors became enraged at some breach of the norm and caused the death. Once the cause of death is known, it is determined what ritual remedies and sacrifices need to be performed. In addition, the lineage consults to know whether the death has "brought anything our way"—e.g. has the soul of the dead man decided to come back into a newborn child of the lineage; has the funeral been pleasing to the ancestors; has any shrine been defiled during the course of the funeral; has the soul *(dima)* of the dead man been successfully incorporated into the village of the ancestors *(lelejang)*? In essence, then, this consultation is performed to clear away any lingering ritual obligations resulting from the death, and to provide an explanation of the death, as well as a means of rectifying any wrongdoing.

Reasons for Consulting a Diviner

The harshness of life leads people to consult diviners quite frequently, although most clients go to a *dalusuntina* [owner of medicine] first, and only when "medicine" fails is a diviner contacted.

Table 1 shows that the modal number of consultations during the month prior to the interview was two, and only 14 percent of the population had not consulted a diviner during that period.

In an environment where almost no scientific medicine exists, it is not surprising that one of the main concerns of the Sisala is health. Table 2

TABLE 1 NUMBER OF TIMES A DIVINER WAS CONSULTED IN THE PREVIOUS MONTH

Consultations	0	1	2	3	4	5	6	7	8	9+	Totals
No. of clients	37	71	90	36	22	6	3	2	1	3	271
Percent	14	26	33	13	8	2	1	1	0	1	100

shows that the modal reason for consulting a diviner is illness. Of the sample interviewed, 38 percent said that illness was their motivation, while another 15 percent of the troubles that led to consultation (e.g. insomnia, childbirth, infertility, and death) were health-related. Clearly over half of the persons who consult diviners do so because of a health problem which is occurring at the time of the consultation. The Sisala say, "We do not consult by heart," meaning that a Sisala man does not consult a diviner unless there is an affliction, and the affliction is usually an immediate one.

The belief in occult causation, and especially in the power of the ancestors, is the primary motivation to consult and the *raison d'être* of divination. These beliefs exist in a milieu where scientific medicine is difficult to obtain, and where traditional medicine is often ineffective. The majority of the population takes refuge in traditional divination, which provides them with a ritual outlet when empirical ones are lacking or fail. Many Sisala admit the superiority of the "white man's medicine" and readily use it when it is available, but when it is not, or when it and/or their own medicines fail, they consult to determine the occult cause of the affliction. Once that is determined, they are provided with a ritual course of action, whereas they had no course of action before.

Fallibility of Divination

The Sisala have a saying: "Diviners tell lies and people die, and they tell lies and the people live," which indicates that there are powers greater than divination. Diviners are fallible because fate (*Wia ne longe*—literally, "what God brings down") is something that a diviner cannot always know. One informant explained that diviners may tell you certain things to do "to have life," but when a person's time to die comes, diviners are useless.

Several factors enter into the belief in the fallibility of diviners. First, it is common knowledge that some diviners are better at their art than others and can communicate with the occult world more effectively. Bascom (1941: 52) also notes this tendency in Ifa divination when he says:

> The diviners themselves admit that some of their number may not be able to answer all questions, and it is to be noted that in placing the blame on the individual's lack of knowledge of Ifa, they shift it from the system itself.

Second, some diviners are believed to tell outright lies to get gain. Third, a diviner's shrine may lose power (*dolung*) if he does not sacrifice on it periodically, or if one of the ancestors who previously owned it is angry with him. Fourth, tradition relates that diviners have been imperfect even in

TABLE 2 REASONS FOR CONSULTING A DIVINER

	No Answer	Journey	Marriage	Child-Naming	Illness	Insomnia	Childbirth	Dreams	Wife Infertility
No. of clients	25	32	33	4	102	12	18	3	7
Percent	9	12	12	1	38	4	8	1	3

	Death	To See Future	Conflict in Compound	Death of Animals	To Foretell Outcome of Harvest	General Trouble	Total
No. of clients	3	3	4	1	1	10	271
Percent	1	1	1	0	0	4	100

TABLE 3   NUMBER OF CONSULTATIONS BY DIVINERS IN THE MONTH PRIOR TO THE INTERVIEW

Consultations	0	1	2	3	4	5	6	7	8	9	10	11	12	13	14	15	16	Total
Diviner																		
Number	12	1	6	10	8	1	5	0	1	0	1	0	9	4	2	0	2	62
Percent	18	2	10	16	13	2	8	0	2	0	2	0	15	6	3	0	3	100
Sisala male																		
Number	37	71	90	36	22	6	3	2	1	3	0	0	0	0	0	0	0	271
Percent	14	26	33	13	8	2	1	1	0	1	0	0	0	0	0	0	0	100

the past, and since *fa fa* is a pattern for the present, even imperfection in *fa fa* is carried into the present world of the living.

Diviners are well aware that people do not consider their pronouncements as final, and they often add a rider to the pronouncement, such as: "If I have spoken the truth, you will hear of a funeral soon" (a very ambiguous statement, and a highly probable event to predict in western Africa). I have many times heard Sisala, by circular, *ex-post-facto* thinking, justify a diviner's pronouncement because such an event transpired. Because a diviner is not considered infallible, more than one is consulted about an important matter. The second consultation is a check on the first, and if the first diviner's edict is confirmed by a second consultation, it is considered to be valid, so that no more divining is needed. However, if the second diviner contradicts the first one, then the client seeks a third diviner to try and match up the third edict with one of the other pronouncements, in which case the inconsistent one will be ignored. In fact, most clients use an institutionalized technique called *dachevung* to test a diviner's edict. Although I was unable to find a suitable translation for the

word *dachevung*, roughly it means "he heard some things." Once a client has "heard some things" from one diviner, he does not have to go through another complete consultation to check the validity of the proclamation. He may merely go to a diviner and tell him that he wants to have *dachevung*. This method of divining is much quicker than a normal consultation, and is used only to confirm or reject another diviner's edict, because with *dachevung* the diviner does not have to open his bag and go through all of its contents; he merely uses a wand. This method is also called *a ga purung* [literally, "to steal the bag"]. The client squats before the diviner and presents silent alternatives in the form of marks on the floor or in the dirt. The diviner points the wand toward one mark or the other without knowing what they mean. For example, if the first diviner has told the client that his affliction was due to a quarrel with his elder brother, he will present that as one possibility. If the second diviner chooses that possibility (without knowing what it is), the client will be satisfied that the first diviner was telling the truth and the *dachevung* will come to an end. The following is an account of a *dachevung*:

TABLE 4   SHRINE OWNERSHIP BY DIVINERS AND BY PAGAN MALES

Number of Shrines	0	1	2	3	4	5	6	7	Total
Diviner									
Number	0	7	10	12	25	5	4	0	62
Percent	0	12	16	19	39	6	6	0	100
Pagan male									
Number	62	25	29	59	78	6	6	6	271
Percent	23	9	11	22	29	2	2	2	100

TABLE 5 Farthest City Visited by Diviners and by Non-Diviners

	No Answer	Tumu	Wa/Bolga	Tamale	Kumasi	Accra	Total
Diviner							
Number	0	11	12	6	24	9	62
Percent	0	18	19	10	39	15	100
Nondiviners							
Number	6	15	55	54	98	33	261
Percent	2	6	21	21	38	13	100

The client entered the room of the diviner and indicated that he would like to have a *dachevung* conducted. He squatted before the diviner and made two marks on the dirt floor. In his mind he had assigned the edict of the first diviner to one of the marks, while the other mark stood for the negation of that edict (he told me this afterwards). When he made the marks he said:

"What has brought me from the house this morning?"

Diviner: "This." (The wand pointed to one of the marks.)

At this point the client made several more marks in silence and said: "What is inside it?"

Diviner: "This."

Client (making new marks): "I've put it down."

Diviner: "No!" (This was an attempt on the part of the client to get the diviner to contradict himself.)

Client: "I've stolen it."

Diviner: "This is what you have stolen."

This type of consultation takes only a few minutes, whereas a normal consultation can take up to an hour.

Although the Sisala are aware that, for one reason or another, diviners do not always tell the whole truth, they view divination as the only legitimate mechanism whereby they can receive feedback from the ancestors. Since diviners are not infallible, and since they are considered the best means of receiving such feedback from the occult world, a client wishing to consult about an important matter may travel some distance to consult an alien, and therefore unbiased, diviner (see also Colson 1970). This diviner is alien only in the sense that he is a stranger, and hence is thought to be less prejudiced than a local diviner. He is normally a Sisala diviner, although Kasena diviners and fairy-callers are also consulted. In any case, he operates within a similar cultural framework as a local diviner.

Divination is a powerful mechanism for the release of anxiety in Sisala society. In a society where illness is unchecked by modern medicine, where wells can go dry or water holes dry up, where crop success is at the mercy of the elements, divination provides answers in a world of questions. Even Moslems, Christians, and the educated elite find it difficult indeed, when faced with affliction, to resist the "concreteness" of divination. More than once I have been sitting with a diviner and had an educated Christian enter the room to consult. In one case I had had a conversation the previous week with this very Christian in which he had passed divination off as a mere superstition of "uneducated pagans," yet when faced with the severe illness of his wife, he resorted to the ways of his forefathers. I have seen men who were very depressed at the onset of the consultation leave happy and content with what they had learned. On the other hand, a consultation may increase one's anxiety, as in the case of a man whose worst suspicions are confirmed. But there is almost always a ritual outlet provided by divination for the release of anxiety. Almost no consultation ends without the client having been instructed to avoid a "danger" before consulting the diviner, but only afterward does the client have means to avoid it. Therefore, even though many consider diviners to be fallible, it is the traditional method *par excellence* of dealing with dangers, problems, and affliction. Also, the internal structure of the institution of divination is ordered so that it copes with this fallibility. Indeed, the belief in fallibility may be partly

TABLE 6   SEX OF DIVINERS

	No Response	Male	Female	Total
Number of respondents	1	54	7	62
Percent	2	87	11	100

responsible for the continued existence of divination. Concerning the repeated consultation of many diviners, Horton (1967: 167) says:

> What is notable in all this is that the client never takes his repeated failures as evidence against the existence of the various spiritual beings named as responsible for his plight, or as evidence against the possibility of making contact with such beings as diviners claim to do. Nor do members of the community in which he lives ever try to keep track of the proportion of successes to failures in the remedial actions based on their beliefs, with the aim of questioning these beliefs. At most, they grumble about the dishonesty and wiles of many diviners, whilst maintaining their faith in the existence of some honest, competent practitioners.

In spite of the belief in fallibility, it must be pointed out that diviners themselves consult each other frequently. In fact, Table 3 shows that they do so more frequently than the average pagan male. Sisala diviners, like their Yoruba counterparts (Bascom 1941: 52–53), believe in divination as a means of communicating with the occult world, and regularly perform postdivinatory sacrifices in an effort to appease the ancestors and thereby avoid or eliminate an affliction.

Diviner Characteristics

Persons who become diviners tend to be traditional, conservative individuals who are oriented toward the past and who adhere to the ways of the ancestors—the true path (wenbiing titi). A comparison of shrine ownership by diviners as against pagan males highlights this conservatism (see Table 4).

Also, diviners appear to be more conservative in that they utilize other diviners more often than do nondiviners (it is also true that they do not have to pay the fee). Table 3 shows that Sisala males have a mode of two consultations per month, whereas the diviners have a mode of three consultations, and many consult as often as twelve times per month.

Diviners also appear to have traveled slightly less than non-diviners (see Table 5). Disinclination to travel is an indication of conservatism.

Most diviners are males, but some very old women, who "are like men because they can no longer bear children," do practice divination (see Table 6).

My sample included no diviners below the approximate age of twenty, and the greatest number of diviners were between the ages of thirty and forty (see Table 7).

Divining is not a full-time occupation (see Table 8). Most diviners are full-time farmers, who take clients in the early morning hours before they go to their farms, and sometimes (but rarely) at night.

Summary

While the Sisala have other kinds of divination, the traditional method predominates. The institution

TABLE 7   AGE OF DIVINERS

	20–30	31–40	41–50	51–60	61–70	71–80	81–90	Total
Number of respondents	12	21	15	8	1	3	2	62
Percent	19	34	24	13	2	5	3	100

TABLE 8 Occupation

	None*	Farmer	Trader	Hunter	Laborer	Educated	Total
Diviner							
Number	8	51	2	0	0	1	62
Percent	13	82	2	0	0	2	99
Nondiviner							
Number	7	224	2	3	26	6	268
Percent	3	83	1	1	10	2	100

*The "None" category largely contains old men, most of whom were farmers when young.

of divination provides a customary way of communicating with the ancestors who control the power of the universe. Ancestors use this power to afflict the living, and divination allows the living to determine the cause and to remedy this affliction. Most diviners are males, and the rest are old women and therefore have shown their support for the gerontocratic order. Diviners appear to be traditionalists who have inherited a position in the social order which functions to orient the Sisala toward the "true path" of the ancestors. Divination, therefore, acts as a social control mechanism.

Deviant behavior is handled in the context of affliction-divination-sacrifice. Affliction leads a client to consult a diviner, who provides an institutionalized occult cause, as well as a sacrificial remedy, to his problem. Thus, divination is a conservative mechanism which reinforces the established social order, and it is not surprising to find that ordinarily Sisala diviners are older males who own a higher than average number of shrines, who have had little travel experience, and who tend to engage in farming rather than non-farming economic pursuits.

Rational Mastery by Man of His Surroundings

Bronislaw Malinowski

Rare is the anthropology course that sometime during the semester is not directed to the thought and writings of Bronislaw Malinowski (1884–1942). This world-famous Polish anthropologist was trained in mathematics, but shifted his interests to anthropology after reading Sir James Frazer's The Golden Bough. *Malinowski's field work in the Trobriand Islands of Melanesia influenced the direction of anthropology as an academic discipline. He is recognized as the founder of functionalism, an anthropological approach to the study of culture that believes each institution in a society fulfills a definite function in the maintenance of human needs. His major works include* Crime and Customs in Savage Society *(1926),* The Sexual Life of Savages *(1929), and* Coral Gardens and Their Magic *(1935). Malinowski was professor of anthropology at the University of London from 1927 until his death in 1942. In this classic article Malinowski asks two important questions: do pre-literate people have any rational mastery of their surroundings; and can primitive knowledge be regarded as a beginning or rudimentary type of science, or is it merely a crude hodgepodge devoid of logic and accuracy?*

Reprinted from *Magic, Science and Religion* (New York: Doubleday, 1955), pp. 25–35, by permission of the Society for Promoting Christian Knowledge.

THE PROBLEM OF PRIMITIVE KNOWLEDGE HAS been singularly neglected by anthropology. Studies on savage psychology were exclusively confined to early religion, magic, and mythology. Only recently the work of several English, German, and French writers, notably the daring and brilliant speculations of Professor Lévy-Bruhl, gave an impetus to the student's interest in what the savage does in his more sober moods. The results were startling indeed: Professor Lévy-Bruhl tells us, to put it in a nutshell, that primitive man has no sober moods at all, that he is hopelessly and completely immersed in a mystical frame of mind. Incapable of dispassionate and consistent observation, devoid of the power of abstraction, hampered by "a decided aversion towards reasoning," he is unable to draw any benefit from experience, to construct or comprehend even the most elementary laws of nature. "For minds thus orientated there is no fact purely physical." Nor can there exist for them any clear idea of substance and attribute, cause and effect, identity and contradiction. Their outlook is that of confused superstition, "pre-logical," made of mystic "participations" and "exclusions." I have here summarized a body of opinion, of which the brilliant French sociologist is the most decided and competent spokesman, but which numbers besides, many anthropologists and philosophers of renown.

But there are dissenting voices. When a scholar and anthropologist of the measure of Professor J. L. Myres entitles an article in *Notes and Queries* "Natural Science," and when we read there that the savage's "knowledge based on observation is distinct and accurate," we must surely pause before accepting primitive man's irrationality as a dogma. Another highly competent writer, Dr. A. A. Goldenweiser, speaking about primitive "discoveries, inventions and improvements"—which could hardly be attributed to any pre-empirical or pre-logical mind—affirms that "it would be unwise to ascribe to the primitive mechanic merely a passive part in the origination of inventions. Many a happy thought must have crossed his mind, nor was he wholly unfamiliar with the thrill that comes from an idea effective in action." Here we see the savage endowed with an attitude of mind wholly akin to that of a modern man of science!

To bridge over the wide gap between the two extreme opinions current on the subject of primitive man's reason, it will be best to resolve the problem into two questions.

First, has the savage any rational outlook, any rational mastery of his surroundings, or is he, as M. Lévy-Bruhl and his school maintain, entirely "mystical"? The answer will be that every primitive community is in possession of a considerable store of knowledge, based on experience and fashioned by reason.

The second question then opens: Can this primitive knowledge be regarded as a rudimentary form of science or is it, on the contrary, radically different, a crude empiry, a body of practical and technical abilities, rules of thumb and rules of art having no theoretical value? This second question, epistemological rather than belonging to the study of man, will be barely touched upon at the end of this section and a tentative answer only will be given.

In dealing with the first question, we shall have to examine the "profane" side of life, the arts, crafts and economic pursuits, and we shall attempt to disentangle in it a type of behavior, clearly marked off from magic and religion, based on empirical knowledge and on the confidence in logic. We shall try to find whether the lines of such behavior are defined by traditional rules, known, perhaps even discussed sometimes, and tested. We shall have to inquire whether the sociological setting of the rational and empirical behavior differs from that of ritual and cult. Above all we shall ask, do the natives distinguish the two domains and keep them apart, or is the field of knowledge constantly swamped by superstition, ritualism, magic or religion?

Since in the matter under discussion there is an appalling lack of relevant and reliable observations, I shall have largely to draw upon my own material, most unpublished, collected during a few years' field work among the Melanesian and Papuo-Melanesian tribes of Eastern New Guinea and the surrounding archipelagoes. As the Melanesians are reputed, however, to be specially magic-ridden, they will furnish an acid test of the existence of empirical and rational knowledge among savages living in the age of polished stone.

These natives, and I am speaking mainly of the Melanesians who inhabit the coral atolls to the N.E. of the main island, the Trobriand Archipelago and the adjoining groups, are expert fishermen, industrious manufacturers and traders, but they rely mainly on gardening for their subsistence. With the most rudimentary implements, a pointed digging-stick and a small axe, they are able to raise crops sufficient to maintain a dense population and even yielding a surplus, which in olden days was allowed to rot unconsumed, and which at present is exported to feed plantation hands. The success in their agriculture depends—besides the excellent natural conditions with which they are favored—upon their extensive knowledge of the classes of the soil, of the various cultivated plants, of the mutual adaptation of these two factors, and, last not least, upon their knowledge of the importance of accurate and hard work. They have to select the soil and the seedlings, they have appropriately to fix the times for clearing and burning the scrub, for planting and weeding, for training the vines of the yam plants. In all this they are guided by a clear knowledge of weather and seasons, plants and pests, soil and tubers, and by a conviction that this knowledge is true and reliable, that it can be counted upon and must be scrupulously obeyed.

Yet mixed with all their activities there is to be found magic, a series of rites performed every year over the gardens in rigorous sequence and order. Since the leadership in garden work is in the hands of the magician, and since ritual and practical work are intimately associated, a superficial observer might be led to assume that the mystic and the rational behavior are mixed up, that their effects are not distinguished by the natives and not distinguishable in scientific analysis. Is this so really?

Magic is undoubtedly regarded by the natives as absolutely indispensable to the welfare of the gardens. What would happen without it no one can exactly tell, for no native garden has ever been made without its ritual, in spite of some thirty years of European rule and missionary influence and well over a century's contact with white traders. But certainly various kinds of disaster, blight, unseasonable droughts, rains, bush-pigs and locusts would destroy the unhallowed garden made without magic.

Does this mean, however, that the natives attribute all the good results to magic? Certainly not. If you were to suggest to a native that he should make his garden mainly by magic and scamp his work, he would simply smile on your simplicity. He knows as well as you do that there are natural conditions and causes, and by his observations he knows also that he is able to control these natural forces by mental and physical effort. His knowledge is limited, no doubt, but as far as it goes it is sound and proof against mysticism. If the fences are broken down, if the seed is destroyed or has been dried or washed away, he will have recourse not to magic, but to work, guided by knowledge and reason. His experience has taught him also, on the other hand, that in spite of all his forethought and beyond all his efforts there are agencies and forces which one year bestow unwonted and unearned benefits of fertility, making everything run smooth and well, rain and sun appear at the right moment, noxious insects remain in abeyance, the harvest yields a superabundant crop; and another year again the same agencies bring ill luck and bad chance, pursue him from beginning till end and thwart all his most strenuous efforts and his best-founded knowledge. To control these influences and these only he employs magic.

Thus there is a clear-cut division: there is first the well-known set of conditions, the natural course of growth, as well as the ordinary pests and dangers to be warded off by fencing and weeding. On the other hand there is the domain of the unaccountable and adverse influences, as well as the great unearned increment of fortunate coincidence. The first conditions are coped with by knowledge and work, the second by magic.

This line of division can also be traced in the social setting of work and ritual respectively. Though the garden magician is, as a rule, also the leader in practical activities, these two functions are kept strictly apart. Every magical ceremony has its distinctive name, its appropriate time and its place in the scheme of work, and it stands out of the ordinary course of activities completely. Some

of them are ceremonial and have to be attended by the whole community, all are public in that it is known when they are going to happen and anyone can attend them. They are performed on selected plots within the gardens and on a special corner of this plot. Work is always tabooed on such occasions, sometimes only while the ceremony lasts, sometimes for a day or two. In his lay character the leader and magician directs the work, fixes the dates for starting, harangues and exhorts slack or careless gardeners. But the two roles never overlap or interfere: they are always clear, and any native will inform you without hesitation whether the man acts as magician or as leader in garden work.

What has been said about gardens can be paralleled from any one of the many other activities in which work and magic run side by side without ever mixing. Thus in canoe building empirical knowledge of material, of technology, and of certain principles of stability and hydrodynamics, function in company and close association with magic, each yet uncontaminated by the other.

For example, they understand perfectly well that the wider the span of the outrigger the greater the stability yet the smaller the resistance against strain. They can clearly explain why they have to give this span a certain traditional width, measured in fractions of the length of the dugout. They can also explain, in rudimentary but clearly mechanical terms, how they have to behave in a sudden gale, why the outrigger must be always on the weather side, why the one type of canoe can and the other cannot beat. They have, in fact, a whole system of principles of sailing, embodied in a complex and rich terminology, traditionally handed on and obeyed as rationally and consistently as is modern science by modern sailors. How could they sail otherwise under eminently dangerous conditions in their frail primitive craft?

But even with all their systematic knowledge, methodically applied, they are still at the mercy of powerful and incalculable tides, sudden gales during the monsoon season and unknown reefs. And here comes in their magic, performed over the canoe during its construction, carried out at the beginning and in the course of expeditions and resorted to in moments of real danger. If the modern seaman, entrenched in science and reason, provided with all sorts of safety appliances, sailing on steel-built steamers, if even he has a singular tendency to superstition—which does not rob him of his knowledge or reason, nor make him altogether prelogical—can we wonder that his savage colleague, under much more precarious conditions, holds fast to the safety and comfort of magic?

An interesting and crucial test is provided by fishing in the Trobriand Islands and its magic. While in the villages on the inner lagoon fishing is done in an easy and absolutely reliable manner by the method of poisoning, yielding abundant results without danger and uncertainty, there are on the shores of the open sea dangerous modes of fishing and also certain types in which the yield greatly varies according to whether shoals of fish appear beforehand or not. It is most significant that in the lagoon fishing, where man can rely completely upon his knowledge and skill, magic does not exist, while in the open-sea fishing, full of danger and uncertainty, there is extensive magical ritual to secure safety and good results.

Again, in warfare the natives know that strength, courage, and agility play a decisive part. Yet here also they practice magic to master the elements of chance and luck.

Nowhere is the duality of natural and supernatural causes divided by a line so thin and intricate, yet, if carefully followed up, so well marked, decisive, and instructive, as in the two most fateful forces of human destiny: health and death. Health to the Melanesians is a natural state of affairs and, unless tampered with, the human body will remain in perfect order. But the natives know perfectly well that there are natural means which can affect health and even destroy the body. Poisons, wounds, burns, falls, are known to cause disablement or death in a natural way. And this is not a matter of private opinion of this or that individual, but it is laid down in traditional lore and even in belief, for there are considered to be different ways to the nether world for those who died by sorcery and those who met "natural" death. Again, it is recognized that cold, heat, overstrain, too much sun, overeating, can all cause minor ailments, which are treated by natural remedies such as massage, steaming, warming at a fire and certain potions. Old age is known to lead to bodily decay and the explanation is given by the natives that very old people grow weak, their oesophagus closes up, and therefore they must die.

But besides these natural causes there is the enormous domain of sorcery and by far the most cases of illness and death are ascribed to this. The line of distinction between sorcery and the other causes is clear in theory and in most cases of practice, but it must be realized that it is subject to what could be called the personal perspective. That is, the more closely a case has to do with the person who considers it, the less will it be "natural," the more "magical." Thus a very old man, whose pending death will be considered natural by the other members of the community, will be afraid only of sorcery and never think of his natural fate. A fairly sick person will diagnose sorcery in his own case, while all the others might speak of too much betel nut or overeating or some other indulgence.

But who of us really believes that his own bodily infirmities and the approaching death is a purely natural occurrence, just an insignificant event in the infinite chain of causes? To the most rational civilized men health, disease, the threat of death, float in a hazy emotional mist, which seems to become denser and more impenetrable as the fateful forms approach. It is indeed astonishing that "savages" can achieve such a sober, dispassionate outlook in these matters as they actually do.

Thus in his relation to nature and destiny, whether he tries to exploit the first or to dodge the second, primitive man recognizes both the natural and the supernatural forces and agencies, and he tries to use them both for his benefit. Whenever he has been taught by experience that effort guided by knowledge is of some avail, he never spares the one or ignores the other. He knows that a plant cannot grow by magic alone, or a canoe sail or float without being properly constructed and managed, or a fight be won without skill and daring. He never relies on magic alone, while, on the contrary, he sometimes dispenses with it completely, as in firemaking and in a number of crafts and pursuits. But he clings to it, whenever he has to recognize the impotence of his knowledge and of his rational technique.

I have given my reasons why in this argument I had to rely principally on the material collected in the classical land of magic, Melanesia. But the facts discussed are so fundamental, the conclusions drawn of such a general nature, that it will be easy to check them on any modern detailed ethnographic record. Comparing agricultural work and magic, the building of canoes, the art of healing by magic and by natural remedies, the ideas about the causes of death in other regions, the universal validity of what has been established here could easily be proved. Only, since no observations have methodically been made with reference to the problem of primitive knowledge, the data from other writers could be gleaned only piecemeal and their testimony though clear would be indirect.

I have chosen to face the question of primitive man's rational knowledge directly: watching him at his principal occupations, seeing him pass from work to magic and back again, entering into his mind, listening to his opinions. The whole problem might have been approached through the avenue of language, but this would have led us too far into questions of logic, semasiology, and theory of primitive languages. Words which serve to express general ideas such as *existence, substance,* and *attribute, cause* and *effect,* the *fundamental* and the *secondary*; words and expressions used in complicated pursuits like sailing, construction, measuring and checking; numerals and quantitative descriptions, correct and detailed classifications of natural phenomena, plants and animals—all this would lead us exactly to the same conclusion: that primitive man can observe and think, and that he possesses, embodied in his language, systems of methodical though rudimentary knowledge.

Similar conclusions could be drawn from an examination of those mental schemes and physical contrivances which could be described as diagrams or formulas. Methods of indicating the main points of the compass, arrangements of stars into constellations, co-ordination of these with the seasons, naming of moons in the year, of quarters in the moon—all these accomplishments are known to the simplest savages. Also they are all able to draw diagrammatic maps in the sand or dust, indicate arrangements by placing small stones, shells, or sticks on the ground, plan expeditions or raids on such rudimentary charts. By co-ordinating space and time they are able to arrange big tribal gatherings and to combine vast tribal movements over extensive areas. The use of leaves, notched sticks, and similar aids to memory is well known and seems to be almost universal. All such "diagrams" are means of reducing a complex and unwieldy bit of reality to a simple and handy form. They give

man a relatively easy mental control over it. As such are they not—in a very rudimentary form no doubt—fundamentally akin to developed scientific formulas and "models," which are also simple and handy paraphrases of a complex or abstract reality, giving the civilized physicist mental control over it?

This brings us to the second question: Can we regard primitive knowledge, which, as we found, is both empirical and rational, as a rudimentary stage of science, or is it not at all related to it? If by science be understood a body of rules and conceptions, based on experience and derived from it by logical inference, embodied in material achievements and in a fixed form of tradition and carried on by some sort of social organization—then there is no doubt that even the lowest savage communities have the beginnings of science, however rudimentary.

Most epistemologists would not, however, be satisfied with such a "minimum definition" of science, for it might apply to the rules of an art or craft as well. They would maintain that the rules of science must be laid down explicitly, open to control by experiment and critique by reason. They must not only be rules of practical behavior, but theoretical laws of knowledge. Even accepting this stricture, however, there is hardly any doubt that many of the principles of savage knowledge are scientific in this sense. The native shipwright knows not only practically of buoyancy, leverage, equilibrium, he has to obey these laws not only on water, but while making the canoe he must have the principles in his mind. He instructs his helpers in them. He gives them the traditional rules, and in a crude and simple manner, using his hands, pieces of wood, and a limited technical vocabulary, he explains some general laws of hydrodynamics and equilibrium. Science is not detached from the craft, that is certainly true, it is only a means to an end, it is crude, rudimentary, and inchoate, but with all that it is the matrix from which the higher developments must have sprung.

If we applied another criterion yet, that of the really scientific attitude, the disinterested search for knowledge and for the understanding of causes and reasons, the answer would certainly not be in a direct negative. There is, of course, no widespread thirst for knowledge in a savage community, new things such as European topics bore them frankly and their whole interest is largely encompassed by the traditional world of their culture. But within this there is both the antiquarian mind passionately interested in myths, stories, details of customs, pedigrees, and ancient happenings, and there is also to be found the naturalist, patient and painstaking in his observations, capable of generalization and of connecting long chains of events in the life of animals, and in the marine world or in the jungle. It is enough to realize how much European naturalists have often learned from their savage colleagues to appreciate this interest found in the native for nature. There is finally among the primitives, as every field worker well knows, the sociologist, the ideal informant, capable with marvelous accuracy and insight to give the *raison d'être*, the function and the organization of many a simpler institution in his tribe.

Science, of course, does not exist in any uncivilized community as a driving power, criticizing, renewing, constructing. Science is never consciously made. But on this criterion, neither is there law, nor religion, nor government among savages.

Baseball Magic

George Gmelch

In the preceding article, Malinowski observed that in the Trobriand Islands magic did not occur when the natives fished in the safe lagoons but when they ventured out into the open seas: then the danger and uncertainty caused them to perform extensive magical rituals. In the following article, anthropologist George Gmelch demonstrates that America's "favorite pasttime" is an excellent place to put the test to Malinowski's hypothesis about magic. Anyone who has watched baseball, either at a ballpark or in front of a television set, is aware of some of the more obvious rituals performed by the players; but Gmelch, drawing upon his own experiences as a one-time professional baseball player, provides an insider's view of the rituals, taboos, and fetishes involved in the sport.

We find magic wherever the elements of chance and accident, and the emotional play between hope and fear have a wide and extensive range. We do not find magic wherever the pursuit is certain, reliable, and well under the control of rational methods.
—Bronislaw Malinowski

PROFESSIONAL BASEBALL IS A NEARLY PERFECT arena in which to test Malinowski's hypothesis about magic. The great anthropologist was not, of course, talking about sleight of hand but of rituals, taboos and fetishes that men resort to when they want to ensure that things go their own way. Baseball is rife with this sort of magic, but, as we shall see, the players use it in some aspects of the game far more than in others.

Everyone knows that there are three essentials of baseball—hitting, pitching and fielding. The point is, however, that the first two, hitting and pitching, involve a high degree of chance. The pitcher is the player least able to control the outcome of his own efforts. His best pitch may be hit for a bloop single while his worst pitch may be hit directly to one of his fielders for an out. He may limit the opposition to a single hit and lose, or he may give up a dozen hits and win. It is not uncommon for pitchers to perform well and lose, and vice versa; one has only to look at the frequency with which pitchers end a season with poor won-lost percentages but low earned run averages (number of runs given up per game). The opposite is equally true: some pitchers play poorly, giving up many runs, yet win many games. In brief, the pitcher, regardless of how well he performs, is dependent upon the proficiency of his teammates, the inefficiency of the opposition and the supernatural (luck).

But luck, as we all know, comes in two forms, and many fans assume that the pitcher's tough losses (close games in which he gave up very few runs) are eventually balanced out by his "lucky" wins. This is untrue, as a comparison of pitchers' lifetime earned run averages to their overall won-lost records shows. If the player could apply a law of averages to individual performance, there would be much less concern about chance and uncertainty in baseball. Unfortunately, he cannot and does not.

Hitting, too, is a chancy affair. Obviously, skill is required in hitting the ball hard and on a line. Once the ball is hit, however, chance plays a large role in determining where it will go, into a waiting glove or whistling past a falling stab.

With respect to fielding, the player has almost complete control over the outcome. The average fielding percentage or success rate of .975, compared to a .245 success rate for hitters (the average batting average), reflects the degree of certainty in fielding. Next to the pitcher or hitter, the fielder has little to worry about when he knows that better than 9.7 times in ten he will execute his task flawlessly.

If Malinowski's hypothesis is correct, we should find magic associated with hitting and pitching, but none with fielding. Let us take the evidence by category—ritual, taboo and fetish.

Ritual

After each pitch, ex-major leaguer Lou Skeins used to reach into his back pocket to touch a crucifix, straighten his cap and clutch his genitals. Detroit Tiger infielder Tim Maring wore the same clothes and put them on exactly in the same order each day during a batting streak. Baseball rituals are almost infinitely various. After all, the ballplayer can ritualize any activity he considers necessary for a successful performance, from the type of cereal he eats in the morning to the streets he drives home on.

Usually, rituals grow out of exceptionally good performances. When the player does well he cannot really attribute his success to skill alone. He plays with the same amount of skill one night when he gets four hits as the next night when he goes hitless. Through magic, such as ritual, the player seeks greater control over his performance, actually control over the elements of chance. The player, knowing that his ability is fairly constant, attributes the inconsistencies in his performance to some form of behavior or a particular food that he

ate. When a player gets four hits in a game, especially "cheap" hits, he often believes that there must have been something he did, in addition to his ability, that shifted luck to his side. If he can attribute his good fortune to the glass of iced tea he drank before the game or the new shirt he wore to the ballpark, then by repeating the same behavior the following day he can hope to achieve similar results. (One expression of this belief is the myth that eating certain foods will give the ball "eyes," that is, a ball that seeks the gaps between fielders.) In hopes of maintaining a batting streak, I once ate fried chicken every day at 4:00 P.M., kept my eyes closed during the national anthem and changed sweat shirts at the end of the fourth inning each night for seven consecutive nights until the streak ended.

Fred Caviglia, Kansas City minor league pitcher, explained why he eats certain food before each game: "Everything you do is important to winning. I never forget what I eat the day of a game or what I wear. If I pitch well and win I'll do it all exactly the same the next day I pitch. You'd be crazy not to. You just can't ever tell what's going to make the difference between winning and losing."

Rituals associated with hitting vary considerably in complexity from one player to the next, but they have several components in common. One of the most popular is tagging a particular base when leaving and returning to the dugout each inning. Tagging second base on the way to the outfield is habitual with some players. One informant reported that during a successful month of the season he stepped on third base on his way to the dugout after third, sixth and ninth innings of each game. Asked if he ever purposely failed to step on the bag he replied, "Never! I wouldn't dare, it would destroy my confidence to hit." It is not uncommon for a hitter who is playing poorly to try different combinations of tagging and not tagging particular bases in an attempt to find a successful combination. Other components of a hitter's ritual may include tapping the plate with his bat a precise number of times or taking a precise number of warm-up swings with the leaded bat.

One informant described a variation of this in which he gambled for a certain hit by tapping the plate a fixed number of times. He touched the plate once with his bat for each base desired: one tap for a single, two for a double and so on. He even built in odds that prevented him from asking for a home run each time. The odds of hitting a single with one tap were one in three, while the chances of hitting a home run with four taps were one in 12.

Clothing is often considered crucial to both hitters and pitchers. They may have several athletic supporters and a number of sweat shirts with ritual significance. Nearly all players wear the same uniform and undergarments each day when playing well, and some even wear the same street clothes. In 1954, the New York Giants, during a 16-game winning streak, wore the same clothes in each game and refused to let them be cleaned for fear that their good fortune might be washed away with the dirt. The route taken to and from the stadium can also have significance; some players drive the same streets to the ballpark during a hitting streak and try different routes during slumps.

Because pitchers only play once every four days, the rituals they practice are often more complex than the hitters', and most of it, such as tugging the cap between pitches, touching the rosin bag after each bad pitch or smoothing the dirt on the mound before each new batter, takes place on the field. Many baseball fans have observed this behavior never realizing that it may be as important to the pitcher as throwing the ball.

Dennis Grossini, former Detroit farmhand, practiced the following ritual on each pitching day for the first three months of a winning season. First, he rose from bed at exactly 10:00 A.M. and not a minute earlier or later. At 1:00 P.M. he went to the nearest restaurant for two glasses of iced tea and a tuna fish sandwich. Although the afternoon was free, he observed a number of taboos such as no movies, no reading and no candy. In the clubhouse he changed into the sweat shirt and jock he wore during his last winning game, and one hour before the game he chewed a wad of Beechnut chewing tobacco. During the game he touched his letters (the team name on his uniform) after each pitch and straightened his cap after each ball. Before the start of each inning he replaced the pitcher's rosin bag next to the spot where it was the inning before. And after every inning in which he gave up a run he went to the clubhouse to wash his hands. I asked him which part of the ritual was most important. He responded: "You can't really tell what's most important so it all becomes important. I'd be afraid to change anything. As long as I'm winning I do everything the same. Even when I can't wash my hands [this would occur when he must bat] it scares me going back to the mound. . . . I don't feel quite right."

One ritual, unlike those already mentioned, is practiced to improve the power of the baseball bat. It involves sanding the bat until all the varnish is removed, a process requiring several hours of labor, then rubbing rosin into the grain of the bat before finally heating it over a flame. This ritual treatment supposedly increases the distance the ball travels after being struck. Although some North Americans prepare their bats in this fashion it is more popular among Latin Americans. One informant admitted that he was not certain of the effectiveness of the treatment. But, he added, "There may not be a God, but I go to church just the same."

Despite the wide assortment of rituals associated with pitching and hitting, I never observed any ritual related to fielding. In all my 20 interviews only one player, a shortstop with acute fielding problems, reported any ritual even remotely connected to fielding.

Taboo

Mentioning that a no-hitter is in progress and crossing baseball bats are the two most widely observed taboos. It is believed that if the pitcher hears the words "no-hitter" his spell will be broken and the no-hitter lost. As for the crossing of bats, that is sure to bring bad luck; batters are therefore extremely careful not to drop their bats on top of another. Some players elaborate this taboo even further. On one occasion a teammate became quite upset when another player tossed a bat from the batting cage and it came to rest on top of his. Later he explained that the top bat would steal hits from the lower one. For him, then, bats contain a finite number of hits, a kind of baseball "image of limited good." Honus Wagner, a member of baseball's Hall of Fame, believed that each bat was good for only 100 hits and no more. Regardless of the quality of the bat he would discard it after its 100th hit.

Besides observing the traditional taboos just mentioned, players also observe certain personal prohibitions. Personal taboos grow out of exceptionally poor performances, which a player often attributes to some particular behavior or food. During my first season of professional baseball I once ate pancakes before a game in which I struck out four times. Several weeks later I had a repeat performance, again after eating pancakes. The result was a pancake taboo in which from that day on I never ate pancakes during the season. Another personal taboo, born out of similar circumstances, was against holding a baseball during the national anthem.

Taboos are also of many kinds. One athlete was careful never to step on the chalk foul lines or the chalk lines of the batter's box. Another would never put on his cap until the game started and would not wear it at all on the days he did not pitch. Another had a movie taboo in which he refused to watch a movie the day of a game. Often certain uniform numbers become taboo. If a player has a poor spring training or a bad year, he may refuse to wear the same uniform number again. I would not wear double numbers, especially 44 or 22. On several occasions, teammates who were playing poorly requested a change of uniform during the middle of the season. Some players consider it so important that they will wear the wrong size uniform just to avoid a certain number or to obtain a good number.

Again, with respect to fielding, I never saw or heard of any taboos being observed, though of course there were some taboos, like the uniform numbers, that were concerned with overall performance and so included fielding.

Fetishes

These are standard equipment for many baseball players. They include a wide assortment of objects: horsehide covers of old baseballs, coins, bobby pins, protective cups, crucifixes and old bats. Ordinary objects are given this power in a fashion similar to the formation of taboos and rituals. The player during an exceptionally hot batting or pitching streak, especially one in which he has "gotten all the breaks," credits some unusual object, often a new possession, for his good fortune. For example, a player in a slump might find a coin or an odd stone just before he begins a hitting streak. Attributing the improvement in his performance to

the new object, it becomes a fetish, embodied with supernatural power. While playing for Spokane, Dodger pitcher Alan Foster forgot his baseball shoes on a road trip and borrowed a pair from a teammate to pitch. The night he pitched a no-hitter and later, needless to say, bought the shoes from his teammate. They became his most prized possession.

Fetishes are taken so seriously by some players that their teammates will not touch them out of fear of offending the owner. I once saw a fight caused by the desecration of a fetish. Before the game, one player stole the fetish, a horsehide baseball cover, out of a teammate's back pocket. The prankster did not return the fetish until after the game, in which the owner of the fetish went hitless, breaking a batting streak. The owner, blaming his inability to hit on the loss of the fetish, lashed out at the thief when the latter tried to return it.

Rube Waddel, an old-time Philadelphia Athletic pitching great, had a hairpin fetish. However, the hairpin he possessed was only powerful as long as he won. Once he lost a game he would look for another hairpin, which had to be found on the street, and he would not pitch until he found another.

The use of fetishes follows the same pattern as ritual and taboo in that they are connected only with hitting or pitching. In nearly all cases the player expressed a specific purpose for carrying a fetish, but never did a player perceive his fetish as having any effect on his fielding.

I have said enough, I think, to show that many of the beliefs and practices of professional baseball players are magical. Any empirical connection between the ritual, taboo and fetishes and the desired event is quite absent. Indeed, in several instances the relationship between the cause and effect, such as eating tuna fish sandwiches to win a ball game, is even more remote than is characteristic of primitive magic. Note, however, that unlike many forms of primitive magic, baseball magic is usually performed to achieve one's own end and not to block someone else's. Hitters do not tap their bats on the plate to hex the pitcher, but to improve their own performance.

Finally, it should be plain that nearly all the magical practices that I participated in, observed or elicited, support Malinowski's hypothesis that magic appears in situations of chance and uncertainty. The large amount of uncertainty in pitching and hitting best explains the elaborate magical practices used for these activities. Conversely, the high success rate in fielding, .975, involving much less uncertainty, offers the best explanation for the absence of magic in this realm.

7

Ethnomedicine: Religion and Healing

If a single pervasive thought were to be singled out in this chapter, it would be the importance of culture in determining the etiology and treatment of disease and mental disorders. Just as humans have always suffered from disease, so too have we always responded to it, seeking ways to reduce its debilitating nature or, we hope, to banish it completely. All human societies have belief systems and practices that people turn to in order to identify disease and effect a cure. The integration of the study of these systems of beliefs and practices into the study of non-Western societies has created medical anthropology, the most recent addition to the discipline of anthropology.

Explanations and cures of illnesses may be either natural or supernatural (a naturalistic response would not involve supernatural aid). As P. Stanley Yoder has clearly pointed out, one of the medical anthropologist's most important tasks is to distinguish between different types of causation and to understand the relationship between them, especially because "different types of causal explanations may be

Bacham dance mask from Cameroun.

involved at different points during the process of diagnosis and treatment, or may characteristically demand differing treatments" (1982: 15). Moreover, because the range and variability of medical beliefs and practices among the non-literate peoples of the world is immense, there will be no easy explanation or simple generalization regarding causation and treatment of diseases. But always it will be possible to see the close relationship between medicine and religion, a cultural bonding that occurs in non-literate, non-industrialized cultures as well as in modern, technological cultures.

The importance of our understanding of ethnomedical systems is made clear by the fact that a great percentage of the non-Western world's population reside in areas that are not exposed to Western medical treatment. Primary among the concerns of such international groups as the World Health Organization is the role that improved health care can play in the socioeconomic development of Third World countries. The lack of implementation of modern medical care in these areas of the world is caused by a lack both of available funds and of information. Partly in response to the dearth of funding, some health planners have proposed that the most effective way to expand modern primary care would be for Western-trained practitioners to collaborate with traditional practitioners (Bichmann 1979: 175); however, lack of information is the greatest barrier to assessing the feasibility of such proposals in relation to national health goals and planning (Good 1977: 705). Because little substantive information concerning indigenous health care systems is available for non-Western countries, the identification and use of agents of change such as local curers to improve the quality of life in rural areas is extremely difficult.

It is noteworthy to point out also that intercultural contact seems to have caused an increase in both physical and psychological Western-based diseases among non-Western populations; the frustrations of not being able to cure these modern illnesses are liable to increase the use of traditional methods of healing. Other problems of contact also exist. Western-trained medical practitioners find little in traditional systems of health care they consider effective in either the physical or mental realms. On the other hand, modern

medical treatment is also often rejected by those in the culture. For example, in rural contemporary Kenya modern medical technology is not interfering with the pervasive "ancestor spirit-sorcery theory" of disease causation that has traditionally been used to account for all major misfortunes (Kramer and Thomas 1982: 169): as late as 1969 there was still no indication among the rural Kamba of Kenya that modern medicine had made prominent inroads at the level of prevention, either in effecting behavioral change or in modifying etiological beliefs, despite their long exposure to Western techniques.

Determining why the ill choose to accept or reject a system of treatment not only would define who the people in the culture perceive as the proper healer but also would delineate their etiology of disease and their perception of appropriate treatment. What applied anthropologists are attempting to determine are the advantages and disadvantages of each of the health care systems —traditional and modern—in the eyes of the patients, as well as the nature of the knowledge healers and their clients draw upon in the process of selecting treatment. Unfortunately, previous research in traditional medical systems has essentially ignored the studied people's own explanations of these criteria, criteria that ordinarily include both natural and supernatural explanations.

Knowledge of the naturalistic treatments and ethnopharmacological systems of non-Western societies is also important, for much of the pharmacopoeia administered by traditional healers does work. (Societies everywhere, including preliterate peoples, possess naturalistic explanations and treatments. Cures derived from hundreds of wild plants were used by the North American Indians, for example, and techniques for treating headaches and stomachaches, setting broken bones, bloodletting, lancing, cauterization, and other naturalistic skills are well known to the non-literate world.) However, since the effectiveness of the traditional healer is dependent upon more than the use of proper chemical treatment, diagnosis is made not only at the empirical level but also at the psychological and social levels as well. In speaking of Africa, for example, Wolfgang Bichmann notes that illness does not mean so much an individual event but a disturbance of social relations (1979: 177), and M. F. Lofchie points out that "African medical research has much to contribute to Western medicine: its wholism, emphasis on treatment of the entire family as well as the 'ill' person, and its encyclopedic lore of information about the curative properties of items available in nature—all of these principles are now working their way into Western medical vocabulary" (1982: vii).

For years it was widely believed that only "civilized" peoples were subject to mental illness, while the pre-literates of the world led a blissful life free of neuroses and psychoses. It did not take anthropology long to prove that Rousseau's Noble Savage was just as susceptible to the major disorders of the mind as was the individual coping with life in the so-called civilized societies of the world. Anthropologists have sought answers to such important questions as whether mental illness rates differ in pre-literate and modern societies; whether styles and types of illnesses vary; and whether it is more difficult to adjust to life in modern cultures than in pre-literate cultures. Anthropologists and others have shown, moreover, that traditional healers are particularly effective in the treatment of mental illness, and that their approaches to curing are beneficial to physical diseases as well. Not only are traditional healers' services readily available to the ill, for example, but their system of care is also non-disruptive to those in the culture, and the patient has the support of family members who are nearby or in actual attendance during the treatment. Beyond these advantages, and in contrast with the Western world, Third World countries frequently are much more accepting of those having mental illnesses. Sufferers of these disorders are often stigmatized in the West, and often attempt to hide their medical history.

In a seven-year multi-cultural pilot study of severe mental illness by the World Health Organization reported in the magazine *Science '80* it was shown that relatively fast and complete recoveries from major psychoses are achieved in developing countries like Nigeria and India. In the United States and other Western countries, however, almost one-half of those who suffer psychotic breakdowns never recover. For example, whereas 58 percent of the Nigerians and 51 percent of the Indians studied had a single

psychotic episode and were judged cured after treatment, the cure rate in the industrialized countries ranged from only 6 percent in Denmark to a high of 27 percent in China (1980: 7). Certainly non-Western healing techniques are effective in the treatment of the mentally ill; however, the treatment of physiological diseases cannot match that of the West. The fact that many non-Western pharmaceuticals may be effective in one society and not in another demonstrates the important relationship of beliefs and cures, in particular the interaction of the healer and the supernatural.

Throughout the world it is possible to place supernaturally caused illnesses into five categories: (1) sorcery, (2) breach of taboo, (3) intrusion of a disease object, (4) intrusion of a disease-causing spirit, and (5) loss of soul (Clements, 1932: 252). It is important to note that these categories may not be recognized by certain societies. Indeed, it is a difficult task to determine the frequency and incidence of illnesses, especially mental illnesses, in non-Western, non-industrialized countries. Native peoples may avoid seeking medical help from a modern health facility, for example; or, if they do seek treatment, there may be a question of accurate recordkeeping.

Anthropologists have correctly noted that the types of cures sought are based not only on the cause but also on the severity of the illness in terms of level of pain and difficulty of curing. Treatment based on cause and severity varies greatly; some non-Western groups maintain that most diseases are of natural origin, whereas others blame the supernatural realm for the misfortunes.

It is apparent that anthropologists must understand the integration of ethnomedical systems with the other areas of culture if they are successfully to conduct comparative studies. Ethnomedical systems are deeply ingrained in the structure of societies, functioning in ways that create a positive atmosphere for health care. No longer can we view pre-literate medical methods as inferior; indeed, Western society owes much to traditional medicine, not the least of which is the support given to the patient by the family and the community.

The selection of readings in this chapter for the most part deal with supernaturally caused diseases and mental illnesses and their etiology and treatment. Charles Hughes opens the chapter with an analysis of the basic categories of diseases, theories of treatment, and the roles played by medical specialists in the non-Western, non-industrialized world. Robert Bergman's article, "A School for Medicine Men," helps us see the similarities and dissimilarities between Navajo medicine men and Western-trained psychiatrists. Bergman also discusses the establishment of a school for Navajo medicine men. Robert Edgerton describes the training and psychiatric approach used by one particular Hehe traditional psychiatrist from Tanzania. Although this traditional psychiatrist normally emphasizes witchcraft and magic, invoking the aid of the supernatural when necessary, he remains primarily a pragmatic psycho-pharmacologist, always ready to use botany and pharmacology to cure his patients. Claude Lévi-Strauss reminds us of the power of belief and faith in understanding certain psycho-physiological mechanisms underlying death and illness caused by magic. In the final selection, Madeleine Leininger discusses the increase in witchcraft behavior in the United States, pointing out that mental health clinics and hospitals may not know how to aid victims. Dr. Leininger also describes a therapy plan she devised to treat victims of witchcraft among urban U.S. families.

References Cited

Bichmann, Wolfgang
1979 "Primary Health Care and Traditional Medicine—Considering the Background of Changing Health Care Concepts in Africa." *Social Science and Medicine*, 13B: 175–82.

Clements, Forrest E.
1932 "Primitive Concepts of Disease." University of California *Publications in American Archaeology and Ethnology* 32, No. 2: 252.

Good, Charles M.
1977 "Traditional Medicine: An Agenda for Medical Geography." *Social Science and Medicine* 11: 705–13.

Lofchie, M. F.
1982 "Foreword." In P. Stanley Yoder, ed., *African Health and Healing Systems: Proceedings of a Symposium*, pp. vii–ix. Los Angeles: Crossroads Press, African Studies Association.

"World Psychosis." *Science '80*, Vol. 1, no. 6, p. 7.

Yoder, P. Stanley
1982 "Issues in the Study of Ethnomedical Systems in Africa." In P. Stanley Yoder, ed., *African Health and Healing Systems: Proceedings of a Symposium*, pp. 1–20. Los Angeles: Crossroads Press, African Studies Association.

Medical Care: Ethnomedicine

Charles C. Hughes

Any relationship between a culture's magical, religious, and scientific systems becomes apparent during illness. This is especially true in the world's underdeveloped cultures, where the diagnosis and treatment of illness are always based on an understanding of beliefs about God and man, about the supernatural and the empirical. Indeed, the success or failure of a modern medical program in an underdeveloped culture may very well depend on understanding that culture's beliefs about such malevolent forces as witchcraft and sorcery.

In the following article Charles Hughes applies the term "ethnomedicine" to "those beliefs and practices relating to disease which are the products of indigenous cultural development and are not specifically derived from the conceptual framework of modern medicine." Although Hughes's article is directed primarily to non-Western, non-industrialized cultures, it is well to remember that many people in Western culture relate disease and its treatment to the supernatural realm.

Reprinted by permission of the publisher from the *International Encyclopedia of the Social Sciences*, David L. Sills, Editor. Vol. 10, pp. 87–93. Copyright © 1968 by permission of Crowell Collier and Macmillan, Inc.

JUDGING FROM PALEOPATHOLOGICAL EVIDENCE, diseases of one kind or another have always afflicted man. Indeed, given the nature of life and the nature of disease, it could not be otherwise; for disease is but an expression of man's dynamic relationship with his environment. And even as there has always been sickness, accident, deformity, and anxiety to trouble man, so, too, has there been an organized, purposeful response by society to such threats. In all human groups, no matter how small or technologically primitive, there exists a body of belief about the nature of disease, its causation and cure, and its relations to other aspects of group life. There also exist therapeutic and preventive practices, many of which are empirically efficacious by standards of modern medicine, although often not for the reasons advanced by folk belief. The variability of societies and cultural systems impedes easy generalization about the nature of "primitive" or "folk" medicine (cf. Ackerknecht 1942b), but one common characteristic is its close integration with other institutions of the society. Religion, medicine, and morality are frequently found together in the behavioral act or event, and "folk medicine" becomes "social medicine" to an extent not found in industrialized societies.

The term "ethnomedicine" will be used to refer to those beliefs and practices relating to disease which are the products of indigenous cultural development and are not explicitly derived from the conceptual framework of modern medicine. In this light, most of the following discussion focuses on the non-Western, non-industrialized societies of the world, although it is clear that in "modern" societies as well there exist beliefs and practices relating to disease and its treatment which are based on magical or religious conceptions rather than on those of scientific medicine.

Theory of Disease

Man, everywhere, devises or divines causes for the significant events in his life. The afflictions which beset body and mind are explained in both naturalistic and supernaturalistic terms. A cut finger, a broken limb, a snake bite, a fever, the halting speech and wandering mind of senility—all may be regarded as sometime hazards in life. To explain such events there is always some conceptual framework founded in common-sense empiricism. But often a wound does not heal, a sickness does not respond to treatment, and the normally expected and predictable does not happen. In such cases another order of explanation is employed, one which attempts to come to terms with the more basic meaning of the event in metaphysical perspective. For most non-Western societies this transcendent explanation for the occurrence of disease tends to figure more pervasively in the total body of medical lore and practice than does the empirical framework. One reason is the greater incapacitation and mortality from disease in the underdeveloped world than in highly industrialized societies. In addition, this reality is coupled with the comparative inadequacy of ethnomedical techniques and knowledge for dealing with these common threats to the existence of the group and the person.

Widespread throughout the world are five basic categories of events or situations which, in folk etiology, are believed responsible for illness: (1) sorcery; (2) breach of taboo; (3) intrusion of a disease object; (4) intrusion of a disease-causing spirit; and (5) loss of soul (Clements 1932). Not every society recognizes all five categories; indeed, many groups are selective in the emphasis placed upon one or a combination of causes. For example, the Eskimo most frequently trace the origin of diseases to soul loss and breach of taboo, while the malevolence of sorcerers or witches is especially emphasized in many African cultures. Usually, however, these categories are more useful in analytically characterizing the etiological beliefs of a particular group than in describing the content of an entire belief system. This would be the case where a disease is believed to be caused by the intrusion of an object which contains a spirit, and it is the latter to which primary causative influence is attributed (e.g., Hallowell 1935).

The Greeks were not alone in viewing disease as a manifestation of disharmony in man's overall relation to the universe. "Health" is rarely, if ever, a narrowly restricted conception having its locus only in the well-being of the individual body. In discussing conceptions of illness among a west African people, Price-Williams gives a modern illustration:

> In common with a great many other people, Tiv do not regard "illness" or "disease" as a completely separate category distinct from misfortunes to compound and farm, from relationship between kin, and from more complicated matters relating to the control of land. But it would be completely erroneous to say that Tiv are not able, in a cognitive sense, to recognize disease. As Bohannan has said: "The concept of a disease is not foreign to the Tiv: mumps, smallpox, . . . yaws and gonorrhea are all common and each has a name." What is meant is that disease is seldom viewed in isolation. (1962, p. 125)

Such a notion is widely found, as in certain American Indian groups, where bodily or mental affliction is often viewed as an indicator of moral transgression, in thought or in deed, against the norms of society. Indeed, man is frequently thought of as continuous with both the social and nonsocial aspects of his environment, and what happens in his surroundings affects his bodily well-being. Not only a person's own actions, therefore, but also those of kinsmen or neighbors can cause sickness. Such an etiological conception has obvious implications for treatment. For example, if the curative technique includes magically based dietary restrictions, they may apply to all members of the patient's family; a breach of the restriction by any of these people will undermine the patient's health. Similarly, as among the Thonga of South Africa, sexual relations between any of the inhabitants of the patient's village can aggravate his condition, and some Eskimo groups feel that the patient's family should do no work during the period of convalescence for fear of giving offense to the spirit causing the sickness.

The belief that by his own actions a man can influence the state of his fellow's health also has malevolent implications, as in the practice of witchcraft and sorcery. Frequently this may be an important factor deciding the success or failure of attempts at introducing new medical programs in underdeveloped societies. Cassel (1955) cites as an illustration the Zulu, who believe that only sorcerers and witches have the ability to transmit disease, particularly diseases which show themselves in symptoms normally associated with pulmonary tuberculosis. Progress in one community's acceptance of a Western-styled health program was brought to an abrupt halt when a physician tried to introduce the medical concept of contagion. He traced the course of tuberculosis through a family, showing how one person had been the original source of the disease in the group and had therefore been the agent responsible for sickness in all the others. The cautious cooperation of the family elder immediately turned into a hostile rejection, which was assuaged only after the doctor had retracted his apparent accusation that the daughter of the family was a witch.

A theory of disease implies a theory of normality. Yet the "normal" is in no way easy to define for all times and places. Aside from the questions of a "statistical" versus a "functional" basis for normality, there is the cultural definition. Afflictions common enough in a group to be endemic, though they be clinical deformities, may often be accepted simply as part of man's natural condition. Ackerknecht (1946), for example, has noted that the Thonga believe intestinal worms, with which they are pervasively affected, to be necessary for digestion; the Mano, also of Africa, feel that primary and secondary yaws are so common that they say, "That is no sickness; everybody has that." North Amazonian Indians, among whom dyschronic spirochetosis is prevalent, accept its endemicity to such an extent that its victims are thought to be normal, and individuals who have not had the disfiguring disease are said to be looked upon as pathological and consequently unable to contract marriage. It is culture, not nature, that defines disease, although it is usually culture and nature which foster disease.

Recent behavioral science research has attempted to go beyond a "phenomenological" orientation in investigation of cultural theories of disease and has sought analytic categories which would relate particular emphases in a theory of disease to other aspects of social and cultural life. A striking example of this type of investigation is the work of John Whiting and Irvin Child (1953).

Using a wide sample from the ethnographic "laboratory," these investigators found high correlations between certain aspects of child-rearing practices and dominant themes in etiological beliefs related to disease, more particularly, between the hypothesized degree of anxiety generated during the socialization process—the degree of "negative fixation"—and a theory of disease which reflects these anxieties. Thus, harsh weaning is highly associated with oral explanations for onset of disease: these would include consumption of food, drink, or poison by the sick individual or oral activity on the part of others, such as incantations and spells. Societies in which independence training is characteristically fraught with emotional hazards tend also to have "dependence" explanations of illness. These include soul loss or spirit possession. "Aggression explanations" for disease are highly associated with societies in which training for handling aggressive impulses leaves a residue of unresolved anxiety, and they are expressed in theories which ascribe the cause of a disease to the patient's disobedience or aggression toward spirits, to aggressive wishes on the part of the patient or another person, to introjection of poison other than by mouth, or to harm by magical weapons or objects.

Theory and Practice of Treatment

Therapeutic practices in ethnomedicine address themselves to both supernatural and empirical theories of disease causation. Ackerknecht has said that primitive medicine is "magic medicine" (1942a); certainly much of it is, and, insofar as supernatural causes are involved, therapeutic regimens are based on countervailing supernatural powers or events. Thus, the powerful shaman or healer attempts to recover the soul lost or stolen by a human or supernatural agent. The intrusion of a disease object or disease-causing spirit is treated by extraction or exorcism, and diseases which come as punishment for breach of taboo are usually treated by divination or confession of the infraction. Forgiveness and re-establishment of harmony with the moral and supernatural order are thus important outcomes of the therapy.

In folk medicine, however, there is more to treatment than magical or religious ritualization, however effective this may be psychosocially in providing emotional catharsis and reassurance. All human groups have a pharmacopoeia and at least rudimentary medical techniques; some groups, indeed, are exceptional in their exploitation of the environment for medicinal purposes and in the degree of their diagnostic and surgical skills (Ackerknecht 1942a; Sigerist 1951; Laughlin 1963). The trephining done by the Inca, Masai surgery, the anatomical knowledge of the Aleut and the Eskimo, and the extensive drug repertory of west African tribes are familiar examples. In addition to trephining, numerous other types of surgery and bonesetting are found, as well as massages, bloodletting, dry cupping, bathing, inoculation, and cauterization. It has been estimated that from 25 to 50 percent of the non-Western pharmacopoeia is empirically effective. In fact, our knowledge of the therapeutic efficacy of a large number of modern drugs is derived from the experience of primitive peoples: opium, hashish, hemp, coca, cinchona, eucalyptus, sarsparilla, acacia, kousso, copaiba, guaiac, jalap, podophyllin, quassia, and many of the tranquilizers and psychotomimetics now used in psychiatric therapy and research.

A great part of the task of folk medicine, however, and especially of preventive medicine, is borne by cultural practices which, although oriented to different social purposes, have important functional implications for health. Thus, notable hygienic purposes are served by many religious and magical practices, such as avoidance of the house in which a death has occurred, theories of contagious "bad body humors" which necessitate daily bathing, distinctions of "hot" and "cold" food and water which require boiling or cooking, hiding of fecal and other bodily waste through fear of their use by sorcers or witches, and numerous others.

Other cultural practices inadvertently relevant to health have a more general ecological basis. These may include customs regarding cosmetics and clothing or house styles and settlement patterns. Regardless of their value to the archeologist, the middens of ancient sedentary communities have rather baleful implications for the public health of the times. Changing economic incentives and circumstances which disrupt the adaptation of a cultural activity to its environment frequently create health hazards. May (1960) provides a striking illustration of the intersection between cultural

and ecological factors in North Vietnam. Dwellers on the plains lived in low, squat houses in which they sheltered their cattle on one side and did their cooking on the other. When these rice growers moved into the hills they constructed houses according to the same general plan. In the hills, however, the incidence of malaria among them became so high as to limit further such movement, despite governmental encouragement. The people themselves ascribed the calamity to the ill will of the hill deities. In fact, however, the incidence of malaria was low among the indigenous hill people, who constructed their houses on stilts, sheltered their animals underneath, and did their cooking inside the house. Several factors were apparently instrumental in the latter case in keeping down the spread of malaria from the mosquito vector found in the hills; flight ceiling of Anopheles Minimus is restricted to about ten feet above the ground, and, despite its preference for human blood, the presence of animals underneath the house and of smoke inside the house (where the cooking was done) created an unrealized protection for human inhabitants.

The study of folk medicine has important theoretical implications for the persistent question of a "magical" versus a "scientific" orientation among non-Western peoples. Erasmus (1952), utilizing data from South American Indian populations, contends that the inductive epistemological framework of folk medicine is essentially similar in structure to that of modern scientific medicine, but that the latter differs chiefly in its amenity to generalization and degree of predictive success. In folk medicine the chances of "natural" recovery are in favor of predictive successes, but, more often than in modern medicine, the theoretical propositions lying behind such predictions are merely coincidentally rather than functionally related to the phenomenon in question. Thus, the recooking, before eating, of food that has been left standing overnight is done on the basis of the need to dispel the dangerous quality of "coldness" in the food, but in fact such recooking destroys enterotoxin-producing staphylococci.

The possible implications for a sociology of knowledge are apparent: so long as any activity or set of activities produces a sufficiently high proportion of predictive successes, there will be little elaboration or alteration of the conceptual framework orienting the activity. Cognitive frameworks relating to disease are instruments in the total process of adaptation; they change, evolve, and respond when their viability and acceptability are challenged. Only when folk etiology fails too often and in too many areas to give pragmatic and especially psychodynamic satisfaction does it yield to other frameworks, autochthonous or adopted from outside.

Disease, Medicine, and Culture

Some knowledge of diseases, their classification and etiology, is part of all cultural systems (e.g., Lieban 1962; Rubel 1960; Price-Williams 1962). Investigators have analyzed disease categories in an attempt to understand the structure of the conceptual world of different peoples. The use of componential analysis, the investigation of semantic interrelationships of terms, has been applied to words for sickness (cf. Frake 1961). Aside from illustrating the extent to which concern with disease is elaborated in a folk nosology, such work also emphasizes a more general point: an effective cultural response to disease requires patterned discrimination and categorization of disease symptoms, even if treatment is based largely on methods of trial and error. Diagnostic categories, however crude, serve the purpose of directing sustained attention and reflection to the appearance of disease syndromes; thus providing empirical data for inferences about the probable effectiveness of one type of treatment or another. Undoubtedly this constitutes a kind of inadvertent experimental approach (see, e.g., Laughlin 1963; Erasmus 1952).

Theories of disease generally have major relevance to the moral order, that is, to the control of man's behavior in society. Disease is frequently seen as a warning sign, a visitation from punishing agents for a broken taboo, a hostile impulse, or an aberrant urge to depart from the approved way. In a series of classical papers, Hallowell (e.g., 1963) has analyzed the function of anxieties over sickness among the Ojibwa Indians of North America, and other investigators have looked at the same problem in different cultural settings (e.g., Lieban 1962). Sickness is often interpreted as the supernaturals' way of indicating an act or intention of socially disruptive behavior. Especially in societies lacking strong centralized sociopolitical institutions, the occurrence and imminence of disease—with the belief that it represents punishment for aberrant, dissocial impulse or action—can be functionally important in maintaining group cohesion and restraining disruptive tendencies.

The therapeutic practices attendant upon occurrence of disease may also have socially cohesive results. Although such therapy may often be medically effective, it may serve ancillary functions in the total organization of the society. Typically, the curative session (and often the diagnostic occasion as well) involves not only the patient and the healer, but also the patient's family and neighbors. Often the therapy involves confession by the patient, and under such conditions the confession may well relieve him of diffuse as well as focused anxieties and guilt. When followed by concrete expiatory acts, it may also give him a chance to participate in his own treatment through action. (It is doubtful whether such curative rites do more than provide temporary symptom relief—but the same can be said of much modern psychotherapy.) At the same time group cohesion is often enhanced, for such confessions dramatize fundamental social values by illustrating the harm that can come from social deviance. They provide a setting in which all participants are enveloped in the aura of forgiveness and, through stress on the protection afforded by adherence to group values, assurance of good health. In short, the therapeutic context is usually explicitly a social context, and during the course of the therapy the reciprocal psychosocial involvement of the patient with his fellows is ritually underscored. As noted above, if therapeutic directives for behavior are issued, they frequently apply to the group, or selected members of the group, as well as to the patient; and if successful recovery is as dependent upon good thoughts as upon effective techniques—as frequently happens—then the assembled company must be devoid of ill wishes and hostilities toward not only the patient but also each other. The curative rite thus may serve in multiple ways as an occasion for reintegration of the group around common social values.

The practice of folk medicine is variously institutionalized. In all societies some rudimentary medical knowledge is an aspect of enculturation, but beyond this general protection there is always a specialist. Sometimes the specialist's role is a full-time activity, but more frequently it is combined with other principal roles appropriate for the practitioner. In some societies there are more complex social arrangements than the simple dyadic relationship between healer and patient. Even as the kin and covillagers of the patient may be explicitly involved in the curative process, so too there may be a society of healers or several societies of healers devoted to diagnosis and cure of various diseases. In west Africa there are found, for example, specialized associations of healers of smallpox or snake bite; each association possesses its own rules of qualification, initiation, and procedure (Hardley 1941).

Folk Medicine in Change

Folk medicine does not easily change under the impact of sustained contact with the industrialized world, or even as a result of deliberate attempts to introduce new conceptions of disease and hygiene. Paul (1955), Foster (1962), and others have documented the variety of factors that may impede or altogether prevent the successful introduction of a modern health program, even of so simple an innovation as the boiling of drinking water. Such factors include ecological considerations, as well as functional efficiency in domestic tasks, the social structure, the status and prestige of the innovator, and the perception of threat or advantage to the recipient. The proper role of the healer may be differently defined; in India, for example, the medical practitioner must assure the patient of recovery, and any admission of uncertainty (even couched in the form of probability) is not allowed. Rudimentary physical testing may be impossible or difficult in a non-Western context. In societies where blood, for example, is thought of as a nonregenerative substance, to take samples for testing is tantamount to inflicting deliberate harm.

It has been found to be easier to introduce behavioral changes than changes in belief about the nature of illness, its cause, and prevention. Domestic hygiene and community health may be bettered by the public health worker who influences a change in habits while not disturbing the underlying belief system. One reason for this has been mentioned above: belief systems, particularly those centered on critical areas of social value, serve more than a single cognitive function. Because they interrelate with religious and magical systems, as well as with the moral order of the society, they impart a deeper sense of resignation and acceptance of events than does an alien concept treating of a germ theory of illness. The value system of a culture provides a more satisfying answer to the question, "Why did I and not my neighbor get sick?" than does an explanation phrased in terms of communicability of a disease, thresholds of resistance, host, agent, and environment.

Yet in many instances modern medicine does get accepted; and one of the reasons is its demonstrably greater effectiveness in the treatment and prevention of many diseases. But even such acceptance is often compromised by the existence of alternative diagnostic and therapeutic frameworks: One relating to those diseases for which it is felt modern medicine is more effective, and the second relating to diseases conceived to be unamenable to modern medical treatment. The first is often applied to sicknesses introduced by Europeans (such as tuberculosis, measles, smallpox, and others of a communicable nature), while in the second group are traditionally endemic diseases and, especially, ailments having a large component of psychological or psychophysiological involvement.

But in the extremity of fear for a patient's life even such distinctions as these are often disregarded, and the ill person may be taken to a modern medical facility after indigenous healers have done their best—taken either to be cured or left to die. Every hospital, and not just those in non-Western, "underdeveloped" countries, will admit patients brought too late for the course of disease to be halted even by the most advanced techniques of scientific medicine. Disease being an unequivocal threat to life, adaptive responses are many and sometimes override ingrained belief, either of folk medicine on the one hand or modern medicine on the other. In this light, given the avowedly limited role of scientific medicine in society—together with the inevitability of disease—elements of folk medicine will no doubt everywhere persist, even as they do in Europe and the United States, so long as there is uncertainty of outcome or technical ineffectiveness in alleviating pain, prolonging life, and guaranteeing cure.

A School for Medicine Men

Robert Bergman

The anthropological study of mental illness demonstrates that the types and frequency of mental disorders vary from one culture to another, as do the diagnosis and treatment of the illness. In this article Robert Bergman discusses a training school for Navajo medicine men founded by the Navajo themselves at Rough Rock, Arizona, a community on the Navajo reservation. As a non-Indian psychiatrist working for the Indian Health Service, the author volunteered his professional services to the fledgling school. Working side-by-side with the Navajo medicine men, or "singers," as they are called, Bergman analyzed the nature of Navajo curative ceremonies and their effects on patients. The clash of folk medicine and modern scientific medicine has received considerable attention by anthropologists, and reports of fear and grief felt by non-Western patients undergoing modern medical treatment are common. If pre-literate patients and their curers are ignorant of the procedures and philosophies underlying modern medicine, so too are those trained in modern medicine ignorant of folk medicine and its accomplishments.

Reprinted from the *American Journal of Psychiatry*, Vol. 130, no. 6 (1973), pp. 663–66, by permission of the author and the American Psychiatric Association. Copyright 1973 the American Psychiatric Association.

THIS PAPER IS AN ACCOUNT OF HOW A NAVAJO community set up its own medical school and how a non-Indian psychiatrist became involved in it. In order to understand what happened one must have some acquaintance with the nature of Navajo medicine. This subject has received an enormous amount of attention from anthropologists and other behavioral scientists. I will make no attempt here to review the extensive anthropologic literature except to recommend the great works of Haile (1), Reichard (2), and Kluckhohn and associates (3–6). The psychiatric literature is less extensive. It includes the early article of Pfister (7), which seems to me to be remarkably insightful and sound in spite of having been based on very little and quite second-hand evidence. The Leightons (8) in 1941 described Navajo ceremonials beautifully and explained many of their beneficial elements. Sandner (9) reported his work with Navajo medicine men to the APA three years ago. Almost everyone agrees that the ceremonies work.

Background

Navajo practitioners generally fall into three categories. The herbalists know a variety of medicinal plants, which are used primarily for symptomatic relief. The diagnosticians are shamans who work by inspiration. By one of several techniques, such as hand trembling, crystal gazing, or star gazing, they divine the nature and cause of an illness and make an appropriate referral to a member of the third and highest status group, the singers. The singers (I will use the terms "ceremonialist," "medicine man," and "singer" synonymously) do the only truly curative work, and it is a school to train them that I will be discussing.

Navajo nosology classes diseases by etiology; identical illnesses often have similar symptoms, but they need not. Note that psychiatric nosology is similar, e.g., depression is often characterized by insomnia, but sometimes the reverse can be true. A seriously oversimplified statement of Navajo etiology is that disease is caused by a disharmony with the universe, including the universe of other men. A singer restores this harmony by performing a ceremony proper to the case. Little or no reliance is placed on herbs or other medicines and, as is the case with psychiatry (at least from the psychoanalytic viewpoint), this absence of organic measures confers high status.

No one seems to know precisely how many ceremonies there are, but there are many. Important ones last five or nine nights and are difficult and elaborate to a degree approached among us physicians, I think, only by open heart surgery. The proper performance of a major sing requires the presence of the entire extended family and many other connections of the patient. The immediate family must feed all of these people for days. Many of the people present have important roles in the performance, such as chanting, public speaking, dancing in costume, leading group discussions, and many other prescribed activities of a more or less ritualized nature. For the singer himself the performance requires the letter-perfect performance of 50 to 100 hours of ritual chant (something approaching the recitation of the New Testament from memory), the production of several beautiful and ornate sand paintings, the recitation of the myth connected with the ceremony, and the management of a very large and difficult group process.

Non-Navajo explanations of why all this effort helps anyone tend to be rather offensive to the medicine men themselves, and *their* explanations, if they should feel like giving any, tend to be unsatisfying to us since they are based on the supernatural. The difference may not be as great as it appears, however. Traditional Navajos talk frequently in symbols: "We are glad you came from Washington to talk with us. There are many mountains between here and Washington," which translates as, "Communication with the federal government is difficult. We are glad you are making an effort to improve it." They also reject the notion that they are using figures of speech. They do not attach as much significance to the distinctions among different levels of reality as we do, and like some poets, they reject as stupid and de-structive any attempt to translate their words into ordinary language. Though it seems to me that their myths and chants are symbols of human social-psychological forces and events, they would regard such a statement as silly and missing the point. Nevertheless, I will make a slight attempt in that direction.

The Rituals

For the past six years, I have been practicing psychiatry among the Navajo people. I have often referred patients to medicine men (who in turn occasionally refer patients to me). I have also often consulted medicine men, and patients have often told me about the medicine men's traditional cures and their feelings about these cures. It seems to me, although my knowledge of the sings is very limited, that the ceremony performed is almost always symbolically appropriate to the case. Pathologically prolonged grief reactions, for example, are almost always treated with a ceremony that removes the influence of the dead from the living and turns the patient's attention back toward life. "Treatment of a dream by a dream," Pfister called it.

It seems to me that the singers and we psychiatrists are the converse of one another with regard to our attitude toward ritual. To them ritual is the main focus: What is unvaryingly their practice from one case to another is at the center of their thought. Informal interaction with the patient and his family is considered important in an informal sort of way. This kind of interaction is not what is taught explicitly but only what is taught by the by. Our ritual, which I would argue is fairly elaborate, is not taught as the central part of psychiatry; rather, the more varying interaction is taught explicitly to psychiatry residents—ritual being taught by the by. In any event the singers do manage an intricate family interaction that, I think, has several important effects: (1) the patient is assured that his family cares for him by the tremendous effort being made; (2) the prolonged and intense contact makes it inevitable that conflicts are revealed and, if things are handled skillfully, resolved; and (3) a time of moratorium and turning point are established.

At the time I first heard of the medicine-man school in 1967, I was already quite convinced of the value of Navajo medicine. Aside from the cases I had seen, I was greatly influenced by my contact with a singer named Thomas Largewhiskers. Mr. Largewhiskers, who is now 100 years old, agreed to be my consultant and to teach me a little of what he knew. I first looked him up after seeing a formerly psychotic patient who attributed her remarkable and well-documented improvement to him. At the time of our first meeting I tried to explain what I do and said that I wanted to learn from him. He replied, "I don't know what you learned from books, but the most important thing I learned from my grandfathers was that there is a part of the mind that we don't really know about and that it is that part that is most important in whether we become sick or remain well." When he told me some of his life story it impressed me that he had become interested in being a singer when, as a young man, he had had an accident and the singer who took care of him explained that it had been unconsciously determined.

Mr. Largewhiskers and many other extremely old men are still practicing very actively. There is a growing demand for their services—growing because the population is increasing and their belief in traditional medicine is continuing. The trouble is that younger people are not becoming singers. The reasons behind the lack of students are largely economic. To learn to perform even one short ceremony takes at least a year of full-time effort. To learn a major ceremony takes much longer, and many medicine men know several. Since the end of the old herding economy, almost no one can afford to give up earning a living for such a long time. At the time of starting the school for medicine men Yazzie Begay, one of its founders, said "I have been acquainted with several medicine men who have recently died. They were not able to teach the ceremonies which they knew to their grandchildren or to anyone else. Today their sacred instruments and paraphernalia are sitting unused."

The School

The school is at Rough Rock, Ariz., a community near the center of the Navajo Reservation. It is part of the Rough Rock Demonstration School, the first community-controlled Indian school. The Demonstration School was started in 1965, when the Bureau of Indian Affairs (BIA) gave the buildings and

equipment to a nonprofit corporation of Navajo leaders called Dine, Inc. Dine helped the Rough Rock chapter of the tribe set up and elect its own board of education (no one on the original board could speak English and all were ceremonialists) and then contracted with the board to operate an elementary boarding school. BIA contributed funds that would have been equal to the budget of such a school if they had been operating it; funds also came from the Office of Economic Opportunity (OEO) and other sources. Soon after the school began operations in 1966, the people became convinced that their ideas really were taken seriously in its daily workings, and several local people suggested setting up the medicine-man school to the board. It was pointed out at a board meeting that white people have medical schools and give students scholarships to attend them and that what was needed most on the reservation were new medicine men. Therefore they felt Rough Rock should set up a school for singers and provide scholarships.

The idea was taken up enthusiastically by the board, and the details, were worked out over the course of the next year. It was decided to alter the traditional method of teaching and learning sings as little as possible. (The old way is by apprenticeship and takes place in the teacher's home.) It was also decided that each medicine man would teach two apprentices of his own selection; that is, application for admission to the school would be made by trios consisting of a medicine man and two trainees. The school board would select among them on the basis of the medicine man's reputation, the trainees' apparent ability, and the importance of and threat of extinction to the ceremony that was proposed to be taught. The medicine men were to be paid a very modest salary and the trainees considerably less for their subsistence.

Obtaining Funds

Ever since the Demonstration School started, I had been going there once a month or more to consult with the guidance counselor and teachers. At one time the school administration, at the direction of the board, was preparing a project proposal in an attempt to obtain funds; I was asked to attend a meeting about the project, and here my support for the proposal was enlisted. This was the first of several project discussions in which I took part, and ultimately the board kindly included me in the proposal. It was decided that I should meet regularly with the trainees to discuss non-Navajo medicine, particularly psychiatry. I strongly suspect that my inclusion was a move to make the project look more reasonable to funding agencies.

I flatter myself that from time to time my colleagues in the school and the trainees have been glad to have me around, but I am sure that I have gained much more from this than they have. Before the project could materialize, however, we had to obtain funds.

The first proposal was made to OEO, which turned it down. The second proposal went to the Training and Special Projects Branch of the National Institute of Mental Health (NIMH). This one was accepted, although not, I suspect, without some trepidation. At the time of the site visit by NIMH it became apparent how many mountains there really were between Rough Rock and Bethesda, Md. First of all, the weather became very bad and the site visitors felt they were stranded in Albuquerque, which is 250 miles away from Rough Rock. Luckily the school board was able to go to Albuquerque, so we had a meeting. Two incidents seemed to me to epitomize the meeting. The first was a question from the visitors: "How can a project that supports the continuance of superstition promote mental health?" The reaction of the ceremonialist school board members was more restrained than I had expected. They answered at length, and I added my endorsement. The visitors seemed satisfied. Later one of them, in leafing through the documents, said, "The project director is to be full-time, and the salary listed here is $5000. Can that possibly be right?" When that question had been translated, Mr. John Dick, the director in question, who was a medicne man and a former school board member, asked anxiously, "Is it too much?" I am very grateful that the project was funded, and I know that the board is also appreciative.

The Training Program

The work began in September 1969 and is still continuing. There are six medicine men and 12 trainees. Most of the original trainees are still in the program. One of the faculty members died during the first year and was replaced. The ceremonies being taught so far have been one and two nights in length, and almost all of the trainees have completed learning them. Soon they will be performing them for the first time. They will then go on to major ceremonies. Although the lessons (excluding the ones I teach) are conducted at various homes scattered over considerable territory in which there are no paved roads, Mr. Dick as director maintains close supervision. He travels to each home and watches over the teaching and its results. As the trainees have progressed, he and other medicine men have tested them. My only criticism has been that Mr. Dick's supervision seems rather harsh at times. He has demanded continuous effort and has been very hard on some people whom he surprised when he thought they should be working and they weren't. Still, apart from minor professional jealousy, the group's morale seems high. The program has been well accepted, and there clearly will be a demand for the services of the graduates. Other communities are trying to start similar schools. Recently one of the medicine men had one of his students perform a sing over him.

My sessions are a full day every two weeks. Before I started holding them I met with the medicine men to describe what I intended to do and to ask their permission. To my great pleasure they not only agreed to my plans but said they would like to attend along with the trainees. Attendance has varied from time to time, but usually most of the trainees are present as well as three to five of the medicine men. During the first year I talked about somatic medicine, attempting to cover elements of anatomy, physiology, pathology, diagnosis, and treatment. I discovered that the entire group, including the trainees, had considerable knowledge of anatomy and some of physiology. The sessions were lively. The medicine men and the trainees enjoyed trying out stethoscopes, otoscopes, opthalmoscopes, and blood-pressure cuffs. Microscope slides of blood smears and pathology specimens were also very popular. In return I was learning more about ceremonial practice, although not as much as I was to learn the next year when we began discussing psychology.

One of the high points of the first year was a visit that the group made to the Gallup Indian Medical Center. It was characteristic, I thought, that the two things the medicine men most enjoyed seeing at the hospital were an operation and a particularly good view of a sacred mountain peak from the windows of the psychiatric ward. They also had criticisms and suggestions. They were horrified by the pediatric ward because the children were so lonely. They kept asking, "Where are the parents?" They urged that better provisions be made for parents to stay with their children. They also suggested that we build two hogans at the hospital for ceremonial purposes. They remarked that they all had performed brief ceremonies in the hospital but that they could do more in a real hogan. They said that the medical staff could see the patients during the sing and could go back and forth if necessary. Their suggestion still has not been followed, but I hope that it will be soon.

During the second year I began discussing psychiatry, and in this area there has been more of a two-sided interchange. We have spent much time on European and Navajo notions of the unconscious, a subject in which difficulties in translation have been great. Navajo metapsychology still largely eludes me, but it is clear that the medicine men know about the dynamic interpretation of errors and dreams. We spent a great deal of time discussing dreams and were pleased to discover that all of us followed the same custom with regard to them. We all, it turned out, spend our first waking moments in the morning contemplating and interpreting our dreams. One of the medicine men gave an example. He had dreamt about an automobile accident and said that that kind of a dream meant something serious was going on within him and that in order to prevent some disaster from happening to him, it was important to perform a chant about it.

There has been a good deal of case presentation on both sides, particularly, for some reason not clear to me, regarding returned Viet Nam veterans. My feeling of trust and closeness to this group ultimately became such that I presented my own case, describing some things that had led me to enter my analysis and something of the analysis itself. When I finished this rather long account, one of the singers asked me the name of my analyst and where he is now. When I told him, he said, "You were very lucky to find a man who could do so much for you. He must be a very intelligent person."

Another high point for me was demonstrating hypnosis. The group ordinarily looks half asleep—as seems to be the custom with medicine men in meetings. This was unnerving at first, until I found out from their questions and comments that they had been paying very close attention. When hypnosis was demonstrated, however, they were obviously wide awake, although at times I wondered if they were breathing. Working with a carefully prepared subject (I was unwilling to face failure before this audience), I demonstrated a number of depth tests, somnambulism, age regression, positive and negative hallucinations, and some posthypnotic suggestions. When I was done, one of the faculty members said, "I'm 82 years old, and I've seen white people all my life, but this is the first time that one of them has ever surprised me. I'm not surprised to see something like this happen because we do things like this, but I am surprised that a white man should know anything so worthwhile." They also pointed out the resemblance of hypnosis to hand trembling, a diagnostic procedure in which the shaman goes into a trance and his hand moves automatically and indicates the answers to important questions. After we had discussed the similarity, they asked that my subject, a young Navajo woman, diagnose something. I objected, saying that neither she nor I knew how to do this and that it was too serious a matter to play with. They insisted that we try, however, and finally we decided that a weather prediction was not too dangerous to attempt. They were particularly interested in the weather at that time because we were in the midst of an especially severe drought, and someone in the community had predicted that it would continue for another year. When my subject was in a deep trance, I instructed her to visualize the weather for the next six months. She predicted light rain within the week, followed by a dry spell of several months and finally by a good rainy season in late summer. I make no claim other than the truthful reporting of facts: She was precisely correct.

My involvement in this project has, of course, been extremely interesting to me. It is hard, however, to assess the effects of the project on the medicine men and on me. The medicine men say that they know better when and how to refer patients to the white doctors, and I think they feel more kindly toward us. In turn, I feel better able to understand my Navajo patients and know better when to refer them to medicine men. I have adopted some Navajo styles of thought, I think. I use hypnosis more than I used to. And one of my Navajo colleagues in the Indian Health Service Mental Health Program claims that I try to act like a medicine man all the time.

A Traditional African Psychiatrist

Robert B. Edgerton

Tracing the education of an African traditional doctor from his early training to his mature status as an effective man of medicine, Robert Edgerton in the following article characterizes Hehe shamans as rational, logical empiricists and keen observers and diagnosticians. Edgerton demonstrates that the Hehe make no clear distinction between shamanism and Western science and that Hehe shamans recognize a host of physical and mental illnesses. The shaman Abedi, for example, recognizes five psychotic conditions that, depending on their origin, are treated either magically or with pharmaceuticals, physical therapy, or actual removal of the patient from the situation causing the psychological distress. Illustrating the interaction of healers and their clients, Edgerton well shows the importance of traditional doctors in Africa, where a permanent lack of funds has prevented the implementation of Western-type medical systems.

Reprinted from the *Southwestern Journal of Anthropology*, Vol. 27, no. 3 (1971), pp. 259–78, by permission of the author and the *Journal of Anthropological Research*.

INTEREST IN NON-WESTERN PSYCHIATRY IN THE past decade has produced a substantial literature, much of it relating to Africa. Nevertheless, the coverage of African societies has only begun, and the preliminary findings that we now possess may be one-sided. Thus, despite the sometimes positive evaluations of such men as Prince (1964), Collis (1966) and Lambo (1964) in Nigeria, and Gelfand (1964) and Loudon (1960) in Southeast Africa, many writers continue to feel that traditional African psychiatric practices have little instructive value for Western psychiatry. Others have been even more critical, believing that the magical practices of African healers are inimical to science. For example, Margetts (1965: 115) writes that native healers "can do little good in a mental health programme and may do harm. They have no rational place in the modern technological world . . ."; however, he adds that analyses should be made of their folk medicines.

Before any considered opinion on the nature of traditional African medicine or "psychiatry" can be reached, we not only need more research from additional areas of Africa, but research which adopts additional perspectives. The following report is offered because its practitioner, a Hehe of Tanzania, is a specialist in psychiatry, and his beliefs and practices, particularly as they emphasize botanical and pharmacological empiricism, complement our knowledge of African ethnopsychiatry as it is practiced in other parts of Africa.

The Hehe

The Hehe are a Bantu-speaking people located in the Southern Highlands Region of Tanzania, formerly Tanganyika. Their territory stretches from the Great Ruaha River on the north and west to the escarpment of the Kilombero Valley on the south and east. Most of this area is high rolling woodland or grassland, but some Hehe occupy arid lowland savanna areas and others live at higher elevations in the mountain rain forest. The Hehe were a congeries of small chieftancies until they were united by the aggressive military and diplomatic actions of Muyugumba and his son, Mkwawa. By extending Hehe hegemony over much of southcentral Tanganyika, these men established the Hehe as a kingdom of considerable military and political power. After early victories over the Germans, Mkwawa was defeated and killed in 1894. The Germans restored the independence of territories conquered by the Hehe and confined the Hehe state to its present boundaries.

The Hehe, who now number over 200,000, live in dispersed homesteads which are organized into neighborhoods. A homestead is typically occupied by a man, his wife or wives, and their children. It is surrounded by its fields of maize, millet, beans, cassava, and squash and by small numbers of cattle, sheep, and goats. Each Hehe neighborhood is bound together by ties of kinship and friendship, by ceremonial activities, and by cooperative work parties. In addition to the strong ties of kinship, the Hehe recognize a hierarchy of lesser and greater chiefs who possess considerable traditional authority and have obligations to the British administration.

When the Hehe fall ill, as they often do, they may attribute their misfortune to any of several sources: to natural phenomena such as worry, impure water, or faulty inheritance, to witchcraft, or to legitimate retribution for the violation of Hehe norms. If the source of illness is seen as natural, a Hehe may seek help from a European-trained physician or medical helper in a nearby town. But even for "natural" illnesses, the patient is likely also to seek out a traditional doctor—an *mbombwe* —and where the source of illness is other than natural, he is certain to do so. There are many such doctors (the Swahili term is *mganga*) throughout Hehe territory, and their advice is continually sought. Some, of course, are more highly regarded than others. The best known native doctor in the Iringa area was a man whom I shall name Abedi. Unlike most traditional Hehe doctors who attempt to treat any disorder, Abedi is a specialist in mental disorders—he is a Hehe psychiatrist.

Abedi's Training

Abedi was the headman *(jumbe)* of an area near Iringa until early in the 1950's when he encountered some sort of difficulty with the British administration. Accused of malfeasance, he left the post in 1955 and turned to full-time practice as an *mbombwe*. Abedi was born around 1910 to a man who had been a renowned *mbombwe*, a doctor to the King, Mkwawa, himself. Thus Abedi's father had access to the traditional medicine not only of the royal clan and court of the Hehe, but also from those neighboring tribes whom the Hehe conquered. Abedi's mother was also an *mbombwe*, who, like Abedi, was known as a specialist (her specialty was female disorders).

Abedi's formal training as an *mbombwe* did not begin until he was an adult, by which time his father was quite elderly. Abedi learned primarily from his father, but also studied with his mother who gave him intensive instruction in botany. Much of his training was highly practical, giving attention to the method of diagnosis and treatment, observation of symptoms, collection of plants and roots, knowledge of inherited disorders, etc. But an equal emphasis was placed upon the supernatural. Abedi inherited his father's *lyang'ombe*, a small metal object that appeared to be an old European belt buckle. Through prayer, the *lyang'ombe* could be imbued with God's power to cure. Abedi learned to pray to God (*Nguluvi*), to practice divination, to discover the cause of witchcraft, to defend against witchcraft, and to employ magic. His father also gave him protection against the malevolence of witches, who might be angered because he cured those whom they had sickened, by rubbing a secret medicine (*gondola*) into a series of cuts (*nyagi*). These cuts are located on the thumb of the right hand, the third joint of the small finger of the left hand, the wrist, elbow, both temples, forehead, hairline, sternum, chest, neck, nipples, ribs, spine, ankles, knees, and toes. Abedi must reinforce this protection from time to time by reopening the cuts and adding fresh *gondola*. Abedi has also purchased magical knowledge and herbal medications from other traditional doctors over a large area of southern Tanzania.

Abedi's specialization in mental illnesses began during his apprenticeship when he first hallucinated ("hearing voices of people I could not see") and ran in terror to hide in the bush. He was discovered and returned to his father's care, but lay ("completely out of my senses") for two weeks before being cured. The cause was diagnosed as witchcraft and since the cure, Abedi has never been sick again. This experience initiated Abedi's interest in mental illness, and the subsequent mental disorders of his sister and his wife reinforced it. At different times, both women became violently psychotic, but Abedi quickly cured them both. These two cures not only heightened Abedi's interest in psychiatric phenomena, but they led to his reputation as a skillful psychiatrist.

Diagnosis, Etiology, and Prognosis

Although, as we shall see later, Abedi sometimes makes home visits, almost all of his patients came to him in what we might call his "office." The office is a small house, 10 by 20 feet, flimsy and poorly thatched, unlike ordinary Hehe houses, which are massive and solid structures. It has the look of a temporary building, but Abedi has been practicing medicine in it for eight years. The inside of his "office" is remarkably cluttered, with large pots, baskets, and gourds in every corner and hanging from the walls. These containers are filled with the roots and leaves from which Abedi mixes his medicines on a small table in one corner of the office. In his small office he stores, sorts, grinds, and boils his medications before packaging them in a variety of bottles, leaves, horns, small gourds, and leather pouches.

Seeking treatment from Abedi in his office often requires interrupting him in the course of preparing his medications, but he always greets a patient warmly as he asks him (and the usual family members or kinsmen who attend him) to be seated by the fireplace before he begins his diagnostic routine.

In proceeding with his diagnosis, Abedi must keep in mind his nosology of disorders (the catalogue of illness categories that he knows), the signs and symptoms, and the patient's biography —including past illnesses and, especially, antagonists who might want to bewitch him. In short, Abedi is concerned with the entire social context of the patient and his illness—a context which Abedi enters and typically alters—for while successful treatment pleases some, it may displease others (Winans and Edgerton 1964).

In a general way, Abedi recognizes a great variety of illnesses such as impotence, venereal infections, infertility, stomach and bowel ailments, respiratory disorders (including pneumonia and asthma), orthopedic malfunctions, and fevers. He also recognizes more specific diseases such as trachoma, tetanus, malaria, and smallpox. While he may choose to treat all such disorders with specific medications he has developed for that purpose, it is only when the disorders are "mental" (when the locus of disorder, in his perspective, is in the mind) that his diagnosis categories achieve any prognostic differentiation. Indeed, his categories of mental illness are defined by criteria that are based far less upon symptoms than they are upon etiology and prognosis.

Hehe men and women who live in the area near Abedi typically described mental illness in behavioral terms, perceiving its onset as sudden, with aggressive behavior that can result in human injury, but rapidly "cooling" to a fearful and stuporous retreat from human interaction (Edgerton 1966). They made no distinctions among psychotics. Abedi's views of mental illness were more complex. He recognized two symptoms as being indicators of excessive worry: headache and stomach pain. He felt that both responded well to removal of the source of worry and to his herbal medications. For extreme cases, he recommended that the patient move away from his neighborhood for a prolonged vacation with kinsmen. He denied, however, that worry was a common cause of psychotic conditions. He also recognized epilepsy by its *grand mal* seizures, and mental retardation by the fact that intellectual ability was deficient from birth. Mental retardation he deemed untreatable, but he felt that epilepsy, which he said was an inherited condition, was curable by medication if treatment were begun in the first few days after the initial seizure.

Among psychotic conditions, he recognized five: *litego, mbepo, lisaliko, kuhavila* and *erishitani*. *Litego* is marked by depression and guilt, by fever and headache, and sometimes by unusual or bizarre behavior. It never produces thought disturbances. Because it is caused by moral retributive magic brought on by wrong-doing, it cannot be treated medically (or the *mbombwe*, too, would be sickened by the moral magic). Instead it requires confession, apology, and the payment of compensation. Without such restitution, *litego* can be fatal (Winans and Edgerton 1964).

Mbepo is marked by disturbances of behavior (running wildly, destroying property, and assaulting people) as well as by thought disturbances (inability to concentrate, hallucinations, visions, and a loss of touch with reality). It is a product of evil—in this case, witchcraft—and hence it can be cured without wrongdoing by a skilled and protected *mbombwe* (the protection is essential lest the thwarted witch turn his evil upon the doctor).

Lisaliko is indistinguishable from *mbepo* in its symptoms but its causes are natural, not supernatural. These causes include faulty inheritance, febrile illness, poisoning, and, very rarely, excessive worry. It is curable if treated early.

Kuhavila is a particularly violent sort of psychosis, even more so than *mbepo*. Persons afflicted with *kuhavila* actually kill others, and abuse them violently if unable to kill them. They also have prolonged fevers, go naked, eat feces, and run about without apparent purpose except to attack others. The disorder is caused by a specific sort of magic, which can only be acquired by a woman who has intercourse with her father. Such women must continue the incestuous relationship to maintain their power, but their male offspring may inherit the power without continuing the incestuous relationship. This form of psychosis is easily cured by a native doctor who possesses the appropriate magic to "see" the witch and establish protective magic, as well as the requisite medications.

Erishitani is produced only by Muslims who direct "devils" (*erishitani*) to enter the body of their victim, and "like the wind, squeeze out a person's blood, leaving him mad." The symptoms are an affectlessness and mental vacuity—literally, an emptiness. It can only be cured successfully by other Muslims; Abedi attempted two such cures and failed both times.

In his diagnostic search for symptoms, Abedi never touches the patient. He observes carefully, although usually unobtrusively and he carefully questions the patient and any available kinsmen or friends. The questioning is often lengthy, involving what appears to the patient (or kinsmen) to be nothing more than an exchange of pleasantries and a concern for mutual acquaintances. In reality, it appeared that Abedi was probing carefully for an understanding of the social context of the illness.

Who might be an enemy? What is the patient fearful about? Has he had a similar problem before? Do such illnesses run in his family?

Following the period of informal conversation, Abedi initiates his formal divinatory procedures. He begins by praying to *Nguluvi* to give him the power to see the cause of the sickness and to understand what ought to be done. He then takes out his *lyang'ombe*, kisses it to imbue it with God's power, and begins to divine by means of his *bao*. The *bao* is a paddle-shaped board about 8 inches long and 3 inches wide, with a groove in which a small wooden cylinder is rubbed running diagonally along its upper surface. Abedi places the board on the ground, puts the *lyang'ombe* on its narrow end, and holds both objects down with his foot. He then sprinkles water on the groove and begins rubbing the wooden cylinder in it. As he manipulates the *bao*, he chants in a low liturgical voice interrupted from time to time by a question he addresses to the *bao*. As the water in the groove dries up, the counter moves less easily and at some point it will stick. This is taken as an affirmative answer to the last question addressed to the *bao*. As long as the counter moves freely, the answers to questions addressed to it are usually taken to be negative. In any case of illness, Abedi asks five preliminary questions: Did the patient commit adultery? Did he steal? Did he borrow money and refuse to repay it? Did he quarrel with someone? Did he actually have a fight with someone? In some instances, the answer to all the questions is negative. This indicates that the patient has become ill for no good reason and hence the cause is natural. Or, it means that effective counter magic must be made against the evil person who has performed magic or witchcraft against the patient without cause. This Abedi determines by further questions. He then asks specific questions about his ability to cure the patient, alternating "yes" and "no" questions until the *bao* answers. Finally he asks about the effectiveness of various medicines until the *bao* selects for him the medicine favored by God.

Throughout the investigations and supplications Abedi takes great care, for both he and his patient realize that the treatment of illness is dangerous, involving as it does not merely natural phenomena but such critical matters as moral magic, witchcraft, spirits, and the like. All realize that a faulty diagnosis endangers the doctor as well as the patient.

Treatment

Although Abedi's treatment routine varies somewhat depending upon the diagnosis he reaches, for almost all of the "mental illnesses" that he recognizes (*mbepo, lisaliko,* etc.), his treatment follows a prescribed course. First, the patient must be made tractable. Only a few patients are quiet enough that Abedi will begin their treatment without subjecting them to some degree of restraint. Most patients are agitated and difficult to manage, and they are either tied sitting to the center post of Abedi's office or, if treated at home, they are shackled to a bed. Next, all patients are purged. For this purpose Abedi maintains a ready supply of purgatives and emetics. The emetic is administered first; if the patient will not cooperate by swallowing the medication, a liquid preparation, his nose is held until he is compelled to swallow. If vomiting should not quickly ensue, Abedi assists by tickling the patient's throat with a feather. As soon as vomiting has taken place, a purgative is given with almost universal success within a few hours. Once purged, the patient is allowed to rest but is usually permitted only water until Abedi's specific medications have been prepared and administered.

As we have seen, Abedi's *bao* has already identified the appropriate medications, but it may take Abedi several hours, or even overnight, to prepare the prescriptions. In some cases, the necessary ingredients have already been collected, ground into powder, and stored, but in other instances Abedi must sort out the correct mixture of leaves, roots, patent medicines, and other substances before mixing them. Occasionally, he must actually go out to collect the ingredients. Some medications cannot even be selected until Abedi has gone to a crossroad (a place where village footpaths intersect or, ideally, trisect), stood naked at midnight, and used his magical powers to "see" the correct medicine (the *bao* is not involved in this form of divination). Sometimes the medication must be mixed at the crossroad as well, and in rare circumstances, the patient must ingest the medicine at the same crossing. Where selection of a medication has

proven particularly difficult, and where the cause of the psychosis has been diagnosed as witchcraft, the patient himself may be made to act as an oracle in the selection of his own medication. This is done by burning a mass of *Cannabis sativa,* covering the patient with a blanket, and forcing him to inhale the smoke for a period of an hour or more. The patient identifies the person who has bewitched him, and by answering Abedi's questions with "yes" or "no," selects an effective medicine.

Once assured that the medication of choice is known and available Abedi "cooks" it by boiling the powdered ingredients over a fire in full view of the patient and his kinsmen. Most of the resulting medications are taken as liquids, usually drunk in a glass of tea. A few medications are rubbed on the skin as ointment, others are rubbed into shallow linear incisions, and a few are inhaled. Before the medicine is actually given, Abedi offers a brief *sotto voce* prayer for the success of the medicine and spits once or three times upon the patient's head as a blessing for good luck. Doses of medicine are repeated at varying intervals until a cure is effected. Abedi accepts no payment for his treatment (except a small retainer for house calls) until such time as the patient has recovered.

An Illustrative Case

The following case is one which I was able to follow closely from its inception to its remission. A 17-year-old boy, related to a Hehe man whom I knew, was stricken with a high fever. When his fever continued for six days his parents took him to a nearby hospital for European medical care. Once in the hospital, he lay in a coma for the better part of six days, occasionally returning to consciousness with violent efforts to escape his bed and flee. He became so violent in his delirium that he was tied to his bed, but it was not until his struggles tipped the bed over that he would lie quietly. No sedatives calmed him and no diagnosis was made, although malaria was suspected. At no time was he able to speak coherently, although he did mutter to himself.

His parents complained that he was receiving inadequate care (the European medical officer was on leave) and that his condition had not improved. They took him home where he continued to be delirious. When he showed no improvement and refused food by the seventh day of treatment, his parents and his uncle asked me if I would take them to see Abedi, who was some 45 minutes away by automobile. This we did immediately. Abedi could have had no warning that we were coming, and it is difficult to believe that he knew anything about so distant a family and their sick child. After customary greetings, the sick boy's uncle said, "I want to ask you about a sick person." Abedi sat down with his *bao* and after a few minutes he announced that the person was male, about 18 years old. The uncle was suitably impressed and asked Abedi to undertake treatment. Abedi asked to see the patient, but was told that the boy could not be moved. Abedi accepted this necessity and began at once his prayer to *Nguluvi* to give him the power to see and to cure. After praying in his monotonous manner for four minutes, he began to divine, sliding the piece of wood along his *bao* while asking the routine questions.

After five minutes of divination, Abedi found an answer: the boy had been bewitched by someone in a mountainous area several miles from his home. The witch's identity could not be seen, but it was known that the boy's illness was *mbepo*, caused by eating a "medicine" which was lodged in his chest making breathing difficult, disorienting his mind, and threatening his life. When he heard this, the uncle asked that Abedi go and treat the boy without delay. Abedi said that he had made plans to be elsewhere and such a trip would be most inconvenient. The uncle then threw one shilling (14 cents) at Abedi's feet. He picked it up, committing himself to walk over 25 miles round trip.

Once this matter was settled, Abedi again consulted his *bao*, asking which of his medicines would cure the boy. The *bao* chose first the usual emetic and purgative, next, a "tranquilizer" called *ngambe* ("to cool his heart and stop his wildness"), and then another to counteract the evil "medicine." Each medication was already available in Abedi's containers so he poured out the correct amounts, perfunctorily tasting each with his tongue ("to prove that it is not a poison") before wrapping each separately in a corn husk and tying it with bark. Before leaving, Abedi again consulted his *bao*, this time to determine the order in which the medications should be given. The answers

were given quickly and the order was the standard one used with most patients.

I then offered to take everyone to see the sick boy. Abedi probably knew that I would do so on this occasion, but he must also have known that I could not be counted upon to do so on subsequent days. When we arrived, the boy lay bound to a bed. Seven days without food had left him emaciated. He stared at me, the only non-African, but did not speak. He had a massive facial tic and there was a marked tremor of his extremities. Abedi approached him without any ceremony and attempted to force the emetic past his lips. The boy struggled and moaned and it was only with assistance and by holding the boy's nose that Abedi compelled him to swallow. The purgative followed without delay. Abedi then unwrapped his second medication—the "tranquilizer"—and mixed it with water, creating a cup full of a foul-smelling, rather slimy, green liquid. Filling his mouth with this preparation, Abedi spat three times on the boy's head. Briefly reciting his prayer for healing, Abedi rubbed the remainder of the medication on the boy's head, pulling three hairs as he did so. To these three hairs he added the green paste that he next scraped off the boy's head, tying them together in a rag that was tied to the patient's wrist. Later, the same medication would be given internally, but first the patient must vomit.

While waiting for the emetic to take effect, Abedi unwrapped his third medicine, a powder to provide protection against witchcraft. It was rubbed into the boy's nostrils; it too he would later take by mouth. Although Abedi said that the emetic usually takes effect in ten minutes, this time nothing happened. Abedi and the assembled kin agreed that the boy's seven day fast was the reason for the delay. Abedi instructed everyone to wait, deciding not to tickle his throat with a feather, or to administer more of the emetic. Everyone waited quietly, sometimes leaving the room to talk in the courtyard. After two hours, the boy vomited, and all gathered around to examine the two long yellow strands of vomitus carefully. All agreed that the vomitus was unique—not mucous, not worms, nor any normal contents of the stomach. They agreed that it must be as Abedi said: the boy had vomited the "medicine" that was the source of his illness.

Abedi next gave the second and third medication by mouth, saying that the patient would sleep and that he need not be tied any longer—"his heart has been cooled." At this point, Abedi left to walk back to his office where he would see other patients. The boy slept all afternoon, awakening at about six o'clock to ask for food. He ate, to the joy of everyone, then slept quietly all night. Abedi returned each morning to see his patient and to repeat applications of the second and third medications. For two more days the boy slept and ate without speaking. On the fourth day of treatment he spoke rationally. By the eighth day he was able to leave the bed for short periods. After 15 days Abedi pronounced him cured, and the boy did indeed appear to be normal.

Abedi said, following the cure, that the original diagnosis had been incorrect (Edgerton 1969). The boy suffered from *kuhavila*, not *mbepo*, because there is no fever with *mbepo*. When asked how the *bao* could be wrong he said, "It happens sometimes." He explained further that he could have cured the boy in one day had he seen him on the initial day of illness, but that once the "medicine" had time to take effect the recovery was always protracted. The parents were said to have paid Abedi 100 shillings for his services, but I do not know how the fee was settled upon or whether it was paid in several installments.

Discussion

The foregoing case is intended to illustrate some of the typical features of Abedi's therapeutic routine, but it is also directed to the point that his therapy for "mental" illness is often, perhaps even usually, rewarded by the remission of symptoms. There are obvious reasons why this pattern of apparent remission should not be construed as a "cure." For one thing, the symptoms presented by Abedi's patients are so diverse as to challenge the therapeutic arsenal of any doctor, African or Western. What is more, while my four week study of his practice revealed striking success in the remission of symptoms, it would be naive to suppose that failures could not have been hidden from me had Abedi chosen to do so. Finally we have no way of knowing how often the symptoms would have vanished under differing treatment or with no treatment at all. We do know, however, that rapid and seemingly complete recovery from apparently psychotic

conditions has been reported from several parts of Africa. Any discussion of the efficacy of Abedi's treatment must await properly designed research of the sort begun in West Africa by Collis (1966). The purpose of this discussion is to compare Abedi's treatment routine with principles of treatment reported from other parts of Africa and to ask why his therapeutic practices have taken their particular form.

Analysts of "primitive medicine" from Ackerknecht (1943) to Frank (1961) have emphasized the role of suggestion in treatment. Recently, Kiev (1964) concluded that two universals of non-Western psychiatry were suggestion and confession. Others have expanded this list to include faith, catharsis, group support, and suggestion (Kennedy, MS). Let us examine the role of each of these in Abedi's psychiatric practice.

Faith

By faith I mean the generalized expectation on the part of the patient that treatment of the sort offered by the traditional doctor *can* be effective. These expectations are difficult to determine and research reports regarding them are generally superficial. The Hehe data are also superficial, although here at least some quantification and comparison is possible. For example, 36 of 123 Hehe respondents in a neighborhood near Abedi's office said that psychotic patients could be cured, 12 said that they could not, and 75 were unsure. This degree of expressed faith was much greater than that shown by the Pokot of Kenya or the Sebei of Uganda, but less than that indicated by the Kamba of Kenya (Edgerton 1966: 416). We can probably conclude that while the Hehe have some faith in psychiatric treatment they also maintain ample skepticism. Turning now to Abedi, who is certainly the most highly regarded doctor in this area, we see that even where his ability is concerned, a degree of what might be considered skepticism remains. For example, in the case presented earlier of serious and prolonged illness, the boy's parents were in no hurry to see a native doctor and while they had heard of Abedi's reputation, they had no blind faith in his ability. They, as did others, began their contact with Abedi by testing him—could he identify the sick boy and his illness? And all patients withhold payment until a cure has taken place (a practice which is as unusual in Africa as in the West). Thus while Hehe patients approach

Abedi with some faith in his reputation as a doctor, most enter treatment with an attitude that combines hope and doubt. For his part, Abedi does nothing to foster or require a testimonial of faith before treatment begins. Instead he is content to rely upon his treatment itself.

Catharsis

For the Hehe, as for other African peoples, catharsis through confession is a commonplace. In childbirth, as in many forms of illness, both Hehe patient and spouse or other kinsmen must confess and apologize for wrongful thoughts or acts before birth or recovery can take place (Winans and Edgerton 1964). Nevertheless, Abedi makes virtually no use of catharsis in his practice. He never asks a patient or kinsman to act out any hidden desire and only very infrequently do his questions to the *bao* elicit any sort of confession from a patient. Asked about this anomaly, Abedi said, "Talking cures nothing. Medicines cure."

Group Support

There are reports from several African societies that point to the importance of group support in the treatment of mental illness. In West Africa, for example, group support may be supplied by religious cults (Prince 1964), secret societies (Dawson 1964), or by elaborate "discharge" ceremonies that ritualize the patient's cleansing of illness, death, and rebirth into a new life (Prince 1964). Elsewhere, the patient may receive support by moving from one area and social network to another. Among the Ndembu of Northern Rhodesia, the patient's kinsmen may join with hostile persons in what amounts to group therapy, complete with catharsis and social reintegration (Turner 1964).

While Abedi permits kinsmen of his patients to be present throughout his diagnosis and treatment he does nothing to solicit group support. As with his disavowal of confession, this neglect of group concern is remarkable, for just such group support is a regular feature of childbirth and the recovery from many illnesses. As with catharsis, other Hehe doctors I knew did require that their patients undergo treatment within a larger social nexus.

Suggestion

Research on African psychiatric practice has emphasized the role that suggestion plays in treatment. For example, Prince (1964: 110), writing about the Yoruba, refers to a "continuous barrage of suggestions at all levels from the most intellectual to the most concrete and primitive." Others have attributed whatever success the African therapies may have had entirely to suggestion, noting that Africans are highly suggestible. There can be no doubt that suggestion plays an important part in Abedi's practice, and yet Abedi makes little or no use of a variety of practices widely employed in Africa to heighten suggestibility or to implant specific ideas. For example, Abedi never alters his own personality to indicate special powers, nor does he claim direct communication with supernatural powers through dissociation or possession. Neither does he employ special effects through legerdemain or ventriloquism. He makes no attempt at indirect communication by means of allegory, simile, traditional, or sacramental stories. He never gives commands, nor does he attempt to change his patient's consciousness through hypnosis, drumming, or dancing to exhaustion (cf. Whisson 1964). What is more, he utilizes none of the many versions of body contact common in Africa such as rubbing, sucking, bathing, or such stressful ones as whipping, burning, or steaming.

Kennedy (MS) and others have noted the significance of dramatic rituals and powerful symbolism in psychiatric practice in Africa and throughout the non-Western world. For example, Gelfand (1964) notes the flamboyant regalia of Shona "medicine men"; the Yoruba, Luo, and Ndembu all enact potent rituals in the service of therapy. However, Abedi's use of ritual is minimal, being confined almost entirely to a few ritual acts on the first day of treatment. Others have noted that non-Western psychiatrists rely upon settings so suffused by religious or magical symbolism that they are set apart from the ordinary world (Kennedy MS). Again, nothing could be more prosaic than the settings in which Abedi works.

Abedi's principal uses of suggestion lie in his appeals for supernatural guidance or power and in his utilization of potent medications. Although Abedi's frequent prayers for divine assistance are understated and humble, they nonetheless must serve to impress patients, as must also the divine and magical power that resides in his *lyang'ombe*. And, of course, the *bao* is an impressive divinatory device, especially when it reveals information about the patient that would seem to be inaccessible to Abedi by normal means. It is possible that Abedi maintains an "intelligence system" in the form of boys who inform him of matters relevant to actual or prospective patients, but I saw no evidence that he did so. Abedi's knowledge of magic and his occasional visits to crossroads and the like must also contribute to the supernatural aura that he is able to establish.

Probably of equal importance, however, is the placebo effect of Abedi's medications. Several of his preparations contain copper sulphate which has the impressive property of turning from blue-green to white when heated. The patients whom I watched during their first exposure to this transformation were visibly startled. Similarly, his infrequent but copious use of *Cannabis sativa* may produce impressive psychological changes, and the reliable effects of his standard emetics and purgatives must alike create in a patient a sense of the dramatic power of Abedi's medications. The resulting alteration of psychological and bodily states should produce a heightening of suggestibility. Such effects from the use of herbal remedies by African doctors have been widely noted. However, in recognizing the prominent place of suggestion in Abedi's use of drugs, we should not overlook the possibility that some of his medications possess specific psychopharmacological action that may have value in the treatment of mental illness (Gelfand 1964).

Abedi as Pharmacologist

Abedi's pharmacopoeia is extensive. In addition to emetics, purgatives, and his specific preparations for mental illness or epilepsy, he keeps on hand many drugs for gastro-intestinal disorders, as well as a variety of aphrodisiacs for men, and, for women, various drugs specific for infertility, miscarriage, menorrhagia, and the like. Most of the botanical knowledge that underlies his drugs was inherited from his father and mother, but some knowledge was purchased and some preparations were purchased ready-made (e.g., copper sulphate). I collected seven preparations said to be specific for mental illness or epilepsy. Of these, several were described by Abedi as (and were seen by me to have the apparent effect of) soporifics or

tranquilizers. Of these, the most potent was called *mwini*.

Following this lead, the botanist, Mildred Mathias, and the pharmacologist, Dermot Taylor, visited Abedi. Concentrating their collection upon plants that might affect the central nervous system, they went with Abedi while he collected the plants essential to his medications for mental illness and epilepsy. They traveled throughout the Southern Highlands Province, finding medicinal plants in all of the micro-habitats in that diverse area. In all, 37 species of plants were collected, representing 35 genera in 26 plant families. Some individual medications contained as many as 11 species of plants (Mathias 1965: 87–88).

Abedi's empirical knowledge of the botany of Hehe territory was considerable, and so was his pharmacological skill in preparing and administering these medications. For example, several of these plants contain violent emetics and purgatives which can produce death in overdose (Mathias 1965: 87). Yet, of over 120 Hehe questioned, none had heard of so much as an accusation that Abedi's medications had ever killed a patient. Recall, too, that Abedi refused to increase the standard dosage of his emetics and purgatives when they did not have an immediate effect upon the boy in the previous case. In the mixing of each medication, Abedi takes care to prepare and measure each ingredient, and he does so with the secular manner of a pharmacist, not that of a magician. Yet his preparations are not confined to the leaves and roots of plants with at least potential psychopharmacological effect. He often adds to his medicine such magical substances as the aforementioned copper sulphate, powdered rock from the sea coast, corn flour, the blood of a black cock, and the urine or powdered bones of a sheep. Abedi insists that these latter substances are as essential to certain of his medications as the plant components. In this sense, he is not without full commitment to the Hehe world of supernatural belief. But other medications contain only leaves and roots. For these, no magic in preparation, content, or administration is employed. Abedi's pharmacopoeia has its supernatural elements, but they are relatively few, and may be relatively unimportant.

Neither is there evidence that he regularly employs his medications in the manner of a charlatan. To be sure, we can point to the fact that he feels the need for copper sulphate, which he says that he regards as just another vital ingredient, and that he sometimes uses *Cannabis sativa* to evoke witchcraft accusations from his patients. But unlike doctors among the Yoruba, he does not use hallucinogenics to worsen a patient's condition simply in order to achieve a spectacular treatment success by withdrawing the toxin (Prince 1964: 118). Nor does he employ *Datura* to evoke confessions of witchcraft or to induce psychosis, although he knows of its properties, is aware that it grows in many accessible places, and knows that other "medicine men" in Tanzania, including those among the nearby Mtumbi, use it for those purposes (Lienhardt 1968: 75–76). He said, "*Datura* can cause madness but it cannot cure it." I agree with Lienhardt (1968: 74) that the medications used or sold by many a *mganga* in Tanzania are known to be useless by the so-called doctor himself. Abedi stands apart from fraud. He believes in the efficacy of his medications.

Demonstrating that Abedi is a serious empiricist about his medications is one thing; demonstrating that the medicines have any specific effect upon the central nervous system is quite another. The final word here must await complete pharmacological analysis, of course, but we might note that Abedi's treatment regimen follows that of the Yoruba of Nigeria—emetics and purgatives followed by a drug that seems to induce sleep and tranquility. For the Yoruba, this drug is *Rauwolfia*, the source of reserpine (Prince 1964: Hordern 1968). Abedi's "tranquilizing" drugs, especially the one he calls *mwini*, were observed to induce both sleep and, following sleep, tranquility. These effects may be a product of verbal suggestion, but if this is so, then the suggestion must be very subtle, for I have witnessed the use of this drug on ten occasions, and on none of these occasions could I detect any verbal suggestion that would lead to sleep or tranquility. My Hehe-speaking interpreter also failed to discover any such cues. On the other hand, this drug (and others he employs) *could* have soporific or tranquilizing effects since Abedi's pharmacopoeia included 19 alkaloid-producing plant families.

Although the pharmacological analysis of *mwini* has proven difficult in research with laboratory animals, psychopharmacological activity (some of it soporific) has been noted. The drug had a quieting effect upon mice, reducing their activity noticeably. It also doubled the barbiturate sleeping time (modern tranquilizers will increase it six or seven times). Because of difficulties in acquiring sufficient quantities of the plant and in developing techniques for the assay of this plant material, a more active fraction from the plant could not be obtained. The plant involved was *Limosella major* Diels, a member of the Scrophulariaceae. The family has not been noted for its medicinal properties.

Conclusion

In his practice as a traditional African psychiatrist, Abedi not only must, but does, live within the belief systems of his culture, and these beliefs center around the etiological and prognostic significance of magic and witchcraft. Abedi diagnoses and treats mental disorders within the constraints posed by this supernatural system, constraints that emphasize his vulnerability to danger in equal measure to that of his patients. He believes in supernatural causes of illness, and he excels in discovering and in thwarting such causes. At the same time, however, he recognizes natural causes of illness and he seeks medication that will cure, not merely impress. He has stated this conviction, and his actions have given his convictions legitimacy. Only extensive botanical and pharmacological research can determine to what extent he has succeeded in locating medications whose successes are due to specific action and not to the placebo effect. If future analyses should show that the medications have specific actions upon the central nervous system, it would be an error to conclude that such action is a fortuitous product of the more or less random collection of leaves and roots. Abedi, and other Hehe doctors before him, have believed not only in supernatural causation and treatment of illness, but also in herbal remedies.

For example, Mkwawa, the King, and members of his court, were highly pragmatic men who displayed a keen interest in innovation. Their empiricism was especially notable in regard to botany. Mkwawa imported several plants to his kingdom from other parts of East Africa, seeking not only better medicinal plants but better food sources and even superior shade trees. He also experimented with cross-breeding cattle. At the same time,

Mkwawa and his court retained their traditional beliefs in witchcraft, divination, and the like. Abedi's father, as physician to Mkwawa, was a member of this elite, among whom traditional belief in supernatural causation coexisted with an intense pragmatic interest in natural cause and effect. Years of empirical effort have yielded Abedi's pharmacopoeia and his knowledge of it. It would be surprising indeed if his medications did not possess some specific pharmacological effectiveness.

In comparison to traditional doctors in other parts of Africa, as well as among the Hehe, Abedi is notable for his secular approach to medicine. He does not reject the supernatural beliefs or practices of his culture. On the contrary, he excels in their use. But he does attempt to go beyond them by formulating principles of natural causation and by empirically discovering chemical cures. In this sense, he has transcended his culture, and such transcendance is an achievement for any man. Yet, whether Abedi's success in treating mental illness has anything to do with the pharmacological action of his drugs or not, he possesses the essential attitude of a scientist—a belief in natural causes and effects, and an empirical method of seeking out causal relationships. His story is worth recording simply because he has made the effort to find useful drugs, to continue the beginnings of science within a pre-scientific system of medicine.

There is nothing necessarily contradictory about Abedi's continuing commitment to a world of supernatural cause and effect. As Koestler (1963) has pointed out, such beliefs were very much a part of the lives of Kepler, Galileo, Newton, and others who nevertheless brought about scientific revolution. Abedi is no Newton either in intent or accomplishment, but neither is he simply a magician-herbalist. He believes that supernatural practices are necessary but not sufficient for a cure. Only medicines are sufficient, and he is devoted to the discovery of more effective chemical agents. Abedi's own words best reflect this quest: "I became a doctor to cure people. Medicines cure, nothing else works. I have some very strong medicines, but I always hope to find better ones. I would like to be able to travel to a place where roots stronger than those around here grow. My medicines cure some things. If I had stronger roots I could cure more." Abedi undoubtedly undervalues the importance of suggestion in his practice of psychiatry, just as he no doubt overvalues the efficacy of his medications. His commitment to empiricism is botanical, not psychological.

Abedi is not the first of his kind in pre-scientific societies: curare, quinine, digitalis, atropine, reserpine, and many other valuable drugs attest to that. The dominant presence of a scientific ethos does not exclude magical practices in modern Western psychiatry. This we realize all too well. We should remind ourselves that the dominance of a supernatural ethos in non-Western psychiatry does not exclude the presence of beliefs and practices that are of significance for science.

The Sorcerer and His Magic

Claude Lévi-Strauss

Lévi-Strauss, the leading exponent of the French structural school of anthropology, here analyzes the elements of the "shamanistic complex" and demonstrates by example their reliance on one another. The overall effectiveness of the sorcerer's treatment relies on the integration of his own belief in the effectiveness of his powers, the patient's belief in therapy, and the support of and faith in the shaman and his herbal and supernatural powers by members of society. An important component of the success or failure of shamans is directly related to the powerful elements of suggestion that pervade the interaction of shamans with patients and society. The marked difference between the confidence, indeed omnipotence, of the shaman, on the one hand, and the anxiety of the patient and his family, on the other, is important to the cure. So too is the sorcerer's secret knowledge of formulas, incantations, and other methods of control over supernatural agents who work at his command to help effect the cure. The final element in suggestion is the homogeneous belief system of the members of the patient's society, who reify and validate the power of the sorcerer. All these elements aid the sorcerer and demonstrate a marked difference between Western and non-Western treatment of psychophysical ailments.

SINCE THE PIONEERING WORK OF CANNON, WE understand more clearly the psycho-physiological mechanisms underlying the instances reported from many parts of the world of death by exorcism and the casting of spells. An individual who is aware that he is the object of sorcery is thoroughly convinced that he is doomed according to the most solemn traditions of his group. His friends and relatives share this certainty. From then on the community withdraws. Standing aloof from the accursed, it treats him not only as though he were already dead but as though he were a source of danger to the entire group. On every occasion and by every action, the social body suggests death to the unfortunate victim, who no longer hopes to escape what he considers to be his ineluctable fate. Shortly thereafter, sacred rites are held to dispatch him to the realm of shadows. First brutally torn from all of his family and social ties and excluded from all functions and activities through which he experienced self-awareness, then banished by the same forces from the world of the living, the victim yields to the combined effect of intense terror, the sudden total withdrawal of the multiple reference systems provided by the support of the group, and, finally, to the group's decisive reversal in proclaiming him—once a living man, with rights and obligations—dead and an object of fear, ritual, and taboo. Physical integrity cannot withstand the dissolution of the social personality.

How are these complex phenomena expressed on the physiological level? Cannon showed that fear, like rage, is associated with a particularly intense activity of the sympathetic nervous system. This activity is ordinarily useful, involving organic modifications which enable the individual to adapt himself to a new situation. But if the individual cannot avail himself of any instinctive or acquired response to an extraordinary situation (or to one which he conceives of as such), the activity of the sympathetic nervous system becomes intensified and disorganized; it may, sometimes within a few hours, lead to a decrease in the volume of blood and a concomitant drop in blood pressure, which result in irreparable damage to the circulatory organs. The rejection of food and drink, frequent among patients in the throes of intense anxiety, precipitates this process; dehydration acts as a stimulus to the sympathetic nervous system, and the decrease in blood volume is accentuated by the growing permeability of the capillary vessels. These hypotheses were confirmed by the study of several cases of trauma resulting from bombings, battle shock, and even surgical operations; death results, yet the autopsy reveals no lesions.

There is, therefore, no reason to doubt the efficacy of certain magical practices. But at the same time we see that the efficacy of magic implies a belief in magic. The latter has three complementary aspects: first, the sorcerer's belief in the effectiveness of his techniques; second, the patient's or victim's belief in the sorcerer's power; and, finally, the faith and expectations of the group, which constantly act as a sort of gravitational field within which the relationship between sorcerer and bewitched is located and defined. Obviously, none of the three parties is capable of forming a clear picture of the sympathetic nervous system's activity or of the disturbances which Cannon called homeostatic. When the sorcerer claims to suck out of the patient's body a foreign object whose presence would explain the illness and produces a stone which he had previously hidden in his mouth, how does he justify this procedure in his own eyes? How can an innocent person accused of sorcery prove his innocence if the accusation is unanimous—since the magical situation is a consensual phenomenon? And, finally, how much credulity and how much skepticism are involved in the attitude of the group toward those in whom it recognizes extraordinary powers, to whom it accords corresponding privileges, but from whom it also requires adequate satisfaction? Let us begin by examining this last point.

It was in September, 1938. For several weeks we had been camping with a small band of Nambicuara Indians near the headwaters of the Tapajoz, in those desolate savannas of central Brazil

where the natives wander during the greater part of the year, collecting seeds and wild fruits, hunting small mammals, insects, and reptiles, and whatever else might prevent them from dying of starvation. Thirty of them were camped together there, quite by chance. They were grouped in families under frail lean-tos of branches, which give scant protection from the scorching sun, nocturnal chill, rain, and wind. Like most bands, this one had both a secular chief and a sorcerer; the latter's daily activities—hunting, fishing, and handicrafts—were in no way different from those of the other men of the group. He was a robust man, about forty-five years old, and a *bon vivant*.

One evening, however, he did not return to camp at the usual time. Night fell and fires were lit; the natives were visibly worried. Countless perils lurk in the bush: torrential rivers, the somewhat improbable danger of encountering a large wild beast—jaguar or anteater—or, more readily pictured by the Nambicuara, an apparently harmless animal which is the incarnation of an evil spirit of the waters or forest. And above all, each night for the past week we had seen mysterious campfires, which sometimes approached and sometimes receded from our own. Any unknown band is always potentially hostile. After a two-hour wait, the natives were convinced that their companion had been killed in ambush and, while his two young wives and his son wept noisily in mourning for their dead husband and father, the other natives discussed the tragic consequences, foreshadowed by the disappearance of their sorcerer.

Toward ten that evening, the anguished anticipation of imminent disaster, the lamentations in which the other women began to join, and the agitation of the men had created an intolerable atmosphere, and we decided to reconnoiter with several natives who had remained relatively calm. We had not gone two hundred yards when we stumbled upon a motionless figure. It was our man, crouching silently, shivering in the chilly night air, disheveled and without his belt, necklaces, and arm-bands (the Nambicuara wear nothing else). He allowed us to lead him back to the camp site without resistance, but only after long exhortations by his group and pleading by his family was he persuaded to talk. Finally, bit by bit, we extracted the details of his story. A thunderstorm, the first of the season, had burst during the afternoon, and the thunder had carried him off to a site several miles distant, which he named, and then, after stripping him completely, had brought him back to the spot where we found him. Everyone went off to sleep commenting on the event. The next day the thunder victim had recovered his joviality and, what is more, all his ornaments. This last detail did not appear to surprise anyone, and life resumed its normal course.

A few days later, however, another version of these prodigious events began to be circulated by certain natives. We must note that this band was actually composed of individuals of different origins and had been fused into a new social entity as a result of unknown circumstances. One of the groups had been decimated by an epidemic several years before and was no longer sufficiently large to lead an independent life; the other had seceded from its original tribe and found itself in the same straits. When and under what circumstances the two groups met and decided to unite their efforts, we could not discover. The secular leader of the new band came from one group and the sorcerer, or religious leader, from the other. The fusion was obviously recent, for no marriage had yet taken place between the two groups when we met them, although the children of one were usually betrothed to the children of the other; each group had retained its own dialect, and their members could communicate only through two or three bilingual natives.

This is the rumor that was spread. There was good reason to suppose that the unknown bands crossing the savanna belonged to the tribe of the seceded group of which the sorcerer was a member. The sorcerer, impinging on the functions of his colleague the political chief, had doubtless wanted to contact his former tribesmen, perhaps to ask to return to the fold, or to provoke an attack upon his new companions, or perhaps even to reassure them of the friendly intentions of the latter. In any case, the sorcerer had needed a pretext for his absence, and his kidnapping by thunder and its subsequent staging were invented toward this end. It was, of course, the natives of the other group who spread this interpretation, which they secretly believed and which filled them with apprehension. But the official version was never publicly disputed, and until we left, shortly after the incident, it remained ostensibly accepted by all.

Although the skeptics had analyzed the sorcerer's motives with great psychological finesse and political acumen, they would have been greatly astonished had someone suggested (quite plausibly) that the incident was a hoax which cast doubt upon the sorcerer's good faith and competence. He had probably not flown on the wings of thunder to the Rio Ananaz and had only staged an act. But these things might have happened, they had certainly happened in other circumstances, and they belonged to the realm of real experience. Certainly the sorcerer maintains an intimate relationship with the forces of the supernatural. The idea that in a particular case he had used his power to conceal a secular activity belongs to the realm of conjecture and provides an opportunity for critical judgment. The important point is that these two possibilities were not mutually exclusive; no more than are, for us, the alternate interpretations of war as the dying gasp of national independence or as the result of the schemes of munitions manufacturers. The two explanations are logically incompatible, but we admit that one or the other may be true; since they are equally plausible, we easily make the transition from one to the other, depending on the occasion and the moment. Many people have both explanations in the back of their minds.

Whatever their true origin, these divergent interpretations come from individual consciousness not as the result of objective analysis but rather as complementary ideas resulting from hazy and unelaborated attitudes which have an experiential character for each of us. These experiences, however, remain intellectually diffuse and emotionally intolerable unless they incorporate one or another of the patterns present in the group's culture. The assimilation of such patterns is the only means of objectivizing subjective states, of formulating inexpressible feelings, and of integrating inarticulated experiences into a system.

These mechanisms become clearer in the light of some observations made many years ago among the Zuni of New Mexico by an admirable fieldworker, M. C. Stevenson. A twelve-year-old girl was stricken with a nervous seizure directly after an adolescent boy had seized her hands. The youth was accused of sorcery and dragged before the court of the Bow priesthood. For an hour he denied having any knowledge of occult power, but this defense proved futile. Because the crime of sorcery was at that time still punished by death among the Zuni, the accused changed his tactics. He improvised a tale explaining the circumstances by which he had been initiated into sorcery. He said he had received two substances from his teachers, one which drove girls insane and another which cured them. This point constituted an ingenious precaution against later developments. Having been ordered to produce his medicines, he went home under guard and came back with two roots, which he proceeded to use in a complicated ritual. He simulated a trance after taking one of the drugs, and after taking the other he pretended to return to his normal state. Then he administered the remedy to the sick girl and declared her cured. The session was adjourned until the following day, but during the night the alleged sorcerer escaped. He was soon captured, and the girl's family set itself up as a court and continued the trial. Faced with the reluctance of his new judges to accept his first story, the boy then invented a new one. He told them that all his relatives and ancestors had been witches and that he had received marvelous powers from them. He claimed that he could assume the form of a cat, fill his mouth with cactus needles, and kill his victims—two infants, three girls, and two boys—by shooting the needles into them. These feats, he claimed, were due to the magical powers of certain plumes which were used to change him and his family into shapes other than human. This last detail was a tactical error, for the judges called upon him to produce the plumes as proof of his new story. He gave various excuses which were rejected one after another, and he was forced to take his judges to his house. He began by declaring that the plumes were secreted in a wall that he could not destroy. He was commanded to go to work. After breaking down a section of the wall and carefully examining the plaster, he tried to excuse himself by declaring that the plumes had been hidden two years before and that he could not remember their exact location. Forced to search again, he tried another wall, and after another hour's work, an old plume appeared in the plaster. He grabbed it eagerly and presented it to his persecutors as the magic device of which he had spoken. He was then made to explain the details of its use. Finally, dragged into the public plaza, he had to repeat his entire story (to which

he added a wealth of new detail). He finished it with a pathetic speech in which he lamented the loss of his supernatural power. Thus reassured, his listeners agreed to free him.

This narrative, which we unfortunately had to abridge and strip of all its psychological nuances, is still instructive in many respects. First of all, we see that the boy tried for witchcraft, for which he risks the death penalty, wins his acquittal not by denying but by admitting his alleged crime. Moreover, he furthers his cause by presenting successive versions, each richer in detail (and thus, in theory, more persuasive of guilt) than the preceding one. The debate does not proceed, as do debates among us, by accusations and denials, but rather by allegations and specifications. The judges do not expect the accused to challenge their theory, much less to refute the facts. Rather, they require him to validate a system of which they possess only a fragment; he must reconstruct it as a whole in an appropriate way. As the field-worker noted in relation to a phase of the trial, "The warriors had become so absorbed by their interest in the narrative of the boy that they seemed entirely to have forgotten the cause of his appearance before them." And when the magic plume was finally uncovered, the author remarks with great insight, "There was consternation among the warriors, who exclaimed in one voice: 'What does this mean?' Now they felt assured that the youth had spoken the truth." Consternation, and not triumph at finding a tangible proof of the crime—for the judges had sought to bear witness to the reality of the system which had made the crime possible (by validating its objective basis through an appropriate emotional expression), rather than simply to punish a crime. By his confession, the defendant is transformed into a witness for the prosecution, with the participation (and even the complicity) of his judges. Through the defendant, witchcraft and the ideas associated with it cease to exist as a diffuse complex of poorly formulated sentiments and representations and become embodied in real experience. The defendant, who serves as a witness, gives the group the satisfaction of truth, which is infinitely greater and richer than the satisfaction of justice that would have been achieved by his execution. And finally, by his ingenious defense which makes his hearers progressively aware of the vitality offered by his corroboration of their system (especially since the choice is not between this system and another, but between the magical system and no system at all—that is, chaos), the youth, who at first was a threat to the physical security of his group, became the guardian of its spiritual coherence.

But is his defense merely ingenious? Everything leads us to believe that after groping for a subterfuge, the defendant participates with sincerity and —the word is not too strong—fervor in the drama enacted between him and his judges. He is proclaimed a sorcerer; since sorcerers do exist, he might well be one. And how would he know beforehand the signs which might reveal his calling to him? Perhaps the signs are there, present in this ordeal and in the convulsions of the litle girl brought before the court. For the boy, too, the coherence of the system and the role assigned to him in preserving it are values no less essential than the personal security which he risks in the venture. Thus we see him, with a mixture of cunning and good faith, progressively construct the impersonation which is thrust upon him—chiefly by drawing on his knowledge and his memories, improvising somewhat, but above all living his role and seeking, through his manipulations and the ritual he builds from bits and pieces, the experience of a calling which is, at least theoretically, open to all. At the end of the adventure, what remains of his earlier hoaxes? To what extent has the hero become the dupe of his own impersonation? What is more, has he not truly become a sorcerer? We are told that in his final confession, "The longer the boy talked the more absorbed he became in his subject. . . . At times his face became radiant with satisfaction at his power over his listeners." The girl recovers after he performs his curing ritual. The boy's experiences during the extraordinary ordeal become elaborated and structured. Little more is needed than for the innocent boy finally to confess to the possession of supernatural powers that are already recognized by the group.

We must consider at greater length another especially valuable document, which until now seems to have been valued solely for its linguistic interest. I refer to a fragment of the autobiography of a Kwakiutl Indian from the Vancouver region of Canada, obtained by Franz Boas.

Quesalid (for this was the name he received when he became a sorcerer) did not believe in the power of the sorcerers—or, more accurately, shamans, since this is a better term for their specific type of activity in certain regions of the world. Driven by curiosity about their tricks and by the desire to expose them, he began to associate with the shamans until one of them offered to make him a member of their group. Quesalid did not wait to be asked twice, and his narrative recounts the details of his first lessons. a curious mixture of pantomime, prestidigitation, and empirical knowledge, including the art of simulating fainting and nervous fits, the learning of sacred songs, the technique for inducing vomiting, rather precise notions of auscultation and obstetrics, and the use of "dreamers," that is, spies who listen to private conversations and secretly convey to the shaman bits of information concerning the origins and symptoms of the ills suffered by different people. Above all, he learned the *ars magna* of one of the shamanistic schools of the Northwest Coast: The shaman hides a little tuft of down in the corner of his mouth, and he throws it up, covered with blood, at the proper moment—after having bitten his tongue or made his gums bleed—and solemnly presents it to his patient and the onlookers as the pathological foreign body extracted as a result of his sucking and manipulations.

His worst suspicions confirmed, Quesalid wanted to continue his inquiry. But he was no longer free. His apprenticeship among the shamans began to be noised about, and one day he was summoned by the family of a sick person who had dreamed of Quesalid as his healer. This first treatment (for which he received no payment, any more than he did for those which followed, since he had not completed the required four years of apprenticeship) was an outstanding success. Although Quesalid came to be known from that moment on as a "great shaman," he did not lose his critical faculties. He interpreted his success in psychological terms—it was successful "because he [the sick person] believed strongly in his dream about me." A more complex adventure made him, in his own words, "hesitant and thinking about many things." Here he encountered several varieties of a "false supernatural," and was led to conclude that some forms were less false than others—those, of course, in which he had a personal stake and whose system he was, at the same time, surreptitiously building up in his mind. A summary of the adventure follows.

While visiting the neighboring Koskimo Indians, Quesalid attends a curing ceremony of his illustrious colleagues of the other tribe. To his great astonishment he observes a difference in their technique. Instead of spitting out the illness in the form of a "bloody worm" (the concealed down), the Koskimo shamans merely spit a little saliva into their hands, and they dare to claim that this is "the sickness." What is the value of this method? What is the theory behind it? In order to find out "the strength of the shamans, whether it was real or whether they only pretended to be shamans" like his fellow tribesmen, Quesalid requests and obtains permission to try his method in an instance where the Koskimo method has failed. The sick woman then declares herself cured.

And here our hero vacillates for the first time. Though he had few illusions about his own technique, he has now found one which is more false, more mystifying, and more dishonest than his own. For he at least gives his clients something. He presents them with their sickness in a visible and tangible form, while his foreign colleagues show nothing at all and only claim to have captured the sickness. Moreover, Quesalid's methods gets results, while the other is futile. Thus our hero grapples with a problem which perhaps has its parallel in the development of modern science. Two systems which we know to be inadequate present (with respect to each other) a differential validity, from both a logical and an empirical perspective. From which frame of reference shall we judge them? On the level of fact, where they merge, or on their own level, where they take on different values, both theoretically and empirically?

Meanwhile, the Koskimo shamans, "ashamed" and discredited before their tribesmen, are also plunged into doubt. Their colleague has produced, in the form of a material object, the illness which they had always considered as spiritual in nature and had thus never dreamed of rendering visible. They send Quesalid an emissary to invite him to a secret meeting in a cave. Quesalid goes and his foreign colleagues expound their system to him: "Every sickness is a man: boils and swellings, and itch and scabs, and pimples and coughs and con-

sumption and scrofula; and also this, stricture of the bladder and stomach aches. . . . As soon as we get the soul of the sickness which is a man, then dies the sickness which is a man. Its body just disappears in our insides." If this theory is correct, what is there to show? And why, when Quesalid operates, does "the sickness stick to his hand"? But Quesalid takes refuge behind professional rules which forbid him to teach before completing four years of apprenticeship, and refuses to speak. He maintains his silence even when the Koskimo shamans send him their allegedly virgin daughters to try to seduce him and discover his secret.

Thereupon Quesalid returns to his village at Fort Rupert. He learns that the most reputed shaman of a neighboring clan, worried about Quesalid's growing renown, has challenged all his colleagues, inviting them to compete with him in curing several patients. Quesalid comes to the contest and observes the cures of his elder. Like the Koskimo, this shaman does not show the illness. He simply incorporates an invisible object, "what he called the sickness" into his head-ring, made of bark, or into his bird-shaped ritual rattle. These objects can hang suspended in mid-air, owing to the power of the illness which "bites" the house-posts or the shaman's hand. The usual drama unfolds. Quesalid is asked to intervene in cases judged hopeless by his predecessor, and he triumphs with his technique of the bloody worm.

Here we come to the truly pathetic part of the story. The old shaman, ashamed and despairing because of the ill-repute into which he has fallen and by the collapse of his therapeutic technique, sends his daughter to Quesalid to beg him for an interview. The latter finds his colleague sitting under a tree and the old shaman begins thus: "It won't be bad what we say to each other, friend, but only I wish you to try and save my life for me, so that I may not die of shame, for I am a plaything of our people on account of what you did last night. I pray you to have mercy and tell me what stuck on the palm of your hand last night. Was it the true sickness or was it only made up? For I beg you have mercy and tell me about the way you did it so that I can imitate you. Pity me, friend."

Silent at first, Quesalid begins by calling for explanations about the feats of the head-ring and the rattle. His colleague shows him the nail hidden in the head-ring which he can press at right angles into the post, and the way in which he tucks the head of his rattle between his finger joints to make it look as if the bird were hanging by its beak from his hand. He himself probably does nothing but lie and fake, simulating shamanism for material gain, for he admits to being "covetous for the property of the sick men." He knows that shamans cannot catch souls, "for . . . we all own a soul"; so he resorts to using tallow and pretends that "it is a soul . . . that white thing . . . sitting on my hand." The daughter then adds her entreaties to those of her father: "Do have mercy that he may live." But Quesalid remains silent. That very night, following this tragic conversation, the shaman disappears with his entire family, heartsick and feared by the community, who think that he may be tempted to take revenge. Needless fears: He returned a year later, but both he and his daughter had gone mad. Three years later, he died.

And Quesalid, rich in secrets, pursued his career, exposing the impostors and full of contempt for the profession. "Only one shaman was seen by me, who sucked at a sick man and I never found out whether he was a real shaman or only made up. Only for this reason I believe that he is a shaman; he does not allow those who are made well to pay him. I truly never once saw him laugh." Thus his original attitude has changed considerably. The radical negativism of the free thinker has given way to more moderate feelings. Real shamans do exist. And what about him? At the end of the narrative we cannot tell, but it is evident that he carries on his craft conscientiously, takes pride in his achievements, and warmly defends the technique of the bloody down against all rival schools. He seems to have completely lost sight of the fallaciousness of the technique which he had so disparaged at the beginning.

We see that the psychology of the sorcerer is not simple. In order to analyze it, we shall first examine the case of the old shaman who begs his young rival to tell him the truth—whether the illness glued in the palm of his hand like a sticky red worm is real or made up—and who goes mad when he receives no answer. Before the tragedy, he was fully convinced of two things—first, that pathological conditions have a cause which may be discovered and second, that a system of interpretation in which personal inventiveness is important

structures the phases of the illness, from the diagnosis to the cure. This fabulation of a reality unknown in itself—a fabulation consisting of procedures and representations—is founded on a threefold experience: first, that of the shaman himself, who, if his calling is a true one (and even if it is not, simply by virtue of his practicing it), undergoes specific states of a psychosomatic nature; second, that of the sick person, who may or may not experience an improvement of his condition; and, finally, that of the public, who also participate in the cure, experiencing an enthusiasm and an intellectual and emotional satisfaction which produce collective support, which in turn inaugurates a new cycle.

These three elements of what we might call the "shamanistic complex" cannot be separated. But they are clustered around two poles, one formed by the intimate experience of the shaman and the other by group consensus. There is no reason to doubt that sorcerers, or at least the more sincere among them, believe in their calling and that this belief is founded on the experiencing of specific states. The hardships and privations which they undergo would often be sufficient in themselves to provoke these states, even if we refuse to admit them as proof of a serious and fervent calling. But there is also linguistic evidence which, because it is indirect, is more convincing. In the Wintu dialect of California, there are five verbal classes which correspond to knowledge by sight, by bodily experience, by inference, by reasoning, and by hearsay. All five make up the category of knowledge as opposed to conjecture, which is differently expressed. Curiously enough, relationships with the supernatural world are expressed by means of the modes of knowledge—by bodily impression (that is, the most intuitive kind of experience), by inference, and by reasoning. Thus the native who becomes a shaman after a spiritual crisis conceives of his state grammatically, as a consequence to be inferred from the fact—formulated as real experience—that he has received divine guidance. From the latter he concludes deductively that he must have been on a journey to the beyond, at the end of which he found himself—again, an immediate experience—once more among his people.

The experiences of the sick person represent the least important aspect of the system, except for the fact that a patient successfully treated by a shaman

is in an especially good position to become a shaman in his own right, as we see today in the case
of psychoanalysis. In any event, we must remember that the shaman does not completely lack empirical knowledge and experimental techniques,
which may in part explain his success. Furthermore, disorders of the type currently termed psychosomatic, which constitute a large part of the
illnesses prevalent in societies with a low degree of
security, probably often yield to psychotherapy. At
any rate, it seems probable that medicine men, like
their civilized colleagues, cure at least some of the
cases they treat and that without this relative success magical practices could not have been so
widely diffused in time and space. But this point is
not fundamental; it is subordinate to the other
two. Quesalid did not become a great shaman because he cured his patients; he cured his patients
because he had become a great shaman. Thus we
have reached the other—that is, the collective—
pole of our system.

The true reason for the defeat of Quesalid's rivals must then be sought in the attitude of the
group rather than in the pattern of the rivals' successes and failures. The rivals themselves emphasize this when they confess their shame at having
become the laughingstock of the group; this is a
social sentiment *par excellence.* Failure is secondary,
and we see in all their statements that they consider it a function of another phenomenon, which
is the disappearance of the *social consensus,* re-
created at their expense around another practitioner and another system of curing. Consequently, the fundamental problem revolves
around the relationship between the individual
and the group, or, more accurately, the relationship between a specific category of individuals and
specific expectations of the group.

In treating his patient the shaman also offers his
audience a performance. What is this performance? Risking a rash generalization on the basis
of a few observations, we shall say that it always
involves the shaman's enactment of the "call," or
the initial crisis which brought him the revelation
of his condition. But we must not be deceived by
the word *performance.* The shaman does not limit
himself to reproducing or miming certain events.
He actually relives them in all their vividness,
originality, and violence. And since he returns to
his normal state at the end of the séance, we may

say, borrowing a key term from psychoanalysis,
that he *abreacts.* In psychoanalysis, abreaction refers to the decisive moment in the treatment when
the patient intensively relives the initial situation
from which his disturbance stems, before he ultimately overcomes it. In this sense, the shaman is a
professional abreactor.

We have set forth elsewhere the theoretical hypotheses that might be formulated in order for us
to accept the idea that the type of abreaction specific to each shaman—or, at any rate, to each shamanistic school—might symbolically induce an
abreaction of his own disturbance in each patient.
In any case, if the relationship is that between the
shaman and the group, we must also state the
question from another point of view—that of the
relationship between normal and pathological
thinking. From any non-scientific perspective (and
here we can exclude no society), pathological and
normal thought processes are complementary
rather than opposed. In a universe which it strives
to understand but whose dynamics it cannot fully
control, normal thought continually seeks the
meaning of things which refuse to reveal their significance. So-called pathological thought, on the
other hand, overflows with emotional interpretations and overtones, in order to supplement an
otherwise deficient reality. For normal thinking
there exists something which cannot be empirically
verified and is, therefore, "claimable." For pathological thinking there exist experiences without object, or something "available." We might borrow
from linguistics and say that so-called normal
thought always suffers from a deficit of meaning,
whereas so-called pathological thought (in at least
some of its manifestations) disposes of a plethora
of meaning. Through collective participation in
shamanistic curing, a balance is established between these two complementary situations. Normal thought cannot fathom the problem of illness,
and so the group calls upon the neurotic to furnish
a wealth of emotion heretofore lacking a focus.

An equilibrium is reached between what might
be called supply and demand on the psychic level
—but only on two conditions. First, a structure
must be elaborated and continually modified
through the interaction of group tradition and individual invention. This structure is a system of oppositions and correlations, integrating all the
elements of a total situation, in which sorcerer, pa-

tient, and audience, as well as representations and procedures, all play their parts. Furthermore, the public must participate in the abreaction, to a certain extent at least, along with the patient and the sorcerer. It is this vital experience of a universe of symbolic effusions which the patient, because he is ill, and the sorcerer, because he is neurotic—in other words, both having types of experience which cannot otherwise be integrated—allow the public to glimpse as "fireworks" from a safe distance. In the absence of any experimental control, which is indeed unnecessary, it is this experience alone, and its relative richness in each case, which makes possible a choice between several systems and elicits adherence to a particular school or practitioner.

In contrast with scientific explanation, the problem here is not to attribute confused and disorganized states, emotions, or representations to an objective cause, but rather to articulate them into a whole or system. The system is valid precisely to the extent that it allows the coalescence or precipitation of these diffuse states, whose discontinuity also makes them painful. To the conscious mind, this last phenomenon constitutes an original experience which cannot be grasped from without. Because of their complementary disorders, the sorcerer-patient dyad incarnates for the group, in vivid and concrete fashion, an antagonism that is inherent in all thought but that normally remains vague and imprecise. The patient is all passivity and self-alienation, just as inexpressibility is the disease of the mind. The sorcerer is activity and self-projection, just as affectivity is the source of symbolism. The cure interrelates these opposite poles, facilitating the transition from one to the other, and demonstrates, within a total experience, the coherence of the psychic universe, itself a projection of the social universe.

Thus it is necessary to extend the notion of abreaction by examining the meanings it acquires in psychotherapies other than psychoanalysis, although the latter deserves the credit for rediscovering and insisting upon its fundamental validity. It may be objected that in psychoanalysis there is only one abreaction, the patient's, rather than three. We are not so sure of this. It is true that in the shamanistic cure the sorcerer speaks and abreacts *for* the silent patient, while in psychoanalysis it is the patient who talks and abreacts *against* the listening therapist. But the therapist's abreaction, while not concomitant with the patient's, is nonetheless required, since he must be analyzed before he himself can become an analyst. It is more difficult to define the role ascribed to the group by each technique. Magic readapts the group predefined problems through the patient, while psychoanalysis readapts the patient to the group by means of the solutions reached. But the distressing trend which, for several years, has tended to transform the psychoanalytic system from a body of scientific hypotheses that are experimentally verifiable in certain specific and limited cases into a kind of diffuse mythology interpenetrating the consciousness of the group, could rapidly bring about a parallelism. (This group consciousness is an objective phenomenon, which the psychologist expresses through a subjective tendency to extend to normal thought a system of interpretations conceived for pathological thought and to apply to facts of collective psychology a method adapted solely to the study of individual psychology.) When this happens—and perhaps it already has in certain countries—the value of the system will no longer be based upon real cures from which certain individuals can benefit, but on the sense of security that the group receives from the myth underlying the cure and from the popular system upon which the group's universe is reconstructed.

Even at the present time, the comparison between psychoanalysis and older and more widespread psychological therapies can encourage the former to re-examine its principles and methods. By continuously expanding the recruitment of its patients, who began as clearly characterized abnormal individuals and gradually become representative of the group, psychoanalysis, transforms its treatments into conversions. For only a patient can emerge cured; an unstable or maladjusted individual can only be persuaded. A considerable danger thus arises: The treatment (unbeknown to the therapist, naturally), far from leading to the resolution of a specific disturbance within its own context, is reduced to the reorganization of the patient's universe in terms of psychoanalytic interpretations. This means that we would finally arrive at precisely that situation which furnishes the point of departure as well as the theoretical validity of the magico-social system that we have analyzed.

If this analysis is correct, we must see magical behavior as the response to a situation which is revealed to the mind through emotional manifestations, but whose essence is intellectual. For only the history of the symbolic function can allow us to understand the intellectual condition of man, in which the universe is never charged with sufficient meaning and in which the mind always has more meanings available than there are objects to which to relate them. Torn between these two systems of reference—the signifying and the signified—man asks magical thinking to provide him with a new system of reference, within which the thus-far contradictory elements can be integrated. But we know that this system is built at the expense of the progress of knowledge, which would have required us to retain only one of the two previous systems and to refine it to the point where it absorbed the other. This point is still far off. We must not permit the individual, whether normal or neurotic, to repeat this collective misadventure. The study of the mentally sick individual has shown us that all persons are more or less oriented toward contradictory systems and suffer from the resulting conflict; but the fact that a certain form of integration is possible and effective practically is not enough to make it true, or to make us certain that the adaptation thus achieved does not constitute an absolute regression in relation to the previous conflict situation.

The reabsorption of a deviant specific synthesis, through its integration with the normal syntheses, into a general but arbitrary synthesis (aside from critical cases where action is required) would represent a loss on all fronts. A body of elementary hypotheses can have a certain instrumental value for the practitioner without necessarily being recognized, in theoretical analysis, as the final image of reality and without necessarily linking the patient and the therapist in a kind of mystical communion which does not have the same meaning for both parties and which only ends by reducing the treatment to a fabulation.

In the final analysis we could only expect this fabulation to be a language, whose function is to provide a socially authorized translation of phenomena whose deeper nature would become once again equally impenetrable to the group, the patient, and the healer.

Witchcraft Practices and Psychocultural Therapy with Urban U.S. Families

Madeleine Leininger

In Chapter 5, it was pointed out that in the last few decades there has been a rise in witchcraft and its related behavior in the United States. Leininger observes in the following article that witchcraft victims are being admitted to clinics and hospitals staffed by professionals who may not be aware of witchcraft behavior, beliefs, and practices. With the goal of helping victims, Leininger presents a theoretical framework based on empirical data regarding witchcraft behavior and its function in selected urban families in the United States. Showing her anthropological perspective, Leininger views witchcraft as an expression of psychological, socio-cultural stresses that can be understood only in the victim's own cultural context.

Reprinted from *Human Organization*, Vol. 32, no. 1 (1973), pp. 73–83, by permission of the author and the American Anthropological Association.

WITCHCRAFT, A PSYCHOCULTURAL AND SOCIAL interactional phenomenon, continues to hold the interest of cultural anthropologists, humanists, and many lay persons. Until recently in this country, witchcraft has been a fairly taboo topic and has not been discussed in an open manner in public educational and service institutions. For many health professionals, witchcraft is a new and intriguing subject and they have a limited understanding of its nature and dynamic process. Many persons in our society characterize witchcraft as demon possession, superstition, antireligious, nonscientific, and as a mystical power over human and supernatural phenomena. Some persons find the idea of witchcraft very frightening, others find it amusing, and still others remain sufficiently intrigued to explore the phenomenon with an open-minded attitude.

In recent years, adolescents, religious groups, and individuals interested in mysticism, astrology, and transcendental media have shown increased interest in witchcraft. As a consequence, magazine and newspaper articles, television and radio programs, and film productions have provided information about witchcraft. In addition, educational institutions have offered special courses, group discussions, and public sessions on witchcraft. Thus witchcraft has become a more common and open topic of public discourse than it was a decade ago. Furthermore, witchcraft has generated sufficient interest in several settings to become a topic for systematic investigation.

In this paper, witchcraft refers to the psychocultural and sociological process by which an individual and group(s) subtly and skillfully influence the behavior of others primarily in a harmful way, but there is also evidence of *posi-*

tive secondary consequences which may alleviate life stresses for the persons involved in witchcraft. In general, witchcraft is viewed as a malevolent phenomenon and as a situational misfortune to cope with psychocultural problems and social stresses. Witchcraft practices have been generally characterized as involving mysterious actions, the use of impersonal powers, reliance upon supernatural beliefs, and the use of symbolic modes of communication to affect the behavior of others in a harmful way. From a structural-functional analysis, however, social scientists have also identified some *positive* functions or consequences related to witchcraft practices.

For several decades, Kluckhohn (1944), Nadel (1952), Evans-Pritchard (1937), and other anthropologists have studied witchcraft behavior in Western and non-Western societies and have presented theoretical interpretations and descriptive accounts of witchcraft from cultural, psychological, and social viewpoints. Anthropological findings and explanations of witchcraft have been the primary source for understanding witchcraft, especially in non-Western societies. There is, however, an urgent need to study and understand the prevalence of witchcraft in modern American society, giving fresh thought to the psychocultural forces and changing social structure features which influence the development of witchcraft. Accordingly, efforts should be made to use these insights to help anxiety-ridden witchcraft victims and their families and to make known the means by which therapists can help them. The purpose of this paper is, therefore, to make a modest contribution toward these latter efforts.

Contrary to popular belief, witchcraft is *not* a unique behavior phenomenon restricted to primitive, nontechnological, or non-Western societies. Forms and processes of witchcraft continue to be found in highly developed and technological cultures such as that of the United States. Moreover, witchcraft practices and victims have been reported recently in almost every part of the United States in mental health clinics, general hospitals, community health agencies, educational institutions, and in social gatherings. Unfortunately, statistical data on precise witchcraft occurrences are not available; however, the author received reports of nearly 200 witchcraft cases in a three-year period through her work with and interest in witchcraft

victims. Since witchcraft is generally a highly secretive ingroup experience, and because victims fear that witchcraft may not be accepted by professional health workers, it often goes undetected and unreported.

The author contends that there may be several significant reasons for the increased interest in and prevalence of witchcraft. First, the very rapid movement in this country over a short period of time to reduce inequities and to provide equal rights and opportunities for all ethnic, cultural, and social groups has produced tensions and a fertile climate for witchcraft accusations. Signs of unrest and distrust and challenges between and among different groups who may have never interacted with one another until recently are evident.

Second, there has been a heightened interest and involvement in extrasensory perceptual experiences, transcendental media, and other forms of special psychic experiences, particularly by adolescents. These youths have also been actively involved in the use of a wide variety of drugs and other stimuli in an attempt to obtain special psychophysiological "release experiences" to assuage current societal problems and stresses.

Third, there is evidence of an increased use of secretive and highly symbolic forms of communication in order to relate differently and intimately with humans, superhumans, animals, and nature. The use of special modes, mediums, and seemingly strange forms of communication provides the climate for witchcraft practices which are secretive, mystical, and symbolic in form and function.

Fourth, in recent years there has been a marked increase in a belief in astrology as a guide for one's actions and thought patterns. Many people today will not leave their homes or begin a day's work without checking their horoscope reading. This reading often provides a perceptual set and a psychosocial guide for one's thinking and action. Witchcraft behavior is frequently linked with horoscope readings and astrological predictions, especially with predictions of what forces may cause a witchcraft victim harm.

Fifth, there is also an increase in the use of magical explanations by people who are nonscientifically disposed to explain unusual and unknown scientific findings. Undoubtedly, these magical explanations have arisen because of the tremendous gap in understanding highly scientific and technological data and they are used to cognitively bridge two different perceptual worlds, namely, the highly scientific and the nonscientific. Supernatural and mystical explanations are important means to reduce conceptual incongruencies and to understand complex phenomena and the many unknowns in our society.

Sixth, many youths today are actively seeking and testing what is "real" and "not real," and in so doing, they may test witchcraft spells and incantations with their peers. The youth are faced with trying to understand divergent cultural norms, and conflicts in value systems, and witchcraft practices are used to test such value orientations and to make life more congruent with one's interests and identity.

Finally, witchcraft practices may be increasing in our society in order to cope with problems related to acculturational stresses which may be exceedingly troublesome for some individuals and groups. The necessity for rapid and sudden adjustments to groups with different life styles is producing obvious psychocultural stresses on various groups. Witchcraft behavior, as discussed in this paper, reveals the psychocultural struggle of certain groups to adjust to rural-urban acculturational situations.

Theoretical Framework and Empirical Phases

Using a theoretical framework which was inductively developed through direct participant-observation experiences with witchcraft victims, the author focused primarily upon Spanish-speaking (Spanish and Mexican-Americans) families and a few Anglo-American students attending college in a large univesity setting in the United States. In the process of providing therapy to four of the Spanish-speaking families and two Anglo-American families as well as observing and studying 40 additional Spanish-speaking families (the latter without being involved in therapy), the author developed the following theoretical formulation which was used as a guide for helping the bewitched victim and his family.

Witchcraft behavior reflects the process by which some individuals and groups experience psychocultural and social stresses which arise within a designated primary group (to be referred to as the ingroup). Later, these stresses are perceptually and cognitively displaced to a secondary group (to be referred to as the outgroup) which the primary group has known for some time. Figure 1 depicts this conceptual framework with the three phases which will be discussed shortly. Throughout this paper, the terms "ingroup" and "outgroup" are used in a general sense to represent all the cases studied. Furthermore, the term, ingroup or primary, refers to the initial locus of the family stresses and the term, outgroup or secondary, to the group receiving the displaced stresses of the ingroup.

Phase One: The Prewitchcraft Stress Period

Phase one of the prewitchcraft period was characterized by the intended victim and his family (primary ingroup) experiencing intense interpersonal conflicts which arose from identifiable social, economic, and acculturational problems. One of the early signs of prewitchcraft stress was a decrease in the traditionally shared verbal communication among family members and a general distrust of each other's behavior. As the communication problems increased and the interpersonal stresses became more evident, the family members began to distort and misinterpret one another's behavior.

Since the majority of families had shifted from a rural to an urban way of life, economic stresses related to maintaining an adequate income to live in the city were often a basis of quarrels and subtle antagonisms among the family members.

But most importantly, the families were in conflict with and/or ambivalent about "new" cultural values encroaching upon their traditional values. Generally, some of the younger family members, in an annoying and semi-hostile manner, would "try on" the new values to which they had been recently exposed. Sometimes the "new" ways of acting were openly challenged or verbally suppressed when the behavior appeared completely out of harmony with past behavior modes.

Scapegoating behavior was clearly evident in the ingroup with one family member serving as the victim. This victim was frequently blamed for matters which were generally unresolved problems or conflicts which the total family needed to

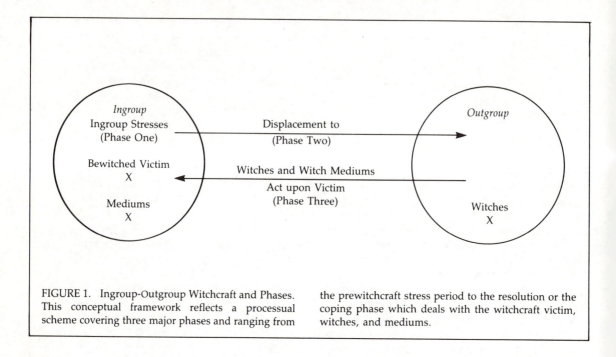

FIGURE 1. Ingroup-Outgroup Witchcraft and Phases. This conceptual framework reflects a processual scheme covering three major phases and ranging from the prewitchcraft stress period to the resolution or the coping phase which deals with the witchcraft victim, witches, and mediums.

face. Many unresolved family problems could be identified, and most of them were related to discrepancies in "new" and "old" cultural values and family practices. Because of the intense and largely covert interpersonal tensions and communication problems along with the economic concerns and conficting values, no family member was able to assume a group leadership role to discuss these problems openly. Instead, the intrafamily tensions increased with the scapegoat victim being harrassed more and more by all family members. The family accusations became formalized, the tension mounted, and later (phase three) the scapegoat victim became legitimately the witchcraft victim. By the time phase three occurred, the victim had been emotionally and socially conditioned to take the bewitched victim role.

Phase Two: Displacement to the Outgroup

Phase two was characterized by the family ingroup members becoming increasingly angry with and distrustful of one another and finally displacing their feelings and problems to a known outgroup.

The ingroup members continued to openly accuse each other of not helping and of not being concerned about one another's most urgent needs, e.g., food, sleep, clothing, and money. Although all ingroup members tended to blame each for their problems, the scapegoat member continued to receive the greatest share of blame. There was evidence that family members denied their feelings about one another, especially when directly confronted about them. As the ingroup members became increasingly angry with one another, they withdrew to their bedrooms or left the house. Their silent periods reflected passive hostility to one another. In general, the ingroup members were afraid to express their pent-up feelings openly to one another, except for some periodic blasts of anger at the scapegoat family member.

Soon the primary ingroup began to cognitively displace its problems and feelings to a secondary outgroup. In all cases studied, the ingroup knew the outgroup, whose members were distant kinsmen—for example, "second or third cousins." In some cases, the outgroup was a social group whom the ingroup had known for at least six months, and in most cases, the ingroups and out-groups had been socially and economically dependent upon one another prior to the displacement phenomenon.

After the displacement of feelings and problems to the outgroup occurred, the ingroup and outgroup marked decreased their contact with each other. Gradually, they showed increased fear and open anger toward one another and accusatory statements were secretively passed between the two groups. The intense fear and anger between each group led to avoidance behavior, and soon the groups began to talk cautiously and secretively about one another. The "terrible" ways and "horrible" witches in the outgroup were commonly discussed by the ingroup for a number of months and during the third phase.

Phase Three: Identification of the Bewitched Victim, the Witches, and the Witch Mediums

The third phase was characterized by intense ingroup-outgroup antagonisms and by identification of the bewitched victim, the witches, and the witch mediums. At this time, the scapegoat victim in the ingroup was clearly victimized and identified as the bewitched person. In all cases studied, the bewitched member was a female who was conditioned to assume the role because she had been the scapegoat family member, as described in phase one. The bewitched person became increasingly ill (emotionally and physically) as the witches in the outgroup were perceived to be affecting her in a covertly destructive manner. As the witchcraft accusations increased, the victim felt more and more frightened, helpless, and controlled by the outgroup witches. She would remain silent and angry and would often stay in bed for hours with the door closed or locked. The witchcraft accusations and the perceived malevolent acts were talked about by both groups in a cautious, angry manner, but without direct verbal exchanges. As the malevolent acts were perceived to increase, the ingroup noted that the bewitched victim became more acutely ill; as the acts decreased, the victim got better. The bewitched victim was sometimes brought to a hospital or to a mental health clinic for relief of her symptoms during the intense period of witchcraft accusations between the two groups.

During the third phase, *witchcraft mediums* who had the power to transmit covert messages from the outgroup witches into the body or mind of the bewitched victim were also identified. As these frightening auditory and visual messages were relayed to the bewitched victim, she became extremely tense or openly aggressive to those near her. The witch mediums (usually one or two) were found in the ingroup and were thought to have been "chosen" by the outgroup witch to transmit her malevolent directives to the bewitched victim. That the witch medium was in the ingroup and near the bewitched person was terrifying to the medium himself as well as to the victim. It was almost an untenable situation since neither the medium nor the victim thought they could change their roles—they, too, were helpless in influencing the witches to be less destructive and horrible. In all cases studied, the witch medium was usually a female who was terribly distraught that she had been "picked" as the medium because it pinpointed her as the immediate person causing harm to the victim. Often the witch medium was the mother or an older sister of the victim. Thus one can envision the tense daughter-mother relationships that existed, accompanied with feelings of intense fear, helplessness, and hostility. Occasionally, the witch medium would use her indirect power upon other ingroup family members to threaten and control their behavior when family relationships seemed out of control. All family members greatly feared the power of the witch mediums as well as the witches and thought that they themselves might become bewitched at any moment.

Psychocultural Approach and Therapy

The author attempted psychocultural therapy with six families (four Spanish-speaking and two Anglo-American families) in their homes. She saw each family about three hours each week (two sessions) and for a period of four to eight months of therapy. The therapy with the four Spanish-speaking families will be described in this first section, followed by a brief account of one of the two Anglo-American families.

In working with all cases, the author was identified as a professional nurse who had come into the home to help and study the sick member of the family. The Spanish-speaking families identified her as a *medicas*—a person who combined indigenous practitioner skills with professional practices; whereas the Anglo-American families saw her as someone providing help in a "crisis situation." In working with the families I used a similar psychocultural nursing therapy approach, employing psychotherapy methods and cultural data such as kinship ties, ethnohealth beliefs, economic aspects, social concerns, and religious beliefs. The families seemed responsive to this comprehensive and multidimensional approach.

The Spanish-Speaking Families

As the author began working with the six Spanish-speaking families, she learned that two of the young females (20 and 25 years of age) had been in psychiatric hospitals for varying periods of time, one for seven months and another for one year. In each case, the victims' conditions had been diagnosed as "paranoid schizophrenia" and they had been dismissed with a "guarded prognosis." Their families felt that the hospital's professional staff had not helped their daughters and commented: "She is worse than before she went to the hospital. They did not seem to understand our situation. It was hard to tell them about it." One of the Spanish-speaking patients had made a serious suicidal attempt three months before the author began working with her. A number of the psychiatric staff were baffled about the patient's "secretive behavior" and the meaning of her communication referents.

The Spanish-speaking families seemed desperate for help since the bewitched victim in each family had not improved and the indigenous curers had "given up on the victim." Thus the climate for helping them seemed favorable. Fortunately, the author had known two of these families through her study of an urban Spanish-speaking community and its health care system (Leininger 1969)—and it was important to these families that they knew the author.

At the start of therapy with the four Spanish-speaking families, the author focused upon their family ties and past relationships and took their genealogies. The latter seemed to be extremely important to the families, enabling them to tell about each family member and what had happened to them in recent months as well as to their family

and friends. Furthermore, the genealogies were the key means for discovering the male and female witches as well as the witch mediums. When the families spoke about the witches, they whispered their names and always spoke of them with intense fear because of their great power and malevolent ways.

After the initial warm-up sessions using the genealogies and other relevant sociocultural data, the family members gradually became more at ease in talking about their family concerns and the sick members in the family. In a short time, they discussed the anger, fear, and distrust which existed among them. The author listened attentively to each family member's concerns, fears, and conflicts with no attempt to modify their behavior. It was felt that this approach was important in this initial phase of the therapy so that the members could openly express their feelings to an outsider who was actively interested in them, but who was not trying to suppress their feelings. Family members made direct and hostile accusations to one another, but especially to the bewitched victim. Initially, the victim was completely overwhelmed at these accusations and occasionally cried or left the room. Gradually, the author interceded in behalf of the victim and offered her emotional and social support by protecting and defending her feelings. When this occurred, the victim's ego became stronger and more confident. She would talk in a more coherent manner and would try to handle the accusations that she felt were unfair. For example, one victim stated: "You (family) 'caused' me to become ill. You have picked on me too long in this family. I did not do everything you said I did. Whenever I tried something different, I was pounced upon. I don't know why you always pick upon me."

During the course of the family "talk-out" sessions, the members discussed their past and current problems in adjusting to different "kinds of people and new ways in the city." There was evidence of conflict between their traditional cultural norms and the different sets of norms they were being exposed to in the urban community. Several common themes became evident in the family therapy sessions and will be highlighted and summarized below.

First, there had been unresolved family problems related to value changes and their ambivalence about changing traditional family relationships. For example, in one Mexican-American family the daughter was very angry with her mother for not permitting her to be more independent and "to be like other teenagers in the city." From a cultural viewpoint, this mother believed in maintaining close surveillance on her daughter, but after the family moved to the city, the daughter wanted to try some of the urban norms and to "live a different life." The mother, however, was extremely reluctant to let her daughter be so free and felt she needed even greater surveillance and protection than when they had lived in the rural area.

Second, the ingroup families were feeling the impact of the diverse ideologies of the different people encountered in their work and school settings and they were experiencing ambivalence about changing their own values. The families talked about how much they valued the warm, friendly, and generous attitudes which they had maintained traditionally with their extended family kinsmen. Lately, they felt these values were changing and that even their distant kinsmen (the outgroup) were becoming "cold, impersonal, and ungenerous people like the rest of these city people." The ingroup family members gave several examples of how their outgroup kinsmen or friends (toward whom they now felt hostile and frightened) had become extremely selfish and inconsiderate. In fact, the ingroup members were highly critical of the outgroup's behavior and were unwilling to forgive or forget such inconsiderate behavior. They said the outgroup had been stingy in giving gifts, loaning money, and helping them with occasional family celebrations. It was, therefore, no wonder that the outgroup became the ingroup's target for the displacement of its angry, distrustful, and suspicious feelings.

Third, a series of traditional cultural norms had been broken in each of the family ingroups, and the witchcraft victim was blamed for breaking them. And since the victim was perceived in each family to have violated the norm most flagrantly, she was vulnerable to most of the witchcraft accusations. In addition, the ingroup had become emotionally tense with one another because of a "cultural awkwardness" in changing their life style from one set of norms to another. They did not seem to know how to act as they "tried out" new or different behaviors in the family context and they were uncomfortable with the new ways.

Fourth, as the ingroup families spoke about their angry and antagonistic feelings toward the outgroup, they were oblivious to the dynamics of their own internal family relationships and their displacement of family problems and hostilities to the outgroup. None of the families studied were aware of this important aspect of their behavior until the author helped them to see such relationships. In time, some of their anger, which had been displaced to the outgroup, subsided as the author focused therapy upon ingroup behavior and explored ways to resolve family conflicts.

In the process of working with the families, the specific incidents, problems, and feelings of the ingroup that seemed to have precipitated the cycle of events were dealt with. As a consequence, it was observed that as feelings of anger and hostility shifted from the ingroup to the outgroup, the ingroup members became more comfortable with one another and gradually began to work on their own problems. It was also apparent that as the ingroup dealt with their problems as a group, family unity and solidarity increased. It was, however, a difficult task for the therapist to help the ingroup see the relationship between their own behavior and the displacement of problems to the outgroup. This goal was not achieved until after the ingroup learned to trust each other and work as a family unit again.

During the therapy, the victim challenged the family members who called her "sick" for she felt *all* the family members were involved in similar stresses and were also "sick." As she made these counter-challenges, the author encouraged her to express other feelings and reassured her that other family members would not be allowed to harm her.

The families also talked about the economic pressures they had experienced and how they had to work long hours to meet the monthly costs of urban living. They had expected their outgroup friends to help them economically, however, the outgroup was also feeling economic pressures and was unable to provide the gifts, food, or help that they had earlier. Hence, the ingroup began to realize that their expectations of the outgroup were probably unrealistic and that they would have to deal with their own problems as best they could.

The author talked with some outgroup members who were accused of acting malevolently toward the group. Interestingly, the outgroup members were aware of their culturally defined role in witchcraft and that there were witches among them who were causing harm to the ingroup victim and his family. They were, however, very cautious in talking with the author as they were uncertain about her role since they had never experienced an "outside-professional" person who wanted to help them with "their witchcraft." Two outgroup "witches" said that they were acting protectively in order to control the behavior of the ingroup whom they greatly feared—and so, they did not mind being accused of being witches since they felt they were protecting their families.

Occasionally, members of the ingroup would meet or see a member of the outgroup at the store, church, or school. There was always great fear of each other and efforts were made to avoid direct contacts—even if it meant walking or driving several blocks away from the person. In one instance, a male "witch" from the outgroup boarded a bus driven by a member of the victim's ingroup. The "witch" started to enter the front of the bus, quickly recognized the ingroup member driving the bus, and then entered the bus at the rear. He sent another person to the front to pay his fare. Later, the driver said he had been extremely frightened to have the "witch" riding "his bus" and wanted to leave his job. The author was able to help this ingroup member retain his job, and in time, he gradually changed his feelings, but only after his sister (the bewitched victim) showed signs of health improvement. In general, the ingroup and outgroup members were not able to confront one another about their actions and feelings. The author chose not to work with the outgroup members but rather to help the ingroup members modify their behavior so that they themselves could deal with the outgroup in time—which did occur in the majority of families.

With two of the Spanish-speaking families, a large black cat was the symbol which indicated that the family and home were bewitched. For example, in one of these families the ingroup believed that the black cat had been sent by the outgroup witches who desired to cause them evil. They contended that the outgroup had broken the window and dropped the cat in their basement. Initially, they were terrified of removing the cat because they feared it would cause the victim's death or provoke outright family revenge toward them. Instead, they kept the cat well cared for and fed each day. Finally, as their group unity increased, they decided to release the cat from the basement, after which the victim's husband repaired the window. The decision to remove the cat was a major one and caused great fear; however, once they felt "strong enough" to remove the cat, the ingroup became greatly relieved and more relaxed in their home. Symbolically, it meant that the outgroup was no longer living in their basement since the cat was the symbol of oppressive witchcraft practices from the outgroup which brought harm to the bewitched victim and the family. Removal of the cat was a significant factor in achieving a positive direction in the family therapy. The ingroup used the author to support them in their decision because in the past they had had to wait until the outgroup "released" the cat from their house. Having the cat in the house clearly sustained the illness associated with witchcraft behavior.

Since the goals of the therapy for both the Spanish-speaking and the Anglo-American families were similar, with only slight modification according to symbolic referents, they are presented now. The therapy or treatment goals were based upon empirical cultural, psychological, economic, and social data which were conceptualized into a theoretical framework as described earlier. The author attempted to: (1) provide expressive therapy for the ingroup members by focusing upon their social tensions and daily living problems, (2) provide an emotional supportive relationship using cultural referents for an extremely harrassed bewitched victim, (3) assist the group to cope with acculturation changes and the concomitant shift in value orientations, and (4) help the family to function again as a viable and cohesive social group under the duress of cultural changes.

Anglo-American Families

Turning briefly to the two Anglo-American families I worked with for approximately six months, I found similar dynamics in operation as noted above with the Spanish-speaking families.

Although there were some variation in the linguistic expression and symbolic cultural forms, the same ingroup-outgroup theoretical model was used and similar therapy goals were applied. While both Anglo-American cases were similar, only one of the families will be discussed.

Reo, a fictitious name, was a 21-year-old college student who had lived in a small midwestern rural community. According to Reo and her family, she had been "hexed" by two college students (referred to as the "hex-witches") at the end of her first year of college in a large urban community. The family had taken Reo to a psychiatric clinic because "she was acting strangely toward us and her classmates." During the interview with the clinic staff she said she had been "hexed" by some classmates who were distant friends, but with whom she had quarreled prior to being bewitched. Since then, Reo felt that these two "witches" were acting unfriendly toward her and influencing her behavior "from a distance." With her closest classmates and family she felt she was being accused of things she did not do. (Scapegoat behavior toward Reo was evident within her family and close ingroup classmates and was based upon social tensions and interpersonal antagonisms.)

Reo said that previously her "close classmates" and family had been good, dependable persons, but lately they seemed to be suspicious, unfriendly, cold, and even fearful of her. She told the clinic staff that one friend, who was now a terrible "hex-witch," was forcing her roommate and also her sister to influence her (Reo's) thoughts and actions by using "McLuhan's medium techniques" and by making her feel strange and sick. The clinic staff were baffled by "the hexing" phenomenon, but diagnosed her case as "paranoid schizophrenia with a guarded prognosis." She was sent home after two weeks of hospitalization (largely on a medication regimen) with some mild tranquilizers and was told to return "if things got worse for her and the family." Things did seem to get worse and they returned to the outpatient clinic where the author agreed to provide therapy in the home.

There was no difficulty in working with this Anglo-American family because they viewed the author as another "Anglo" and as a professional nurse who had worked with other families with similar difficulties. The family members desperately wanted help because they were frightened of what Reo might do to herself or to them and commented that "we believe she is being influenced by that college group (outgroup), but we don't know what to do about it and what she might do."

After Reo was "hexed," she attended some of her classes, but gradually withdrew from them as she became more emotionally disturbed and experienced periodic episodes of nausea and vomiting. Reo also feared she would encounter the hex-witches on the campus and she was most fearful of them and what they might do to her—ranging from being haunted mentally to being killed by the witches.

As I worked with Reo and her family in their home, using indirect interview therapy techniques similar to those used with the Spanish-speaking families, Reo explained how she had been initially victimized by a large black spider. She said her distant college "hex-witches" had put the spider on her dormitory door, after which "she knew they were going to cause her harm." She also told how this college outgroup had once been kind to her, but had become harsh and unkind. She said that they used to have snacks with her, but suddenly became angry and hostile toward her after they "hexed" her. Reo felt her older sister was also involved in making her ill since her sister also knew this college outgroup. Reo thought the latter were sending messages through her sister.

The changes taking place in Reo's family life were similar to those taking place in the Spanish-speaking families. Reo's family also had moved from a rural to an urban community about three years before, and they were encountering acculturational stresses and conflicts in rural-urban value systems. They were able to identify some of the differences they were experiencing between rural and city life, but were unable to cope with their ambivalence about "which ways would be better for them." They found rural life with its many warm and friendly neighbors a real asset in contrast with their cold and busy city neighbors whom they really did not know. Nor could they depend upon their city neighbors in times of crises like they did with their rural counterparts. They had had many ambivalent feelings about sending Reo to college and they "just knew something would happen to her there and that is why the oldest daughter did not go to college." They had two other daughters who would soon be ready for college (the reason they had moved to an urban community), and they did not know how to handle this problem.

Also, all adult family members were employed in semiskilled and unskilled jobs in the city. They often left the house at 7 a.m. and returned at 6 p.m., and had little time to discuss their family problems and be together as a group as they had been previously in their rural community. Economic problems were evident and they were deeply concerned about how to make a living in the city. There was no question that many of the initial problems which were related to witchcraft had begun with ingroup family problems and interpersonal tensions. Even before Reo was "hexed" at college, the family relationships had become tense with the family members growing increasingly irritable, impatient, and suspicious of one another. They were not fully aware of what was happening to their family relationships, except that "it was not going well." Reo was the family scapegoat member who received their accusations. Moreover, Reo revealed in the family therapy sessions that she had decided to go to college to "get away from all this family bickering and the unfair accusations placed upon me—I just could not take it any longer." The displacement phenomenon to the college outgroup occurred after the family social tensions had become unbearable and the family members were unable to talk with one another without quarreling or physically fighting.

Fortunately, the author was able to talk with Reo's college outgroup who also spoke about the noticeable change in Reo's behavior. They said they had become frightened of her and decided to "leave her at a distance" since "they could no longer understand her." They did feel that they sent "wave lengths"to her and were influencing her behavior unfavorably by the use of "transcendental power communication modes." Later they asked about Reo's health and wondered if they could "use their power to help her get well." They had been very angry with her because "she did not treat us fairly and was unkind, scary and uncharitable to us." They also admitted that they had placed the black spider on her door because "we wanted to scare her."

In working with Reo and her family, the same approach and goals described above were used over a period of four months. Most of the time was spent talking about: changes in rural-urban values and what to do about them; perceptions and anxieties about college life; and how to cope with social, economic, interpersonal family problems in the future in a city way of life with different cultural norms. The family also was extremely sensitive and, hence, secretive about sharing their "family problems with the whole hospital staff or psychiatric group" as they were sure the staff "would not believe" their daughter was hexed, and did not know "how to help her." Because Reo's behavior became worse, they had decided to try the clinic but were disappointed that she did not improve while in the hospital.

Perhaps because they desperately wanted help, this family responded quite readily to family therapy. They liked that therapy was given in their home. The author also worked with Reo on other hostilities and offered her emotional support as she talked about her role as a scapegoat member of the family. Family antagonisms gradually subsided and the family was still functioning as a group one year after the author left them. Reo subsequently completed a college degree and another daughter has enrolled in college.

General Observations and Functional Analysis of Witchcraft Dynamics

The author observed that as the initial tensions and conflicts mounted in the family ingroup, there seemed to be *no* traditional institutionalized norms and practices which the family could rely on to cope with its problems. Moreover, the family contacts to obtain help from outside groups were limited because of the differing cultural norms involved. In general, the family members felt socially and culturally alienated and alone with their problems with no way to deal with them or resolve them.

Although most of the ingroup families had been living in an urban community for at least two years, it was apparent that their traditional values had been challenged only recently by their own family members and by outsiders. The exposure to a number of individuals and groups through work, school, and church seemed to increase their insecurity about themselves as a social group and about the values that they held. Interestingly, each family member was trying to resolve his value conflicts by himself and was afraid to talk openly about them with other family members. In time, the unresolved cultural value differences and social tensions increased so that the family members were unable to converse with one another in an acceptable manner.

The displacement of anger and the maintenance of stresses between the ingroup and the outgroup were dynamic features of the witchcraft practices and had several important social, cultural, and psychological functions which can be summarized here.

First, the displacement of angry feelings from the ingroup to the outgroup helped the ingroup become socially and psychologically more comfortable with one another and kept them united during the heightened ingroup conflict period.

Second, the identified witches in the outgroup (who were perceived to be highly destructive and powerful) were important in explaining the sick victim's behavior to the ingroup. While this temporarily served to relieve the ingroup family members by focusing their group problems on one family member, it also disguised the family's critical problems which ultimately had to be dealt with in the family therapy sessions. Concomitantly, the witches functioned as a powerful external threat to the ingroup and brought them together from fear in order to prevent the witches from generating more "deadly power" upon the sick victim.

Third, the scapegoating behavior exerted upon an ingroup member not only localized the emotional and social conflicts of the family in one member, but it also prepared and conditioned the victim and the others for the roles they would play in the witchcraft practices. Most importantly, the bewitched victim knew the role she would be expected to play, and she served as a barometer for determining the strength and nature of the ingroup-outgroup relationships by the degree of her illness.

Fourth, witchcraft practices were clues to natural, social, economic, and psychological stresses which were extremely difficult for the ingroup to handle and required a nonfamily member to be helpful and objective. Reports of other victims who

had not been helped in this way revealed either a prolonged illness in the hospital or increased social pathology in the family.

Fifth, symbolic referents such as cats and lizards served the important function of legitimizing the witchcraft phenomenon and of alerting the victim and the family to difficulties with an outgroup.

Summary

In this paper, the author has presented a theoretical framework, based upon empirical data, regarding witchcraft behavior and its functions in selected urban families in the United States. Through an intensive study and the provision of psychocultural therapy to four Spanish-speaking and two Anglo-American families, the author was able to help the bewitched victims and their families.

An analysis of the six families, plus other families who did not receive therapy, disclosed that ingroup tensions and problems (which were largely a consequence of acculturation and the ensuing economic, social, and psychocultural stresses) were dispatched in time to a known outgroup whose witches acted upon the scapegoat or bewitched victim in the ingroup. Witchcraft practices in these families were important psychocultural and social mechanisms to cope with ingroup problems generated by external societal concerns.

The theoretical model with three major phases served as an important guide in providing psychocultural nursing therapy to the six families. The therapy was largely supportive and expressive in form involving the use of cultural value orientations adapted to the current life and environmental situation of the families. Although witchcraft behavior has been described in the anthropological literature since the early part of this century, there have been no known reports of professional groups attempting to relieve bewitched victims and their families through psychocultural therapy. However, with the reported increase of interest in witchcraft in this country and the increase of bewitched victims seeking help, it seems important that professional staff (and especially mental health personnel) become more knowledgeable of the witchcraft phenomenon and explore ways to relieve victims and their families of such stress.

8

Ghosts, Souls, and Ancestors: Power of the Dead

Religions universally promise believers that there is life after death. Although the worship of ancestors is not universal, a belief in the immortality of the dead occurs in all cultures. There is variation among cultures in the degree of interaction between the living and the dead, however, as well as in the intensity and concern a people may have for the deceased. Eskimos are never free of anxieties about ghosts, while Pueblo Indians are seldom bothered by them; the Plains Indians of North America constructed elaborate ghost beliefs, while the Siriono of South America, although believing in ghosts, paid little attention to them.

Perhaps humans have some basic need that causes us to believe in ghosts and to worship ancestors: to seek verification that although the mortal body may die, the soul survives after death. The nineteenth-century sociologist Herbert Spencer speculated that the beginnings of religion were in ancestor worship—the need

Ivory pendant mask from Benin, Nigeria.

284

for the living to continue an emotional relationship with their dead relatives. A major problem with Spencer's argument is that many societies at the hunting-and-gathering level do not practice ancestor worship. The Arunta of Australia, for example, worshiped their totemic plants and animals, but not their human ancestors. This objection to Spencer's belief notwithstanding, ancestor worship does remind the living of a vital continuing link between the living and the dead.

One writer has pointed out that two major attitudes are widely held about the dead: that they have either left the society or remain as active members (Malefijt 1968: 156–59). In societies that separate the dead from the living social group, any possibility of the dead returning is regarded as undesirable because they could disrupt the social order and the daily routine of life. In such cultures, Malefijt believes, the dead are likely to be greatly feared, and an elaborate belief system —a cult of the dead—is constructed and practiced in order to separate them from the living. The primary function of cults of the dead is to aid the survivors in overcoming the grief they may feel about the dead. Such cults are not found in societies where the dead are seen as active members of the group; instead, funeral ceremonies are undertaken with the hope the deceased will return to society in their new status. These beliefs, according to Malefijt, result in the development of ancestor cults instead of cults of the dead.

Ancestor cults and the ritual that surrounds them may also be seen as an elaboration of cults of the dead. The Bantu of Africa, for example, outline distinct ancestral deities for each lineage and clan. All of these ancestral gods are gods to their living relatives, but not to individuals who belong to other kinship organizations. Further elaboration of Bantu ancestor worship may be seen in Bantu beliefs about the supernatural beings believed to head their royal clans. Gods of such royal clans are worshiped by the entire kingdom, not just the royal clan itself.

The study of ancestor worship among American and British anthropologists has emphasized the connection between the identity and behavioral characteristics of the dead, on one hand, and the distribution and nature of their authority in both domestic and political domains of the society, on the other (Bradbury 1966: 127). Al-though the belief in ghosts of ancestors is universal, the functions ancestors play vary greatly among societies. It is also clear that variations in ancestor worship are directly related to social structure and that this relationship is not based on mere common religious interests alone: rather, the structure of the kin group and the relationships of those within it serve as the model of ancestor worship (Bradbury 1966: 128). Among the Sisala of Ghana, for example, only a select number of Sisala elders, based on their particular status and power within the group, can effectively communicate with the ghosts of ancestors (Mendonsa 1976: 63–64). In many other parts of the non-Western world, non-elder ritual specialists, such as heads of households, are responsible for contacting the ancestors. A cross-cultural study of fifty societies found that where important decisions are made by the kin group, ancestor worship is a high probability (Swanson 1969: 97–108).

Many, but certainly not all, non-Western societies believe ancestors play a strong and positive role in the security and prosperity of their group, and anthropological data is full of these kinds of examples. It is important, however, to recognize that ancestors are but one of several categories of spirits whose actions directly affect society. John S. Mbiti's study of East and Central Africa shows that the status of spirits may change through time. Ancestor spirits, the "living dead," are those whose memory still exists in the minds of their kin, and who are primarily beneficial to the surviving relatives. When the living dead are forgotten in the memory of their group and dropped from the genealogy as a result of the passing of time (four or five generations), they are believed to be transformed into "nameless spirits," non-ancestors, characterized as malicious vehicles for misfortune of all kinds (1970). In keeping with Mbiti's model, the Lugbara of Uganda recognize two types of dead. The first group, simply called "ancestors," comprises nameless, all deceased relatives; these are secondary in importance to the recently deceased, called "ancestor spirits" or "ghosts," who can be invoked by the living to cause misfortune to befall those whose acts threaten the solidarity of the kin group (Middleton 1971: 488).

Clearly spirits, ghosts, and ancestors are often

given unique statuses in the afterlife, and are viewed as having different functions and effects on the living. In many respects the relationship of fear and responsibility of elders toward ancestors is mirrored by the son-father relationship among the living. The ancestral world in many cases is an extension or model of the real world. The supernatural status of the ancestors exhibits major differences, for although one can argue to a point with an elder, no one questions the wisdom and authority of an ancestor.

The power of the dead is an important aspect of religion and social control. If, for example, a Lugbara man threatened the solidarity of the clan or lineage in any of a number of ways, the elder may invoke ghosts to punish the troublemaker (Middleton 1971: 488–92). Without doubt this veneration of the ancestors and the fear of their power functions importantly to help control many societies. Interestingly, ancestor worship also contributes to the conservative nature of those cultures where it is practiced. Typically, dead ancestors do not smile favorably on any kind of change in the cultures of their living relatives. Because ghosts are capable of severely punishing an earthly mortal desirous of change, the force for conformity is strong.

Not all societies assign power to ancestors. In many cultures, North America included, a high god (monotheism) or gods (polytheism) exert authority over the living, punishing those who violate religious tenets, rules that often are duplicated in civil law and serve as the bases of appropriate social behavior. In these groups ancestor cults and worship of the deceased are not found, although the spiritual nature of ancestors and belief in the afterlife persevere.

Among peoples where the deceased are believed to take an active role in society, the living are understandably concerned with the welfare of ancestors. Customs are established to assure the comfort of the dead in their life after death. Most commonly, rituals carried out at funerals, burials, and in some cases reburial or cremation, insure that loved ones arrive safely at what the living believe is the proper abode of the dead. The care taken in preparing the deceased for the afterlife is an important reinforcement of the society's customs and an expression of unity among its members. Participation helps insure that the same care

can be expected to be given at the time of one's own death. Beyond this motivation, however, the power to rain down misfortunes is a major reason for carefully following customs surrounding the preparation, interment, and propitiation of the dead. No one wants to be subjected to supernatural punishment by vengeful and angry ghosts.

To most people in Western culture the word "ghost" brings forth an image of a disembodied spirit of a dead person swooping through dark halls, hovering frighteningly over a grave, or perhaps roaming aimlessly through damp woods. Typically, the ghost is observed wearing white sheets—an image that undoubtedly arises from the shroud or winding sheet used to wrap the corpse for its placement in the grave. There is a wide variety of shapes available to would-be ghosts, however. Some are transparent; some are lifelike apparitions of their former selves; others appear with horribly gaunt, empty faces, devoid of eyes and lips. Not all ghosts take a human or even vaguely human shape: horses frequently appear in phantom form, as do dogs and large birds, and ghost lore is full of accounts of ghost trains, stagecoaches, and, of course, such phantom ships as the Flying Dutchman.

Very few peoples do not support the idea of a separate spirit world—a land of the dead. It is to this other world that souls will travel and, once there, will rest in eternal peace. At some point in history, however, the notion arose that not all souls deserved an easy trip to a blissful spiritual world. Murder victims, miscreants, and evil people, for example, might become ghosts doomed to wander the earthly world. Inadequate funerals also might give rise to restless ghosts: thus, the attention paid by cultures everywhere to meticulously preparing and dressing the corpse for burial, and to placing gifts, food, and weapons in the grave or at the gravesite to enhance the spirit's journey to the place of eternal rest.

In the first article of this chapter, Shirley Lindenbaum explores the problem of why some New Guinea societies show little interest in ghosts and sorcery, while others seem preoccupied with both. The granting of the first gun permits to another New Guinea group and the resulting formation of a cult is the subject of the article by William Mitchell. Mitchell shows how the cult's belief in vengeful spirits helps them understand why they sometimes experience unsuccessful hunting. James F. Downs examines some of the basic concepts of Washo religious life, noting that the spirits of the dead were to be greatly feared and avoided among this North American Indian tribe. In the final selection, Peter Metcalf compares American and Berawan funeral rites. As Metcalf learned to see Berawan funerary customs as natural, American treatment of the dead began to seem exotic.

References Cited

Bradbury, R. E.
1966 "Fathers, Elders, and Ghosts in Edo Religion." In Michael Banton, ed., *Anthropological Approaches to the Supernatural*, pp. 127–53. London: Tavistock Publications, Ltd.

Malefijt, Annemarie de Waal
1968 *Religion and Culture: An Introduction to Anthropology of Religion*. New York: Macmillan.

Mbiti, John S.
1970 *African Religions and Philosophies*. Garden City, N.Y.: Doubleday.

Mendonsa, Eugene L.
1976 "Elders, Office-Holders and Ancestors Among the Sisala of Northern Ghana." *Africa* 46: 57–64.

Middleton, John
1971 "The Cult of the Dead: Ancestors and Ghosts." In William A. Lessa and Evon Z. Vogt, eds., *Reader in Comparative Religion: An Anthropological Approach*, 3rd ed., pp. 488–92. New York: Harper and Row.

Sorcerers, Ghosts, and Polluting Women: An Analysis of Religious Belief and Population Control

Shirley Lindenbaum

Concentrating on three important components of New Guinean culture, Shirley Lindenbaum here analyzes the roles that sorcery, ancestral ghosts, and female pollution play in maintaining social structural integrity. Emphasis on varying ecological conditions led her to the construction of a continuum in which groups could be located and compared in terms of the relative importance they placed on these elements. Taking a structural-functional approach, her data and the resulting model clarify why some groups differ so radically in their beliefs surrounding incest, adultery, chastity, and the relative importance of witches, sorcerers, and ghosts in enforcing the institutionalization of male-female relationships and reproduction.

Reprinted from *Ethnology*, Vol. 11 (1972), pp. 241–53, by permission of the author and the Department of Anthropology, University of Pittsburgh.

THE PROBLEM OF WHY SOME NEW GUINEA societies evince little interest in sorcery while others seem preoccupied with sorcery as an explanation for disease and death has been examined in recent publications (Hogbin 1958; Lawrence and Meggitt 1965; Lindenbaum 1971). Analyses have focused on the structural features of society. It has been suggested that sorcery accusations are a necessary means of easing tension between individuals who lack the security of membership in solidary groups. Sorcery also acts as a mechanism whereby permanently settled descent groups maintain their identity in the absence of wars for economic aggrandizement (Lawrence and Meggitt 1965: 17). It has been noted that these theories do not account for the absence of a great interest in sorcery among the Mae Enga and the Ngaing, and it was suggested that these peoples have an alternate means of channelling aggression through warfare and ceremonial exchange (Lawrence and Meggitt 1965: 18). This paper continues the discussion, but relates the presence of sorcery to ecological variables. The polluting woman is also seen to inhabit a particular form of social and material environment; an examination of the interaction of the two accounts for her presence.

Enga and Fore

Two societies in the Highlands of New Guinea illustrate the variations which exist at each end of the range; the Enga in the West and the Fore in the East. It has been noted that Enga, for instance, believe misfortune and death to be the result of attacks by malicious ghosts of the dead rather than by living sorcerers. Enga, moreover, do not simply fear ghosts in general; they fear male ancestral ghosts. As the degree of danger is judged more serious—such as the death of a socially important victim or an epidemic of illness—Enga turn from appeasing particular domestic ghosts to the placation of all the ancestral ghosts of a clan. There is, as Meggitt (1965b: 131) points out, an isomorphism of the structures of the lineage system and the religious system. A hierarchical order runs through them both.

Fore beliefs about the etiology of disease also reflect structural features of their society. Fore use the idea of sorcerers rather than of ancestral ghosts to define the boundaries of their social groups and to maintain their internal cohesion. The composition of South Fore political groups provides the basis for mutual mistrust. The political unit of widest span, the parish, is an aggregate of people residing on a defined territory. Parish membership is not based on common descent; rather, the parish may be described as a temporary coalition of factions united by a common desire for security and defence. The parish section is similarly a residential rather than a genealogical unit. The smallest parish subdivision, the "people of a place," is based on genealogical criteria, although the permitted adoption of outsiders disqualifies it as a strictly unilineal group. The social system at all levels is thus characterized by flexibility and expediency. Every parish includes immigrants who have fled conflict in their original parish. Newcomers are readily incorporated, given gardening land, and if necessary are bound to their new co-residents by ties of fictional kinship. The ambiguity felt about the loyalty of people with ties to an outside parish is expressed in sorcery beliefs and activities. Sorcery is thus a political institution peculiarly suited to the organizational problems of South Fore society. Fore do not enjoy the comfort of genealogical unity, and sorcery discussions are endemic (Lindenbaum 1971).

I wish to argue here that the choice between ancestral ghosts or sorcerers as an explanation for death from disease may be ecologically determined. If disease is considered to result from the anger of ancestors, the society in which such a religious belief is held is one in which there is population pressure on scarce resources. The implication is that members of the society regard disease sent by one's own former kinsmen as an acceptable form of population control. Enga typify this position. Enga land is scarce, and the relative scarcity of arable land is a significant determinant of the rigidity of lineage structure in the society. Enga religion is also one in which agnatic ghosts are believed to control the fertility of the land and the people (Meggitt 1965b: 105–131). Disease and death are attributed to angry ghosts. This philosophical viewpoint appears to be a Malthusian acceptance of the realities of the Enga man-land ratio.

Fore, on the other hand, do not hold such beliefs. They have ample land for a small population. Their problems are not focused on restricting the access of outsiders to group resources. The opposite is the case—how to maintain group strength in the face of aggressive neighbors. South Fore groups readily admit newcomers and provide them with fertile land. Fore view illness and death as an attack by jealous enemy sorcerers who not only endanger the viability of small groups, but who may be attempting to wipe out the entire society. The presence of *kuru*, a fatal neurological disorder which mainly kills women, gives rise to realistic fears for survival, expressed in terms of the assault of particularly malignant sorcerers.

Illness and Death

The hypothesis may be illustrated by examining the behavior provoked by illness and death in Enga and Fore societies. Meggitt (1965b: 113) describes Enga response to the illness and death of an adult man. The victim's brothers or sons kill a pig and give its essence to the ghost they think is causing the misfortune, distributing the meat to both maternal and paternal kinsmen. If the sick man does not recover, his agnates consult a diviner to locate the identity of the angered ghost, and again kill pigs to propitiate the ghost. If the victim is an important person, all the men of his patrilineage, with pigs contributed by subclan and even parallel subclan members, may perform a ritual to placate the ancestral ghosts of a clan. The clan fertility stones are rubbed with pig grease. If the patient then dies, his relatives mourn briefly and publicly. Close relatives of the deceased slice their ear lobes or cut off finger joints. For the next two or three weeks the immediate family members do not tend their pigs or gardens. They subsequently return to everyday life after holding a feast.

The Enga response thus appears to be controlled and orderly. The source of attack is assumed to come from within the group itself—not a disrupting idea for Enga. It is assumed that an invisible agnatic ghost attacks the internal agnatic spirit of the victim, and at the same time injures the victim's maternally acquired flesh and vitality. Both paternal and maternal kinsmen are thus offered pork in compensation for their loss. Enga attempt to avert the loss of an important man by ceremonial treatment of the clan fertility stones, but the death itself elicits only a brief, public mourning period. The family's loss of a productive member is indicated by injury to body extremities, an important mutilation of the domestic group but not of the body of the lineage. The family group, in a realistic acknowledgment of its decreased size, does not attempt to increase its food production for the following two or three weeks. Meggitt (1965a: 187) also notes that the deaths of women and children are rarely the subject of inquiry.

Fore response to illness and death is markedly more excited. Sorcery accusations arise over the severe illness or death of any adult male or female. Most sorcery accusations occur between men residing in different parish groups. The location of a sorcery challenge thus indicates the extent of mutual distrust felt by allies and neighbors; if an accusation occurs within parish borders, it signals the possibility of incipient political fission. Sorcery challenges are therefore socially disruptive, particularly as the sorcerer is assumed to be within a close range. In the past, sorcery challenges led to fighting and migration; now charges and counter-charges are adjudicated in indigenous courts and cases heard by the Administration.

Fore do not accept severe illness with equanimity. Much day-to-day behavior is concerned with preventing a sorcerer from acquiring the material he needs for attack. Men, women, and children make use of deep pit latrines for feces and food scraps. They also hide hair cuttings and nail parings. Women, in particular, scrupulously eliminate menstrual blood, the emissions from childbirth, and an infant's umbilical cord; that is, they conceal evidence of their fertility in response to the high incidence of *kuru*, a sex-biased disease. Fore use the image of the human body to make symbolic statements about the body politic (Douglas 1966). They monitor substances entering and issuing from the body; the small South Fore groups fear population decline resulting from social intermingling. South Fore both protect the body's boundaries and police the borders of their social groups (Lindenbaum 1972).

When an adult falls ill, Fore resort to a variety of cures, part of which involves a divination test to reveal the identity of the sorcerer. Opossum meat, an environmental mediator, is used as an oracle to screen suspected groups, and after many tests the malicious actor is finally identified. Relatives of the victim try to persuade or threaten the sorcerer to reverse his actions, to remove his hidden sorcery materials, and to allow the patient to recover. This acrimonious political activity, in the case of *kuru* victims, may last for a year or more. The victim's supporting group, her husband, and his kinsmen and friends, are also involved in expensive, time-consuming visits to foreign curers who live outside Fore territory.

At this point the patient may die. In the past, most deceased persons were eaten. Rules of the cannibal consumption of dead bodies are somewhat undefined, because cannibalism was a relatively late custom in Fore society and has been forbidden since the mid 1950s. In general, however, body parts were distributed along the same lines as were traditional death payments in pork and valuables—large payments to matrilateral kinsmen and smaller payments to age-mates and classificatory brothers and friends. That is, kinship cannibalism among the Fore appears to underline the recognition of responsibility for loss to those who generated the body and to those who see themselves as its equivalents.

Little ideology was associated with the consumption of dead bodies. If the body was buried, the Fore say "the ground ate him"; that is, bodies fertilize the ground. Dismemberment of a corpse for consumption was carried out in a kinsman's garden. The association between cannibalism and fertility has also been noted by Berndt (1962: 271). Kinship cannibalism among the Fore suggests that a society in biological decline may attempt regeneration by eating itself. A wife expects to eat her husband's buttocks and penis (Berndt 1962: 273). It may be significant that South Fore society has a marked imbalance in the sex ratio; *kuru* decimates adult women, and women were in the main the cannibals. In contrast, cannibalism is repugnant to the Enga (Meggitt 1965b: 120). Cannibalism does occur, according to Enga, among demons who inhabit the inhospitable forest. Some demons with an appetite for human flesh eat solitary bush travelers; others appear as snakes to abduct men from the men's houses, or as sexually appealing women whose false promises of wealth lead to property dissipation and dementia (Meggitt 1965b: 122). For Enga, fertility and cannibalism present the same kinds of danger.

The responses to epidemic illness in Enga and Fore societies are markedly different. If Enga are troubled by an increase in the death rate of children or important men, or by an increase in the incidence of disease, they turn their attention to clan ghosts. The same response is elicited by a sudden rise in the death rate of pigs, or by a clan-wide crop failure, resources on which man depends (Meggitt 1965b: 114). To deal with this threat, they perform rituals which require peace to be observed among neighboring clans. During part of the rituals, a bachelor and a spinster sit on the roof of a cult house which protects the clan stones. The ancestral ghosts are believed to have temporarily removed their potency from men and land, withdrawing into the stones. Each clansman is offered a fragment of pork fat bespelled in the presence of the ancestral ghosts. Married men may eat it; bachelors may only smell the fat. Black opossums, used in another part of the ritual, are offered to the oldest men of the clan, but some refuse to eat, fearing it may hasten their deaths. For a month or two following the rituals, clansmen should not copulate or prepare new gardens; such activities would, it is said, "antagonize the ancestors." The cult house may be left to disintegrate, or neighboring clans may be invited to destroy it. This contest to destroy the cult house generates much ill will against the triumphant clan, which boasts its superiority (Meggitt 1965b: 114–120).

The rituals may be interpreted as a cultural mechanism by which Enga accept a population or a subsistence loss. The performance of the rituals requires a truce amongst warring clans, a regulation which precludes further depletion of numbers. Although the purpose of the rituals is ostensibly to restore the good humor of ancestral ghosts so that they will cease meting out punishment in the form of illness and death, the central actors are persons whose generative powers are recognized to be temporarily inactive—bachelors and spinsters—as are the generative powers of the clan stones. Nor does the impetus of the ritual seem to suggest great renewal of fertility. Indeed, Meggitt (1965b: 118) comments that "the propitiatory rituals . . . are not thought to be immediately efficacious . . . it is assumed that revitalisation of the clan and its land may take some time." Ritual symbolism seems to have more to do with death, and a recognition of temporary stasis, than with renewed fertility. Some old men are afraid to eat the large black opossums which may propel them beyond life to join the body of ancestors. For one or two months following the rituals there is a ban on copulation and new gardening of which the ancestors might disapprove—an indication that there will be no new additions to society and no provision for them.

In similar rituals held by Western Enga, ceremonies surround the clan pool (Meggitt 1965b: 118–119). Again the theme is a separation of men and women, the use of a pair of bachelors as central actors, and a temporary ban on copulation and gardening. The young boys selected to participate in the clan pool rituals are moreover considered inducted into the bachelors' association, which prescribes prolonged avoidance of contact with women.

Thus the response to epidemic illness or unusual loss of life and resources results in ceremonies which do not emphasize fertility, or symbolize creative behavior. Rather, the depletion of clan membership is publicly accepted in a number of ceremonies whose content emphasizes instead the spacing of men and women, the importance of men whose sexual capacities are socially constrained, and an acceptable stasis in the relationship between men and land. Enga clans appear to repair damaged relationships with the ghosts of their ancestors lest they decline in relation to similar groups. The clan which successfully demolishes the cult house—a symbol of withdrawn fertility—threatens others with its suggestion of superiority and imbalance.

Fore response to illness is another matter. Fore rituals concern protection and unity; groups close their ranks against the sorcerer. Annual ceremonies are observed for the safety of children and pregnant women. Infants and future mothers eat special foods, and receive a share of the feast before other women and all men. The ceremonies are held if there is news of infant illness in surrounding areas, or at the beginning of the dry season, presumably a time of increased sickness. During the early 1960s, the South Fore responded dramatically to the high incidence of *kuru* among the population. From November, 1962, to March, 1963, mass meetings took place almost daily throughout the entire region. Men from hostile parishes faced each other in compact opposing groups and demanded an end to *kuru* sorcery and the mending of the male-female sex imbalance. Reputed sorcerers made public confessions of their past activities; men sought to purge themselves of ill feeling in a context of beneficial ritual forces at a time when mutual suspicion and hostility were disrupting social life. To the often expressed fears of extinction through the loss of the reproductive capacity of the women was now added the fear of internal disorder so great that society itself was felt to be endangered. Persuasive orators gave moral discourses on good behavior and appealed to those sorcerers who had not come forward to relinquish all future activities. The meetings had a formal, ritual quality in seating arrangement, orderly speechmaking, and food distribution. Sometimes they culminated in peacemaking rituals that signaled an end to hostile action. Men clapped hands and poured water on *kuru* victims—symbolic actions common to ceremonies calling for a truce between enemies, whether warriors or sorcerers.

Ritual emerged as a device by which the society attempted to create an illusion of unity. Orators recalled a golden past of supposedly less divisive times when their ancestors were not troubled by *kuru*. Men, they said, must halt their present intergroup strife and realize that they are one people. They named little-known all-inclusive groups to which they said they belonged. The meetings sought to redefine and enlarge the moral boundaries of the assembled groups. To survive the epidemic, the Fore thus offered the fiction of a united community.

Sorcerers, the Fore noted, had plainly exceeded the concept of self-limitation that men recognize in wartime. In the past, peace ceremonies were arranged when the toll of deaths met a certain limit

of propriety. Fore accused sorcerers of aiming to eliminate all women, of perpetrating a crime against society, a breach of the natural order. Women of the host group were present to listen to the discussion, sometimes angrily taking part. At some meetings, borrowing symbolism from recent mission exposure, men pledged their commitment to the future by washing their right hands in soapy water and raising the purged hand for all to see. They promised thenceforth, to forego sorcery.

The Fore image of society, then, is that of a body under attack. Illness, like warfare, endangers the viability of small groups whose cohesion is constitutionally unsound. Fore therefore attempt to enlarge their moral boundaries to avert further loss. Debates emphasize renewal, a new order, a society without sorcerers.

For the Enga, interpretation of disease as a form of ghost attack is an acknowledgment that the attack is coming from within one's own political group. It is internal and invisible, and not subject to identification in living human form. A population or resource reduction caused by the ancestors is socially acceptable; they are assumed to have the proper balance in mind. On the other hand, when Fore interpret disease as a consequence of attack by sorcerers they assume that aggression is coming from known living enemies outside the viable political units. It is unacceptable, and the ritual underlines this. The choice between the two interpretations is related to the man-resource ratio.

Sorcery is therefore a political instrument whereby antagonistic political groups recognize and adjust to a competitive advance or decline in strength. In societies where sorcery is an overwhelming issue—Tangu (Burridge 1960: 122), Dobu (Fortune 1963: 312), and Fore—epidemic disease has created alarming population problems. Sorcerers in these societies not only kill people; they are also wife stealers. Men are in competition for the sexual productivity of the women. Sorcerers are thus predators of the scarcest resource. This throws into relief other New Guinea societies where sorcery is not a central issue, but where the predominant theme is fear of women and their powers of contamination. The concept of female pollution in the latter societies would therefore appear to be a cultural regulator impressing on men their need to keep distant from the women.

Female Pollution

In a paper on female pollution in New Guinea, Meggitt (1964) outlined a complex of social attitudes and practices characteristic of certain parts of the Highlands. Meggitt (1964: 219) pointed out, without suggesting any causal sequence, that certain attitudes and practices clustered together.

> We might expect, therefore to find the notion of female pollution emphasized in societies where affinal groups are seen—for whatever reason—as inimical to one's own group, but absent or of little significance where marriages usually occur between friendly groups. Moreover, as a logical extension of this argument, associations devoted to male purification, seclusion, or initiation should be more sharply defined among the former. Finally, it follows that where male-female hostility exists in societies of the second category—those favouring inter-marriage among friendly groups—it will differ markedly from that of the first category.

He defined a regional variation in the phenomenon, noting two main kinds of intersexual conflict or opposition, the "Mae type" and the "Kuma type," reflecting the Western and Central Highlands social arrangements. The Mae reflect the anxiety of prudes to protect themselves from contamination by women, the Kuma the aggressive determination of lechers to assert control over recalcitrant women (Meggitt 1964: 221). In addition, Meggitt noted that Eastern Highlands societies appear to display both sets of characteristics simultaneously or in parallel form.

The argument pursued here would add causality to the analysis. The idea of female pollution is used as a cultural whip in societies where available resources are endangered by further population increase. Pollution is of less concern (Eastern Highlands) or absent (Central Highlands) where population expansion is not an environmental threat and is generally desired. Fear of pollution is a form of ideological birth control. Fear of female contamination thus declines with the introduction of new technologies and food sources.

Enga, Kaulong, and Sengseng are New Guinea societies with the most acute fear of female pollution yet recorded (Meggitt 1964; Goodale and Chowning 1971). Enga pressure on resources and pollution fears are well documented (Meggitt 1965a, 1965b), fears that lead to male postponement of marriage and to conflict over the need for heirs (Meggitt 1964: 210). Kaulong and Sengseng, neighboring societies in the Passismanua Census Division of Southwest New Britain, also live in a taxing environment, one subject to rapid flooding. Shifting taro cultivation is a major subsistence activity, while "at least 60% of the food consumed comes from the forest" (Goodale and Chowning 1971: 3). The "lack of any strong demarcation of sex roles in basic subsistence," noted as an unusual feature of New Guinea societies, suggests the need for an equal labor contribution by both men and women. Fear of female pollution and male avoidance of marriage are "one of the most distinctive aspects of Passismanua culture" (Goodale and Chowning 1971: 6). Kaulong and Sengseng males, like Enga, marry late. Some avoid sexual union until their 60s, and permanent bachelors are allowed a place of prestige in society. Until Mission and Administration interference, widows were strangled and buried 24 hours after the death of their husbands, thus seriously limiting their reproductive years. Kaulong and Sengseng manifest no strong desire for heirs, and practice infanticide. Belief in the contaminating powers of women, together with certain socially accepted behavioral manipulations, appears to have resulted in an effective cultural barrier to human reproduction. The population density of two to three persons per square mile is reported to have been held constant for many generations (Goodale and Chowning 1971: 2).

In Enga, Kaulong, and Sengseng societies the cultural sanctions against sexual congress are expressed in biological terms. An Enga husband refrains from frequent copulation, equating the loss of semen with a depletion of male vitality. Overindulgence will "dull his mind and leave his body permanently exhausted and withered" (Meggitt 1964: 210). The Enga bachelor, who should remain chaste, is kept from socially disapproved sexual congress by the belief that contact with a menstruating woman "will, in the absence of counter-magic sicken a man and cause persistent vomiting, turn his blood black, corrupt his vital juices so that his skin darkens and wrinkles as his flesh wastes, permanently dull his wits, and eventually lead to a slow decline and death." (Meggitt 1964: 207). That is, socially approved sexual congress within marriage is a biological danger; sexual contact outside the severe limits imposed by society leads to premature withering of the society.

Kaulong and Sengseng similarly resort to threats of biological disaster to enforce behavioral compliance. Shortly after her husband's death, a widow should be strangled by a close male kinsman—her son, brother, or father (Goodale and Chowning 1971: 8). The widow goads the reluctant murderer by suggesting that his restraint is based on a desire to copulate with her (Goodale: personal communication). This is not only a taunt of incest, but also an open reference to sex which is an affront in this prudish culture. The feeling of guilt is sufficient to force the murderer's hand. Enga, Kaulong, and Sengseng thus appear to be telling us their problems. For Enga, to contemplate nonapproved sexual activity leads to the dispatch of the actor. Kaulong and Sengseng males face a similar threat to their health; in addition, a male who fails to carry out a socially approved execution is contemplating an improper addition to society.

People are also telling us something of their problems by the way they mix or separate sex and the staple crop. Enga men, with magic to protect them from female pollution, copulate with their wives in the bush. Moreover, a husband "should not enter his gardens on the day he copulates, lest the female secretions adhering to him blight his crops" (Meggitt 1964: 210). Nor should he attempt to cook meat on that day, for it would spoil. In addition, Enga believe the menstrual blood destroys the *Acorus calamus* plants men use for wealth, pig, and war magic. Enga thus fear that increased female fertility would upset the delicate balance between men and their resources. Fore males, in contrast, purchase love magic to enchant the women they desire, and they copulate in the gardens.

Initiation

Initiation and bachelor associations also differ markedly in the Eastern and Western Highlands. The theme of Enga initiation rites concerns the shielding of males "from femininity, sexuality and impurity" (Meggitt 1964: 123). The men's behavior is prudish; they refrain from looking at each other's sexually provocative body areas and keep their conversations free of reference to sex or natural functions. Boys enter the bachelor associations when they are fifteen or sixteen, and remain members until marriage at a modal age of 25 to 27 (Meggitt 1965a: 86). The rituals require bathing to purify the youths from female influence, and ceremonies to keep alive the *Acorus* plants, the joint heritage of the subclan. A bachelor who breaks the sex rules prescribing chastity endangers not only his own health but also the welfare of the bachelors of the entire subclan. The iris plant would consequently die. Subclan members then beat the wayward youth and demand from him pig compensation "for the injury he has done them." The subclan thus exerts strong sanctions against unregulated additions to its size.

Courtship ceremonies in Enga society are "drearily proper gatherings," unlike the licentious functions in other parts of the Highlands, and girls attend with their chaperones (Meggitt 1964: 212). The playful culmination, where girls seize favored bachelors, is "not a betrothal" but a sign of willingness to pursue future acquaintance. The bachelors use the left hand to touch the penis throughout the unmarried period, thus keeping it from the fertilizing dangers of the right hand which has had contact with women (Meggitt 1964: 223–224). The bachelors themselves, the purificatory rituals, and the bog-iris leaves are all referred to as *sanggai*, "that which is hidden." That which is hidden would seem to be the penis, a fact recognized by the frustrated women who exert no restraint on public reference to sex, and taunt men about the smallness of their penises (Meggitt 1964: 214, 210).

The stress throughout the ceremonies is on male chastity and the aggregation of clan groups. The rituals culminate in a potentially explosive period, as the bachelors in each clan group shout mutually aggressive and boastful songs at other clans. Their earlier songs indicate the problems and ultimate dangers in Enga society; they tell of the shortage of the bog-iris plants for the many bachelors of the clan, and their dreams of territorial conquest (Meggitt 1964: 215).

Fore initiation is another matter. The ceremonies emphasize fertility and stress the rapid maturity of the youths. Rituals center on symbolic and imitative biological reproduction. In place of the bog-iris, which must be protected by the chastity of the bachelors, Fore men in seclusion reveal a pair of flutes, one male and one female. For men the flutes are a symbol of their virility, but the women refer to them as "flute-women" or co-wives (Berndt 1962: 70). Like the flutes, age-mates in Fore society are ideally pictured as matched pairs, men with an interest in the same women. The two must protect each other in life and are pledged to avenge each other's death. They are sexual confidants, and each has the right to inherit the other's widow (Lindenbaum and Glasse 1969).

The flutes are thus potent symbols of fertility, and during rituals are rubbed with pig blood, as are the male and female participants. Pig blood is also splashed on the earth. The ritual also requires that the youths undergo forced nose-bleeding, an imitative menstruation (Berndt 1962: 65–73, 104), believed to strengthen them and hasten maturity. Moreover, the same nose-bleeding ritual is performed for girls to strengthen them after menstruation and childbirth and before marriage (Berndt 1962: 106). This illuminates the danger men fear most. It seems that women represent two different kinds of danger in the Eastern and Western Highlands. Enga men fear women for the dangers of excess fertility. Fore men fear sexual inadequacy in the face of aggressively demanding females. Fore fear for their powers of reproduction; men and women alike must protect and increase their fertility with rituals which celebrate the physiological events of menstruation and childbirth (Berndt 1962: 105). Male-female relationships in the Eastern Highlands express complementarity rather than conflict (cf. Newman 1964: 265–266).

The tone of Fore society would shock the Enga. Male initiation ceremonies include men dressed as women, enacting scenes of copulation as a lesson on the dangers of adultery (Berndt 1962: 103). Female initiation presents women dressed as men, causing vaginal bleeding with mock coitus (Berndt 1962: 106). Fore women's songs, predictably, do not include frustrated reference to penises the size of tiny mushrooms (Meggitt 1964: 214) but extol the irresistible attraction of the penis-flutes (Berndt 1962: 70). Erotic farces are also frequently enacted, dramatizing incidents from myth or everyday life (Berndt 1962: 148).

Fore boys undergo initiation at a tender age (Berndt 1962: 106 photo) and continue until past adolescence. Participation in the rituals, however, does not rule out sexual adventure. Rather the ceremonies stimulate an interest in sex and carry the message that society awards prestige to the sexually active male. Moral rules during initiation stress protection of the political unit by aggressive behavior in both war and sex (Berndt 1962: 110), while negative lessons deal emphatically with stealing property and adultery, thefts which endanger internal solidarity. The negative lessons are hardly effective, for adultery is a common source of conflict. Berndt (1962: 328–380) records 107 indigenous court hearings among Fore and their neighbors. Most cases concern adultery, and there was no case of homicide. Punishment in one adultery case required the forced re-enactment of the crime by the adulterous pair, after which the husband received a compensation payment and also kept his wife. In contrast, Enga beat adulterous wives and then transfer them to the adulterer in return for a compensation payment of pigs, a scarce resource.

Although Fore may talk about female pollution, they lack the Enga sense of horror. Premarital and extra-marital affairs abound, and Fore are cavalier in their approach to incest. Faced with a shortage of women, South Fore redefine classificatory sisters as marriageable partners; the new wife's father then becomes a mother's brother, and her brothers the husband's cross-cousins (Glasse 1969: 29–30).

Conclusion

Gross differences thus emerge in the relationship of men to women throughout New Guinea. It may be possible to construct a continuum whereby Enga, Kaulong, and Sengseng typify societies in which the man-resource ratio is unusually high, giving rise to a certain cultural complex. Here death from disease is accepted as the punishment of ancestral spirits, pollution ideas limit the meeting of men and women during their fertile years, and there is an emphasis on male chastity. Other cultural features also seem to cluster at this end of the spectrum: a severe attitude towards incest and a view that adulterers are no great threat. Cannibalism in these societies is considered repulsive to the living, but may occur among ogres and other inhabitants of the pantheon.

At the other end of the spectrum are societies where population increase is desired—Fore, Daribi, Tangu, Dobu, Bena-Bena, and Orokaiva. Here disease is interpreted as an external attack by sorcerers, pollution ideas are not strenuously used to curb the access of men to women, the incest rule may be loosely observed, adultery is the serious theft of a scarce resource, and cannibalism may be present as a form of symbolic self-generation.

Few societies are found at these extremes. Kyaka, for instance, who are neighbors of the Enga but with a lower population density, have a cultural complex that includes malicious ghosts of the dead, together with a fertility goddess and more emphasis on sorcery (Bulmer 1965: 132–161). It is suggested that witches appear in the middle of the continuum, where population densities rise, altering the ratio of people to resources. Witches are not connected with the important survival issues but are concerned with the lesser dangers of infant mortality, small property less, and constitutional conflicts. Important survival issues are left to gods or to sorcerers.

A New Weapon Stirs Up Old Ghosts

William E. Mitchell

In the following article, William E. Mitchell describes the Wape shotgun cult, a belief and behavioral system that sprang up in New Guinea after the introduction of guns to the area in the late 1940s and early 1950s. Mitchell tells how Wape villagers pool their money to collectively purchase a shotgun, and then select a candidate from within their ranks to take the firearm test administered by officials. If the applicant is successful, a permit is issued and the individual must agree to shoot game for his village. Of special interest for this chapter is the role of ancestral ghosts in the system. Among the Wape, the dead are believed not only to protect the living from harm but also to supply them with meat and punish anyone who may have wronged them. Thus, a dead male relative becomes an invaluable aide to the hunter. The author shows how the cult's belief in vengeful spirits helps them understand why they sometimes experience unsuccessful hunting.

Reprinted with permission from *Natural History*, Vol. 82, no. 10 (December 1973), pp. 75–84. Copyright the American Museum of Natural History, 1973.

WHEN, IN 1947, THE FRANCISCAN FRIARS WENT to live among the nearly 10,000 Wape people of New Guinea, the principal native weapons were bone daggers and the bow and arrow. Even then, game was scarce in the heavily populated mountains where the Wape live, and the killing of a wild pig or a cassowary, New Guinea's major game animals, was an important village event. The Wape live in the western part of the Sepik River Basin. Their small villages lie along the narrow ridges of the Torricelli Mountains, above the sago palm swamps where women process palm pith, the Wape staff of life.

Today the Wape hunter's principal weapon is still the bow and arrow and game is even scarcer. This is partially the result of a new addition to the hunter's armory—the prosaic shotgun—which has had a profound moral impact on Wape village life.

The first guns were brought into this area in the late 1940s and early 1950s by missionaries, traders, and Australian government officials. Although natives were not permitted to own guns, they could use them if employed by a white man to shoot game for his table. This was a very prestigious job.

In 1960, government regulations were changed to permit natives to purchase single-shot shotguns. At first only a few Wape men, living in villages close to the government station and helpful to government officials, were granted gun permits. Eventually more permits were issued, but today, in hopes of preserving the remaining game, one permit is issued for every 100 people.

Within ten years of the granting of the first gun permits, a belief and behavioral system had evolved around the shotgun. It was based on traditional Wape hunting lore but had distinctive elaborations stemming from native perceptions of the teachings of government officials and missionaries. For descriptive purposes I call this system of formalized beliefs and ritual the "Wape shotgun cult." It is one of several Wape ceremonial cults, but the only one originating after contact with Europeans. Although the specific practices of the shotgun cult vary from village to village, the underlying beliefs are the same.

In creating the shotgun cult the Wape faced the challenge of adapting an introduced implement to their culture. Unlike steel axes and knives, which replaced stone adzes and bamboo knives, the shotgun has never replaced the bow and arrow. The shotgun is a scarce and expensive machine. This, together with the European sanctions imposed upon its introduction, places it in a unique position, both symbolically and behaviorally, among the Wape.

The cult is a conservative institution. It breaks no new cognitive ground by challenging established Wape concepts. Instead it merges traditional hunting concepts with European moral teachings to create a coherent system. The cult upholds traditional beliefs, accepts European authority, and most important, provides an explanation for unsuccessful hunting.

In 1970, my family and I arrived in Lumi, a small mountain settlement, which is the government's subdistrict headquarters in the middle of Wapeland. For the next year and a half, we lived in the village of Taute, near Lumi. There my wife and I studied Wape culture.

Taute, which has a population of 220, is reached by narrow foot trails, root strewn and muddy, passing through the dense, damp forest. The low houses—made of sago palm stems and roofed with sago thatch—are scattered about in the sandy plaza and among the coconut palms and breadfruit trees along the ridge. Towering poinsettias, red and pink hibiscus, and multicolored shrubs contrast with the encircling forest's greens and browns. A few small latrines perch on the steep slopes, concessions to Western concepts of hygiene. In the morning, flocks of screeching cockatoos glide below the ridge through the rising mists. When the breadfruit trees are bearing, giant fruit bats flop across the sky at dusk.

Since the mid-1950s the Franciscan friars have maintained off and on, a religious school in Taute. There, Wape boys are instructed by a native catechist in Catholicism, simple arithmetic, and Melanesian Pidgin. A priest from Lumi visits the village several times a year, and the villagers, Catholic and heathen alike, are proud of their affiliation with the Franciscans and staunchly loyal to them. But their Catholicism is nominal and superficial—a scant and brittle frosting that does not mask their own religious beliefs, which dominate everyday life.

The ethos of Wape society is oriented around sacred curing rituals. Whereas some Sepik cultures aggressively center their ceremonial life around headhunting and the raising of sturdy and brave children, the Wape defensively center theirs in the ritual appeasement of malevolent ghosts and forest demons, who they believe cause sickness. Most men belong to one of the demon-curing cults where, once initiated as priests, they are responsible for producing the often elaborate curing ceremonies for exorcising the demon from the afflicted.

The little money that exists among the Wape is earned primarily by the men, who work as two-year contract laborers on the coastal and island copra plantations. Because of the lack of money to buy canned meats, the scarcity of game, and the paucity of fish in the mountain streams, the protein intake of the Wape is exceedingly low. The most common meal is sago dumplings and boiled leaves. Malnutrition is common among youngsters, and physical development is generally retarded. According to studies by Dr. Lyn Wark, a medical missionary who has worked widely among the Wape, the average birth weight of the Wape baby is the lowest recorded in the world. Correspondingly, secondary sex characteristics are delayed. For example, the mean age for the onset of menses is over eighteen years.

Before contact with Westerners, Wape men were naked and the women wore short string skirts. Today most men wear shorts and the women wear skirts purchased from Lumi's four small stores. To appear in a semblance of European dress, however meager or worn, is a matter of pride and modesty to both sexes. "Savages" do not wear clothes, but white men and those who have been enlightened by white men do. In this sense, the Wape's Western-style dress represents an identification with the politically and materially powerful white man. The identification is with power; it is an ego-enhancing maneuver that permits the Wape to live with dignity, even though they are subservient to Western rule and influence. The tendency of the Wape to identify with, and incorporate, the alien when it serves to preserve their culture will help us to understand how they have woven diverse cultural strands into the creation of the shotgun cult.

From the first day I arrived in Taute, the men repeatedly made two urgent requests of me. One was to open a store in the village, saving them the difficult walk into Lumi; the other was to buy a shotgun to help them kill game. This was the least, they seemed to indicate, a fair-minded and, in Wape terms, obviously rich neighbor should do. One of the hardest things the anthropologist in the field must learn is to say "no" to deserving people. To be stingy is almost to be un-American, but we had come half-way around the world to learn about the Wape way of life, not to introduce stores and shotguns that would alter the established trading and hunting patterns.

After several months the people of the major Taute hamlets, Kafiere, where we lived, and Mifu, a ten-minute walk away, each decided to buy a group-owned shotgun. The investment was a sizable forty-two Australian dollars; forty dollars for the gun and two dollars for the gun permit. Each hamlet made a volunteer collection from its members and I, as a fellow villager, contributed to both guns. A week later the villagers purchased the guns from one of the Lumi stores, and I began to learn about the shotgun's ritual and moral importance to the Wape. The villagers were already familiar with the significance of the shotgun for they had purchased one seveal years before. The cult ended, however, when the gun broke.

The shotgun, like Melanesian Pidgin, is associated by the Wape with Europeans and modernity. Not surprisingly, Pidgin is favored for shotgun parlance. The licensed gunman is not only called *sutboi* ("shootboy") but also *laman* ("law man"), the latter a term that connotes his official tie to European law and government as perceived by the villagers.

When a candidate for a gun permit appears before the government official in Lumi, he is examined orally on the use of firearms, then given an unloaded shotgun and tested on his handling knowledge. Under the direct and questioning gaze of the examining official, candidates sometimes become flustered. One inadvertently aimed the gun first toward the wife of the assistant district commissioner and then toward a group of observers. His examination ended ignominiously on the spot.

If the candidate passes the test and the examining official approves of his character, he is then lectured on the use of the gun: only the candidate can fire it, he must willingly shoot game for his fellow villagers, and the gun must be used exclusively for hunting. He is strongly warned that if any of these rules are broken or if there is trouble in the village, he will lose the gun and the permit and will be imprisoned.

The candidate's friends and the inevitable audience are present for the lecture. Here, as in many spheres of native life, the official's power is absolute, and the Wape know this from long experience. Guns have been confiscated or destroyed without reimbursement and gunmen have been jailed.

The official's charge to the candidate is willingly accepted. Henceforth, he will never leave the village without carrying his gun. He is now a *laman*, and he has the gun and permit, printed entirely in English, to prove it.

The government official's strong sanctions against village quarrels are motivated by his fear that the gun might be used in a dispute among villagers. The sanctions are further upheld by the missionaries' and catechists' sermons against quarreling and wrongdoing as they attempt to teach the Christian doctrine of brotherly love. The message the villagers receive is this: To keep the white man's gun, they must follow the white man's rules. This the Wape do, not in servile submission, but with some pride because the presence of the gun and the public focus on morality mark the village as progressive and modern. The licensed gunman, therefore, is not only the guardian of the gun but of village morality as well.

Rain or shine, he is expected to go into the forest without compensation to hunt for his fellow villagers, who give him cartridges with some personal identifying mark upon them. After a gunman makes a kill, the owner of the cartridge receives the game and distributes it according to his economic obligations to others. But the gunman, like the bow and arrow hunter, is forbidden to eat from the kill; to do so would jeopardize further successful hunting.

In the hamlet of Kafiere, the clan that had contributed the most money toward the gun and on whose lands the most game was to be found appointed Auwe as gunman. But Auwe's wife, Naiasu, was initially against his selection. Her previous husband, Semer, now dead several years, had been Kafiere's first *sutboi* and she argued that the heavy hunting responsibilities of a *sutboi* took too much time, forcing him to neglect his own gardening and hunting obligations.

When Auwe first requested a gun permit he was turned away. The villagers believed that the ghost of Naiasu's dead husband, Semer, had followed Auwe to Lumi and influenced the examining official against him. Semer's ghost was acting to fulfill Naiasu's wish that her young son, now Auwe's stepson, would have a stepfather who was always available. This was the first of many stories I was to hear about the relationship between ghosts and the gun. When Auwe returned to Lumi for a second try, he passed the examination and was given the official permit.

The hamlet now had its own gun and hunting could begin in earnest. The first step was an annunciation feast called, in Pidgin, a *kapti* ("cup of tea"). Its purpose was to inform the villagers' dead ancestors about the new gun. This was important because ancestral ghosts roam the forest land of their lineage, protecting it from intruders and driving game to their hunting descendants. The hunter's most important hunting aide is his dead male relatives, to whom he prays for game upon entering his hunting lands. The dead remain active in the affairs of the living by protecting them from harm, providing them with meat, and punishing those who have wronged them.

The small sacrificial feast was held in front of Auwe's house. Placing the upright gun on a makeshift table in the midst of the food, Auwe rubbed it with sacred ginger. One of Auwe's elderly clansmen, standing and facing his land, called out to his ancestors by name and told them about the new gun. He implored them to send wild pigs and cassowaries to Auwe.

Several men spoke of the new morality that was to accompany hunting with a gun. The villagers should not argue or quarrel among themselves; problems must be settled quietly and without bitterness; malicious gossip and stealing were forbidden. If these rules were not obeyed, Auwe would not find game.

In traditional Wape culture there is no feast analogous to the *kapti*. Indeed, there are no general community-wide feasts. The *kapti* is apparently modeled on a European social gathering.

For the remainder of my stay in Taute, I followed closely the fortunes of the Taute guns and of guns in nearby villages as well. All seemed to be faced with the same two problems: game was rarely seen; and when seen, was rarely killed. Considering that a cartridge belongs to a villager, not the gunman, how was this economic loss handled? This presented a most intriguing and novel problem for there were no analogs to this type of predicament within the traditional culture. By Wape standards, the pecuniary implications of such a loss, although but a few Australian shillings, could not graciously be ignored by the loser. At the very least the loss had to be explained even if the money for the cartridges could not be retrieved.

Now I understood the concern about the ancestral ghosts. If the hunter shot and missed, the owner of the fired shells was being punished by being denied meat. Either he or a close family member had quarreled or wronged another person whose ghost-relative was securing revenge by causing the hunter to miss. This, then, was the functional meaning of the proscription against quarreling. By avoiding disputes, the villagers were trying to prevent the intervention of ancestral ghosts in human affairs. In a peaceful village without quarrels, the gunman could hunt undisturbed by vengeful ghosts chasing away game or misrouting costly shells.

Although a number of factors in European culture have influenced the shotgun cult, the cult's basic premise of a positive correlation between quarreling and bad hunting is derived directly from traditional Wape culture. In bow and arrow hunting, an individual who feels he was not given his fair share of a hunter's kill may punish the hunter by gossiping about him or quarreling openly with him. The aggrieved person's ancestral ghosts revenge the slight by chasing the game away from the offending hunter or misdirecting his arrows. But this is a private affair between the hunter and the angered person; their quarrel has no influence upon the hunting of others. And it is rare for an issue other than distribution of game to cause a ghost to hinder a bowman's success. The hunter's prowess is restored only when the angered person performs a brief supplication rite over the hunter.

This, then, is the conceptual basis for the tie between quarreling and bad hunting. Originally relevant only to bow and arrow hunting, it was then broadened to accommodate the government's pronouncements about the shotgun and keeping the village peace. And it applies perfectly to the special circumstances of shotgun hunting. Because the shotgun is community owned and many villagers buy cartridges for it, the villagers are identified with both the gun and the gunman. As a proxy hunter for the villagers, the gunman is potentially subject to the ghostly sanctions resulting from their collective wrongs. Thus gun hunting, unlike bow and arrow hunting, is a community affair and the community-wide taboo against quarrels and personal transgressions is the only effective way to prevent spiteful ghosts from wrecking the hunt.

No village, however, even if populated by people as disciplined and well behaved as the Wape, can constantly live in the state of pious peace considered necessary for continuous good gun hunting. When the hunting is poor, the gunman must discover the quarrels and wrongs within the village. After having identified the individuals whose ancestral ghosts are sabotaging the hunting, the gunman must also see to it that they implore the ghosts to stop. Embarrassed by the public disclosure, they will quickly comply.

The common method for detecting points of friction within the village is to bring the villagers together for a special meeting. The gunman will then document in detail his misfortunes and call on the villagers to find out what is ruining the hunting. If confessions of wrongdoing are not forthcoming, questioning accusations result. The meeting, beginning in Pidgin, moves into Wape as the discussion becomes more complex and voluble. It may last up to three hours; but even if there is no resolution, it always ends amiably—at least on the surface. For it is important to create no new antagonisms.

The other technique for locating the source of the hunting problem is to call in a professional clairvoyant. As the villagers must pay for his services, he is usually consulted only after a series of unsuccessful meetings. Clairvoyants have replaced the shamans, who were outlawed by the government and the mission because they practiced sorcery and ritual murders. The Wape do not consider a clairvoyant a sorcerer; he is a man with second sight who is experienced in discovering and treating the hidden causes of intractable problems. As such, shotguns are among his best patients.

Mewau, a clairvoyant from a neighboring village, held a "shotgun clinic" in Taute to examine the Mifu and Kafiere guns. For about an hour he examined the two guns and questioned the villagers. Then he declared the reasons for their misfortune.

Kapul, a dead Mifu shaman, was preventing the Mifu gun from killing game because a close relative of the gunman had allegedly stolen valuables from Kapul's daughter. Because of the family ties between the gunman and the thief, Kapul's ghost was punishing the gunman.

The Kafiere gun, Mewau declared, was not able to find game because a widow in the village felt that her dead husband's clan had not previously distributed game to her in a fair way. By interfering with the Kafiere gun, her husband's ghost was punishing his clan for the neglect of his family.

Once the source of trouble is named, there are several possible types of remedial ritual depending upon the seriousness of the situation. For example, the circumstances surrounding the naming of the husband's ghost were considered serious, and a *kapti* was held to placate him. Another, simpler ritual involves the preparation of taro soup, which the gunman consumes. But the simplest, commonest remedial rite is the supplication ritual without sacrificial food offerings, a ritual in which I became involved.

Mifu's gunman had shot a pig with one of his own cartridges but did not give me the small portion due me as a part owner of the gun. Partly as a test to see if my ancestors counted for anything in Taute and partly because I did not want to let this calculated slight go unchallenged, I, in typical Wape fashion, said nothing to the gunman but gossiped discreetly about his selfishness. The gunman continued to hunt but had no further success. When his bad luck persisted, a meeting was called to find out the reason. The gunman asked me if I was angry because I had not been given my portion of the pig. When I acknowledged my anger, he handed the shotgun to me and I dutifully spoke out to my ancestors to stop turning the game away from the gun.

But the gunman still had no success in the hunt, and the villagers decided there were other wrongs as well. The search for the offending ghosts continued. Eventually the villagers became so discouraged with the Mifu gun that they stopped giving cartridges to the gunman. The consensus was that a major undetected wrong existed in the hamlet, and until it was uncovered and the guilty ghost called off, hunting with the gun was senseless and extravagant. Thus the propriety of a remedial rite is established if there is success on the next hunt. The system is completely empirical: if no game is seen or if seen, is not killed, then the search for the wrong must continue.

Wape people are generally even tempered, and their villages, in contrast to many in New Guinea, strike the newcomer as almost serene. But the social impact of the guns at this time was pervasive, and life in Taute literally revolved around the guns and their hunting fortunes. Whereas the villagers previously had kept to their own affairs, they now became embroiled in meeting after meeting, seeking out transgressions, quarrels, and wrongdoing. As the gunman continued to have bad luck, his efforts to discover the cause became more zealous. A certain amount of polarization resulted: the gunman accused the villagers, the men accused the women, and the adults accused the young people of hiding their wrongs. And a few who had lost many cartridges wondered if the *sutboi* was keeping the game for himself. But no one ever suggested that he was an inexperienced shotgun hunter. The gunman was generally considered to be blameless; in fact, the more game he missed, the more self-righteous he became and the more miscreant the villagers.

Six months of poor hunting had gone by; the villagers felt that the only recourse left to them was to bring a bush demon named *mani* into the village from the jungle for a festival. The *mani's* small stone heart is kept enshrined in a rustic altar in a corner of Kafiere's ceremonial house and after a kill the animal's blood is smeared upon it. The *mani* will reward the village with further kills only if he is fed with blood. *Mani* is the only spirit, other than ghosts, who can cause both good and bad hunting depending upon the way he is treated. Soon after the shotgun arrived in Taute, the gunman and some other men left their homes to sleep in the men's ceremonial house to keep *mani's* stone heart warm. They thought *mani*, in appreciation, would send game to the gunman.

When little game was killed, the villagers decided on the hunting festival. In a special house outside of the village, men constructed the great conical mask that depicts *mani*. For several weeks they worked to cover the mask's frame with the spathes of sago palm fronds painted with designs traditional to *mani*. Finally, a priest of the *mani* cult, wearing a 20-foot-high mask festooned with feathers and leaves, pranced into the village to the thunderous beat of wooden drums.

For the next week and a half men from other villages who wished us well came and joined in the all-night singing of the *mani* song cycle. In the morning, if the weather was clear, *mani* led the bow and arrow hunters and the gunman to the edge of the village and sent them on their way to hunting success. But in spite of the careful attentions the villagers directed toward *mani*, he rewarded them with only one wild pig. The villagers became openly discouraged, then annoyed. Finally the hunters, disgusted and weary from numerous long futile hunts, and other men, their shoulders sore and bloody from constantly carrying the heavy mask around the plaza, decided that *mani* was simply taking advantage of them; all of their hard work was for nothing. Disgusted, they decided to send *mani* back to his home in the forest.

One late afternoon the *mani* appeared in the plaza but he did not prance. He walked slowly around the plaza, stopping at each house to throw ashes over himself with his single bark cloth arm. The villagers said he was in mourning because he had to leave by dusk and would miss the company of men. Silently the people watched the once gay and graceful *mani* lumber out of the village. The men and boys followed him into the forest. Then the gunman split open the mask, to insure the spirit's exit and eventual return to his forest home, and hurled it over the edge of the cliff into the bush below.

A few months after the *mani* hunting festival, the shotgun cult as I had known it in Taute ceased to function. All but one of the able young men of the hamlet of Kafiere went off to work on a coastal plantation for two years. With no young men, the ceremonial activities of the hunting and curing cults were suspended and the fault-finding meetings halted until their return. The drama and excitement of the previous months had vanished with the men.

Spirits, Power, and Man

James F. Downs

Religion among the Washo of California and Nevada was interwoven into nearly every act of the day. Ritual occurred everywhere and at all times—in food-getting, childbirth and childrearing, dreams, the treatment of animal remains, interaction with the environment, games, gambling, and even in courtship—and Washo religion seldom required specialists for these activities, but rather placed the responsibility for ritual on the individuals within a particular family group. The two basic components of Washo religion were the spirits of the dead and the power of the living. The preceding article showed how Wape ancestral ghosts provided invaluable aid to hunters, and how a person's ancestral ghosts could sabotage the hunting of an adversary: in other words, Wape family ghosts were generally considered to be helpful. Among the Washo, however, ancestral ghosts were feared and avoided. Spirits of the dead were angry and vengeful, always ready to return and terrorize the living.

WITHIN THE SCOPE OF HIS LIMITED TECHnology, the Washo was a rational person, well aware of cause and effect and prepared to handle the exigencies of his position. However, the precarious balance of Washo society often made survival seemingly dependent on chance. Why should a well-trained hunter locate his quarry only to have it escape him at the last moment? How could a well-made and well-aimed arrow miss an easy shot? Why should one man on a raid be wounded or killed and another escape unscathed? Why should the pine nut tree be fruitful one year and not at all the next? How was it that sickness struck down one person and passed over another? Why indeed should a man, unwounded and unhurt, die at all? These questions plague all societies and in many, including our own, are more or less successfully resolved in sophisticated theologies. Among many primitives, the basis of religion is an explanation of both the how and the why of the vagaries of life. The ritual of many primitive peoples, including those of the Washo, are both expressions of the Washo view of cause and effect and an attempt to maintain an understandable order to life.

The Washo did not articulate a complete philosophy or theology. Their religious life dealt with the practical day-to-day events: hunting, war, love, birth, health, and death. Yet we can present an organized picture of Washo religious life. We must remember, however, that a systematic presentation of Washo religion is a device which helps us understand a foreign and confusing point of view. It does not reflect the minds of the Washo as they go about their daily tasks, scarcely separating the sacred and the profane.

Power

To many of the questions posed above the Washo's answer was "power." A successful hunter was more than skilled and careful, he was aided by a special power. A man who dreamed of rabbits or antelope was more than simply lucky, he was a possessor of a special power. The nature of this power is not clearly defined in all cases. We can see how power works most clearly if we learn how a man becomes a "doctor," or shaman, among the Washo. The shaman was expected to carry his share of the burden of living, but his special powers set him apart from his fellows and contributed to his livelihood because his services were valuable and demanded payment. The shaman's special power was the ability to diagnose and cure illness.

Illness might come from three sources. A ghost, angry because some piece of his property was being used by the living, might make the user sick. A sorcerer might cause illness by using magic to "shoot" a foreign body into his victim. Or a person might become ill because he had violated some taboo such as mistreating pine nuts or piñon trees. To affect a cure, a shaman was called to perform a ceremony over the patient. The cure was felt to be brought about not by the shaman's skill but by his "power" which was felt to be apart from the person of the shaman himself. The shaman served as a medium through which the power could be used to the benefit of the sick person. A treatment required that the shaman work for four nights. In addition to the shaman, the patient's family and a number of friends gathered. On each of the nights the shaman prayed to his power to assist him, smoked tobacco, frequently a sacred or semi-sacred act among Indians; and sang special songs which were his alone. Accompanying his singing with a rattle made of dry cocoons, he passed into a trance and while in this state located the site of the illness and identified the cause. If a ghost was the cause, the shaman would identify the contaminating object and instruct the patient as to whether he should get rid of it or perhaps simply treat it differently. If, on the other hand, an enemy had "shot" a sickness into the patient, the shaman would remove it by sucking, employing an eagle feather and tobacco smoke to make the extraction easier. When the object was removed and shown to the patient and his guests, the shaman would lecture it and then throw it away into the night. He was able to produce an object by means of legerdemain. He did not, however, feel that this was in any way hypocritical. His ability to perform these sleight-of-hand tricks was part of the exercise of his power. We might compare his use of sleight-of-hand to instill confidence in his power to the bedside manner of a modern doctor attempting to instill confidence in his patients. For his services a shaman was paid in food and valuable objects. The process of becoming a doctor illustrates the nature of power as the Washo conceived it.

The power to become a shaman was not sought by the Washo, it came unsought and often unwelcomed. The first signs of receiving power were often a series of dreams. In these dreams an animal, a bear, an owl, a "ghost" or some other being would appear. The vision would offer him power and assistance in life. The Washo feared power; it was dangerous for one who had it and the greater and more clearly defined the power, the more dangerous it was. The trancelike state which was part of the curing ceremony seemed to many Washo to be akin to death, a loss of spirit. Because of this, a young man might ignore the offers of spiritual power. But a spirit being, or *wegaleyo*, frequently refused to be ignored. It would begin to inflict a series of ailments upon its chosen vehicle. Although it was not considered good social form to brag of having power or to openly seek it, some men did secretly hope for power. Men of this type today invariably complain of a long series of illnesses, seizures, and ailments. To the outsider such a person might appear to be simply a hypochondriac, but the Washo recognized this as a veiled claim to power. Under pressure from the *wegaleyo*, a man would usually succumb and accept his power. Once he had made this secret decision, his dreams would become instruction sessions. The *wegaleyo* would tell him where he could find a special spring or pool. This was "his water" to be used in ceremonies or for ritual bathing or to decontaminate sacred articles collected by the shaman in his career. The spirit also taught his pupil a special song which he would remember word for word when he awoke. In later years a shaman might learn many such songs from his spirit. He would also receive instructions as to what equipment to collect. This would always include a rattle and eagle feathers. Individuals might also possess special stones, shell jewelry, or animal skins. These objects were usually obtained under unusual or miraculous circumstances. One shaman, for instance, had a stone shaped like a human molar which attracted his attention by whistling until he located the stone. In addition to his instructions direct from his spirit, a prospective shaman would seek out an established practitioner and apprentice himself to the older man. The tutor would instruct his apprentice in the arts of legerdemain, ventriloquism, and such feats as smoking several pipefulls of tobacco without allowing the smoke to escape from his lungs. In time, after his powers were known through participation in ceremonies held by his mentor, a shaman would be asked to perform cures of his own.

Shamans were always considered to be potential sorcerers. Their power was neither good nor bad in itself and could be used for whatever ends the shaman sought. The ability to use power against others is illustrated in a traditional Washo tale, which also points out the basic suspicion held by southern Washo toward northern Washo. According to the story, a northern Washo appeared at a camp in Carson Valley and there asked for food. Because he was a stranger, he was refused by all but one old woman. She fed the stranger and allowed him to sleep in her camp. The man left the camp determined to work vengeance on the people who had been so miserly with him. Walking west from Carson Valley, the northerner rested at the hot springs near Markleville. There performing some unknown magic, he pointed his finger in the direction of the camp. The power he controlled killed all the members of the camp, save the old woman who had been generous to him. Modern Washo insist that one can see a barren line in the earth stretching from Markleville to Carson Valley. They also insist that the campsite is covered with skeletons and abandoned equipment. This winter camp may well have been struck by the plague or some other epidemic disease.

Tradition describes other uses of shamanistic power. In what might be described as advertising contests, shaman engaged in tests of power, particularly at gatherings such as the *gumsaba*. The most common demonstration of power was said to be setting a number of stakes in a line. The shaman would point at the sticks and the winner of the contest was the shaman who could knock down the most sticks. Shamans are reported to have engaged in casual displays of power by offering an unsuspecting victim a pipe, or in later times, a cigarette. The shaman's power would remain in the pipe or cigarette and the smoker would be knocked flat or perhaps unconscious. To possess such power was dangerous and inconvenient. A person who received his power from the deer, for instance, could no longer eat deer meat. If he did, he would become ill and perhaps die. The possession of power also made one subject to frightening and mysterious experiences. A well-known shaman in the early part of this century staged a curing ceremony during which he fell into the fire while in a trance. Burning his trousers off, he had to go home wearing his shirt as a loin cloth although he was not hurt. On his way the shaman stopped at a stream to bathe. As he bent over the water, he fell into a faint and was taken down into the water. There he was greeted by Water Baby, a spirit creature said to inhabit all bodies of water in the Washo country. The Water Baby took the shaman into a strange land to meet the king of the Water Babies who lived in a large stone house. There the shaman was entertained by five young girls who taught him a special song. The Water Baby guide then took the shaman back to the surface and left him where the frightened man awoke floating in the water.

If a shaman lost his sacred paraphernalia or it was destroyed, he would most certainly become seriously ill. Because of these dangers, many men tried to avoid power if it was thrust upon them and would employ a shaman to help them rid themselves of the persistent spirit. If this was successful they could resume the normal Washo life. If not, they had little choice but to quiet the spirit and accept its gift.

The nature of power is most clearly seen in the complex of Washo shamanism, but *wegelayo* often provided special powers of a less general nature. Some men with a water *wegelayo* were believed to be able to bring rain. Others who had been visited by the bear-*wegelayo* might on occasion act like a bear and be particularly brave or notably short tempered. Others might have the power to handle rattlesnakes with impunity and cure rattlesnake bites. The Water Baby might act as a *wegelayo* and give a person the power to walk under water. There is said to be a broad road of white sand cross the bottom of Lake Tahoe. This was the special route of men with Water Baby *wegelayo* who wished to visit the beds of wild poison parsnips on the north shore of the lake. These poison plants used to be eaten with impunity as a demonstration of power. Some specially powerful men received their power from a number of different sources all of which helped in curing or performing other miracles.

The most dangerous task for a shaman was to recover the soul of a person who had apparently died. It was believed that with the help of his *wegelayo* a shaman could go into a trance and, in spirit form, follow the soul of the dead person into the land of the dead. This was described as a place in the sky to the south of Washo country. Its approaches were guarded by a number of fierce warriors. Behind these sentries was a spring. If the shaman could overtake the soul before it had drunk from the spring he could return it to its earthly body and revive his patient. This land of the dead was said to be a happy place where people played games and gambled and danced unless they had committed a murder. Murderers were banned by the other shades and placed in a kind of heavenly coventry.

We have spoken of shamans as being males, but women could also become shamans and many did. Their experiences and training did not differ from those of men. Power was not exclusively a gift of the spirit beings to humans. In a general way, everything was viewed as having some power. Merely to live required some supernatural assistance. Successful survival was a sign of power and thus old people had demonstrated that they were powerful. There was a widespread belief that old people were dangerous and should not be offended or harmed lest they retaliate by using their power. This belief worked to assure that an ancient Washo in his final years would receive support from those who were obligated to him. Even though he might be unable to share the burdens of life, he could avenge himself on those who did not behave ethically. This general power was extended to all living things, animals, and plants and, as we have seen, was the basis of many of the behavior patterns associated with hunting, fishing, and gathering.

Ghosts

The spirits of the dead were to be greatly feared and avoided. No Washo ever thought of his ancestors as benign figures concerned with his happiness and welfare. Instead they were angry and vengeful. If their property was used or misused, if their burial was not properly conducted, or for any one of a dozen other sins of omission or commission, the dead might return to plague the living. Therefore Washo funerals were not ceremonies designed to honor the dead or comfort the living. They were ways of making sure the dead person's spirit would not return. It was for this reason that his home was burned or abandoned. If he returned to familiar haunts, the house and family would be gone. For the same reason his clothing and personal property were burned or buried with him. A person using some possession of a dead man was always liable to a visit from the ghost who had located his property and found the user. The brief Washo burial prayers were really exhortations to the dead person to accept his death and leave the living alone. He was told that no one had killed him and that no one was angry at him. Association with the dead was slightly contaminating and upon returning from funerals people washed themselves before handling food or touching children lest the contamination spread and attract the ghost. The Washo argue that it is the nature of things that the dead should remain dead and not bother the living. For this reason they say a rain storm always occurs after a death to wipe out the footprints of the deceased and thus remove all traces of his existence. The taboo on using the name of the dead was another such precaution. Despite all these precautions, the dead did return. Sometimes they came on specific missions of vengeance and on other occasions to simply wander in the vicinity of human beings. The twirling dust devils so common in the summer in this region were thought to be ghosts, and a sudden puff of warm air on a still summer night was most certainly a shade. The belief in ghosts and personal power was an important factor in Washo child raising practices. Parents avoided spanking or striking a child for fear of angering some dead relative. In this instance the ghost seemed to have some friendly concern for the living, but the manner of showing it was to cause the death of the child as a punishment to the parents. The fear of sorcery led the Washo to encourage their younger children to remain within their own family group. Associating with strangers, particularly old strangers, could be dangerous. This belief is obviously related to the development of deep ties of dependence on one's close relatives and the strengthening of the all-important Washo family unit. The two major concepts of Washo religion are: ghosts, to be feared, avoided, and appeased; and power, to be used to accomplish the business of living. But, these were not all the facets of Washo religion. Like most people the Washo had explanations for the natural and human environment in which they found themselves. These explanations were preserved in a body of mythology. The corpus of myth was not an elaborate and involved body of scripture. Rather, it consisted of a number of rather simple tales, many of which seem confused and inconsistent to foreigners.

Creation

Two myths deal with creation and although they are quite different, the inconsistency seems not to trouble the Washo who use whichever set of tales seems most appropriate at the time. The world is described in one set of myths as having gone through a number of stages. In each stage there was a different set of inhabitants, the modern Indians representing the fifth inhabitation of the earth. The creation of the various cultural groups known to the Washo is attributed to "Creation Women" who made the Washo, the Paiutes, and the Diggers (a generic term for California Indians) out of the seeds of the cattail. Still another tale tells of how a different personage, "Creation Man," formed the three groups by separating his three sons so they would not quarrel. The natural features of the Washo country are usually explained by reference to a pair of weasels. These two, *Damalali* (short-tailed weasel) and *Pewetseli* (long-tailed weasel), traveled together. The wiser *Pewetseli* usually managing to save the day threatened by the impulsive behavior of the rascal *Damalali*. The general structure of these tales is reminiscent of a common theme of adventuresome twin brothers found throughout much of western North America. The many lakes in the mountain region are, for instance, said to be caused by one such misadventure of the weasels. *Damalali*, the story says, came upon a Water Baby and took it prisoner. The water creature at first begged for his freedom and finally threatened to flood the world. When neither pleading nor threats moved the wea-

sel, the Water Baby made good his threat and caused a flood to come which covered the mountains to their tips. *Pewetseli*, furious at his companion's irresponsibility, forced him to release the water spirit and begged the creature to lower the waters. This the Water Baby did, but in every mountain valley a lake remained. The adventures of this pair are seemingly endless, many of the incidences are virtually meaningless to the outsider, and in many cases the modern Washo appear to have forgotten the real significance of the episode. In other cases they appear to be simply humorous or sometimes salacious stories told for amusement.

Other Figures

A number of other miraculous figures appear in Washo mythology, all of them threatening and dangerous at least in part. *Hanglwuiwui*, a great one-eyed, one-legged giant, is said to have hopped from hilltop to hilltop in search of his favorite food, Indians. Near Gardenerville, Nevada, there is a cave called by the Washo *Hanglwuiwuiangl*, the dwelling of Hanglwuiwui, which is still avoided or approached with caution, although most Washo say that the giant has been dead for a long time.

Another fearsome feature of Washo mythology was the *Ang*, a great bird which carried off human victims and terrorized the world. Birds such as this figure in many Indian myths. The *Ang* is said to have died and fallen into Lake Tahoe where its skeleton formed a reef, which the Washo insist can be seen by anyone flying over the lake. The failure of white airplane pilots to report the reef is felt to be a conspiracy to discredit Washo belief.

The coyote, a figure found almost universally in Indian mythology, was prominent in Washo legends. As is true in other tribes, the nature of coyote is exceedingly difficult to define. In some episodes he is a dangerous and threatening force, in others quite benevolent, and in yet others a rather stupid fellow given to jokes and tricks and generally finding himself the laughing stock. One such tale describes the coyote attempting to seduce a young woman who thwarts him by inserting a seed pot between her legs and injuring coyote in an embarrassing and painful manner. Most coyote tales still told emphasize his lecherous and rascally nature and are told as salacious stories rather than moral fables. Some persons were felt to be able to turn themselves into coyotes and threaten their fellow men. Stories of such occurrences are not unknown today.

In addition to the one-legged giant, the Washo believed that the mountains were inhabited by another race, possibly human but possessed of much more power than ordinary people. These giants or wild men figure in many stories of disappearance or mysterious occurrences while on hunting trips. Occasionally, they directly attacked humans, trying to steal food from them or otherwise bother them. In most cases in stories dealing with these direct confrontations, the wild man was bested by the cleverness or courage of the Washo. In 1911 an Indian appeared in Oroville, California, attempting to steal scraps from a local slaughterhouse. He was eventually identified as Ishi, the last survivor of a small band of southern Yana who had maintained a furtive and fearful freedom in the Sierra foothills. His appearance caused a minor sensation as the "last wild Indian" in the United States. Modern Washo believe that he was not an Indian but one of the wild men of their myths.

One Washo tale tells of a great battle between the Washo and the giants in which the giants, who had no bows, were defeated after building a fort and throwing stones at the Washo. It is possible that the wild men represent some previous culture inhabiting the region. References to them and to a great battle in which they were exterminated are found in the mythologies of many groups in the Great Basin. Many of the Washo myths have been forgotten or have become garbled as the Washo world changed and the conditions that they have described and explained disappeared. One figure has maintained its vitality and dominates the supernatural life of the modern Washo as it did that of the aboriginal tribe. This is the Water Baby mentioned previously. These little creatures are described as being two or three feet tall with long black hair that never touches the ground but instead floats behind the Water Baby when it walks. They are grey in color and soft and clammy to the touch and possess immense power. Every body of water, lake, river, stream, pond, sink, or modern irrigation ditch is occupied by Water Babies. There is, according to Washo tradition, a tunnel from Lake Tahoe to the Carson Valley used by the Water Babies when they travel. All Washo today have heard the high mewing call of the Water Baby luring them toward some body of water at night. When they hear such a summons they hide in their houses and resist the temptation to follow.

In aboriginal times certain springs and lakes were considered to be favorite haunts of the Water Babies. Persons seeking their assistance, in curing an illness for instance, made or purchased an especially fine basket and deposited it in the lake or pond as a gift. Water Baby was a frequent *wegelayo* for the most powerful shamans. As individuals, Water Babies visited human beings. Some Washo believed that simply to see a Water Baby brought illness or death. Others felt it was a good omen, a chance to obtain power. Some others argue that a Water Baby did not give power but instead exchanged it for a human life. A gift of Water Baby was repaid with the life of a relative.

While many of the figures of Washo mythology have grown vague, their stories half forgotten and their place in Washo life reduced, the Water Baby has demonstrated an amazing vitality. Stories of visitations, or hearing Water Baby calls from streams or ponds, of seeing Water Baby footprints are still told. In fact, the Water Baby has kept abreast of the times and one informant with whom I talked stubbornly insisted he could tell a female Water Baby's footprints because she wore high-heeled shoes! Almost all the Washo are somewhat fearful of the consequences of the ignorance of white men in the matter of Water Babies. Fishermen or hunters, they fear, might catch or kill a Water Baby by mistake. One such misadventure is said to have resulted in the San Francisco earthquake of 1906. A fisherman caught a Water Baby and gave it to the San Francisco aquarium. Despite the warnings of a famous Indian leader who went to San Francisco to talk to the mayor, the creature was kept in the aquarium. It remained there until the earth shook and the water came up over the city. When the water receded the Water Baby, of course, was gone.

A most important element of the Washo world was the view that animals were not really any different than human beings. That is, they had societies of their own and languages and a special place in nature and a supernatural power which in some cases was greater than man's. The large and ferocious animals like the bear were considered to be intrinsically more powerful than men and we have seen that to kill a bear was an act which conferred power. Other animals, like men, might or might not have power. But the old buck who successfully eluded the hunter and even a wily rabbit who would not be killed were considered to have special power and to be *mushege* or "wild animals." But the term was not limited to animals alone. A man of particular fierceness or power, one who hunted successfully or was a renowned fighter or who simply had an unpredictable temper, was also called *mushege*. This partial equation of men and animals and the behavior which it engendered, as we shall see, was particularly important in developing the contacts between the Washo and white invaders of their land.

Summary

In this chapter we have examined some of the basic concepts and figures of Washo religious life. Washo religion was not based on a well-developed theological scheme but instead must for the most part be analyzed from the behavior of people in day-to-day life. There were few, if any, purely religious acts. Instead, we see ritual reflecting a Washo view of the supernatural woven through nearly every act of the day. Hunting ritual, dreams of rabbits and fish and antelope, special power to obtain food, respectful treatment of the remains of animals, the minor ceremonies of childbirth and childhood were all viewed as essential parts of the activities with which they were associated. To go hunting without taking the proper ritual steps would be as foolish in Washo eyes as failing to take a bow or using a crooked arrow. To try and hunt with a weapon contaminated by a menstruating woman would be as hopeless as going into the field with a bow but no bowstring. Another feature of Washo religion was that its observance seldom required the participation of specialists or of special groups of people. The ritual of life was the ritual of individuals or individuals within the family group. Certain occasions when people could come together for extended periods were also times when religious rituals were performed. But they were also occasions for games and gambling and courtship and could not be considered purely religious occasions. Even in curing, when a specialist was needed, any shaman would do, if his power was great enough. There was no special caste of priests and any person, man or woman, might become a shaman. Shamans said to have Water Baby power were believed to have a secret cave which could be entered by sinking into Lake Tahoe and then rising inside a great rock. This is the nearest thing to an association or guild of specialists.

In short, Washo religion offered an explanation for the universe as it existed and for the accidents and misadventures of life. It also provided a system of ritual to be used in the business of life which probably allayed some of the fear and uncertainty of the hunting and gathering existence. Because each step in ritual was associated with practical matters, the sacred actions may have provided a framework within which the practical actions could be more easily learned and remembered. As simple as it might be, Washo religion played an important role in aboriginal life and was, as we shall see, a cornerstone of Washo cultural survival in the modern world.

Death Be Not Strange

Peter A. Metcalf

In this article Peter A. Metcalf compares American and Berawan funeral and mortuary rites and shows why Western practices so shocked the Berawan. To the Berawan we trap the deceased in a suspended condition between life and death, producing evil, not beneficent spirits. "For the Berawan, America is a land carpeted with potential zombies." Metcalf's field work not only explains the fate of the Berawan dead and demonstrates their beliefs to be as coherent and reasonable as any, but also draws attention to the exotic nature of American funerary practices. His comparison reminds us that our level of ethnocentrism both leads us to view the beliefs of others as illogical and sometimes reprehensible and causes us to ignore our own death rituals and practices.

Reprinted with permission from *Natural History*, Vol. 87, no. 6 (1978), pp. 6–12. Copyright the American Museum of Natural History, 1978.

THE POPULAR VIEW OF ANTHROPOLOGY IS THAT it is concerned with faraway places, strange peoples, and odd customs. This notion was neatly captured by a nineteenth-century wit who described the field as "the pursuit of the exotic by the eccentric." In recent decades many anthropologists have tried to shake this image. They see the exotic as dangerously close to the sensational and, therefore, a threat to the respectability of a serious academic discipline. They argue that anthropology has solid theoretical bases, and that some anthropologists routinely work in cities right here in America. And they are right. Nevertheless, anthropologists are as much involved with the exotic as ever, and I think that this concern actually works to scholarship's advantage.

This continuing involvement is a result of the characteristic *modus operandi* of anthropologists. First, we seek out the exotic, in the sense of something originating in another country or something "strikingly or excitingly different," as my *Webster's* puts it. Second, we try to fit this alien item—culture trait, custom, piece of behavior—into its social and cultural context, thereby reducing it to a logical, sensible, even necessary element. Having done that, we feel that we can understand why people do or say or think something instead of being divorced from them by what they say, think, or do.

Sir James Frazer, whose classic study of primitive religions *The Golden Bough*, was first published in 1890, provides an excellent example of the eccentric in pursuit of the exotic. For him, the process of reducing the mysterious to the commonplace was the very hallmark of scientific progress. Like many anthropologists of his time, Frazer assumed that some societies were superior and others inferior, and that anthropology's main task was to describe how the latter had evolved into the former. To Frazer, Europe's technological achievements were proof of social, intellectual, and moral superiority. The dominance of the West represented the triumph of science, which in Frazer's evolutionary schema, superseded even the most rational of world religions. Science's clear light was to shine far and wide, driving superstition, the supernatural, and even God himself back into shadows and dimly lit corners.

But Frazer might have found a second aspect of the anthropological *modus operandi* less to his taste. In the course of making sense of someone else's behavior or ideas, we frequently begin to observe our own customs from a new angle. Indeed, this reflexive objectivity is often acclaimed as one of the great advantages of our methods and cited as a major justification for the long, expensive physical and psychic journeys that we make, seeking out societies far removed from our own cultural traditions. Less often remarked upon, however, is that the exotic possesses its own reflexive quality. As we learn to think of other peoples' ways as natural, we simultaneously begin to see our own as strange. In this sense, anthropologists import the exotic, and that, I suppose, puts us on the side of the angels.

An incident that occurred about four years ago during my fieldwork in north-central Borneo brought home to me the depth and subtlety of anthropologists' involvement with the exotic. I was working with the Berawan, a small tribe comprising four communities, each made up of several hundred people living in a massive wooden longhouse. The four longhouses stand beside the great rivers that are the only routes into the interior of Borneo. Berawan communities live on fish and on rice planted in clearings cut anew in the rain forest each year. In the late nineteenth century, which was a stormy period of tribal warfare, each longhouse was a fortress as well as a home, and the Berawan look back with pride on the military traditions of that era.

Among the things that interested me about the Berawan were their funeral rites, which involve what anthropologists call "secondary burial," although the Berawan do not usually bury the dead at all. Full rites consist of four stages: the first and third involve ritual preparation of the corpse; the second and fourth make up steps in storage of the remains. The first stage, lasting two to ten days, consists of rites performed immediately after death. During the second stage, the bereaved family stores the corpse in the longhouse or on a

simple platform in the graveyard. This storage lasts at least eight months and sometimes for several years if the close kin cannot immediately afford to complete the expensive final stages. Third, if the corpse has been in the graveyard, the family brings it back to the longhouse, where it is kept for six to ten days, while the family lavishly entertains guests who have been summoned from far and wide. Finally, the remains are removed to a final resting place, an impressively proportioned mausoleum.

Within this four-part plan, details of the corpse's treatment vary considerably. During the first storage stage, the family may place the corpse in a large earthenware jar or in a massive coffin hewn from a single tree trunk. For secondary storage, the family may use a valuable glazed jar or the coffin left over from the first stage. During the third-stage rites, the family may take out the bones of the deceased and clean them. As the corpse decomposes, its secretions may be collected in a special vessel. Some neighbors of the Berawan reportedly consume liquids of decomposition mixed with rice—a variety of endocannibalism.

For anthropologists, this intimate interaction with the corpse is certainly exotic. For Americans not professionally trained in the niceties of cultural relativism, Berawan burial is no doubt disgusting: keeping corpses around the house, shuttling them between the graveyard and the longhouse, storing them aboveground instead of burying them, manipulating the bones, and, to Western eyes, paying macabre attention to the process of decay itself. My Berawan informants were aware that some phases of their ritual bothered Europeans. They soon learned, moreover, that I had a lot of questions about their funerals. One of the pleasures of working in Borneo is that people soon begin to cross-examine their interviewer. They are as curious about the stranger as he or she is about them. So before long, they began to quiz me about the death ways of my country.

On one memorable occasion, during a lull in ritual activity, I responded to one of these questions by outlining American embalming practices —the treatment of the corpse with preservative fluids and its display in an open coffin. I was well into my story, concentrating on finding the right words to describe this unfamiliar topic, when I became aware that a sudden silence had fallen over my audience. They asked a number of hesitant questions just to be sure that they had understood me correctly and drew away from me in disgust when they found that they had. So shocked were they that I had to backtrack rapidly and change my story. The topic was never broached again.

At the time, I did not understand why American embalming practices had so unnerved the Berawan. Now, having thought about the meaning of Berawan death rituals, I think that I do understand.

The death rituals of central Borneo early attracted the interest of explorers and ethnologists. In 1907, Robert Hertz, a young student of French sociologist Emile Durkheim, wrote an essay about these rites that has become a classic. Never having set foot in Borneo, Hertz relied on the accounts of travelers. Had he not been killed during the First World War, he might well have undertaken firsthand research himself. Nevertheless, his analysis is still routinely cited in discussions and comparisons of funeral customs. Yet, oddly, Hertz's central thesis has received very little attention. Hertz hypothesized that peoples who practice secondary burial have certain beliefs about the afterlife, namely, that the fate of the body provides a model for the fate of the soul.

Since Hertz did not know of the Berawan, they provided me with an appropriate test case for his hypothesis. I collected data on everything related to Berawan death rites: the people involved, mourning practices, related rituals, myths and beliefs, and so on. I also pressed my informants for interpretations of rituals. All the material I accumulated revealed a consistent set of ideas very similar to those described by Hertz. The Berawan believe that after death the soul is divorced from the body and cannot reanimate the already decaying corpse. However, the soul cannot enter the land of the dead because it is not yet a perfect spirit. To become one of the truly dead, it must undergo a metamorphosis. As the body rots away to leave dry bones, so the soul is transformed slowly into spirit form. As the corpse is formless and repulsive until putrefaction is completed, so the soul is homeless. It lurks miserably on the fringes of human habitation and, in its discomfort, may affect the living with illness. The third stage of the mortuary sequence, which Hertz called the

"great feast," marks the end of this miserable period. The soul finally passes to the land of the dead, and the mortal remains of the deceased join those of its ancestors in the tomb.

But before this happy conclusion is reached, the hovering soul is feared because it may cause more death. Even more dread surrounds the body itself, caused not by the process of rotting, for that releases the soul of the deceased from the bonds of the flesh, but by the possibility that some malignant spirit of nonhuman origin will succeed in reanimating the corpse. Should this occur, the result will be a monster of nightmarish mien, invulnerable to the weapons of men, since it is already dead.

I once witnessed an incident that dramatically demonstrated how real is the Berawan fear of reanimated corpses. Toward sunset, a group of mourners and guests were chatting casually beside a coffin that was being displayed on the longhouse veranda in preparation for primary storage. Suddenly there was a tapping sound, apparently from inside the coffin. The noise could have come from the house timbers, contracting in the cool of the evening, but the people present saw a different explanation. After a moment of shock, the women fled, carrying their children. Some panic-stricken men grabbed up what weapons were handy, while others tied up the coffin lid with yet more bands of rattan. Calm was not restored until later in the evening when a shaman investigated and declared that nothing was amiss.

We can now see why American mortuary practices so shock the Berawan. By delaying the decomposition of corpses, we commit a most unnatural act. First, we seem to be trying to trap our nearest and dearest in the unhappiest condition possible, neither alive nor in the radiant land of the dead. Second, and even more perverse and terrifying, we keep an army of undecomposed corpses, each and every one subject to reanimation by a host of evil spirits. For the Berawan, America is a land carpeted with potential zombies.

After a couple of years of field work, and an application of the ideas of Hertz and others, I can offer a relatively full account of Berawan death ways: what they express about Berawan notions of life and death; how they are manipulated by influential men in their struggles for power; how they relate to their sense of identity, art forms, and oral history. Meanwhile, I have also explored the literature on American death ways—and have found it wanting. For the most part, it is restricted to consideration of psychological variables—how people react to death, either the possibility of their own or that of close relatives and friends. None of these studies begins to explain why American funerals are the way they are; why they differ from British funerals, for instance.

Jessica Mitford, author of *The American Way of Death*, tried to explain the form that American funerals take by arguing that they are a product of the death industry's political power. But Mitford's theory does not explain the tacit support that Americans give to this institution, why successive immigrant groups have adopted it, or why reform movements have failed.

I have tried to relate American practices to popular ideas about the nature of a fulfilling life and a proper death. Despite these intellectual efforts, I am left with a prickly sense of estrangement. For, in fact, I had spared my Berawan friends the more gruesome details of embalming: replacement of the blood with perfumed formaldehyde and other chemicals; removal of the soft organs of the chest and abdomen via a long hollow needle attached to a vacuum pump; injection of inert materials. I did not mention the American undertaker's elaborate restorative techniques: the stitching up of mutilated corpses, plumping out of emaciated corpses with extra injections of waxes, or careful cosmetic care of hands and face. Nor did I tell the Berawan about the padded coffins, grave clothes ranging in style from business suits to negligees, and other funeral paraphernalia. Had I explained all this, their shock might have been transformed into curiosity, and they might have reversed our roles of social scientist and informant.

In the meantime, something of their reaction has rubbed off on me. I have reduced the celebrated mortuary rites of remote and mysterious Borneo to a kind of workaday straightforwardness, only to be struck by the exotic character of an institution in our very midst.

9

Old and New Religions: The Search for Salvation

Anthropologists have long studied cultural stability and change and agree that all cultures have continuous change, although the rate of change can vary dramatically. Whereas American society has an unmatched cultural dynamism, other cultures change so gradually as to appear static. The types and rates of cultural changes are functions of many factors originating from within the society itself or from external pressures and influences.

> Internal conditions affecting the rate of change include the relative degree of cultural receptivity to new ideas, the amount of freedom of inquiry and competition, the degree of cultural elaboration, the population size and density, the presence of innovators and inventors, and—perhaps most important—the degree of harmony between cultural and social values. Among the external conditions affecting culture change, the degree of contact with other groups is the outstanding factor (Malefijt 1968: 329).

Protective mask from the Sepik River region, New Guinea.

What anthropologists have discovered is that religious change occurs for the same reasons as general culture change and, as is the case with change generally, religious change is both continuous and universal.

One of the most dramatic classes of change, and one that has strong religious content, is what Anthony F. C. Wallace termed "revitalization movements": "a deliberate, organized, conscious effort by members of society to construct a more satisfying culture" (1956: 265). This chapter presents three examples of revitalization movements (Wallace writes of nativism and revivalism and Worsley of cargo cults), and Wallace (1956) outlined several other major types of revitalization movements that are clearly religious in nature (vitalistic movements, millenarian movements, and messianic movements). It is important to recognize that these kinds of cultural change phenomena are not mutually exclusive; several may be at work within a single society at any one time, all simultaneously contributing to change in the cultural gestalt. Wallace's article, for example, combines nativism and revivalism, but there are cases in which these types of changes in a single society are accompanied by messianic and millenarian movements as well. All revitalization movements have in common a reactionary character; all are the result of real or imagined conditions that create a demand for change.

Wallace's categories and definitions have been broadly accepted. Nativistic movements are characterized by a strong emphasis on the elimination of alien persons, customs, values, and material from the "mazeway," which Wallace defines as the mental image an individual has of the society and its culture, as well as of his own body and its behavioral regularities, in order to act in ways to reduce stress at all levels of the system. Revivalistic movements emphasize the readoption of customs, values, and even aspects of nature in the mazeway of previous generations. Cargo cults emphasize the importation of alien values, customs, and material into the mazeway, these being expected to arrive, metaphorically, as a ship's cargo. Vitalistic movements also emphasize the importation of alien elements into the mazeway, although not via a cargo mechanism. Millenarian movements emphasize changes in the mazeway

through an apocalyptic world transformation engineered by the supernatural. Messianic movements emphasize the actual participation of a divine savior in human flesh in bringing about desired changes in the mazeway (1956: 267). (This categorization of revitalization movements, however, is only one of many schemes used by ethnographers, and as John Collins has noted, "any such scheme, basically, is merely a device to initiate thought and comparison" [1978: 137]).

The religious nature of revitalization in the non-Western world, particularly in Melanesia, is made clear not only by the expectation of a messiah and the millennium in some of the movements, but also by the very structure of movement phenomena, in which prophets play an indispensable role. I. C. Jarvie maintains that the religious character of these movements may be explained by the fact that traditional institutions are not able to adopt and respond to social changes, and that the only new organizational system offered these societies by European colonialists is Christianity. Melanesians, for example, have learned more about organization from religion than from any other foreign institution, and it is logical for them to mold revitalization movements in religious form in order to accommodate, indeed combat, the impact of European society (1970: 412–13).

Revitalization in the broad sense of bringing new vigor and happiness to society is certainly not restricted to traditional groups or to the religious realm. Edward Sapir, for example, spoke of cultures "genuine" and "spurious": in the former, individuals felt well integrated into their culture, and in the latter they experienced alienation from the mainstream of society. Examples of attempts to change Western cultures abound. Political and economic conditions have frequently moved modern prophets to seek power to change, sometimes radically, the institutional structure and goals of society.

Throughout the readings in this chapter, reference is frequently made to cults and sects. These are terms that have been used in the anthropology and sociology of religion to describe particular types of religious organizations. Typically, the word *church* is applied to the larger community's view of the acceptable type of religious organization, whereas the term *sect* is used to refer to a protest group. Sects are generally small, express defiance of the world, or sometimes withdrawal from the world. Sect members are strict believers who usually experience some sort of conversion experience before becoming members. Bryan Wilson, (1959, 1961) has described four different types of sects based on their ideologies: (1) the conversionist sect is hopeful of converting others; (2) the adventist sect anticipates a drastic divine intervention; (3) the introversionist sect is very pious and eager to develop its inner spirituality; and (4) the gnostic sect possesses esoteric religious knowledge. The word *cult* is not as clearly defined as sect and church, and appears to refer to a more casual, loosely organized group. Cults seem to have a fluctuating membership whose allegiance can be shared with other religious organizations. (It is well to remember, however, that the terms *church, sect,* and *cult* are best seen as scholarly descriptions of ideal, theoretical concepts.)

During the last decade this country has witnessed an immense growth in the number of religious cults. The Children of God, Hare Krishna, the followers of Bhagwan Shree Rajneesh, the Maharaj Ji's Divine Light Mission, and, of course, the largest and most controversial group of all, the Reverend Sun Myung Moon's Unification Church, are a few examples of groups that have attracted thousands disenchanted with traditional religious organizations. The history of the world is replete with examples of new religious groups springing to life as spiritually dissatisfied peoples seek alternatives to traditional religious organizations.

What appeal do these movements have for people? What social forces underlie the development and rapid growth of religious movements? Many sociological and psychological analyses have attempted to answer these important questions (see especially Glock and Stark, 1965; Eister, 1972; Zaretsky and Leone, 1974; Talmon, 1969). Briefly, these studies draw a picture of people who have become attracted to cults because of such lures as love, security, acceptance, and improved personal status. Unstable and rapidly changing social and political situations in contemporary technological countries also provide a rich seedbed for the emergence and blossoming of religious movements. Charles Y. Glock (1964) has listed five types of deprivation that may result in the establishment of a new sect or that may lead individuals to join one: (1) *economic* deprivation, which is suffered by people who make less money, have fewer material goods, and are financially beholden to others; (2) *organismic* deprivation, which applies to those who may exhibit physical, mental, and nutritional problems; (3) *ethical* deprivation, which grows out of a perceived discrepancy between the real and the ideal; (4) *psychic* deprivation, which can result in the search for meaning and new values (and which is related to the search for closure and simplicity); and (5) *social* deprivation, which results from a society's valuation of some individuals and their attributes over others.

The articles in this chapter have been selected to demonstrate how religion can help people living in cultures undergoing sudden and disruptive social change. The selections also show the wide extent of ritual used by religious groups in their quest and deep longing for holiness. Anthony F. C. Wallace describes revivalistic and nativistic movements, using as examples the Ghost Dance of 1890 among certain North American Indian tribes and the Paliau Movement in the Admiralty Islands. Peter Worsley points out that throughout history people who have felt themselves to be oppressed and deceived have always been ready to pour their hopes and fears into a belief in a coming golden age. Worsley's article describes a cargo cult, a revitalization movement among the peoples of New Guinea and adjacent islands. Mary Lee Daugherty discusses serpent handlers in West Virginia, who base their particular religious practice on the Gospel of Mark: "they shall speak with new tongues; they shall take up serpents." In the final article Berkeley Rice describes Reverend Sun Myung Moon's Unification Church, the most controversial psychoreligious cult of the several that have mushroomed across the United States in the last decade.

References Cited

Collins, John J.
1978 *Primitive Religion.* Totowa, N.J.: Rowman and Littlefield.

Eister, Allen
1972 "An Outline of a Structural Theory of

Cults." *Journal for the Scientific Study of Religion* 11: 319–33.

Glock, Charles Y.
1964 "The Role of Deprivation in the Origin and Evolution of Religious Groups." In R. Lee and M. E. Marty, eds., *Religion and Social Conflict.* New York: Oxford University Press.

Glock, Charles Y., and Rodney Stark
1965 *Religion and Society in Tension.* Chicago: Rand McNally.

Jarvie, I. C.
1970 "Cargo Cults." In Richard Cavendish, ed., *Man, Myth and Magic,* pp. 409–12. New York: Marshall Cavendish Corporation.

Malefijt, Annemarie de Waal
1968 *Religion and Culture: An Introduction to Anthropology of Religion.* New York: Macmillan.

Sapir, E.
1924 "Culture, Genuine and Spurious." *American Journal of Sociology* 29: 401–29.

Talmon, Yonina
1969 "Pursuit of the Millennium: The Relation Between Religious and Social Change." In Norman Birnbaum and Gertrude Lenzer, eds., *Sociology and Religion: A Book of Readings.* Englewood Cliffs, N.J.: Prentice-Hall.

Wallace, A. F. C.
1956 "Revitalization Movements." *American Anthropologist* 58: 264–81.

Wilson, Bryan R.
1959 "Role Conflicts and Status Contradictions of the Pentecostal Minister." *American Journal of Sociology* 64: 494–504.
1961 *Sects and Society: A Sociological Study of the Elim Tabernacle, Christian Science, and Christadelphians.* Berkeley, Calif.: University of California Press.

Zaretsky, Irving S., and Mark P. Leone, eds.
1974 *Religious Movements in Contemporary America.* Princeton, N.J.: Princeton University Press.

Nativism and Revivalism

Anthony F. C. Wallace

As a social movement, nativism and revivalism have the goal of reconstituting a way of life that has been destroyed for one reason or another and retaliating against the group responsible for the loss. In this selection Anthony F. C. Wallace explores the history of the concept, the four major schools of thought concerning the conditions under which these movements arise, and the current status of research that seeks to explain them. Finally, Wallace offers two examples of revivalistic and nativistic movements: the Ghost Dance of 1890 among the Plains Indians of North America and the Paliau movement in the Admiralty Islands of Melanesia following World War II. Wallace's article is an excellent selection to show how people use religious principles to cope with a cultural crisis that has prevented them from achieving a more satisfying culture.

Reprinted by permission of the publisher from the *International Encyclopedia of the Sciences*, David L. Sills, Editor, Vol. 11, pp. 75–80. Copyright © 1972 by Crowell Collier and Macmillan, Inc.

NATIVISM AND REVIVALISM ARE TWO FORMS OF social movements. Like several other forms of social movements—such as millenarism, cargo cults, and utopian communities—revivalism and nativism have been considered to be aspects of the same class of phenomena. This larger class has been termed "revitalization movement" and has been defined as a conscious, deliberate, organized effort on the part of some members of a society to create a more satisfying culture. In revivalism, the aim of the movement is to return to a former era of happiness, to restore a golden age, to revive a previous condition of social virtue. In nativism, the aim of the movement is to purge the society of unwanted aliens, of cultural elements of foreign origin, or of both. Frequently, a movement is both revivalistic and nativistic.

The term nativism has also been used to refer not to social movements but to a widespread attitude in a society of rejection of alien persons or culture. In this second sense of the term, nativism is a form of utopian thought (Mannheim 1929–1931). It is thus comparable to such popular beliefs as faith in the existence of a land without evil, or in the ultimate arrival of a messiah or mahdi, or in the coming of a millennium or of the ancestors with cargo. All of these beliefs are pervasive "myth-dreams" (Burridge 1960), which suffuse a society or culture area over considerable periods of time; but although the code of a movement may incorporate such a myth-dream, the myth-dream, as well as the general social policy, of nativism, millennial expectation, revivalistic nostaliga, etc., does not in itself constitute a movement.

Natural History

Revivalistic, nativistic, and other kinds of revitalization movements have been generally observed to go through certain processual stages.

These stages, if effectively fulfilled, are characterized by the initiation of certain functional tasks without which the movement cannot achieve its aim, the transformation of society. Manifestly, all movements do not complete the cycle, sometimes because the movement is suppressed by force, because its millenarism or messianic hopes are disappointed, or because it cannot attract or retain a sufficient membership. The successful movement, however, passes through the following stages:

(1) Premovement phase.

(a) *Steady state*. The society is satisfied with itself; no major group is experiencing sufficient stress or is sufficiently disillusioned to be seriously interested in radical change.

(b) *Period of increased individual stress*. As a consequence of one or more of many possible circumstances—depression, famine, conquest by an alien society, acculturation pressures, or whatever leads to the awareness of a growing discrepancy between life as it is and life as it could be (and is for someone else)—growing numbers of people experience psychological and physical stress.

(c) *Periods of cultural distortion*. As increasing numbers of individuals, singly and in small groups, find their situation both intolerable and without hope of relief by the use of available, culturally sanctioned means, they turn to idiosyncratic or systematically deviant means. This period of anomie (Merton 1949) leads to the distortion of the cultural fabric by the institutionalization of such socially dysfunctional customs as drug and alcoholic addictions, organized crime, excessive corruption of officials, mob violence, sabotage, and vandalism, etc.

(2) Movement phase.

(d) *Prophetic formulation of a code*. A prophet formulates a code, frequently (in religious movements) as a result of a vision in which he is instructed by supernatural beings and in which he and his people are promised salvation if the instructions are followed. The code defines what is wrong with the existing culture, delineates a goal that is described as better than the existing culture (if not utopian), and outlines a cultural transfer, by the use of which the people can move from the bad existing culture to the good future culture.

(e) *Communication*. The prophet preaches his revelation to the people, promising salvation to the convert and to the society if his code is accepted.

(f) *Organization*. Special disciples and then mass followers join the prophet. As the number of members in the group increases and as the complexity of the mission grows, a division of labor develops. Different disciples take over the responsibility for various aspects of the movement's activities.

(g) *Adaptation*. The movement will encounter resistance from vested interests. These must be either defeated in political or military combat or converted; sometimes conversion is accomplished by making modifications in the code that will remove the fears of the reluctant.

(h) *Cultural transformation*. As the whole, or a controlling portion, of the population comes to accept the new code, the system of cultural transfer, and perhaps even the goal culture, is instituted.

(3) Postmovement phase.

(i) *Routinization*. Once the cultural transformation has been accomplished, or is well under way, the organizational structure is divested of executive control of many spheres of the culture and contracts, maintaining responsibility only for the maintenance of doctrine and for the performance of ritual. It thus ceases to be a movement and becomes, in effect, a church or a political party.

(j) *Steady state*. Once the cultural transformation has been accomplished and the movement's organization has been routinized in its activities, a new steady state may be said to exist. Even if the professed aim of the movement was revivalistic, this new state will almost certainly be different from the initial steady state. Now the cycle is ready to begin again.

History of the Concept

Anthropological interest in revivalistic and nativistic movements can be considered to have begun with the work of Lewis Henry Morgan. In his book *League of the Iroquois* (1851), which is considered to be the first systematic ethnography of a primitive people, Morgan devoted considerable space to a study of the New Religion of Handsome Lake. This was a religious movement, beginning in 1799, that was only mildly nativistic and even more mildly revivalistic, but it did represent an effort to rebuild a healthy way of life among the reservation Iroquois of New York state. Following Morgan's work, the next major contribution was James

Mooney's study of the Ghost Dance among the Plains Indians (Mooney 1896). The Ghost Dance was both enthusiastically revivalistic and vehemently nativistic.

Comparable phenomena were soon reported by anthropologists working in other parts of the world. In 1923 Williams published his study of the Vailala Madness, a cargo cult among a native people in New Guinea. Later workers have described other cargo cults in the Melanesian area and in general found them, as Williams found the Vailala Madness, to be revivalistic in native theory (in that the followers of the cult believe that they are restoring a golden age in which they will be reunited with their ancestors) and to be nativistic in social policy (in that whites are to be driven away). But inasmuch as the "cargo" is composed principally of European goods, and native goods and rituals are abandoned, both the nativistic and revivalistic aspects of cargo cults are qualified by a strong motive toward acculturation.

By the 1940s, it was possible to recognize that what were then generally called "nativistic movements" occurred within almost all of the areas of primitive culture known to anthropologists, among North and South American Indians, African Negroes, the peoples of the Pacific, and the tribal peoples of Europe and Asia as well. (The only major culture area in which revitalization movements are not known to have occurred on a wide scale is the aboriginal culture area of Australia and Tasmania.) In 1943 Ralph Linton published a brief paper on nativistic movements that served to establish the phenomenon as a special topic in anthropological studies of culture change.

Because communication among the various social science disciplines has been fitful, anthropological workers did not at first take full cognizance of studies of comparable movements by sociologists, historians, Biblical scholars, classicists, and classical archeologists. Sociologists have been concerned with such contemporary social movements in complex societies as the Father Divine cult in urban areas of the United States; historians have dealt with millenarian movements and utopian communities of the past, with major anti-Western movements in Africa (e.g., the Mahdi in Sudan) and in Asia (e.g., the Taiping Rebellion), and with the origins of the great religious and political movements in both Western and Oriental tradi-

tions; Biblical scholars have studied the origin of Christianity as a social movement; and classicists and classical archeologists have investigated the new religion of Ikhnaton in ancient Egypt and the pre-Christian Essene cult memorialized by the Dead Sea scrolls. These materials, together with anthropological observations, now make possible sophisticated field and historical studies as well as generalizations about the phenomenon of rapid culture change.

Schools of Thought

Concerning the conditions under which these movements arise, there would seem to be four major schools of thought.

The Absolute Deprivation Theory

Perhaps the most common, and least sophisticated, theory is the view that absolute deprivation, in the sense of a low material standard of living, leads to dissatisfaction with the *status quo* and eventually to the adoption of a revolutionary ideology. This viewpoint, in political application, leads to a "bread and circuses" theory of social control. Mere material deprivation, however, does not inevitably prompt the deprived to revolt: on the one hand, under some circumstances, such as war, both civilian and military personnel may maintain high morale while hungry, cold, and uncomfortable; on the other hand, the response to extreme deprivation, as in concentration camps, may be profound apathy, dependence, and suggestibility. Furthermore, it may be empirically observed that social movements sometimes occur not in the least fortunate class or nation, nor in the most, but in a middle station.

The Acculturation Theory

Many nativistic and revivalistic movements have occurred among tribal peoples in contact with European civilization. This has sometimes led to the impression that acculturation pressure leads directly to fanatical social movements. This pressure, it is implied, produces a state of "culture shock," in which the tribal people experiences a sort of collective hysterical syndrome characterized by ecstatic, but unrealistic, commitment to a utopian social movement. The nature of the trauma inflicted by the higher civilization upon the lower may be conceived as the imposition of a competitive way of life, or as the requirement of an unfamiliar pattern of culture, or simply as interference with tradition. The code of the movement will, it is argued, represent some sort of compromise between withdrawal from, and approach to, the higher civilization. Although this viewpoint has merit as far as it goes, its relevance appears to be restricted largely to tribal populations in culture-contact situations; and even here it is only a partial explanation, since it fails to account for many kinds of social responses to acculturation pressure which are not fanatical, hysterical, or unrealistic at all, such as rationalistic political and economic movements or wholesale adoption of major portions of the higher culture.

The Social Evolutionary Theory

Scholars working in the tradition of social criticism and analysis founded by Karl Marx have pointed out that in many revivalistic and nativistic movements it is possible to discern the expression of social protest by disadvantaged classes or groups. Furthermore, the historical significance in a program of social evolution of a given kind of movement may be defined by Marxian theory. Thus, millenarian movements in early modern European history and the Taiping Rebellion in nineteenth-century China have been interpreted as premature popular protests against oppressive social conditions, and the cargo cult in Melanesia as an early, naive, supernaturalistic effort to overturn a social order that can be effectively challenged only by a more rational revolution. As Worsley (1957) has indicated, the organization and tactics of even primitive social movements can be usefully analyzed by applying the Marxist model of revolutionary procedure. The rigid application of a class-revolutionary model in an evolutionary perspective, however, can obscure both general sociopsychological principles and also particular local and temporal conditions.

The Relative Deprivation Theory

The most generally acceptable theory of revivalistic, nativistic, and other types of revitalization movement would seem to be one that recognizes, on the one hand, the influence of local and temporal circumstances and, on the other, the effect of a situation of increasing discrepancy between level of aspiration and level of realization. This theory has been called the "relative deprivation theory" (Aberle 1962). According to this view, the *content* of the movement, as expressed in the code promulgated by the prophet or other leaders, will be determined by the cultural materials locally available at the time, including in particular the myth-dream, the traditional customs of the society, and the customs of the society that may be exerting the acculturation pressure. The *occurrence or nonoccurrence and timing* of the movement will be determined by the degree of disillusionment of a significant number of members of the society with the way of life now available to them. This disillusionment must be based on an awareness of extreme discrepancy between some available image of the good life and the prevailing image of life as it is. The good life will be conceived as the life of a happier past era if present circumstances contrast unfavorably with nostalgic memory, or it will be conceived as the life of another group (a higher class, an acculturating alien society, or a foreign nation). The good life, however, generally is defined not only as a materially more comfortable existence but also as a life with self-respect and the respect of significant others. The precise moment at which the movement crystallizes is difficult to predict, and even the content is not easy to foretell in detail, because these features will be heavily determined by the knowledge, personality, and circumstances of the prophet and other leaders of the movement. Paradoxically, individual variability in society thus plays a crucial role in determining the nature and timing of a movement whose motivation derives from widespread social and cultural conditions.

Current Status of Research

There now exists a considerable literature describing nativistic, revivalistic, and similar kinds of movements, and, in view of the commonness of the phenomenon, there will be no dearth of future studies. Comparative analysis and theory, however, are slight in quantity and uneven in quality. Because there is no general consensus concerning the classification of movements, it is difficult to relate the definitive characteristics of the various types of movements to other classes of phenomena. Thus, a principal research need is the establishment of a taxonomy of social movements. Even though such a taxonomy will very likely require modification as experience with its use reveals inadequacies, it will serve to focus research problems more effectively than in the present system, which is a combination of culture area types (e.g., Melanesian cargo cults, South American *terre sans mal* migrations, Judaeo-Christian Messianic movements), and nonindependent general attributes (e.g., revivalism, nativism, millenarism).

The technical problem in establishing a reasonable classification of revitalization movements is the same as in most areas of the social sciences: there are so many variables of interest that the inclusion of all of them in one taxonomic matrix generates a very large number of classes, each defined by a large number of criteria. Thus the investigator is forced to choose between a simple rule-of-thumb typology convenient to his own interests but of little value as an absolute classification, or a complex classification too cumbersome for convenient use as a typology and too demanding for general use as a guide to observation. Until this problem is solved, this area of investigation, like many others in the social sciences, must remain imprecise.

Among the research questions of particular interest in the current state of understanding, the following may be mentioned.

(1) *Psychological processes.* It has been often observed that new codes formulated by prophets have a paranoid quality and that in the case of religious movements they often occur in hallucinatory visions. To what extent do "psychopathological" processes actually occur in prophets in the genesis and development of such movements? In particular, to what extent and under what conditions are the prophets and leaders of the movement necessarily dependent upon paranoid and hallucinogenic modes of thought? It has also been observed that the behavior of followers has a suggestible, even hysterical, quality. Is the hysterical conversion process a necessary feature of successful social movement?

(2) *Cultural processes.* Successful revitalization movements are able to induce coordinated change in large areas of culture in a short period of time. To what extent does evolutionary culture change depend upon this rapid process, as opposed to slower processes of invention, diffusion, and acculturation? What is the relative importance of cultural syncretism and of radical innovation?

(3) *Social processes.* The social structure of revitalization movements is often inadequately described. What are the relationships among the members of the movement, and between them and nonmembers (including both potential converts and enemies)? To what extent are these relationships determined by available cultural models, and to what extent are they developed in response to the exigencies of the movement itself?

Examples

Finally, two examples of revivalistic and nativistic movements may suffice to convey the quality of these phenomena.

The Ghost Dance of 1890

Among the Plains Indians of North America during the last quarter of the nineteenth century, a religious movement emerged under the leadership of the prophet Wovoka (Mooney 1896). The central tenets of the prophet's teaching were both revivalistic and nativistic: the existing world was soon to be destroyed by fire, flood, and upheaval, and in the holocaust the intruding whites would be annihilated, and along with them those Indians who followed their ways. Salvation, however, was assured for those who participated in certain prescribed dances, who led pure lives, and who abandoned white customs and returned to Indian ways. The new world, which was to follow the apocalypse, would see America returned to the surviving "Ghost Dance" followers and to their Indian ancestors, who would lead together lives of virtue and happiness. The Ghost Dance swept across the Plains and into neighboring culture areas, with various modifications from place to place. Although the Ghost Dancers planned no violence, American frontier settlers and military authorities feared an armed uprising. These suspicions led directly to the notorious massacre at Wounded Knee, in which U.S. troops killed a band of Sioux Indians who had fled their reservation after the "medicine man," Sitting Bull, was shot while resisting arrest. Indian interest in the Ghost

Dance subsided gradually in the face of white hostility and the failure of the millennium to arrive.

The Paliau Movement in the Admirality Islands

Following World War II, the Manus, a coastal people residing near New Guinea in the Australian Trust Territory, developed a new religious, political, and economic system under the leadership of a secular prophet named Paliau (Schwartz 1962). The Paliau movement was not a cargo cult and did not aim at the categorical expulsion of all whites. It was nativistic, however, to the extent that the movement sought to secure for Melanesians a greater degree of economic and political sovereignty than they had hitherto enjoyed under either the Japanese or Australian administrations. The "New Fella Fashion," as the movement was termed in pidgin, dispensed with many of the traditional religious beliefs and observances, reorganized the settlement pattern and economy, and proposed new standards of family organization, political structure, and economic activity. In effect, the Paliau movement was an effort by a native population to bring itself into the main stream of world cultural development by a rationally conceived reorganization of its entire culture. Although Australian authorities were suspicious of Paliau, and his movement suffered administrative setbacks, and although a short-lived cargo cult temporarily interrupted its progress, the Paliau movement has survived and contributed substantially to the furtherance of the general aims of the Trust Territory itself: the development of self-respecting, self-supporting, and self-governing native communities linked to the rest of the modern world by mutually satisfying economic and political ties (Mead 1956).

Cargo Cults

Peter M. Worsley

A cargo cult, one of the several varieties of revitalization movements, is an intentional effort on the part of the members of society to create a more satisfying culture. Characteristic of revitalization movements in Melanesia, but not restricted to that area, cargo cults function to bring scattered groups together into a wider religious and political unity. These movements are the result of widespread dissatisfaction, oppression, insecurity, and the hope for fulfillment of prophecies of good times and abundance soon to come. Exposure to the cultures and material goods of the Western world, combinations of native myth with Christian teachings of the coming of a messiah, and belief in the white man's magic—all contributed to the New Guinean's faith that the "cargo" would soon arrive, bringing with it the end of the present order and the beginning of a blissful paradise. Worsley's article depicts a movement that often was so organized and persistent as to bring government work to a halt. Cargo cult movements still occur in Melanesia, where they are often intermixed with other types of revitalization movements.

Reprinted with permission from *Scientific American*, Vol. 200 (May 1959), pp. 117–28. Copyright © 1959 by Scientific American, Inc. All rights reserved.

PATROLS OF THE AUSTRALIAN GOVERNMENT venturing into the "uncontrolled" central highlands of New Guinea in 1946 found the primitive people there swept up in a wave of religious excitement. Prophecy was being fulfilled: The arrival of the Whites was the sign that the end of the world was at hand. The natives proceeded to butcher all of their pigs—animals that were not only a principal source of subsistence but also symbols of social status and ritual preeminence in their culture. They killed these valued animals in expression of the belief that after three days of darkness "Great Pigs" would appear from the sky. Food, firewood, and other necessities had to be stockpiled to see the people through to the arrival of the Great Pigs. Mock wireless antennae of bamboo and rope had been erected to receive in advance the news of the millennium. Many believed that with the great event they would exchange their black skins for white ones.

This bizarre episode is by no means the single event of its kind in the murky history of the collision of European civilization with the indigenous cultures of the southwest Pacific. For more than one hundred years traders and missionaries have been reporting similar disturbances among the peoples of Melanesia, the group of Negro-inhabited islands (including New Guinea, Fiji, the Solomons, and the New Hebrides) lying between Australia and the open Pacific Ocean. Though their technologies were based largely upon stone and wood, these peoples had highly developed cultures, as measured by the standards of maritime and agricultural ingenuity, the complexity of their varied social organizations, and the elaboration of religious belief and ritual. They were nonetheless ill prepared for the shock of the encounter with the Whites, a people so radically different from themselves and so infinitely more powerful. The sudden transition from the society of the ceremonial stone ax to the society of sailing ships and now of airplanes has not been easy to make.

After four centuries of Western expansion, the densely populated central highlands of New Guinea remain one of the few regions where the people still carry on their primitive existence in complete independence of the world outside. Yet as the agents of the Australian Government penetrate into ever more remote mountain valleys, they find these backwaters of antiquity already deeply disturbed by contact with the ideas and artifacts of European civilization. For "cargo"—Pidgin English for trade goods—has long flowed along the indigenous channels of communication from the seacoast into the wilderness. With it has traveled the frightening knowledge of the white man's magical power. No small element in the white man's magic is the hopeful message sent abroad by his missionaries: the news that a Messiah will come and that the present order of Creation will end.

The people of the central highlands of New Guinea are only the latest to be gripped in the recurrent religious frenzy of the "cargo cults." However variously embellished with details from native myth and Christian belief, these cults all advance the same central theme: the world is about to end in a terrible cataclysm. Thereafter God, the ancestors, or some local culture hero will appear and inaugurate a blissful paradise on earth. Death, old age, illness, and evil will be unknown. The riches of the white man will accrue to the Melanesians.

Although the news of such a movement in one area has doubtless often inspired similar movements in other areas, the evidence indicates that these cults have arisen independently in many places as parallel responses to the same enormous social stress and strain. Among the movements best known to students of Melanesia are the "Taro Cult" of New Guinea, the "Vailala Madness" of Papua, the "Naked Cult" of Espiritu Santo, the "John Frum Movement" of the New Hebrides, and the "Tuka Cult" of the Fiji Islands.

At times the cults have been so well organized and fanatically persistent that they have brought the work of government to a standstill. The outbreaks have often taken the authorities completely by surprise and have confronted them with mass opposition of an alarming kind. In the 1930's, for example, villagers in the vicinity of Wewak, New Guinea, were stirred by a succession of "Black King" movements. The prophets announced that the Europeans would soon leave the island, abandoning their property to the natives, and urged their followers to cease paying taxes, since the government station was about to disappear into the sea in a great earthquake. To the tiny community of Whites in charge of the region, such talk was dangerous. The authorities jailed four of the prophets and exiled three others. In yet another movement, that sprang up in declared opposition to the local Christian mission, the cult leader took Satan as his god.

Troops on both sides in World War II found their arrival in Melanesia heralded as a sign of the Apocalypse. The G.I.'s who landed in the New Hebrides, moving up for the bloody fighting on Guadalcanal, found the natives furiously at work preparing airfields, roads and docks for the magic ships and planes that they believed were coming from "Rusefel" (Roosevelt), the friendly king of America.

The Japanese also encountered millenarian visionaries during their southward march to Guadalcanal. Indeed, one of the strangest minor military actions of World War II occurred in Dutch New Guinea, when Japanese forces had to be turned against the local Papuan inhabitants of the Geelvink Bay region. The Japanese had at first been received with great joy, not because their "Greater East Asia Co-Prosperity Sphere" propaganda had made any great impact upon the Papuans, but because the natives regarded them as harbingers of the new world that was dawning, the flight of the Dutch having already given the first sign. Mansren, creator of the islands and their peoples, would now return, bringing with him the ancestral dead. All this had been known, the cult leaders declared, to the crafty Dutch, who had torn out the first page of the Bible where these truths were inscribed. When Mansren returned, the existing world order would be entirely overturned. White men would turn black like Papuans, Papuans would become Whites; root crops would grow in trees, and coconuts and fruits would grow like tubers. Some of the islanders now began to draw together into large "towns"; others took Biblical names such as "Jericho" and "Galilee" for their villages. Soon they adopted military uniforms and began drilling.

The Japanese, by now highly unpopular, tried to disarm and disperse the Papuans; resistance inevitably developed. The climax of this tragedy came when several canoe-loads of fanatics sailed out to attack Japanese warships, believing themselves to be invulnerable by virtue of the holy water with which they had sprinkled themselves. But the bullets of the Japanese did not turn to water, and the attackers were mowed down by machine-gun fire.

Behind this incident lay a long history. As long ago as 1857 missionaries in the Geelvink Bay region had made note of the story of Mansren. It is typical of many Melanesian myths that became confounded with Christian doctrine to form the ideological basis of the movements. The legend tells how long ago there lived an old man named Manamakeri ("he who itches"), whose body was covered with sores. Manamakeri was extremely fond of palm wine, and used to climb a huge tree every day to tap the liquid from the flowers. He soon found that someone was getting there before him and removing the liquid. Eventually he trapped the thief, who turned out to be none other than the Morning Star. In return for his freedom, the Star gave the old man a wand that would produce as much fish as he liked, a magic tree and a magic staff. If he drew in the sand and stamped his foot, the drawing would become real. Manamakeri, aged as he was, now magically impregnated a young maiden; the child of this union was a miracle-child who spoke as soon as he was born. But the maiden's parents were horrified, and banished her, the child, and the old man. The trio sailed off in a canoe created by Mansren ("The Lord"), as the old man now became known. On this journey Mansren rejuvenated himself by stepping into a fire and flaking off his scaly skin, which changed into valuables. He then sailed around Geelvink Bay, creating islands where he stopped, and peopling them with the ancestors of the present-day Papuans.

The Mansren myth is plainly a creation myth full of symbolic ideas relating to fertility and rebirth. Comparative evidence—especially the shedding of his scaly skin—confirms the suspicion that the old man is, in fact, the Snake in another guise. Psychoanalytic writers argue that the snake occupies such a prominent part in mythology the world over because it stands for the penis, another fertility symbol. This may be so, but its symbolic significance is surely more complex than this. It is the "rebirth" of the hero, whether Mansren or the Snake, that exercises such universal fascination over men's minds.

The nineteenth-century missionaries thought that the Mansren story would make the introduction of Christianity easier, since the concept of "resurrection," not to mention that of the "virgin birth" and the "second coming," was already there. By 1867, however, the first cult organized around the Mansren legend was reported.

Though such myths were widespread in Melanesia, and may have sparked occasional movements even in the pre-White era, they took on a new significance in the late nineteenth century, once the European powers had finished parceling out the Melanesian region among themselves. In many coastal areas the long history of "blackbirding"—the seizure of islanders for work on the plantations of Australia and Fiji—had built up a reservoir of hostility to Europeans. In other areas, however, the arrival of the Whites was accepted, even welcomed, for it meant access to bully beef and cigarettes, shirts and paraffin lamps, whisky and bicycles. It also meant access to the knowledge behind these material goods, for the Europeans brought missions and schools as well as cargo.

Practically the only teaching the natives received about European life came from the missions, which emphasized the central significance of religion in European society. The Melanesians already believed that man's activities—whether gardening, sailing canoes, or bearing children—needed magical assistance. Ritual without human effort was not enough. But neither was human effort on its own. This outlook was reinforced by mission teaching.

The initial enthusiasm for European rule, however, was speedily dispelled. The rapid growth of the plantation economy removed the bulk of the able-bodied men from the villages, leaving women, children, and old men to carry on as best they could. The splendid vision of the equality of all Christians began to seem a pious deception in face of the realities of the color bar, the multiplicity of rival Christian missions and the open irreligion of many Whites.

For a long time the natives accepted the European mission as the means by which the "cargo" would eventually be made available to them. But they found that acceptance of Christianity did not bring the cargo any nearer. They grew disillusioned. The story now began to be put about that it was not the Whites who made the cargo, but the dead ancestors. To people completely ignorant of factory production, this made good sense. White men did not work; they merely wrote secret signs on scraps of paper, for which they were given shiploads of goods. On the other hand, the Melanesians labored week after week for pitiful wages. Plainly the goods must be made for Melanesians somewhere, perhaps in the Land of the Dead. The Whites, who possessed the secret of the cargo, were intercepting it and keeping it from the hands of the islanders, to whom it was really consigned. In the Madang district of New Guinea, after some forty years' experience of the missions, the natives went in a body one day with a petition demanding that the cargo secret should now be revealed to them, for they had been very patient.

So strong is this belief in the existence of a "secret" that the cargo cults generally contain some ritual in imitation of the mysterious European customs which are held to be the clue to the white man's extraordinary power over goods and men. The believers sit around tables with bottles of flowers in front of them, dressed in European clothes, waiting for the cargo ship or airplane to materialize; other cultists feature magic pieces of paper and cabalistic writing. Many of them deliberately turn their backs on the past by destroying secret ritual objects, or exposing them to the gaze of uninitiated youths and women, for whom formerly even a glimpse of the sacred objects would have meant the severest penalties, even death. The belief that they were the chosen people is further reinforced by their reading of the Bible, for the lives and customs of the people in the Old Testament resemble their own lives rather than those of the Europeans. In the New Testament they find the Apocalypse, with its prophecies of destruction and resurrection, particularly attractive.

Missions that stress the imminence of the Second Coming, like those of the Seventh Day Adventists, are often accused of stimulating millenarian cults among the islanders. In reality, however, the Melanesians themselves rework the doctrines the missionaries teach them, selecting from the Bible what they themselves find particularly congenial in

it. Such movements have occurred in areas where missions of quite different types have been dominant, from Roman Catholic to Seventh Day Adventist. The reasons for the emergence of these cults, of course, lie far deeper in the life-experience of the people.

The economy of most of the islands is very backward. Native agriculture produces little for the world market, and even the European plantations and mines export only a few primary products and raw materials: copra, rubber, gold. Melanesians are quite unable to understand why copra, for example, fetches thirty pounds sterling per ton one month and but five pounds a few months later. With no notion of the workings of world-commodity markets, the natives see only the sudden closing of plantations, reduced wages and unemployment, and are inclined to attribute their insecurity to the whim or evil in the nature of individual planters.

Such shocks have not been confined to the economic order. Governments, too, have come and gone, especially during the two world wars: German, Dutch, British, and French administrations melted overnight. Then came the Japanese, only to be ousted in turn largely by the previously unknown Americans. And among these Americans the Melanesians saw Negroes like themselves, living lives of luxury on equal terms with white G.I.'s. The sight of these Negroes seemed like a fulfillment of the old prophecies to many cargo cult leaders. Nor must we forget the sheer scale of this invasion. Around a million U.S. troops passed through the Admiralty Islands, completely swamping the inhabitants. It was a world of meaningless and chaotic changes, in which anything was possible. New ideas were imported and given local twists. Thus in the Loyalty Islands people expected the French Communist Party to bring the millennium. There is no real evidence, however, of any Communist influence in these movements, despite the rather hysterical belief among Solomon Island planters that the name of the local "Masinga Rule" movement was derived from the word "Marxian"! In reality the name comes from a Solomon Island tongue, and means "brotherhood."

Europeans who have witnessed outbreaks inspired by the cargo cults are usually at a loss to understand what they behold. The islanders throw away their money, break their most sacred taboos, abandon their gardens, and destroy their precious livestock; they indulge in sexual license, or, alternatively, rigidly separate men from women in huge communal establishments. Sometimes they spend days sitting gazing at the horizon for a glimpse of the long-awaited ship or airplane; sometimes they dance, pray and sing in mass congregations, becoming possessed and "speaking with tongues."

Observers have not hesitated to use such words as "madness," "mania," and "irrationality" to characterize the cults. But the cults reflect quite logical and rational attempts to make sense out of a social order that appears senseless and chaotic. Given the ignorance of the Melanesians about the wider European society, its economic organization and its highly developed technology, their reactions form a consistent and understandable pattern. They wrap up all their yearning and hope in an amalgam that combines the best counsel they can find in Christianity and their native belief. If the world is soon to end, gardening or fishing is unnecessary; everything will be provided. If the Melanesians are to be part of a much wider order, the taboos that prescribe their social conduct must now be lifted or broken in a newly prescribed way.

Of course the cargo never comes. The cults nonetheless live on. If the millennium does not arrive on schedule, then perhaps there is some failure in the magic, some error in the ritual. New breakaway groups organize around "purer" faith and ritual. The cult rarely disappears, so long as the social situation which brings it into being persists.

At this point it should be observed that cults of this general kind are not peculiar to Melanesia.

Men who feel themselves oppressed and deceived have always been ready to pour their hopes and fears, their aspirations and frustrations, into dreams of a millennium to come or of a golden age to return. All parts of the world have had their counterparts of the cargo cults, from the American Indian Ghost Dance to the Communist-millenarist "reign of the saints" in Münster during the Reformation, from medieval European apocalyptic cults to African "witch-finding" movements and Chinese Buddhist heresies. In some situations men have been content to wait and pray; in others they have sought to hasten the day by using their strong right arms to do the Lord's work. And always the cults serve to bring together scattered groups, notably the peasants and urban plebeians of agrarian societies and the peoples of "stateless" societies where the cult unites separate (and often hostile) villages, clans, and tribes into a wider religio-political unity.

Once the people begin to develop secular political organizations, however, the sects tend to lose their importance as vehicles of protest. They begin to relegate the Second Coming to the distant future or to the next world. In Melanesia ordinary political bodies, trade unions and native councils are becoming the normal media through which the islanders express their aspirations. In recent years continued economic prosperity and political stability have taken some of the edge off their despair. It now seems unlikely that any major movement along cargo-cult lines will recur in areas where the transition to secular politics has been made, even if the insecurity of prewar times returned. I would predict that the embryonic nationalism represented by cargo cults is likely in future to take forms familiar in the history of other countries that have moved from subsistence agriculture to participation in the world economy.

Serpent-Handling as Sacrament

Mary Lee Daugherty

In this article Mary Lee Daugherty discusses serpent-handlers in West Virginia. The author, raised in the area she writes about, maintains that the handling of serpents as a religious act reflects the geographic and economic harshness of the environment in which the snake-handlers live. Professor Daugherty has been studying religious behavior and beliefs throughout Appalachia as well as West Virginia. It is a mark of her professional ability that she has been allowed by the members of several Holiness-type churches to conduct her research. Although many people in this country are appalled at the thought of religious behavior that encourages the handling of poisonous snakes and the drinking of such poisons as strychnine and lye, West Virginia's defeat of a 1966 bill that would have made serpent-handling illegal serves as an indication of religious freedom in the United States.

Reprinted from *Theology Today*, Vol. 33, no. 3 (October 1976), pp. 232–43, by permission of the author and Princeton Theological Seminary.

"And he [Jesus] said unto them, Go ye into all the world, and preach the gospel to every creature. He that believeth and is baptized shall be saved; but he that believeth not shall be damned. And these signs shall follow them that believe; In my name shall they cast out devils; they shall speak with new tongues; they shall take up serpents; and if they drink any deadly thing, it shall not hurt them; they shall lay hands on the sick, and they shall recover."

—Mark 16:15–18 (AV)

THE SERPENT-HANDLERS OF WEST VIRGINIA WERE originally simple, poor, white people who formed a group of small, independent Holiness-type churches. Serpent-handlers base their particular religious practices on the familiar passage from the "long-conclusion" of the Gospel of Mark. (They are unaware of the disputed nature of this text as the biblical scholars know it.)

The handling of serpents as a supreme act of faith reflects, as in a mirror, the danger and harshness of the environment in which most of these people have lived. The land is rugged and uncompromisingly grim. It produces little except for coal dug from the earth. Unemployment and welfare have been constant companions. The dark holes of the deep mines into which men went to work every day have maimed and killed them for years. The copperhead and rattlesnake are the most commonly found serpents in the rocky terrain. For many years mountain people have suffered terrible pain and many have died from snake bite. Small wonder that it is considered the ultimate fact of faith to reach out and take up the serpent when one is filled with the Holy Ghost. Old timers here in the mountains, before the days of modern medicine, could only explain that those who lived were somehow chosen by God's special mercy and favor.

Today serpent-handlers are experiencing, as are other West Virginians, great economic improvement. Many now live in expensive mobile homes that dot the mountain country side. They purchase and own among their possessions brand new cars and modern appliances. Many of the men now earn from twelve to eighteen thousand dollars a year, working in the revitalized mining industry. Most of the young people are now going to and graduating from high school. I know of one young man with two years of college who is very active in his church. He handles serpents and is looked upon as the one who will take over the pastor's position sometime in the future. What the effect of middle-class prosperity and higher education will be among serpent-handlers remains to be seen. It may be another generation before the effects can be adequately determined.

I

Knowing serpent-handlers to be biblical literalists, one might surmise that they, like other sects, have picked a certain passage of Scripture and built a whole ritual around a few cryptic verses. While this is true, I am persuaded, after years of observation, that serpent-handling holds for them the significance of a sacrament.

Tapestry paintings of the Lord's Supper hang in most of their churches. Leonardo da Vinci's *Last Supper* is the one picture I have seen over and over again in their churches and in their homes. But in West Virginia, the serpent-handlers whom I know personally do not celebrate the Lord's Supper in their worship services. It is my observation and hypothesis that the ritual of serpent-handling is their way of celebrating life, death, and resurrection. Time and again they prove to themselves that Jesus has the power to deliver them from death here and now.

Another clue to the sacramental nature of lifting up the serpents as the symbol of victory over death is to be observed at their funerals. At the request of the family of one who has died of snake bite, serpents may be handled at a funeral. Even as a Catholic priest may lift up the host at a mass for the dead, indicating belief that in the life and death of Jesus there is victory over death, so the serpent-handlers, I believe, lift up the serpent. Of course,

none of this is formalized, for all is very spontaneous. But I am convinced that they celebrate their belief that "in the name of Jesus" there is power over death, and this is what the serpent-handling ritual has proved to them over and over again. This is why I believe they will not give up this ritual because it is at the center of their Christian faith, and in West Virginia, unlike all the other States, it is not illegal.

Many handlers have been bitten numerous times, but, contrary to popular belief, few have died. Their continued life, and their sometimes deformed hands, bear witness to the fact that Jesus still has power over illness and death. Even those who have not been bitten know many who have, and the living witness is ever present in the lives of their friends. If one of the members should die, it is believed that God allowed it to happen to remind the living that the risk they take is totally real. Never have I heard any one of them say that a brother or sister who died lacked faith.

The cultural isolation of these people is still very real. Few have traveled more than a few miles from home. Little more than the Bible is ever read. Television is frowned upon; movies are seldom attended. The Bible is communicated primarily through oral tradition in the church or read at home. There is little awareness of other world religions. Even contacts with Roman Catholics and Jews are rare. Most of their lives revolve around the local church where they gather for meetings two or three times a week.

When one sees the people handling serpents in their services, the Garden of Eden story immediately comes to mind. In the Genesis story, the serpent represents evil that tempts Adam and Eve and must be conquered by their descendants. But the serpent means something far different to West Virginia mountain people; it means life over death. There is never any attempt to kill the snake in Appalachian serpent-handling services. Practitioners seldom kill snakes even in the out of doors. They let them go at the end of the summer months so that they may return to their natural environment to hibernate for the winter. They catch different snakes each spring to use in their worship services. When you ask them why, they tell you quite simply that they do not want to make any of God's creatures suffer. The serpent is always handled with both love and fear in their services, but it is never harmed or killed. Handlers may be killed from bites, but they will not kill the snake. Neither do they force the handling of serpents on any who do not wish to do so.

The snake is seldom handled in private, but usually in the community of believers during a church service. Members may encourage each other to take the risk, symbolically taking on life and testing faith. Their willingness to die for their beliefs gives to their lives a vitality of faith. Handlers usually refuse medicine or hospital treatment for snake bite. But they do go to hospital for other ilnesses or if surgery is needed. In the past, they usually refused welfare. They revere and care for their elderly who have usually survived numerous snake bites. Each time they handle the serpents they struggle with life once more and survive again the forces that traditionally oppressed mountain people. The poverty, the unemployment, the yawning strip mines, death in the deep mines have all been harsh, uncontrollable forces for simple people. The handling of serpents is their way of confronting and coping with their very real fears about life and the harshness of reality as experienced in the mountains in years gone by and, for many, even today.

Yet in the face of all this, they seek to live in harmony with nature, not to destroy it or any of its creatures, even the deadly serpent. It is only with the Holy Ghost, however, that they find the sustenance to survive. They live close to the earth, surrounded by woods, streams, and sky. Most live in communities of only a few hundred people or less.

II

The deep longing for holiness of these Appalachian people stands out in bold relief in the serpent-handling ritual of worship. The search for holiness is dramatized in their willingness to suffer terrible pain from snake bite, or even death itself, to get the feeling of God in their lives. The support of their fellow Christians is still with them. In their experience, God may not come if you don't really pray or ask only once. The person in the group who has been bitten most often and who has suffered the most pain or sickness is usually the leader. While it is the Holy Ghost who gives the power, those who have survived snake bite do get recognition and praise for their courage and their faith from the group. They have learned to cope

with their anxieties by calling upon the name of Jesus and the power which he freely offers. Support is given to each member through the laying on of hands in healing ceremonies, through group prayers, and through verbal affirmations, such as: "Help her Jesus," "Bless him, Lord," "That's right, Lord." Through group support, anxiety about life is relieved. They feel ennobled as God becomes manifest in their midst.

The person of the Holy Ghost (they prefer this to Holy Spirit), enables them not only to pick up serpents, but to speak in tongues, to preach, to testify, to cure diseases, to cast out demons, and even to drink strychnine and lye, or to use fire on their skin when the snakes are in hibernation during the winter months. In these dramatic ways, the mountain folk pursue holiness above all else. They find through their faith both meaning and encouragement. Psychological tests indicate that in many ways they are more emotionally healthy than members of mainline Protestant churches.

Having internalized my own feelings of insecurity and worthlessness for many years because I was "no count" having been born from poor white trash on one side of my family, I have in my own being a deep appreciation and understanding of the need of these people to ask God for miracles accompanied with spectacular demonstrations. Thus they are assured of their own worth, even if only to God. They have never gotten this message from the outside world. They know they have been, and many still are, the undesirable poor, the uneducated mountain folk, locked into their little pockets of poverty in a rough, hostile land. So the Holy Ghost is the great equalizer in the church meeting. One's age, sex, years of schooling are all of less value. Being filled with the Holy Ghost is the only credential one needs in this unique society.

III

The Holy Ghost creates a mood of openness and spontaneity in the serpent-handling service that is beautiful to behold. Even though there is not much freedom in the personal lives of these people, there is a sense of power in their church lives. Their religion does seem to heal them inwardly of aches and pains and in many instances even of major illnesses. One often sees expressions of dependence as men and women fall down before the picture of Jesus, calling aloud over and over again, "Jesus . . . Jesus . . . Jesus . . ." The simple carpenter of Nazareth is obviously a person with whom mountain people can identify. Jesus worked with his hands, and so do they; Jesus was essentially, by our standards, uneducated, and so are they; Jesus came from a small place, he lived much of his life out of doors, he went fishing, he suffered and was finally done in by the "power structure," and so have they been in the past and often are today.

As I think about the mountain women as they fall down before the picture of Jesus, I wonder what he means to them. Here is a simple man who treated women with great love and tenderness. In this sense, he is unlike some of the men they must live with. Jesus healed the bodies of women, taught them the Bible, never told jokes about their bodies, and even forgave them their sexual sins. In the mountains, adultery is usually punished with beatings. Maybe it should not surprise us that in a State where the strip miners have raped the earth that the rape of the people has also taken place, and the rape of women is often deeply felt and experienced. Things are now changing, and for this we can be grateful.

IV

In the serpent-handlers' churches, the Bible usually remains closed on the pulpit. Since most older members cannot read very well and have usually felt shy about their meager education, they did not read the Bible aloud in public, especially if some more educated people were present. They obviously read the Bible at home, but most remember it from stories they have heard. The Bible is the final authority for everything, even the picking up of serpents and the drinking of poison. It is all literally true, but the New Testament is read more often than the Old Testament.

In former years, their churches have given these poor and powerless people the arena in which they could act out their frustrations and powerless feelings. For a short time, while in church, they could experience being powerful when filled with the Holy Ghost. Frustrated by all the things in the outside world that they could not change, frustrated by the way the powerful people of the world were running things, they could nevertheless run their own show in their own churches. So they gathered three or four times a week, in their mod-

est church buildings, and they stayed for three to five hours for each service. On these occasions, they can feel important, loved, and powerful. They can experience God directly.

I am always struck by the healing love that emerges at the end of each service when they all seem to love each other, embrace each other, and give each other the holy kiss. They are free from restrictions and conventions to love everyone. Sometimes I have the feeling that I get a glimmer of what the Kingdom of God will be like as we kiss each other, old and young, with or without teeth, rich and poor, educated and uneducated, male and female. So I have learned much and have been loved in turn by the serpent-handlers of West Virginia. As they leave the church and go back to their daily work, all the frustrations of the real world return, but they know they can meet again tomorrow night or in a few days. So they have faith, hope, and love, but the greatest message they have given to me is their love.

V

There are thousands of small Holiness churches in the rural areas of West Virginia. While four-fifths of all Protestants are members of mainstream denominations, no one knows just how many attend Holiness churches. Membership records are not considered important to these people, and although I personally know of about twenty-five serpent-handling churches, there may be others, for those in one church often do not know those in another. They laugh and makes jokes about churches that give you a piece of paper as you enter the door, telling you when to pray and what to sing. They find it difficult to believe that you can "order around" the worship of the Holy Ghost on a piece of paper.

Those who make up the membership of the serpent-handling churches are often former members of other Holiness churches or are former Baptists or Methodists. In the Holiness churches, the attainment of personal holiness and being filled with the Spirit is the purpose and goal of life. Members view the secular world as evil and beyond hope. Hence they do not take part in any community activities or social programs.

Fifty-four percent of all persons in the state of West Virginia still live in communities of 1,000 people or less. Freedom of worship is the heritage of the Scotch-Irish, who settled these mountains 200 years ago. In more recent times, among Holiness groups there were no trained ministers. So oral tradition, spontaneous worship, and shared leadership are important.

Holiness church members live by a very strict personal code of morality. A large sign in the church at Jolo, W. Va., indicates that dresses must be worn below the knees, arms must be covered, no lipstick or jewelry is to be worn. No smoking, drinking, or other worldly pleasures are to be indulged in by "true believers." Some women do not cut their hair, others do not even buy chewing gum or soft drinks. For years, in the mountains, people have practiced divine healing, since medical facilities are scarce. Four counties in West Virginia still do not have a doctor, nurse, clinic, dentist, or ambulance service.

In a typical serpent-handling church service, the "true believers" usually sit on the platform of the church together. They are the members who have demonstrated that they have received the Holy Ghost. This is known to them and to others because they have manifested certain physical signs in their own bodies. If they have been bitten from snakes, as many have, and have not died, they have proved that they have the Holy Ghost. And those who have been bitten many times, and survived, are the "real saints." The "true believers" also demonstrate that they have the Holy Ghost by speaking in tongues, by the jerking of their bodies, and by their various trance-like states. They may dance for long periods of time or fall on the floor without being hurt. They may drink the "salvation cocktail," a mixture of strychnine or lye and water. They may also speak in tongues or in ecstatic utterances. Usually this is an utterance between themselves and God. But sometimes members seek to interpret the language of tongues. They lay their hands upon each other to heal hurts or even serious illnesses such as cancer. They sometimes pass their hands through fire. I have witnessed this activity and no burn effects are visible, even though a hand may remain in the flame for some time. A few years ago, they picked up hot coals from the pot bellied stoves and yet were not burned. They apparently can block out pain totally, when in a trance or deep into the Spirit of God.

One woman who attended church at Scrabble Creek, W. Va., experienced, on two occasions, the stigmata as blood came out of her hands, feet, side and forehead. This was witnessed by all present in the church. When asked about this startling experience, she said that she had prayed that God would allow people to see through her body how much Jesus had suffered for them by his death and resurrection.

A local church in the rural areas may be known as "Brother So and So's" or "Sister So and So's" church to those who live nearby, but the sign over the door will usually indicate that the church belongs to Jesus. Such names as "The Jesus Church," "The Jesus Only Church," "The Jesus Saves Church," and "The Lord Jesus Christ's Church" are all common names. The churches do not belong to any denomination, and they have no written doctrines or creeds. The order of the service is spontaneous and different every night. Everyone is welcome and people travel around to each other's churches, bringing with them their musical instruments, snakes, fire equipment, poison mixtures, and other gifts.

Often the service begins with singing which may last thirty to forty-five minutes. Next, they may all pray out loud together for the Holy Ghost to fall upon them during the service. Singing, testifying, and preaching by anyone who feels God's spirit may follow. Serpents then will be handled while others are singing. It is possible that serpents will be handled two or three times in one service, but usually it is only once. Serpents are only handled when they feel God's spirit within them. After dancing ecstatically, a brother or sister will open the box and pull out a serpent. Others will follow if there are other snakes available. If only one or two serpents are present, then they may be passed around from believer to believer. Sometimes a circle may be made and the snakes passed. I have only once seen them throw snakes to each other. Children are kept far away.

There is much calling on the name of Jesus while the serpents are being handled, and once the "sacrament" is over, there is a great prayer of rejoicing and often a dance of thanksgiving that no one was hurt. If someone is bitten, there is prayer for his or her healing and great care is taken. If the person becomes too ill to stay in the church, he or she may be taken home and believers will pray for the person for days, if necessary. Even if the person does not die, and usually he or she doesn't, the person is usually very sick. Vomiting of blood and swelling are very painful. Some persons in the churches have lost the use of a finger or suffered some other deformity. But in many years of serpent-handling, I believe there are only about twenty recorded deaths.

VII

The symbolism of the serpent is found in almost all cultures and religions, everywhere, and in all ages. It suggests the ambiguity of good and evil, sickness and health, life and death, mortality and immortality, chaos and wisdom. Because the serpent lives in the ground but is often found in trees, it conveys the notion of transcendence, a creature that lives between earth and heaven. And because it sheds its skin, it seems to know the secret of eternal life.

In the Bible, the serpent is most obviously associated with the Adam and Eve temptation (Gen. 3:1–13), but we also read of the sticks that Moses and Aaron turned into snakes (Ex. 7:8–12), and of Moses' bronze serpent standard (Num. 21:6–9). The two entwined snakes in the ancient figure of the caduceus, symbolizing sickness and health, has been widely adopted as the emblem of the medical profession. And sometimes in early Christian art, the crucifixion is represented with a serpent wound around the cross or lying at the foot of the cross (cf. John 3:14). Here again good and evil, life over death, are symbolized.

In early liturgical art, John the Evangelist was often identified with a chalice from which a serpent was departing, a reference to the legend that when he was forced to drink poison, it was drained away in the snake. Among the early Gnostics, there was a group known as Ophites who were said to worship the serpent because it brought "knowledge" to Adam and Eve and so to all humanity. They were said to free a serpent from a box and that it then entwined itself around the bread and wine of the Eucharist.

But, of course, this ancient history and symbolic lore are unknown to the mountain serpent-handlers of West Virginia, and even if they were told, they probably would not be interested. Their own tradition is rooted in their literal acceptance of what they regard as Jesus' commandment at the conclusion of Mark's Gospel. The problems of biblical textual criticism, relating to the fact that these verses on which they depend are not found in the best manuscript evidence, does not bother them. Their Bible is the English King James Version, and they know through their own experience that their faith in the healing and saving power of Jesus has been tested and proven without question. In any case, their ritual is unique in church history.

What the future holds for the serpent-handlers, no one can tell. Although the young people have tended to stay in their local communities, the temptation in the past to move out and away to find work has been very great. Now many of the young people are returning home as the mining industry offers new, high-paying jobs. And a new era of relative economic prosperity is emerging as the energy problem makes coal-mining more important for the whole Appalachian area. In the meantime, serpent-handling for many mountain people remains a Jesus-commanded "sacrament" whereby physical signs communicate spiritual reality.

Honor Thy Father Moon

Berkeley Rice

*Reverend Sun Myung Moon's Unification Church,
the most controversial psychoreligious cult of the
several that mushroomed across the United States in
the last decade, described vividly here by Berkeley
Rice, still holds the allegiance of thousands of
Americans. Rice explores the major tenets of the
religion, its appeal to certain youth, and why, in
terms of growth, wealth, organization, and
discipline, it is the most controversial manifestation
of the new evangelism. Considered both fraud and
saint, the Reverend Moon utilizes a training
system, not unlike that of other new sects, which
offers to the initiate the strength of an unbreachable
family, the removal of worldly cares, and a path to
salvation.*

Reprinted with permission from *Psychology Today
Magazine* (January 1976), pp. 36–47. Copyright ©
1976 American Psychological Association.

HELLFIRE, DAMNATION, SALVATION! THE MESS-
iah is here. Sun Myung Moon has come from
Korea to save our country, and thousands of
young Americans have left their homes and
schools to join his evangelical crusade, one of
several religious cults that have mushroomed in
the last decade. Thousands of other youths have
joined Hare Krishna, the Children of God, the
Jesus People, and the Maharaj Ji's Divine Light
Mission. Hundreds of others have attached
themselves to lesser-known sects, gurus and
mystics.

In a time of recession and turmoil, the cults
are a growth industry, their leaders successful
entrepreneurs of salvation for the young. None
of these new psychoreligious cults threatens to
sweep the country, and probably none commands more than 5,000 full-time members. But
in a country in which many of the young have
recently tripped out on drugs and radical politics, the cults have become a new opiate for the
youth of the 70s.

In terms of growth, wealth, organization and
discipline, the Reverend Moon's Unification
Church is the hottest and most controversial
manifestation of the new evangelism. Founded
in Korea in 1954 as The Holy Spirit Association
for the Unification of World Christianity, it now
claims a worldwide membership of 500,000 to
two million, based mainly in Korea and Japan,
with a modest following in Europe. Moon
moved his headquarters to America in 1973 because he believes it to be God's chosen land, and
possibly because it looked like promising territory. It has been. This article concentrates on the
movement's activities in the United States.

Starting with only a few hundred members in
1970, the Unification Church now claims a U.S.
following of 10,000 to 30,000, with a core of 2,-
000 to 10,000 full-time members. The movement
now takes in about $10 million a year from fund
raising and contributions. It is difficult for any

outsider to measure its size or wealth with full confidence, since the numbers vary wildly from one supposedly official estimate to another. As of the fall of 1975 the Church operated 120 communal recruiting and fund-raising centers in cities across the country, with recruiting teams covering 150 college campuses. Teams of Moon's missionaries bring word of the new Messiah to the heathen in other parts, and a Church-run publishing company spreads his message in pamphlets, paperbacks and leaflets.

Professional "Deprogrammers"

Moon has been denounced as a religious fraud and hustler, an antichrist who threatens established Christianity. He has also been accused of manipulating and ripping off the innocent young "Moonies" who serve him. His recruiters have left behind a trail of irate or hysterical parents who claim he has stolen their children and brainwashed them into conversion and slavery.

Many parents have tried to rescue their sons and daughters from Moon's communes, but often the kids can't be found, or refuse to come home. Some parents have hired professional "deprogrammers" to kidnap their children and free them from Moon's spell. Some have sued the Church for holding the youths against their will, a charge difficult and humiliating to prove when the kids swear they prefer Moon's Family to their own.

Many other parents either approve of or don't seem to mind their children joining Moon's movement. Some feel it may be better than drugs or drifting aimlessly around the country. Others look with favor upon it as a Christian youth movement, without understanding exactly what the members do or believe.

While Church members easily accept Moon's theology as revealed truth, outsiders tend to find it a mind-boggling mixture of Pentecostal Christianity, Eastern mysticism, anticommunism, pop psychology and metaphysics. According to *Divine Principle,* Moon's book of revelations, God intended Adam and Eve to marry and have perfect children, thereby establishing the Kingdom of Heaven on Earth. But Satan, embodied in the snake, seduced Eve, who in turn passed her impurity on to Adam, bringing about the Fall of Man. God then sent Jesus to redeem mankind from sin, but Jesus blew it too. He died on the cross before he could marry and father a new race of perfect children. The time has now come for a second Christ who will finally fulfill God's original plan. Moon doesn't identify the new Messiah, but like Moon, He just happens to have been born in Korea in 1920.

A short, stocky, moon-faced man of great energy, this 55-year-old millionaire industrialist-evangelist remains unfamiliar to most Americans. He speaks little English, grants almost no interviews, and makes infrequent public appearances at Unification rallies and banquets, usually surrounded by a phalanx of husky Moonie bodyguards. Since Moon addresses his American followers only in Korean, outsiders cannot understand his charisma, which depends mostly on his dynamic delivery and the members' belief in his semidivinity.

Since settling in the U.S., Moon has lived near Tarrytown, N.Y., in a $620,000 25-room mansion overlooking the Hudson River, with his wife, seven children, and a personal staff of 35 Moonies. The estate was called "Exquisite Acres" by the brassiere tycoon who built it; Moon has renamed it "East Garden"—a Garden of Eden for the new Adam from the East.

When not looking after his religious and corporate affairs, Moon spends a good deal of time out fishing on his 50-foot cabin cruiser, *New Hope.* Church officials bristle at criticisms of Moon's luxury. "Why must a religious leader be an ascetic?" one of them responded recently. "Look at the Pope." When I raised the issue with Farley Jones, a 29-year-old Princeton graduate who handles the Church's press relations, he said, "Followers of many religions honor their spiritual leader with physical comforts worthy of the dignity of his position. I trust the Reverend Moon's relationship with God, so I don't object to his lifestyle."

Moon's dealings with God began soon after his birth in North Korea. "From childhood I was clairvoyant," Moon once told his followers. "I could see through people, see their spirits." When he was 12 he began praying for "extraordinary things," and must have caught God's attention. On an Easter Sunday morning when Moon was 16, he had a vision in which Jesus appeared and told him to "carry out my unfinished task."

THE QUOTATIONS OF SUN MYUNG MOON

"I am your brain."

"What I wish must be your wish."

"My mission is to make new hearts, new persons."

"Of all the saints sent by God, I think I am the most successful one."

"The time will come . . . when my words will almost serve as law. If I ask a certain thing it will be done."

"The whole world is in my hand, and I will conquer and subjugate the world."

"By putting things in order, we can accomplish God's will. All obstacles to this world must be annihilated."

"Our strategy is to be unified into one with ourselves, and with that as the bullet we can smash the world."

Shining Dragon

Moon prepared for his divine mission by carrying on visionary chats with other prominent Biblical figures, and studying religious sects and cults then popular in Japan and Korea. In 1946 he began preaching his own version of Messianic Christianity, and gradually attracted a small, devoted following. He also changed his name from Yong Myung (Shining Dragon) Moon to a more celestial Sun Myung (Shining Sun) Moon. Moon, in Korean, means moon.

As his sect grew, Moon ran afoul of the authorities. He was excommunicated by the Presbyterian Church in 1948 and arrested various times by the police—on morals charges according to his Korean critics; for anticommunist activities according to Moon. Church legend tells how Moon was imprisoned, tortured and starved, yet shared his faith and his food with fellow inmates. Upon his escape or release in 1950 he led a band of followers on the mountainous trek to South Korea. He demonstrated his supernatural strength by carrying a crippled comrade on his bicycle—400 miles on the handlebars, according to one account; 600 miles on his back, according to another.

Reestablished in the South at the end of the Korean War, Moon founded the Unification Church,

which has flourished under the military dictatorship of General Park Chung Hee.

Since moving to the United States in 1973, Moon has proclaimed his new age of Christianity at lectures, banquets and mass rallies in every major city in the country, culminating in a rally at New York City's Madison Square Garden in 1974. This spring he hopes to gather 250,000 people at a rally in Yankee Stadium.

Moon's crusades feature performances of the Korean National Folk Ballet, a Korean children's dance troupe called the "Little Angels," the New Hope Singers and a rock group called "Sunburst."

As a build-up for the Garden rally, 2,000 Moonies (about half flown in from Japan and Europe) spent weeks thrusting out leaflets on crowded street corners, and plastering virtually every bare wall in the city with posters announcing the coming of Sun Moon.

"Kung-Fu Tantrum"

In a two-hour speech punctuated by kicks, jumps, karate chops and tears (one reporter called it a "kung-fu tantrum") the Reverend Moon spewed forth a torrent of hellfire and brimstone in Korean, which was translated by a heavily accented Korean interpreter as Moon stood smiling beatifically. Moon told of the fall of man, recounted the history of Christianity, warned of the approaching apocalypse and announced the arrival of a second Christ who would offer the world one last chance at salvation. "You can be the citizens of the Kingdom of Heaven if you meet the coming Messiah," he told a packed audience that thinned considerably before he finished. "He is your hope . . . and the only hope of America and this world." As usual, Moon stopped just short of actually proclaiming himself the Messiah, but he left little doubt in anyone's mind.

At other rallies the Unification Church's President Neil Salonen holds forth. Salonen, 30, is a smooth New Yorker who managed a psychiatric hospital in Washington, D.C. before his life was "transformed" by Sun Moon. Salonen tells Americans how the country is going to hell because of all the crime, suicide, alcoholism, divorce, sex, drug abuse, college radicals and foreign communists. He says God has sent the Reverend Moon to the

U.S. to solve these problems, and to "mobilize an ideological army of young people . . . to unite the world in a new age of faith."

The immediate goal of the crusades, rallies and street-corner evangelism is the recruitment of new members for the movement. Wherever the clean-cut, smiling Moonies can find them—on city streets or college campuses—they engage young Americans in discussions of the state of the country or their souls. As one U.C. official told me, "If someone's lonely, we talk to them. There are a lot of lonely people walking around."

The discussions almost invariably end with an invitation to an introductory lecture at the nearest Unification center. After these lectures come invitations to other lectures and dinners at the center. Along with dinner, potential converts get a diet of relentlessly hearty friendship from the brothers and sisters of what soon becomes the Family instead of the Church.

Those attracted to Moon's Family or his religion get invited next to a weekend "workshop" devoted to further study and friendship. The weekends follow an exhausting and rigidly structured pattern with little time for sleep and none for private reflection. Recruits get a daily dose of six to eight hours of mind-numbing theology based on Moon's *Divine Principle*. By the final lecture they learn that God has sent Sun Moon to save the world in general, and themselves in particular.

After each lecture, recruits and Moonies join in small discussion groups to answer questions but also to explore any personal problems, and to offer comforting attention. The rest of the days are filled with group activities: calisthenics, meals, sports, and lots of singing and praying. After dinner, and often lasting well past midnight, there's more group singing and praying, with testimony by Moonies of how they came to find peace, purpose, love and joy in the Family. Never left alone, the recruits are encouraged to pour out their hearts to their new brothers and sisters. Many do.

By Sunday night the conversion process turns hard-sell, with each recruit pressed to make a commitment to a week-long workshop, the next stage in the initiation process. About one out of four does. Those who don't often receive phone calls or visits afterward by Moonies who don't give up easily.

No Time for Relatives

For most of those who sign up for the seven-day workshop, the next stop is the Church's training headquarters at Tarrytown, N.Y., about 90 miles up the Hudson from New York City. Tarrytown is big time. Indoctrination there becomes more serious, the study more rigorous, and the life more spartan than that of the cadets just down the river at West Point. The program leaves neither time nor opportunity for contacting relatives or friends on the outside.

At the end of the week comes the pressure for commitment to full-time membership in the Family. The recruits reach this moment of decision worn out from lack of sleep, numbed by the endless lectures, cut off from the advice of family or friends, and softened up by the embracing warmth of the group. "It was like being taken care of," one ex-Moonie recalled. "The people were very friendly, and you really thought they did love you. . . . Also, I was kind of afraid of going out into the world. . . . It was an escape from the outside world." Some seem to have been ready for just such a commitment. "I've been looking for something like this for years," one told me. "It answers all the questions I was asking."

About half of those who complete the week-long seminar join the movement. Some join as "followers," remaining at their jobs or at school, and working evenings or weekends on Church projects. Some contribute part of their salaries. Those who join as full-time members either move into a local commune or stay at Barrytown and go on to increasingly intense seminars of three to 16 weeks.

During their first few months in the movement, new members often get phone calls or letters from parents or friends, urging them to drop out or at least come home to talk it over. Those who even waver, or who consider leaving are often told that their parents and others who oppose the Church are acting on behalf of Satan. A few do eventually drop out, but usually over the strenuous objections of their leaders. An evening of intense prayer and guidance frequently brings such wayward sheep back to the fold.

Once they move in, new members often give what possessions they have to the Church. While this rarely involves much money, some wealthy converts have donated considerable sums. At Barrytown or the communal centers, the Moonies no longer need money anyway. The Church takes care of all their daily needs, from toothpaste to trousers. Except for a few senior officials, every member who needs a new pair of shoes or eyeglasses has to ask the local director or team leader for the money to buy them. Directors of the bigger centers sometimes buy up large lots of nearly identical clothes for their resident members, thereby increasing the degree to which groups of smiling Moonies look as though they were cloned rather than recruited.

Life in a Moonie commune offers a welcome refuge to those unwilling or unable to face the daily frustrations of life on the outside: no drugs, no drinks, no sex, no money, no problems, no choices, no decisions. From the team leader's cheerful "Rise and shine!" in the sexually segregated dormitories to the last group songs and prayers at midnight, the Moonies rarely have to think for themselves. Full of religious fervor and new-found purpose, they follow orders and perform chores with gusto.

When not out recruiting, fund raising or working for the movement's various commercial enterprises, Moonies spend most of their remaining hours in group prayer. While they sometimes pray to God, they frequently pray to "Father." I asked one church official who "Father" was, and he replied, "Reverend Moon." One ex-Moonie feels the Church uses prayer as a means of emotional control over its members. "Everyone else is praying, like 'Heavenly Father, help us, help us. Oh, we're so lost Father.' They tell you that in order to reach God, you have to scream as loud as you can, and work up emotionally. . . . You're supposed to pray so fervently that you cry."

Spiritual Highs

I once watched a few dozen Moonies kneel in prayer at "the holy rock" at Barrytown. It got the title because Moon often stands on it to preach. Most were crying, some sobbing, as they prayed loudly and independently, but with the same general plea: "Father, oh Father, please help us." Some jerked spasmodically, in spiritual transport, like participants in a voodoo ceremony.

Those who observe Moonies closely often notice a glassy, spaced-out look in their eyes, which, combined with their everlasting smiles, makes them look like tripped-out drug freaks. Many are indeed on a high, but they are tripping out on God, not drugs. Some of that glassy-eyed look may also be attributable to lack of sleep.

Like the Unification Church, the other religious cults also produce highs without the aid of drugs or liquor. The Jesus People urge potential converts to "turn on with Jesus," or to "take a trip with Jesus." The Hare Krishna movement advertises: "Stay high forever." The mother of a Child of God gave this description of her son's cult-mates: "Their eyes are fully dilated, and they glitter. . . . Although they talk to you, and they smile at you, you don't feel that it's the whole person."

To learn how the Church creates such spiritual fervor I visited the Barrytown training center recently with Michael Warder, a 29-year-old Stanford graduate who joined the Church seven years ago and now serves as its director of training. The center occupies a former Catholic seminary the Church purchased a few years ago for $1.5 million.

As we toured the buildings and grounds at Barrytown, I saw dozens of Moonies servicing the center's cars and vans, preparing meals for hundreds of trainees, and doing all the chores involved in running a sizable education institution.

Wherever we went in the buildings, photos of Moon smiled down on us. In one office I met a spry, gray-haired lady of 67 who was led into the movement in 1974 by her son. She admits to having been negative at first, "but once I saw the light I quit my job, sold my house, and joined the Church." When I asked her what her son had been doing before he joined, she replied, "Spacing out. He didn't know what to do with his life." In another office I met a girl who said she'd been "a strong hippie radical at Berkeley" where she spent two years at college. "I didn't like the world the way it was. I wanted to change it. I had tried several Christian groups, and the Guru Maharishi. This was the first movement I tried that offered real answers."

Warder and I tried to look in on the three-week and six-week groups, but they were both away recruiting or fund raising as part of their training. The four-month trainees spend about one month out fund raising, but we found them at Barrytown just as their afternoon session began with several stirring hymns and a prayer to "Father" Moon for the "strength to understand his teaching."

The 120 well-dressed novitiates then sat through a four-hour lecture on predestination, which they followed attentively, taking notes in detail. When I asked if four hours without a break wasn't a bit long for such a topic, a staff member sitting next to me explained, "That is part of our training."

Diverting Energies

As I had noticed at other Church activities, the male and female members sat on separate sides of the hall. Warder explained that all activities at Barrytown and other Church centers are carefully segregated by sex. "We find that way everyone feels more comfortable in their study and in their search for the truth. As soon as they're mixed you find the boys and girls begin thinking about other things."

The Church's puritan attitudes toward sex govern every minute of the training and lives of its members. Perhaps as a way to divert libidinal energies, group leaders encourage various forms of asexual but segregated physical contact: touching, massaging, backslapping and general horseplay.

In one of the Reverend Moon's "Master Speaks" training lectures, he warned the young men and women against holding hands or even sitting next to each other because it might lead to sin: "You must keep your purity and chastity. You must think of it as more valuable, more important than your own life. . . . Purity is something like a blossom before it is opened. So before you are blessed, you must be like a blossom shut tight, and bear the fragrance deep within you."

Before they can become eligible for marriage, Moonies must put in seven years of faithful service to the Church and even then they need Moon's personal approval. Eligible members may propose mates of their own choice, but Moon makes the final selection, often pairing couples completely unknown to each other.

As a generous and efficient father, Moon likes big weddings. Last year, at an all-day affair held in a Seoul sports arena, he married 1,800 member couples from 24 countries, including 70 couples from the United States.

As in the outside world, marriage does not bring immediate bliss. Newlywed Moonies must live separate and celibate lives for at least 40 days, and up to three years for younger members, which allows them time to achieve a proper level of spiritual perfection. Even after the period of enforced celibacy, Church couples tend to live as brothers and sisters in the Family, rather than as husband and wife. By enforcing celibacy and permitting only the distant prospect and eventual facade of marriage, Moon's movement follows a long tradition of American communes. The successful ones generally encouraged free love or enforced celibacy, thereby preventing the formation of family units that could threaten the cohesiveness of the communal family and the authority of its leader [see "Individualism Busts the Commune Boom" by Laurence Veysey, pt, December 1974].

In addition to warnings on the evils of sex, trainees at Barrytown receive a heavy indoctrination in the dangers of communism. According to Moon, communism equals satanism, and every good Christian should be willing to give up his life to fight it anywhere in the world, particularly in defense of South Korea, the movement's "Fatherland."

Since he arrived in America, Moon has continued to mix politics with his religion. The Church has a political affiliate in Washington, D.C. called the Freedom Leadership Foundation (FLF), dedicated to "ideological victory over communism in the United States." The FLF's rallies, seminars, lectures and publications stress America's moral obligation to provide military and economic support for General Park's government in South Korea.

God Chose Nixon

Like his competitor Billy Graham, the Reverend Moon has demonstrated considerable flair for political publicity. With bipartisan agility he has had his picture taken (and used repeatedly in Church publications) with Senators Hubert Humphrey, Edward Kennedy, Strom Thurmond and James Buckley.

When Richard Nixon was under siege during the final months of his presidency, Moon, acting upon what he called direct instructions from God, took out full-page ads in major newspapers across the country urging public support of the President.

Blending piety and patriotism, Moon proclaimed: "This nation is God's nation. The office of the President of the United States is therefore sacred. . . . God has chosen Richard Nixon to be President of the United States."

The following month Moon mobilized 1,000 of the faithful for a Washington prayer fast and vigil in the President's support. They marched on Capitol Hill carrying signs that read: "PRAY FOR NIXON" and "GOD LOVES NIXON."

Except for their anticommunist indoctrination, most Moonies seem uninterested in politics. Besides, few have much time or energy left over from fund raising and recruiting. During much of their life in the Family, the brothers and sisters put in grueling dawn-to-dusk days peddling candles, peanuts, dried flowers or anything else the Church feels will inspire donations.

Moonies work in pairs at street corners or shopping plazas; others go out in teams selling door to door in suburban neighborhoods. When asked what they're raising money for, they give vague or misleading answers like "Christian youth work," "youth counseling," or "a drug-abuse program."

The young solicitors rarely mention the Church or Sun Moon. They are polite, but remarkably persistent. Success at fund raising becomes a test of devotion to the Church. Team leaders send their troops off in the morning with songs, prayers and pep talks, encouraging competition among each other and with other teams. Stoked up like Marine recruits for a bayonet drill, the Moonies charge out and work the streets with a fervor no profit motive could ever inspire. Those who fail to meet a respectable daily quota often spend the evening praying for God's help the following day.

Except for the spartan food, clothing and shelter it provides for its members, the Church seems to invest most of its funds in real estate. It bought the former Columbia University Club in New York for $1.2 million, for its national headquarters, and owns another $10 million worth of property along the Hudson River.

In addition to its real-estate holdings, the movement also runs cottage industries in dozens of communes around the country, with members turning out candles and other items used for fund-raising drives. The Church also owns and operates other member-run commercial enterprises: a ranch, gas station, printing company, travel agency, landscape service, home-cleaning service and tea house. While these hardly amount to a financial empire, they grow fast on tax exemptions and free labor.

From similarly modest beginnings, Moon has built up a $15 million-a-year industrial conglomerate in Korea, drawing largely on churchmembers' labor. His factories turn out heavy machinery, titanium, paint, pharmaceuticals, marble vases, and shotguns.

"He Has a Right"

Current plans call for U.S. distribution of a ginseng tea produced in Korea by Moon's Ilhwa Pharmaceutical Co. An old Oriental favorite brewed from a powdered root, Moon's ginseng tea reputedly "lowers blood sugar, prevents degeneration of human cells, and stimulates the gonads." It sells for $24 for seven ounces, and tastes like boiled chalk.

To arouse consumers in this country, Moon has hired a high-priced public-relations firm (whose other accounts include General Motors, Gulf and Exxon) to promote his tea and to repair the Church's image in the U.S., which even its own officials admit is pretty bad.

Newspapers around the country have run stories about tearful parents who have tried in vain to free their children from Moon's cult; ex-Moonies have appeared on televised press conferences to denounce the Church for brainwashing them into conversion and turning them against their parents. Rabbi Maurice Davis, of white Plains, N.Y., has formed a national organization of several hundred parents who have lost their children to Sun Moon and other religious cults.

"Moon's theology is nonsense," says Rabbi Davis, "but he has a right to preach whatever nonsense he wants. What I hold against the Moon movement is that they take kids and treat them as things. They use the kids as slaves, as workers. They don't really care about these kids, and they do nothing to make the world better."

Church officials often argue they are making the world better by getting wayward youths off drugs and away from crime. But few of their recruits look like ex-junkies, and most come from middle-class schools and homes rather than crime-ridden ghettos. For all its talk about crime, drugs, alcohol and other social ills, the movement runs few programs aimed at solving such problems, or at helping non-members. Most of its resources are directed inward, producing more money and more members, who in turn will recruit more members and raise more money. Rather than helping society, the movement siphons off the energy and idealism of its members. When I asked one official how this would benefit society, he replied, "we can change the world by changing men's hearts." When I countered that such a policy would solve society's problems only if everyone joined the Unification Church, he smiled.

Americans may not all join the Unification Church, but many are joining its competitors, which share similar policies and practices. The Children of God also spend much of their time selling various articles and soliciting donations, turning all receipts over to their leader Moses David. The movement is often accused of "brainwashing," and teaches recruits to regard anyone who challenges it as an agent of the devil. "They give you the answers for everythng," one ex-member recalled. "The leader does your thinking for you."

Pattern of Vulnerability

The 5,000-member Hare Krishna Society is run by a successful businessman from India, who, like Moon, has organized his followers into a band of devoted fund raisers willing to live a life of ascetic denial. Membership requires insulation from the outside world, surrender of prior identity, strict standards of dress and behavior, and a great deal of group chanting which helps create the high. Instead of drugs, sex, or personal pleasure, the members substitute dedication, endurance, and self-sacrifice.

Psychologists who have studied the Jesus People movement found a pattern of vulnerability among the members. On a personality test they scored significantly lower than average on self-confidence and personal adjustment. The conversion process at Jesus People communes follows a rigid pattern, involving subtle and overt pressure, and a rewarding warmth, and acceptance from new "brothers" and "sisters" upon conversion. Converts must make a total commitment, and give up all material possessions and outside contacts with family or friends.

The charge of "brainwashing" deserves attention. Much of what happens to Moon's converts during the weekend and week-long initiation workshops does follow the classic steps of brainwashing: isolating them from all past and outside contacts; surrounding them with new instant comrades and a new authority figure; wearing them down physically, mentally and emotionally; then "programming" them with new beliefs and pressuring them into total commitment.

But the term brainwashing implies force and captivity, conditions that do not apply to Moon's recruits. Church members may use heavy-handed emotional or psychological pressure, but they do not force anyone to join or believe. While one might question the independence of a convert's mind, no one has proven the Church holds its members against their will. It might be fairer to use the term conversion instead of brainwashing. If conversion requires the suspension of critical faculties, at least the Moonies do so willingly.

In his classic study of *The Varieties of Religious Experience*, William James described religious conversion in a manner strikingly similar to the tales told by Moonies. James wrote that conversion occurs most often among those beset by a "sense of incompleteness and imperfection," and frequently during a "state of temporary exhaustion." He told how conversion brings "a new level of spiritual vitality" in which "new energies and endurances are shown. The personality is changed, the man *is* born anew . . . perceiving truths not known before," a sense of peace and harmony in themselves and in the world.

Instant Salvation

Through a process of self-selection Moon's movement probably attracts only those youths already seeking some form of total commitment. Many Moonies have been drifting from cults to communes for years, sampling the spiritual fare like diners at a smorgasbord. The Church may be capitalizing on their loneliness, but it can hardly be blamed for their vulnerability. However remarkable the experience seems to the convert and his family, James described it as essentially an "adolescent phenomenon, incidental to the passage from the child's small universe to the wider intellectual and spiritual life of maturity."

While one can commiserate with parents whose children leave home to join religious cults, it's hard to condone the desperate attempts to recover the children by kidnapping and deprogramming, a process openly based on the techniques of brainwashing. Youths of legal age have a right to practice any religion they choose. Whether or not their choice is wise has nothing to do with their right to exercise it. Eighteen-year-olds who join the U.S. Marines may be using equally rash judgment, and their boot-camp training subjects them to group discipline, exhaustion and "brainwashing" that match anything that the Moonies endure. One could easily question the judgment of grown-ups who seek instant salvation in such socially acceptable adult cults as TM, Arica, est, primal therapy, or encounter groups.

While its critics describe the Unification Church as authoritarian, Church leaders prefer to call their approach "loving and parental." They may be right. To thousands of young Americans threatened by the approach of life as an adult, Moon's Family offers the security of perennial childhood. To lonely young people drifting through cold, impersonal cities, it offers instant friendship and communion, a sense of belonging. To college students suffering the rigors of academic competition, it offers an egoless life of cooperative group spirit. To those troubled by personal problems with drugs or sex, it offers a drugless, sexless world of militant puritanism. To those troubled by our materialistic society, it offers a life of disciplined asceticism. To those who have no faith in the traditional institutions of society, it offers the comfort of belief. To those hungering for truth and meaning in a complicated world, it offers simple answers.

Critics may call Moon's movement a religious fraud, and accuse it of exploiting innocent youths but, except for those who drop out, most Moonies seem genuinely happy in their service to Moon and the Church. In exchange for their labor, devotion and commitment, the Church has given them a home, a family, and a purpose. Critics may call that exploitation or slavery, but the Moonies consider it a bargain. No more problems, no more hassles, no more doubts. Just honor thy Father Moon.

10

The Occult: Paths to the Unknown

The occult, from the Latin *occulere*, meaning to conceal, is a non-specific term for things magical and mystical—a kind of esoteric knowledge available only to those initiated into the secrets of acquisition. As the authors of the following selections make clear, the study of the occult properly falls into the realm of the study of magic, witchcraft, and religion. In addition, the tremendous recent interest in the occult has made it a worthy subject for study. Wuthnow (1978) cites evidence that the occult has become an even more popular supernatural belief than is the belief in God. The popularity of the occult serves as an index of social strain, of rebellion against tradition, and of the need for small-group reinforcement.

This chapter emphasizes occult practices in contemporary America and demonstrates that even Western groups seek wisdom and knowledge unavailable through science or established religions. The articles incorporated here will also demonstrate that occult practices in America appear to many to be more exotic in nature

Goat mask of a modern witch high priestess.

345

than the traditional religious practices of members of non-Western societies.

Most attempts at determining how believers in the occult feel about religion are met with difficulty. Some occultists see themselves as philosophers, whereas others describe themselves as scientists or even as religious practitioners—the latter in spite of the usual disdain occultists have for the teachings of established religions. In regard to this point, Harriet Whitehead (1974: 561) believes the rejection by occultists of Christian theodicy does not mean a denial of Christian morality, for there is evidence that contemporary occult publications reflect a "generalized" Christian morality. What is being rejected by the occultists, according to Whitehead, is the doctrine of atonement and the belief that the unrepentant will be consigned to some sort of eternal punishment. Whitehead sums up the basis of American occultism in the following way:

> Occultism seeks to reunite the separate pieces of the intellectual, emotional, and apprehensional jig-saw puzzle by surveying and abstracting from all the traditions that address themselves to the task of *understanding* things, whether this understanding be directed at practical mastery or a passive acceptance. Occultism posits an underlying singular Truth, the search for which cannot be confined to a particular style and the content of which cannot exclude any dimension of human experience, however "irrational" it may seem (Whitehead 1974: 587).

As is the case with all religions, occultists have developed systems of beliefs that guide true believers, but because occult practices appear exotic to most observers, they are viewed with skeptical interest and suspicion. Astrology is the most popular and accepted of the occultist traditions in the Western world. The growing popularity of witchcraft, however, and the fact that witchcraft is still well embedded in traditional beliefs in various parts of the pre-industrial world, offer an opportunity for cross-cultural comparison (see Chapter 5 on "Witchcraft, Sorcery, and Other Forces of Evil").

Modern witches, according to Frank Smyth, "refer to their religion as 'wicca,' the feminine form of an Old English word, 'wicce,' meaning a witch, possibly a derivative of the verb 'wiccian,' to practice witchcraft. Wicca is a largely urban cult. . . . In common with more orthodox religions, wicca has worship as its main object, but the additional element of magic lends the cult an illicit and undoubtedly attractive aura" (Smyth 1970: 1866). Wicca has a matriarchal character, and while in most cases both men and women are referred to as witches, local organizations of witches, called covens, are made up of more women than men. Indeed, the high priestess is symbolic of the mother goddess and not dissimilar to the Virgin Mary; the mother goddess is the principal deity of witchlore. Wicca is basically a fertility cult with its great festivals geared to the seasons (Smyth 1970: 1866). The elements of sexuality that sometimes appear as part of initiation and the symbolic or actual intercourse of members have brought wicca into disrepute in many quarters, but the explanation that it is a fertility cult has been used as a justification for these acts. Whatever the accusations made or answers given, it has provided the media with tantalizing copy.

The popular press in this country typically portrays believers in the occult as a single group. This is an incorrect assessment. Marcello Truzzi (1974: 628–32) provides a more accurate analysis of the occult by dividing practitioners into three broad categories. At the first level are people whose involvement in the occult is minimal—who do not see themselves as occultists per se but as concerned individuals interested in explaining such strange occurrences as flying saucers, assorted land and sea monsters, and various parapsychological phenomena. Typically their activities are characterized by an absence of mysticism, supernaturalism, and anti-scientific thought; in fact, scientific support for their beliefs is highly valued. On Truzzi's second level of occultism are people who seek to understand mysterious causal relationships between events—who express an interest, for example, in numerology, sun-sign astrology, and palmistry. Knowledge gained at this level is more likely to be *a*scientific or *extra*-scientific rather than *anti*-scientific. Truzzi's third level of occultism is concerned with those complex belief systems—witchcraft, Satanism, ritual magic, and other mystical traditions—that combine elements from the first two levels. Third-level believers often question or contradict scientific validation of an event or relationship, and thus may see themselves as competitors to science. Truzzi concludes that although some occult believers exist in "pure form," most are a combination of all three types.

This final chapter is a departure from the preceding ones in that every article is based on American society. This is because the subject matter, the occult, constitutes a set of beliefs and practices that become distinctive only in cultures steeped in a scientific tradition of problem-solving. What the scientific world regards as occult would possibly constitute a "correct" system of knowledge or of technical arts in a non-Western culture. The formulas, the spells, the paraphernalia, the reliance upon the supernatural—all aspects of the occult world—fall quite acceptably into a culture that relies on magic as a logical system of explaining events or getting something done.

There can be no doubt that from the very beginning a cloud of controversy has hung over occultism. Yet, through all the controversy its appeal has attracted scholars, scientists, and philosophers, as well as the general public. Freud at one time was fascinated by certain numerological theories, but apparently discarded them as well as the entire subject of occultism. The conflict between Freud and Jung over the occult is caught in the following quotation from Jung (1961: 150):

> I can still recall vividly how Freud said to me, "My dear Jung, promise me never to abandon the sexual theory. This is the most essential thing of all. You see, we must make a dogma of it, an unshakeable bulwark." He said that to me with great emotion, in the tone of a father saying, "and promise me this one thing, my dear son: that you will go to church every Sunday." In some astonishment I asked him, "A bulwark —against what?" To which he replied, "Against the black tide of mud"—and here he hesitated for a moment, then added—"of occultism."

Margaret Mead's article is an excellent selection to open the chapter. Mead defines the occult and offers some reasons why so many people are fascinated by forms of wisdom that originated in Babylonia and ancient Egypt and by beliefs and practices known in Europe in the Middle Ages and earlier. Barry Singer and Victor Benassi also examine the popularity of the occult in an age of science, and then speculate about the social mechanisms that may have given rise to the recent widespread interest in the occult. John Fritscher believes that what witches say about themselves is more revealing than what non-witches say about them. Accordingly, Fritscher presents the personal revelations of Anton Szandor LaVey, high priest and founder of the Church of Satan in San Francisco. In the final article of this book, Marcello Truzzi assesses the rising tide of occultism in the United States. Truzzi, who has done extensive research on contemporary occultism, concludes that for most Americans the interest in the occult is a leisure-time activity and a fad of popular culture rather than a serious religious movement.

References Cited

Jung, C. G.
1961 *Memories, Dreams, Reflections.* New York: Vintage Books.

Smyth, Frank
1970 "Modern Witchcraft." In Richard Cavendish, ed., *Man, Myth and Magic,* Vol. 14, pp. 1865–70. New York: Marshall Cavendish Corporation.

Truzzi, Marcello
1974 "Towards a Sociology of the Occult: Notes on Modern Witchcraft." In Irving I. Zaretsky and Mark P. Leone, eds., *Religious Movements in Contemporary America,* pp. 628–45. Princeton, N.J.: Princeton University Press.

Whitehead, Harriet
1974 "Reasonably Fantastic: Some Perspectives on Scientology, Science Fiction, and Occultism." In Irving I. Zaretsky and Mark P. Leone, eds., *Religious Movements in Contemporary America,* pp. 547–87. Princeton, N.J.: Princeton University Press.

Wuthnow, R.
1978 *Experimentation in American Religion.* Los Angeles: University of California Press.

The Occult: On the Edge of the Unknown

Margaret Mead

Margaret Mead's knowledge of Western society serves as the basis for her explanation of the popularity of the occult among contemporary youth. Providing a number of sociological and psychological explanations for the phenomena, Mead advocates a combination of the abilities of open-minded scientists and open-minded occultists to gain entry to the unknown through experiments carried out in an atmosphere of skeptical but meticulously careful exploration. She rejects the value of extremists of either camp in this attempt to contact other intelligences in the universe, and argues for expansion of knowledge of our own human capacities and senses.

"On the Edge of the Unknown—March 1977" from *Aspects of the Present* by Margaret Mead and Rhoda Metraux. Copyright © 1980 by Mary Catherine Bateson Kassarjian and Rhoda Metraux. By permission of William Morrow & Company.

How do you define the occult?

I asked a group of my students that question not long ago. Their answers were both knowledgeable and puzzling—and very different from what they would have been only a few years ago.

All of them—somewhat to my surprise—said correctly that the occult has to do with things kept "secret" or "hidden" from those not initiated, and with the mysterious and perhaps the supernatural. But their examples encompassed the ancient and the modern, the East and the West; they included subjects nowadays studied by scientists, and other subjects believed to be beyond the reach of empirical science as we understand it today. They ranged from astrology and alchemy to witchcraft, from medieval cabalism to modern Theosophy, from Taoism to Yoga, from geomancy to numerology, from palm reading and fortune telling with tarot cards to clairvoyance and telekinesis and telepathy, from the magical to the mystical. Altogether it was an extraordinary mélange of ideas, beliefs, practices and forms of both prescientific and scientific exploration and explanation, held together by the idea of mystery and of some relationship to what we call the supernatural.

None of the students rejected the idea of the occult out of hand, and the diversity of the subjects mentioned suggests the paths on which their curiosity had taken them and, further, the extent to which the idea of the occult has captured the imagination not just of these students but of so many of their generation.

Why should this be? How is it that so many of our young people are fascinated by forms of wisdom that originated long ago in Babylonia and ancient Egypt, by conceptions of life and arts developed in the distant past in China and India, by beliefs and practices known in Europe in the Middle Ages and earlier?

It is certainly strange and unexpected that in a generation that belongs by birth to the space age, so many young people have turned away from the sciences that have made possible the world they live in and the extraordinary expansion of our knowledge about our universe. Instead there are, all around the world, very large numbers of young people who spend long, solitary hours in silent meditation; others who gather in groups to chant mystical syllables in monotonous, dreamlike repetition; others who concentrate on learning complex and difficult body disciplines; and still others who scan numbers minutely to work out the relationship between the day and the hour of their birth and the astrological potentialities of a day on which they propose to make a journey or marry or take an examination.

How can we explain all this?

It is useful, I think, to bear in mind that since the earliest times and in the simplest cultures of which we have any knowledge, members of human societies have tried to understand the past—where they came from and who they are and how the world came to be as it is—and to discover how to predict the future so as to order their lives more safely. And as far as we know, this kind of striving often has been a compound of two very different things: careful, accurate observations of the part of the world in which a people lived, and imaginative explanations of *why* and *how* that often were closer to dreams than anything we think of as science.

People have observed the movements of the sun and the moon, the configurations of the fixed stars, the motions of the visible planets, the changing seasons, the migrations of birds or whales or salmon or the monthly appearance of fish over the reef. They have mused on the way sleepers seem to leave their inert bodies and travel to far places, and on the way a person's shadow grows and shrinks and dances in the flickering firelight; and they have concluded that there must be some part —perhaps more than one part—of the self that is separable from the body and may have existed before birth and may endure after death. And some peoples have solved, with a belief in an endlessly turning circle of reincarnation, the problem of life and death in which past and future are linked. But however differently human beings have tried to explain what they could observe, thinking about

our relationship to the cosmos has been a distinctive, universal human activity.

Through long ages, workable knowledge slowly accumulated and was passed from one people to another—as, for instance, the idea of zero treated as a number passed from Hindu to Arabian and finally to European mathematicians in the later Middle Ages, making modern mathematics possible. But almost invariably ancient wisdom was embedded in magical, religious or ideological systems. Such systems enfolded the knowledge that made it possible, for instance, for the ancient Egyptians to work out quite accurately the length of the solar year or, using simple geometric principles, to measure land accurately and design great structures such as the pyramids.

Sometimes an element has escaped from its magical matrix, but without losing a kind of aura of the mysterious, the marvelous. There is, for example, the number 7. This was the number of the luminaries in the sky (the sun, the moon and the five visible planets) that were observed in their courses by the ancient Babylonians and were believed to control the fate of all human beings. So 7 became embedded as a key number in astrology, but it also broke free of its matrix and time and again has been associated in a marvelous way with great things. So we have Rome built on seven hills; we have the seven seas and the Seven Wonders of the World, the seven ages of man, the seven deadly sins, the seventh heaven, where, according to Islamic belief and the cabala, God and the most exalted angels live. There is also the seventh son (or the seventh son of the seventh son), variously believed to be gifted with healing powers or to be clairvoyant or telepathic or simply lucky, and among Gypsies the seventh daughter who always tells true fortunes.

People can get into a fine state of confusion over beliefs like those that relate numbers to the events of life. And their belief that there is a real relationship can easily affect their expectations and their acts, and so the outcome of events. The belief that 13 is an unlucky number, a number that foreshadows disaster, is still potent enough to cause a hand to slip, a bolt to be left unfastened, a mission to fail on the 13th day. Yet the Thirteen Colonies stood together against England to form a new country.

When people go back through degraded superstition and the veils of a religious symbolism to trace a magic number or a whole number system to its oldest matrix, there is a very good chance that they will feel they are finding out something secret and wonderful, something that puts them in touch with the deep wisdom of the ancients, something that can give them power too. And they may begin to think that numbers matter—like the Pythagoreans, who built a kind of religion on the belief that the essence of all things is number and that the most complex ideas could be expressed as relations between numbers.

Tracing back such a philosophical conception of how the universe is constructed and how human beings are related to the universe and one another, people may easily come to endow numbers (or, equally, some other set of emotionally highly charged symbols) with extraordinary powers. And when they find that there is working knowledge embedded in such a matrix (for the Pythagoreans were innovative mathematicians as well as philosophers and religious cultists), they may well take it as proof that the special view of the universe, the religious belief, also is "true."

This is, it seems to me, one important ingredient in the current fascination with the occult. And because so many of these old beliefs have been superseded as obsolete, outlawed religiously, or politically (sometimes, 1,000 or more years ago), driven underground and carried through generations by tiny groups or carried in writings buried in obscure libraries and rediscovered by accident, there is also the fascination of secretly resuscitating and secretly joining with others in practices known only to an initiated few. This identifies the practitioner at one and the same time as an individual who is different and as someone who belongs to a group with a unique identity. In a world in which individuals continually see themselves classified anonymously as one in a category of thousands— or millions—the search for personal identity can become crucial to survival.

But there is another aspect to the search that guides modern young people in their choices of what to look for in ancient beliefs and practices. Modern science and its application—for example in medicine—has become increasingly impersonal and detached from the problems that beset individuals as they grow and mature, suffer disappointment and loss and try to find satisfaction and happiness—or simply health and quiet. So in their search for some alternative life-style a great many young people turn to those occult beliefs and disciplines in other cultures—Chinese or Indian, Japanese or Persian in origin—that promise both a greater understanding of one's own self and some sense of unity between one's private, personal self and the infinite, impersonal universe. In the predicament in which these young people find themselves, the familiar disciplines of Christianity and Judaism have become bonds to be cast off and only the unfamiliar disciplines of Zen or Yoga or one of the new cultist groups have the imaginative power to give them access to their own minds and bodies and a sense of participation in some larger, spiritual whole.

This is, I think, a use of the occult that is quite different from anything in the past, for it is a specific response to needs unmet in our very troubled present. For many it has great fascination; for some it is a way out of the present.

However, there are also points of real contact between certain ideas of great importance in the occult—telepathy, for example—and the thinking of scientists whose experiments have taken these ideas to the very edge of science. Here the extraordinary engineering capacities of scientific instruments are being brought to bear in more and more refined ways to explore and characterize the infinitely small and the vastly distant, the extremely delicate and the extremely complex. With the use of infrared photography and under certain conditions, today we can take a picture of a car that was parked in a parking place yesterday; we can "look" at the land surface of Mars; we can "see" with the radio telescope unimagined distances into the universe. And on this growing edge of knowledge, scientists are devising experiments that may—almost certainly *will*—give us, in time, new insight into the powers attributed to seers and clairvoyants, to those who have the power to "see" auras, to communicate with plants, to dream or visualize events outside the bounds of time.

Instead of a world in which scientists, who have been by definition unbelievers in all that the great religions have ever claimed, are divided by a deep, unbridgeable gulf from blind believers, who insistently reject all that science has learned, we are in the process of discovering a middle ground. Here the most open-minded scientists and the most open-minded believers in occultism can meet to plan and carry out experiments in an atmosphere of expectant, skeptical but also meticulously careful exploration. We are living on the edge of the unknown not only in terms of possible communication with other intelligences somewhere in the universe but also with renewed and greatly expanded knowledge of our own human sensibilities and capacities.

It can be said that in some sense we have come full circle. And it may be that among those young people who seem to be lost in some unreal relationship to the magical thinking or the miraculous beliefs of the past, there will be some who will shake themselves loose of inappropriate beliefs, past and present, and will help to shape a world society in which women and men know what human beings in the past could see only through a glass darkly, know only in part.

Occult Beliefs

Barry Singer
Victor A. Benassi

In the following article Barry Singer and Victor A. Benassi maintain, as did Mead, the social and scientific importance of understanding the occult; although they show these beliefs to be based on psychological and sociological rather than on rational determinants, they do not totally reject their validity. According to Singer and Benassi, media distortion, social uncertainty, and the deficiencies of human reasoning seem to be the basis of occult beliefs. They also maintain that occult phenomena are a possible index of fluctuations in religious belief or social dislocation. The article addresses the question of the origins and mechanism of the individual's occult beliefs and speculates about the social mechanisms that may have given rise to the recent widespread involvement with the occult.

Reprinted from *American Scientist*, Vol. 69, no. 1 (1981), pp. 49–55, by permission of the authors and the Scientific Research Society.

WHY IS AN UNDERSTANDING OF OCCULT BELIEFS scientifically and socially important? One reason is their current prevalence in Western societies. Occult beliefs have increased dramatically in the United States during the last two decades (Freedland 1972; Godwin 1972). Far from being a "fad," preoccupation with the occult now forms a pervasive part of our culture. Garden-variety occultisms such as astrology and ESP have swelled to historically unprecedented levels (Eliade 1976). Belief in ESP, for instance, is consistently found to be moderate or strong in 80–90% of our population (Gallup 1978; Polzella et al. 1975); in one survey it ranked as our most popular supernatural belief, edging out belief in God in strength and prevalence (Wuthnow 1978). Ouija boards overtook Monopoly as the nation's best-selling board game in 1967.

As indexed by audience tallies and book sales, more exotic occultisms such as spoon bending, the Bermuda Triangle, biorhythms, psychic healing, and hauntings have also increased dramatically in variety and popularity since the early 1960s. Von Däniken's book *Chariots of the Gods?*, a vivid account of ancient astronauts' bestowing their technology and spermatozoa upon human beings, has become the best-selling book of modern times. Occult beliefs are salient not only among the lay public, but also among college students, including those at some of our science-oriented campuses. The occult trend shows no signs of diminishing.

The current high level and strength of occult beliefs, which at least implicitly constitute a challenge to the validity of science and to the authority of the scientific community, may be a cause for our concern. This growing trend is also intrinsically of scientific interest as a psychological and sociological phenomenon. The psychological mechanisms involved in occult beliefs may represent more dramatic forms of some mundane pathologies of reasoning. To the extent that occult and mundane beliefs have similar determinants, the study of occult beliefs, which are at the outer limits of irrationality, may throw light on more ordinary reasoning pathologies.

From a sociological point of view, the occult phenomenon is of interest as a possible index of fluctuations in religious belief or social dislocation. Moreover, the study of occult beliefs may further our understanding of scientific belief systems as they are explicitly constructed to compensate for the cognitive shortcomings which characterize many occult beliefs. This article will address the question of the origins and mechanisms of the individual's occult beliefs, a topic which psychological research is beginning to illuminate. We will also speculate about the social mechanisms that may have given rise to the recent widespread involvement with the occult.

Let us make clear at the outset of this discussion that we do not assume the beliefs and practices termed "occult" or "paranormal" to be totally without validity. They seem rather to span a range from the objectively unsupportable at present to the demonstrably absurd. Therefore, to the extent that such beliefs are held widely and strongly, they are probably based on psychological and sociological rather than rational determinants.

A variety of methodological cautions are appropriate in this inquiry. It is likely that differing occult beliefs have different determinants. Evidence suggests, for instance, that those occult beliefs which are institutionalized and are organized around a social community of believers may serve functions similar to those of traditional religions, whereas other beliefs cluster with factors related to escapist entertainment, such as interest in fantasy and science fiction (Bainbridge 1978). Still others may be personally insignificant beliefs acquired desultorily through media misinformation. Determinants may contribute differently at various levels of strength of a particular belief. Further, it has been shown for astrology and spiritualism, for instance, that several disparate demographic populations tend to entertain these beliefs for differing reasons (Jahoda 1969; Robbins et al. 1978).

Research on occult beliefs has not reached the scope and precision necessary to address these complexities in full. A complete account of the rise in occult beliefs will have to explain the concomitant rise of such beliefs in other industrialized nations for which data are available (Jahoda 1969), and probably should also account for recent social movements which appear correlated with the occult trend, such as the development of a youth counterculture and the recent spread of pentacostal and charismatic religions through a considerable portion of the world. Social science has provided a number of plausible explanations for these social trends, but little relevant data. However, we believe we can identify at present a number of causal or contributing factors involved in occult beliefs, keeping in mind the strictures discussed above.

Media Promotion of the Occult

It is not clear how great a role promotion by the popular media played in starting the occult inflation of the early 1960s. The present treatment of the occult by the media, however, may account for much of the near universality of belief. The public is chronically exposed to films, newspaper reports, "documentaries," and books extolling occult or pseudoscientific topics, with critical coverage largely absent. Our most trusted and prestigious sources of information are no exception. When the layperson hears about New Zealand UFOs from Walter Cronkite or reads about new frontiers in psychic healing in a front-page article in the *Los Angeles Times* (1977), he has prima facie reasons for believing such phenomena valid. Such uncritical coverage may be due in part to the inherent difficulties of science reporting in a popular medium. However, media coverage of the occult may sometimes be deceptive and monetarily motivated. It is our impression that the public is not aware of the extent to which First Amendment privileges permit such practices. The public seems to trust the printed word implicitly.

Research has consistently shown that people attribute most of their occult beliefs to the popular media and/or to personal experiences (Evans 1973). In a survey of several hundred college students, we were surprised to find that "scientific media" was also listed as a source of occult beliefs—more frequently than popular media, personal experience, personal faith, or logical arguments. When the students were asked afterwards to list examples of the scientific media in question, however, not one mentioned even a single genuinely scientific source. Instead, *Reader's Digest* and the *National Enquirer* were occasionally cited as "scientific media," as were such films as *The Exorcist* and *Star Wars* (i.e. "the Force"). Television "documentaries" were also frequently mentioned, with the documentary "Chariots of the Gods?" being the single most frequently cited "scientific" source. Scientists have recently brought lawsuits against the television networks in protest of misleading occult documentaries. In response, the networks have claimed that their pro-occult coverage was formerly billed as "entertainment" rather than as a "documentary," and that the public can and does make this discrimination. Our evidence does not support these claims.

Although scientists who wish to rebut paranormal claims are sometimes denied access to the media, it also seems to be true that scientists have not extended themselves to gain media access and to issue public rebuttals. Those few scientists who do visibly protest may thus be perceived as stodgy and prejudiced isolates who have not yet climbed on the bandwagon of scientific acceptance of the occult. In addition, scientists have generally not cared to monitor or rebut occult claims issuing from their own academic institutions. Uncritical courses on occult topics are frequently found in the extension division of even our most reputable universities. In our experience the public invariably perceives the university as having then placed its stamp of approval upon the occultism, perhaps as having an entire department devoted to the topic, and understands that the extension instructor is "on the faculty."

The promotion of the occult by the popular media probably serves to heighten the general cognitive "availability" of the occult as an explanatory category in the culture. Puzzling events for which explanations might otherwise be conceived in terms of scientific phenomena or of fraud may tend to be explained as paranormal phenomena when the media bring this category so obtrusively to our attention.

Cognitive Biases and Heuristics

With occult beliefs currently so prevalent as to constitute, perhaps, part of what it means to be human, we might be justified in speculating on the basic quirks inherent in human psychological structure that support such beliefs. Current re-

search in an area of cognitive psychology termed "cognitive biases and heuristics" has revealed deficits in human inference so universal and so stubborn that they can plausibly account for many of our errant beliefs, including occult ones. This recent spate of research, focusing on human problem-solving and judgmental processes, has resulted in an unflattering portrait of intuitive human reasoning (Nisbett and Ross 1980).

Briefly stated, the findings are that when presented with an array of data or a sequence of events in which they are instructed to discover an underlying order, subjects show strong tendencies to perceive order and causality in random arrays, to perceive a pattern or correlation which seems a priori intuitively correct even when the actual correlation in the data is counterintuitive, to jump to conclusions about the correct hypothesis, to seek and use only positive or confirmatory evidence, to construe evidence liberally as confirmatory, to fail to generate or to assess alternative hypotheses, and, having thus managed to expose themselves only to confirmatory instances, to be fallaciously confident of the validity of their judgments (Jahoda 1969; Einhorn and Hogarth 1978). In the analyzing of past events, these tendencies are exacerbated by selective memory and by failure to appreciate the pitfalls of post hoc analyses.

As an illustration of these tendencies, Wason (1960) asked subjects to try to discover a rule he had in mind for generating series of three numbers, where an example of the rule was the series "2, 4, 6." Subjects were to discover the rule by generating their own three-number series and receiving feedback on whether or not each series was an instance of the rule in question. The correct rule was "Any ascending sequence of whole numbers." Subjects typically generated sequences, such as "8, 10, 12, 14, 16, 18, etc.," repeatedly, for the duration of the experiment. They then expressed the rule as, for instance, "Even numbers increasing by two," and, having been consistently confirmed, were highly confident that this rule was the correct one.

When a judgment involves data that are probabilistic or minimally complex, people behave as if they do not possess the concept of probability, basing their estimates on a simple enumeration of positive instances rather than on the ratio of positive to negative instances. In addition, they adopt simplifying judgmental heuristics which can easily result in misconceptions (Tversky and Kahneman 1974). Thus, an instance is judged to be a number of a larger class on the basis of whether or not it seems intuitively to "represent" that class, rather than on the basis of the known number of times the instance in fact falls either in or out of the class; or hypotheses are chosen simply on the basis of their "availabiity," circumstances which have made them more vivid or salient. For instance, personal experience is more potent in influencing judgments than is abstract data (Nisbett and Ross 1980). When tested in experimental situations, scientists and mathematicians as well as laypersons have displayed the above tendencies (Kahneman and Tversky 1973; Mahoney 1976).

On the whole, then, our everyday intuitions do not seem to serve us well in the understanding of probabilistic or complex patterns in our environment. Under what circumstances will such cognitive biases and limitations lead to occult beliefs? Given that through media or other influences occult ideas are highly available in the culture, and given that there is a tendency to trust intuitive rather than scientific judgments, Marks and Kammann (1979), Myers (1980), and Singer (in press) have shown how occult beliefs can easily be acquired and supported through our cognitive biases and heuristics. For instance, due to our cognitive quirks it is predictable that we will notice and be impressed by the coincidence of a dream and an external event, will overlook the disconfirming instances of failures to match our dreams with reality, and will have difficulty appreciating the concept of random occurrence as an explanation for the coincidences. Even when informed that such matches are predicted to occur occasionally on the basis of the large number of opportunities for dreams and external events to coincide by chance, we fail to appreciate intuitively the mathematics of rare events. A rare event is seen as one that seldom occurs, regardless of the number of opportunities for its occurrence. As a result of our natural tendency to misunderstand the probabilities involved in a match of dreams and reality, the hypothesis of clairvoyance is apt to be a more intuitively compelling explanation for such an occurrence than the concept of chance.

As another example of cognitive bias, an event that seems mysterious, or difficult to explain through ordinary causes, will seem to us to "represent" a mysterious cause. When an abandoned ship is found floating intact off the coast of Florida, causes such as freakish weather, geysers, or sharks are often dismissed because they seem too rare and therefore inherently unlikely. An explanation in terms of some malevolent occult force in the Bermuda Triangle, however, seems intuitively to represent or "fit" the event better. The representativeness heuristic thus fails entirely to consider the very large number of opportunities for rare but natural causes to determine the event.

In the "illusion of control," another common cognitive fallacy, a random process such as rolling of dice is perceived as under personal control to the extent that it seems to incorporate elements of skill. At Long Beach we have shown (Benassi et al. 1979) that subjects who were permitted practice sessions or active physical involvement in a dice-rolling task reported greater belief in their ability to produce psychokinesis than subjects who were instructed to "influence" the dice but were not permitted such involvement.

Experiments which have attempted to encourage disconfirmation of occult or illusory beliefs by motivating subjects to think through their judgments more carefully or by providing blatant disconfirmatory input have uniformly revealed an astonishing resistance to change of such beliefs. Marks and Kammann (1979), in attempting to reduce the impression of validity of generalized personality descriptions, provided subjects with negatively toned, highly specific, and inherently unlikely statements about their personality, but found only a slight reduction of belief in their accuracy.

In a series of experiments (Benassi and Singer, in press; Benassi et al., in press) we arranged for an amateur magician to perform three psychic-like stunts—blindfold reading, teleportation of ashes, and mental bending of a metal rod—in front of six introductory psychology classes. Under one condition, the instructors skeptically introduced the performer as an alleged psychic, and under the other as an amateur magician. Belief was assessed through written feedback from the students to the performer. We expected to demonstrate a difference in occult belief depending on the introductory descriptions, but found instead that three-quarters of the subjects in both conditions believed strongly that the performer was psychic; more than a few, in fact, displayed an agitated conviction that the performer was an agent of Satan.

We then added a third condition in which the instructors quite emphatically repeated six different times that the performer was an amateur magician and that the students would be seeing only tricks, and not psychic phenomena. A written check attested that the students had heard and understood their instructors. This manipulation succeeded in reducing the occult belief, but only to the level where 50% of the class believed the performer to be psychic.

In follow-up studies with other subjects we provided neutral written descriptions of the performer and asked for an assessment of whether the performer was genuinely psychic. Again we found a majority of subjects judging that he was. We then asked whether magicians could also perform such stunts as described, and do so in identical fashion, and found near-unanimous agreement that they could; when asked how many people who performed such stunts were likely to be fakes and magicians, instead of genuine psychics, students agreed that the vast majority were likely to be tricksters and magicians. Finally, we asked students to re-estimate the likelihood that the particular performance described was in fact psychic, in light of the information they themselves had just generated. Once again the performer was judged to be psychic.

Such astonishing stubbornness of illusory and occult beliefs is typical rather than exceptional (Nisbett and Ross 1980). There may be several reasons for this intransigence. First, our intuitive reasoning errors may be like visual illusions. At some abstract level we may suspect that our perceptions are in error, but the error remains just as intuitively compelling. To the extent that we get "lost in the details" of a mental problem, as was probably the case with our subjects who watched or read about our magic act above, the problem becomes increasingly difficult to reason about abstractly. Second, to the extent that our cognitive structuring of our environment is "theory-driven," interpreted through a personal hypothesis, we may be all but blind to any evidence disconfirming our theory.

Finally, in the laboratory reasoning tasks described above, our subjects may not be strongly motivated to reason and behave at their rational best. If we had told them that they must reason accurately or be taken out and shot in the morning, they might have performed better. It may be that occult beliefs, both in the laboratory and in everyday life, surface mainly when they entail little personal cost to the believer. The following section discusses such motivational factors in occult beliefs.

Environment and Motivation

Studies in the laboratory and in naturalistic settings have indicated that, in general, superstitions (including occult beliefs) are likely to form under two conditions: environmental uncertainty (roughly conceived as the product of the unpredictability and the magnitude of an event) and low "cost" of the superstition (Jahoda 1969). The erroneous belief may thus alleviate feelings of helplessness and anxiety under uncontrollable or unpredictable circumstances, and in this sense may be functional. Superstitions seldom supplant or intrude upon rational, empirical approaches, where such approaches will serve. In his classic example, the anthropologist Malinowski (1954) described the Trobriand islanders as showing no superstitious behavior when fishing in their lagoon, where the task was routine and the returns relatively certain, but much superstitious behavior when fishing in the open sea, a more uncertain and dangerous enterprise.

As a modern example, Gmelch (1978) has recently documented the plethora of superstitions surrounding batting (a highly uncertain activity) in baseball, and the absence of superstitions in fielding, where skill and practice can virtually guarantee success. Similarly, Malinowski noted superstitious ritual in the launching of South Sea canoes and the impressive development of the science of navigating them. The islanders had done all they could empirically and rationally in developing their sailing practices, and the added superstitious behavior "cost" little and probably allayed their anxiety. Malinowski has pointed out furthermore that the supernatural and the empirical were typically emphatically compartmentalized from each other: "The body of rational knowledge and the body of magical lore are incorporated each in a different tradition, in a different social setting, and in a different type of activity" (pp. 86–87). This deliberate distinguishing of the non-rational may serve to validate, through contrast, the general validity of rational approaches.

In inspecting modern occultisms, we find that most offer an alleged ability to increase predictability and control, especially under uncertain circumstances. Thus, Tarot cards, clairvoyance, or astrology allow us to "know" the future; biorhythms and psychic healing allow us to regulate our often capricious bodies and health. It is further clear that occultisms in this category "cost" little and do not make many demands on our lives. Despite their often fervidly avowed beliefs in psychic healing, the clients of a psychic surgeon do not go to the "healer" as their first choice, but usually after all else has failed; nor do law enforcement agencies seek the aid of psychics before they have attempted traditional police methods.

Moreover, as with superstitions in South Seas cultures, the occultisms are compartmentalized. On the personal level, people seem easily able to be less than rational in their occult beliefs while being hard-headed where rational approaches are strategic. We are willing to use astrology in determining our partners for social dating, because nothing else seems to work well, but would not contemplate trusting to the stars if we were making legal and financial arrangements with these same partners. On the societal level, and particularly in America, limited and scaled involvement with the occult may be achieved through commercialization—packaging of the occult as a commodity in graduated quantities. Thus, many occult beliefs seem to be instances of superstitious or magical thought patterns. Cognitive heuristics and biases may serve as a mental substructure which leads to and rationalizes the maintenance of such beliefs, while the circumstances under which they are maintained may be defined by how dearly they cost us.

An explanation in terms of environmental determinants for the rise in occult beliefs since the early 1960s must show that, like other superstitions, occult beliefs increase as a function of environmental uncertainty, and that uncertainty has in fact increased in the last two decades. To begin with, we do have evidence that many occult beliefs are a function of shifting levels of environmental uncertainty. For example, Hyman and Vogt (1979) have shown that the practice of water dowsing was more prevalent in locations where finding water was difficult, and Sales (1973) has found that astrology beliefs increased in the United States during the years of the Depression. Lamar Keene (1976, pp. 70–71), who was once a famous and fraudulent medium, writes: "All mediums would agree. . . . Wars, depressions, personal and national disasters spell prosperity for us. The present economic stresses in the United States are good news for mediums."

There is also evidence that environmental uncertainty in the United States and other Western countries has increased markedly since the early 1960s.

Constructing a working definition of variables such as "environmental uncertainty" at the level of a society is a decidedly complex and ambiguous task. Like the subjects in our experiments, we can find confirming evidence through post hoc analyses, depending on how assiduously we search for it and on the liberality of our interpretations. It is clear, however, that social change, which may have resulted from or given rise to feelings of uncertainty, has been marked since 1960. The past two decades have seen a decline of membership in the traditional religions in the United States and Europe, though not a decline in private religious belief; increased membership in fundamentalist, charismatic, and pentacostal religions; a proliferation of cults, paganism, and Eastern religions; a 29% rise in belief in the Devil; the development of a youth counterculture; disruption of traditional patterns in marriage and the family; a feminist movement; an alternative lifestyles movement and change in sexual ethics; the development of a drug culture; and the rise of a "human potential movement" (Glock and Bellah 1976; Wuthnow 1976).

These social trends overlap with the occult belief trend not only in time, but also in structural characteristics and in populations (Gallup 1976; Greeley 1975; Jahoda 1969; Johnson 1979; Wuthnow 1978). The evidence thus suggests that social trends may have caused, or may share causes with, the rise in occult beliefs. A long and unpopular war, political assassinations, and other events of the turbulent 1960s may have contributed to such trends. Other plausible determinants of these social changes include the recent increase in the youth population cohort, a long-term economic decline dating from 1965, and a devaluing of conventional meaning systems through the rising influence of social science. Thus, the prima facie case for an increase in environmental uncertainty since the early 1960s, while only partially substantiated in concrete detail, is a strong one.

Beit-Hallahmi (unpubl.) has pointed out that occultisms are not the only form of magical belief that has recently increased. The *National Enquirer*, which has become one of the best-selling newspapers in the United States, features articles not only on UFOs and ESP, but also on various miracle discoveries in health, dieting, cure of disease, and getting rich quickly. Whether such ideas are labelled "occult" is somewhat arbitrary, but they have similar superstitious qualities.

We have so far neglected to consider a category of occult beliefs that do make demands on believers' lives and extract heavy costs of belief. Occultisms such as Scientology, Theosophy, Satanism, and UFO cults resemble religions rather than ordinary superstitions, and there is evidence that they serve needs usually associated with religions, such as affiliation, moral direction, and an occasion for profound emotion (Bainbridge and Stark 1980). Such belief systems often demand total commitment, monetary and otherwise, from their members.

An explanation for the recent proliferation of such cults is then best couched in terms of developments in American religious practices. Stark and Bainbridge, at the University of Washington, have provided such an explanation, along with compelling documentation. A marked decline in membership in traditional religions over the past two decades has coincided with their theological retreat toward a more abstract, less personal deity, and with an orientation of these religions toward civil rights and other secular concerns, with consequently less investment in individual parishioners' needs (Bainbridge and Stark 1980; Stark and Bainbridge, in press; Glock and Bellah 1976). However, private belief in and need for the supernatural has not declined, and thus we infer that there has been a large population pool available for conversion to new, unorthodox religions, including those of the occult variety. In support of this interpretation, Bainbridge and Stark (1980) have found a negative correlation between membership in organized occult groups or reports of mystic psychic experiences, and membership in traditional religions.

In general, we do not adopt superstitions or fall prey to cognitive biases in areas, where empirical approaches bear fruit and where illusory beliefs would be costly. As Sagan (1979, p. 93) observes, "A people going to war may sing over their spears in order to make them more effective. If there ever have been people who felt they could defeat an enemy in war merely by singing and who therefore dispensed with spears, we have not heard of them; they were, undoubtedly, all dispatched."

In areas where judgments under uncertainty are important, we self-consciously avoid biases and fallacies. Thus, we have institutionalized elements of the scientific method, including meticulous weighing of alternative hypotheses, into police work, criminal law, and medical diagnosis. Under conditions of uncertainty, and where the cost of illusory belief is low, however, superstitions will surface and will be maintained through the aid of our somewhat faulty cognitive apparatus. In the last two decades it has become socially permissible to entertain occult beliefs as well as many other deviant beliefs and values, and conventional meaning systems and social orders have changed rapidly, perhaps generating widespread feelings of uncertainty and occult beliefs in the process. In addition, occultisms in the form of religious cults have moved into the void created by the recent decline of traditional religions.

Deficiencies in Science Education

There remains the question of how people maintain occult beliefs in the face of contravening scientific opinion. Granted that the popular media present a distorted picture, and that dependence upon our intuitive cognitions can also result in occultisms. The public nevertheless does seem to recognize that science emphatically rejects most occultisms. The layperson usually accepts scientific opinion unquestioningly, even when it is strikingly counter to his own intuitive understandings, as in the case of the atomic structure of matter or the astronomy of the solar system. Why are occult beliefs an exception to this customary deference to scientific authority?

One general explanation rests on the observation that people seem adept at compartmentalizing incongruent beliefs. We can comfortably live with disparate scientific, religious, and common sense approaches to different beliefs, and employ the belief approach most suitable to the personal need at hand. Personal needs which support occult beliefs may include, for instance, a need to assert the validity of one's own common-sense judgment vis-à-vis scientific "authority," needs for feelings of control and predictability, and a need for affiliation with a religious community. If the need to maintain an irrational belief outweighs any cost associated with maintaining it, the fact that the belief is not rational or scientifically supportable does not usually enter the equation. If cognitive dissonance does occur in maintaining an occult belief in spite of scientific debunking, any number of simple rationalizations, such as "Scientists are prejudiced about paranormal phenomena," will serve to reduce the cognitive tension. It is thus not really inexplicable that widespread occult beliefs exist within our most scientifically advanced societies.

Nevertheless it is our impression that the occult trend cannot be attributed wholly to innate cognitive flaws and emotional needs, but that current practices in the field of science education itself facilitate the rationalizing and compartmentalizing of occult beliefs. We have examined three major aspects of this problem.

First, from elementary school through graduate training, science seldom seems to be taught as a cognitive tool, a way of reaching deeper understanding of our environment. It is taught instead as a set of facts and concepts to be acquired by the same rote methods used in other academic subjects (Godfrey 1979). Even at graduate schools, research methodology appears to be taught as a set of advanced laboratory techniques, specific to the subject matter at hand. From elementary school onward the student does not seem to learn about the validity of scientific approaches vis-à-vis his intuitive understandings, but is simply heavily socialized to accept certain counterintuitive facts—the earth is round and rotates, matter is structured atomically—as items of culturally given common sense. Science is taught in the context of a specific, often technical subject matter, such as chemistry or botany; religious claims, occult claims, everyday problems are seldom examined in the science classroom. The student is thus encouraged to compartmentalize science as a set of facts or at best a dry, technical methodology within a limited number of narrow domains, and to trust his intuitions in the

larger spheres remaining. The occult is then naturally viewed as outside the domain of science, to be apprehended intuitively instead.

Second, many occult claims could be countered with even an elementary knowledge of scientific facts, but even elementary knowledge may be largely lacking. Morison (1969) has questioned whether science has in fact had any effect in raising the cognitive sophistication of the lay public above prehistoric levels, and suggested as one test asking people whether all objects fall at the same rate. We have tested hundreds of college sophomores over the past several years (Singer, in press) with the problem of estimating the duration of flight of a 4-lb and a 2-lb lead weight dropped simultaneously from the same 16-ft height. Over half the students gave different estimates for the flight durations of the two weights. Fifteen percent gave estimates in the range of 4–50 seconds, perhaps envisioning them floating down like paper airplanes. On the same test we found that over half the students did not know that water in a tipped glass remains level, and many believed that islands float in the ocean and that the moon remains fixed in the sky over them, but is only visible at night. This is not a useful armamentarium for evaluating occult claims.

Third, many students have the impression that science is entirely subjective and unable to assess or predict the validity of ideas, apparently on the basis of limited exposure to philosophers such as Polanyi, Hansen, and Kuhn. In presenting perspectives on science in our classrooms, we have perhaps overdone the critical view of the validity of our knowledge. In a series of paradoxical confusions, students attribute more empirical validity to philosophy than to science itself, and the fact that science "changes its mind" is regarded as a totally discrediting weakness. We do not read these philosophers as subscribing to the total subjectivity of science, and we do not believe they would subscribe to such a position. It would seem a service to speak more plainly and more assertively about science's track record.

One benefit of studying the mechanisms of occult beliefs is that we can thereby highlight the characteristics of science, considered as a belief process. That is, we can look at science as a cognitive system deliberately constructed to avoid or compensate for the mechanisms involved in occult beliefs. For instance, we can say that science in theory trusts data and distrusts intuition, generates alternative hypotheses, systematically attempts disconfirmation of favored hypotheses, uses mathematically calculated probabilities, and conscientiously engages in self-examination to determine whether values and motives are influencing beliefs. The question then arises whether the compensatory mechanisms of science are as comprehensive and effective as is feasible. Although the scientific enterprise is obviously successful, we have evidence that its compensatory mechanisms are not complete.

Einhorn and Hogarth (1978), Mahoney (1976), and Kahneman and Tversky (1973) have all found confirmatory cognitive biases, at a level approaching that of a layperson's, in scientists and mathematicians who were administered simple conceptual problems. Recent work in the psychology of science, particularly that of Mahoney (1976) and Mitroff (1974), has demonstrated the operation of confirmatory bias in actual scientific processes. In our own discipline, psychology, we have seen numerous cases of scientists operating in ways which seem intuitively correct to them on the basis of their personal experience, though objectively contraindicated. For example, scientifically trained clinicians continue to rely on personal interviews and clinical judgment in prediction and diagnosis of mental illness, despite twenty years of consistent evidence that simple actuarial techniques are more predictive (Dawes 1979).

Some scientists develop occult beliefs. Surveys have indicated, for example, that over half the natural and social scientists in the United States believe ESP to be established or likely (*Psychology Today* 1978; Wagner and Monnet 1979) and are either unaware of the small fraction of research psychologists who hold such a view, or convinced that their own intuitive understandings are somehow more correct than the scientific ones in this case. In addition, now as throughout the history of science there is a sprinkling of scientists, including eminent ones, who have been duped by the fraudulent practices of "psychics."

The evidence just presented raises the question of the locus of the norms of science and the mechanisms by which they are maintained. It is quite possible, for instance, that scientific rules of belief formation operate primarily at a system level. Such rules may affect scientists' cognitive behavior or public statements under particular contingencies as enforced by the scientific community, but this public attitude may not be completely internalized by the scientist as an individual. There may be tensions between the beliefs uttered by the scientist as a professional person operating within a professional community and those entertained by him as a private person who is still humanly prone to the flaws of intuition. Such tensions may substantively affect the conduct of science or the formation of scientific belief.

How should the scientific community respond to the upsurge of popular interest in the occult? The interest in occultism and pseudoscience may in fact be dangerously distracting from rational solutions to social problems and corrosive to rationality, as some scientists have feared. It seems to us, however, that occult beliefs are more symptomatic of dislocating social trends than causal of them, and that they are usually compartmentalized well enough that they do not in themselves corrupt a practical rationality, any more than does a monotheistic faith or a belief that Moses parted the Red Sea. The most serious side effect of occult beliefs may be that they are inherently discrediting of science, although the evidence does not indicate that this outcome has been realized. While recent public disaffection with science and technology is often mentioned as a stimulus to occult belief, hard evidence for such disenchantment is lacking (Marshall 1979). Further, correlational studies have more often than not found no relation between negative feelings toward science and occult beliefs (Wuthnow 1978).

The most convincing rationale for a scientific response to the occult preoccupation may simply be scientific self-integrity. The following steps seem appropriate: issuing rebuttals to fraudulent or unsubstantiated occult claims—far from being beneath our dignity, this can be considered a compelling social responsibility; increasing the availability to the media of scientific expertise on the occult; helping the public recognize which media sources speak with scientific authority and which do not; treating occult concepts in science education, including perhaps, introductory textbooks; examining policies relating to occult courses and concepts that appear in the name of a university, and relating to the selection of books and films for public school reading and science classes; and reorienting science education so that science becomes more personal, more life-oriented, and more easily apprehended as a highly useful mode of inquiry.

Straight from the Witch's Mouth

John Fritscher

John Fritscher's article presents the thoughts of Anton Szandor LaVey, the founder and high priest of the Church of Satan in San Francisco. Although LaVey's personal theology, the basis of Satanism, has attracted few to the church, the exotic nature of his views has drawn the attention of many. LaVey, author of the Satanic Bible, *maintains that Satanism is the reverse of Christian values: that God is evil and the Prince of Darkness good, and that Lucifer will ultimately triumph over the Christian God. LaVey's scathing attacks on would-be Satanists are an enlightening exposé of other occultists, pseudo-occultists, and miscellaneous pretenders who profit from what he considers the true religion—a theology that requires anarchy and chaos before Satanic morality can prevail.*

Reprinted from *Popular Witchcraft* by John Fritscher (Bowling Green, Ohio, 1972), pp. 89–90 and 107–123, by permission of the author and Bowling Green University Popular Press.

As men's prayers are a disease of the will, so are their creeds a disease of the intellect.

Emerson, *Self-Reliance*

WITCH-HUNTING THESE DAYS IS A SNAP. IN fact, new inquisitors have it easy since witches advertise. Where advertisement is lacking, ask the manager of the local occult bookstore. If he is not a witch, he'll know who is. Check out the backwater boutiques and the slightly-off campus shops with window signs reading "Occult Records." Catch up on occult symbolism and casually confront anyone wearing mystic insignia during a rock concert. (The median age of witches has lowered drastically. Crones are out.) Read the classifieds of the local college newspaper or the advertising in the local TV guides (free for the taking at supermarkets). Clip addresses from the Wanton Ads of the Underground Press or from overground tabloids like *The National Enquirer*.

Let your fingers do the walking through the Bell System's Yellow Pages (pop culture's surest and handiest index): check listings for astrologers, astrology schools, and palmists. In every instance, ask the persons listed what they think about witchcraft. (What they're advertising is often not what they're selling. Witches advertise as palmists because of Dis(ney)-crimination against witches. After all, in the popular mind what does a witch do? *Witch* is too indirect a come-on. *Palmist, astrologer, numerologist* are titles specific of what the consumer expects and will get.) In any group of seven or more people, interrupt the conversation to ask, "Has anyone here any American Indian blood?" Always there will be someone. Try the same with: "Does anyone here know a witch?" Once a witch is found, ask for a referral to his or her friends in the Craft.

If all else fails, join a psychic encounter group or better yet the Psychic Club of Dayton, Ohio. For ten dollars this club, which advertises itself as the place "where witches and warlocks abound," will give you—besides what you deserve—an astro-twin pen pal, a Free Location Service for correspondence with others with the same interests, and a one year subscription to the Psychic Club Bulletin.

In the last analysis, witches like beauty and smut are in the eye of the beholder. What they say about themselves though at times repetitious is often more revealing that what we say.

◇ ◇ ◇

Anton Szandor LaVey, High Priest and Founder of The Church of Satan; San Francisco, California

I don't feel that raising the devil in an anthropomorphic sense is quite as feasible as theologians or metaphysicians would like to think. I have felt His presence but only as an exteriorized extension of my own potential, as an alter-ego or evolved concept that I have been able to exteriorize. With a full awareness, I can communicate with this semblance, this creature, this demon, this personification that I see in the eyes of the symbol of Satan—the goat of Mendes—as I commune with it before the altar. None of these is anything more than a mirror image of that potential I perceive in myself.

I have this awareness that the objectification is in accord with my own ego. I'm not deluding myself that I'm calling something that is disassociated or exteriorized from myself the godhead. This Force is not a controlling factor that I have no control over. The Satanic principle is that man willfully controls his destiny; if he doesn't, some other man—a lot smarter than he is—will. Satan is, therefore, an extension of one's psyche or volitional essence, so that that extension can sometimes converse and give directives through the self in a way that mere thinking of the self as a single unit cannot. In this way it *does* help to depict in an externalized way the Devil per se. The purpose is to have something of an idolatrous, objective nature to commune with. However, man has connection, contact, control. This notion of an exteriorized God-Satan is not new.

My opinion of succubi and incubi is that these are dream manifestations of man's coping with guilt as in the case of nocturnal emissions with a succubus visiting a man or of erotic dreams with an incubus visiting a woman. This whole idea of casting the blame off one's own sexual feelings onto convenient demons to satisfy the Church has certainly proved useful in millions of cases. When the priest is confronted one morning by a parishioner holding a stiffened nightshirt, a semen-encrusted nightgown, the priest can tell him about this "terrible" succubus who visited him in the night. They proceed to exorcise the demon, getting the parishioner off the sexual hook and giving the priest a little prurient fun as he plays with the details of its predication on some pretty girl in the village. This, on top of it all, leaves the girl suspect of being a witch.

Naturally the priest can keep his eyes open as to who fits the succubi descriptions that he's heard in the confessional. Of course, the concept of incubi and succubi has also been used by people who have engaged in what they would consider illicit sexual relations. More than one lady's window has been left open purposely for the incubus to enter—in the form of some desirable male. This can then be chalked up the next day to demonic possession. All these very convenient dodges have kept Christianity and its foibles alive for many hundreds of years.

The birth of a satanic child is another manifestation of the need to extend the Christ-myth of the virgin birth to an antithetical concept of a demonic birth, a Devil-child. *Rosemary's Baby* wasn't the first to use this age-old plot. The Devil's own dear son or daughter is a rather popular literary excursion. Certainly the Devil walks in the sinews and marrow of a man because he is the representation of fleshly deity. Any animal heritage, any natural predilections, any real human attributes would be seen in the personification of the Devil. Consequently the Devil would have offspring and be proud of them, antithetic as they are to Christianity. Instead of being ashamed the child was conceived in sin and baptized out of sin, the Devil revels in the lust-conception of his child. This child would be involved much more magically than one who was the by-product of an environment that sought to negate at first opportunity the very motivating force—carnal desire—that produced him.

Religious artists' desexualizing of the birth process (Christ coming out of the bowels of Mary) has caused women to suffer childbirth pains much more than they need to because of the age-old collective unconsciousness that they must suffer this and the periodic suffering that comes every 28 days. Both these are attempts to stamp out or discredit what is in the animal world the most passionate feelings when the animal comes into heat at that time of the month. The "curse" of the menstrual cycle is a manufactured thing, manufactured by society that recognizes this period as one of great desire. Automatically, we have overemphasized its pains, tensions, turmoil, cramps. This taboo is not just Christian. Women have been placed in huts outside many villages. Every culture has thought she'd cause more jealousy and turmoil at this time because of this increase in her passions. Male animals fight more when the female is in heat. Having been a lion tamer, I know even the females are more combative at this time.

Christianity has put women at this time in more need of self-recrimination. This is the big difference between tribal customs and Christian: in the tribe, the woman is considered bleeding poison; in Christianity the woman is not only considered taboo, but she has to endure her pain as a "moral" reminder of her mortality and guilt. The primitive woman can give birth relatively painlessly and return to the fields. She goes through the physical act, but not through the moral agonies of the Christian woman. Such is the compounding of guilt. This kind of hypocrisy is my enemy number one.

I don't think young people can be blamed too much for their actions and antics. Although they coat their protests in ideological issues, I think what they resent most is not the actions of older adults, but the gross hypocrisy under which adults act. What is far worse than making war is making war and calling it peace and love and saying it's waged under the auspices of God or that it's the Christian thing to do. Onward, Christian soldiers and all that. I think that the worst thing about Christianity is its gross hypocrisy which is the most repugnant thing in the world to me. Most Christians practice a basic Satanic way of life every hour of their waking day and yet they sneer at somebody who has built a religion that is no different from what they're practicing, but is simply calling it by its right name. I call it by the name that is

antithetical to that which they hypocritically pay lip service to when they're in church.

Take for example, the roster of people executed for witchcraft in the Middle Ages. They were unjustly maligned because they were free-thinkers, beautiful girls, heretics, Jews, or people who happened to be of a different faith than was ordained. They were mercilessly tortured and exterminated without any thought of Christian charity. The basic lies and propaganda of the Christian Fathers added to the torment of the people. Yet the crime in today's streets and the mollycoddling of heinous criminals is a byproduct of latter-day Christian charity. Christian "understanding" has made our city streets unsafe. Yet helpless millions of people, simply because they were unbelievers or disbelievers, were not "understood." They were killed. It's not right that a mad dog who is really dangerous should be "understood" and those who merely dissent from Christianity should have been killed. At the Church of Satan we receive lots of damning letters from people condemning us in the most atrocious language. They attest they are good Christians; but they are full of hate. They don't know if I'm a good guy or a bad guy. They only know me by the label they've been taught: that Satanism is evil. Therefore they judge me on the same basis those people did in the thirteenth through sixteenth centuries. These very same people hardly ever get worked up over a murderer.

I think, in short, that Christ has failed in all his engagements as both savior and deity. If his doctrines were that easily misinterpreted, if his logic was that specious, let's throw it out. It has no place. It is worthless to a civilized society if it is subject to gross misinterpretation. (I'm not just protesting the "human element" in Christianity the way Christians do when something goes wrong with their system. I void the whole of the system that lends itself to such misinterpretation.) Why the hell didn't the writers mean what they said or say what they meant when they wrote that stupid book of fables, the Bible? This is the way I feel about it.

Anybody who takes up the sanctimonious cult of white light is just playing footsy with the Christian Fathers. This is why the bane of my existence are these white witches, white magicians, people who'd like to keep their foot in the safety zone of righteousness. They refuse to see the demonic in themselves, the motivations Satan's Majesty and Nature has placed inside them for their terrestrial goal. Materialism is part of Satanism, but a right kind of materialism. Everyone wants to acquire. The only thing wrong with money is it falls into the wrong hands. This makes it a curse, a disadvantage rather than an advantage. The marketplace is full of thieves. Easy wealth may be something would-be Faustian Satanists would like to get ahold of. In my experience people have come to me after I had opened doors for them. They come back wanting to know how to turn "it" off as they have more troubles than they had before. Once I offer to people what they think they want, given a week to think it over, they get cold feet. Success is a threat. Threatened by success, most people show their true colors. They show they need a god or an astrological forecast to really lay the blame on for their own inadequacy in the threatening face of imminent success.

Man needs religion, dogma, ritual that keeps him exteriorized outside of himself to waylay his guilt and inadequacy. Men will always, therefore, search for a god. We should, however, be men in search of man. The man in search of God is the masochist: he is the world's masochist. There are more than we imagine.

In the beginning I may not have intended Satanism to evolve into an elitist movement. But experience has taught me that Satanism can be a mass movement insofar as its basic pleasureseeking premise is concerned. You build a better mousetrap, and people are going to flock to it. A pleasure principle is going to be more popular than a pleasure denying. I can't help attracting the masses. As for the people who practice a truly Satanic way of life, you can't expect the masses to transcend mere lipservice to the pleasureseeking principle and get into the magical state of the Absolute Satanist. The Absolute Satanist is totally aware of his own abilities and limitations. On this self-knowledge he builds his character.

The Absolute Satanist is far removed from the masses who look for Satanic pleasure in the psychedelics of the headshops. We Satanists are magically a part of all this surface. I realize what my magical lessons have done, the things I've stumbled upon. We necessarily spawn our neo-Christian masses seeking their sense of soma through pills and drugs. Certainly I don't oppose this for other people who get stoned out of their minds. When they do this, the more material things there will be for me and my followers since all those people who freaked themselves out on drugs will be satisfied with their pills and will move off to colonies based on drugs. The rest of us, the Materialists, will inherit the world.

Actually, I'm very much opposed to drugs from a magical point of view, from a *control* point of view. I feel drugs are antithetical to magic. The pseudo-Satanist or pseudo-witch or self-styled mystic who predicates his success on a drug revelation is only going to suceed within his drugged peer group. His miracles go no farther than his credibility. This type of witchery is limited. This, I say, despite the fact that the druggies are no longer just a marginal group, but are a very large subculture which threatens to be the New Spirituality or the New Mysticism or the New Non-Materialism. They don't realize the whole concept of witchery is manipulation of other human beings. Druggies are not manipulative witches. To manipulate someone you've got to be able to relate to that someone. Their idea of witchery is not witchcraft so much— in the sense of witchery being manipulative magic —as witchery equalling revelation of a spiritual nature. Their superego gets developed through the use of drugs. This superego can be the earmark of a new world of drones who, through soma, would attain superegos which allow them while so controlled to think they have superiority over those really enjoying the fruits of the earth. This is why as the leader of the Satanic movement I have to examine these popular movements in the culture from a very pragmatic point of view.

The point is there will always be, among the masses, substitutes for the real thing. A planned way of life—not drugs—gets the materialist what he wants. There's nothing wrong with color TV and cars in the garage as long as the system which provides them respects law and order—a terribly overworked term. But as long as people don't bother other people, then I think this is an ideal society. I'm in favor of a policeman on every corner as long as he doesn't arrest people for thinking their own way or for doing within the privacy of their own four walls what they like to do.

We haven't been hassled too much by the law because we have so many policemen in our organization. I'm an ex-cop myself. I worked in the crime lab in San Francisco and I've maintained my contacts. They've provided for me a kind of security force. But all in all we have a very clean slate. We are very evil outlaws in theological circles, but not in civil.

How could we murder? We—unlike Christians—have a real regard for human bodies. The Satanist is the ultimate humanist. The Satanist realizes that man can be his own worst enemy and must often be protected against himself. The average man sets up situations for himself so he can be a loser. We Satanists have ancient rituals which exorcise these needs for self-abasement before they happen. We wreck Christians' tidy little dreams. When you have somebody rolling orgasmically on the floor at a revival meeting claiming an ecstasy, you tell them they're having a "forbidden" orgasm and they hate you for enlightening them. You've robbed them of their "succubus," of their freedom from guilt. They push their evilness on to us. In this sense, then, we are *very* evil.

I needn't send my child to a private school. Why should I when children are, in fact, all Satanists. She has no trouble at school. Ironically enough, the majority of our members are that often-attacked silent middle class. At least fifty percent of our members have children; the other fifty percent are not rebels, but they're not losers.

I was very liberal in my younger years. I would have been thrown into prison during the McCarthy purge had I been of any prominence. I was ultra-liberal, attending meetings of the Veterans of the Spanish Civil War, the Abraham Lincoln Brigade, the Revisionist Movements of Israel's founding. This was all very liberal at the time. I was always for civil rights. I had Negro friends when Negro friends weren't fashionable. A man should be judged on his accomplishments, his kindness and consideration for others. A certain planned form of bigotry may be a little healthy. I mean, if a person is the worst that his race has produced, he should be prevented from using his race unless he is a credit to his race, religion, whatever it is.

Martin Luther King was killed because he was an articulate gentleman, concerned about his wife and family. He tried to do things in a mannerly way. A man like that belongs on a pedestal. But these loud baboons—and I choose the term—are nothing but rabblerousers, spewing venom. The

more a person has at stake the more he watches his p's and q's. This is my test of a person's sincerity. The public is no judge. The public is not too particular in its choosing of heroes.

I voted for Wallace to act out a magical ritual. I performed it—knowing he would not win, but wishing simply to cast my runes. Wallace's advantage was he would have been helpful in the inert area between action and reaction. The pendulum is swinging. I've been misinterpreted when I've said people like Reagan and Nixon are doing a lot to help Satanism because they are causing tremendous popular reaction whereby we're getting off the hook in Vietnam.

Popular opinion is simply a reaction against the leaders who have made their stand so heinous that the protesters don't realize they're doing exactly what the masters want them to do: they're getting the masters off the hook. The masters are using the old magical technique of allowing the people to think it's their idea. This explains the government's permissive attitude toward protest. The idealists of the early fifties during the McCarthy era were certainly just as against violence; but the Government posture did not lie in that direction so they had to be shut up fast. Currently the show of rebellion is, therefore, a very magical ritual.

The new emphasis will be placed on staging. Life is a game and we'll realize it's a game. Life is not "God's Will." We have to go to the point of no return before we can return. We will get to the point where anybody who is establishment oriented is suspect as being the worst kind of individual. This will happen before we return to a rather safe normality, to a sane discrimination as to who are really the contributing members of society and who are the cancerous tissue.

Satanically speaking, anarchy and chaos must ensue for awhile before a new Satanic morality can prevail. The new Satanic morality won't be very different from the old law of the jungle wherein right and wrong were judged in the truest natural sense of biting and being bitten back. Satanic morality will cause a return to intrigue, to glamour, to seductiveness, to a modicum of sexual lasciviousness; taboos will be invoked, but mostly it will be realized these things are fun.

The various Liberation Fronts are all part of the omelet from which the New Satanic Morality will emerge. Women's Liberation is really quite humorous. Supposedly women were liberated after the Industrial Revolution when they got out of the sweatshops. They're going to defeat themselves because they're not using the ammunition of their femininity to win as women. They're trying to reject their femininity which is their greatest magical weapon.

They're parodying themselves.

Speaking of parody, the historical Black Mass is a parody of a parody. The Black Mass parodies the Christian service which parodies a pagan. Every time a man and woman go to church on Sunday they are practicing a Black Mass by parodying ancient earth rituals which were practiced by their ancestors before they were *inverted* by the Christian Fathers. Our Satanic mass captures the beauty of the self and ritualizes that; the Satanic mass is no parody. It is catharsis. The Women's Libists should simply use their femininity by taking the Devil's name and using it and playing the Devil's game. They should take the stigma that cultural guilt has thrown at them and invert the values, making a virtue in their semantic reversal. This is what we have done in Satanism. What theologians have supplied in stigma, we use as virtue. We therefore have the attraction of the forbidden. This has greatly aided our success.

I know I have been rumored to have cursed Jayne Mansfield and caused her death. Jayne Mansfield was a member of the Church of Satan. I have enough material to blow sky-high all those sanctimonious Hollywood journalists. She was a priestess in the Church of Satan. I have documentation of this fact from her. There are many things I'll not say for obvious reasons. Her lover, who was a decidedly unsavory character, was the one who brought the curse upon himself. There was decidedly a curse, marked in the presence of other people. Jayne was warned constantly and periodically in no uncertain terms that she must avoid his company because great harm would befall him. It was a very sad sequence of events in which she was the victim of her own—as we mentioned earlier—inability to cope with her own success. Also the Demonic in her was crying out to be one thing and her Apparent Self demanded that she be something else. She was beaten back and forth in this inner conflict between the Apparent Self and the Demonic Self. He was black-mailing her. I have definite proof of this. She couldn't get out of his

clutches. She was a bit of masochist herself. She brought about her own demise. But it wasn't through what I had done to curse *her*. The curse was directed at *him*. And it was a very magnificent curse.

The dedication of my *Satanic Bible* to Marilyn Monroe and Tuesday Weld was, in Marilyn's case, homage to a woman who was literally victimized by her own inherent witchery potential which was there in her looks. I think a great deal of the female mystique of beauty which was personified in Marilyn's image. In the case of Tuesday Weld it's part of the magical ritual. She is my candidate of a living approximation of these other two women. Unlike them, Tuesday has the intelligence and emotional stability to withstand that which Marilyn Monroe could not. For this reason Tuesday is not in the public eye as much. Her own better judgment has cautioned her not to bite off more than she can chew.

I'd like to point out that another popular American, Ben Franklin, was a rake without question. He was a sensual dilettante. He joined up with the British Hellfire Club. Their rituals came to them from the Templars and other secret societies. We practice some of these same rituals secretly in the Church of Satan. Not only did Ben Franklin influence the activities of the Hellfire Club, his very association sheds some light on the *quality* of members of what would appear to be a blasphemous group of individuals. This proves the Devil is not only a gentleman but a cultured gentleman.

Throughout history the witch most feared is the witch most antithetical to the physical standards. In Mediterranean cultures, anyone with blue-eyes would have been the first to be named as a witch. The black woman Tituba in Salem was antithetical to New England physical standards. Anyone who is dark has an edge because of all the connotations of black arts, black magic, the dark and sinister side of human nature. Tituba probably was not only more feared but also more sought after. She was set apart physically from the rest of the people. She was the magical outsider.

The Church of Satan does not employ males as altars simply because the male is not considered to be the receptacle or passive carrier of human life. He possesses the other half of what is necessary to produce life. Woman is focal as receiver of the seed in her recumbent role as absorbing altar. A male would defeat the purpose of receptor unless he were fitted out with an artificial vagina and were physically and biologically capable of symbolizing the Earth Mother.

We do, however, accept homosexuals. We have many in the Church of Satan. They have to be well adjusted homosexuals—and there *are* many well adjusted homosexuals who are not on the daily defensive about their sexual persuasion. Many have a great amount of self-realization. Of course, we get the cream of the crop. Since they cannot relate to the basic heterosexuality of the Church of Satan whatever they do must be modified. If the homophile were involved in defining the dogma of our Church it would be very imbalanced for the masses of people with whom we deal. The homophile would very easily like to substitute a male for the female altar. It's a fact that a heterosexual can accept homosexuality more readily than a homosexual can accept heterosexuality. Relating to the existence of the other sex is something that MUST be in evidence. Women cannot be denied their function in our Satanic Church. Needless to add, man-hating women cause us a great lack of sensual scintillation.

My book *The Complete Witch; or What to Do When Virtue Fails* is a guide for witches. It doesn't stress the drawing of pentacles on the floor. It smashes all the misconceptions that women have had, not only about witchery but about their own sexuality. I think of this book like de Beauvoir's *The Second Sex*. Even if a woman is a man-hater, she can use her femininity to ruin that man. This book tells her how to do it. If she wants to enjoy men, this book will open her eyes to a few things.

Sexual fetishes we find natural. Everybody has one. These should be catered to. Sexual deviations are only negative factors when they present an obstacle to one's success. They present an obstacle when they are carried out of the ritual chamber, out of the fantasy room into the world where others will see them disapprovingly.

I must tell you something quite amusing. *Rosemary's Baby* did for us what *The Birth of a Nation* did for the Ku Klux Klan. I never realized what that film could do. I remember reading at the premiere of Griffith's *Birth of a Nation* recruiting posters for the KKK in southern cities. I chuckled because at the premiere of *Rosemary's Baby* there were posters of the Church of Satan in the lobby. Here at the

San Francisco premiere there was a great deal of consternation, but the film started an influx of very worthwhile new members. Since *Rosemary* the quality of membership has gone up. Immeasurably.

Since that film with Polanski, I am constantly confronted with scripts by thick-skulled exploitation producers who want me either to be technical advisor or play the role of the Devil or the Satanic doctor in their new films. They think to one-up *Rosemary*. What they don't realize is that *Rosemary's Baby* was popularly successful because it exploded a lot of the preconceptions of Satanism: it didn't chop up the baby at the end. It threw all the crap down the drain and showed the public who was expecting the sensational the real image of the Satanist. It will remain a masterpiece.

The allegory of the Christ child in reverse is simply the birth of the new Satanic Age, 1966. The year 1966 was used in *Rosemary's Baby* because it was our Satanic Year One. The birth of the baby was the birth of Satanism. *Rosemary's Baby* stands foursquare against the popular image of child sacrifice. The role that I played in the picture—the devil in the shaggy suit was not from my point of view anything other than it should have been: man, animal, bestial, carnal nature coming forth in a ritualized way. The impregnation of Rosemary in that dream sequence was to me the very essence of the immodest, the bestial in man, impregnating the virginal world-mind with the reawakening of the animalism within oneself. This impregnation was very meaningful because it spawned literally the Church of Satan. Among all the rituals in the film, this was the big ritual in *Rosemary's Baby*.

These others who want my opinion on their scripts are simply producing more trash of the blood-sacrifice variety. In *Rosemary's Baby*, the girl who went out the window and landed on the pavement died in the pure Satanic tradition. She had made it clear—although the people who saw the film didn't realize it—that she was a loser. Everything she said pointed to it. She'd been kicked around. She'd been on the streets. She'd been on dope. She was obviously the wrong girl to be a carrier. Satan saw her lack of maternal instinct, of winning instinct, of spunk to carry this baby out into the world. She therefore, sort of fell "accidentally" out the window. The end of the film shows Rosemary throw away her Catholic heritage and cherish the devil-child. The natural instinct of Satanism wins out over man-made programming.

Even though I have done the consulting for *Mephisto Waltz* for Twentieth Century Fox, that film still has the old elements of witchery. It's going to take a lot to come up with a film that's as much a blasphemy as *Rosemary's Baby*. Polanski's other film *The Fearless Vampire Killers* is like nothing else that's ever been done before in the film world. The film explodes all the puerile Christian myths about vampires. The old professor, sort of a Count Dracula, is shown to be not only the doddering old fool he really is but also the real victim at the end. The fact that all those unfortunate murders took place at Polanski's—his wife Sharon Tate and all the rest—was used by the press to highlight Polanski's interest in witchery and Satanism. The deaths had nothing to do with the films. The Polanskis were simply plagued with hippies and drug addicts. If I were to allow it, my house would be full of the sychophantic loungers. If I neglected them, they'd be paranoid. I would have been put in the same position as those people at Polanski's house had I allowed it. He attracted, as people in Hollywood do, all the creeps, kooks, and crackpots. He wasn't around to stop it or was too nice to put his foot down. He, in a sense, put himself in much the same position as Jayne Mansfield.

Those people that were killed were all freaked out of their minds anyway. They were people who were only a little better than the killers. As far as their warped outlooks on life, their senses of values, it was a case of the blind destroying the blind. Sharon was probably the victim of her environment, but I can't find it in myself to whitewash these people. I know firsthand how the people at the Factory and the Daisy and these other nightclubs behave. They're quite indiscriminate as to the people they take up with.

The devil in *Rosemary's Baby* was depicted as a combination of many anthropomorphic ideals of the bestial man: the reptilian scales, the fur, claws. A combination of animal kingdom. It was not a red union suit with a pitchfork. Nor was it Pan transmogrified by Christians into a cloven-hoofed devil. *The Cloven Hoof* title of our newsletter was chosen precisely for its eclectic image in the popular mind as one of the devil's more familiar and acceptable traits. Cloven-hoofed animals in pre-Christian times had often been considered sacred in their association with carnal desire. The pig, goat, ram —all of these creatures—are consistently associated with the devil. Hence our title.

The truest concept of Satan is not in any one animal but is in man, the evolutionary accomplishment from many animals.

The historical note that Satan has an icecold penis is a very pragmatic thing because when Satan had to service the witches who would come to him to draw from his power at the Sabbaths, he could actually remain erect either with those who stimulated him—that is the magician who portrayed Satan—or until he became expended of his sexual vigor. Naturally then, under his fur cloak or garb he had to strap on something of an artificial nature, a bull's pizzle, a dildo. In the night air, it would cool off. The witches all swore that it was cold. He would have to use something like this to maintain his position as the devil.

It is of interest to me that hippies and Hell's Angels tattoo themselves with the markings of Satanism and other symbols of aggression. Tattooing is an ancient and obscure art. One of the few books on it is called *Pierced Hearts and True Love* by Ebensten. There's also George Burchett's *Memoirs of the Tattoist*. Certainly much needs to be said of the relation of Satanism and witchery to tattooing. We have members that were tattooed long before the Hell's Angels made it fashionable. One man has the Goat of Bathona, the Satanic Goat, tattooed across his back. Beautifully done. The devil-headed eagle is on his chest. Then on each thigh he has the figure of Seth. He's quite spectacular. He has a shaven head and the build of a professional wrestler. He is extremely formidable when he is in ceremony wearing only a black pair of trunks with a very small mask across his eyes. His are very symmetrically contrived attempts at using tattoos for ritualistic purposes.

Witchcraft has a lot of show business in it. Religious ritual after all was the first theater. For this reason, I think, *Dark Shadows* and *Bewitched* are fine. White witches think these TV shows are terrible because they play the witch as a pretty girl who can snap her fingers and get things done. They try to impress the world that a *wicca* is not up to that sort of thing. They try to play that they're an intellectually justified "Old Religion." The popular image of the witch is a gal who can get things done in apparently supernatural ways. Like *I Dream of Jean-*

nie. Why not take advantage of the glamorized witch? If this has been the very element that has brought witchraft out of a stigmatized, persecuted stereotype, then why put it down? It is the glamorization of witchraft that gives the erstwhile white witches the free air in which to breathe. Why knock it?

This gets me to Gerald Gardiner, whom I judge a silly man who was probably very intent on what he was doing; he had to open a restaurant and get it filled with customers. He took over a not too successful teashop and turned it into a museum. He had to say he was a research scholar. He got the term *white witch* from a coinage in *Witchcraft's Power in the World Today*. Gardiner used the term because witchery was illegal in England at the time. To avoid persecution he opened his museum under the guise of research. He stated he wasn't a witch until the repeal of the laws in 1953. Then he made it very clear he was a white witch. That's like saying, "Well, I'm a good witch. The others are bad witches. So don't persecute me." Gardiner did what he had to do, but I don't think he was anymore of an authority on the true meaning of witchcraft than Montague Summers. I think that he simply followed Summers' crappy rituals of circles and "Elohim" and "Adonai." They used the name of Jesus and crossed themselves.

I have broken the barrier. I have made it a little bit fashionable to be a black magician. A lot of them, therefore, are trying to say now that their horned god is not a Devil. It is just a horned god. Well, let me tell you, until five or six years ago they wouldn't even admit to a horned god. Suddenly they like to intimate that perhaps they have made pacts with the Devil. For many years the old Religionists used Albertus Magnus, the Sixth and Seventh Books of Moses, The Book of Ceremonial Magic, crossing themselves as they turned the pages, denying theirs was a Christian based faith. Why in the hell did they use all these accoutrements? White witches are no more than a by-product of Christianity, or they wouldn't have to call themselves white witches in the first place. I don't think white witches have the courage of their convictions.

I have said that Aleister Crowley had his tongue jammed firmly in his cheek. I think Crowley was a pragmatist. He was also a drug addict. The demons he conjured were the products of a be-

numbed mind. Basically he was a sweet, kind man who was trying to emancipate himself from the throes of a very strict upbringing. He can't be blamed for anything he did from a psychoanalytical point of view. He wasn't really that wicked of a man. He had to work overtime. All the arbitrary numbers, dogma, and so on of his magical curriculum were constructs he invented to answer the needs of his students. Crowley's greatest wisdom was in his *Book of Lies*. The particular page can be paraphrased: "My disciples came to me, and they asked, Oh Master, give us your secret." He put them off. They insisted. He said it would cost them ten thousand pounds. They paid, and he gave them his words: "A sucker is born every minute." This says more for Crowley than all his other work. His judgment of the popular follower was accurate; most of the public wants gibberish and nonsense. He alluded to this in his numbering of his *Libers* which are not immense volumes but just a few bound sheets of paper. He's saying the real wisdom is about ten lines long.

Like Crowley, Gerald Gardiner probably knew a good thing when he saw it and got something going that turned out to be more sanctimonious than it should be. Ray Buckland began the same way. Now he admits to once being part of the more mundane rather than the complete esoteric he was made out to be. Ray Buckland certain knows a great deal about the occult. He has a good synthesis of the Arts. But sanctimony still comes through. His famous chapter on black magic threatens that if a curse is not performed properly it will return to the sender. He defines things like good and bad, white and black magic for those who—as I say in my *Satanic Bible*—are frightened by shadows. I maintain that good like evil is only in the eyes of the beholder. Ray Buckland has guts, though, to sit in his Long Island home conducting his rituals and not caring what the neighbors think.

I don't know whether Sybil Leek is as big a fool as she sometimes seems, or whether she's laughing up her sleeve. Sybil is a good business woman. I don't want to judge her—if she is a good business woman she knows on which side her bread is buttered! My only complaint with Sybil—and I do know her personally—is she has done nothing to dispel all the crap about black and white witches. If she's after the little old ladies in tennis shoes, fine. But she is a dispenser of misinformation.

Alex Sanders has become more public in proclaiming himself the king of the Witches. He is a dispenser of misinformation too. He's not too bad; in the stifling climate of England he's a forward man among a backward people. He's got a big load. For this I admire him. He's great enough to claim himself King. I don't put much credence in astrology—it's a case of the tail wagging the dog. A competent sorcerer, however, should know his astrology because it is a motivating factor for many people. Sydney Omarr, the popular syndicated astrologer, is basically a level headed guy who sees through a lot of the fraud.

I'll be the first to give Sybil Leek and Louise Huebner and all these people their due. They don't say, "We witches don't want publicity." That takes moxie in a sanctimonious society. They're not like these damn cocktail party witches who can't defend their self-styled reputations when called to do it. These people give me a pain. It's part of being a witch, the ego gratification of being a witch, to want to talk about it in detail in public.

The Occult Revival as Popular Culture: Some Observations on the Old and the Nouveau Witch

Marcello Truzzi

How can the rising tide of occultism in the United States be assessed? In this article Marcello Truzzi observes that the revival of interest in the occult shows how certain religious events can reflect serious social conflict in a culture. After identifying four major categories of occult interest, Truzzi devotes most of his article to an analysis of the two areas that he believes dominate occult interest in this country—astrology and witchcraft-Satanism. Truzzi concludes that for most Americans the involvement in the occult is more a fad of popular culture than a serious religious commitment.

Reprinted from *Sociological Quarterly*, Vol. 13 (Winter 1972), pp. 16–36, by permission of the author and the Midwest Sociological Society, Department of Sociology, Southern Illinois University.

IN HIS CLASSIC ARTICLE ON FASHION, EDWARD Sapir noted that:

> There is nothing to prevent a thought, a type of morality or an art form from being the psychological equivalent of costuming the ego. Certainly one may allow oneself to be converted to Catholicism or Christian Science in exactly the same spirit in which one invests in pewter or follows the latest Parisian models in dress (Sapir, 1937: 143).

Although religion holds a somewhat exalted position in many of the prominent macro theories of societies (e.g., those of Durkheim, Weber, etc.), it is often a rather mundane phenomenon, satisfying a wide variety of idiosyncratic needs for society's many groups and their members. The functions of a religious phenomenon will often vary for its different actors and audiences, and they need not necessarily reflect a single fundamental fact or crisis of social life. This point is nicely exemplified by Ogden Nash's delightful poem describing the sequential religious affiliations of Mrs. Marmaduke Moore. He reminds us that her changes in religion might result from causes other than those of some set of central social structural origins (e.g., anomie, status inconsistency). Describing her many conversions from Methodism to Bahai, he concluded:

> When seventy stares her in the face
> She'll have found some other state of grace.
> Mohammed may be her Lord and Master
> Or Zeus, or Mithros, or Zoroaster.
> For when a woman is badly sexed,
> God knows what god is coming next.
>
> Nash, 1945: 12

The revival of interest in the occult and the

supernatural is a current example of religious events that some have seen as being of great cultural significance and as reflecting serious social conflicts and strains of macroscopic import. (For good examples of this alienation-argument, see Staude, 1970; Greeley, 1969. For a somewhat similar view, see Harris, 1970). A wide variety of indicators shows that we are in the midst of a widespread boom of things occult. As *Time* magazine (1968: 42) noted: "A mystical renaissance is evident everywhere, from television to department stores." In late 1969, The *Wall Street Journal* reported that the boom continued and "mysticism is becoming a big business. A New York book store specializing in the occult says sales have zoomed 100% in the past three years" (Sansweet, 1969: 1, for the British counterpart, see Williams, 1970). In 1968, 169 paperback books dealing with occult topics were in print [see *Paperbound Books in Print* (June 1968), under the headings "Psychology: Occult Sciences," "Parapsychology," and "Astrology,"] and, by 1969, the figure had jumped to 519 books (see *Paperbound Books in Print*, October 1969). In 1969, 364 hardback volumes dealt with occultism, which represented an increase both from 261 volumes in 1968 and from 198 volumes in 1967 (Prakken and Shively, 1967, 1968, 1969). A final indicator of this boom has been the sales of Ouija boards. After some forty years of poor sales, companies reported over two million sold in 1967 (Pileggi, 1970: 63), thereby outdistancing the sales of *Monopoly* (Buckley, 1968: 31). (An excellent history of the Ouija and its family can be found in Jastrow, 1962: 129–143. For a discussion of the mechanisms involved, see Rawcliffe, 1959: 134–151; and for an interesting case study, see Wenger and Quarantelli, 1970. On the earlier Ouija board fads, see Sann, 1967: 139–144.)

The revival of occultism has been heavily touted as (and, in large part, certainly does represent) an important part of the current youth culture (see Greeley, 1969; Levin, 1968; and Gams, 1970; and on the concept of "youth culture," see Berger, 1963). Certain facts and assumptions, however, indicate that a broad spectrum of persons has been involved in this boom. My own teaching experiences and the wide variety of magazines now giving space to this subject (from *McCall's* and *The Ladies Home Journal* to *Playboy* and *Esquire*) show that many persons outside the youth culture are interested in the occult. A 1969 survey of *Fate* magazine readers, which then had about 94,000 monthly readers, showed that 88 percent of them were over 34 years old, 37.9 percent being over 55 years old (Consumer Communication Corporation). A 1963 Gallup Poll showed that one in five persons reported some sort of sudden or dramatic "religious or mystic experience." The study further showed no relationship between the respondent's experience and his level of education (Gallup, 1963; for a detailed analysis of this report, see Bourque, 1969; and Bourque and Back, 1968). It is safe to assume that even though they were not sudden or dramatic, a great many other Americans have had comparable religious experiences. It is also likely that even though today's social scientists have only superficially examined the subject, a vast reservoir of magical and superstitious thought exists in the American population. (Such studies of magic in modern America would include Henslin, 1967; Hyman and Vogt, 1967; McCall, 1964; Lewis, 1963; Blumberg, 1963; Whitten, 1962; Vogt and Golde, 1958; Roth, 1957; Vogt, 1956; Simpkins, 1953; Levitt, 1952; Zapf, 1945–1946, and 1945; Belanger, 1944; Weiss, 1944; Passin and Bennet, 1943; Caldwell and Lundeen, 1937; Dudycha, 1933; Hurston, 1931; Grilliland, 1930; Wagner, 1928; Park, 1923; Conklin, 1919; and Shotwell, 1910). These facts and assumptions plus the well-known concern held by the elderly about occultisms relating to healing and survival of bodily death (see Buckner, 1968) indeed indicate that interest in the occult is not an unique phenomenon with the youth culture.

Despite the widespread interest in occultism throughout the population, this current revival seems to be primarily a youth phenomenon. Some facts support this claim. The mass media portray youth as adherents of occultism. Occult bookstores have emerged around the academic campuses. Even many institutions in the nation, including so-called Free-Universities, have offered numerous courses dealing with occult topics.

Empirical research on the prevailing attitudes of the occult among youths is nearly non-existent. During the past three years, my investigations of the national occult scene reveal four rather distinct foci of interest, foci sometimes intersecting but basically quite separate. Three major sources of data provided the basis for my interpretation of the integrated pattern of existing occult belief-systems: extensive readings in the available literature, interviews with hundreds of students, and interviews or exchanged communications with numerous major occult figures, writers, and publishers. The four major foci of occult interest currently dominating the youth culture are (1) astrology, (2) witchcraft-satanism, (3) parapsychology and extrasensory perception, and (4) Eastern religious thought. Classified as a "waste-basket variety," a fifth category encompasses a large number of esoteric items of occult interest, including among others, prophets (Edgar Cayce, Nostradamus, etc.), strange monsters (sea serpents, snowmen, werewolves, vampires, etc.), unidentified flying objects, and many others. Because the interests in the fifth category either have small scope and influence or are in an actual state of decline, the interests in the four major categories represent the dominant factors or motifs currently in fashion. At times, these four interest-areas do intersect among some believers. (For example, some witches, as Sybil Leek, also believe in astrology.) This, however, is not necessarily the case and indeed is relatively uncommon.

Of the four major foci of occult interest, the first two are most clearly central in the current revival. Parapsychology does not seem to be undergoing any significant increase in popularity. Interest in Eastern religious thought seemingly passed its peak as a topic of mass interest when interest in Zen Buddhism, which the so-called "beat-generation" writers of the 1950's made popular, began to decline (for sociologically relevant works on this subculture, see Regney and Smith, 1961; Moore, 1960; and Feldman and Gartenberg, 1958). Both parapsychology and Eastern religious thought act not as central values in the youth occult world, but as *bolsters* or legitimizing linkages to the broader and more generally accepted cultural areas of science and religion. One becomes receptive to an analysis of witchcraft-satanism with their generally unacceptable magical elements if he remembers two facts. First, the current limits of scientific understanding have been highlighted by the parapsychologists conducting "respectable" laboratory investigations. Second, in the process of establishing their own identity, some proponents of Western philosophical naturalism may have become rather parochial in their own views toward

the older and more mystical traditions of the East. I will now devote the rest of this paper to an analysis of these two major foci of occult interest currently dominating the scene—astrology and witchcraft-satanism.

Astrology

Certain existing indicators of occult preferences clearly reveal the predominant interest in astrology. In 1969, 252 or 68 percent of the 373 books printed on occultism dealt with astrology (Prakken and Shively, 1969). In 1969, 33 of 40 articles dealing with occultism covered the topic of astrology [in *Readers Guide to Periodical Literature* (New York: H. W. Wilson Co.), for January 17, 1969, to January 29, 1970]. Paperbound books on astrology increased from 35 in 1968 to 102 in 1969 (see *Paperbound Books in Print*, October 1969, June 1968). Even the popular press (Time, 1969; Jennings, 1970; Robinson, 1970; and Buckley, 1968) has widely reported the phenomenal growth of interest in this ancient pseudoscience (for good reviews of the scientific repudiation of astrology, see, Bok and Mayakkm, 1941; Thorndike, 1955; Hering, 1924: 18–37; de Camp and de Camp, 1966: 20–31; Lewinsohn, 1962: 90–114; and, especially, Gauquelin, 1970); such interest has become a marketing bonanza. Twenty years ago only about 100 papers carried horoscope columns, but today 1200 of the 1750 daily newspapers regularly carry such columns (Buckley, 1968: 31; and Jennings, 1970: 104). Because of their public endorsement of astrology, a wide variety of celebrities, which range from Hollywood stars (e.g., Marlene Dietrich, Robert Cummings, Susan Hayward), to members of the political (e.g., Ronald Reagan) and intellectual (e.g., Marshall McLuhan) communities, have added to its attractiveness to their admirers. The popular musical *Hair* with its hit song of *Aquarius* and its own well publicized company-astrologist gave special impetus to the movement (Buckley, 1968: 136). The Dell publishing company alone had some 49 horoscope publications in press and sold over 8,000,000 copies of its annual astrological dopesheet in 1969 (Jennings, 1970: 104). About 10,-000 full-time and 175,000 part-time astrologers in the United States serve some 40,000,000 persons in their American audience (Jennings, 1970: 154). One only has to look around at the shops in any semi-urban community to see astrological recordings, calendars, ashtrays, hairstyles, sweatshirts, and thousands of merchandized items linked to the zodiac. As one leading figure in the occult world, who himself does not endorse astrology, succinctly put it: "The stars may affect no one, but astrology affects everyone" (LaVey, 1968).

How, then, are we to account for the renewed popularity of this ancient and scientifically discredited belief system? No one who is familiar with the rules of scientific evidence or with the history of both astrology and astronomy over the centuries can accept the interpretation of the manifest functions of astrology, that it represents a scientifically true explanation and predictive framework for understanding man and his actions. Of course, some followers of astrology claim acceptance of their "science" for just such reasons. Such rigid scientific justification, however, is rare among the practitioners. Most astrology-believers place their credence in their system for reasons, at least partly, beyond what they themselves see as a legitimate science. To them, the heart of the matter is not that they use science as the basis for their acceptance of astrology as truth but that science must catch up with their truth. We, thus, might look at the latent functions of astrological beliefs, both for the social system (group) in which they exist and for the needs of the social actors involved in the system. One must, however, recognize that the involvements of those "into" astrology are quite varied. One can meaningfully speak of at least three, somewhat oversimplified and "ideal typical," levels of involvement. Each level of involvement manifests somewhat different consequences for the actors.

At the first, most superficial level of involvement, we find the occasional reader of the newspaper and magazine astrology-columns. This person knows next to nothing about the "mechanics" of astrology. From my interviews and preliminary explorations, I found that most of the middle-aged (over 35 years old) population who follow astrology fall into this category. These astrology-followers were largely present before the astrology-revival of these past five years. Because horoscopes do not normally take into account the subject's (client's) exact time and place of birth, those more advanced than are others in astrology perceive this level of astrology-believers as highly superficial. Even the noted newspaper-astrologer, Sidney Omarr, was quoted as conceding that "daily columns provide entertainment rather than enlightenment" (Buckley, 1968: 31). The overwhelming majority of astrology-believers fall into this first level. Consideration of the latent functions for the individual involved at the first level would have to take into account the following factors: (1) the familiarity with astrology, its ancient and pervasive character; (2) the quasi-scientific character of astrology that acts as legtimating astrology to those not scientifically critical put personally concerned about the present explorations of the heavens; (3) the usually positive character of astrological advice that makes it ego-boosting; (4) the ego-directed attention of the advice; (5) the element of mystery, of the esoteric that makes the advice exciting and entertaining; (6) the ambiguity of the message that makes it amenable to interpretation and difficult to falsify; and (7) the self-fulfilling nature of many astrological predictions. (This phenomenon may operate in the following way: a person who reads that he is in good spirits becomes so, or a person who reads that he should be cautious acts so and then finds a justifying event.) Some latent functions on the group (societal) level might include the following factors: (1) tension-management of anxieties within the social system; (2) fulfillment of economic goals that the mass merchandising of an astrology-fad affords; and (3) the availability of a cognitive belief-system that transcends science and is "safe" from the sanctions of or overt conflict with the major religions. (This is true today, but it was not always so.)

At the second level of involvement with astrology, we find those people who have some knowledge of the "mechanics" of astrology. These people usually have their own personal horoscopes cast. They do this through a variety of ways, ranging from personal visits with a consulting astrologer to a computer-analysis of their horoscopes. Unlike those in the first level of involvement, the astrology-believers in the second level have some knowledge of the special language and of the astrological reasoning; they are able to speak about other people astrologically. Like those in the first level, most astrology-believers in the second level seek advice and predictions from their excursions into astrology. I have observed that *the astrology-believers in the second level primarily repre-*

sent those of college-age, and this level has had the greatest relative increase during the current revival. Some latent functions for the individual involved at the second level might include the following factors: (1) all functions available to those involved at the first level; (2) the enhancement of the *personal* and ego-gratifying character of the involvement; (3) an increased commitment to astrology [by means of the expense and trouble of getting a personal horoscope, by means of a direct interpersonal relation with the astrologer, and by means of a personal investment (dissonance) strongly motivating the person to act upon the belief-system]; and (4) the enhancement of the believer's self-esteem among his friends and colleagues. (This phenomenon operates in the following way: because of its special language, astrology is an excellent topic of conversation; because the believer can direct the substance of astrology to another's ego as well, he gains great interpersonal merit in his interactional process.) Some latent functions on the group (societal) level might include the following factors: (1) all functions available to those involved in the first level; (2) the creation and maintenance of an in-group cohesiveness and an out-group exclusion by means of the special language of astrology; and (3) the presence of a highly interpersonally binding conversational framework that often centers around a highly personal and ego-centric discourse. (Astrology and psychoanalysis both share this and many other common features.)

At the third level of involvement with astrology, we find those people who have become really involved in the literature of the field and usually cast their own horoscopes. Until relatively recently, this level was composed of only a very small number of elderly people; it now consists of many youthful advocates. Persons involved this deeply in astrology are still comparatively few. (For example, the approximately 30,000 students at the University of Michigan have enough interest in astrology to support an occult-astrology bookstore; yet only about 20 such serious adherents are reportedly around that campus.) Unlike those in the first two levels of involvement, the astrology-believers in the third level are not primarily concerned with advice or prediction. For them, astrology represents a highly complex and symbolically deep conceptual scaffolding which offers them a *meaningful* view of their universe and gives

them an *understanding* of their place in it. They use astrology as a means of establishing their identity (Klapp, 1969). They usually acknowledge the great difficulties in establishing any predictive statements from astrology. To them, astrology represents a world view far more reminiscent of religion than of science. In fact, they most likely speak of their belief-system, not as a science like physics or astronomy, but as an art or as one of the "occult sciences." The latent functions for the individual involved at the third level may well include many of the features found in the first two rather superficial levels of involvement. The major latent function, however, is that the adept astrologer obtains an ideological integration of his self with his perception of the universe. Of course, other benefits may occur. He may, for example, become a leader in his astrology-oriented circle of friends. He may even become a professional astrologer and earn his living from his involvement; for the social actor, however, the central function is that the astrological belief-system operates as a grand conceptual-philosophical scheme. (Because the actor is aware of the consequences of his belief in astrology, this central function may now become manifest, not latent.) On the group (societal) level, this intensity of involvement may well act as a "sacred canopy" (see Berger, 1967) for the social group. Composed of only a few thousand astrology-believers, this level of involvement clearly follows the depiction of the astrological belief-system as a social reaction against the normlessness of modern life. It is at this level of involvement that we see the search for identity and for new sacred elements. We should, however, see these relatively extreme astrology-believers in their true perspective: they represent a very small minority of those involved in the massive revival of interest in astrology. I would argue, in fact, that the vast majority of those involved with astrology, those at the first two levels, take a highly irreverent, almost playful attitude toward astrology. To most of these people, astrology is fun; it is a non-serious, leisure-time element of popular culture, *not* a spiritual searching for Karmic meaning.

Witchcraft and Satanism

Witchcraft and Satanism follow astrology as the second most popular focus of current attention in occultism. The large number of recent popular books and articles dealing with these subjects attests to this upsurge of interest in them. (Often these publications are reprints of much older volumes.) Although witchcraft and Satanism are commonly linked together, they actually represent very different belief-systems, and each has an existing variety of forms.

The alleged difference between so-called *white* versus *black* magic is one major distinction discussed in much of the occult literature. While white magic is supposed to be the use of magic for socially beneficent ends, black magic is supposed to be the use of magic for malevolent ends. Even though some ritual forms of black magic clearly involve calling upon such malevolent forces as the Devil or his demons, most magicians basically view magic as a value-free "technology-of-the-supernatural" (or *super-normal*, a term preferred by many magicians). They believe that their own motives really determine whether their use of magic is for good (white), or for evil (black). Most contemporary witches stress that they perform only white magic (e.g., Leek, 1968: 3–5; or Holzer, 1969: 19) as an attempted antidote for the stereotypes usually portraying them as evil workers of the devil. The distinction between black and white magic is essentially a matter of the user's intent rather than of his technique.

Contemporary witches usually do not consider themselves to be Satanists. Satanism is basically a worship of the Judaeo-Christian Devil, which is, at times, only a symbol and, at other times, very literally real. (Varying degrees of fundamentalism exist among Satanists. For these varieties, see Truzzi, 1972; and Lyons, 1970). Practitioners in witchcraft do not usually view themselves as an heretical offshoot of Christianity, but Satanists do view themselves, either literally or symbolically (since many Satanists are atheists), as members in league with the Christian's Devil. Most witches perceive witchcraft as a folk tradition of magical beliefs. Many, if not most of them, further perceive it as an ancient, pre-Christian fertility religion that the Christian churches sought to suppress: primarily through the Catholic inquisitions and the Protestant witch trials. They believe that their religion became misrepresented and distorted as an heretical worship of the Devil. [For the early Catholic image, see Kramer and Sprenger, 1948. Most Catholics no longer accept the orthodox picture of the witch, but some Catholic scholars do; e.g., see Pratt, 1915, and Cristiani, 1962. The leading writer presenting the strictly orthodox (medieval) Catholic viewpoint in recent years was the late Montague Summers (1946, 1956, and 1958).] On the other hand, Satanists do often constitute a kind of inverted Christian sect. (Most of the presently vast literature on Satanism is quite unreliable. Some reliable sources include Hartland, 1921; Spence, 1960: 123–124; Carey, 1941; and Murray, 1962. For the official views of the Church of Satan, centered in San Francisco, see LaVey, 1969. For good historical commentaries, see Carus, 1969; Langston, 1945; Coulange, 1930; and Garcon and Vinchon, 1929. And for the classic occult view on Satanism, see Huysmans, 1958; and Waite, 1896). Oddly enough, most of history's Satanisms seemed to be direct outgrowths of the Christian churches' misrepresentations of early witchcraft practices. The inquisitors so impressed some individuals with the fantastic and blasphemous picture of Satanism that they apparently decided that they also would "rather reign in hell than serve in heaven."

Several different varieties seem to depict the non-heretical, non-Satanic or white witches. The major division of great importance to the sociologist is between those witches who are individual practitioners and those who belong to organized witch groups or *covens*. Most frequently encountered, the former variety represents the independent or solitary witches. This variety can be further subdivided into two, somewhat oversimplified, classes: (1) one represents those who, having learned the secrets of the art through some special kinship-relation to another solitary witch, practice witchcraft as a culturally inherited art from kin; (2) the other represents those who, having invented their own techniques or having obtained their practices from the occult literature, practice witchcraft as self-designated witches. My investigations show that the vast majority of witches are in the second class: they belong to no organized group and have obtained their knowledge from their readings and conversations with others uninitiated into coven-held secrets. The typical person of this class is a young high-school or college-age girl who, for a variety of reasons, self-designates herself as a witch to her peers; because her status is attractive to her friends but elicits fear in her enemies, it produces many social rewards for her. Yet this type of witch is "illegitimate" in terms of the very criteria that she herself may accept for being a witch. Most of the major works on witchcraft state that before one becomes a true practitioner of the craft, he must obtain initiation into a coven and learn the group (coven) secrets. These secrets, however, are not available in such public works as the occultism-volumes in most public libraries or occult bookstores.

A number of varieties exist among the organized white witch groups. A rather clear division seems to exist between the witch covens formed before and after the 1951 repeal of witchcraft-laws in England or, especially, after the 1954 publication of the late Gerald Gardner's first book on witchcraft (also, see Gardner, 1959, and Bracelin's biography on Gardner, 1960). Gardner's works were very influential in British occult circles, and many contemporary witches, sometimes called Gardnerites, received their credentials through Gardner's Witchcraft Museum on the Isle of Man. The question of legitimacy among British witches is still raging, each accusing the other of concocting his own rituals. *Pentagram: A Witchcraft Review*, the publication of the Witchcraft Research Association in London, prominently featured this debate in its first five issues (for an example of a lively exchange, see issue number 5, December 1965: 18–19). The much publicized witch, Monique Wilson, who with her husband inherited Gardner's museum, has stated that she holds a secret register of covens existing around the world (Wilson, 1968). This, however, seems to include only the Gardnerite covens, which according to Mrs. Wilson, numbered several hundred at that time. In 1969, another well publicized witch, Mrs. Sybil Leek, estimated to me that approximately 300 covens were then operating in the United States. The facts are that covens, especially those in existence before 1951, have little communication with one another. Members sometimes migrate from an area and join or begin a new coven, but no central hierarchy or witchcraft-organization actually exists. Except for Mrs. Wilson and Mrs. Leek, most witches know little about those in the other parts of the country. These women are somewhat unusual because their extensive publicity and travel about the world have brought them into contact with a great many witches wanting interaction with them. It is, therefore, impossible to obtain any sort of accurate estimate of the number of covens now in operation. Because a great number of new covens did begin after 1951, they certainly appear to represent the bulk of the *known* witchcraft-groups about which we read today. Even though more could exist, I did locate three pre-1951 covens in Michigan. I thus estimate that at least 150 such traditional covens probably exist in Great Britain and the United States.

According to Murray, the maximum number of persons in a coven is thirteen: Thus, Great Britain and the United States probably can claim no more than 1950 coven members. These cultists represent a rather small part of the mass market currently devouring the many marketable witchcraft items and books. Coupling the number of coven members with that of the solitary witches (many of whom are really not very serious about witchcraft) still leaves us with a relatively small number of witches in the United States, the maximum being probably less than 3000. Like their interest with astrology, the popular interest of the general public toward this form of occultism is very superficial. From my observations of many people's reactions toward witches during public occasions, I know that most people show interest in meeting a witch for the novelty rather than for any occult enlightment. Like astrology, witchcraft also represents a play-function for the major portion of its current popular audience.

Like the witches, the Satanists also represent two distinct types of individuals: those acting as solitary agents and those operating in groups. We know next to nothing about the former. If some individuals in the world believe that they have made contractual arrangements with the Devil, then they probably would prefer that this not be widely known: this seems likely, especially if they are really doing evil things. Much diversity exists among the Satanic groups; these groups have at least four major varieties. Probably the least frequent, the first variety represents Satanic groups who follow some non-heretical (to them) interpretation of Christianity in which Satan is perceived as an angel still to be worshipped. These may represent some sort of Gnostic tradition which the members claim to follow.

A second variety about which one can read a great deal in the "soft-core" pornographic literature (e.g., Moore, 1969) consists of sex clubs that incorporate Satanism and some of its alleged rituals. Here we find, as an attraction or embellishment, the celebrated but usually artificial "black mass" (for the best work on this topic, see Rhodes, 1954). Many of these groups are sado-masochist clubs or flagellation societies.

Probably more frequent than the previous two, a third variety of Satanic group is an outgrowth of the current narcotics or "acid-culture" now found in various parts of the country [even though the author seems to confuse it with traditional Satanism, Burke (1970) presents a good description of one of these groups]. Epitomized by the much publicized Charles Manson group that allegedly killed Sharon Tate in 1969, this sort of group has received much publicity. It is, however, much more rare than newspaper headlines would imply. More importantly, most of these groups are almost completely untraditional, and they make up their brand of Satanism as they go along (Burke, 1970; and Kloman, 1970). Like the sex club, their central focus is not occultism at all; in their case, it is narcotics. Ironically enough, many traditional Satanists commonly complain that the sex and acid cultists give a "bad name" to "real Satanism."

Clearly dominant today, the fourth variety of Satanic group consists of members of the Church of Satan in San Francisco. High Priest Anton Szandor La Vey founded this church, which is, in fact, a church, not a cult. Only La Vey knows the exact number of members in the Church of Satan, but on numerous occasions he has stated that over 7000 were contributing members. He gave this figure before mid-1969: since then, La Vey's book *The Satanic Bible* has had national circulation (125,000 copies in its first of now four printings), and two movies that prominently feature the Church of Satan have been released nationally. The figure of 7000 appears reasonable, if not conservative, for several reasons; because La Vey does remarkable public relations work and because *Rosemary's Baby*, the movie with which he was associated, has been a great success, the Church of Satan has received vast international publicity over the past five years.

The church has been remarkably successful during its short life. Although it still depends heavily upon the charisma of its founder, it is hierarchically governed and now has two other churches (Grottos) in the Bay Area plus a number of still secret (to the general public) branches scattered around the country. By the end of 1971, La Vey hopes that Grottos will exist in every state of the Union. At the current rate of growth, achievement of his goal is not impossible. Because contributing members pay an initial fee of twenty dollars for their lifetime membership, the church has a relatively prosperous economic beginning.

Although the Church of Satan believes in the practice of magic, it simply defines magic as "obtaining changes in accordance with one's will." The church perceives magic not as supernatural (i.e., forever scientifically inexplicable), but simply as supernormal (i.e., not yet fully understood by science but amenable to eventual scientific explanation). The church actively rejects spirituality and mysticism of any sort; it espouses an elitist, materialist, and basically atheistic philosophy. Satan constitutes a worship of one's own ego. Unlike most atheisms, the position of the Church of Satan is that these symbolic entities are powerful and indispensable forces in man's emotional life and that these forces are necessary conditions for the success of greater (Ritual) Magic.

In its major features, the Church of Satan takes the position of extreme Machiavellianism and cynical-realism toward the nature of man. It has many philosophical parallels with philosophies as divergent in sophistication as the Superman views of Friedrich Nietzsche and the Objectivist ideals of Ayn Rand. Its major feature, however, is its emphasis upon the importance of myth and magic and upon their impact in a world of people who can still be manipulated through such beliefs and emotions. This Satanist, then, is the *ultimate pragmatist*.

This predominant form of Satanism does not represent a new mysticism at all. It not only denies the existence of anything supernatural or spiritual, but it even condemns any narcotics, hallucinogens, or other agents that might act to separate rational man from his material environment. This Satanist does not seek escape from reality; he wishes full control of reality and is even willing to use all forces—including irrational elements—that help him in achieving his desired ends. Unlike the acid-culture Satanist who seeks identity through mysticism and other levels of "consciousness," this Satanist is very much opposed to the hippie culture of acid and altruism.

Thus, I argue that, like those interested in astrology, the major followers of Satanism represent not a search for a new spiritual meaning, but only a disenchantment with religious orthodoxy.

Conclusion

How are we to assess this rising tide of interest in the occult? I have shown three major facts in this paper. First, the interest in the occult is multidimensional, and it is not the simple, integrated, and consistent "bag" that many, especially the writers in the popular press, have described it to be. Second, many persons involved in the following of today's occultisms are not the simple identity-seeking variety that some have portrayed them to be; these occultisms serve a variety of functions quite apart from offering new normative structures as an escape from alienation for the anomie. Third, most of those involved in supporting the current occult revival have a relatively superficial connection with it, a connection that is usually more one of play than one of seriousness. For most Americans, the involvement in the occult is a leisure-time activity and a fad of popular culture rather than a serious religious involvement in the search for new sacred elements.

Dr. Donald Kaplan has made a very insightful observation about astrology: "It's pop science . . . It has the same contempt, in a playful way, for science that pop art has for academic art" (quoted in Buckley, 1968: 133). I believe that we may even go further and refer to the mass version of occultism as *pop religion*. I would argue that it shows a playful contempt for what many once viewed seriously (and some still view thusly). I further would argue that the current mass interest in occultism represents, in fact, a kind of victory over the supernatural. What we are seeing is largely a demystification-process of what were once fearful and threatening cultural elements. Most significant is the very playfulness in the attitudes of most of the people involved in the occult revival. What were once fearful and awe-inspiring dark secrets known

only through initiation into arcane orders are now fully exposed to the eyes of Everyman.

I illustrate this point by the example of the probable contemporary reaction to the allegation that a house in the neighborhood is haunted. Years ago, few would dare enter the house; all would whisper in fear about it. Now, such an allegation would bring a rush of inquisitive teenagers who desire to spend the night there just to see the ghost. Would it be proper to interpret this direct interest as a renewed belief in ghosts? It is precisely because we no longer believe in the fearsome aspects of the occult that we are willing to experiment with them. Most of those who would willingly draw a proper pentagram on the floor to invoke a demon would do so precisely because they do not really believe that some Devil's emissary who might just pluck their souls down to Hell would possibly ever visit them. If we fully believed in demons, we certainly would not want to call them up.

This assessment does not deny that a growth has occurred in the number of true believers in the occult. It also does not deny that other non-occult phenomena, which indicate a growing number of persons seeking new religious meanings, have occurred. Certain factors, however, would alone cause an expected increase in occult activity: (1) the increase in our general population, (2) some disillusionment with the dominant religions, (3) our lack of fear of the occult or an involvement with it, (4) the present lack of social sanctions against involvement with the occult, and (5) the increased saliency of the occult resulting from the revival itself. *I must stress that I am concerned more with the mass character of the occult than with its small but significant minority of serious advocates.* As long as these *mass* phenomena represent a playful and non-serious confrontation with the supernatural elements, they then represent a possible cleansing or purging of the old fears and myths still present in our society. The more we eliminate these old fears and myths, the more we develop a naturalistic rationalism, a scientific view of the universe.

Glossary

Acculturation: Culture change occurring under conditions of close contact between two societies. The weaker group tends to acquire cultural elements of the dominant group.

Age-Grade: An association that includes all the members of a group who are of a certain age and sex (for example, a warrior age-grade).

Age-Set: A group of individuals of the same sex and age who move through some or all of the stages of an age-grade together.

Ancestor Worship: A religious practice involving the worship of the spirits of dead family and lineage members.

Animatism: The attribution of life to inanimate objects.

Animism: The belief in the existence of spiritual beings (Tylor's minimal definition of religion).

Anthropomorphism: The attribution of human physical characteristics to objects not human.

Anthropophagy: The consumption of human flesh (cannibalism).

Associations: Organizations whose membership is based on the pursuit of special interests.

Astrology: The practice of foretelling the future by studying the supposed influence of the relative positions of the moon, sun, and stars on human affairs.

Avoidance Rules: Regulations that define or restrict social interaction between certain relatives.

Berdache: A French term for North American Indian transvestites who assume the cultural roles of women.

Bull-Roarer: A flat board or other object that is swung at the end of a cord to produce a whirring sound; commonly used in religious ceremonies around the world.

Bundu: A women's secret society among certain tribes of West Africa (also known as Sande).

Cannibalism: See *Anthropophagy*.

Caste: An endogamus social division characterized by occupational or ritual specialization ascribed by birth.

Ceremony: A formal act or set of acts established by custom as proper to a special occasion, such as a religious rite.

Charisma: A divine gift that endows an individual with the ability to prophesy, perform miracles, and carry out other divinely inspired acts; it often results in a religious following.

Churinga: Sacred objects used by Australian aborigines in a variety of rituals.

Cicatrization: Ritual and cosmetic scarification.

Clan: A unilineal descent group based on a fictive ancestor.

Communitarianism: A secular or religious lifestyle in which groups share beliefs and material goods; these groups are ordinarily isolated from the general population.

Cosmogony: A theory or account of the creation or origin of the world.

Cosmology: Theory or philosophy of the nature and principles of the universe.

Couvade: Culturally prescribed behavior of a father during and after the birth of his child; for example, mimicking the mother's labor pains.

Coven: An organization of witches with a membership traditionally set at thirteen.

Creationism: The doctrine of divine creation. Opposed to evolutionism.

Cult: An often loosely organized group possessing special religious beliefs and practices.

Cultural Relativism: The concept that any given culture must be evaluated in terms of its own belief system.

Cultural Universals: Aspects of culture believed to exist in all human societies.

Culture: The integrated total of learned behavior that is characteristic of members of a society.

Culture Trait: A single unit of learned behavior or its product.

Curse: An utterance calling upon supernatural forces to send evil or misfortune to a person.

Demon: A person, spirit, or thing regarded as evil.

Diffusion: A process in which cultural elements of one group pass to another.

Divination: The process of contacting the supernatural to find an answer to a question regarding the cause of an event or to foretell the future.

Emic: Shared perceptions of phenomena and ideology by members of a society; insiders' views.

Ethnocentrism: A tendency to evaluate foreign beliefs and behaviors according to one's own cultural traditions.

Ethnography: A detailed anthropological description of a culture.

Ethnology: A comparison and analysis of the ethnograhic data from various cultures.

Ethnomedicine: Beliefs and practices relating to diseases of the indigenous peoples of traditional societies.

Ethos: The characteristic and distinguishing attitudes of a people.

Etic: An outside observer's viewpoint of a society's phenomena or ideology.

Exorcism: The driving away of evil spirits by ritual.

Familiar: A spirit, demon, or animal that acts as an intimate servant.

Fetish: An object that is worshipped because of its supernatural power.

Folklore: The traditional beliefs, legends, myths, sayings, and customs of a people.

Functionalism: An analytical approach that attempts to explain cultural traits in terms of the uses they serve within a society.

Ghost Dance: A nativistic movement among several tribes of North American Indians during the late nineteenth century.

Ghosts: Spirits of the dead.

Glossolalia: The verbalizing of utterances that

depart from normal speech, such as the phenomenon of "speaking in tongues."

God: A supernatural being with great power over humans and nature.

Hallucinogen: Any of a number of hallucination-producing substances, such as LSD, peyote, ebene, and marijuana.

Holistic: The anthropological approach that emphasizes the study of a cultural and bio-ecological system in its entirety.

Idolatry: Excessive devotion to or reverence for some person or thing.

Incest Taboo: The prohibition of sexual relations between close relatives as defined by society.

Invocation: The act of conjuring or calling forth good or evil spirits.

Legend: A folkloric category that relates an important event popularly believed to have a historical basis although not verifiable.

Magic: A ritual practice believed to compel the supernatural to act in a desired way.

Magic, Contagious: A belief that associated objects can exert an influence on each other—for example, a spell cast using the intended victim's property.

Magic, Imitative: A belief that imitating a desired result will cause it to occur.

Magic, Sympathetic: A belief that an object can influence others that have an identity with it—for example, a bow symbolizes the intended victim.

Mana: A sacred force inhabiting certain objects and people giving them extraordinary power.

Mazeway: Anthony F. C. Wallace's term for an individual's cognitive map and positive and negative goals.

Monotheism: A belief that there is only one god.

Mysticism: A contemplative process whereby an individual seeks union with a spiritual being or force.

Myth: A sacred narrative believed to be true by the people who tell it.

Necromancy: The ability to foretell the future by communicating with the dead.

Neurosis: A mild psychological disorder.

Oath: An appeal to a deity to witness the truth of what one says.

Occult: Certain mystic arts or studies, such as magic, alchemy, and astrology.

Ordeal: A ritual method to supernaturally determine guilt or innocence by subjecting the accused to a physical test.

Pantheism: The worship of several gods.

Participant Observation: An anthropological field technique in which the ethnographer is immersed in the day-to-day activities of the community being studied.

Peyote Cult: A cult surrounding the ritual ingestion of any of a variety of mescal cactuses; commonly associated with certain Native American religious beliefs.

Polytheism: See *Pantheism*.

Possession: A trance state in which malevolent or curative spirits enter a person's body.

Primitive: A term used by anthropologists to describe a culture lacking a written language; cultures also characterized by low-level technology, small numbers, few extra-societal contacts, and homogeneity (sometimes referred to as pre-literate or non-literate cultures).

Profane: Not concerned with religion or the sacred; the ordinary.

Prophet: A religious leader or teacher regarded as, or claiming to be, divinely inspired who speaks for a god.

Propitiation: The act or acts of gaining the favor of spirits or deities.

Psychosis: A psychological disorder sufficiently damaging that it may disrupt the work or activities of a person's life.

Reciprocity: A system of repayment of goods, objects, actions, and sometimes money, through which obligations are met and bonds created.

Reincarnation: The belief that the soul reappears after death in another and different bodily form.

Religion: A set of beliefs and practices pertaining to supernatural beings or forces.

Revitalization Movements: According to Wallace, a deliberate, organized, conscious effort by members of a society to construct a more satisfying culture.

Rites of Passage: Ritual associated with such critical changes in personal status as birth, puberty, marriage, and death.

Ritual: A secular or sacred, formal, solemn act, observance, or procedure in accordance with prescribed rules or customs.

Sacred: Venerated objects and actions considered holy and entitled to reverence.

Sacrifice: The ritualized offering of a person, plant, or animal as propitiation or in homage to the supernatural.

Sect: A small religious group with distinctive beliefs and practices that set it apart from other similar groups in the society.

Secular: Not sacred or religious.

Shaman: A religious specialist and healer with powers derived directly from supernatural sources.

Society: A group of people sharing a common territory, language, and culture.

Sorcery: The use of magical paraphernalia by an individual to harness supernatural powers ordinarily to achieve evil ends.

Soul: Immortal or spiritual part of a person believed to separate from the physical body at death.

Structuralism: An anthropological approach to the understanding of the deep, subconscious, unobservable structure of human realities that is believed to determine observable behavior (a leading exponent: Claude Lévi-Strauss).

Supernatural: A force or existence that transcends the natural.

Symbol: An object, gesture, word, or other representation to which an arbitrary shared meaning is given.

Syncretism: A process of culture change in which the traits and elements of one culture are given new meanings or new functions when they are adapted by another culture—for example, the combining of Catholicism and African ancestor worship to form Voodoo.

Taboo: A sacred prohibition put upon certain people, things, or acts that make them untouchable, unmentionable, and so on (*also* tabu, tabou, tapu).

Theocracy: Rule by religious specialists.

Totem: An animal, plant, or object considered related to a kin group and viewed as sacred.

Trance: An altered state of consciousness induced by religious fervor, fasting, repetitive movements and rhythms, drugs, and so on.

Transcendence: The condition of being separate from or beyond the material world.

Voodoo: A syncretic religion of Haiti that combines Catholicism and African ancestor worship; sometimes referred to as Tovodun or Vodun.

Witchcraft: An evil power inherent in certain individuals that permits them, without the use of magical charms or other paraphernalia, to do harm or cause misfortune to others.

Zombie: A corpse brought to a state of trance-like animation and made to obey the commands of the person exercising the power; see also *Familiar*.

Index

Page numbers in italics indicate a selection by this author.